CENSORSHIP

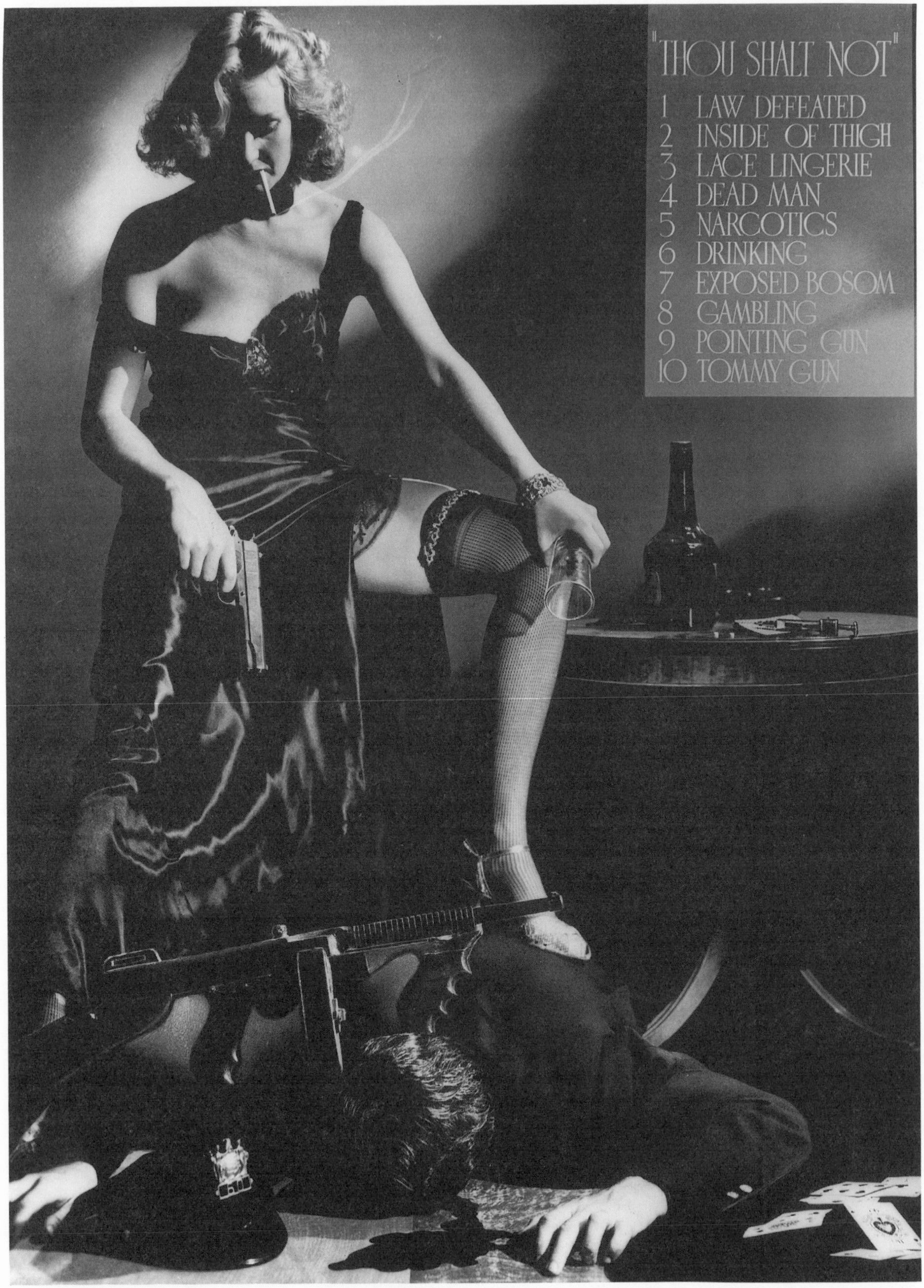
"THOU SHALT NOT"
1 LAW DEFEATED
2 INSIDE OF THIGH
3 LACE LINGERIE
4 DEAD MAN
5 NARCOTICS
6 DRINKING
7 EXPOSED BOSOM
8 GAMBLING
9 POINTING GUN
10 TOMMY GUN

Ready Reference

CENSORSHIP

Volume II

Gabler, Mel, and Norma Gabler – President's Commission on Obscenity and Pornography

Consulting Editors

Lawrence Amey
Dalhousie University

Timothy L. Hall
University of Mississippi Law School

Carl Jensen
Project Censored
Sonoma State University

Charles May
California State University,
Long Beach

Richard L. Wilson
University of Tennessee at Chattanooga

Project Editor

R. Kent Rasmussen

Salem Press, Inc.
Pasadena, California   Englewood Cliffs, New Jersey

Frontispiece: UPI/Corbis-Bettman

∞ The paper used in these volumes conforms to the American National Standard for Permanence of Paper for Printed Library Materials, Z39.48-1984.

Library of Congress Cataloging-in-Publication Data

Censorship / consulting editors: Lawrence Amey, Timothy L. Hall, Carl Jensen, Charles May, and Richard L. Wilson; project editor, R. Kent Rasmussen

p. cm. — (Ready reference)

Includes bibliographical references and index.

ISBN 0-89356-444-3 (set : alk. paper). — ISBN 0-89356-446-X (vol. 2 : alk. paper).

1. Censorship—United States—Encyclopedias. 2. Censorship—Encyclopedias. I. Amey, L. J., 1940- . II. Rasmussen, R. Kent. III. Series.

Z658.U5C38 1997
363.3'1—dc21 97-14245
CIP

First Printing

PRINTED IN THE UNITED STATES OF AMERICA

CONTENTS

ALPHABETICAL LIST OF ENTRIES

Volume I

Volume II

Volume III

CENSORSHIP

G

Gabler, Mel

Born: January 5, 1915, Houston, Texas

Gabler, Norma

Born: 1923?

Identification: Husband and wife leaders of a grassroots movement to review school textbook adoptions

Significance: The Gablers have achieved remarkable success in their self-proclaimed mission to cleanse the nation's public schools of ideas that threaten their own conservative religious and patriotic beliefs

Mel Gabler, a retired Exxon employee, and his wife, Norma, began their crusade in 1965, when they first observed a "weakening of the moral fiber" and a "lack of patriotic reinforcement" among public school students in their home state of Texas. According to their own account, they awakened to the faults in school textbooks one day when their son brought home a history text that discussed only the powers that are held by the federal government, without addressing states' rights. Although neither Gabler claimed expertise in any academic discipline, they founded Educational Research Analysts, which operated out of their home in Longview, Texas.

Within a few years, the Gablers claimed to be "recognized authorities on textbook content," as well as the voices for millions of persons in mainstream America. From their organization's humble beginnings as a mom-and-pop textbook review service, Educational Research Analysts grew into a full-time operation and took up most of the space in the Gablers' home. Eventually, the Gablers would be featured on such national television broadcasts as *The Phil Donahue Show*, *Nightline*, and *The Today Show.* They would also become subjects of articles in periodicals as diverse as *Fundamentalist Journal*, *People*, and *The Wall Street Journal*. They would even receive a variety of awards, such as the Texas Senate Award of Appreciation, and Mel Gabler would become a national delegate to the White House Conference on Families.

The Gablers' speaking engagements across the United States, donations from an estimated sixteen thousand like-minded activists, and dissemination of photocopied information packets earned their nonprofit organization more than $100,000 each year. The Gablers received a hundred letters a day from supporters throughout the United States and from more than forty other countries; some correspondents requested as many as two hundred copies of their information packets. The Gablers' speaking tours addressed concerned parents and community leaders, who were encouraged to become more involved in the education of the nation's children and to monitor reading materials more closely, even in religious schools.

Texas Textbook Adoptions. Because the state of Texas had a universal adoption policy for textbooks and a $45 million annual budget for purchasing textbooks, it was a force to be reckoned with in the textbook publishing business. Its state board of education encouraged public discussion to provide students with less-biased sources of information. Each year open textbook hearings were held in the state capital of Austin; however, these hearings focused only on objections to textbook adoptions, and not comments in support of particular books. After examining hundreds of textbooks and appraising their presumed educational value, the Gablers attended the state hearings, armed with hundreds of pages of objections to particular texts. Gabler later claimed that before he and his wife became involved in Texas' textbook-adoption process, textbooks had been considered "classroom ready"; after they became involved, the books were listed as merely "format finished."

Although the Gablers stated that they were only patriotic citizens seeking to save the children, they almost singlehandedly forced several companies to rewrite textbooks for the entire country. One such set of books was a series entitled *Justice in America*, designed for use in eighth-grade citizenship classes. Some of the Gablers' objections to that series were that one volume featured an illustration of a person burning a flag, and another depicted a mock welfare application without providing information that reinforced the work ethic.

Many people have charged that the Gablers institutionalized textbook censorship in Texas. Indeed, in 1979 the *American School Board Journal* cited them as perhaps the two most powerful individuals in American education. In 1983 the *Encyclopedia Britannica Book of the Year* included the Gablers among ninety-five persons it judged as having had a worldwide impact the previous year.

Secular Humanism. The Gablers have argued that "secular humanism" has pervaded public school systems, purging the textbooks of traditional American values, such as Christianity, patriotism, free enterprise, and traditionally prescribed gender roles in marriage. Furthermore, they have claimed that textbooks—in conjunction with proselytizing teachers—have been indoctrinating students in secular humanist beliefs, promoting values change, and contributing to a permissive society. According to Mel Gabler, "the only thing the humanists [were] absolute about is that there [were] no absolutes." He insisted that schoolchildren were being forced to discover their own values, based on individual situations and, often, peer pressure. In addition, he cited time spent on wasted activity, such as values change, discussions of modern literature, and the reinforcement of self-esteem, as the root of lowered academic skills and Scholastic Aptitude Test (SAT) scores.

The Gablers have particularly objected to books containing lengthy discussions of topics such as women's suffrage, the women's movement, slavery, the Civil Rights movement, trade unions, ecology, world hunger, the American Indian experience, the Watergate scandal, poverty, one-world government, world peace, and communism. For them, textbooks should be conduits of moral, thus sacrosanct, education, and they have argued that the books should teach only absolute—not relativistic—values. Perhaps surprisingly, the Gablers have not championed any one theory of creation over another—whether biblical, evolutionary, or mythological. They have insisted only that the teaching of evolution as a scientific theory is permissible only so long as contrary theories are given equal time.

The Gablers as Opponents of Censorship. Mel Gabler has claimed that traditional American values had been deleted from textbooks before they ever reached his office. After examining hundreds of textbooks, line by line, that were considered suitable for kindergarten through high school, he asserted that "we can unequivocally state that the values and beliefs held by the vast majority of Americans have been censored from textbooks. Censorship has resulted in textbooks with biased content. Students receive only one side of an issue but believe they are receiving enough pertinent information to give them a balanced education." He emphatically asserted that he and his wife were not censors, but rather fighters against censorship. He felt that textbooks should not point to America's weaknesses; instead, they should point to America's strengths. *—Joyce Duncan*

See also Evolution; Pressure groups; Secular humanism; Textbooks.

Bibliography

The Gablers' views are presented in James C. Hefley's *Are Textbooks Harming Your Children?* (Milford, Mich.: Mott Media, 1979), and in their own book, *What Are They Teaching Our Children?* (Wheaton, Ill.: Victor Books, 1985). More objective assessments of the Gablers can be found in "Behind the Move to Ban More Books," in *Changing Times* (June, 1982), and in David Bollier's essay "The Witch Hunt Against 'Secular Humanism'" in *The Humanist* (September-October, 1984). *Books Under Fire* (Wilmette, Ill.: Films, Inc., 1983) is an hour-long film on censorship that features the Gablers at home and in public lectures.

Gag order

Definition: A trial judge's order requiring attorneys, police, and parties involved in a criminal proceeding not speak to the news media concerning the proceeding

Significance: A gag order, or rule, is designed to protect a defendant's right to a fair trial while at the same time providing for a press free from more extreme censorship

Since the U.S. Supreme Court overturned Samuel H. Sheppard's murder conviction in 1965 because a trial judge had permitted a media circus to deny him a fair trial, judges have sequestered juries during trials and issued gag orders, or rules, to the parties, attorneys, police, and potential witnesses barring them from talking to the press outside court before the trials begin. Such gag orders, while a form of censorship, minimize excessive pretrial publicity that might damage a court's ability to find a jury untainted by prejudicial remarks, while avoiding a direct prior restraint or censorship of the press.

In *Nebraska Press Association v. Stuart* (1976) the trial judge, believing that pretrial hearings, as trials, were required to be open to the press and public under the Sixth Amendment, allowed the press in a pretrial hearing without realizing how damaging information in a dramatic sex/murder case would be. The judge then imposed a gag order banning members of the press from printing what they had learned. However, the Supreme Court ruled that this was an impermissible prior restraint on the press. The Court balanced press freedom against the defendant's right to a fair trial by allowing judges to issue gag orders to keep material secret, but it did not permit them to impose gag orders on the press even if they acquire prejudicial information on the defendant. Similarly, the Court has allowed military secrecy, but has forbidden prior restraints after secrets have reached the press.

See also Courtrooms; Criminal trials; Judicial publication bans; *Pentagon Papers, The*; Prior restraint.

Galileo Galilei

Born: February 15, 1564, Pisa, Republic of Florence (Italy)

Died: January 8, 1642, Arcetri, Republic of Florence (Italy)

Identification: Italian astronomer and philosopher

Significance: One of the most significant figures in the history of science, Galileo provided conclusive evidence of Copernicanism, but his challenge to orthodoxy contradicted religious dogma, and he was silenced by the Roman Inquisition

For centuries Europeans believed the explanation of the second century C.E. cosmos of the astronomer Ptolemy that the earth is the center of the universe, around which all heavenly bodies revolve. The sun's revolution around the earth explained night and day. Moreover, the official worldview of Roman Christianity since the thirteenth century—a Christian version of Aristotelianism—held the heavens to be perfect and unchanging, with only the earth imperfect.

The Copernican Challenge to Ptolemaism. The Ptolemaic system, and by implication Aristotelianism, along with literal interpretations of certain biblical passages, were challenged by the research of Polish astronomer Nicolaus Copernicus. By assuming that the earth revolves around the sun, he was able to work out in mathematical detail observations of the positions of known planets. Fearing persecution by the Church, however, Copernicus delayed publication of his findings. When he did publish them, he presented the notion that the earth revolves around the sun merely as a device to facilitate his calculations of planetary positions, rather than as a fact that he actually believed—which he did.

Galileo and Copernicanism. Active in a number of fields of science in the first decades of his career, Galileo was teaching mathematics at the University of Pisa in the 1590's when he found his views of physics at odds with the reigning Aristotelian orthodoxy around him. However, he was reluctant to deny Aristotle's physics openly. By 1597 he adopted Copernicanism but remained publicly silent on the subject, influenced, no doubt, by the execution in 1600 of Giordano Bruno for heresies that had included belief in Copernicanism. When a new star (a nova sighted by German astronomer Johannes

Kepler) appeared in 1604, Galileo began to argue openly that the appearance of the star disproved the Aristotelian view of the heavens' immutability.

Galileo became publicly involved in the Copernican controversy after hearing about lenses being ground in Holland that magnified distant objects in 1609. After inventing his own lens-grinding the tools, he fashioned telescopes and began to scour the heavens nightly. First he studied the moon, finding its surface to be rough, not smooth—contrary to currently held beliefs. The astronomical observations that Galileo made through his telescopes provided irrefutable evidence supporting Copernicanism.

In 1610 Galileo made his most spectacular discovery—four of Jupiter's moons, known to posterity as the Galilean moons. The fact that they revolved around Jupiter proved that all heavenly bodies do not revolve around the earth. Galileo now set about sharing his discoveries with educated Europe. He personally made a hundred telescopes and sent them to strategically chosen individuals, among them Kepler. He also published his findings in *Starry Messenger* (1610), arguably the most important scientific work of the century. It caused great excitement and evoked comparisons between Galileo and Christopher Columbus. Of similar significance was Galileo's discovery of sun spots, whose motion across the solar disk, he argued, was evidence of the sun's rotation.

The revolutionary potential of Copernicanism led to Galileo's eventual humiliation and silencing by the Roman Catholic church and to the temporary triumph of censorship and obscurantism over the findings of the new science of astronomy. Galileo might have succeeded in carrying on his scientific work unimpeded had he not begun commenting openly on the theological implications of his work. Blinded by arrogance, he managed to arouse a formidable array of hostile forces against him: the Jesuits, the Aristotelian professors, and the church hierarchy, who found his science a threat to its monopoly on interpretation of the universe and humanity's place in it.

Galileo's First Silencing. In 1614 Galileo was accused of heresy for his defense of Copernicanism, and the Roman Inquisition entered the fray. In 1615 he was relieved to hear that the Church's foremost intellectual, Cardinal Robert Bellarmine, the inquisitor of Bruno, thought that Copernicanism would not be prohibited, but would be treated as supposition or hypothesis, not fact.

In 1616, however, the situation for Galileo became more serious. In February the Inquisition met, and the pope ordered Cardinal Bellarmine to silence Galileo on Copernicanism. Accordingly, Bellarmine met with Galileo and warned him not to "hold, teach, or defend [Copernicanism] in any way orally or in writing." Disobedience would result in formal charges before the Inquisition, which meant imprisonment or death. An unsigned memorandum on the meeting that played a key role in his trial in 1633 stated that Galileo agreed to obey. Soon afterward, the pope formally pronounced Copernicanism heretical.

The Inquisition's Chill and Galileo's Trial. The papal pronouncement and Bellarmine's message to Galileo dealt a massive setback to astronomy in Italy from which the country would not recover for centuries. Though Galileo continued his scientific research, his dissemination of his Copernican work suffered a severe chill. In 1619 a "Discourse on the Comets" published under a disciple's name, deeply antagonized the Jesuits, who in 1633 would seek to square accounts. Meanwhile, in 1623, Galileo's hope for the new science was renewed when an old acquaintance known to respect him became Pope Urban VIII. Galileo tried unsuccessfully to have the papal decree on silencing him nullified. Nevertheless, he began a master work on Copernicanism, *Dialogue on the Two Chief Systems of the World* (1632). A brilliant work of science and literary polemics, this book sealed Galileo's fate when the pope was led to believe that Galileo intentionally ridiculed his views. The book was banned and Galileo was ordered to Rome for trial before the Inquisition.

Old, sick, and terrified, Galileo was tried in secret and, on June 22, 1633, forced under threat of torture to kneel and recant his belief in Copernicanism. The story that upon rising he murmured "Eppur si muove" ("nevertheless, it does move") is apocryphal. Sentenced to perpetual house arrest, Galileo never wrote on astronomy again. Scientific knowledge was retarded in Italy, and the reputation of the Roman church was stained for centuries. Writers subject to Vatican scrutiny feared to tread upon this dangerous subject. Thus, René Descartes postponed publication of his own Copernican views in light of Galileo's fate.

Placed on the *Index Librorum Prohibitorum*, Galileo's works were not removed until 1825; Copernicanism could not be taught in Catholic schools until 1925. In 1992 an inquiry into the affair resulted in a papal statement admitting the truth of Galileo's Copernican beliefs but stopping short of apology. In 1995 an interplanetary probe named in his honor approached Jupiter and successfully sent invaluable data back to Earth. *—Charles F. Bahmueller*

See also *Areopagitica*; Aristotle; Astronomy; Brecht, Bertolt; Bruno, Giordano; Copernicus, Nicolaus; Darwin, Charles; Descartes, René; Heresy; *Index Librorum Prohibitorum*; Mercator, Gerardus; Political correctness; Science; Vatican; Vesalius, Andreas.

BIBLIOGRAPHY

Galileo's life, work, trial, and ordeal have inspired a large literature. A good starting point is the classic biography by J. J Fahie—*Galileo: His Life and Work* (London: John Murray, 1903). Karl von Gebler was the first modern scholar to examine the Vatican archives; the book he wrote in 1879 is still worth consulting: *Galileo Galilei and the Roman Curia*, translated by Mrs. George Sturge (repr., Merrick, N.Y.: Richwood Publishing, York, 1977). The many important Italian-language works translated into English include Ludovico Geymonat's *Galileo Galilei: A Biography and Inquiry into His Philosophy of Science*, translated by Stillman Drake (New York: McGraw-Hill, 1965). James Reston, Jr., *Galileo: A Life* (New York: HarperCollins, 1994), reexamines the principal issues of Galileo's life, trial, and punishment. James Brophy and Henry Paolucci, eds., *The Achievement of Galileo* (New York: Twayne, 1962), is a useful collection of Galileo's own writings. Isaac Asimov provides a useful overview of Galileo's scientific achievements in *Asimov's Biographical Encyclopedia of Science and Technology* (2d ed. New York: Doubleday, 1982).

Gangster films

DEFINITION: Motion pictures treating organized crime activities

SIGNIFICANCE: Gangster films faced censorship from religious, civic, and ethnic groups for depictions of graphic violence, amoral behavior, and negative ethnic stereotyping

From their inception and throughout the twentieth century, gangster films have often encountered censorship. Storylines depicting criminals committing senseless violent acts, police brutality, political corruption, and amoral sexuality have conflicted with the values of many communities and individuals. Religious and civic groups have been quick to protest against gangster films. As early as 1905 state and local censor boards were established across the country to restrict violence and immorality in films such as *The Black Hand* (1906) and *The Ex-Convict* (1905). Cross-denominational religious groups objected to sympathetic attitudes shown toward criminals in gangster films. Protesters contended that such films undermined the values of youthful audiences and contributed to immorality and rising crime rates.

Filmmakers argued that violent portrayals were more realistic and demonstrated the ruthlessness of criminal behavior. Studios tried to find a balance between profitability and the audience appeal of striking violent scenes and the possibility of damaging public protests. By the end of the 1920's thirty-six states had censorship bills ready to be voted into law. Religious and civic groups worked together to boycott particularly objectionable movies and were successful in reducing profits. Roman Catholics banded together by the millions to boycott films not approved by the newly formed Legion of Decency.

Sound brought additional excitement to the gangster film genre in the 1930's. Audiences could now hear quick-witted dialogue, police sirens, machine-gun volleys, and screeching automobile tires. The popularity of gangster films soared with graphic, well-written movies such as *Little Caesar* (1930), *Public Enemy* (1931), and *Scarface* (1932). These films contained scenes of human bodies riddled with bullets, legs amputated, dead bodies, and even women being slapped, hit, or punched in the face.

In an effort to ward off increasing demands for censorship by state and federal authorities, studio moguls hired U.S. Postmaster General Will H. Hays to help censor the film industry. Under the Hays Code, gangster films could no longer sympathize with criminals. Murder and other criminal acts, such as arson, theft, safecracking, and smuggling, could no longer be presented in detail so as to "teach" crime to audiences.

In 1966 Jack Valenti, the president of the Motion Picture Association of America, eliminated the Hays Code. In an effort to recapture audiences lost to television, films resumed offering patrons explicit scenes of sex and violence that television could not broadcast into homes. Films about the St. Valentine's Day Massacre, sympathetic biographies of Bonnie and Clyde and John Dillinger, and director Francis Ford Coppola's *Godfather* series enraged many filmgoers. Protesters were joined by ethnic pressure groups such as the National Italian-American League to Combat Defamation and Americans of Italian Descent. Such groups objected to the large numbers of Italian Americans who were depicted as criminals in films, charging that such portrayals denigrated and defamed twenty-two million Italian Americans.

As special effects technology improved, film violence became more graphic and realistic. Religious and civic groups, industry critics, and Parent Teacher Associations protested against the relentless graphic violence, and criticism of gangster films continued unabated.

See also Film censorship; Hays Code; Legion of Decency; Motion Picture Association of America; *Pulp Fiction*; Snuff films; Violence.

García Márquez, Gabriel

BORN: March 6, 1928, Aracataca, Colombia

IDENTIFICATION: Colombian novelist

SIGNIFICANCE: García Márquez's novels are considered to be anti-Christian; they contain incidents of casual sex, possible pederasty, open marriage, incest, and cannibalism

Popularly known as "Gabo," Gabriel García Márquez has often been called the peoples' writer in the Hispanic world. He has been compared to Leo Tolstoy, Fyodor Dostoevski, Charles Dickens, and, especially, William Faulkner. His rich literary mixtures of myth and fantasy paint a picture of Latin American people not as idealized heros or piteous victims, but as ordinary people in opposition to powerful forces. This opposition García Márquez portrays in his often bawdy and humorous accounts of everyday work, play, and romantic and erotic love. Known for their political radicalism, his novels contain the underpinnings of irreverence toward all things official. A declared foe of Western imperialism, he is recognized as one of the twentieth century's great political writers. In addition to U.S. imperialists, this 1982 Nobel Prize winner's satirical targets have included lawyers, doctors, political hierarchies, and church officials. His novels involve such incidents as civil wars, labor strikes, military repression, and heroic revolutions. In a stylistic blend of Caribbean folklore and modernistic Western technique, García Márquez explores life in all its manifestations, even if these manifestations include casual sex, incest, ménage à trois, and even cannibalism.

His work has been translated into at least thirty languages, and censorship problems have followed in the wake of his international success. In 1986, for example, his *One Hundred Years of Solitude* (1967), which reveals the history of the little Colombian town of Macondo through its love affairs, marriages, and deaths, was criticized as "garbage being passed off as literature," and purged from use at Wasco, California, Union High School. This novel, the school board stated, was "anti-God, anti-religion and anti-personal dignity." In 1987 English teacher Lee McCarthy, filed suit claiming that the board's decision was made on religious, and not educational, grounds. The case was dismissed, but a Fresno, California,

Gabriel García Márquez accepts the Nobel Prize in Literature from Swedish king Carl Gustav in December, 1982. (AP/Wide World Photos)

appellate court ordered the *McCarthy v. Fletcher* case reinstated. A settlement allowed García Márquez's book to remain in the library, but forbade teachers from assigning it. In 1991 the Darlington, South Carolina, school board voted to remove *One Hundred Years of Solitude* from the advanced English placement reading list at St. John's High School, following a parental complaint that the book was "garbage," profane, and anti-Christian.

García Márquez's other well-known novels include: *The Autumn of the Patriarch* (1976), *Love in the Time of Cholera* (1988), and *Chronicle of a Death Foretold* (1982).

A resident of Mexico City since 1975, García Márquez is known as a convinced socialist giving time and money to left-wing causes. The U.S. State Department has placed him on its immigration subversives list.

See also Faulkner, William; Libraries; Literature; Sex in the arts; South America.

Garden of Eden, The

TYPE OF WORK: Film

RELEASED: 1957

DIRECTOR: Max Nosseck (1902-1972)

SUBJECT MATTER: A widow rescued by nudists discovers a new and welcome way of life in their colony

SIGNIFICANCE: More of a documentary than a drama, this film helped to create a more acceptable legal atmosphere for nudity

After the New York State censorship board screened *The Garden of Eden*, it labeled the film's contents to be "indecent" for public viewing and ordered that the film not be shown unless the scenes displaying residents of the nudist colony were deleted. The word "indecent" was disputed when the film was reviewed by the New York Court of Appeals, which ruled that the term was too broad for censorship purposes. In his decision, Judge Charles S. Desmond wrote that because the film contained no scenes depicting sexual immorality it could not be labeled obscene. In making his determination the judge read the court the findings of the U.S. Supreme Court in the 1952 case of *The Miracle* which referred to the description of obscenity under the First and Fourteenth amendments. As stipulated a film had to be obscene in a "traditional, historic sense of the term," which *The Garden of Eden* was not. In addition the court concluded that the film had not violated any part of the state's penal code on nudity because it had not glorified any criminal act.

See also Film advisory board; Film censorship; First Amendment; Fourteenth Amendment; *Miracle, The*; Morality; Nudity.

Garvey, Marcus

Born: August 17, 1887, St. Ann's Bay, Jamaica
Died: June 10, 1940, London, England
Identification: Jamaican American black nationalist leader
Significance: U.S. federal officials placed Garvey under surveillance, and both U.S. officials and European colonial officials in the Caribbean and Africa curtailed his organizing and propaganda campaigns

Garvey founded the Universal Negro Improvement Association (UNIA) in Jamaica and brought the organization to Harlem in 1917, during the radical New Negro era that followed World War I. Through this period, radical African American intellectuals and nationalists were speaking out for black rights, through street-corner oratory, newspaper articles, and mass meetings. Garvey became part of this political milieu and quickly won fame as a street speaker.

Garvey also published and edited *The Negro World* newspaper and led weekly UNIA meetings in New York. He conducted several successful organization tours of the United States and traveled to Europe, the West Indies, and Central America, spreading a philosophy of racial separatism and uplift. Through speeches and editorials, he called for pan-African unity, black self-help, and black enterprise, inspiring the formation of hundreds of local UNIA divisions internationally. Despite the importance of African investment and colonization schemes to the UNIA platform, Garvey never visited Africa—primarily because European colonial officials feared his influence and prohibited his entering their colonies.

Garvey's success in organizing led government officials to perceive him as a threat. European officials in particular saw his rhetoric as instigating anticolonial sentiments and fostering possible black independence movements in areas of Africa and the Caribbean then under European control. In the United States, Garvey's association with radicalism led to the infiltration of the UNIA by Bureau of Investigation agents. J. Edgar Hoover and Bureau of Immigration officials attempted to bar Garvey from re-entering the United States after he toured the Caribbean on a major organizing tour in 1921. Meanwhile, *The Negro World* was banned as seditious in many countries under colonial rule in the Caribbean and Africa. Copies were confiscated in South Africa, Trinidad, British Guiana, Costa Rica, and elsewhere. In August, 1919, the British governor of Jamaica ordered that copies of the newspaper be routinely delayed and censored when they arrived on the island.

A printer and journalist by training, Jamaican Marcus Garvey used his writing and oratorical powers to build the first mass African American movement in the United States. (Library of Congress)

In Africa, Garveyite organizers were detained for questioning and subjected to searches and seizures. In New York, pressure was repeatedly applied to Garvey by the district attorney's office. After efforts to trap Garvey on income tax evasion charges failed, federal officials arrested and tried the UNIA leader on mail fraud charges stemming from the improper sale of stock in the UNIA's shipping company, the Black Star Line. After being convicted in 1923, Garvey was incarcerated in Atlanta's federal penitentiary on February 8, 1925. His sentence was commuted by President Calvin Coolidge in November, 1927, but he was deported directly to Jamaica. Despite lobbying efforts in his behalf, he was never allowed to return to speak in the United States.

Garvey and his publications continued to be censored by colonial officials as he pursued a political and publishing career in Kingston and London in the late 1920's and 1930's. He served a three-month sentence for contempt of court stemming from a campaign speech he gave critical of the Jamaican justice system in 1929.

See also African Americans; Colonialism; Farrakhan, Louis Abdoul; Hoover, J. Edgar; Immigration laws; Malcolm X; Newspapers, African American; Street oratory.

Gautier, Théophile

BORN: August 31, 1811, Tarbes, France
DIED: October 23, 1872, Neuilly-sur-Seine, France
IDENTIFICATION: French writer and critic
SIGNIFICANCE: Gautier's brazen challenges to French literary and social values provoked censorship of his writings

Central to the acceptance of romantic artists and writers in nineteenth century France, Gautier was a fervent promoter of such figures as Victor Hugo and Charles-Pierre Baudelaire. His key role in the development of Parisian literary bohemia put him in direct conflict with the emerging stuffiness of French bourgeois life. As the art critic for *La Presse* from 1838-1845, and as the literary commentator for the *Journal Officiel* (until 1870) and other publications, Gautier rejected prevailing aesthetic notions and attacked the hypocrisy of French culture and morality.

Gautier rejected the notion that art has an ideological mission, and called for art for art's sake, the truest possible expression of truth and beauty. He also rejected prevailing mores and became a figure of popular revulsion and moral approbation. Having two mistresses and three children, Gautier outraged polite society by turning his own life into a work of bohemian expression.

Gautier's novel *Mademoiselle de Maupin* (1835) was his most acerbic attack on the mediocrity of the bourgeoisie. That novel daringly explored bisexual relationships, opening Gautier to charges of promoting immorality. The legal battle that ensued cleared him but sealed his fate in the eyes of the French literary establishment. It was the first major case of the century involving an attempt at literary censorship on moral, rather than political grounds.

Mademoiselle de Maupin established Gautier's reputation for the scandalous, a reputation that transcended both his century and his country. Gautier was denounced and rejected by the French Academy three times, his works were banned in Russia, and as late as 1917 the New York Society for the Suppression of Vice sought to purge him from the public libraries.

See also Baudelaire, Charles; Dumas, Alexandre, *père*; France; Hugo, Victor; Literature; Morality; Society for the Suppression of Vice, New York.

Genet, Jean

BORN: December 19, 1910, Paris, France
DIED: April 15, 1986, Paris, France
IDENTIFICATION: French writer and filmmaker
SIGNIFICANCE: Because many of Genet's writings glorify criminals and contain homosexual eroticism, several of them have been banned, and one of his films provoked a landmark obscenity case in American law

Abandoned by his mother, Genet was handed over to foster parents when he was only one year old. At fourteen he apprenticed himself to a typographer near Paris. He ran away first from the typographer and then from other homes and institutions in which he was placed, beginning a life of wandering and stealing. In order to get out of an agricultural penitentiary in 1929, he joined the French army. After serving one full tour of duty, he re-enlisted, only to desert in 1936. This was followed by years of stealing and being sentenced to prison terms.

While in prison, Genet started to write poetry and to work on a novel, *Our Lady of the Flowers* (1944), an autobiographical fiction about criminal life and homosexual passion that was secretly printed and circulated by admirers of his work. In 1944, having spent most of his life in and out of prisons, he was freed as a result of support from the admirers of his writing. After World War II ended, he published numerous poems, novels, and plays, and the philosopher Jean-Paul Sartre began to champion his writing.

Despite Genet's literary success, his work remained highly controversial. In 1948 French authorities banned his radio script "The Criminal Child." In 1951 all of his books were legally prohibited from sale in the United States, and when *Our Lady of the Flowers* was finally published in the U.S., in 1963, his American publishers worried about censorship.

Un Chant d'amour (*A Song of Love*), a film written and directed by Genet in 1950, became an important part of the history of American law regarding obscenity. Copies of this silent black and white film, showing masturbation, oral copulation, and other sexual acts, were circulated in the United States. In New York an avant-garde filmmaker who publicly screened the film in 1964 was beaten by police. When a Californian, Sol Landau, showed the film at the University of California at Berkeley in the same year, the local police department warned him that if he persisted in screening it, it would be confiscated and all involved in its showing would be arrested. With the assistance of the American Civil Liberties Union, Landau sued to be free of police interference.

Despite testimony from expert witnesses such as critic Susan Sontag, a California district court of appeals found that *Un Chant d'amour* had no redeeming artistic value and that it should be banned as pornography. Landau appealed to the U.S. Supreme Court, which, by a bare majority, upheld the California court's decision, condemning and suppressing the film.

See also Books and obscenity law; Film censorship; France; Free Speech Movement; Homosexuality; Redeeming social value; Sartre, Jean-Paul.

Genetic research

DEFINITION: Scientific investigation into the nature of heritable physical, physiological, and behavioral traits of living organisms
SIGNIFICANCE: Genetic research aims to elucidate the origin of innate differences among organisms; despite the potential benefits of such research, some critics advocate censorship because of the possibility that genetic researchers may discover material bases for human social inequality or create new recombinant organisms

Questions about the causes of similarities and differences among individuals, and on the interaction between innate and acquired characteristics, have probably been asked by all peoples at all times in human history. Genetic research attempts to provide scientific answers to these questions. Although many genetic researchers investigate these questions solely for the purpose of gaining understanding, other scientists and social activists hope that genetic research will produce understanding and technology for the purpose of improving human biological, ecological, and social conditions. Arguments about the relative importance of "nature" and "nurture" have persisted in the intellectual history of Western civilization, but these arguments provoked little censorship until the mid-nineteenth century, following the publication of Charles Darwin's controversial evolutionary theory on the origin of differences in species. Societal censorship of genetic research intensified during the twentieth century, when powerful genetics tools became available to scientists trained to formulate hypotheses and produce data that can influence social policy.

Mechanisms of Genetic Research Censorship. Censorship of genetic research can occur through one of two processes. The first is the denial of funds for certain genetic research topics. In the United States, this is a very effective mechanism by which the federal government, operating through agencies that support most academic scientific research, such as the National Science Foundation (NSF) and the National Institutes of Health (NIH), can influence the direction of genetic research. For example, in 1993, President Bill Clinton issued an executive order barring federal funds from being applied to research into genetic engineering (cloning) of human reproductive (germ-line) cells. It is important to note that genetic research thus "censored" by the federal government can still be conducted with private funds.

The second process through which genetic research can be censored is by preventing publication of research results. This mechanism provides an opportunity for editors to reject publication of studies perceived to be unethical or inadequate in any way. Publication censorship is not as effective as withdrawal of research funds, because only the formal dissemination of research results is inhibited. Ethical standards vary among journal editors who exercise discretion in accepting or rejecting a research manuscript, and controversial genetic research can be published in non-peer-reviewed books, where topical marketability often prevails over ethical considerations.

Origins of Genetic Research Censorship. The origin of overt censorship of genetic research can be traced to the end of World War II when the German Nazi regime's extremist policies on heredity, racial identity, and social desirability became widely discredited. The roots of the Nazi policy on genetics and social status were embedded in the development of eugenics, a term coined by Francis Galton in 1883 to describe the scientific study of stock-quality improvement. Galton proclaimed that human eugenics must not be confined to judicious mating but must also include deliberate enhancement of factors that give superior races a better chance of increasing their population at the expense of inferior races. The founding of the English Eugenics Society by Galton and others supported the incorporation of the eugenicist agenda into political and scientific programs in Great Britain and the United States.

By the beginning of the twentieth century, well-known genetic researchers such as Charles B. Davenport, Hermann J. Muller, and Julian Huxley were publishing books and perpetuating opinions in support of eugenics. In 1904 Davenport influenced the Carnegie Institution in Washington, D.C., to establish an organized database for genetic information. The Eugenics Records Office was officially opened in 1910 at Cold Spring Harbor Long Island, New York, with funds provided by John D. Rockefeller and others. The Immigration Restriction Act of 1924 and involuntary sterilization laws passed by the U.S. Congress were based on data accumulated by the Eugenics Records Office. By 1935 more than twenty thousand people in the United States had been forcibly sterilized under compulsory sterilization laws; by 1941 eugenic extermination practices involving procedural "selection and eradication" of "inferior" types by the Nazi regime in Germany was in full operation. A direct consequence of popular revulsion against the Nazi eugenics policies was the acute decline in scientific interest in the idea of genetic "purification" of human races. Funding for human genetic research became scarce, and publication of studies highlighting genetic differences between individuals or races of humans became difficult after World War II.

Dynamics of Genetic Research Censorship. Following the war, developments in the study of population genetics and the birth of molecular genetics (highlighted by James Watson and Francis Crick's announcement of the molecular identity of the gene in 1953) ushered in a new age of genetic research, far more powerful in diagnostic and manipulative capabilities than that available to the original eugenics program. Throughout the 1980's, attempts to censor the teaching of genetic evolutionary theory in schools were still noticeable, and many individuals and groups such as Jeremy Rifkin of the Foundation on Economic Trends in Washington, D.C., protested the use of genetic engineering to create new and chimeric life forms. Molecular genetic research led directly to a proposal to map and sequence the entire human genome beginning in 1990. The Human Genome Project, as it became known, precipitated new fears among some genetic researchers and social scientists regarding human intervention in the natural course of evolution. An attempt in 1994 by the NIH to fund a scientific symposium aimed at examining the genetic basis for violent human behavior drew widespread criticism from social activists and some members of Congress. Subsequent to the public outcry, the project was suspended, pending careful reevaluation of the agenda in order to eliminate ideas that might be misconstrued as eugenic in nature.

—Oladele A. Ogunseitan

See also Darwin, Charles; Human Genome Project; Medical research; Race; Science; Technology; Unprotected speech.

Bibliography

Carl F. Cranor's *Are Genes Us?* (New Brunswick: Rutgers University Press, 1994) contains essays on institutional attempts to protect genetic research from censorship and discusses why genetic research affects all aspects of social institutions. Troy Duster's *Backdoor to Eugenics* (New York: Routledge, 1990) explores the social and ethical issues surrounding modern genetic research, inviting social scientists to participate in guiding the direction of genetic research. Ruth Hubbard and Elijah Wald's *Exploding the Gene Myth* (Boston: Beacon Press, 1993) focuses on over-geneticization of human physical and social conditions and how genetic information is produced and manipulated by scientists, physicians, employers, insurance companies, educators, and law enforcers. Richard C. Lewontin, Steven Rose, and Leon Kamin's *Not in Our Genes* (New York: Pantheon Books, 1984) provides a critique of modern genetic determinism. Edited by Robert F. Weir, Susan Lawrence, and Evan Fales, *Genes and Human Self-Knowledge* (Iowa City: University of Iowa Press, 1994) discusses moral, legal, and practical issues surrounding modern genetic research.

Georgia

DESCRIPTION: Southeastern state of the United States

SIGNIFICANCE: Like many of its fellow southern states, Georgia has often prosecuted obscenity cases

Censorship has taken many paths in Georgia's history. The state's 1833 slave code, for example forbade teaching slaves to read or write. In 1908 a preacher at a revival meeting urged a large woman to move her "big rump" so that the meeting could continue. Georgia's supreme court found that remark obscene, noting that the setting of the speech made it obscene; such speech might be allowed in a bordello, but not at a revival meeting. In 1953 the state's General Assembly created the Georgia State Literature Commission to censor cheap paperback novels. The commission was most successful in censoring material that it considered pornographic, and in censoring materials relating to race. During the height of the Cold War, a loyalty oath was imposed on all state employees, including teachers. Julian Bond, who was elected three times to the Georgia House of Representatives, was refused a seat by that body because his expressed antiwar views violated the state's loyalty oath.

In 1969 the U.S. Supreme Court decided, in *Stanley v. Georgia*, that private possession of materials considered obscene was not illegal. Georgia police, suspecting bookmaking activity, had raided a private home and found films judged obscene. Justice William J. Brennan, Jr., wrote in support of the unanimous decision: "If the First Amendment means anything, it means that the state has no business telling a man, sitting alone in his own house, what books he may read or what films he must watch." However, the Court argued against interpreting the *Stanley* decision too broadly.

In *Bowers v. Hardwick* (1986), the Supreme Court, with new justices appointed by President Ronald Reagan, demonstrated in another case arising from Georgia that *Stanley* was, in fact, not being interpreted broadly. Police arrived at the home of Hardwick, a gay Atlanta bartender, and were allowed in by another resident to serve a warrant for Hardwick's arrest. They found Hardwick in his bedroom engaged in oral copulation with another man, in violation of Georgia's law against sodomy. Hardwick, charged but not prosecuted for the crime (the Atlanta prosecutor perhaps foreseeing that the sodomy law might be struck down under the Eighth Amendment if Hardwick were prosecuted), sued in civil court to challenge the constitutionality of Georgia's sodomy law. Finding nothing in the U.S. Constitution that defended the right to commit sodomy, the Supreme Court upheld the Georgia statute. Justice Harry Blackmun, in a dissenting opinion, wrote that the *Bowers* case was no more about sodomy than the *Stanley* case had been about obscene films, but rather that the case was about "the most comprehensive of rights . . . the right to be let alone."

See also Brennan, William J., Jr.; Homosexuality; Ku Klux Klan; Loyalty oaths.

Germany

DESCRIPTION: Western European nation created from Prussia and many small principalities during the late nineteenth century

SIGNIFICANCE: Germany's history of censorship reflects attempts of authoritarian and conservative regimes to manipulate public opinion and repress progressive and democratic aspirations

Ecclesiastical and governmental efforts at suppressing religious freedom and freedom of expression reached a high point in the Holy Roman Empire with the Diet of Worms in 1521. Emperor Charles V condemned the writings of the Protestant reformer Martin Luther and ordered them burned and prohibited their further publication, purchase, or possession. After that, governmental censorship became institutionalized at the Imperial Diet of Speyer in 1529. Later imperial diets, however, rejected some of the more stringent prohibitions on heretical writings demanded by the papacy. During the seventeenth and eighteenth centuries political censorship focused increasingly on newspapers as witnessed by the edicts of 1749 and 1772 issued by Prussia's Frederick the Great.

From Confederation to Empire. After the failure of a German national state to form after the end of the Napoleonic Wars in the early nineteenth century, liberal students and intellectuals expressed their discontent in several rallies such as the Wartburg Festival of 1817. In 1819 a theology student named Karl Sand killed the playwright and suspected Russian spy August von Kotezbue. Prince Clemens Lothar Wenzel von Metternich, the guiding spirit of the German Confederation, responded by trying to stifle further nationalist and liberal agitation with the Carlsbad Decrees. In addition to banning student societies (*Burschenschaften*), the decrees ordered supervision of university lectures. Also, a specific Press Decree introduced prepublication censorship of all newspapers, journals, and books. Both decrees remained in effect until 1848. In other instances, censorship manifested itself in the dismissal of seven prominent professors at the University of Goettingen in 1847. The dismissed professors included philologist Jakob Grimm—who had protested the dissolution of the parliament of Hannover and the banning of the works of writers who included Heinrich Heine.

The 1848 revolution in Germany brought to an end many of the repressive features of the preceding period. A new constitution guaranteed freedom of expression and specifically forbade any form of precensorship. However, the ultimate failure of the republican experiment resulted in reestablishment of conservative regimes and caused the flight of scores of liberals and democrats, many of them to the United States.

The constitution of the German Empire of 1871 guaranteed

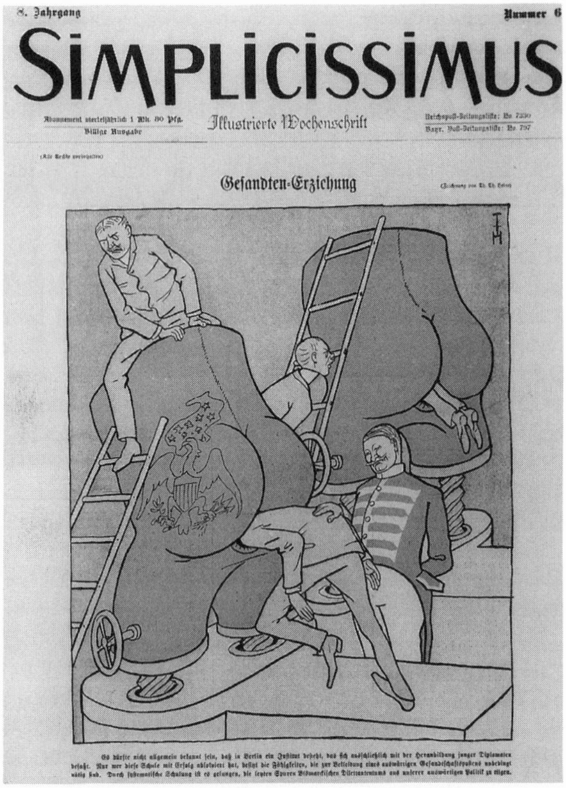

The subversive power of caricature is evident in this 1903 magazine cover ridiculing Germany's deference to U.S. foreign policy objectives. It depicts an imaginary diplomatic training school that German ambassadors attend to qualify for their foreign posts. (Robert J. Goldstein)

freedom of the press and outlawed censorship, while permitting government control of materials deemed harmful to youth. Despite such guarantees, Chancellor Otto von Bismarck managed to reduce the influence of the Catholic Center Party by means of the so-called "pulpit paragraph." This law made it a crime for clerics to comment unfavorably on matters of state. A few years later, increasing fears of radicalism from the Left coupled with the growing strength of the Social Democratic Party led to the passage of antisocialist legislation. The new laws allowed the government to dissolve organizations considered threats to public safety, and to confiscate their newspapers and pamphlets. Under Bismarck's prompting the legislation survived until 1890. The government also was in a position to affect freedom of expression at universities through its right to nominate heads of universities and to appoint professors. With the outbreak of World War I, free speech was further abrogated, and opponents of the war such as socialist leader Karl Liebknecht were arrested for delivering treasonous speeches.

From Weimar to Adolf Hitler. With the defeat of Germany in the war and the subsequent establishment of the Weimar Republic, Germany entered briefly on a more liberal course. Freedom of the press was again constitutionally guaranteed. Of crucial importance was article 48 of the postwar constitution. It provided that basic freedoms such as freedom of the press could be suspended temporarily by the president in cases of threats to public safety. In 1933 article 48 provided the legal basis for a decree suspending civil and individual liberties that gave the rising National Socialist Party (Nazis) a free hand.

The assumption of power by the National Socialists in 1933 began an era of ever-increasing government control of all forms of expression. At the outset the Nazis eliminated all socialist press organs and began to screen all working journalists as to their racial "purity" and ideological reliability. By September, 1936, Joseph Goebbels, the minister of propaganda, had forged the press into an instrument of public education controlled by his Reich Press Chamber. At the same time artists whose ideas were not in line with National Socialist ideals were prevented from publishing, exhibiting, or performing. Many of them, including Thomas Mann and Bertolt Brecht, chose exile in the United States. Artists who remained in Germany were subject to control by such organizations as the Reich Theater Chamber and Reich Music Chamber.

Post-World War II Germany. With the defeat of Adolf Hitler's Third Reich in World War II, a measure of censorship in Germany was continued by the Allied occupation forces, largely in an effort to prevent the spread of pro-Nazi or anti-Allied propaganda. In the summer of 1949 all such licensing requirements were abolished, however, and freedom of the press was reestablished. The constitution of the new Federal Republic of Germany (West Germany), the Basic Law, guaranteed freedom of expression and prohibited censorship. This provision applied to the press as well as to the broadcast industry. Freedom of expression was, however, restricted by a number of regulations of general law and regulations pertaining to protection of juveniles. The constitutional guarantees were put to a major test in 1962, when the publisher of the newsmagazine *Spiegel* was briefly imprisoned for an alleged breach of state security. The affair ended with the resignation of the minister of defense, who had ordered the publisher's arrest.

Other laws limiting freedom of expression prohibited the publication of material designed to incite racial hatred, or material openly glorifying violence or threatening the democratic order. Neo-Nazi and other parties seeking to overthrow the government were outlawed. However, many of these provisions were only sporadically enforced and could be challenged in the federal constitutional court. Enforcement of the laws differed among individual states. Although there has been no censorship of motion pictures, the "Voluntary Self-Control of the Film Industry" has effectively played a censorship role.

The approach to freedom of expression in the former German Democratic Republic (East Germany) was similar to that in other communist nations in Eastern Europe. Unification of East and West Germany in 1990 required the former East German state to accept the Basic Law of the Federal Republic.

—*Helmut J. Schmeller*

See also Brecht, Bertolt; Degenerate Art Exhibition; Grosz, George; Heine, Heinrich; Jehovah's Witnesses; Luther, Martin; National Socialism; Reformation, the.

Bibliography

Gordon A. Craig, *The Germans* (New York: Putnam, 1982), is a highly acclaimed work on modern German history. Oron J.

Hale's *The Captive Press in the Third Reich* (Princeton, N.J.: Princeton University Press, 1964) remains the best treatment of censorship under National Socialism. Jarrell C. Jackman and Carla M. Borden, eds., *The Muses Flee Hitler: Cultural Transfer and Adaptation, 1930-1945* (Washington, D.C.: Smithsonian Institution Press, 1983), contains essays on intellectuals who fled Nazi Germany. For a useful survey of German press history, see Kenneth E. Olson, *The History Makers: The Press of Europe from Its Beginnings Through 1965* (Baton Rouge: Louisiana State University Press, 1966). Fritz Stern's *Gold and Iron: Bismarck, Bleichroder, and the Building of the German Empire* (New York: Alfred A. Knopf, 1977) is particularly strong on Bismarck's relations with the press.

Ghazzali, al-

Born: 1059, Tus, Khurasam, Iran
Died: December 18, 1111, Tus, Khurasam, Iran
Identification: Islamic philosopher
Significance: Known as the "Great Renewer," al-Ghazzali advocated the censorship of rationalistic philosophers

A member of a family distinguished for its knowledge of Islamic law, al-Ghazzali completed his education at Nishapur and became a professor at the Nizamite Academy in Baghdad in 1091. He wrote against the Ishma'ilites (Assassins). In 1095 he experienced a spiritual crisis, abandoned his professorship, and become an ascetic Sufi until his death. Beginning as a rationalist skeptic, who doubted true religious knowledge was possible, al-Ghazzali ended as a mystic fideist. In numerous works he sought to correct influences that he believed were corrupting Islamic society. With serious study he mastered Islamic philosophy, then wrote against the philosophers, especially al-Farabi and Avicenna (Ibn-Sina), systematically demonstrating their "heresies" in his *Incoherence* (or *Destruction*) *of the Philosophers*. He regarded such philosophers as unbelievers, who stood outside orthodox faith.

In his autobiographical *Deliverance from Error* al-Ghazzali called for censorship. Philosophical works were to be kept from common people, who lacked the skill to discern the errors. He believed that it was necessary to use rigorous methods to bar the door to reading "the books of the misguided," otherwise the weak in the general public would be corrupted. His writings remained an important source for orthodox Muslim traditionalists for eight centuries after his death.

See also Heresy; Iran; Islam; Rushdie, Salman.

Gibbon, Edward

Born: May 8, 1737, Putney, Surrey, England
Died: January 16, 1794, London, England
Identification: English historian
Significance: One of the most influential historians of the eighteenth century, Gibbon was constrained by British blasphemy laws to express his negative views of Christianity through irony

The author of *The History of the Decline and Fall of the Roman Empire* (1776-1788), Gibbon is most renowned for his thesis that Christianity played a leading role in the Roman Empire's fall. His views on Christianity ran from skepticism to outright denial of its central claims. In openly expressing such views, he risked falling afoul of England's Blasphemy Act of 1698. To avoid prosecution, he adopted the protective coloring of a dispassionate literary style, indirect expression, and artful construction of passages designed to disguise—though not fully conceal—his cynical attitude toward Christianity. Speaking of this technique in his autobiography, he wrote that he learned from the *Provincial Letters* of Blaise Pascal "to manage grave and temperate irony, even on the subjects of ecclesiastical solemnity"—more accurately, especially on religious subjects. In *Childe Harold's Pilgrimage* (1818), Lord Byron later wrote, appropriately, of Gibbon's treatment of Christianity, that it constituted "sapping a solemn creed with a solemn sneer."

Gibbon's stratagems succeeded, for he was never prosecuted, nor were his works officially censored. He was subjected, however, to furious theological criticism from clerics, who had little difficulty penetrating his flimsy literary veil. Gibbon's ill-concealed cynicism about religion is most apparent in such passages as this ironic "explanation" of Christianity's triumph in the Roman Empire:

> When the promise of eternal happiness was proposed to mankind on condition of adopting the faith, and of observing the precepts of the Gospel, it is no wonder that so advantageous an offer should have been accepted by great numbers of every religion, of every rank, and of every province, in the Roman Empire.

Shortly after publication of the first of the six volumes of *The History of the Decline and Fall of the Roman Empire* in 1776, Gibbon wrote to his mother from the safety of Lausanne, Switzerland, that he was enduring a theological "cannonade" the like of which might be aimed at the revolutionary George Washington. Other writers of Gibbon's time were brought to trial for blasphemy, but Gibbon escaped, evidently, because he did not—unlike Thomas Paine and others—launch direct, emotionally stirring attacks on religion aimed at the common person. The fact that his volumes, unlike Paine's, were not published in cheap editions calculated to maximize circulation was also an important consideration to the authorities.

Three decades after he died, Gibbon was subjected to an informal form of censorship when Thomas Bowdler—later notorious for his sanitized editions of William Shakespeare—published his own version of Gibbon's history. By this time, too, Gibbon was coming under increasing attack, for his hypocrisy, by courageous publishers who defied the blasphemy laws by reprinting works such as Paine's *The Age of Reason*, which blatantly derided Christianity.

Britain's Society for the Suppression of Vice, a private morality police, initiated a long series of prosecutions that sent dozens of publishers—and in one instance a publisher's wife, in-law, assistant, and assorted friends—to jail for periods ranging from months to years. The accused denounced Gibbon's immunity from prosecution, saying it was because the historian "was a sinecure placeman [that is, a do-nothing] and an advocate for the American war."

See also Blasphemy laws; Christianity; Historiography; Paine, Thomas; Pascal, Blaise; Roman Empire; Society for the Suppression of Vice, U.K.

Giddings, Joshua Reed

Born: October 6, 1795, Tioga Point (now Athens), Bradford County, Pennsylvania

Died: May 27, 1864, Montreal, Quebec, Canada

Identification: American abolitionist and politician

Significance: As a member of the U.S. House of Representatives, Giddings fought against all attempts to gag opponents of slavery and prevent them from exercising their right to free speech

Giddings moved to Ohio with his family when he was ten and worked long hours on the family farm while pursuing an education in the winter months. In 1821 he was admitted to the bar, and he afterward maintained a successful practice in Jefferson, Ohio. He was elected to the House of Representatives in 1838 as an antislavery Whig. There he joined former president John Quincy Adams in vigorous opposition to the "gag" rule. Petitions were normally referred to a committee for discussion and possible action, but in 1836 the House added to its rule a provision that any petitions dealing with slavery would be tabled and not given consideration. Adams argued that this rule violated the right to petition Congress guaranteed in the First Amendment to the Constitution. Not until 1844, however, did the House abandon the gag rule, as changes in public opinion led Northern Democrats to stop supporting it.

In 1842 Giddings introduced a resolution criticizing the government for pressuring Great Britain to return the *Creole* mutineers—slaves who had seized a ship in the open Atlantic and reached Nassau and freedom. When the House censured him for raising the issue of slavery, Giddings immediately resigned and was triumphantly re-elected.

In 1861 President Abraham Lincoln appointed Giddings U.S. consul general in Canada, where he served until his death.

See also Abolitionist movement; Civil War, U.S.; Douglass, Frederick; Gag order; Helper, Hinton.

Gide, André

Born: November 22, 1869, Paris, France

Died: February 19, 1951, Paris, France

Identification: French novelist and Nobel Prize winner

Significance: Gide's work, banned at various times on three continents, was noted for its frank portrayal of homosexual love and other behaviors deemed unacceptable by the Roman Catholic church; it was also the subject of an obscenity case in New York

The work of André Gide was censored at various times during his lengthy career, especially after 1920, when he began to reach a large readership. After his earliest works had received little critical notice, he printed limited editions of his later work, and he sent out few review copies. These strategies may explain why such an important work such as *The Immoralist* (1902) received little critical notice. A novella with autobiographical overtones, *The Immoralist* details the North African honeymoon of a man who discovers that he prefers sex with boys. The book drew attention less for its subject matter than for the spare exactitude of Gide's prose. Gide's preface closes: "Finally, I have tried to prove nothing, but to paint my picture well and light it properly."

Critical notice of Gide's work increased with publication in 1926 of his masterpiece, *The Counterfeiters*, a narrative tour de force that recounts the lives, lies, and romantic dalliances of French schoolboys. In contrast to Marcel Proust's *Remembrance of Things Past* (1913-1927), which disguises the author's homosexuality, Gide's novel proclaims it openly. That same year a charge of obscenity was brought against another Gide novel, *If It Die*, in New York, which had law prohibiting "any obscene, lewd, lascivious, filthy, indecent or disgusting book." However, a New York court cited a precedent in *St. Hubert Guild v. Quinn* (1909) to rule that it was not the court's duty to censor literary production, because works of art and literature require "latitude."

Gide prided himself on being the literary champion of social outcasts, including criminals, the underprivileged, and indigenous peoples in French colonies. He also considered himself a communist through the middle years of his life; however, a visit to the Soviet Union in 1936 disillusioned him. After he wrote several books criticizing the Soviet Union, the Soviet government banned all his works.

Gide's reputation peaked in 1947 when he received the Nobel Prize in Literature. In 1952, a year after he died, the Roman Catholic church placed his complete works on its *Index Librorum Prohibitorum*. The church's accompanying decree characterized Gide as a "committed anti-Christian" whose work exhibited a "customary obscenity" and "imprudence." (The church formally abolished the *Index* in 1966.) In the years since Gide's death, his reputation as a major figure in twentieth century French literature has become secured.

See also Banned Books Week; France; Homosexuality; *Index Librorum Prohibitorum*; Intellectual freedom; Literature.

Ginsberg, Allen

Born: June 3, 1926, Newark, New Jersey

Died: April 5, 1997, New York, New York

Identification: American poet

Significance: Ginsberg's first collection of poems was the subject of an obscenity trial in San Francisco in 1957

In 1954, Allen Ginsberg, a former Columbia University student, moved to California to meet the West Coast contingent of the Beat movement. On October 13, 1955, he gave a reading of "Howl," a long Whitmanesque poem, at Six Gallery, an outlet for Beat visual and literary arts. His poem chronicled the depressed state of post-World War II Americans who felt alienated from a prevailing materialistic and technological culture and tried to escape through alcohol, drugs, and sex. It contained language and descriptions of sexual activities that tested the mores of the 1950's. After Lawrence Ferlinghetti, a local poet and publisher, heard Ginsberg's reading, he offered to publish "Howl."

Ferlinghetti owned City Lights Bookshop, which stayed open until midnight during the week and even later on weekends, making it a popular hangout for young writers. Earlier in 1955, Ferlinghetti had founded City Lights Books, which printed inexpensive paperback editions of the works of emerging poets in a series titled Pocket Poets. Since its books were printed in England, they had to pass through U.S. Customs

Poet Allen Ginsberg speaking in 1982. (AP/Wide World Photos)

before their distribution in the United States. The first printing of *Howl and Other Poems* occurred in October, 1956, without incident. The second printing, however, was seized by customs officials on March 25, 1957. A local customs officer, Chester MacPhee, called the volume obscene, citing a section of the Tariff Act of 1930 to support his decision to hold the books. A week later the American Civil Liberties Union (ACLU) contested the seizure. In late May, Customs released the impounded texts after the U.S. Attorney in San Francisco convinced the Customs office that it had no case. A few days later, however, the San Francisco police entered City Lights Bookshop and arrested Ferlinghetti and one of his employees on obscenity charges for selling Ginsberg's book.

This was not Ginsberg's first encounter with censorship. At Columbia University he had been chastised by a creative writing professor and a dean for writing a fictionalized version of a murder at Columbia involving a student. Ginsberg had also been suspended for writing graffiti critical of Columbia's president on a dormitory window.

Ginsberg's trial lasted through the summer and into the fall of 1957. The ACLU defense team called local critics, reviewers, and professors to testify on the literary merits of his poems. The defense also cited *Roth v. United States* (1957), arguing that the First Amendment of the Constitution prohibited the suppression of literature unless it is utterly without social or literary value. On October 3 Judge Clayton Horn read a thirty-nine-page decision that favored the defense. Far from condemning "Howl," Judge Horn's opinion described the poem as presenting "a picture of a nightmare world" that offers an "indictment of those elements of modern society destructive of the best qualities of human nature," such as "materialism, conformity, and mechanization leading toward war."

After that decision, Ginsberg's poems, including "Howl," became standard inclusions in literary anthologies used in universities throughout the United States.

See also American Civil Liberties Union; Customs laws, U.S.; Ferlinghetti, Lawrence; Obscenity: legal definitions; Poetry; *Roth v. United States*; Whitman, Walt.

Ginzburg, Ralph

BORN: October 28, 1929, New York, New York
IDENTIFICATION: American magazine publisher
SIGNIFICANCE: Ginzburg's unsuccessful appeal on a federal obscenity conviction led to the U.S. Supreme Court's amending its test for defining obscenity to include a pandering clause

In 1963 New York publisher Ralph Ginzburg was convicted of violating the Comstock Act in the U.S. District Court for the Eastern District of Pennsylvania. He was sentenced to five years in prison. The Justice Department had indicted Ginzburg at the height of the Civil Rights movement in the South. The decision to prosecute was initiated when the head of the department, Robert F. Kennedy, became incensed with Ginzburg for publishing a series of color photographs depicting, as lovers, a nude black male and nude white woman in the fourth issue of *Eros* magazine.

Eros, billed as the magazine of sexual candor, was first published on Saint Valentine's Day in 1962. It was an expensive and well-designed, hardcover periodical that received, among other honors, the Art Directors Club of New York gold medal for graphic design. The magazine showcased erotic masterpieces by Edward Degas, Albrecht Durer, Rembrandt, and Pablo Picasso, as well as work by well-regarded contemporary illustrators and photographers. *Eros* also featured venerable erotic tales and essays, such as Guy de Maupassant's *Madame Tellier's Brothel* and Mark Twain's *1601*, alongside the work of established authors and noted sex researchers. Ginzburg was also convicted of mailing not only *Eros*, but also *Liaison*, a biweekly newsletter of sexology, and a memoir, *The Housewife's Handbook on Selective Promiscuity*.

Ginzburg's appeal to the Supreme Court was decided on March 21, 1966. Voting 5-4, the justices sustained the lower court's conviction, even though they did not find *Eros* or the other publications to be obscene. Instead, while avoiding the question of whether Ginzburg's publications were in themselves obscene, the Court ruled that Ginzburg was guilty of pandering because he had written provocative advertisements for his wares suggesting they were obscene. The Court called attention to Ginzburg's attempts to have circulars for *Eros* postmarked from the Amish Pennsylvania communities of Blue Ball and Intercourse, while eventually posting the advertisements from Middlesex, New Jersey. The Roth test, the federal standard for obscenity from 1957 to 1973, was thus amended to include a pandering clause that made it illegal to advertise products in a manner designed to appeal to prurient interest.

Justice William J. Brennan, Jr., who wrote the majority opinion in the Ginzburg case, later claimed that this decision was the worst he ever made. The private papers of Justice Abe Fortas, who also voted against Ginzburg, reveal that Fortas' personal dislike for Ginzburg lead him to vote to sustain the publisher's conviction. In strong dissent, Justice Potter Stewart argued that sustaining Ginzburg's conviction deprived the publisher of due process of law, as the Court had found Ginzburg guilty of committing a crime for which he was neither charged nor tried.

Ginzburg's conviction was subsequently reduced from five years in prison to three. In 1972 he served eight months in the Lewisburg, Pennsylvania, federal penitentiary.

See also Brennan, William J., Jr.; Comstock Act of 1873; Courts and censorship law; Magazines; Men's magazines; Miscegenation; Obscenity: legal definitions; *Roth v. United States*.

Girodias, Maurice

BORN: 1919, Paris, France
DIED: July 3, 1990, Paris, France
IDENTIFICATION: French publisher
SIGNIFICANCE: Girodias published sexually explicit books, many of outstanding literary merit, under the imprint of Olympia Press

Girodias was the son of French publisher Jack Kahane, whose Obelisk Press had published works by such writers as Henry Miller and James Joyce that had been too experimental or sexually explicit for other commercial publishing houses. Kahane died in 1939, but his son revived the company after World War II. As head of Obelisk Press, Girodias was prosecuted twice, once for libel (in a politically sensitive case) and once for obscenity after he published a French edition of Henry Miller's novel *Tropic of Capricorn* (1939). Girodias won both cases.

In 1953 Girodias established Olympia Press, a firm that was to have a significant impact on contemporary literature. Its headquarters were in Paris, but it published works in English that, in theory at least, were not to be introduced into the United States or the United Kingdom. Among Olympia's titles were Terry Southern and Mason Hoffenberg's comic novel *Candy* (1958), as well as such highly regarded works as Vladimir Nabokov's *Lolita* (1955) and William Burroughs' *Naked Lunch* (1959). Olympia Press also published a number of salaciously titled works of little literary merit.

Beginning in 1956, Girodias was repeatedly prosecuted for obscenity by the French government, and a number of his firm's books were banned. He moved Olympia Press to New York in 1967 but met with only marginal success in the United States. Many of the works he had first pioneered had since been picked up by other publishers and were openly available throughout the English-speaking world.

See also Book publishing; France; *Lolita*; Miller, Henry; *Naked Lunch*; Southern, Terry.

Elinor Glyn, author of Three Weeks, *one of the most censored novels of the early twentieth century.* (Library of Congress)

Glyn, Elinor

BORN: October 17, 1864, Jersey, Channel Islands, England
DIED: September 23, 1943, London, England
IDENTIFICATION: English novelist and Hollywood film writer
SIGNIFICANCE: The suppression of Glyn's popular novel *Three Weeks* led to a U.S. court judgment that an immoral work was not entitled to copyright protection

Glyn published *Three Weeks* in 1907 in London. The novel's story about a young man's seduction by a sexually experienced and aggressive older woman (who was a member of the royal family) so shocked society that King Edward VII would not allow the book to be mentioned in his presence. By 1916, when the book's first inexpensive edition appeared, it had sold almost two million copies in the United States and the British Empire, despite frequent attempts to ban it. Glyn's stage adaptation was performed privately in 1908 but was denied a license for commercial production by Britain's Lord Chamberlain.

In 1915 Glyn brought suit for copyright infringement against a burlesque of her novel called *Pimple's Three Weeks*. The court ruled that immoral works did not have copyright protection and urged suppression of Glyn's novel. Glyn wrote the screenplay for the 1924 Hollywood film version; in England the original title of the novel was banned, so the film was released there as *The Romance of a Queen*. In 1932 censors in Ohio reportedly banned a Mickey Mouse cartoon that showed a cow reading the novel. In 1934 a proposed sound version starring Gloria Swanson was shelved as a result of censorship pressures.

See also Copyright law; Disney films; Examiner of plays; Film adaptation; Lord Chamberlain.

Goethe, Johann Wolfgang von

BORN: August 28, 1749, Frankfurt am Main, Saxony
DIED: March 22, 1832, Weimar, Saxe-Weimar-Eisenach
IDENTIFICATION: German writer, dramatist, scientist, and political administrator
SIGNIFICANCE: Arguably the greatest German writer, Goethe had some of his early works censored, and he occasionally advocated moderate censorship himself

Goethe lived through tumultuous times in politics and, consequently, in censorship. He had seen the coronation of Joseph II in 1764, deplored the French Revolution from afar in 1789, witnessed the end of the Holy Roman Empire in 1803, met Napoleon in 1808, heard of Napoleon's defeat in Leipzig in 1813, and witnessed the establishment of the German Confederation of thirty-nine states at the Congress of Vienna in 1815. Throughout Goethe's life censorship varied in extent and degree in each of the many German principalities, city states, and territories (in 1749 several hundred, and in 1832 thirty-nine).

When Napoleon summoned Goethe to Erfurt, Thuringia, in 1808, he wanted to meet the famous author of *The Sorrows of Young Werther* (1774). This epistolary novel, Goethe's first, describes a man madly in love with a woman whom he cannot marry because she is engaged to another man. Out of desperation, he eventually commits suicide. The novel was first published anonymously in Leipzig. Because of its sympathetic description of a suicide, the Roman Catholic as well as the Lutheran churches banned it in several states and cities, including Austria, Denmark, Milan, Hamburg, Dresden, and Leipzig. Despite the suppression of the novel it became the first post-Enlightenment best-seller of German literature throughout Europe.

Goethe's first play, *Götz from Berlichingen* (1774), experienced a similar reception. The knight Götz is portrayed as a rebel with a just cause. The play was censored mainly for its coarse and blasphemous language, characteristic of the *Sturm und Drang* movement. After it was published anonymously, it went through twelve editions in a single year—after its language was "amended." Goethe later repudiated the language of his *Sturm und Drang* works and wrote a new version of *Götz* when it was staged for the first time in 1804 in Weimar, where Goethe was stage director from 1791 to 1817. In Vienna the play could only be staged in censored versions. When Goethe's *Faust I* (1808) was performed for the first time—in honor of Goethe's eightieth birthday in 1829—in Braunschweig, Dresden, Leipzig, and Weimar, its vulgar language and offensive parts regarding religion had to be toned down.

Certain works by Goethe were censored for religious and moral reasons, for example, his *Venetian Epigrams* (1796) and some of the poems in his *Roman Elegies* (1795), which were considered too erotic. Goethe's poem "The Diary" could not be published in the nineteenth century without the risk of confiscation. This poem was even omitted from the "unabridged" Weimar edition of 133 volumes (1887-1919), and is absent from the heavily used modern fourteen-volume Hamburger edition (1948-1964).

Although some of Goethe's early writings, such as *Götz* and *Egmont* (1788) implied political positions that opposed the *ancien régime*, Goethe was a life-long supporter of enlightened feudalism who advocated not revolutionary but evolutionary change. He favored moderate reforms to enhance humanistic ideals. As a minister of the four small states of Saxony, he wrote two legal drafts (1799, 1816) in which he advocated paternalistic and moderate censorship. When in 1816 Saxony's constitution abolished censorship, and Professor Oken edited the journal *Isis* promoting liberal and constitutional rights of a democratic society, Goethe tried to mediate between "press anarchy" and "despotism of censorship." From Goethe's elitist point of view freedom of the press seemed "anarchic." At the same time his works promoted the ideal of a well-educated humanist, and therefore opposed "despotism."

See also Drama and theater; Germany; Heine, Heinrich; Schiller, Friedrich von.

Gogol, Nikolai Vasilyevich

BORN: March 31, 1809, Sorochintsy, Ukraine, Russia
DIED: March 4, 1852, Moscow, Russia
IDENTIFICATION: Russian novelist and short-story writer
SIGNIFICANCE: One of Russia's great authors during its literary "Golden Age," Gogol won both praise and criticism for his work

Born in the Ukrainian region of the Russian Empire, the youthful Gogol absorbed the images of country life and social classes which he later portrayed in his novels and short stories. Alexander Pushkin, prior to Gogol's early death, spoke highly of Gogol's potential as a writer. Gogol's brief career in teaching was a notable failure; however, residence in St. Petersburg and extensive travel in Europe broadened his knowledge and shaped his literary skills.

Despite Gogol's success with an early novel, his dramatic and florid style was not widely popular. His later novels and plays often endured public criticism. A hypochondriac, Gogol responded with periodic bouts of depression, and he occasionally destroyed his own manuscripts and contemplated suicide.

Gogol's writings included a variety of plots, themes, and styles ranging from comedic stories, such as *The Inspector-General* (1836), to pathos, as in "The Overcoat." *Dead Souls* (1842), his novel best known to twentieth century readers, deals with the institution of Russian serfdom. Gogol never thought of himself as a reformer, and his literary characterization of Russian society occasionally evoked opposition among his reform-minded contemporaries. His *Correspondence with Friends* (1847) portrayed serfdom and the class system sympathetically, leading other writers to accuse Gogol of supporting those repressive social conditions.

See also Dostoevski, Fyodor; Literature; Nicholas I; Russia.

Goldman, Emma

BORN: June 27, 1869, Kovno (now Kaunas), Lithuania
DIED: May 14, 1940, Toronto, Ontario, Canada
IDENTIFICATION: Russian American anarchist and social activist
SIGNIFICANCE: Goldman was stripped of U.S. citizenship and deported, in part because of her outspoken views on labor, free speech, women's rights, and military conscription

Goldman was one of the most controversial women in American public life from the late nineteenth century until her death. In pursuing her lifelong commitment to social advocacy, she repeatedly confronted formal and informal types of censorship. Throughout much of her adult life, she faced opposition and even persecution from both the government and the public because of her beliefs and practices.

Goldman emigrated to the United States in 1885, joining the anarchist movement in 1889. She adopted the anarchist traditions of a community of German-speaking immigrants in New York City. After a brief marriage, Goldman formed what was to be a lifelong relationship with the anarchist Alexander Berkman. Two events particularly affected the development of her ideology. During a labor strike in 1892, Goldman's circle of allies planned to initiate an anarchist uprising by assassinating an antilabor industrialist. This effort backfired miserably, generating a backlash in public opinion. She was later forced underground after President William McKinley was assassinated by an anarchist in 1901. Many by then viewed Goldman as a terrorist.

Upon her return to public life after McKinley's assassination, Goldman rejected her earlier, more violent beliefs and dedicated herself to fighting the evils of exploitation, which she saw as threats to individual freedom. Embarking on a passionate crusade, Goldman lectured, published the magazine *Mother Earth* with Alexander Berkman, and led demonstrations calling attention to such issues as labor rights, free speech, and access to birth control for women. She was critical of marriage and monogamy and was even an early voice for gay rights. Anarchism, for Goldman, was a means of resisting society's practices of coercion, domination, and hierarchy.

Such social advocacy and her hybrid philosophy of progressivism, libertarianism, and anarchism did not endear Goldman to authorities or to the general public. There were repeated attempts to silence her. In 1917, while protesting U.S. involvement in World War I and opposing the draft, she was arrested and imprisoned for two years. After her release in 1919, Goldman, Berkman, and 249 others were deported to the Soviet Union. Her deportation, however, did not stop her social activism. Disillusioned by Bolshevik repression, she left the Soviet Union in 1921. Unable to obtain an American visa, she subsequently lived in Stockholm, Berlin, and London, where she continued her fight for individual freedoms. After supporting anarchists during the Spanish Civil War, she spent the final years of her life in Toronto, assisting refugees fleeing World War II. Her autobiography, *Living My Life* (1931), provides a full account of her activities and beliefs.

See also Bakunin, Mikhail Aleksandrovich; Birth control education; Draft resistance; Harris, Frank; Immigration laws; Labor unions; Women; World War I.

Goldsmith, Oliver

BORN: November 10, 1728 or 1730, Pallas, County Langford(?), Ireland

DIED: April 4, 1774, London, England

IDENTIFICATION: Anglo-Irish novelist, playwright, poet, and hack writer

SIGNIFICANCE: An abridgment of Goldsmith's *History of England* was listed on the *Index Librorum Prohibitorum* in 1823 because it presented an unfavorable view of the Roman Catholic church

Goldsmith is best known for his novel *The Vicar of Wakefield* (1766), his play *She Stoops to Conquer* (1773), and his poem *The Deserted Village* (1770). It was, however, an abridged version of his *A History of England* (1764) that raised the ire of the Roman Catholic church. That abridgment—which contributed nothing to Goldsmith's literary reputation—was first published shortly after he died in 1774, and it was often revised and republished in Great Britain and North America during the eighteenth and nineteenth centuries. In 1823, an Italian translation of the text was listed on the *Index Librorum Prohibitorum* with the proviso *donec corrigatur* ("until it is corrected").

Goldsmith's negative remarks about the Catholic church at the time of the Reformation, were doubtless a primary reason for his book's condemnation. He wrote that the "vices and impositions of the church of Rome were now almost come to a head; and the increase of arts and learning among the laity . . . began to make them resist that power which was originally founded in deceit." The book also discusses how Pope Leo X's greed led to the hated practice of selling of indulgences, which were easily purchased "at taverns, brothels and gaming houses," and it emphasizes base financial squabbles among Catholic monastic orders. In Goldsmith's view, the Catholic church was petty and weak, and thus an easy mark for England's forceful and astute King Henry VIII. Goldsmith's account of Pope Innocent III's interdict against England in the reign of King John is also notable for its unflattering portrayal of Catholic leadership: "This instrument of Terror in the hands of the See of Rome was calculated to strike the senses, and to operate on the superstitious minds of the people, in the highest degree."

See also Henry VIII; *Index Librorum Prohibitorum*; Reformation, the; Sterne, Laurence; Vatican.

Gorbachev, Mikhail

BORN: March 2, 1931, Privalnoye, Soviet Union

IDENTIFICATION: Last leader of the Soviet Union

SIGNIFICANCE: Gorbachev's efforts to overturn decades of government secrecy helped to end communist rule and to dissolve the Soviet Union itself

In March, 1985, Gorbachev was named general secretary of the Soviet Union's Communist Party after the death of Konstantin Chernenko. Within weeks, he embarked on a campaign referred to as *glasnost*, or openness, by which he hoped to end the decades-long atmosphere of suspicion, secrecy, and fear. Another purpose behind this policy was to engage the support of the people for his economic reforms. The most logical and efficient way to bring his new programs to the citizenry was through the media. Gorbachev saw a vital need for poetry, novels, plays, movies, and television programs that would popularize and convey his programs to the Soviet people.

Gorbachev soon mandated lifting official bans on all outlawed books, poems, films, and plays. Books such as Boris

Pasternak's *Doctor Zhivago* (1985), Anatoli Rybakov's *Children of the Arbat* (1967), Vasili Grossman's *Life and Fate* (1985), and Alexander Solzhenitsyn's *Gulag Archipelago* (1978)—all of which had been published years before in the West—became available for the first time in the Soviet Union. Considered by many in the Soviet Union as the single most significant work symbolizing the end of an era of repression and the birth of a new age of intellectual and artistic freedom was the film *Repentance*. As a graphic, bitter denunciation of Joseph Stalin and his reign of terror, it marked the inauguration of an anti-Stalinist movement in literature, cinema, and historical works. Film archives were opened and thirty years of censored films were released.

Gorbachev also pushed to free the mass media from Party control and restraints. He encouraged open debate and criticism of the stagnation and corruption of the Soviet regime. To accomplish these goals, he allied himself with intellectuals without whom economic and political reforms would be impossible. Many of the writers and editors of the numerous papers and journals had been victims of Stalin's purges, or had been in self-imposed exile in Siberia prior to the Gorbachev era.

The news media would serve as his chief tool for exposing, describing, and criticizing problems in the Soviet Union, such as corrupt managers and officials, inefficient industry, apathy, drugs, AIDS, juvenile crime, alcoholism, slipshod workmanship, homelessness, gangs, and police brutality. *Pravda* and *Izvestia*, former Party and State newspapers, began to shatter old taboos with their reports on these subjects. *Novy Mir* became the most significant publication for the presentation of Gorbachev's views. It published *Doctor Zhivago* as well as works by Vladimir Nabokov and Joseph Brodsky for the first time in the Soviet Union. Novosti Press Agency published *Moscow News*, which printed numerous articles and exposés revealing the new, freer atmosphere.

Television also experienced a revolution. Many programs made their appearance covering news stories which would have previously been banned or censored. Reports of disasters such as the 1986 Chernobyl tragedy and the 1988 Armenian earthquake, and documentaries on the Soviet war in Afghanistan were shown with candor. Programs combining interviews, rock music, and the news became very popular.

Gorbachev ordered an end to the "blank spots" in Soviet history. Openness demanded rewriting history textbooks that were based on truth, not on Party distortions and gaps. All history examinations in the schools were canceled in 1988 while new books and tests could be written.

The line between official and unofficial art was diminished with *glasnost*. Considerable artwork proscribed during the earlier years was now exhibited and auctioned. Abstract art previously labeled as decadent was accepted and exhibited.

See also Communism; Historiography; Pasternak, Boris; Russia; Solzhenitsyn, Aleksandr; Soviet Union; Stalin, Joseph; TASS.

Gorky, Maxim

Born: March 28, 1868, Nizhni Novgorod, Russia
Died: June 18, 1936, Gorki, near Moscow, Russia
Identification: Russian writer and political activist
Significance: Gorky's life and literary work reveal deep sympathies for the oppressed and forgotten lower classes of Russia, and he believed V. I. Lenin's Bolshevik Party would serve the needs of the Russian people

Growing up in poverty, Aleksey Peshkov was forced to work from an early age. His interest in writing fortunately caught the eye of writers and publishers, who encouraged him during the 1890's. Leading literary figures of the period, including Anton Chekhov and Leo Tolstoy, praised his talent. Under the pseudonym of "Gorky," he wrote short stories, plays (notably *The Lower Depths*, 1902), and novels. By the early twentieth century his work was translated and became known in the West.

Gorky's reputation in literature was matched by his social activism and his criticisms of Russia's society and imperial political system. Czarist bureaucrats periodically kept him under surveillance, and he was briefly imprisoned on several occasions. Tolstoy's personal intercession with the authorities gained Gorky's release in one instance. Gorky was elected to the prestigious Russian Academy of Sciences in 1902, but academy officers overruled his selection because of his objectionable political reputation. Chekhov resigned from the academy in protest.

Gorky briefly participated in Russia's 1905 revolution, and once again was imprisoned. Widespread public support from the West helped gain his release. Admired as a champion of freedom and democracy, he traveled through Europe and the United States. A controversy occurred in New York in 1906, however, when it became known his female traveling companion was not his wife—from whom he had long been separated, but not divorced. This wounding of American moral sensibilities undercut the success of his visit, as Gorky had to cancel several public lectures and meetings with prominent figures, including President Theodore Roosevelt. American support for Russian reform suffered as a consequence. Gorky left the United States, angered by the public intrusion into his private life.

Later years saw Gorky participate in the revolutionary movement in Russia, including membership in the Bolshevik faction of the Social Democratic Party. The party took full advantage of having a literary figure of national reputation as one of its leading advocates. Gorky's hopes for the creation of a just society sustained his support of the Bolshevik movement, but he occasionally questioned V. I. Lenin's ruthless leadership during and after the 1917 revolution.

After the revolution Gorky sponsored and directed numerous social and cultural projects. He wished to protect and encourage Russia's vibrant and valuable culture. But he observed the pressures and restrictions imposed on both ordinary citizens and intellectuals under the new Soviet regime, as Bolshevism proved to be oppressive and destructive, even as it was taking Russia out of the czarist era. Gorky left the Soviet Union in 1921, but returned home in 1928.

Gorky spent his final years in the repressive cultural atmosphere of Joseph Stalin's dictatorship. He supported the theory of Socialist Realism in literature in the 1930's, with its sympathetic proletarian emphasis, and he directed the national writers' association. This organization, shaped by communist ideology, became notorious for its repression of literary independence. Gorky's death in 1936 raised suspicions of foul play at the hands of the secret police, but available evidence has not supported them.

See also Bulgakov, Mikhail Afanasyevich; Communism; Lenin, Vladimir Ilich; Literature; Mayakovsky, Vladimir; Socialist Realism; Soviet Union; Stalin, Joseph.

Gouzenko, Igor Sergeievich

BORN: 1917

DIED: June 29, 1982, Ottawa, Ontario, Canada

IDENTIFICATION: Soviet government intelligence officer

SIGNIFICANCE: After defecting to Canada, Gouzenko exposed the Soviet government's espionage network and had to be hidden for his own protection; revelations convinced U.S. and British leaders that more elaborate security measures were needed to protect atomic secrets

As the principal cipher clerk in the Soviet embassy in Ottawa, Canada, Gouzenko decoded all embassy cables and had access to the most sensitive secret intelligence. When he was informed that he was about to be recalled to Moscow, he decided to seek asylum in Canada, revealing to government officials his knowledge of extensive Soviet spy networks in Canada, the United States, and Great Britain.

Gouzenko's files proved that prominent scientists such as Klaus Fuchs and Alan Nunn May had divulged military secrets to the Soviets, much of it derived from infiltration of the Los Alamos, New Mexico, atomic bomb project. Eighteen persons were eventually brought to trial in Canada, and eight were sent to prison.

The Gouzenko case caused a public sensation in Canada, raising suspicions that Canadian, American, and British citizens had collaborated with Soviet agents. The specter of a real communist conspiracy convinced Western government leaders that they should strengthen their national security, which carefully controls and even censors the information it imparts to citizens and monitors suspected spies. Security agencies such as Britain's MI5 and MI6, and the U.S. Central Intelligence Agency, conducted internal investigations searching for "moles" (American and British spies in the employ of the Soviet Union), and censoring what the public could learn about the activities of security agencies.

Gouzenko himself had to live the rest of his life in seclusion, appearing in public only under the protection of a mask.

See also Canada; Canadian Access to Information Act; Central Intelligence Agency; Classification of information; Espionage; Nuclear research and testing; Official Secrets Act (Canada); Witnesses, protection of.

Graffiti

DEFINITION: Uninvited—and often unwelcome—writing and drawing on public surfaces, such as walls

SIGNIFICANCE: In some communities efforts to stop or remove graffiti have been called censorship

As a form of public art graffiti has existed for thousands of years, and can be found throughout the world. It has appeared in caves and pyramids and on vehicles, buildings, walls, and other surfaces. Often it is a form of cultural production reflecting the ideas, values, beliefs, and experiences of people and cultures. It frequently contains images and information regarding a social system and its relationship to specific cultural groups. Graffiti also can reflect the identity of individual artists. It can, accordingly, be positive to the extent that it affirms an artist's individuality or reflects the cultural identity of its creators as members of a particular community. Graffiti can either be socially approved or negatively sanctioned depending on its message and the elements used as well as the edifice on which it appears.

Modernism. Some observers have associated the gradual devaluation of graffiti with societal values related to capitalism. Accordingly, a greater emphasis on financial interests and materialism gave rise to the presentation and exhibition of art that increased its profitability as a commodity. Therefore, graffiti, with its focus on social values, became deemphasized. Graffiti or public art in its many forms became replaced with galleries and museums.

During the 1960's and 1970's murals were widely accepted and supported by the U.S. federal government. Governmental support of public art was evidenced by the Art-in-Architecture Program administered by the General Services Administration. The primary reason for the government's sponsorship of public art was related to the desire to place art in federal buildings. Consequently, the government adopted various art forms in its facilities such as murals, lightworks, kinetic art, and so forth. Much of the public art during the 1960's and 1970's reflected social issues related to the demand for social equality inherent in the Civil Rights movement, as well as other themes of social protest relative to the U.S. involvement in the Vietnam War. Other social issues reflected unity among diverse peoples and urban issues for which government intervention was sought. For example, in the 1960's African American artists painted a collage of portraits, photographs, and poems that featured African Americans in the areas of literature, music, sports, and politics. Public art—or graffiti that conforms to Western culture's definitions of suitability—is frequently funded by the government or receives support from individuals who reside within the community in which the graffiti is presented. When graffiti fails to engender social approval regarding its content, its medium, or its projected location, efforts may be undertaken to prevent its production.

Censorship. Public disapproval and censorship of graffiti is common, particularly within the inner cities of major metropolitan areas. Many people view graffiti that appears on public buildings, subways, bathroom stalls, and on billboards as inappropriate, unattractive, and unwarranted. When graffiti takes the form of angry insults, profanity, or social commentaries that challenge or fail to conform to social norms within the larger society, it is usually considered unacceptable.

Public and government opposition to graffiti increased greatly in the U.S. during the 1980's. The efforts of authorities in New York City to prevent graffiti received national attention. The local government in New York used what some

Community volunteers paint over graffiti in a Los Angeles, California, suburb in 1993. (AP/Wide World Photos)

considered extreme measures to prevent graffiti on public structures and transportation vehicles. Graffiti artists were subject to arrest and in some cases were chased by dogs. As legal sanctions and efforts to prevent graffiti artists from expressing themselves increased, they often developed ingenious and surreptitious methods of producing their work. Defenders of graffiti have charged that the notion that some forms of public art are socially acceptable while others are not is based on cultural value judgments. Such arguments raise the question of what groups' values should define acceptable public art in a given community.

Many graffiti artists live in inner-city communities, which are characterized by declining resources, substandard housing, poverty, and other forms of marginalization. The powerlessness of their existence and isolation from America's mainstream often means that they have limited opportunities to be included. It might therefore be argued that their graffiti represents significant forms of self-expression.

Graffiti or public art can be valuable to society by providing information expressing the collective and personal identities of various cultures. Graffiti can also inform the public of the status and experiences of peoples who are marginal to society.

—K. Sue Jewell

See also Art; Mural art; Wall posters.

BIBLIOGRAPHY

Volker Barthelmeh's *Street Murals* (New York: Alfred A. Knopf, 1982) presents a discussion and pictorial illustration of murals in the 1970's and 1980's in the United States. Yoko Clark and Chizu Hama's *California Murals* (Berkeley: Lancaster-Miller, 1979) presents murals produced in California. Eva Sperling Cockcroft and Holly Barnet-Sanchez's *Signs from the Heart: California Chicano Murals* (Albuquerque: University of New Mexico Press, 1993) examines the mural movement that began in the 1960's and that reflected the collective vision and experiences of Chicano artists. In *Public Art: New Directions* (New York: McGraw-Hill, 1981) Louis G. Redstone and Ruth R. Redstone discuss both public art and illustrated projects from the United States, Canada, and other countries. David Robinson's *Soho Walls: Beyond Graffiti* (New York: Thames and Hudson, 1990) contains many photographs of graffiti in New York City.

Grapes of Wrath, The

TYPE OF WORK: Book

PUBLISHED: 1939

AUTHOR: John Steinbeck (1902-1968)

SUBJECT MATTER: Novel about Oklahoma tenant farmers trekking to California during the Great Depression hoping to escape from their poverty, only to encounter degradation, dehumanization, and starvation

SIGNIFICANCE: This novel is one of the most widely suppressed and censored modern novels in American literature; many critics regard it as a social document instead of fiction

From the moment of its publication in 1939, no twentieth century American novel has provoked more controversy and criticism for its social philosophy, alleged atheistic beliefs,

Harsh depictions of rural poverty were among the reasons that conservative elements condemned John Steinbeck's The Grapes of Wrath. (Museum of Modern Art/Film Stills Archive)

and profane language than has John Steinbeck's *The Grapes of Wrath*.

Born in Salinas, California, in 1902, Steinbeck published his first novel, *Cup of Gold* in 1929. Many other novels followed, including *The Grapes of Wrath.* Many critics consider this his finest work; it won him the Pulitzer Prize in 1940. *The Grapes of Wrath* became an instant best-seller despite vehement attacks by critics, who were not limited to Californians and Oklahomans. Efforts by school boards from Kansas City, Kansas, to Buffalo, New York, to censor the book in public libraries on pornographic and political grounds were successful. Chambers of commerce and religious groups throughout the United States tried to prevent filming of the novel by producer Darryl F. Zanuck. Because of the intense furor, Zanuck sent a film crew to California to discover whether Steinbeck had exaggerated the plight of the migrants. What they discovered was worse than Steinbeck depicted, so they proceeded with the film—which later received seven Academy Award nominations.

However, Zanuck did alter certain parts of the novel, including the ending. Instead of having Rose of Sharon breast-feed a starving man after she delivered a stillborn child, the film ended with Ma Joad reaffirming the belief that common people would endure despite their hardships.

While *The Grapes of Wrath* was accused of exploiting the poor, using lewd and obscene language, and portraying life in a bestial, mean way, most criticism focused on two misconceptions: The novel's alleged espousal of atheism—largely through the character of Jim Casy—and its supposedly sympathetic view of communism. Such accusations were made by critics who misunderstood the two basic American concepts underlying the novel, Transcendentalism and Jeffersonian Agrarianism.

Steinbeck's characters of Jim Casy, Tom Joad, Ma Joad, and Rose of Sharon convey spiritual, rather than atheistic, attitudes toward life. Although Casy is a defrocked preacher, he believes in the universal presence of a deity in every facet of life and relies on his conscience to guide his behavior. In a Christ-like gesture, Casy sacrifices his life for the good of all displaced people. Tom Joad, too, sacrifices himself at the end of the novel for the same goal. The two main female characters exhibit the Christian qualities of self-sacrifice, uncompromising love, and strength in the face of tragedy.

Charges that the novel is sympathetic toward communism are equally unfounded. Its story calls for unity among migrant workers in order to preserve rather than restrict their rights. The collective efforts of the poor farmers against the power structure are based on pragmatic objectives, not Marxist concepts. Representing yeoman farmers in the Jeffersonian tradition, the migrant workers believe that working and owning the land gives meaning and purpose to their lives. Because of ideas such as these, *The Grapes of Wrath* remains a classic depiction of humanity's struggle against oppression.

See also Communism; Film censorship; Libraries, school; Literature; Steinbeck, John; *Uncle Tom's Cabin*.

Greek junta

Date: April 21, 1967-July 24, 1974

Place: Greece

Significance: The rule of the junta, with its policies of repression and censorship, tarnished Greece's democratic reputation

Since its independence in 1830 Greece has experienced incidents of censorship and abuse of human rights. War, enemy occupation, and civil unrest brought the country to its darkest hours between 1940 and 1952. Aware, however, of being the cradle of democracy, Greece has always valued basic freedoms, which the 1952 constitution guaranteed. It, therefore, came as a shock to many when on April 21, 1967, a military junta deposed the legitimate government.

Knowing they would face opposition, the colonels, as the leaders of the military junta were called because of their lower rank, instituted a repressive program of censorship and abuse of human rights, including torture and illegal confinement. All media, including the classical theater, were placed under strict censorship. Prominent civil servants were forced to resign and other civil servants required to take an oath of loyalty to the government; hundreds of senior military officers were forcibly retired; trade unions were restricted; gatherings by more than five persons were prohibited; thousands of persons were detained or imprisoned without trial; other prominent figures, including artists, were placed under house arrest. To facilitate their repressive program, the junta created a powerful secret police.

Late in 1967 King Constantine II attempted to dismiss the leaders of the junta but was himself forced into exile. The departure of the king strengthened the hand of Colonel George Papadopoulos, who emerged as the leader of the junta. He appointed a regent, declared himself prime minister, and continued the policy of censorship and human rights abuse. To appease public opinion, a new constitution, never ratified, was to go into effect in 1968, which it did not.

In 1969 the government moved against the judiciary, the military, academicians, and intellectuals. Twenty-one senior judges and public prosecutors, including the president of the Council of State, the country's highest judicial office, were removed from office. Academicians critical of the junta were dismissed and military deferment withdrawn from students suspected of disloyal activities. Papadopoulos, meanwhile, assumed the title of prime minister and regent.

In November, 1973, students of the Athens Polytechnic staged a sit-in protest strike. The government sent in the army with tanks to break the strike. In the ensuing confrontation ten students were killed and dozens wounded. It was the beginning of the end of the junta. Papadopoulos was replaced by the head of the secret police. Hoping to stabilize itself by successful military action, the junta interfered in Cyprus, an island they wished to join to Greece. The government of the island was to be replaced by one sympathetic to union. Turkey, to protect its minority, landed troops on Cyprus on July 20, 1974. Greek attempts to mobilize were a failure. On July 24, former prime minister Constantine Karamanlis was invited to return from exile and form a new government which brought the leaders of the junta to justice and restored democracy. In 1975 Greece was declared a republic.

See also Athens, ancient; Turkey.

Green Sheet, The

Type of work: Newsletter

First published: 1933

Author: Film Board of National Organizations

Subject matter: Monthly film ratings designed to help parents guide their children's viewing

Significance: In an effort to avoid outside censorship, the Motion Picture Producers and Distributors Association (MPPDA) underwrote this publication

Designed to guide parents as to which films should be viewed by children, *The Green Sheet* was a monthly newsletter that rated current films according to age groups. Established in 1933, the publication arrived at its findings through the opinions of a ten-member board, which consisted of various religious, special interest, educational, and film groups. Readership was limited and rarely exceeded thirty thousand people. Funding for the publication came from the film industry's MPPDA (later renamed the Motion Picture Association of America), which had been founded in the 1920's as a self-regulating association that deleted film material they thought offensive. Although the MPPDA underwrote *The Green Sheet*, it did not allow the newsletter's film ratings to appear in film advertisements.

Criticized for reviewing less than half of the films released in the United States each year, the newsletter expanded its coverage during the 1960's. Its reviews were originally restricted to domestic films, but after 1963 it began rating foreign films as well. As the publication included more titles it also became more stringent on what it regarded as acceptable for children.

See also Film censorship; Hays Code; Legion of Decency; Motion Picture Association of America.

Greer v. Spock

Court: U. S. Supreme Court

Date: March 24, 1976

Significance: This case upheld the principal that censorship rules on military bases can differ from those in public forums

Fort Dix, New Jersey, an army training facility, long operated under the exclusive jurisdiction of the federal government, which encompassed all state and county roads passing through the facility. Regulations promulgated by the base commander permitted free and open civilian access to certain areas of the base, but simultaneously prohibited distribution of literature without prior approval by military officials. The regulations also banned partisan political speeches and demonstrations anywhere on military property.

In 1972 Dr. Benjamin Spock, the famous pediatrician, author, and antiwar activist, was the left-leaning People's Party candidate for president of the United States. Together with his vice-presidential running mate, several political activists who had previously been evicted from the base for distributing unapproved political literature, and the candidates for president and vice-president of the Socialist Workers Party, Spock petitioned Fort Dix's commanding officers for permission to hold a political meeting on the base and to distribute campaign literature there. Pursuant to standing regulations, the base commander rejected the request and barred the previously evicted activists from re-entering the base. Spock and his cohort filed a lawsuit, seeking to enjoin enforcement of the regulations, alleging violations of the First and Fifth amendments to the U.S. Constitution. They were partially successful when an appeals court enjoined the military from enforcing the regulations to the extent that they prevented the four actual candidates (but not the accompanying activists) from making political speeches and distributing campaign leaflets in the parts of Fort Dix that were otherwise generally open to the public.

On appeal to the Supreme Court, Solicitor General Robert Bork (later an unsuccessful Supreme Court nominee) successfully argued the government's case. Justice Potter Stewart, writing for the majority on the divided court, reversed the appeals court, upholding the right of the military to enforce the regulations that censored political activity and speech on military bases. The Supreme Court ruled that although Fort Dix admitted the public to certain areas of the base, the base had neither abandoned nor ceded control to nonmilitary authorities.

The Court declared that the fundamental business of a military installation was to train soldiers, not to provide a censorship-free public forum. Although municipal streets and parks had "traditionally served as a place for free public assembly and communication of thoughts by private citizens" without government censorship, the Court expressed a fear that if it failed to uphold the military's authority to insulate itself from any appearance of endorsing partisan political causes, the American constitutional tradition of a politically neutral military establishment under civilian control could be undermined. A vigorous dissent, written by Justice William J. Brennan, Jr., and joined by Justice Thurgood Marshall argued that the military's training mission and the important principle of military neutrality could both be protected without such blanket prohibitions and censorship regulations.

See also First Amendment; Free speech; Leafletting; Military censorship; Political campaigning; Vietnam War.

Grenada, U.S. invasion of

Date: October 25-December 15, 1983

Place: Lesser Antilles, Caribbean

Significance: During this surprise invasion, U.S. military leaders kept the press out of Grenada, thus preventing independent news coverage of initial military operations

On October 25, 1983, approximately six thousand U.S. Marines and paratroopers invaded the tiny Caribbean island of Grenada on the orders of President Ronald Reagan. Hostilities ended ten days later, and U.S. combat troops were withdrawn by December 15, 1983. Military commanders, supported by the Reagan Administration, kept all news reporters out of Grenada during the first two days of military operations. Not surprisingly, representatives of the news media bitterly accused the president and the Pentagon of denying freedom of the press and encouraging censorship in the name of national security.

The military's contention that the exclusion of press representation during the initial fighting was motivated solely by concerns for the reporters' safety was promptly challenged. Journalists pointed out that they had always accepted the risks of war as part of their profession, citing the 146 war correspondents killed during World War II and the 53 correspondents killed in the Vietnam War. Management of the news by the Department of Defense was described as a military blackout. This implied that unsympathetic coverage of the war against Grenada should not be available to the American public or the U.S. Congress.

A long tradition of war reporting and the First Amendment's protection of the public's right to know dates back to the U.S. Civil War. In Grenada, however, the Pentagon chose to bar

This picture of U.S. armored personnel carriers rolling through Grenada's capital, St. George, was one of the first "pool" photographs released to the press after the American occupation began. (AP/Wide World Photos)

independent media access by not arranging transportation, allowing unrestricted movement among the troops, or providing communications facilities on the island until the invasion's success was achieved.

This type of censorship differed from that during the British-Argentine Falkland Islands War seven years earlier. In that conflict the British government provided journalists with access to warships, and gave a limited number of journalists access to the ground fighting, but it subjected their reports to official scrutiny, deletion, and revision. In Grenada the U.S. officials did not overtly censor the press; it simply did not bring reporters along during the initial fighting, thereby creating a news blackout. The important exceptions to the blackout were the Pentagon's official statements on the fighting, White House justifications of the invasion, and statements of other officials, who portrayed the "rescue mission" of American medical students and removal of Grenada's communist government in the best possible light.

The relationship between the U.S. press and the military establishment had deteriorated so greatly since the Vietnam War that in the eyes of leading military officers much of the press was viewed as motivated by malevolent intent and lacking any sympathy for a strong military. An attempt to reconcile the media and the press was made by the Sidle Commission report, August 23, 1984. It recommended that the media should be allowed to cover U.S. military operations to the maximum degree possible in the future. If only a few journalists could be accommodated, then "pool" reporters would be selected by the Pentagon who then would share their information with other journalists.

See also Civil War, U.S.; Falkland Islands War; Haiti; Military censorship; National security; Panama, U.S. invasion of; Right of reply; War.

Grosz, George

BORN: July 26, 1893, Berlin, Germany
DIED: July 6, 1959, West Berlin, West Germany
IDENTIFICATION: German graphic artist, painter, and author
SIGNIFICANCE: Noted for its unrelenting exposure of social ills and its scathing depictions of contemporary figures, Grosz's art was a major target of the Nazis' Degenerate Art Exhibition of 1937

Because of his father's business failures in Berlin, Grosz spent much of his early childhood in the Pomeranian town of Stolp, where he developed an intense love of the countryside and nature. After his father died in 1900, his mother moved the family to a working-class quarter of Berlin, but later returned to Stolp, where Grosz, a sensitive but audacious young man, was expelled from high school at the age of fifteen. Encouraged by a local art teacher, he painted and drew assiduously; within a year he obtained admission to the Royal Saxon Academy of Fine Arts at Dresden. In 1911 he returned to Berlin to study at the School of Applied Arts.

Grosz's first caricature appeared in 1910 in a weekly humorous supplement to a major Berlin daily newspaper. In the spring of 1913 he went to Paris and drew models at the Croquis Calarossi for about eight months. In November, 1914, he enlisted in the German army. Though World War I brought Grosz new subject matter for his uncompromisingly critical art, it also shook him to the core. He was temporarily discharged in May, 1915—ostensibly as a result of sinus surgery. He may have been on the verge of a breakdown, however, as he was admitted to a mental hospital in January, 1917. After four months his permanent discharge came through, and he was released. He published a collection of grotesque and darkly satirical drawings from the war that same year (*Klein Grosz-Mappe*), followed by the scathing *Face of the Ruling Class* in 1919. By then he was well on the way to becoming a famous social critic through his aggressive satire, and was a major avant-garde figure of the Weimar Republic period. He became known for his expressionistic portraits of vulgar prostitutes, satiated and parasitic industrialists, bloodstained military officers, and hypocrites of all sorts.

As an avowed leftist and erstwhile member of the Communist Party, Grosz was destined to attract the attention of the National Socialists, whom he quickly and rightly viewed as a serious threat to the Left. Grosz satirized Adolf Hitler and the Brownshirts in his drawings. His painting "Rabble Rouser" (1928) is both a universal allegory of demagoguery and a depiction specifically of the Nazi leader, complete with swastika and a paint pot at the central figure's feet, signifying the derisive epithet "housepainter" for Hitler's failed art career.

In June, 1932, Grosz went to the United States to teach at the Art Students League in New York City. He returned to Germany for a short time, but since he had come to be harassed by the Nazi paramilitary organization known as the SA (*Sturm Abteilung*), he decided to leave Germany for good in January, 1933—eighteen days before Hitler was named chancellor. He continued to publish satirical drawings of the Nazis, casting German fascism in terms of a visual allegory of Cain and Abel. In general, however, his work became less aggressively critical while he lived in America. Nazi persecution did not, however, relent while Grosz was living abroad. He continued to speak out, both verbally and through his art, against all attempts to suppress German art and artists, as well as against Nazi attempts to appropriate German artistic traditions for their own propaganda.

In 1937 Hitler's minister for propaganda, Joseph Goebbels, issued a decree requiring the "cleansing" of avant-garde paintings from German art museums. In the months that followed, more than sixteen thousand works were collected. The Nazis confiscated 285 works by Grosz, of which five oil paintings, two watercolors and thirteen graphic works were displayed in the infamous Degenerate Art Exhibition, which opened in July, 1937. The centerpiece of the Grosz collection in that exhibition was his 1927 portrait of the poet Max Hermann-Neisse, a diminutive seated figure that the Nazis labeled "loathsome subject matter" (Hermann-Neisse was a Jew who had emigrated in 1933). The Nazis also exhibited Grosz's well-known expressionist painting *Metropolis* (1916-1917), a violently red-toned, frenetic vision of city life.

In March, 1938, Grosz learned that his German citizenship was revoked and that his wife's remaining property had been confiscated. During that same year he was granted U.S. citizenship. World War II brought out something of the force of his earlier bitterness about Germany again, and his most famous picture of the period, *Cain* (1944), shows a shabby Hitler in Hell beside a mountain of skeletons.

Grosz published his first autobiographical book in 1946, titled *A Little Yes and a Big No*. Interestingly, his leftist sympathies did not get him into trouble in the United States, either before or after the war, in contrast to other German exiles in America, notably Bertolt Brecht, who had to appear before the House Committee on Un-American Activities in 1947. Nevertheless, Grosz was disillusioned in large measure with his experience in America, although he never really wanted to return to Germany. When he visited Europe in 1954 he was pleased to find interest in his work. His wife wanted to return to Germany for good, which the couple did in 1959. However, there was to be no happy ending; on July 6, within two months of his return home, a heavy drinker, Grosz choked to death after a night of excess.

See also Art; Brecht, Bertolt; Caricature; Degenerate Art Exhibition; Germany; National Socialism; Nolde, Emil; World War I.

Grove Press

FOUNDED: 1949

TYPE OF ORGANIZATION: American book publishing company

SIGNIFICANCE: Grove pioneered in the publishing of experimental, sexually explicit, and politically controversial books

From an obscure reprint house Grove Press grew into a major force in publishing. In the process it altered the moral and intellectual climate of the United States. The press published translations of European avant-garde writers and reprinted such erotic titles as Frank Harris' *My Life and Loves* (1922-1926), the anonymous *My Secret Life* (c. 1890), and D. H. Lawrence's *Lady Chatterley's Lover* (1928). Grove's publication of the latter title was the first unexpurgated edition of the novel in the United States. Copies were seized by the New York Post Office in 1959—an action that Grove and its owner Barney Rosset successfully challenged in court.

The company's publication of Henry Miller's *Tropic of Cancer* (published in France in 1934) resulted in years of legal action. The book was finally declared not obscene by the U.S. Supreme Court in 1964, but only after Grove had spent sizable sums on legal costs. The company subsequently published Miller's other major works, as well as William Burroughs' *Naked Lunch* (1959) and Hubert Selby's *Last Exit to Brooklyn* (1964).

Some of Grove's most controversial titles were political. For example, its publication of works by the Argentine-Cuban revolutionary leader Che Guevara led to the bombing of Grove's headquarters by anti-Castro Cubans in 1968—an action in which Grove charged Central Intelligence Agency involvement.

Grove also published the literary journal *Evergreen Review* from 1957 through 1973. It also distributed the films *I Am Curious—Yellow* (1967) and *Titicut Follies* (1969), both of which were targets of censors.

See also Cerf, Bennett; Harris, Frank; *I Am Curious—Yellow*; *Lady Chatterley's Lover*; *Last Exit to Brooklyn*; Lawrence, D. H.; Miller, Henry; *My Secret Life*; *Naked Lunch*; Postal regulations; *Titicut Follies*; *Tropic of Cancer*.

Grundy, Mrs.

DEFINITION: An offstage character in a play by Thomas Morton

SIGNIFICANCE: Since 1800, Mrs. Grundy has served as a symbol of prudishness, narrow-mindedness, and censoriousness

The best-known play by Thomas Morton (1764-1838) is *Speed the Plough*. Its title comes from a medieval greeting that marked the return to work after the festivities of Christmas. First performed in London in 1800, this play, which blends comedy and melodrama, remained popular for three decades. The play's most famous character, Mrs. Grundy, never appears on stage. Meanwhile, the sympathetic, if comic, farmer's wife Dame Ashfield continually weighs her own and her husband's actions and thoughts against the supposed opinion of Mrs. Grundy, a social superior whom she slightly envies, and measures their success against hers despite Farmer Ashfield's grumbling. Mrs. Grundy quickly became a popular term, used to personify the social and moral consensus of the community.

In 1872 Samuel Butler made "Ygrund" and her disciples, the Ygrundites, the principal religion of the newly discovered country in his novel *Erewhon*. For Butler, she is a kindly goddess, useful in fending off fanatics of all persuasions.

In 1988 David Mamet's Tony-winning *Speed-the-Plough* marked the stage debut of rock star Madonna. As does Morton's play, Mamet's drama deals with the work ethic. Mrs. Grundy is not a character in the play, but its main characters still measure themselves against offstage values, in Mamet's play those of Hollywood and its debased worship of money and success.

See also Community standards; Drama and theater; Fear; Madonna; Morality.

Guthrie, Woody

BORN: July 14, 1912, Okemah, Oklahoma

DIED: October 3, 1967, New York, New York

IDENTIFICATION: American folksinger, composer, and social critic

SIGNIFICANCE: Guthrie established the modern genre of the traveling folk poet while defending himself and his work from a variety of would-be censors

Among other things, Guthrie was a visionary, columnist, author, songwriter, hobo, and—possibly—communist. He was nearly impossible to categorize, being too liberal for the wealthy conservatives who generally controlled the print and electronic media, and too outspoken and undisciplined for the organized Left. Every form of institutionalized power with which he came into contact tried to censor or silence him, but Guthrie simply would not be censored or silenced.

Born into a poor rural family, Guthrie left home at age thirteen and supported himself by singing in brothels, saloons, migrant worker camps, and union halls, and he quickly learned to commiserate with and empathize for society's have-nots. As an untrained but talented musician, Guthrie searched in vain for a recording contract. When this was not forthcoming, he blamed unnamed "capitalists," who, he thought, were trying to suppress his songs—many of which dealt with what he saw as the abuse of entrenched authority. That Guthrie's music was controversial is irrefutable. His song, "Philadelphia Lawyer," for example, describes the murder of an attorney, and "Goin' down the Road Feelin' Bad" deals with the misery caused by the Depression. It was not just the content of his songs, however, that made him controversial. In the mid-1930's, the communist newspaper *The Daily Worker* began publishing a weekly column by Guthrie titled "Woody Sez." He seemed to many leftists to be a prime example of the socially aware working poor—a rural proletarian. He often wrote in non sequiturs, but his general tone was a relatively humorous diatribe against societal inequities. In 1940, without explanation, his column stopped appearing. In later years, he said that the communists dropped his column because he did not always adhere to the party line and had dared to criticize the Soviet Union. There was another possible explanation, however. Guthrie was then performing on a nationally broadcast radio program, *Back Where I Come From*, a popular program that had a difficult time attracting and keeping sponsors. As soon as Guthrie's column stopped appearing in *The Daily Worker*, the program's sponsorship problems disappeared, and Guthrie was able to keep his lucrative radio job.

Controversy and Guthrie were never apart for long. In 1949 he unsuccessfully tried to publish his rambling, sexually explicit autobiography. Guthrie believed that he was being censored again, but the publishing house said the work was too long and too prurient. Later that same year, Guthrie was convicted of sending obscene material through the U.S. mail and was sentenced to six months in prison as a result of a sexually explicit letter that he had written to an offended female acquaintance. He believed his legal problems were instigated by the House Committee on Un-American Activities, then meeting in Washington, D.C. He spent the last fifteen years of his life in and out of hospitals as he fought a losing battle with Huntington's Chorea.

Pictured here in 1943, Woody Guthrie always played a guitar labeled "This Machine Kills Fascists." (AP/Wide World Photos)

See also Baez, Joan; Communist Party of the U.S.A.; Faulk, John Henry; Folk music; House Committee on Un-American Activities; Postal regulations; Protest music; Radio; Recording industry; Seeger, Pete; Weavers, the.

H

"H-Bomb Secret, The"

Type of work: Magazine article
Published: 1979
Author: Howard Morland (1942-)
Subject matter: Description of how to construct and operate a hydrogen bomb
Significance: Publication of this article initiated a legal debate regarding governmental authority to classify information said to be vital to national security

Only a few times in U.S. history has the First Amendment's guarantee of free expression been weighed against the government's interest in classifying information prior to publication in order to protect national security. In 1979 the U.S. District Court for the Western District of Wisconsin faced this question when a small monthly magazine, *The Progressive*, scheduled for publication in its April issue an article by Howard Morland entitled, "The H-Bomb Secret: How We Got It—Why We're Telling It." Government officials sought to restrain publication of the article because it revealed restricted data regarding nuclear weapons production. Eventually the government dropped the case because the information in question had been published elsewhere, so the article was published in the November, 1979, issue of *The Progressive* as "The H-Bomb Secret: To Know How Is to Ask Why."

Background. The Atomic Energy Act of 1954 regulates all information relating to the design, manufacture, or utilization of atomic weapons and to the production or use of nuclear material. Such information is considered to be "born secret"—classified from the moment of its conception—and it can be declassified only by the relevant governing agency—in this case, the U.S. Department of Energy. Intentional disclosure can result in penalties as severe as capital punishment.

Morland sought to demonstrate that anyone with basic scientific understanding could unravel the mystery of the hydrogen bomb—in other words, that the "secret" was no secret at all. He also intended to stimulate public knowledge and debate regarding nuclear weapons. "Secrecy itself," Morland wrote in *The Progressive*, "especially the power of a few designated 'experts' to declare some topics off limits, contributes to a political climate in which the nuclear establishment can conduct business as usual, protecting and perpetuating the production of these horror weapons." Morland gathered material for his article from unclassified sources. Experts agreed that his information was accurate but disagreed in the matter of its potential to injure the United States. Government witnesses claimed that the article's publication would be unprecedented and could assist others in constructing a fusion bomb; defense witnesses argued that the information was already common knowledge among scientists and was readily available in the public domain.

The District Court's Rulings. On March 9, 1979, U.S. District Court Judge Robert W. Warren issued a temporary restraining order enjoining publication of Morland's article, and he moved for a hearing on the issuance of a preliminary injunction as soon as possible. He reflected, "I want to think a long, hard time before I'd give a hydrogen bomb to" a foreign dictator. On March 26 Warren ruled that a preliminary injunction would be issued despite Morland's free-speech claim. He recognized that "the question before the Court is a basic confrontation between the First Amendment right to freedom of the press and national security." He admitted that "a large, sophisticated industrial capability" and teams of "imaginative, resourceful scientists and technicians" are necessary to produce nuclear weapons, and that therefore his prior concerns regarding the possibility of a nuclear "giveaway" had been misplaced. Nevertheless, Warren endorsed the government's request for an injunction because "a mistake in ruling against the United States could pave the way for nuclear annihilation for us all." He apparently agreed with the government that "the danger lies in the exposition of certain concepts never heretofore disclosed in conjunction with one another." He was convinced that the defendants could sacrifice those parts of the article that the government had determined should be classified, without impeding their effort to enhance public understanding of nuclear weapons and to stimulate informed debate on national policy issues. He concluded that the need to protect the security of the nation outweighed the risk of infringing First Amendment rights.

Suppression of Information. As the trial unfolded, the government took unprecedented action in its zeal to classify information. Numerous briefs, affidavits, and exhibits were censored. When an investigator for the American Civil Liberties Union found highly technical reports describing hydrogen bombs publicly available at Los Alamos Scientific Laboratory, the government reclassified the documents and closed the library. Judge Warren responded to *The Progressive*'s request to lift the injunction by issuing an opinion that was itself classified and which the defendants were never permitted to read. The Department of Energy classified a letter written by physicists at the Argonne National Laboratory to Senator John Glenn, identifying public sources of information that revealed the alleged H-bomb secret. Seven newspapers subsequently published the letter. The department also classified a letter written by a concerned citizen, Charles Hansen, to Senator Charles Percy, summarizing technical information derived from public sources regarding the H-bomb. When the Hansen letter was published by one newspaper, several others threatened to do the same. In response, the government dropped its case and the U.S. Seventh Circuit Court of Appeals vacated the district court's injunction. The information was liberated from classification and *The Progressive* published Morland's article.

Aftermath. The government's exercise of its broad powers to classify public and private information at will refocused public attention on censorship concerns. Many critics argued that keeping basic scientific and mathematical theories and processes secret is impossible because the inventiveness of the human mind would always outstrip the power of the censor. The real issue, these critics concluded, was the Department of Energy's authority to withhold legitimate scientific information from the American people. Edward Cooperman of the University of California declared in his trial affidavit: "Governmental policy designed to preserve secrecy with respect to such matters not only is unsuccessful but inhibits research and obstructs the advancement of scientific knowledge." The *Charlotte Observer* noted: "The day when safety was guaranteed by secrecy is long past. . . . The nuclear threat doesn't come from magazines but from governments, including ours." The debate contrasted the government's authority to withhold information with the right of the press to disclose and the right of the people to know. Judge Warren offered his own contribution to that debate when he refused to vacate his opinion of March 26, 1979. "In view of the sparsity of opinions in this area, this Court believes that it is in the best interests of justice and furtherance of the development of the law that its opinions stand and be available for any Court that in the future might be presented with a similar issue." Warren's opinion survives; its potential to influence future judicial decisions when government censorship is challenged became a source of continuing concern among advocates of free expression. *—Richard A. Parker*

See also American Civil Liberties Union; Atomic Energy Act of 1954; Classification of information; Fear; Military censorship; National security; Nuclear research and testing; Prior restraint; Sedition.

BIBLIOGRAPHY

Perhaps the most coherent history of post-Civil War free-speech issues in the U.S. is Margaret A. Blanchard's *Revolutionary Sparks: Freedom of Expression in Modern America* (New York: Oxford University Press, 1992). Richard O. Curry has edited a series of provocative essays for those interested in the censorial authority of government in *Freedom at Risk: Secrecy, Censorship, and Repression in the 1980s* (Philadelphia: Temple University Press, 1988). Herbert N. Foerstel's *Secret Science: Federal Control of American Science and Technology* (Westport, Conn.: Praeger, 1993) analyzes persuasive arguments against scientific secrecy and governmental censorship in general and the attempted suppression of Morland's essay in particular. First Amendment theorist Franklyn S. Haiman, in *Speech and Law in a Free Society* (Chicago: University of Chicago Press, 1981), provides an enduring commentary on *The Progressive* case in his penetrating analysis of the consequences of government secrecy.

Hair

TYPE OF WORK: Musical play

FIRST PRODUCED: 1967

LYRICIST: Gerome Ragni (1942-1991) and James Rado (1939-)

COMPOSER: Galt MacDermot (1928-)

SUBJECT MATTER: Exuberant young American "hippies" express their feelings about the politics and culture of the 1960's

SIGNIFICANCE: *Hair* was censored in many cities for its nudity and its perceived disrespect to prevailing American values

Hair was both the first Broadway show to include total male and female nudity and one of the first to address the conflict between young counterculture rebels and the 1960's establishment. The show encountered such strong opposition in many cities that an extra scene was added in which actors disguised as policemen entered the auditorium and interrupted the performance by pretending to arrest audience members.

In Boston and Chattanooga local and state authorities succeeded in stopping the productions for a time, until the U.S. Supreme Court overruled these actions, citing the chilling effect on free expression that such bans would have. Outside the United States, reactions to *Hair* were mixed. In Mexico City, for example, the production was closed after a single performance, and non-Mexican cast members were expelled from the country. The play's premiere in London coincided with Parliament's abolition of the office of Lord Chamberlain—who had licensed stage plays in England—and passage of the 1968 Theatres Act, which limited criminal prosecution of dramatic works based on content. The musical also encountered controversial receptions in Japan, Argentina, Scandinavia, France, and Germany.

Hair's adaptation to the screen had to wait more than a decade. By the time that director Milos Forman's film version appeared in 1979, the nudity and subject matter of the original play had lost much of their shock value. Michael Weller's screenplay gave the film a new narrative storyline, built around a young Midwesterner (John Savage) who hangs out with a hippie band living in Central Park when he comes to Manhattan to be inducted into the army.

See also Chilling effect; Community standards; Courts and censorship law; Drama and theater; Lord Chamberlain; Nudity; *Oh, Calcutta!*; Theatres Act of 1968.

Haiti

DESCRIPTION: Caribbean nation that shares an island with the Dominican Republic

SIGNIFICANCE: In its nearly two centuries of independence, Haiti has had a series of dictatorial regimes that have ruthlessly suppressed dissent

Since Haiti won its independence from France in 1804, it has experienced chaos in the political arena. Between 1843 until 1915 alone, more than twenty-two presidents held office, replacing one another through coups and bloody civil wars. In 1915 U.S. troops occupied the island nation and remained there until 1934. After the U.S. forces left, a series of elected presidents ruled the country until 1957. That year saw François "Papa Doc" Duvalier assume the presidency. By manipulating the constitution, he had himself designated "president-for-life," establishing a dictatorship that he and his son controlled until the son was disposed in 1986.

During the 1960's the United States cut off foreign aid and military assistance to Haiti because of the regime's political repression, which Duvalier enforced with a brutal personal paramilitary force known as the Tontons Macoutes. Under

Haitians distribute pro-Jean-Bertrand Aristide literature as U.S. armored vehicles move through Port-au-Prince during the U.S. occupation of Haiti in 1994. (AP/Wide World Photos)

Duvalier, government censorship took various forms. All political opposition was outlawed. Independent newspapers, free speech, and group assembly were all forbidden under threats of arrest; even the death penalty was occasionally applied when the government suspected that treasonous ideas had been expressed. Duvalier held power over the impoverished country using the popular fear of Voodoo and black magic to keep people obedient.

Under the Carter and Reagan Administrations, the United States made human rights in Haiti an issue in the world's international agenda. In Haiti's first free elections in nearly four decades, in 1991, Haitians finally chose a president themselves—Jean-Bertrand Aristide. Shortly afterward, however, the army drove Aristide into exile and a new military regime took root under General Raoul Cédras.

After three years of international pressure on Cédras to allow Aristide to return, former U.S. president Jimmy Carter persuaded Cédras to step aside for Aristide. In September, 1994, twenty thousand U.S. troops landed in Haiti and reinstalled Aristide as president. With this new U.S. occupation questions on military censorship of the news media resurfaced. Fearing a return to the type of Vietnam War news coverage that might undermine U.S. troop morale and lose public support, the military closely controlled information made available to the press for reasons of national security.

See also Cuba; Grenada, U.S. invasion of; Military censorship; National security; News media censorship; Panama, U.S. invasion of; Police states; Vietnam War.

Halloween

DEFINITION: Secular holiday celebrated on October 31

SIGNIFICANCE: Some Christian Fundamentalist groups have tried to suppress Halloween believing that it promotes witchcraft and satanism

The Celtic festival of Samhain is probably the source of Halloween, as it is known in the United States. The Celts lived in Great Britain, Ireland, and northern France more than two thousand years ago. Honoring Samhain, the Lord of Death, the celebration marked the beginning of a season of cold, darkness, and decay, so it was naturally associated with death. The Celts believed that Samhain allowed the souls of the wicked who had died during the previous year to return to their earthly homes for this one evening.

The Druids, the priests and teachers of the Celts, ordered the people to extinguish their hearth fires, then built huge bonfires of oak branches, which they considered sacred. They burned animals, crops, and even human beings as sacrifices. Then, each family relit its hearth fire from the community bonfire. During this celebration, people wore costumes made from animal heads and skins, and told fortunes about the coming year by examining the remains of the animals that had been sacrificed.

Many Celtic customs survived even after the Celts became Christians. During the 1800's Roman Catholic churches established All Saints' Day on November 1. People then made the old pagan customs part of this Christian holy day. The Mass that was said on this day was called "Allhallowmas," and the eve before All Saints' Day became known as All Hallows' Eve, or Halloween.

Because many early American settlers had strict Protestant religious beliefs, Halloween celebrations did not become popular until Roman Catholic immigrants from Ireland and Scotland introduced their Halloween customs. Eventually, there was no clear distinction between sacred and secular in Halloween celebrations. Christian Fundamentalists believe that events linked to Halloween violate their rights. Some want to see it banned, especially from the schools because they believe it exposes children to the religion of Satan, and that notions about things such as witches, evil spirits, ghosts, demons, and vampires destroy children's minds. Halloween celebrations heighten awareness of the macabre and pique curiosity about the occult.

Supporters of Halloween celebrations, on the other hand, believe that its pagan history is irrelevant, and that it is a harmless, secular holiday for children. Debates about Halloween have created tensions in public schools, religious schools, churches, and day-care centers.

See also Books, children's; Education; Impressions reading series; Libraries, school; Occult; Parents' Alliance to Protect Our Children.

Hamling v. United States

COURT: U.S. Supreme Court

DATE: June 24, 1974

SIGNIFICANCE: This Supreme Court decision clarified the test for obscenity adopted in *Miller v. California* by ruling that distributors of obscene materials need not know that such materials are in fact obscene

During the early 1970's a small group of individuals and businesses mailed thousands of copies of a brochure advertising a book called *The Illustrated Presidential Report of the Commission on Obscenity and Pornography*—which was described as a companion to the official report of the President's Commission on Obscenity and Pornography. The illustrated report was essentially the same as its nonillustrated counterpart, with the addition of numerous photographs. The brochure itself contained graphic photographs of men and women engaged in a variety of heterosexual and homosexual acts. The distributors of the brochure were convicted of mailing and conspiring to mail obscene material in violation of a federal statute. Some of the defendants received prison sentences, others were fined.

The defendants appealed their convictions on several grounds. Between the time of their conviction and their appeal to the U.S. Supreme Court, the Court issued a decision in *Miller v. California* (1973) that reformulated the test for determining what constituted obscene material. Prior to the *Miller* decision, the test used for obscenity was one that the Court had articulated in *Memoirs v. Massachusetts* (1966). In that case, the Court held that in order for material to be deemed obscene, it must as a whole appeal to a prurient interest in sex. Further, it had to be patently offensive by affronting contemporary community standards relating to descriptions or representations of sexual matters. Finally, it had to be utterly without redeeming social value. In the *Hamling* case the Court concluded that the trial jury had not erred in finding the illustrated brochure obscene under the *Memoirs* test.

The Court reformulated its test for obscenity in its 1973 *Miller* decision, holding that material is obscene if the average person, applying contemporary community standards, would find that the work taken as a whole appeals to the prurient interest. It also had to depict or describe, in a patently offensive way, sexual conduct specifically described by applicable state law. Finally, the work, taken as a whole, had to lack serious literary, artistic, political, or scientific value. The defendants in the *Hamling* case argued that their convictions could not be upheld under the *Miller* test because the trial court had instructed their jury that the community standard against which its members should evaluate the allegedly obscene material was a national one. The Court refused to overturn the convictions on this ground because the instruction regarding the national standard was harmless error.

The defendants also argued that the federal statute under which they had been convicted was unconstitutionally vague because it did not give the same definition of obscenity as the *Miller* decision. However, the Court found that the statute did not need to follow the exact wording of the *Miller* decision and rejected that argument.

Finally, the defendants argued that the government should have been required to show that the defendants knew the materials were unlawfully obscene when they mailed them. The trial court had concluded that the jury must find only that the defendants knew the materials were mailed and knew the character and nature of the materials. The Supreme Court held that whether the defendants believed the materials to be obscene was not relevant. Hence, the Court affirmed the conviction of the defendants and in the process gave greater clarity to its *Miller* decision.

See also Courts and censorship law; *Miller v. California*; Obscenity: legal definitions; President's Commission on Obscenity and Pornography.

Handmaid's Tale, The

TYPE OF WORK: Book

PUBLISHED: 1985

AUTHOR: Margaret Atwood (1939-   )

Subject matter: In a future America which has become a Christian theocracy, the few women capable of becoming pregnant must bear children for infertile members of the ruling elite

Significance: Frequently compared to George Orwell's *Nineteen Eighty-Four* (1949) and Aldous Huxley's *Brave New World* (1932), *The Handmaid's Tale* projects a view of late twentieth century America that many conservative Christians find disturbing

Among the most frequently banned books of the 1990's, *The Handmaid's Tale* won Canada's most prestigious award for fiction, the Governor General's Literary Award. The novel is narrated by a woman known as Offred (Of Fred), a "Handmaid" to a Commander and the Commander's Wife in the fictional Republic of Gilead. As Offred describes events in her highly controlled life, she recalls times before religious fundamentalists assumed political control, a period when she was a wife, mother, and librarian.

Complaints about *The Handmaid's Tale*, which has been used in literature study at the high school level, have included objections to its allegedly despairing themes, depictions of women as sex objects, profanity, sexually explicit scenes, and anti-Christian themes.

See also Canada; Film adaptation; Huxley, Aldous; Libraries; Libraries, school; Orwell, George; Religion.

Harris, Frank

Born: February 14, 1856, County Galway, Ireland

Died: August 26, 1931, Nice, France

Identification: Irish editor, novelist, dramatist, and biographer

Significance: Harris is best known for his revealing multivolume autobiography, a sensational book banned in both Great Britain and the United States

H. L. Mencken described Frank Harris as "happily free from the vanity of modesty." Few who knew Harris would dispute that claim, and just as few who have read his controversial autobiography would attest to its factual accuracy. Harris spent much of his life constructing a persona. Although his birth date is variously recorded as 1854 and 1856, some scholars think he was born in 1855. It has been established convincingly that he was born in Galway, Ireland, although he at times claimed Tenby, Wales, as his birth place.

Educated at the University of Kansas, Harris spent a decade and a half as an editor—of the *Evening News* (1882-1886), *Fortnightly Review* (1886-1894), and *Saturday Review* (1894-1896). His writing career began in 1894 with the collection of *Elder Conklin, and Other Stories*. He also published five volumes of short stories, one play, four novels, three collections of essays, two volumes of literary criticism, a multi-volume autobiography as well as a fictionalized autobiography, and several biographical works, including the four-volume collection *Contemporary Portraits* (1915-1930).

Both as editor and author, Harris faced censorship throughout his life. He was a political activist who supported Oscar Wilde during the latter's trial on sodomy charges. He also wrote *The Bomb* (1908), a muckraking novel about the Haymarket Riots of 1886, and he came to the defense of anarchist Emma Goldman, whose trial he attended during the Red Scare of 1917. Harris was quick to take unpopular stands and did so with a vigor and single-mindedness that generally alienated rather than persuaded people.

Harris' best-known work is his notorious five-volume autobiography, *My Life and Loves* (1922-1926, 1958), which recounts his sexual exploits in such vivid detail that this sprawling work is still often classified as borderline pornography. Unable to find a publisher in England or the United States, Harris had the book printed in Germany and distributed early copies himself from his home in England.

Censors in England and the United States immediately seized the first volume of this book, which was already being pirated in foreign countries. Subsequent volumes suffered a similar fate, as the book was banned in the United States and Britain. In 1925, Harris' New York agent was tried and sent to the workhouse for importing a volume of *My Life and Loves* into the United States.

See also Biography; Book publishing; Goldman, Emma; Mencken, H. L.; Obscenity: sale and possession; Sex in the arts; Wilde, Oscar.

Hatch Act

Enacted: August 2, 1939

Place: United States (national)

Significance: Although designed to protect civil servants from being pressured into undertaking political activities by their superiors, this federal law has been attacked as a violation of the First Amendment rights of government employees

Officially titled "The Act to Prevent Pernicious Political Activities," the Hatch Act took its more common name from its chief sponsor, New Mexico senator Carl Hatch. The law was designed to ensure a politically neutral bureaucracy in the federal government, and it has been imitated in many state laws. It prohibited federal employees from participating in all partisan political activities except voting. Many federal employees have complained that the law violated their rights of free expression. In 1973, however, the U.S. Supreme Court refused to declare the act unconstitutional in *U.S. Civil Service Commission v. National Association of Letter Carriers*. The Court ruled that the law served the best interests of the country by ensuring that federal employment depended upon merit rather than politics.

In 1993 Congress passed, and President Bill Clinton signed into law, a revision of the Hatch Act. The new law permitted federal employees to express opinions about issues and candidates, to participate in campaigns during nonworking hours, to display political stickers and other campaign paraphernalia, to join and hold positions in political parties, and to campaign for or against constitutional amendments. However, the law also forbade federal employees from being candidates for public office, from using their official authority to interfere with or affect elections, from collecting political contributions from subordinate authorities, and from soliciting funds from any persons conducting business in federal offices.

See also Civil service; First Amendment.

Hate laws

DEFINITION: Laws outlawing speech and behavior expressing hatred of ethnic, religious, or other minority groups

SIGNIFICANCE: Some hate laws add penalties to crimes (such as assault) that are motivated by bigotry; others criminalize bigoted forms of expression

The first hate laws were enacted in the United States in the early 1980's. By 1995 all states but three and many cities had passed some kind of hate crime law. These laws are of three types: hate speech laws, which punish offensive speech; hate activity laws, which punish specific hate-motivated acts, such as desecration of a place of worship; and hate crime laws, which increase the punishment for criminal acts that are motivated by the victim's race, religion, or other group membership.

Hate Speech Laws. Hate speech laws have been enacted primarily by cities and towns rather than by states. They are very similar to campus speech codes, in that they punish certain types of offensive speech. The primary difference between campus speech codes and hate speech laws is that the penalties for violation of the campus codes are restricted to disciplinary actions by the schools; violations of hate speech laws, on the other hand, result in criminal penalties.

An example of a hate speech law is the ordinance enacted in St. Paul, Minnesota, in 1990. It read:

> Whoever places on public or private property a symbol, object, characterization or graffiti, including but not limited to, a burning cross or Nazi swastika, which one knows or has reasonable grounds to know arouses anger, alarm, or resentment in others on the basis of race, color, creed, religion, or gender commits disorderly conduct and shall be guilty of a misdemeanor.

In 1992 the U.S. Supreme Court declared St. Paul's hate speech law unconstitutional in the case *R.A.V. v. St. Paul*. In this case, which involved a young man who had burned a cross in the front yard of an African American family, the Court held that St. Paul's ordinance violated the First and Fourteenth Amendments to the U.S. Constitution. The justices disagreed as to why the ordinance was unconstitutional, but they all agreed that cross-burnings and other such displays are forms of expression, rather than mere conduct, which the Constitution does not protect. The Supreme Court clearly indicated that the defendant's actions had been offensive, yet they reiterated the Court's previous holdings that even extremely offensive expression is constitutionally protected. After the *R.A.V.* case, it became highly unlikely that hate speech regulations would pass, on challenge, constitutional muster.

Hate Activity Laws. Several states have enacted laws that prohibit specific activities frequently associated with hate. Wisconsin, for example, has a law that punishes the desecration of cemeteries and places of worship. Vermont prohibits the burning of religious symbols. Connecticut has a law against violating another person's rights while wearing a hood.

These laws have rarely been enforced or litigated. After the decision in the *R.A.V.* case it is likely that any of the laws that prohibit expression, rather than conduct, would be, if challenged, declared unconstitutional. Laws such as Vermont's, for example, which punish cross-burnings and similar activities, would not likely survive appeal to the Supreme Court.

Hate Crime Laws. Most hate crime laws in the United States are based on a model law proposed by the Anti-Defamation League of B'nai B'rith. These laws concern acts that are motivated by the victim's race, religion, national orientation, or other category. They often operate by increasing the punishment for the underlying criminal act. An assault, for example, might be raised from a second degree misdemeanor to a first degree misdemeanor. Therefore, these laws are frequently called "penalty enhancers."

Hate crime laws differ from hate speech laws in that they require more than just offensive expression. For people to be punished for hate crimes, they must commit some act or acts that would be otherwise considered criminal behavior. For example, people could not be prosecuted under a hate crime law merely because they called another person a racially derogatory name, or because they wore shirts containing offensive images, such as swastikas. People could, however, be punished if they trespassed on another person's property in order to burn a cross—in fact, the youth in the *R.A.V.* case was successfully prosecuted for this act under Minnesota's hate crime law—or if they punched another person because of that person's religion. Thus, while speech alone cannot be punished by hate crime laws, the offenders' speech is often used as evidence to prove that they were motivated by hate.

The groups that are protected by hate crime laws vary by jurisdiction. All laws prohibit crimes committed because of race, religion, and national origin. Most, but not all, laws also include crimes committed because of the victims' sexual orientation. A few laws also include gender, disability, age, veteran status, marital status, or political affiliation.

While opposition to hate crime laws has not been as strong

North Dakotans protest against hate crimes committed against Iranian residents of Fargo in late 1995. (AP/Wide World Photos)

as opposition to hate speech laws, many commentators have argued that hate crime laws are unconstitutional in that they punish thoughts, rather than just action. It has also been argued that these laws violate the U.S. Constitution because often the bulk of the evidence that is used when prosecuting people under these laws—and sometimes the only evidence—is the defendants' words or hate group membership. Both bigoted speech and hate group membership, however, are protected by the First Amendment, therefore leading to the argument that the defendant is being additionally punished for legal acts.

The Supreme Court ruled on the constitutionality of hate crime laws in the 1993 case of *Wisconsin v. Mitchell*. In this case, a young African American man urged his friends to attack a white youth who happened to be walking down the street. The youth was severely injured. The prosecution alleged that Mitchell's actions were motivated by racial animosity. Mitchell claimed that Wisconsin's hate crime law—which was very similar to most penalty enhancers—was unconstitutional because it interfered with his freedom of expression, and because it was too vague. The Supreme Court, in a unanimous opinion, disagreed. It found that the law was permissible because, unlike the St. Paul ordinance, it punished conduct, not expression. The offender's speech might have been used as evidence, but it was not the speech itself that was being punished, but rather his actions. The Court concluded that there were good reasons to punish hate-motivated crimes more severely than ordinary crimes, and that the law would still permit people to express bigoted views, so long as they do not act on them. The Court also held that the statute was clear and specific enough to permit ordinary people to understand and therefore was not too vague.

Some people have criticized the Court's decision in the Mitchell case and have argued that hate crime laws infringe upon the right to freedom of expression and of association. Others have expressed fears that hate laws will be used to silence outspoken leaders and others who challenge the status quo.

—*Phyllis B. Gerstenfeld*

See also Anti-Defamation League; Campus speech codes; First Amendment; Hate laws, Canadian; Offensive language; Race; Symbolic speech.

Bibliography

Works giving particularly good descriptions of the history of hate speech laws and of the differing points of view include Samuel Walker's *Hate Speech: The History of an American Controversy* (Lincoln: University of Nebraska Press, 1994) and Rita Kirk Whillock and David Slayden's *Hate Speech* (Thousand Oaks, Calif.: Sage Publications, 1995). A work offering a good international perspective on this subject is Sandra Colliver, ed., *Striking a Balance: Hate Speech, Freedom of Expression, and Non-Discrimination* (London: Article 19, International Centre Against Censorship, 1992). Susan Gellman has written an excellent article on the arguments concerning hate crime laws: "Sticks and Stones Can Put You in Jail, But Can Words Increase Your Sentence? Constitutional and Policy Dilemmas of Ethnic Intimidation Laws," *UCLA Law Review* 39 (1991), summarizes the legal complexities of hate crime laws. For ongoing evidence on hate crimes and hate crime laws, see the annual reports published by the Anti-Defamation League.

Hate laws, Canadian

Definition: Section of the Criminal Code of Canada placing restrictions on certain kinds of expression

Significance: This federal law has been used to prosecute persons accused of wilfully inciting hatred of identifiable groups, particularly Jews

Section 281.2 of the Criminal Code of Canada, which was passed in 1969, makes it a crime for anyone "who, by communicating statements in any public place, incites hatred against any identifiable group where such incitement is likely to lead to a breach of the peace." Since the law's enactment, there have been few prosecutions. Two cases, however, have earned considerable notoriety; both have involved charges of anti-Semitism.

During the mid 1980's, an Alberta social studies teacher named Jim Keegstra, was tried and convicted under the 1969 law for knowingly promoting hatred against Jews. What made Keegstra's case unique was that he regularly expressed his anti-Semitic views as part of the history lessons that he daily gave. Essays written by his students that were entered as evidence during his trial recounted bizarre anti-Semitic conspiracy theories surrounding famous historical events. Keegstra appealed his conviction, which was overturned in 1988. The province of Alberta's Court of Appeal ruled that section 281.2 was unconstitutional because its scope was too broad. The provincial government appealed the decision to the Supreme Court of Canada which, by a four-to-three vote, upheld the antihate laws on the grounds that even though the law did infringe on freedom of speech in Canada, such a restriction benefitted society. The court also reinstated Keegstra's conviction. The Alberta government tried him a second time and once again the former school teacher was convicted. For a second time, however, he appealed and in 1994 a higher court again overturned the conviction on a technicality. The province then appealed the case to the Supreme Court of Canada.

Ernst Zundel, a Toronto publisher, had a long career as an anti-Semitic propagandist before being charged in the early 1980's under the "false news" provision of the Criminal Code of Canada (section 177). This law, which dated back to the 1890's, made it illegal knowingly to publish false information in an effort to single out a particular group. Zundel was charged under this provision instead of section 281.2 because a survivor of the Holocaust swore out a complaint under the former. After a highly publicized trial, Zundel was convicted and sentenced to fifteen months in prison.

Zundel eventually launched an appeal of his conviction. The case slowly progressed through the Canadian legal system until reaching the Supreme Court of Canada in 1995. By another four-to-three vote the court quashed Zundel's conviction on the grounds that the "false news" law violated freedom of speech under Canada's Charter of Rights. Zundel celebrated briefly because in November, 1995, the same Holocaust survivor again swore out a charge against him. This time, however, it was under the previously upheld hate laws section of the criminal code.

See also Canada; Censorship; Criminal trials; Free speech; Hate laws; Holocaust, Jewish; Intellectual freedom.

Havel, Václav

BORN: October 5, 1936, Prague, Czechoslovakia
IDENTIFICATION: Czech author and politician
SIGNIFICANCE: A courageous dissident and important playwright, Havel became the first president of the postcommunist government of the Czech Republic

Havel grew up under the repressive communist regimes imposed on Czechoslovakia after the end of World War II. He was attracted to the avant garde theater, but communist authorities treated it as antisocial and subversive, so he always felt himself an outsider. Alienation became a theme of his earliest plays, *The Garden Party* (1963) and *The Memorandum* (1965). From 1969 through 1989 Havel was a subject of police persecution and was imprisoned several times for terms lasting from two days to nearly four years. By the mid-1970's, he was considered the leading Czech dissident, admired for his outspoken "Letter to Dr. Gustav Husak" (1975), then the country's leader.

A turning point in Havel's public fight against censorship was his founding, in 1976, of Charter 77, a Czechoslovakian civil rights movement. This bold group of writers and intellectuals were constantly harassed and incarcerated by a government determined to silence its opponents. Charter 77 was, in part, a response to the ruthless policies that followed the Soviet occupation of Czechoslovakia in 1968, bringing to an end Alexander Dubček's reform government, which had called for "communism with a human face." Havel and his supporters then embarked on a plan of keeping democratic values and aspirations alive at one of the bleakest points of their country's history.

Keeley Stanley, Mark Harelik, and Lillian Garrett in a scene from a 1989 California production of Václav Havel's play Temptation. (Jay Thompson, Mark Taper Forum)

Havel's imprisonment in January, 1989, provoked a mass revolt in Czechoslovakia, strongly supported by university students, and morally uplifted by Havel's dedication to a peaceful "velvet revolution." By late 1989 he headed an ad hoc political assembly, Civil Forum, and then became the country's president. His task then became the dismantling of more than forty years of communist censorship. After Czechoslovakia split into the Czech Republic and Slovakia, Havel became the former's first president in 1993.

Havel's essays and plays focus on how modern technology and ideology have become tools of enslavement. The materialist ideology of communism, which sought to deprive people of their spiritual or transcendental feelings, established a system of rigid control over human behavior. Havel's plays—sometimes set in the factories where he had performed menial jobs as part of his punishment—show how literally communist governments tried to subdue its intellectuals, forcing them into work that made it difficult, if not impossible, to think.

Havel's writing has counseled individual resistance to governments that seek to deprive people of their identities. Both his plays and his essays suggest that the correct response to censorship is accepting individual responsibility. Individual persons must assert their own values, even at the risk of imprisonment. The greatest danger for thinking persons is to give way to censorship, and to become indifferent or resigned. Havel's characters never lose their wit when confronting government censors, and never forsake a life of the mind that is the antidote to government propaganda and coercion.

See also Drama and theater; Helsinki Agreement; Intellectual freedom; Mandela, Nelson; Police states.

Hays Code

ENFORCED: July 1, 1934-1950's
PLACE: Los Angeles, California
SIGNIFICANCE: This industry production code dictated the content of American films for a quarter of a century

Almost since its beginnings with Thomas A. Edison's primitive kinetoscope, the American film industry has dealt with the specter of censorship. As the industry evolved from a sideshow attraction to a mainstream art form attracting millions of patrons and billions of dollars in revenue, religious groups, citizens' organizations, and governmental entities became increasingly concerned with controlling the content of what was shown to the public—particularly to young children. In its various changing forms the Hays Code was, for many years, the principal tool with which the industry policed itself to avoid being censored by outside organizations. It effectively controlled the content of mainstream American studio films through the mid-1950's.

Early History of Film Censorship. Many of the short films shown in early kinetoscope arcades contained nothing more than interesting current events of their day, such as the famous belly dance of Fatima, the sensation of the 1893 Chicago World's Fair. However, because the fully clothed Fatima's performance was thought too shocking for general audiences, New York censors simply blocked out the offending portions of Fatima's anatomy before allowing the film to be shown. This act began the history of film censorship.

As films grew longer and more complex, censorship efforts grew apace. The most often censored film of the early silent period—and perhaps the most censored film ever—was *The Birth of a Nation* (1915), which provoked a unanimous U.S. Supreme Court decision that motion pictures were "not to be regarded . . . as part of the press of the country or as organs of public opinion," but were instead to be classed with "the theater, the circus, and all other shows and spectacles." This decision effectively denied film producers an argument for protection under the First Amendment, thereby permitting all levels of government to censor or ban films at will.

Will H. Hays and the MPPDA. After World War I the content of American films grew increasingly sophisticated, risqué, hedonistic, and cynical—developments that attracted a growing chorus of criticism from outside the industry. Additionally, several prominent film personalities were involved in widely publicized scandals. In 1921 the popular comic actor Fatty Arbuckle was charged with murdering a young female actor. The following year the president of the Screen Directors Guild, William Desmond Taylor, was found murdered and revealed to have been part of a "love triangle." That same year Wallace Reid, a popular "All-American" screen idol died of a drug overdose.

Under the pressure of negative publicity caused by these scandals, more than thirty-five states and the federal government began considering film censorship laws. This prospect created a major crisis for the industry; that crisis was aggravated by the birth of national commercial radio broadcasting in 1922. Radio threatened to compete with films for the public's time and attention. Steep declines in film attendance in 1922 made the studios anxious to calm public opinion about the "perverted" nature of Hollywood films and filmmakers.

Hoping to stave off outside censorship, leaders of the film industry formed their own organization in March, 1922. Ostensibly designed to control film content, the new Motion Picture Producers and Distributors of America (MPPDA) was headed by Will H. Hays, a noted Indiana conservative who had been postmaster general during the Harding Administration. The Hays Office, as the MPPDA came to be called, developed an initial "Code of Purity" to govern film content that prohibited depictions of certain specific sexual and violent acts, and listed many other acts about which filmmakers were cautioned to "exercise extreme care." (This latter list became informally known as the "Don'ts and Be Carefuls.") The Hays Office also championed the concept of "compensating values," whereby vice (such as murder) could be portrayed, but only if it was properly punished by the end of the film.

A refinement of the industry's original code came in 1930 with the "Code to Maintain Social and Community Values." It, like its predecessor, was voluntary. Because the Hays Office had no powers of enforcement, it engaged in little real censorship. It served mainly as a public relations tool, used by film producers to deflect threats of outside censorship, to manage industry news, and to calm public fears about film content.

The Coming of Sound Films. With the MPPDA as an effective news management tool, film production was barely affected by censorship throughout the 1920's; however, a major change took place in 1927 with the introduction of sound to films. The coming of sound compelled two changes in the film industry that affected censorship: the institutionalization of the studio system and the increasingly violent content of mainstream films. With an entrenched production system, film content came to be more uniform, and the productions veered sharply toward subject matter that best exploited the possibilities of dialogue and sound effects. Musicals and gangster films were new genres that won instant and enduring popularity. At the same time, however, public fears about the effects of films started growing.

In 1928 a study commissioned by a citizen group called the Motion Picture Research Council assessed the impact of film on American youth. Over the next four years the council produced several volumes of findings—all of which indicated that young people were being adversely affected by the values and morals they observed on the screen. Henry James Forman summarized these findings in *Our Movie Made Children* (1933), a book that shocked the country and raised fresh cries for tough censorship. Alarmed film producers were also concerned about the substantial drop in revenue that occurred in 1933—an apparently delayed effect of the Great Depression.

In April, 1934, American bishops of the Roman Catholic church formed the Legion of Decency and called for boycotts of films deemed "indecent" by their church. With the rising storm of protest throughout the country, the film producers were ready to take drastic steps to ensure the profitable continuation of the film medium with American audiences.

Joseph I. Breen and the Production Code. In response to public pressure, Will Hays created the Production Code Administration (PCA) in 1934, placing it under the direction of a prominent Catholic layman, Joseph I. Breen. Along with Father Daniel A. Lord, a Jesuit priest, and Martin Quigley, a Catholic publisher, Breen created the film code that would govern film content for decades. The many things that the code forbade to be shown included "scenes of passion," "excessive or lustful kissing," drunkenness, aberrant sexuality, rape, seduction, cruelty to animals or children, and surgery—especially surgery relating to childbirth. The code also banned even mildly profane words—such as "nuts" and "cripes"—and directed that the sanctity of the home and marriage must be upheld at all times.

In a move designed to target the flourishing gangster film genre, the code's proscriptions on depictions of crime and violence were especially severe. Weapons such as machine guns could not be shown; details of crimes and discussions of crime or weapons were not permitted; police officers were never to be shown killed by criminals; and if any criminal behavior was depicted in a film, it had to punished within the same film.

Unlike earlier incarnations of film production codes, the 1934 code contained enforcement provisions. Scripts had to be

All ten Hays Code prohibitions listed under "Thou Shalt Not" are violated in this tableau staged by Paramount Pictures photographer Whitey Schafter in 1945. (UPI/Corbis-Bettmann)

submitted for PCA approval at every level of production: from purchasing rights to the final cut. Rewrites were approved throughout the production process; scripts either were altered to meet PCA requests for changes, or were scrapped altogether. No studio belonging to the MPPDA could distribute or release a film without Breen's endorsement in the form of a PCA seal of approval. Failure to comply could be punished by twenty-five-thousand-dollar fines—an inducement so strong that no fine was ever levied during the MPPDA's entire history.

Conclusion. Although the Hays Code was later thought by many to have retarded the development of the American film industry through its severe restrictions on content, the fact that it arose at a critical moment in the industry's history helped to ensure the industry's survival by reassuring a worried public that their families could view motion pictures without having to worry about offensive content. By the time the Supreme Court's *Burstyn v. McCaffrey* decision extended First Amendment protections to films in 1952, the public's increasing sophistication, as well as the film industry's solid economic foundations, had eliminated the political need for the Production Code. —*Vicki A. Sanders*

See also Film censorship; Legion of Decency; Motion Picture Association of America.

BIBLIOGRAPHY

Edward de Grazia and Roger K. Newman's *Banned Films: Movies, Censors and the First Amendment* (New York: R. R. Bowker, 1982) gives an overview of the development of film censorship, with detailed discussions of more than 120 films and a list of important court cases. De Grazia's *Censorship Landmarks* (New York: R. R. Bowker, 1969) is a thorough rendering of law-making cases regarding censorship in all media, including film. David A. Cook's *A History of Narrative Film* (2d ed. New York: W. W. Norton, 1990) provides a succinct explanation of the economic and social conditions that led to the hiring of Will Hays and the development of the Production Code, as well as the circumstances surrounding the changes in the code's content and enforcement. Gerald Gardner's *The Censorship Papers: Movie Censorship Letters from the Hays Office, 1934-1968* (New York: Dodd, Mead, 1987) provides examples of letters from censors in the Hays Office to producers detailing reasons why particular films were deemed unacceptable under the Production Code. Finally, Gabe Essoe's *The Book of Movie Lists* (Westport, Conn.: Arlington House, 1981) provides a complete listing of the early code's three main principles, eleven "don'ts," and twenty-five "be carefuls."

Hazelwood School District v. Kuhlmeier

COURT: U.S. Supreme Court

DECIDED: January 13, 1988

SIGNIFICANCE: The Hazelwood decision, giving school administrators the power of prior restraint censorship, reversed a long-time trend of First Amendment support for freedom of expression on high school campuses

This case involved the direct censorship of a school newspaper, the *Spectrum*, at East Hazelwood High School near St. Louis, Missouri, in 1983. The school's principal removed two pages he considered inappropriate from the newspaper prior to its distribution. The pages contained articles about teenage pregnancy and the impact of divorce on children. None of the students quoted in the two articles was identified.

The principal's censorship of the newspaper was upheld by a federal district court but overturned by a court of appeals. The appellate court decision was then reversed by the U.S. Supreme Court in January, 1988, when it ruled that the censorship was permissible under the First Amendment. The Supreme Court's ruling stunned First Amendment supporters, for it reversed a long-time trend of First Amendment support for freedom of expression issues on high school campuses. Further, it joined the Pentagon Papers case and *The Progressive*'s "H-bomb" case as a classic example of a particularly onerous form of censorship by prior restraint.

In writing for the majority of the Court in the 5-3 decision, Justice Byron White said: "We hold that educators do not offend the First Amendment by exercising editorial control over the style and content of student speech in school-sponsored expressive activities so long as their actions are reasonably related to legitimate pedagogical concerns." The ruling opened the door for widespread censorship by giving administrators the power to censor student publications and other school-sponsored activities, such as drama productions, in advance. The decision also contradicted the earlier landmark ruling in *Tinker v. Des Moines Independent School District* (1969), which had permitted campus censorship only if it served to protect the rights of other students or to quell a threatened campus disruption—neither of which was the case with *Hazelwood*.

Justice William J. Brennan, Jr., wrote the dissenting opinion, in which he and two other justices condemned the message by the court's majority: "Instead of teaching children to respect the diversity of ideas that is fundamental to the American system . . . the Court today teaches youth to discount important principles of our government as mere platitudes."

If the intent of the 1988 *Hazelwood* ruling was to intimidate student journalists, it appears to have succeeded. An analysis of high school journalism by the Freedom Forum in 1994 reported that 70 percent of 270 high school newspaper advisers admitted that school principals had rejected newspaper articles or required changes. In 1995 the Student Press Law Center reported that many student journalists "harbor feelings of anger or confusion" when they're not permitted to write about issues they feel are important. In many cases, as the censorship becomes routine, such feelings are replaced by indifference.

See also Birth control education; "H-Bomb Secret, The"; Newspapers, student; *Pentagon Papers, The*; Prior restraint; School dress codes.

Health epidemic news

Definition: Media reports of outbreaks of disease and other public health problems

Significance: Although news coverage of public health problems has generally been free of censorship, efforts to educate the public about prevention of sexually transmitted diseases have consistently been censored

News reports of diseases have usually been relatively free from censorship compared to more controversial topics. Exceptions have occurred, however, during wartime. In World War I, for example, the U.S. government censored news of the extent to which American troops were succumbing to the devastating influenza pandemic of 1918. The most commonly censored news reports of health epidemics have involved sexually transmitted diseases (STDs), especially syphilis, gonorrhea, and AIDS (acquired immunodeficiency syndrome).

The first important discussion of STDs in the popular press was published in September, 1908, in *Ladies' Home Journal*,

Schoolchildren line up to be vaccinated in 1910—two years before the United States created the Public Health Service. (National Archives)

in which editor Edward Bok discussed "diseases of immorality." Bok later claimed to have lost seventy-five thousand subscribers because of his article. The term "syphilis" first appeared in a nonmedical publication in the June, 1910, issue of *Popular Science Monthly*. Despite this openness, not all reports of STDs escaped censorship. In 1912 the U.S. Post Office confiscated copies of Margaret Sanger's pamphlet *What Every Girl Should Know* (1912) under the Comstock Act of 1873, which banned transporting "obscene" materials through the mail. Sanger's pamphlet was seized because it mentioned syphilis and gonorrhea. During World War I a U.S. War Department commission on training camps produced the film *Fit to Fight, Fit to Win* (1918), which depicted soldiers contracting gonorrhea and syphilis from prostitutes. In 1919 the New York State Board of Censors declared the army film obscene.

Broadcast media have frequently censored reports of STDs. On November 19, 1934, for example, Thomas Parran, Jr., the New York State health commissioner, canceled his scheduled radio speech on the subject on the Columbia Broadcasting System (CBS) network because CBS had refused to let him mention syphilis and gonorrhea by name. In 1964 the National Broadcasting Company (NBC) network abandoned plans to produce a television drama about STDs because it would not have been approved by the network's own censors

In the 1980's AIDS displaced syphilis and gonorrhea as the most important STD in censored media reports. During the early years of the growing AIDS epidemic news coverage was rare. This was partly due to the fact that the disease then seemed to be limited to male homosexuals, intravenous drug abusers, foreign immigrants, and other categories of people outside the mainstream. News coverage of AIDs increased greatly when it later became clear that other people were also at risk. Nevertheless, newspaper and television news reports censored explicit information of how the disease was being spread by using vague terms such as "contact" instead of explicit explanations of what kinds of contact actually spread the disease. This inaccuracy did little to calm fears about the new disease.

U.S. Surgeon General C. Everett Koop encouraged the use of frank language in discussion of AIDS, but the media were slow to respond to his lead. In 1984 the copy desk of *The New York Times* censored a news story by reporter Katherine Bishop that described in detail the kinds of sex practices that would prevent spreading AIDS. It was not until February 12, 1986, in an article by health columnist Jane E. Brody, that these techniques were openly discussed in *The New York Times*.

Most governments around the world have remained reluctant to inform their citizens about AIDS prevention. A study of public service announcements in North America and Europe showed that three out of the five announcements judged most effective had been rejected for public broadcast.

See also Alcoholic beverages; Automobile safety news; Birth control education; Medical research; News media censorship; Nuclear research and testing; Postal regulations; Project Censored; Sanger, Margaret; Smoking; Toxic waste news.

Hearst, William Randolph

BORN: April 29, 1863, San Francisco, California
DIED: August 14, 1951, Beverly Hills, California
IDENTIFICATION: American newspaper publisher
SIGNIFICANCE: Hearst built the failing *San Francisco Examiner* newspaper into a chain that came to dominate journalism in the United States, using a technique known as "yellow journalism"

Hearst, son of silver baron and U.S. senator George Hearst, grew up in wealth and opulence. Expelled from Harvard, he asked his father to give him the *San Francisco Examiner* as a business opportunity, and transformed the *Examiner* into a sensationalizing, mass-appeal newspaper. Always on the alert for stories that stimulated readers with innuendo and emotional titillation, Hearst increased the entertainment content of his newspapers by adding graphic illustrations, peep-show photography, cartoons, comic strips, and such features as Robert Ripley's "Believe It or Not." Sensational human-interest stories were printed in bold type, front page.

Hearst played a prominent role in the outbreak of the Spanish-American War. During the Cuban resistance to Spanish rule, he used Evangelina Cisneros, an eighteen-year-old imprisoned by the Spanish in Cuba, to create a heroine known as "the Flower of Cuba." Hearst bribed Spanish guards to "rescue" Cisneros, and he brought her to the U.S. After the sinking of the battleship *Maine* in Havana Harbor, Hearst's newspapers accused the Spanish of treachery, fanning the fires of war that finally led to a U.S. war on the Spanish Empire.

By the 1930's, Hearst's publishing empire included twenty-six dailies in eighteen cities, covering 14 percent of the daily U.S. circulation and 23 percent of all Sunday deliveries. His strongest papers were in San Francisco and Los Angeles, but he also controlled a significant share of the markets in Boston, Washington, Chicago, Detroit, and New York.

In his early years, Hearst saw himself as a progressive, championing municipal reform and challenging the monopolistic practices of the Southern Pacific Railroad. However, during the Depression he became a reactionary anticommunist, using his newspapers to accuse college professors of leftist sympathies and to attack officials of President Franklin D. Roosevelt's administration. He enjoyed manipulating public opinion and would twist stories to fit his political opinions. Using his personal views and prejudices, he exercised daily control over the content of the stories covered by his newspaper empire. During the 1934 general strike in San Francisco, for example, he demonized the union leadership, whom he called communist revolutionaries, inciting vigilante attacks. He fired the editor of *The New York Daily Mirror*, Emile Gaureau, in 1935 for publishing a book that Hearst saw as favorable to the Soviet Union. Hearst regarded Nazism as an anticommunist movement, and although he claimed to favor U.S. democracy, his wire service was the main North American conduit for the Nazi regime, publishing numerous news releases, as well as a series of articles by Hermann Göring.

Hearst believed that rich men earned their great wealth. He lived flamboyantly, spending millions of dollars on castles and mansions all over the world. His practice of sensationalistic reporting has since become, for better or worse, a staple of journalism in the United States.

See also *Citizen Kane*; Newspapers; Pulitzer, Joseph; *Sapho*; Spanish-American War; West, Mae.

Heine, Heinrich

BORN: December 13, 1797, Düsseldorf, Germany
DIED: February 17, 1856, Paris, France
IDENTIFICATION: German poet, author, and journalist
SIGNIFICANCE: Heine was the most prominent member of a group of young German authors who opposed the repressive governments of the Metternich era; his writings were censored during his lifetime and burned and banned by the National Socialist regime during the twentieth century

Heine was the oldest son of a Jewish merchant and a mother from a respected academic family. In 1825 he received a doctorate in law, one of the two German professions legally open to Jews—the other was medicine. It was mainly because of such discrimination that Heine converted to Christianity in 1825 and changed his first name from Harry to Heinrich. In 1831 he left Germany, mainly for political reasons, and settled in Paris, where he pursued his preferred career as a poet, journalist, and essayist, but he continued to write in German and for a German audience. From the 1840's on he suffered from the paralysis which rendered him completely bedridden after 1848.

Heine's prose and journalistic articles—even his popular poetry—represent a prime example of censorship in Germany in the first half of the nineteenth century, for virtually every one of his texts was censored in one way or another. From the 1830's on he was the most prominent author of the Young Germany movement, which vigorously opposed the political repression of the Metternich era (1815-1848). After the Congress of Vienna (1815) the Austrian chancellor Clemens von Metternich became the most influential figure of the newly founded German Confederation, a league of thirty-nine German states dominated by Prussia and Austria. In 1819 Metternich persuaded the confederation to sign the Karlsbad Decrees, which required that every book of less than 320 pages be subject to censorship prior to publication. (It was assumed that longer books would interest only the educated class and therefore not threaten the government.) Moreover, each of the thirty-nine confederation members could determine the extent of censorship to be enforced. Consequently, Heine's exclusive publisher, Campe in Hamburg, followed two strategies: he tried to publish Heine's works in one of the more liberal states; then he distributed and sold them from there. He also asked Heine to pad his texts so that they could avoid censorship by being published in larger books. Even so, there was no guarantee that Heine's books when printed would be distributed, because the Karlsbad Decrees also stipulated that books could be confiscated and banned after publication.

Prussia was particularly harsh on Heine's work. In addition to this double censorship of books, the Karlsbad Decrees also prohibited newspapers and journals from printing criticism of dynasties, the nobility, the government, the military, Christianity, and "morality" in order to silence Metternich's opponents. Thus Heine, who served as a foreign correspondent from Paris for the prestigious German daily the *Augsburger Allgemeine* saw his articles censored on a regular basis.

In 1835 the legislative assembly of the German Confederation banned all books by authors of the Young Germany movement, including specifically those by Heine, but could not stop Heine from criticizing the repressive measures by the governments in Germany, although he was never as radical as Karl Marx, whom he met in Paris in 1843. Ironically, Heine became famous because of censorship, particularly after he wrote a political cycle of poems entitled *Germany. A Winter's Tale* in 1844 that was immediately banned throughout the confederation. Heine's style—indirect, witty, ironic, and often polemical—reveals constant awareness that his works would be censored. This explains why, when censorship eased briefly after the Revolution of 1848, he wrote in a letter: "How can anyone who has always lived under censorship write without being subjected to censorship?"

Heine's writings were again banned and also burned in Germany during the Nazi years, not only because he was a Jewish author, but also because of his advocacy of democracy. Works such as *Die Lorelei* that were so popular they could not effectively be banned were listed as "Anonymous" by the Nazis.

See also Book burning; Germany; Goethe, Johann Wolfgang von; Judaism; Marx, Karl; National Socialism.

Helms, Jesse Alexander

BORN: October 18, 1921, Monroe, North Carolina
IDENTIFICATION: American politician
SIGNIFICANCE: Helms has sought to restrict public funding of the arts by creating grant guidelines aimed at eliminating controversial awards

As a senator from North Carolina, Helms has consistently favored legislation to restrict arts award grants. A modern-day Anthony Comstock, he believes it his Christian duty to fight pornography and religious blasphemy. In the late 1980's and early 1990's he led congressional attempts to suppress the work of artists, photographers, and performance artists. In 1984 he was instrumental in having obscenity added as a predicate act under a federal law that would require book and video store owners convicted of selling two or three adult books or videotapes to forfeit their entire inventories.

In 1989 Helms was involved in two major campaigns to clean up the art world. These campaigns involved works by Andres Serrano and Robert Mapplethorpe that appeared in exhibitions funded by the National Endowment for the Arts (NEA). Helms singled out their work to advocate legislation aimed at denying federal grants to arts projects and exhibits deemed to be offensive. He called Serrano's photograph *Piss Christ*, depicting a crucifix immersed in urine, a "sickening, abhorrent, and shocking act by an arrogant blasphemer." He then proposed legislation banning NEA funding for certain types of art, including "obscene or indecent" portrayals and those that are derogatory of "the objects or beliefs of the adherents of a particular religion or nonreligion."

Helms sought to bring his measure to a voice vote in the

Senate "so that whoever votes against it would be on record as favoring taxpayer funding for pornography." His bill, which was attached to the NEA's 1990 funding measure, stated that no NEA funds could be used to produce or disseminate art which in the judgment of NEA was determined to be obscene. The bill defined obscenity as "including but not limited to, depictions of sadomasochism, homo-eroticism, the sexual exploitation of children, or individuals engaged in sex acts and which, when taken as a whole, do not have serious literary, artistic, political, or scientific value."

Critics argued that such legislation would turn the NEA into a ministry of culture, dictating to the American public what is morally acceptable art. In January, 1991, as a result of lawsuits filed by New York's New School for Social Research, the Newport Harbor Art Museum, and others, several federal judges simultaneously ruled the that the bill's NEA restrictions violated the First Amendment rights of grant recipients.

Another significant national arts controversy emerged in 1989 over the photographs of Robert Mapplethorpe. The Mapplethorpe exhibit itself—which included photographs featuring nudity of adults and children, homo-eroticism and sadomasochism—was canceled in 1989 by a Washington, D.C., art gallery because of the controversy. This was the direct result of pressure by Helms. Helms wrote to Patrick Trueman, head of the Justice Department obscenity unit created after the report of the Attorney General's Commission on Pornography, asking whether Trueman would consider prosecuting the Mapplethorpe photographs. His letter included copies of seven Mapplethorpe photographs (including four of African American men with erections) that Helms found objectionable. Helms's outrage appeared to focus particularly on images with interracial and homoerotic themes. As Helms stated: "There's a big difference between *Merchant of Venice* and a photograph of two males of different races on a marble table top."

After its cancellation in Washington, the Mapplethorpe exhibit traveled to seven other sites without incident until it arrived in Cincinnati, Ohio, a stronghold of the antipornography movement. Citizens for Community Values and other local antipornography groups put pressure on the local Contemporary Arts Center's board members to cancel the exhibit, but curator Dennis Barrie prevailed and the show opened as scheduled. Barrie was arrested on the day the exhibit opened, and a trial resulted after seven of the exhibit's 175 photographs were singled out for indictment. When the defense requested to enter the entire 175 photographs into evidence so that the artist's work could be considered as a whole and in context, the judge ruled that each photograph was a whole. Barrie was acquitted.

In 1990 Helms asked the government's General Accounting Office to investigate NEA funds spent on performance art after finding out about Annie Sprinkle's performance. The former pornographic film actress had asked audience members to point at her cervix with a flashlight. Four other performance artists, all known for incorporating strong sexual themes into their work also were investigated. As a result of his efforts, Helms has become one of the frequently criticized and depicted political leaders within the art world.

See also Attorney General's Commission on Pornography; Chilling effect; Comstock, Anthony; Culture ministries; Mapplethorpe, Robert; National Endowment for the Arts; Performance art; Serrano, Andres; Telephone law.

Helper, Hinton

Born: December 27, 1829, Rowan (now Davie) County, North Carolina

Died: March 8, 1909, Washington, D.C.

Identification: Author

Significance: Helper's published attack on slavery infuriated slaveholders, who prevented fellow Southerners from reading it

Helper grew up in straitened circumstances on a small farm in rural North Carolina but was able to complete his education at the Mocksville Academy in 1848. In 1850 he joined the gold rush to California; later he claimed that his experiences with free labor in California led him to take a critical look at slavery. In 1857 he published *The Impending Crisis of the South: How to Meet It*, a book aimed at the nonslaveholding whites of the South. His book used detailed economic statistics to contrast conditions in free and slave states, while arguing that the relative backwardness of the South was due to the negative impact of slavery on whites. Free laborers were doomed to poverty because they had to compete with slaves. In the North where labor was free, laborers prospered, and the whole section gained in wealth. Helper attacked slaveholders in strong language, calling upon nonslaveholders to overthrow the system—by force if necessary—as the only way to improve their economic condition.

After his book was published, Helper moved to New York, which he considered a safer place to live. He was disappointed that few in the South could actually read his work, however, since Southern states suppressed its distribution and some made it a crime even to possess the book. In North Carolina mobs drove out residents suspected of circulating *The Impending Crisis* and a Methodist minister received a one-year jail sentence for attempting to sell it. Helper's book was furiously attacked by Southerners; dozens of articles and books were written rejecting the book, but few actually attempted to answer Helper's arguments. The most common response was a personal attack, accusing Helper of having fled North Carolina to avoid prosecution for stealing money from his employer.

In contrast Helper's book was widely read in the North. Antislavery groups eagerly seized it as support for their assertion that the expansion of slavery into the western territories would adversely affect free labor. They hoped this argument might help convince people who were prejudiced against African Americans to favor the antislavery cause. In 1859 and 1860 Republicans distributed over sixty thousand copies as campaign documents.

In 1861 President Abraham Lincoln appointed Helper U.S. consul at Buenos Aires, where he served until 1866. Helper's writings after the Civil War made it clear that he had not attacked slavery out of compassion for slaves. The three books he published during Reconstruction furiously denounced the former slaves as a menace to the future of white labor in the

South. Helper opposed racial equality and called for the removal of blacks from the United States.

During the 1870's Helper became obsessed with plans for building a railroad from Hudson Bay to the Strait of Magellan. Failure to secure support for the idea left him depressed and contributed to his suicide in 1909.

See also Abolitionist movement; African Americans; Civil War, U.S.; Douglass, Frederick; Giddings, Joshua Reed; Race.

Helsinki Agreement

Date: July, 1973-August, 1975

Place: Geneva, Switzerland, and Helsinki, Finland

Significance: This accord contributed to the creation of European standards on human rights, particularly freedom of critical expression

The Helsinki Agreement, or Helsinki Final Act (HFA), was signed by the leaders of thirty-three European states and the United States and Canada. As the result of nearly three years of meetings in the Conference on Security and Cooperation in Europe (CSCE), the HFA codified essential humanitarian provisions to be applied in relations among states, and to be implemented in the domestic political systems of the states. A prominent clause in the agreement is Principle Seven, entitled "Respect for human rights and fundamental freedoms, including the freedom of thought, conscience, religion or belief," which is located in the first section (or "basket") of the document. It requires all states to respect the universal significance of "freedom of thought, conscience, religion or belief," all of which are essential for "peace, justice and well-being" in European societies. The HFA reaffirms humanitarian provisions that were previously codified in the Charter of the United Nations, the Universal Declaration of Human Rights, and in the Covenants on Human Rights.

Of equal importance is the third section of the HFA, entitled "Co-operation in Humanitarian and Other Fields." Known as "Basket III" it calls for freer movement of people, broader dissemination of printed, oral, filmed, and broadcast information, and improvement of the working conditions of journalists.

Follow-up conferences, prescribed in the HFA, have focused on improving human contacts, broadening exchanges of information, protecting minority rights, and developing democratic institutions. The regular meetings to review implementation of the HFA are known as the Helsinki process.

Until the collapse of the Soviet Union in 1991, implementation of the HFA was hampered by Cold War rhetoric and deeper disagreements over the source, substance, and exercise of human rights. Leaders of Western democratic governments stated that the unrestricted flow of printed, oral, or broadcast information would improve international relations. Soviet commentators and spokespersons for East European states claimed that all decisions on the availability and exchange of information should rest within the domestic jurisdiction of the governments which signed the HFA. Each state could define the parameters of censorship within its own social and political system. Any information which did not contribute to the building of socialism or the socialist way of life was thus censored by the Soviet authorities, regardless of the broader definitions of the HFA.

In 1976 a group of Soviet citizens invoked the HFA to call for an end to censorship in the Soviet Union. Members of these unofficial Helsinki Monitoring Groups were arrested and imprisoned or forced into exile, often for anti-Soviet agitation and propaganda. Under international political and economic pressure, Soviet representatives to HFA follow-up meetings gradually eased censorship.

By 1991 a more universal interpretation of the HFA emerged. Soviet and East European officials ended the jamming of West European radio broadcasts, freed persons imprisoned for expressing their political or religious beliefs, and allowed unprecedented travel between Eastern and Western Europe. All the signatory states to the HFA agreed to international monitoring of their pledges to allow freedom of expression.

See also Communism; Convention for the Protection of Human Rights and Fundamental Freedoms; Democracy; Gorbachev, Mikhail; Poland; Sakharov, Andrei; Soviet Union; TASS; Fundamental Freedoms.

Hemingway, Ernest

Born: July 21, 1899, Oak Park, Illinois

Died: July 2, 1961, Ketchum, Idaho

Identification: American novelist

Significance: A widely read novelist who received a Nobel Prize in Literature, Hemingway produced books that have nevertheless been scrutinized, banned, and censored

Hemingway started his writing career as a newspaper reporter, then volunteered to drive ambulances for Italy during the early part of World War I. Afterward, he returned to journalism, joining the ranks of newspaper correspondents in Europe by writing for the *Toronto Star.* While he was living in Paris, his life was altered when he joined a group of artists and intellectuals known as the lost generation.

With Ezra Pound and Gertrude Stein encouraging him to write, Hemingway published his first collection of stories, *In Our Time*, in 1924. In 1926 his novel about the postwar generation, *The Sun Also Rises*, put his literary reputation on an upward climb. In 1930, however, this book was banned in Boston, Massachusetts; in 1953 it was prohibited in Ireland; and in 1960 the San Jose, California, school system banned the book, and all of Hemingway's books were removed from Riverside, California, school libraries.

Hemingway's "code heroes" and snappy dialogue brought to life the drama of an Italian retreat during World War I in *A Farewell to Arms* (1929). The book drew immediate protests from Italians, who had banned it in their country because its account of the Italian humiliation was too painfully accurate. In the United States, the book's later film adaptation was censored because of Italian pressure. Boston banned the five issues of *Scribner's Magazine* that contained the story. Throughout the years the novel continued to be challenged and condemned by public school systems through the United States.

After Adolf Hitler's National Socialist Party took power in Germany in 1933, Hemingway's works were among the thousands of books publicly burned. Later, in a 1937 address to the Writer's Congress in New York, Hemingway condemned Germany's fascist government, saying that under its system good writers could not exist, and that "fascism is a lie told by bullies." Hemingway's publication of *To Have and Have Not* in 1938 led to more controversy. Detroit, Michigan, bannished the book's sale, and public libraries removed it from circulation. Hemingway's *For Whom the Bell Tolls* (1940) was nominated for a Pulitzer Prize; however, it drew strong objections and no work of fiction received the prize that year. The U.S. Post Office declared the book to be unmailable.

See also American Civil Liberties Union; *Farewell to Arms, A*; Film adaptation; Italy; Literature; Nonmailable matter laws.

Henry VIII

Born: June 28, 1491, Greenwich, England
Died: January 28, 1547, London, England
Identification: King of England (1509-1547)
Significance: Henry was the first English monarch to use censorship of printed books to shape religious and political opinion

Although books printed on the Continent had reached England earlier, William Caxton introduced book printing into England in 1476. Twenty-three years later Henry Tudor ascended England's throne as Henry VIII. From the beginning of his reign, he claimed that the Crown had the right to control printing. Under his rule censorship became a key to the monarchy's molding of political and religious opinion.

Early in his reign, Henry supported traditional Roman Catholicism so strongly that Pope Leo X named him a Defender of the Faith after the king published *Defense of the Seven Sacraments* (1521), a book attacking the Protestant reformer Martin Luther. Shortly afterward there were reports that Luther's own books were publicly burned in Cambridge and London. In 1526 Henry issued a list of eighteen prohibited books, including five by Luther. Three years later, his list of proscribed works had eighty-five titles, including twenty-two by Luther. Henry's may have been the first such list. The Roman Catholic church's *Index Librorum Prohibitorum* was not issued until 1559. Henry also joined with continental forces to suppress William Tyndale's English translation of the Bible. Of the six thousand copies smuggled into England, all but one were seized and burned at St. Paul's Cathedral in London.

By about 1525, however, Henry wanted the Catholic church to free him from his marriage to Catherine of Aragon, who had failed to bear a surviving male heir to his throne. Before Henry had married her, Catherine was married to his elder brother, Arthur, who died shortly after the wedding. Under Roman Catholic law, brothers could not marry the same woman; Henry cited this prohibition to petition the Church to terminate his marriage to Catherine. His unsuccessful attempts lasted until 1533, when Henry married Anne Boleyn, then pregnant by him. In 1534, he named himself head of the English church by an Act of Supremacy, claiming absolute authority in matters both temporal and spiritual.

From that moment, Henry's censorship activities intensified against those who challenged his new authority. His opponents included both Roman Catholic writers and Reformation writers, such as Luther, who questioned Henry's right to dissolve his first marriage. Henry responded with a lengthy series of acts and proclamations designed to control speech and printing. In 1534 "malicious" denial of the king's religious supremacy was made treason, punishable by death. Among those executed were Sir Thomas More. Among the minor figures executed for denying Henry's religious authority was the prophet Elizabeth Barton, known as the Holy Maid of Kent, who was hanged in 1534. Afterward writings by and about her, including some seven hundred copies of *The Nun's Book*, were seized and apparently destroyed.

In 1538 the monarchy declared that all printed works were to be approved by the Privy Council or its agents prior to their printing. Subversive literature continued to flood England, however, so the order was repeated in 1549 and 1551. Even harsher proclamations followed. According to the Six Articles issued in 1539, those who opposed Henry's neo-Catholic church by denying the true presence of Jesus Christ's body and blood in the mass were to be burned as heretics. Those who denied other tenets were to be hanged as felons. In 1546 Henry forbade ownership of certain strongly Protestant books and prohibited importation into England of any books concerning Christianity.

Shortly after the Act of Supremacy in 1534, Henry had encouraged English translations of the Bible. However, the Act for Advancement of True Religion of 1543 forbade men below the rank of "gentlemen" and all women from reading the Bible. Scripture, Henry informed Parliament in 1545, was for the information of men's consciences. The king alone could distinguish between truth and error; these were not matters to be argued in taverns. By the time of Henry's death, however, religious dissent had penetrated every level of society, including the court.

See also Bible; Book burning; Caxton, William; Censorship; *Index Librorum Prohibitorum*; James I; Luther, Martin; Printing; Prior restraint; Reformation, the; United Kingdom; *Utopia*.

Heresy

Definition: Derived from the Greek word for choosing for oneself, heresy originally referred to religious or philosophical ideas arrived at by oneself, rather than from church teachings
Significance: The Old Testament used "heresy" in a nonpejorative sense to refer to factions with Judaism; in the New Testament Saint Paul redefined the word to designate groups professing false doctrines that would threaten Christian unity.

In 1215 the Roman Catholic church's Fourth Lateran Council declared heresy a crime punishable by death. Sixteen years later Pope Gregory IX established an ecclesiastical tribunal, which came to be known as the Inquisition, to seek out alleged heretics and bring them to trial. Those found guilty of heresy were turned over to civil authorities for punishment.

In Protestant churches, primarily because of their denial of ecclesiastical authority in matters of faith and their emphasis upon private interpretation of the Scriptures, punishing people for heresy was never a widespread practice. With the steady growth of religious toleration after the Reformation, the Catholic church came to abandon the idea that heresy was a crime. In modern times the word has come to refer to doctrines that oppose the dogmas of a particular church, especially when such deviating doctrines are held by members of that church. The word is also often used to refer to any ideas that deviate from the dominant ideas of a particular school of thought.

See also Bacon, Roger; Biddle, John; Galileo Galilei; *Index Librorum Prohibitorum*; Lateran Council, Fourth; Reformation, the; Religion; Spanish Inquisition; *Utopia*; Vatican.

Hicklin case

Date: 1868

Place: London, Great Britain

Significance: The decision of the Court of Queen's Bench in *Regina v. Hicklin* established a test for obscenity (the Hicklin rule) that was long used in Great Britain, Canada, and the United States

In 1857 Great Britain's Parliament passed Lord Campbell's Act, which gave magistrates the power to seize and destroy obscene material. The Hicklin case of 1868 tested that act. Henry Scott, a fervent Protestant, published a pamphlet, *The Confessional Unmasked*, that was an exposé of alleged depraved practices within the Roman Catholic church. Magistrates seized 252 copies of the pamphlet and ordered their destruction. When Scott appealed, a court recorder named Hicklin revoked the order. When the government appealed Hicklin's decision, Chief Justice Alexander Cockburn of the Court of Queen's Bench reinstated the order for the pamphlets' destruction. In so doing he defined what was meant by obscenity: "whether the tendency of the matter charged as obscenity is to deprave and corrupt those whose minds are open to such immoral influences and into whose hands a publication of this sort may fall." This definition became known as the Hicklin rule, or Hicklin test. Though British in origin, it was used in the United States until 1957. Because of the breadth of the Hicklin rule, prosecutions for obscenity in the United States were easy to achieve for seventy-five years. Because it required only a "tendency" to deprave or corrupt, it swept broadly. Anyone could come under its scope. Furthermore, by merely hypothesizing into whose hands the material might fall, the rule extended its scope. The Hicklin rule expressly stated that it wanted to protect children. Thus, children who might tend to be depraved or corrupted, or into whose hands obscene materials might fall, were the main beneficiaries of the rule.

Such reasoning was, however, entirely hypothetical. Adult tastes and interests were simply not considered. Therefore under the Hicklin rule, the adult public could be reduced to reading what was deemed fit only for children, or the most susceptible persons. Furthermore, even if only a part of the material were considered obscene, the whole work could be pronounced obscene and thereby censored. Examples of works banned under this rule during its seventy-five year tenure in the United States include *For Whom the Bell Tolls* and *From Here to Eternity*. In 1957, in the cases *Butler v. Michigan* and *Roth v. United States*, the U.S. Supreme Court changed the standard to preclude only that material so obscene that it might have a negative influence on the average person.

See also Books and obscenity law; Ernst, Morris Leopold; *Miller v. California*; Morality; Obscene Publications Acts; Obscenity: legal definitions; Obscenity: sale and possession; *Roth v. United States*.

Hinton, S. E.

Born: 1950, Tulsa, Oklahoma

Identification: American author of novels for young adults

Significance: Hinton introduced a controversial style of young-adult novels characterized by realistic dialogue, unsentimental plots, and frequent violence that became enormously popular with teens

In 1967, at the age of seventeen, S. E. Hinton published *The Outsiders* because, she said, "A lot of adult literature was older than I was ready for. The kids' books were Mary Jane-Goes-to-the-Prom." She portrayed her characters in honest, almost brutal fashion. The book was hailed by critics who felt that, as opposed to many authors, Hinton depicted adolescence not as a mindless, muddle-headed period but as a painful, dangerous time that often had an unhappy ending. Her later books included *That Was Then, This Is Now* (1971), *Tex* (1979), *Rumble Fish* (1977), and *Taming the Star Runner* (1988).

The language, violence, and realism of Hinton's work became targets of school and library censors. In 1986, for example, *The Outsiders* and *That Was Then, This Is Now* were both challenged in the South Milwaukee, Wisconsin, School District for their depiction of teenagers' drug and alcohol use, and because all the characters were from broken homes. The library in Boone, Iowa, also challenged *The Outsiders* in 1992. *That Was Then, This Is Now* was contested in 1983 in Pagosa Springs, Colorado, because of its graphic depiction of violence, its language, and its supposed lack of literary merit. In spite of such attempts, however, Hinton's novels have continued to reach a wide readership of young adults.

See also Books, young adult; Family; Film adaptation; Libraries; Libraries, school; Violence.

Historiography

Definition: Study of the writing of history—as opposed to the study of history itself

Significance: Historical accounts have often, arguably always, been subjected to pressures to align themselves with the views of those in power

George Orwell's novel *Nineteen Eighty-Four* (1949) describes an authoritarian government that distorts history through a Ministry of Truth that constantly changes historical records to meet its government's needs. The authoritarian government in Orwell's novel eliminates all traces of individual lives and past political actions. Although its logic is often contradictory and inconsistent, the Ministry of Truth reveals how control over history can enhance power. Orwell's novel focuses on authoritarian governments; however, similar censorship of history also exists in democratic nations.

Censorship and Higher Education. The onset of the Cold War in the 1950's and the subsequent ideological battle between Soviet-sponsored communism and Western democratic capitalism had a profound impact upon American historiography and ushered in a period of self-censorship in American education. Before World War II, U.S. historians debated the legitimacy of some of the nation's most exalted historical beliefs. Scholars during the 1920's and 1930's questioned the democratic character of American politics, and suggested that American foreign policy was driven by the same economic imperialist motives that shaped European foreign policy.

The Cold War and the subsequent attacks upon the American Left by Wisconsin Senator Joseph McCarthy and others eliminated most overt political dissent from U.S. college campuses. Since the government did not directly control this process, the censorship came from within and serves as a classic example of self-censorship. Universities, faculty, and college administrators viciously attacked any scholar who had been a member of the Communist Party or continued to endorse radical historiography. Hundreds of scholars from all facets of academic life ranging from the Ivy League to large state schools to small private liberal arts colleges were dismissed from their jobs.

This form of censorship had a significant impact on American education. Only historiography that celebrated the supremacy of American cultural values; espoused the sanctity and democratic virtues of the political system; downplayed all evidence of racial, ethnic, and class conflict; and insisted that American foreign policy followed a high moral code of conduct was considered acceptable for publication. American students were required to learn often incorrect views on history that fostered national unity rather than pursue critical inquiries into the nation's past. Criticism of American history was censored for its lack of patriotism. A climate of fear permeated college campuses. Unofficial blacklists prevented dissident scholars from obtaining employment elsewhere, and academic freedom of speech was dramatically curtailed until the 1960's.

Holocaust Denial and War Guilt. Censorship has not targeted only radical historians. Some scholars have suppressed historical evidence in order to alleviate a nation's responsibility for war crimes. The Nazi Holocaust of World War II, for example, resulted in the deaths of approximately six million European Jews. Despite the fact that it is one of the most well-documented acts of genocide in modern history, some people have maintained that it never occurred. They have attacked the accounts of survivors of the Holocaust as being incredulous, and have maintained that such accounts are intended solely to generate international support for the state of Israel. This style of historiography has secured a significant following in some eastern and central European states that collaborated with the Nazis during World War II, as well as in states that ignored Jewish pleas for help as the news of the Holocaust became known.

In Croatia, for example, a state that not only aligned itself with Nazi Germany but participated in the murdering of Jews as well, the overall extent of the Holocaust has been minimalized. In his book *Wastelands—Historical Truth* (1989), Croatian president Franjo Tudjman accuses the survivors of exaggerating and issuing biased stories regarding their experiences in the death camps, also hinting that instead of being murdered, many Jews in Europe may in fact have committed mass suicide. Similar allegations have appeared in Slovakia, France, Great Britain, and Austria. If the Holocaust is viewed as a fabricated exaggeration, then states and people can no longer be morally condemned for their collaboration with the Nazis. In contrast, postwar Germany enacted a law making Holocaust denial a crime.

High school and college teachers in the United States have also been affected by this development. As Holocaust denial has attained some acceptance, students are increasingly questioning the validity of truthful Holocaust accounts and wondering why it is even necessary to study the topic. Deniers fully understand that they cannot eradicate all of the evidence accumulated on this event, but by issuing numerous doubts and accusations, they hope to fan the fires of anti-Semitism. Although opponents of academic censorship insist upon academic freedom of speech, an idea must have some factual legitimacy to be acceptable, and it should adhere to ethical codes of conduct and methodology. Historiography that denies the Holocaust denies fact, evidence, truth, and ethical methods of research and presentation. Such historiography is the worst, but not the only, example of how those who write history may suppress knowledge and distort facts in order to further personal and national interests.

The Soviet Union and Authoritarian Revisionism. In authoritarian regimes, history is rewritten to legitimize control and justify governmental actions. Throughout the twentieth century, the leaders of the Soviet Union frequently revised Marxist-Leninist ideology and Russian history to help explain the need for political repression, wars, and interventions, and personal leadership. This, in turn, led to the suppression and censorship of dissenting views; anyone who challenged official interpretations of history was classified an enemy of the state.

During the 1930's Soviet leader Joseph Stalin's revisionism embodied all of the attributes of Orwell's Ministry of Truth. Often inconsistent and contradictory, Stalin altered the historical record to enhance his role in the formative years of Soviet history. Instead of correctly placing himself on the periphery of V. I. Lenin's revolutionary vanguard movement, Stalin had himself depicted in Soviet textbooks as Lenin's closet aide. He erased the names of all key party officials who were purged from the historical record. Stalin demanded that historians depict his chief rival, Leon Trotsky, as a bandit and betrayer of the revolution, and all books that were either critical of Stalin or his brand of Marxist-Leninist communism were removed from the library shelves.

During the 1980's Communist Party leader Mikhail Gorbachev utilized historical revisionism to defend his reform policy. While still interested in maintaining the party's control over the Soviet Union, Gorbachev realized that the government needed to loosen its control in order to survive. If the party was to maintain its legitimacy, however, this process had to be explained within the context of Marxist-Leninist ideology. Echoing the mood of the Soviet people, he endorsed widespread attacks upon Stalin, depicted Lenin as a social democrat rather than as the absolutely unprincipled dictator that he was, and dismissed the party's goal of egalitarianism.

The demise of the Soviet Union in 1991 ushered in another era of historical revisionism. Freed from the bonds of authoritarian control, Russian historians reexamined the crimes that Stalin had buried years ago. Articles were published on the purges in Byelorussia, for example, where more than two million people were murdered by Soviet secret police during the 1930's. Historical novels critical of authoritarian government and Soviet rule appeared in Russian libraries. Stalin's defenders still attempted to preserve his reputation, but with the end of authoritarian rule, Russian historiography is no longer subjected to strict governmental censorship.

School Systems, Libraries, and Museums. Since history serves as a vehicle for forging national identity, its content is frequently the subject of debates. Some politicians, special interest groups, educators, and parents maintain that students should be taught a certain core curriculum in order to develop a personal sense of patriotism and pride in their nation's accomplishments. Others, however, declare that history should attempt to adhere to certain objective methodological guidelines, and it should not ignore a country's past sins and transgressions.

This conflict has aroused nationalist passions and has generated a fiery discussion over the role of history in education in the United States. In 1995, in commemoration of the fiftieth anniversary of the end of World War II, the Smithsonian Institution's Air and Space Museum organized an exhibit featuring the dropping of atomic bombs on Japan. Instead of portraying the mission of one of the bombers used, the *Enola Gay*, in a celebratory victorious fashion, the museum planned to exhibit photographs of the victims and to mention the devastation inflicted upon the Japanese cities of Hiroshima and Nagasaki. American veteran organizations cried foul and lobbied Congress to prevent what they perceived to be an unjustifiable moral condemnation of U.S. military strategy. As a result, the Smithsonian revamped its presentation.

A similar controversy surfaced in 1994 following the publication of the proposed *National Standards for United States History for Grades 5-12*. Concerned that students were leaving secondary education with an inadequate understanding of history, the National Endowment for the Humanities and the Department of Education funded this project—along with similar projects in other subjects—and hired historians to devise national guidelines for local school districts. The resulting report angered many. Some maintained that the standards were too critical of American institutions and overly sympathetic to other cultures and non-Western exploits. Why, they argued, should American students be required to learn more about the Gupta empire in India than the U.S. Constitution? After repeated attacks, the Senate passed a resolution censuring the standards and declared that the standards would neither be certified nor implemented. Perhaps wishing to avoid future controversy, the Senate also ruled that such projects would no longer be funded by the federal government. Thus, in effect, the senate decreased its power to censor the teaching of history in American classrooms.

Other Countries. Biased historiography can be found outside Europe and the United States. Instead of focusing upon Japan's militaristic expansionism in China during the 1930's, some Japanese nationalist historians have tended to emphasize the postwar devastation in Japan caused by the atomic bombs dropped on the cities of Hiroshima and Nagasaki. They highlight how the Western Allies utilized racist doctrines to justify the destruction of prewar Japanese society. Consequently, they place Japan in the role of victim rather than the aggressor. Critics of this historiography maintain that Japan was also driven by its own racist beliefs, and as a result, Japan must accept its responsibility for the war. This issue has remained controversial in Japan's school systems since it clearly affects whether or not students will develop a positive or negative view of their nation's past.

Historical disputes have always existed, but instead of allowing all interpretations to compete in a free marketplace of ideas, the elite typically have exerted their authority and eliminated opposing or critical views through censorship. In democratic and communist regimes, history has been manipulated for nationalist interests. Instead of being granted the luxury of academic freedom, scholars have often been forced to restructure the historical record in order to accommodate special interests. Ironically, it is the historical record that best indicates that many have attempted and failed to exert control over history through censorship. —*Robert D. Ubriaco, Jr.*

See also Fear; Gorbachev, Mikhail; Holocaust, Jewish; Intellectual freedom; Libraries; Orwell, George; Stalin, Joseph; World War II.

BIBLIOGRAPHY

Saburo Ienaga, *The Pacific War, 1931-1945* (New York: Pantheon Books, 1978), examines the debate surrounding racism and the Japanese in World War II. Mark Leff, "Revisioning U.S. Political History" in *The American Historical Review* 100, no. 3 (June, 1995), outlines the political controversy surrounding the Enola Gay exhibit and the *National Standards for United States History for Grades 5-12*. Deborah Lipstadt, *Denying the Holocaust* (New York: The Free Press, 1993), uncovers the various motives and agendas surrounding Holocaust denial. Peter Novick, *That Noble Dream: The "Objectivity Question" and the American Historical Profession* (Cambridge, England: Cambridge University Press, 1988), describes how censorship and nationalism influence the teaching of history. George Orwell, *Nineteen Eighty-Four* (New York: Harcourt, Brace, 1949), is a classic novel that demonstrates how censorship shapes historiography. Ellen Schrecker, *No Ivory Tower: McCarthyism and the Universities* (New York: Oxford University Press, 1986), reveals how and why communists and political radicals were excluded from academic life during the McCarthy era. Hedrick Smith, *The New Russians* (New York: Random House, 1990), exposes the role of censorship in the writing of Soviet and Russian history.

Hoaxes

DEFINITION: False claims about events or situations designed to deceive people

SIGNIFICANCE: Hoaxes have been used by those who wish to censor in order to convince others that the object of censorship presents serious dangers

Hoaxes are sometimes used in societies with some commitment to freedom of speech; otherwise outright censorship is easier. Even in totalitarian societies, hoaxes can deceive when more official statements do not. Hoaxes have often been used to demonstrate that there is great danger, and that therefore censorship is needed. Hoaxes, in this light, are part of a large pattern for establishing government censorship: Find a credible monster (Jews, Reds, drugs, communism, anarchists, terrorists, pornography) and endow it with frightening powers (perhaps with a hoax, or some alarming statistics), then campaign against it, making freedoms, including freedom of speech, a necessary casualty of the battle. True events can be exaggerated or interpreted in such a manner that they serve to the same effect as a hoax. For example, in 1898, when the U.S. Navy battleship *Maine* suffered a real explosion in Havana harbor, war sentiment leading to the Spanish-American War was whipped up, although who was to blame for the explosion was not determined.

In totalitarian societies, such as Germany during World War II, governments present dangers as present on all sides. The Nazis justified their complete control over books, music, and the visual arts by claiming that their nation was threatened by an international Jewish and communist conspiracy that sought to undermine German culture and the German state. In a sense, therefore, a hoax was the basis of the Nazi state.

In order to convince people to accept censorship, it may be necessary to create the impression of an immediate threat. The French Revolution, at the end of the 1700's, alarmed many people. In England, the writings of some of those sympathetic to the French Revolution were suppressed. In 1797 an opponent of the revolution, a Scottish scientist named John Robison, published a book titled *Proofs of a Conspiracy Against All Religions and Governments of Europe*. In this, Robison claimed that the French Revolution had actually been brought about by a secret conspiratorial organization, known as the Order of the Illuminati, which had plans for overthrowing all existing governments. Robison's claims were used by those wishing to suppress liberal thought in England, and they were also taken up by conservatives in America. Robison's bogus conspiracy was cited by Americans in support of the Alien and Sedition Acts, America's first official attempts at legislative censorship. Much later, after World War II, Robert Welch, founder of the anticommunist John Birch Society, read Robison's book and was influenced by Robison's claims of a worldwide subversive conspiracy.

The Haymarket Bomb Scare. In the United States in the 1880's, most radical anarchist and socialist publications were produced by immigrants in urban areas. In the 1880's opposition to foreigners and to radical ways of thinking became joined in reaction to the Haymarket Bomb Scare, an event that many still believe was staged by authorities who wanted to crack down on leftist immigrants.

Radicals, many of them of German origin, called a demonstration at Chicago's Haymarket Square on May 4, 1886, the day after a striking laborer had been killed by police. Police arrived to disperse the demonstrators. Someone apparently threw a small bomb, although it has never been clear who this was. In response, the police opened fire. When the shooting stopped, eight policemen and many spectators lay dead.

Anarchists in Chicago and elsewhere were accused of having advocated doctrines that had encouraged violence. The police used the event to attack anarchist newspapers, such as the *Arbeiter-Zeitung* and the *Alarm*. A number of radicals were arrested and sentenced to be hanged, although several escaped the noose by committing suicide. One of those who was hanged was August Spies, editor of the *Arbeiter-Zeitung*. There was no evidence to connect Spies to the throwing of the bomb, and the authorities made no effort to claim that he had even known about it. Spies had, the authorities maintained, instigated deadly violence through his inflammatory writings, and this was enough to merit the death penalty. If the bomb that started the riot was thrown by a government agent, then the Haymarket Riot was a hoax, although the riot actually happened. If the bomb was thrown by a private troublemaker, anarchist or not, then the reaction to the riot may be considered as having the effect of a hoax.

The Red Scare. After World War I, fear of radicalism and the desire to suppress radicals had arisen once again among many Americans. In March, 1919, the *Chicago Tribune* announced that a radical plan to plant bombs in Chicago had been discovered. The following month, the U.S. Department of Justice claimed that it had discovered an anarchist conspiracy to seize a government arsenal in Philadelphia and blow up the entire city. It remains unclear whether these conspiracies actually existed, or whether these were pure hoaxes.

In late April, 1919, claims of radical conspiracies began to receive some support when a package was delivered to Mayor Ole Hanson of Seattle. Acid leaked out of the package, and a bomb was found in it before Mayor Hanson or anyone else was injured. The next day, an identical package was delivered to the home of former Georgia senator Thomas Hardwick. The bomb blew off both hands of Hardwick's maid and severely burned Mrs. Hardwick's face. A postal clerk discovered thirty-four other bombs in a New York post office, all addressed to public officials around the country. The timing suggested that the explosions had been intended to coincide with May Day, a radical holiday.

Reaction against radicals was swift. The offices of the *Call*, a left-wing newspaper in New York, were raided by soldiers, civilians, and sailors, who smashed furniture and confiscated books and other literature. Many publications with fairly wide distribution, such as *The Nation*, *The New Republic*, *Dial*, *Public*, and *Survey*, were accused in the popular press of having sympathized with radical socialism and of having advocated revolution. Attorney General A. Mitchell Palmer claimed that the bombings were part of an organized conspiracy to overthrow the United States Government. Palmer began leading raids on radical individuals and organizations, arresting thousands of immigrants and confiscating truckloads of radical propaganda. At the same time, the postmaster general used wartime legislation to suppress radical magazines and newspapers.

McCarthy and the State Department Hoax. Anticommunism has been the basis of much of modern political censorship. Senator Joseph McCarthy was one of the leading anti-communists in the 1950's. McCarthy also perpetrated one of the most notorious hoaxes of modern times in February, 1950, in Wheeling, West Virginia. Brandishing a piece of paper, the contents of which are unknown, McCarthy claimed to have the names of 205 communist subversives working in the U.S. State Department. The senator later reduced this number, and he was never able to provide any evidence of radical employees. Most historians believe that McCarthy simply made up his claim. Nevertheless, the allegation that there were radicals working within the U.S. Government to overthrow it influenced many in McCarthy's day to support the suppression of communism. —*Carl L. Bankston III*

See also Communist Party of the U.S.A.; Democracy; Holmes, Oliver Wendell, Jr.; Holocaust, Jewish; National security; Sedition.

Bibliography

An American Paradox: Censorship in a Nation of Free Speech (Westport, Conn.: Praeger, 1993), by Patrick M. Garry, offers a discussion of the sources of censorship in a free society. The need for an emergency to justify restricting freedom of speech is addressed in Nicholas Capaldi's *Clear and Present Danger: The Free Speech Controversy* (New York: Pegasus, 1969). *The Fear of Conspiracy: Images of Un-American Subversion from the Revolution to the Present* (Ithaca, N.Y.: Cornell University, 1971), by David Brion Davis, provides information on political delusions and hoaxes used to suppress radicalism. Robert K. Murray's *Red Scare: A Study of National Hysteria, 1919-1920* (New York: McGraw-Hill, 1964) gives a comprehensive picture of the bomb scare and the events following it. *McCarthyism* (Hinsdale, Ill: Dryden Press, 1973), by Thomas C. Reeves, gives a picture of Senator McCarthy and his era, including McCarthy's State Department hoax.

Hobbes, Thomas

Born: April 5, 1588, Westport, Wiltshire, England

Died: December 4, 1679, Hardwick Hall, Derbyshire, England

Identification: British philosopher

Significance: Hobbes's publications on metaphysics, morals, and politics were widely interpreted as supporting atheism; as a consequence, all his works were placed on the Roman Catholic church's *Index Librorum Prohibitorum*

The most controversial and vilified philosopher of the seventeenth century, Hobbes was known as the "Monster of Malmesbury" after his presumed birthplace. As a primarily political philosopher, Hobbes tried to set forth a comprehensive doctrine that would help bring peace to an England divided by civil war during the 1640's. The effect of his writings was, however, quite the opposite. His views rested on materialism, and thus directly opposed the Aristotelian scholasticism established by churches and universities. Hobbes was considered an atheist and immoralist, and his writings were attacked and suppressed.

Hobbes lived in an age marked by two powerful intellectual movements, the Protestant Reformation and the emergence of modern natural science. His special genius was his understanding that the philosophical foundation of science might be used to end the religious and political controversies generated by the Reformation. Simply put, he intended to expound a materialism that would discredit any and all independent religious authorities, whether Roman Catholic or Protestant. If everything were material, he reasoned, then "spiritual" authority would not have a philosophical leg on which to stand.

Hobbes's characteristic political doctrine, the absolute sovereignty of the national state, followed from his materialism. Human beings, he argued, are naturally selfish and contentious, and submit to political authority only to preserve their lives. That authority must be complete and undivided, if warring factions are to be avoided. His masterpiece *Leviathan* (1651) utterly subordinates religion to the state, which he termed "that *mortal god*." To preserve peace, the sovereign may take virtually any action, including prohibiting or censoring doctrines believed to be disruptive.

This combination of materialism, anticlericalism, egoistic morality, and near-deification of the state resulted in the view that Hobbes was an atheist, and his writings atheistic. Hobbes denied this, however, evidently in good faith. He engaged in extensive, learned biblical interpretation designed to demonstrate that the term "spirit" is used in Scripture to mean "breath," "wind," and similarly subtle matter. God, therefore, exists but is material.

Hobbes's numerous and powerful critics were unconvinced by his arguments. His simple, bold "modern" doctrines were completely uncongenial to his traditionalist contemporaries. He favored monarchy, but did not ground his opinion on the established divine right of kings theory. His relationship with his former royal pupil, the exiled—and later restored— King Charles II, was thus ambivalent. Charles banished Hobbes from his court in 1652 and later forbade him to publish any further political writings.

Charles was relatively well disposed toward Hobbes, however. Beginning in the 1650's, periodic attempts were made to censor Hobbes's writings. In 1666 a bill outlawing atheism and profaneness, singling out Hobbes's *Leviathan*, passed the House of Commons but not the House of Lords. In 1683 Oxford University condemned numerous Hobbesian doctrines, and banned and burned *Leviathan* and also his *De Cive*. The Roman Catholic church placed *De Cive* on the *Index Librorum Prohibitorum* in 1654. In 1703 all of Hobbes's works were forbidden by the church, and remained prohibited for nearly three centuries.

See also English Commonwealth; *Index Librorum Prohibitorum*; Reformation, the; Science.

Hochhuth, Rolf

Born: April 1, 1931, Eschwege, Germany

Identification: German playwright, novelist, and essayist

Significance: Hochhuth's use of drama to expose the moral and ethical shortcomings of prominent world figures provoked opposition from governments, organizations, and individuals

The premiere of Rolf Hochhuth's first play, *The Deputy*—also known as *The Representative*—in Berlin in February, 1963,

German playwright Rolf Hochhuth holds a copy of his controversial play The Deputy *at a 1964 news conference in New York City.* (AP/Wide World Photos)

initiated a protracted debate over the author's charge that Pope Pius XII had failed to speak out forcefully against the deportation and murder of the Jews of Europe. Massive protests in Basel, Switzerland, required police intervention and the play had to be withdrawn after only seventeen performances. Although *The Deputy* enjoyed a longer run in Paris, performances there were interrupted by stenchbombs and by members of the audience threatening to assault the actors on stage. The play's performance in New York in February, 1964, was preceded by negative publicity from a variety of quarters, including religious leaders of several denominations. Demonstrators at the theater included such diverse groups as representatives of the American Legion and the American Nazi Party.

Leaders of the Roman Catholic church in various countries strongly protested the appearance of the play, accusing the author of character assassination and pointing to the pope's personal efforts to protect Jews wherever he could without incurring reprisals by the Nazis. The Vatican's first official response to the play came in June, 1963, in a letter from future Pope Paul VI, Giovanni Cardinal Montini of Milan, to a British paper.

Hochhuth's second play, *Soldiers: An Obituary for Geneva* received only a lukewarm reception at its 1967 premiere in Berlin, but it caused a major controversy in Great Britain. The director and the dramatic producer of the British National Theater—Sir Laurence Olivier and Kenneth Tynan—were denied permission to stage the play by the Lord Chamberlain, who denounced it as libelous. Opposition to the play focused on its depiction of Sir Winston Churchill as supporting terror-bombing of German civilians and on its suggestion that Churchill was involved in the murder of the Free Polish leader General Wladyslaw Sikorski. The play was staged in London after the Lord Chamberlain's power of censorship was abolished in September, 1968.

Hochhuth's later plays generated little international interest, but they repeatedly brought him into conflict with German authorities. In one instance, his criticism of governmental policies led to charges of malicious incitement of the population.

Hochhuth defended his position on censorship in a number of speeches and published studies. He argued that poets must be active in politics and that authors should "articulate the bad conscience of their nation because politicians have such a good one." He saw the theater as a forum for political expression and for the teaching of timeless moral lessons and justified his often critical treatment of prominent historical figures because of his belief that all persons must assume full responsibility for their actions.

See also Brecht, Bertolt; Drama and theater; Germany; Holocaust, Jewish; Lord Chamberlain; Vatican.

Hollywood Ten

DATE: 1947

PLACE: Hollywood, California

SIGNIFICANCE: The refusal of these film industry figures to answer questions posed by the House Committee on Un-American Activities about their affiliation with the Communist Party led to their being jailed and blacklisted within the industry

The struggle between the House Committee on Un-American Activities (also known as the House Un-American Activities Committee, or the HUAC) and the Hollywood Ten embodied, in a theoretical sense, the struggle between the right to national security and the right to believe, think, and speak without restraint and fear of reprisal. The case also involved the rights of a congressional committee to gather facts versus witnesses' rights not to disclose information.

Background. In the United States membership in the Communist Party was bolstered in the 1930's and 1940's when Joseph Stalin asserted an antifascist stand and when the Soviet Union was a U.S. ally during World War II. With the end of the war, the not entirely unfriendly political climate between the United States and the Soviet Union gave way to the Cold War, a global confrontation between the ideologies of the two nations and, in the United States, between the subsequent conflict between guardians of internal security and protectors of civil rights. In February, 1944, Sam Wood and prominent Hollywood anti-Roosevelts formally founded the Motion Picture Alliance for the Preservation of American Ideals, pledged to fight any effort to divert the loyalty of the film industry from American ideals. On May 9, 1947, J. Parnell Thomas, the chair of HUAC, arrived in Los Angeles and interviewed "friendly" witnesses. Their accusations created indignation in some and fear in others.

The Hearings. On September 21, 1947, Thomas subpoenaed forty-three members of the Hollywood film industry as witnesses before the committee in its October hearings in Washington. In reaction to this assault on civil liberties the Committee for the First Amendment was formed and included some of the most famous names in Hollywood. Among the forty-three were several witnesses eager to cooperate and nineteen commonly viewed as uncooperative. Of these, eleven proclaimed they would not testify. Of these, Bertolt Brecht testified only that he had never been a communist and subsequently fled the country. The others became known as the Hollywood Ten.

Alvah Bessie, a screenwriter who had collaborated on such screenplays as *The Very Thought of You* (1944), *Hotel Berlin* (1945), and *Objective, Burma!* (1945) was an active communist who had fought in the Spanish Civil War. Herbert Biberman, who had directed such films as *Meet Nero Wolf* (1936) and *The Master Race* (1944), was active in the Communist Party. Lester Cole was a credentialed screenwriter, having worked on thirty-six films. He was running for reelection of the Screen Writers Guild executive board. Edward Dmytryk had directed twenty-four films, including two that were anti-anti-Semitic, *Crossfire* (1947) and *Hitler's Children* (1943). He had left the party in 1945. Ring Lardner, Jr., had coauthored the Academy Award-winning screenplay *Woman of the Year* (1942) and was moving away from the party at the time of the hearings. John Howard Lawson, who had founded and was first president of the Screen Writers Guild, was also head of the Hollywood branch of the Communist Party. He had written two of the most celebrated films depicting World War II, *Action in the North Atlantic* (1943) and *Sahara* (1943). Albert Maltz was an O. Henry Award recipient whose short stories had been widely anthologized. Among his screenplays are *This Gun for Hire* (1942), *Pride of the Marines* (1945), and *Destination, Tokyo* (1943). Sam Ornitz had written twenty-five film scripts, not as notable as those of the others. Robert Adrian Scott was a writer-producer whose career was beginning. With Dmytryk he had produced *Crossfire* (1947) and *Cornered* (1946) and *Murder, My Sweet* (1944) on his own. Dalton Trumbo was the highest paid writer in Hollywood. His

Nine members of the "Hollywood Ten" surrender at the U.S. marshal's office in Los Angeles in December, 1947. From left to right: Robert Adrian Scott, Edward Dmytryk, Samuel Ornitz, Lester Cole, Herbert Biberman, Albert Maltz, Alvah Bessie, John Howard Lawson, and Ring Lardner, Jr. (A photograph of Dalton Trumbo appears in the article under his name.) (AP/Wide World Photos)

The Hollywood Ten

1. Alvah Bessie (1904-1985), screenwriter
2. Herbert Biberman (1900-1971), director
3. Lester Cole (1904?-1985), screenwriter
4. Edward Dmytryk (1908-), director
5. Ring Lardner, Jr. (1915-), screenwriter
6. John Howard Lawson (1894-1977), screenwriter
7. Albert Maltz (1908-1985), screenwriter
8. Sam Ornitz (1890-1957), screenwriter
9. Robert Adrian Scott (1912-1973), writer-producer
10. Dalton Trumbo (1905-1976), screenwriter

films included *Kitty Foyle* (1940), *Thirty Seconds over Tokyo* (1944), and *Our Vines Have Tender Grapes* (1945).

Before appearing the ten planned a joint strategy: each would read a prepared critical statement; sidestep questions about their political affiliation under the guise of giving testimony; and only, if necessary, resort to the Fifth Amendment. HUAC's strategy, however, shattered their hopes for a dispassionate airing of controversial views. Thomas commenced the hearings by calling friendly witnesses who volunteered the names of communists and defended Hollywood against the charge of subversion. They were followed by some of Hollywood's top leading men, who cast themselves as concerned patriots defending Hollywood against a conspiracy.

The first of the ten called, Lawson, was not allowed to read his statement. He was gaveled into silence for anything beyond a direct response to the question posed to him and cited for contempt of Congress when he refused to answer a question about his political affiliation. Louis J. Russell then testified to Lawson's communist affiliation. This routine was followed with the other nine.

Aftermath. On November 24, 1947, Congress confirmed the committee's contempt citations. Lawson's trial was first with Trumbo's following. When both were convicted, the remaining eight agreed to accept for themselves the final verdict in these trials after all appeals were exhausted. All appeals failed, and in April, 1950, the U. S. Supreme Court refused to hear the cases. On June 11, the two writers began their one-year prison sentence. The others soon followed. Ironically, Thomas, later convicted of fraud, served time in the same prison with Cole and Lardner. Except for Dmytryk, who later reversed his position, the ten became virtually unemployable. On November 24, 1947, fifty producers met in New York and drafted a document deploring the action of the ten and indirectly encouraging blacklisting and denunciation that would rock Hollywood and curtail civil liberties into the 1960's. In 1951 a second wave of HUAC hearings were held.

—Christine R. Catron

See also Blacklisting; Communism; Communist Party of the U.S.A.; Film censorship; *Front, The*; House Committee on Un-American Activities; Lardner, Ring, Jr.; Trumbo, Dalton.

Bibliography

Larry Ceplair and Steven Englund's *The Inquisition in Hollywood* (Garden City, N.Y.: Doubleday, 1980) argues that despite renewed interest in the repression of radicalism in the Hollywood film industry little attention has been paid to the prior history of the men and women denounced and blacklisted. It gives the background and aftermath of the 1947 hearings. John Cogley's *Report on Blacklisting* (New York: Arno Press, 1972) is a reprint of his 1956 report on blacklisting practices in the radio, television, and motion picture industries. This report attempts to present all points of view. Stefan Kanfer's *A Journal of the Plague Years* (New York: Atheneum Press, 1973) concentrates on those left out of most histories of the period—the blacklisters, their collaborators, and the victims. The case of the Hollywood Ten has a prominent position. Victor S. Navasky's *Naming Names* (New York: Viking Press, 1980) explores how the HUAC hearings transformed the naming of names, once strongly regarded as morally reprehensible in American culture, into an act of nobility. Members of the ten have also left autobiographical accounts, including Ring Lardner, Jr.'s *The Lardners: My Family Remembered* (New York: Harper & Row, 1976), Alvah Bessie's *Inquisition in Eden* (New York: Macmillan, 1965), Edward Dmytryk's *It's a Hell of a Life But Not a Bad Living* (New York: Times Books, 1978), and Dalton Trumbo's *The Time of the Toad* (New York: Harper & Row, 1972)

Holmes, Oliver Wendell, Jr.

Born: March 8, 1841, Boston, Massachusetts
Died: March 6, 1935, Washington, D.C.
Identification: U.S. Supreme Court justice (1902-1932)
Significance: Holmes was a leading exponent of a liberal interpretation of First Amendment protections of free speech

Holmes was one of the twentieth century's most articulate legal minds; among other contributions, he developed and refined the concept of "clear and present danger" as a protection of free speech. Named after his father, who was a famous physician and writer, Holmes was graduated from Harvard College in 1861; he served for three years in the Civil War, during which he was wounded three times and was promoted to the rank of captain. He returned to Harvard to study law; after graduation in 1866, he practiced law in Boston and taught law and jurisprudence at Harvard.

Intrigued with the philosophical and historical aspects of the law, Holmes questioned many common ideas of the age, especially the assumption that established legal doctrines allowed judges to deduce logical answers to new problems. In 1881 he popularized his pragmatic and historical conceptions of the law in the influential classic *The Common Law*. "The life of the law," he wrote, "has not been logic; it has been experience." In 1882 Holmes was appointed to the Massachusetts Supreme Court, becoming chief justice in 1899. Impressed by Holmes's progressive interpretations of labor law, President Theodore Roosevelt named him to the U.S. Supreme Court in 1902.

On the U.S. Supreme Court, Holmes disagreed so often with the conservative majority that he was sometimes called the "great dissenter." He particularly criticized the way that the

Court struck down economic regulations, such as minimum wage laws, as violations of "due process of law," advocating instead the doctrine of "judicial restraint." Holmes insisted that it was the role of elected representatives to determine public policy, and that the courts should not strike down legislation except when it clearly violated the Constitution.

In cases dealing with free expression, however, Holmes gradually became persuaded that the courts should prevent legislatures from suppressing the right of minorities to express dissent. As the Supreme Court examined the limits of free speech in the years following World War I, Holmes argued that the "bad tendency" standard did not sufficiently protect the right to criticize the government and advocate change. While he approved of convictions for circulating antidraft leaflets in *Schenck v. United States* (1919), Holmes based his opinion on the "clear and present danger test," which allowed for restriction of expression only in cases of an imminent threat to the public welfare, such as the shouting of fire in a crowded theater. In his famous dissent in *Abrams v. United States* (1919), Holmes altered his test so that government could punish speech only when it "produces or is intended to produce a clear and imminent danger" of those evils which the government could "constitutionally prevent." Calling for a "free trade in ideas," he wrote that "the best test of truth is the power of the thought to get itself accepted in the competition of the market." Following his death, Supreme Court majorities repeatedly endorsed liberal interpretations of his clear and present danger test, culminating in *Brandenburg v. Ohio* (1969).

See also Clear and present danger doctrine; cummings, e. e.; Espionage Act of 1917; Meiklejohn, Alexander; *Mutual Film Corporation v. Industrial Commission of Ohio*; *Schenck v. United States*; World War I.

Holocaust, Jewish

Date: 1939-1945

Place: Germany and Europe

Significance: Various powers have censored information about the Holocaust; revisionists have denied that it happened

During World War II, millions of European Jews were exterminated by the Nazis. The German leaders attempted to restrict information about the mass killings by locating major extermination camps (such as Treblinka, Sobibor, Belzec, Maidanek, and Auschwitz (Birkenau) in occupied Poland. The Nazis wanted to prevent any repetition of the public criticism that had greeted the euthanasia program in Germany between 1939 and 1941. In public and private meetings euphemisms of "resettlement" and "special treatment" were used to describe plans for mass murder. Even the mass shootings by special execution units in Russia were described as antipartisan measures. The Nazis could not censor all news, and by the autumn of 1942, the Allies knew about the death camps.

The Press and the Holocaust. After 1942 Soviet authorities began to censor press information about mass killings of Jews. For example, in September, 1944, Soviet officials informed reporters in Maidanek that Germans had killed Poles, Russian prisoners of war, political prisoners, and Jews despite the fact that they knew that Maidanek was a death camp that targeted primarily Jews. In early 1945 the American reporter Bill Lawrence posted a story to *The New York Times* describing the massacre of Jews at Maidanek. The word "Jew" never reached New York because the Russians had struck the word from the story. The Soviets explained that they were afraid that too much emphasis on the plight of the Jews would fuel the flames of anti-Semitism. After the war, the official history of the Soviet campaigns in 1944 and 1945 by I. Konev et al., *The Great Campaign of Liberation by the Soviet Army* (1975), refers to Auschwitz's extermination factories but does not mention Jews.

At times, American officials also censored reports about the mass murder of Jews in Nazi extermination camps. Like Soviet officials, American spokesmen claimed that they did not want to emphasize the plight of the Jews because it would enflame anti-Semitism. In October, 1944, John Pehle, who worked for the War Refugee Board, obtained an eyewitness account of the atrocities in Auschwitz. Many American newspapers published this report in November, 1944, even though Elmer Davis, the head of the Office of War Information office, attempted to block publication of this story. The military censors did prevent the story from appearing in *Yank*, the Armed Forces magazine. When Richard Paul submitted a story based on Pehle's report to *Yank*, his superiors urged him to write "a less Jewish story." As a result, *Yank* did not publish the story and Jews were not mentioned when articles in the magazine described the Maidanek extermination camp.

Postwar Historical Revisionism. Even though the Nuremberg Trials clearly, abundantly, and thoroughly documented (including survivor testimony and ample physical evidence) Nazi efforts to exterminate Europe's Jews, the 1970's saw the appearance of organized efforts to deny the Holocaust. The most extreme revisionism appeared in 1980 with the founding of *The Journal of Historical Review*, which was published in Torrance, California. The journal was supported financially by the Willis A. Carto's Liberty Lobby. The first issue of this journal included papers presented at the first Revisionist Convention in Los Angeles, California, in September, 1979. The two most important editors and contributors were Arthur Butz and Austin App. Butz was an associate professor of electrical

Did the Holocaust Really Occur?

Despite efforts of certain groups to deny that the Jewish Holocaust actually occurred, a large majority of Americans have accepted it as a historical fact. In a CNN/*USA Today*/Gallup Poll taken in early 1994, 79 percent of Americans surveyed expressed a belief that the Holocaust "definitely happened." Another 17 percent agreed that it "probably happened." Only 2 percent of those surveyed thought that the Holocaust probably or definitely did not happen; the rest expressed no opinion on the question.

Jewish prisoners arrive at Nazi Germany's Auschwitz concentration camp during World War II. (Simon Wiesenthal Center)

engineering and computer science at Northwestern University and App was an instructor of English literature at various colleges. These anti-Semitic authors attribute the origins of what they call the Holocaust hoax to Zionists, who allegedly utilized the Holocaust to obtain funds and support for Israel. In the leading article of the first issue of *The Journal of Historical Review*, "The International 'Holocaust' Controversy," Butz accepts Nazi euphemisms for the Holocaust and argues that "final solution" meant deportation, not extermination. He denies that gas chambers were used to murder Jews, and he contends that the poison gas that the Nazis used was a disinfectant. In addition, he echoes Nazi claims that the special SS execution units that killed more than one million Jews in Russia were only used to combat partisans.

No historian of any reputation accepts the arguments of the California revisionists. Archival material and the testimonies of survivors make it clear that there was a Nazi plan to exterminate Jews. Some German academic historians have contributed to the dispute by attempting to relativize the Holocaust. Andreas Hillgruber published a book in 1985 in which he equates the Holocaust with the suffering of Germans on the Eastern Front in 1944 and 1945. The most extreme effort to relativize the Holocaust was attempted by the Berlin historian Ernst Nolte. He has argued that the Holocaust was only one of many genocides which include the massacres of Armenians and the murder of kulaks in the Soviet Union. Nolte has maintained that the Holocaust was not a product of Nazi ideology but rather represented a preventive measure against Bolshevik threats of extermination. Although aware of other genocides, most professional historians have rejected the attempt to relativize the Holocaust.

Many countries, and particularly Germany, have banned literature denying the Holocaust. In addition, authors of such works have been prosecuted and imprisoned. Beginning in 1978 West Germany used a law dealing with "youth-menacing" literature to ban works by Arthur Butz. Butz was also prevented from speaking in Munich, Germany, in September, 1977. A legal case against a revisionist author occurred in Canada in 1985. Ernst Zundel, a German "landed immigrant" in Canada, was tried and convicted in a court in Toronto for publishing pamphlets that denied the Holocaust. Like Butz, Zundel called the Holocaust a hoax, and he praised Hitler as a great leader. Zundel was tried for violating section 177 of the Criminal Code of Canada, which prohibits anyone from wilfully publishing material that is known to be false and is likely to cause injury to the public interest. Canada has also prosecuted another denier of the Holocaust, James Keegstra, in Red Deer, Alberta, for violating section 281 of the Canadian criminal code, which prohibits hate literature.

—Johnpeter Horst Grill

See also Archival laws; Armenian genocide; *Diary of Anne Frank, The*; Euphemism; Germany; Hate laws; Judaism; *Mein Kampf*; National Socialism; Simon Wiesenthal Center; World War II.

Bibliography

Deborah E. Lipstadt, *Denying the Holocaust: The Growing Assault on Truth and Memory* (New York: Free Press, 1993), offers the best critical review of Holocaust revisionism. The reaction of the press and the public to news about the Holocaust are examined by Walter Laqueur in *The Terrible Secret: Suppression of the Truth About Hitler's "Final Solution"* (Boston: Little, Brown, 1980), and by Deborah E. Lipstadt in *Beyond Belief: The American Press and the Coming of the Holocaust 1933-1945* (New York: Free Press, 1986). Charles S. Maier's *The Unmasterable Past: History, Holocaust, and German National Identity* (Cambridge, Mass.: Harvard University Press, 1988) reviews the Holocaust debate in Germany. A case study of the trial of a revisionist who denied the Holocaust is examined by Leonidas E. Hill, "The Trial of Ernst Zundel: Revisionism and the Law in Canada" in *Simon Wiesenthal Center Annual* 6 (1989).

Homosexuality

Definition: Same-sex romantic and sexual relationships

Significance: Homosexuality—whether expressed in romantic literary themes or explicit visual homoerotic imagery—has always invited censorship

Homosexuality—whether depicted in literature, visual arts, theater, or film—arguably is the single most-censored form of sexual desire and behavior. During the late nineteenth century's notorious Oscar Wilde trial in England, Lord Alfred Douglas described homosexuality as "The Love that dare not speak its name." In the United States, public discussion or literary treatment of the topic was almost completely curtailed—both voluntarily and legally—for almost four centuries. The position of puritan Reverend Higgeson, who referred to sodomy in 1629 as "wickedness not to bee named," is scarcely distinguishable from the 1897 decision of an Illinois judge that described the practice as "not fit to be named among Christians." By the 1930's, discussions and portrayals of sex had become more common—with the exception of homosexual themes. The extreme stigma attached to homosexual behavior continued, and few authors or publishers dared to deal directly with the subject.

The emergence of an urban gay subculture during World War II and the publication of the widely discussed Kinsey reports provided evidence that homosexual behavior was far more common than had been believed. The knowledge that they were not unique contributed to the first sustained attempt by gay men and lesbians to organize for social and political reasons. *One*, established in Los Angeles in 1953, was the first openly homophile periodical in the United States. It contained fiction, poetry, and book reviews, and it also discussed such issues as police harassment of homosexuals.

One contained no pictures or material which, by later standards, would remotely be considered obscene. It was mailed in a plain brown wrapper to a few hundred subscribers. Yet the entire run of the October, 1954, issue of *One* was seized for a time by the postmaster of Los Angeles as obscene material because it had the phrase "homosexual marriage" on the cover. It was not until January 13, 1958, that the U.S. Supreme Court reviewed the case and unanimously lifted the ban on the October issue. A volunteer columnist for *One* later opined that even though there was no written opinion from the Supreme Court, this ruling "sort of opened the floodgates" to publications with homosexual subject matter. By 1959, more than three thousand copies per issue of *One* were regularly distributed.

Perhaps more important was the 1962 case of *Manual Enterprises v. Day*, which involved magazines containing photographs of male nudes. The court ruled that although this material, which clearly appealed to the prurient tastes of male homosexuals, was "dismally unpleasant, uncouth, and tawdry," it nevertheless lacked "patent offensiveness" and therefore could not be considered legally obscene. During the next decade, the Warren Court would clear the few gay-related "obscene" books that came before it.

Even as legal constraints against gay literature seemed to dissolve, there still was considerable self-censorship by publishers. As more and more was written about homosexuality in the 1950's, for example, most editors and publishers of newspapers and magazines still felt more comfortable with the euphemistic term "sex variant" rather than "homosexual." By 1961, however, the famous personal advice columnist Ann Landers felt able to print a letter from a homosexual for the first time and to discuss it sympathetically in her widely syndicated column.

Film and Theater. Homosexuality as a theme or topic in the theater was virtually unknown before 1920. During the 1920's, the increased openness about sexuality encouraged the production of a few Broadway plays that dealt openly with lesbian themes. In reaction to this, even the relatively liberal state of New York in 1927 passed the Wales Padlock laws, which outlawed theatrical depiction of "sexual degeneracy" or "sexual perversion." These laws were not repealed until 1967.

In 1915, the Supreme Court ruled that motion pictures were not covered by the First Amendment guarantee of freedom of speech, and film censorship laws were passed in a number of states. New York's law, enacted in 1921, provided that a film could not be licensed for public showing if its exhibition would "tend to corrupt morals or incite crime." *Salome*, a 1923 tribute to Oscar Wilde, horrified New York censors, who ordered eliminated a sequence that clearly depicted a homosexual relationship between two Syrian soldiers.

Even more strict was the Production Code, a vehicle of self-censorship operated by the major studios for many decades. The code prohibited the depiction of "sex perversion or any inference of it." In 1933, for example, the word "pansy" was banned from films. Although the power of the code generally waned by the late 1950's, Stanley Kubrick's 1960 hit film *Spartacus* had several lines deleted in which Crassius (played by Laurence Olivier) is being helped out of a bath and discussing with his handsome young slave, Antonious (Tony Curtis), his taste for both men and women. As the historian John D'Emilio observed, "The shifts in sexual mores that occurred throughout the twentieth century had not extended to homosexuality."

In 1961, the Motion Picture Production Association revised its code to allow treatment of "sex deviation" in films. Of course, there had long been rumors about the sexual orientation of more than a few film stars. The famed columnist Hedda Hopper, when advised that homosexuality could now be the subject of Hollywood films, supposedly remarked: "Well, all I've got to say is that our producers shouldn't have any trouble with casting." Yet even as homosexuality emerged from the closet in films, many gay observers complained that it merely came into the shadows. In the 1960's lesbians and gay men were generally portrayed as sick or dangerous, never as sympathetic heroes.

The Emergence of Gays in the Mass Media. The mid- and late 1960's witnessed a proliferation of gay-related material that would have been suppressed in earlier decades. This material ranged from explicit visual pornography, which became far more available, to serious and often less hostile stories in the mass media. These exposed the sexual behaviors and lifestyles of ordinary gay men and women in an unprecedented manner. In 1964, *Life* magazine featured a lead story on gay life in San Francisco, including photographs taken inside gay bars. The situation was similar in academic institutions, and some historians and sociologists dared by the late 1960's to treat gay life as a subject of study. One scholar who surveyed the production of lesbian-related literature found in 1957 only four paperback originals; by 1965, the figure had skyrocketed to 348. Yet *The New York Times* did not begin using the word "gay" as an adjective until 1987, following a confrontation with GLAAD, the Gay and Lesbian Alliance Against Defamation.

Gay-Related Censorship After Stonewall. The increased availability of literary material with homosexual themes contributed to the development of the national gay liberation movement following the famous 1969 Stonewall Inn riots. Sexual preference became for the first time more or less a political cause for hundreds of thousands—if not millions—of gay Americans, who became a significant political force by the 1970's. The city of San Francisco, for example, enacted statutes against "hate crimes" that made it illegal to harass people on the basis of religion, race, or sexual preference. Those who remained convinced that homosexuality is immoral—generally members of the religious right—often opposed such laws, particularly with regard to hate speech; ironically, they would appeal on the grounds of free speech against what they called "special rights" for homosexuals. U.S. senator Jesse Helms, who had earlier threatened to cut funding for the National Endowment for the Arts because the organization had supported exhibits of Robert Mapplethorpe's gay-themed photographs, in January, 1995, introduced a bill to forbid dismissals without public hearings of federal employees who during off-duty hours publicly opposed actual or proposed government policies outlawing discrimination against gays and lesbians. Other gay rights opponents in the 1990's attacked public-school diversity training that urged tolerance of gays and lesbians. In 1995 a Des Moines, Iowa, school board election became a referendum on such a program, and an openly gay board member was defeated.

A large and thriving gay-publications business developed in the decades following Stonewall. A Different Light, the first bookstore chain devoted to gay and lesbian merchandise, opened in 1979. A major publishing trend in the 1990's saw record numbers of gay and lesbian works being published by mainstream publishers, a far cry from the virtual ban on such works in the 1950's and before. On the other hand, with the growing political clout of the religious right, and with most major Republican presidential candidates criticizing "the gay

Participants in a gay rights march on Washington, D.C., in April, 1993. (AP/Wide World Photos)

agenda," there were signs of a backlash. Across America, the growing strength of antigay forces raised the specter of renewed censorship, directed especially at gay-related materials.

—Anthony D. Branch

See also Bryant, Anita; Film advisory board; Ginsberg, Allen; Hate laws; Helms, Jesse Alexander; Mapplethorpe, Robert; *Naked Lunch*; National Endowment for the Arts; Outing; Wales padlock law.

Bibliography

John D'Emilio's *Sexual Politics, Sexual Communities—The Making of a Homosexual Minority in the United States, 1940-1970* (Chicago: University of Chicago Press, 1983) is a scholarly work that describes the growth of gay politics and shows that homosexuality has been historically a prime target of censorship forces in the United States. Jonathan Katz's *Gay/Lesbian Almanac: A New Documentary* (New York: Harper & Row, 1983) uses colorful excerpts from court records, religious writings, journalistic exposés, plays, and fiction to explore American homosexuals in writings from the early 1600's to 1980. Starting with the premise that the struggles for gay and lesbian rights in the last half century have been "almost entirely ignored" by mainstream historians, Eric Marcus in *Making History—The Struggle for Gay and Lesbian Equal Rights, 1945-1990* (New York: HarperCollins, 1992) interviewed a cross section of gay rights activists, including the elderly founders of *One* magazine. In *Gays/Justice—A Study of Ethics, Society, and Law* (New York: Columbia University Press, 1988), Richard D. Mohr focuses on the legal relationship between American government and homosexual citizens. Chapter 3 deals with the rights to privacy and free speech and their application to gay-related issues. Vito Russo's *The Celluloid Closet—Homosexuality in the Movies* (New York: Harper & Row, 1981) explores the use of gay characters and themes in American films as well as the film industry's self-censorship on the subject. A major resource on all aspects of the American gay and lesbian experience is the voluminous work edited by Lynn Witt, Sherry Thomas, and Eric Marcus, *Out in All Directions—The Almanac of Gay and Lesbian America* (New York: Warner Books, 1995). Chapter 2 is a highly readable account of the changing image of the homosexual in twentieth century America.

Hoover, J. Edgar

Born: January 1, 1895, Washington, D.C.

Died: May 2, 1972, Washington, D.C.

Identification: Director of the Federal Bureau of Investigation (FBI)

Significance: Hoover ran the FBI as his personal fiefdom for most of his forty-eight years as director, developing files on thousands of public figures, which he used to blackmail them and to suppress dissident political opinion

The son of a petty government bureaucrat, Hoover lived his entire life in Washington, D.C. During the 1920's, as he was working his way into service with the Bureau of Investigation, as the FBI was then called, he adopted the name J. Edgar Hoover to avoid confusion with a petty criminal who shared his name.

As a youth, Hoover considered entering the Presbyterian ministry. He was commander of his high school's Reserve Officer Training Corps (ROTC), which he managed with ferocious dedication, demanding absolute obedience from his cadets. Completing high school in 1913, Hoover was offered a scholarship to the University of Virginia. He chose instead to remain in Washington to study law in a special evening program that George Washington University offered to government employees. To qualify, he needed a government job, which he soon obtained, becoming a clerk and cataloger at the Library of Congress, where he mastered a classification system that he later used to organize the files of the FBI. By 1917 Hoover had been admitted to the District of Columbia bar. With the United States now at war, he was eligible for a commission in the Army but opted instead to take a job in the Department of Justice.

The Rise to Power. Hoover was compulsive about proving himself. He completed every job assigned to him promptly and well, although he had no qualms about using lies and deceit to achieve his ends. He worked long hours, being particularly diligent about working on weekends and holidays. This behavior quickly brought him to the attention of his superiors, with whom he sought strenuously to curry favor.

Hoover's rise in the Justice Department was swift. His superiors, using the excuse of wartime exigency, had no reluctance to violate citizens' constitutional rights. Hoover, who shared their contempt for legal niceties, enforced such repressive legislation as the Espionage Act of 1917, the Alien Deportation Act of 1918, and the Sedition Act of 1918. Attorney General A. Mitchell Palmer, who had long justified such laws by citing threats to national security, was impressed by the ambitious Hoover. Hoover was soon given his own secretary, Helen Gandy, who remained with him until his death fifty-four years later, and who, after his death, destroyed his secret files, which had been the bane of many of Washington's most powerful politicians, including most presidents under whom Hoover served.

By 1921 Hoover had ingratiated himself with the new attorney general, Harry M. Daugherty, with whom he shared many of the secret files he had collected. Daugherty appointed Hoover assistant director of the Bureau of Investigation; three years later, the next attorney general, Harlan Fiske Stone, gave Hoover a temporary appointment as acting director. Hoover worked so diligently at this job that in December, 1924, Stone appointed him director; Hoover was then only twenty-nine years old.

Use and Abuse of Power. Hoover was in many ways the quintessential bureaucrat—an unimaginative thinker with provincial views, whose overriding concern was the preservation of his own position and power. As a resident of the District of Columbia, he was unable to vote, and therefore there was no record of any political affiliation for him, which was distinctly to his advantage.

When Hoover took over the bureau, it was a disorganized dumping ground for a variety of political appointees for whom other jobs could not be found. He immediately sought to depoliticize and strengthen the bureau. In the early days of his

FBI director J. Edgar Hoover and his top assistant and intimate friend, Clyde Tolson, in 1954. (AP/Wide World Photos)

directorship, Hoover helped the FBI gain considerable public recognition by doggedly tracking down and apprehending such notorious criminals as John Dillinger, Baby Face Nelson, and Al Capone. Before the FBI closed in to arrest such men, Hoover was always careful to arrange attention-getting press coverage of the event.

In 1928 Hoover hired Clyde Tolson as a special agent. Tolson became Hoover's closest friend and confidant as well as his constant companion and sole heir. It was long rumored that the two were lovers, a supposition substantiated by recent research, which has established that Hoover was a transvestite and a homosexual. Evidence of his sexual orientation and activity fell into the hands of the mafia, whose leaders blackmailed him throughout his career as director. As a result, mob activity came to be less strenuously prosecuted than it might have been, although Hoover was diligent in his prosecution of criminals not connected with the mob.

Using FBI surveillance facilities, Hoover spied on thousands of people, using his secret files to intimidate high government officials and other prominent leaders. Many of the presidents under whom Hoover served sought to remove him from office. The threat that Hoover would expose some of their nefarious activities or those of close family members, however, provided the director with a job security unparalleled by any other government bureaucrat. The greatest challenge to Hoover's directorship came from the presidency of John F. Kennedy. Hoover hated the Kennedys and had a particular vendetta against Robert F. Kennedy, who served as attorney general during and after his brother's tenure in office. The assassinations of John and Robert Kennedy removed the threat that had plagued the director.

Hoover was, ironically, the prisoner of his own files. He could not leave office because of the damning material he had collected and stored. Only his death could free him—and the country—from that burden, and following Hoover's death, many of his appalling activities came to light. It was revealed that he had misappropriated public funds and had used public servants for personal services. Legislation was enacted to limit the FBI director's term of office, so that no one could ever again gain the sort of stranglehold that J. Edgar Hoover had held on the FBI and the nation. —*R. Baird Shuman*

See also Berrigan, Daniel, and Philip Francis Berrigan; Civil service; Espionage; Federal Bureau of Investigation; Kennedy, John F., assassination of; National security; Police; Presidency, U.S.

BIBLIOGRAPHY

The most comprehensive biography of Hoover is Curt Gentry's *J. Edgar Hoover: The Man and the Secrets* (New York: W. W. Norton, 1991). Thorough and somewhat sensational is Anthony Summers' *Official and Confidential: The Secret Life of J. Edgar Hoover* (New York: Putnam, 1993). Nelson Blackstock's exposé, *Cointelpro: The FBI's Secret War on Political Freedom* (New York: Vintage Books, 1976), is a hair-raising account of FBI invasion of personal privacy, as is Angela Calomiris' *Red Masquerade: Undercover for the F.B.I.* (Philadelphia: Lippincott, 1950). Ralph de Toledano's *J. Edgar Hoover: The Man in His Time* (New Rochelle, N.Y.: Arlington House, 1973) and Ovid Demaris' *The Director: An Oral Biography of J. Edgar Hoover* (New York: Harper's Magazine Press, 1975) are less thorough than later studies because much information about Hoover was still classified when they were written. Richard Gid Powers' *Secrecy and Power: The Life of J. Edgar Hoover* (New York: Free Press, 1987) remains useful.

Horror series controversy

DATE: March-September, 1995

PLACE: Canada

SIGNIFICANCE: Efforts of Nova Scotia parents to have a series of children's books banned from school libraries provoked a Canada-wide debate on censorship

In February, 1995, three Nova Scotia parents asked the Halifax County-Bedford District School Board to remove a series of children's horror-thriller books from the libraries and classrooms of the district's seventy-five schools. One series particularly targeted by the parents was the "Goosebumps" horror series written by R. L. Stine, whose books have been exceptionally popular among eight- to twelve-year-olds. With overall sales in excess of 100 million copies and ongoing sales of more than a million copies a month, Stine may well be the best- selling author in the world.

Although Stine has occasionally been described as a sort of Stephen King for the young set, the titles of his books—such as *The Horror at Camp Jellyjam*, *Let's Get Invisible*, and *The*

Abominable Snowman of Pasadena—hint at their goofy and only mildly frightening content. His books contain no offensive language or disturbing marital problems, and his protagonists never die. Nevertheless, they have been subjected to censorship challenges in many places throughout North America. The petition of the Nova Scotian mothers to the school board, for example, claimed that books such as his encouraged children "to read books that may develop unhealthy and harmful thoughts and behavior." They also suggested that horror books "erode away moral values like self-respect and respect for other people and property." They accused Stine of hooking "younger children on his more subtle Goosebumps series so they'll move on to the more graphic and perverse themes in the Fear Street series when they are teenagers." They also argued that the school district had a policy of zero tolerance in the schools, and that the horror books violated this policy.

When a motion was made to the Halifax County-Bedford District School Board to remove the books, the board initially seemed inclined to comply. Instead, however, it referred the matter to a committee comprising supervisors, librarians, teachers, and parents. Over the next six months this committee heard evidence from parents, educators, and experts. Meanwhile, the parents' challenge was intensively covered in Canada's national news media. At one point, a Halifax newspaper published an entire page of letters from young readers, most of whom defended the books and expressed their outrage at adult attempts to censor their reading. Some parents also wrote letters describing the positive impact that the books had on their children's reading habits and urging the board to stay out of the censorship business.

In September, 1995, the board accepted the advice of its special committee that the Goosebumps series was appropriate for the age and interest level of elementary school students, and that its books should remain in the libraries. The board also ruled that the Fear Street and other advanced horror series should be restricted to the junior high school libraries.

See also Books, children's; Books, young adult; Canada; King, Stephen; Libraries, school; Violence.

House Committee on Un-American Activities (HUAC)

Founded: 1938

Type of organization: Investigative committee of the U.S. House of Representatives

Significance: This committee was the most powerful U.S. government organization ever to be involved in censorship activities

From the earliest days of Puritan theocracy to the conservative school boards of small-town, late twentieth century America, attempts at censorship by various extensions of municipal, state, and federal government have been an integral and definitive part of American society. No governmental organization, however, has ever attained the power and notoriety of the investigative committee of the U.S. Congress known as HUAC. It began as a special committee in 1938; before being disbanded in 1969, its thirty-year existence was largely dedicated to what it recognized as the need to protect an unsuspecting American public from the subtle infiltration tactics of international communism. Writers, artists, and entertainers, generally perceived to have a wide following and, therefore, ample opportunity to transmit communist ideology, were among its most frequent targets.

Origins and Early Activities. HUAC was an outgrowth of earlier congressional efforts to investigate purportedly seditious ideological organizations actively working to subvert the U.S. government. The rise of Bolshevism after the Russian Revolution of 1917 and what was perceived as the international initiative of communism had led in the United States to the infamous Red Scare of 1919 and 1920 and the political persecution of communists and socialists. In the wake of the stock market collapse in 1929, Congress once again turned its attention to the threat from the Left and created a special investigative committee under the chairmanship of Republican representative Hamilton Fish of New York.

In 1934 a second investigative committee was chaired by Democratic representative John McCormack of Massachusetts. Its investigation produced two laws: the compulsory registration of foreign agents disseminating propaganda in the United States, and the empowering of congressional committees holding hearings outside of Washington to issue subpoenas.

Although both the Fish and the McCormack committees had been formed in response to perceived anti-American activities, the committee of 1938 was the first to be officially known as the Committee on Un-American Activities, and the first to introduce the issue of the committee's responsibility for censorship of the arts. Republican representative J. Parnell Thomas of New Jersey, destined to be HUAC's most infamous chairman, called for a sweeping investigation of the Federal Theatre and Writers projects which were sponsored by the Works Progress Administration created by President Franklin D. Roosevelt. Undoubtedly the two projects were havens for many writers and ideologues of the Left, but they were also a farsighted effort on the part of government to preserve a generation of writers and performers for the future of American arts and letters. Congress, however, faced with the pressing financial strictures of the times, was not inclined to champion the arts when the needs of the country seemed far more basic. In July, 1939, an amendment to save the program was defeated and the Federal Theatre and Writers projects were voted out of existence.

The Cold War. The end of World War II in 1945 introduced the Cold War between the nations of the West and the Eastern Bloc of the Soviet Union. Given what many members of Congress considered its special mission, HUAC was advanced from its special investigative status to become a standing committee, and it continued in that role until 1969.

In the decade following the end of World War II, particularly in 1947 and 1951, the committee gained its greatest national prominence and its greatest notoriety. Under Chairman Thomas, HUAC turned its attention to Hollywood and the film industry and would later expand its investigations into radio and television. In the scripts and scenarios of American films, much of what had been considered instrumental in strengthening the alliance between the Western and Soviet powers working to defeat the Axis was now considered by HUAC to be morally objectionable and politically insidious.

In October, 1947, HUAC began a series of highly publicized hearings into the issue of communist infiltration of the film industry. Chairman Thomas claimed to have a list of Hollywood films that contained scenes and passages of dialogue written for the primary purpose of dispensing communist propaganda to an unsuspecting American public. The list was never produced. The committee finally responded to the call for specific examples by citing three films—*Mission to Moscow* (1943), *North Star* (1943), and *Song of Russia* (1944), all made when the Soviet Union was a war ally—for their decidedly pro-Soviet sympathies. Among the many witnesses called to testify, those deemed least cooperative were the "Hollywood Ten," eight writers, a producer, and a director, who claimed the protection of the First Amendment and what they considered the inherent right to privacy it affords. In response to their position, the Hearst newspaper chain proclaimed nationwide "the need for federal censorship of motion pictures."

The film industry responded with its own preemptive strike. Meeting at the Waldorf-Astoria Hotel in New York in November, 1947, the industry's leading executives voted to discharge or suspend the ten hostile witnesses, at least until each man had purged himself of contempt charges and declared under oath that he was not a communist. This was the beginning of the infamous blacklist.

HUAC returned to motion pictures in 1951, holding extensive hearings from May through early November. These hearings turned from the futile attempt to prove the ideological corruption of motion picture content to the presence of communists and former communists throughout the industry. To avoid the blacklist, witnesses were required not only to testify under oath as to their noncommunist status but also to provide the committee with names of colleagues and coworkers whom they suspected of communist activity or tendencies.

Then-actor Ronald Reagan was one of the "friendly" witnesses to testify before HUAC during the committee's 1947 investigation into suspected communist activities in the film industry. (AP/Wide World Photos)

As a rationale for its actions, HUAC turned from assurance to supposition. "Had these Communist efforts gone unexposed," the committee stated in its 1952 annual report, "it is almost inevitable that the content of motion pictures would have been influenced and slanted and become a medium of Communist propaganda." From 1952 through 1958, HUAC turned from motion pictures to the rest of the entertainment industry, particularly radio, television, and publishing, using the unofficial weapon of the blacklist as a means of coercion. Its attention to media gradually diminished in the 1960's, and after its abolition in 1969, its affairs were taken over by the House Internal Security Committee. —*Richard Keenan*

See also Blacklisting; Communist Party of the U.S.A.; Congress, U.S.; Film censorship; First Amendment; Hollywood Ten; Hypocrisy; Intellectual freedom; Lardner, Ring, Jr.; Trumbo, Dalton.

Bibliography

Two books are essential to any study of HUAC activities: Walter Goodman's *The Committee: The Extraordinary Career of the House Committee on Un-American Activities* (New York: Farrar, Straus and Giroux, 1968), and Stefan Kanfer's *A Journal of the Plague Years* (New York: Atheneum, 1973). Both give thorough and comprehensive—if not entirely objective—overviews of HUAC's career. Goodman's appendix on the dates and subjects of all hearings from 1938 through 1967 is most helpful. John Cogley's "The Mass Hearings" (excerpted from his two-volume *Report on Blacklisting* [New York: Fund for the Republic, 1956]) is reprinted in *The American Film Industry*, Tino Balio, ed. (Madison: University of Wisconsin Press, 1976). It is a thorough and objective analysis, despite the fact that many sources, still fearing the blacklist, refused to be identified. "Hollywood at War for America and at War with Itself," chapter 15 of Robert Sklar's *Movie-Made America: A Cultural History of American Movies* (New York: Vintage, 1994), offers the best concise analysis of the threat of HUAC to the film industry.

How to Eat Fried Worms

Type of work: Book
Published: 1973
Author: Thomas Rockwell (1933-)
Subject matter: Children's story about a ten-year-old boy who accepts a dare to eat worms
Significance: Efforts to keep this book out of libraries reflect a modern trend to censor children's books because of isolated objectionable passages

Billy, the protagonist of this story, proves himself equal to the challenge of eating fifteen worms in fifteen days by devising a variety of dishes to disguise their taste. Thomas Rockwell's graphic descriptions of these dishes is humor of a type that appeals to middle-graders, but it alarmed some parents and adult library users. Parents complained of the book's violence and vulgarity. For example, a Middletown, New Jersey, parent tried to have the book banned from a local library in 1988. This attempt failed; however, the book was removed from the Livelle Elementary School library in La Paz, Indiana, in 1991, after a library patron complained the book used the word "bastard."

See also Books, children's; Libraries; Libraries, school; Offensive language.

Howe, Joseph

Born: December 13, 1804, Halifax, Nova Scotia, Canada

Died: June 1, 1873, Halifax, Nova Scotia, Canada

Identification: Canadian newspaper publisher and politician

Significance: Howe's acquittal on criminal libel charges set a precedent for freedom of the press throughout North America

In January, 1835, Joseph Howe, publisher of the Halifax newspaper the *Novascotian*, printed an anonymous letter claiming that local government authorities were extorting a thousand pounds a year from the poor. Howe was then charged with criminal libel. Not satisfied with merely printing a retraction in his newspaper, Howe took the authorities to court. No lawyer would take his case, however, claiming that because the criminal law would not allow him to defend the truth of his statements, he had no defense. Howe responded by studying libel law himself and preparing a speech in his own defense.

Howe's trial lasted two days. In a brilliantly inspired six-hour speech, Howe appealed to the jury, ingeniously couching direct accusations against the authorities in emotional and eloquent requests for justice and freedom of the press.

Both the judge and the district attorney were appointees of the government, and the judge made a point of instructing the jury to find Howe guilty of libel. Despite this, the jury returned a verdict of not guilty in ten minutes. The trial was heralded throughout both Canada and the United States as a confirmation of true freedom of the press.

See also Canada; Libel; Newspapers.

Hugo, Victor

Born: February 26, 1802, Besançon, France

Died: May 22, 1885, Paris, France

Identification: French novelist and political critic

Significance: Hugo was forced into exile for his political views during France's Second Empire, and he suffered from periodic censorship of his literary works during the mid-nineteenth century because of their republican political content

Although he became a virtual cultural icon in France during the early years of the Third Republic (1871-1885) due primarily to the fame of such novels as *Les Miserables* (1862), *The Hunchback of Notre Dame* (1831), and *The Toilers of the Sea* (1865), Hugo suffered for his political views earlier in his career. He began his political life as a peer under the monarchy of Louis Philippe, but transferred his support to the republicans during 1848 and was elected as a deputy to the constituent assembly that was created shortly after the overthrow of Louis Philippe and establishment of the Second Republic that same year.

Although Hugo originally welcomed the future Napoleon III to France and supported the latter's successful bid for the presidency of the Second Republic in December, 1848, he gradually alienated himself from the Bonapartist camp by his outspoken opposition to the government's policy toward the papacy and uncompromising republicanism. This process was complete by the time Napoleon III launched his coup d'état of December, 1851. Fearing arrest, Hugo went into hiding immediately after the event and was officially sentenced to exile shortly thereafter. He moved first to Belgium (where he stayed for only a few months) and then to the Channel Islands off the coast of France, first Jersey, then Guernsey, where he lived for eighteen years.

While in exile, Hugo wrote a number of works attacking Napoleon III and his destruction of the Second Republic: *Histoire d'un crime* (1852), *Napoleon le petit* (1852), and *Châtiments* (1853). *Histoire d'un crime* would not be published until after Hugo returned to France in 1871. *Napoleon le petit* and *Châtiments* were published by a Belgian house and smuggled into France throughout the Second Empire. Hugo's later exile writings, such as *Les Contemplations* (1856-1857), *La Légende des siècles* (1859, 1877, 1883), and *Les Miserables*, were legally published and distributed in France—but only after government censors determined they were nonpolitical in content. The Russian government of Nicholas I was not as flexible; it banned all of Hugo's work in 1850. The Roman Catholic church also placed his work on its *Index Librorum Prohibitorum*.

Hugo was offered two amnesties during his exile, but he refused to return to France while Napoleon III was in power. He did finally come back the day after the proclamation of the Third Republic in 1871. Ironically, the romantic republicanism that forced him into exile in 1851 now made him a national hero, and he enjoyed a form of secular literary sainthood in his homeland until his death in 1885.

See also Abelard, Peter; Flaubert, Gustave; France; Luther, Martin; Puritans; Religion.

Human Genome Project

Definition: A multinational effort to map out where genes lie on chromosomes, with the goal of allowing researchers and physicians to predict genetic complications and pinpoint gene therapies

Significance: Efforts to patent the information accumulated by the project have threatened to restrict its use and availability to researchers around the world

Every human cell has more than fifty thousand genes—the segments of chromosomes that perform certain functions in the building and regulation of cells, and therefore the entire body. For example, a gene for eye color is in the same place, on the same chromosome, in every cell of every human being. The genetic information, and therefore the eye color, may differ among people, but the location of the gene is the same in each of them.

In 1990 the U.S. National Institutes of Health and the Department of Energy created the National Center for Human Genome Research. Its goal was to determine the exact locations of all genes in their chromosomes, as well as to establish the sequence of nucleotides—estimated to be about three billion pairs—of all the genes. The fifteen-year-project was to be completed by 2005, at an estimated cost of three billion dollars. The project has had a great commercial potential. Genetic treatments for breast cancer, diabetes, or sickle-cell anemia could, for example, yield billions of dollars to hospitals, universities, and pharmaceutical companies—so long as they can corner the market on treatment processes. If every hospital could treat genetically influenced diseases equally, the few that pioneered the techniques would not necessarily profit more than the rest. Therefore, genetic information could be valuable. For this reason, drug companies have filed for patents on genes, and even one-cell microorganisms, for years. This process, a murky area of patent law, has generated fear among some leaders of the Human Genome Project who have worried that if the NIH does not file for patents on the genome, other countries or companies would.

Disgusted with NIH efforts to acquire patents, Nobel Prize-winning scientist James Watson resigned as head of the project in 1992. He argued that withholding scientific data of any kind for nationalistic advantage was distasteful to him. Meanwhile, opposition to the patenting efforts was growing. Biotechnology companies pleaded with the NIH to put its information in the public domain, so that all companies might compete on an equal basis to discover possible therapies. Bioethicists complained that no institution should have a monopoly on information that exists within every human being.

In 1992 the U.S. Patent Office rejected the NIH application to patent the genome. Afterward there were efforts to revise the law or appeal the decision. However, a team of researchers in France, headed by Daniel Cohen, may make the patent question moot. The team has already sketched a preliminary genome, and has pledged to donate the map to the United Nations, which would make the information freely available to everyone.

See also Copyright law; Genetic research; Science.

Hume, David

Born: May 7, 1711, Edinburgh, Scotland
Died: August 25, 1776, Edinburgh, Scotland
Identification: English philosopher
Significance: Hume argued in support of free speech and against press censorship; many of his writings were listed on the *Index Librorum Prohibitorum*

Born in Scotland of Berwickshire parents, Hume lived most of his life in Scotland, with brief stays in England and France. He ranks with John Locke and George Berkeley among the principal English philosophers of the Enlightenment, and his work strongly influenced the German philosopher Immanuel Kant. Hume's major works are *A Treatise of Human Nature* (1739), *An Enquiry Concerning Human Understanding* (1748), and *Dialogues Concerning Natural Religion* (1779). He also wrote a multivolume *History of England* (1754-1763) and a collection of political and economic *Essays, Moral and Political*, also titled *Political Discourses* (1741).

Hume was a skeptic who argued that reason could prove neither the existence of God, the immortality of the soul, nor the truth of miracles. His views scandalized and offended many contemporaries. He wrote at a time when the English press was relatively free of censorship; the last statute licensing printers had expired in 1694. Nevertheless, he was denied a professorship at Edinburgh University because people believed he was an atheist. Hume also agreed not to publish essays on suicide and the immortality of the soul when the publisher was threatened with a libel suit. Publication of *Dialogues Concerning Natural Religion* was deferred until after his death.

Hume discussed censorship in *Essays, Moral and Political*. He defended liberty of the press because only it could prevent dictatorship and arbitrary power. A free press is the easiest way to inform the public about the rise of dictatorial power. It can also arouse the people to oppose such power. Many times the fear of arousing the people will be enough to stop governments in any attempt to reduce liberty. Hume also considered arguments in favor of censorship. One argument in favor of censorship held that publication of a book or article can lead to riot and rebellion. Hume countered that because people usually read alone, even if a publication outrages them, the opportunity for action with enough people to cause riot or rebellion is likely to be missing.

Another argument favoring censorship was the need to counter the spreading of false and pernicious beliefs that full freedom of the press allows. Hume admitted that false and pernicious statements will be spread along with the true. However, censorship will not stop the spread of falsity. People will still talk and there will be rumors even when freedom of the press disappears. Moreover, governments should welcome total freedom of the press. False rumors usually indicate a discontented and unhappy people. A free press will allow governments a chance to remedy the grievances of the people long before riot and rebellion appear.

Freedom of the press also contributes to the maintenance of free governments. People used to reading in a free press are more likely to develop the ability to think critically and to distinguish truth from falsehood. Such people are less likely to be seduced by idle rumors. In the end, such people will be better able to judge wisely on public matters.

See also Atheism; *Index Librorum Prohibitorum*; Kant, Immanuel; United Kingdom.

Hus, Jan

Born: 1372 or 1373, Husinec, southern Bohemia
Died: July 6, 1415, Constance (now in Germany)
Identification: Czech religious reformer
Significance: Hus was burned at the stake by Roman Catholic authorities for refusing to recant his religious beliefs

After Hus was educated at the University of Prague, he was ordained a Roman Catholic priest in 1400. He then taught at the university and became a well-known preacher in Prague. He also soon became a leader in the Czech reform movement, initially attacking the wealth, corruption, and worldliness of the church. Eventually he also questioned church doctrine. After 1401 he was deeply influenced by the writings of John Wyclif, a mid-fourteenth century English church reformer whose beliefs had been denounced as heretical. Hus stated his own position in a variety of theological treatises, including his principal work, *De Ecclesia* (1413).

In 1415 Hus attended the Council of Constance to defend his beliefs. Although traveling under an assurance of safe conduct, he was imprisoned and questioned by hostile authorities. He was charged with having denied several crucial church doctrines, including the indulgences, transubstantiation, the sacerdotal character of holy orders, and the authority of the pope. However, of the thirty articles of which he stood accused, probably none accurately reflected his beliefs. He refused to recant these articles on the legalistic ground that he could not abjure what he did not believe. Hus's confrontational and uncompromising personality served him poorly, as he alienated even his potential allies. The church council condemned Hus as a Wyclifite heretic, ordered his books destroyed, and burned him at the stake.

These contemporary drawings show Jan Hus being burned at the stake and his ashes being removed. (Library of Congress)

See also Book burning; Death; Heresy; Joan of Arc; Luther, Martin; Opera; Reformation, the; Thomas à Kempis.

Hustler

Type of work: Magazine
First published: 1974
Publisher: Larry Flynt (1942-)
Subject matter: Sexually explicit pictures, stories, articles, and humor aimed at adult male readers
Significance: *Hustler* has been involved in many legal battles including two U.S. Supreme Court decisions

Hustler magazine was begun by Larry Flynt, the owner of a string of Ohio nightclubs of the same name. From its inception it has competed against other men's magazines by emphasizing graphic sexual images and vulgar humor. When it first appeared in July, 1974, it sold 160,000 issues; by 1983 its monthly circulation was two and a half million.

The magazine has involved Flynt in many protracted legal battles, including several libel suits brought by *Penthouse* magazine and its publisher Bob Guccione. Kathy Keeton, the vice-chairperson of *Penthouse*, attempted to sue Flynt for remarks he made in 1975 and 1976. When she discovered that the statute of limitations had run out everywhere in the United States except in the state of New Hampshire, she filed a suit against Flynt there. At issue was the question of whether a magazine could be sued in any locality in which it was sold. The case eventually reached the U.S. Supreme Court, which ruled in Keeton's favor. This case established the legal precedent that persons who believed themselves libeled could sue in any jurisdiction where the allegedly libellous material was read.

Hustler's second Supreme Court decision started with a satirical advertisement depicting the television evangelist Jerry Falwell endorsing an alcoholic beverage while describing a sexual experience he once had with his own mother in an outhouse. Falwell sued Flynt for intentionally inflicting emotional distress. When this case reached the U.S. Supreme Court, the Court unanimously ruled that the satirical advertisement was protected speech. This ruling established that targets of satirical attacks could not evade the legal standards of libel by claiming an emotional distress tort. The ruling also reinforced the right of editorial cartoonists and satirists to lampoon public figures.

See also Caricature; *Doonesbury*; Libel; Men's magazines; Moral Majority; *Penthouse*; *Screw*.

Hutchinson, Anne

Born: July 17, 1591, Alford, Lincolnshire, England
Died: August or September, 1643, Pelham Bay, New Amsterdam (later Bronx, New York)
Identification: Colonial American religious leader
Significance: Hutchinson was banished from Massachusetts Bay Colony for expressing religious views that challenged patriarchal authority

Hutchinson's confrontation with colonial authorities in Boston from 1636 to 1638 has often been called the "Antinomian Controversy," after Greek words meaning "against the established order." Shortly after this bright and eloquent woman

Modern painting of Anne Hutchinson preaching in her Boston home. (Library of Congress)

came to the Puritan colony with her husband, she began to express her opinions of Boston church leaders, assessing who was blessed by God and worth heeding and who was not. In such a religious society, she provided not only diversion but stimulation, and soon even the new young governor, Henry Vane, fell under her growing influence.

John Winthrop, who had led the Puritans to establish the Massachusetts Bay Colony in 1630, helped organize a response to the threat that Hutchinson posed, for their colonial experiment emphasized a covenant, or contractual relationship, between God and their community as a whole. Although the Puritan leaders had earlier often challenged church authority over individual belief in England, in Massachusetts Bay they were the church authority; through their prosecution of Hutchinson they intended to show that dissension within their ranks, especially when it challenged the authority of leaders, would not be tolerated. To add insult to injury, Hutchinson was a woman speaking out against men, and thus the patriarchal structure of their culture was also under attack.

Hutchinson's civil trial took place in November, 1637. Winthrop, recently re-elected by coalescing forces against the faction that Hutchinson represented, chaired the panel of judges. As the judges reviewed her lack of deference to church leaders, Hutchinson blurted out an admission that sealed her fate—that God revealed Himself to her directly through revelations. The Puritans believed this to be heresy. If they allowed citizens to claim God spoke to them directly, and that this took precedence over civil and religious laws, chaos would result. Hutchinson was found guilty; Winthrop sent her to jail to await banishment.

Four months later, in March, 1638, Hutchinson underwent a religious trial before her Boston congregation. Since her first trial, her congregation had returned to the fold and accepted Winthrop's position. Although Hutchinson reversed herself near the end, suggesting that perhaps she had erred, they could not forgive her because of the individualism she represented. She was formally excommunicated and cast out by the congregation. The judge passing sentence intoned, "In the name of Christ I do deliver you up to Satan."

Banished and excommunicated, Hutchinson was offered sanctuary in Rhode Island by Roger Williams. There she led some followers and founded the town of Portsmouth. A few years later she and some followers settled near Pelham Bay in New York, where in August, 1643, she and five of her fifteen children were killed by Indians.

See also Heresy; Joan of Arc; Puritans; Williams, Roger; Women.

Huxley, Aldous

BORN: July 26, 1894, Godalming, Surrey, England

DIED: November 22, 1963, Los Angeles, California

IDENTIFICATION: Novelist and essayist

SIGNIFICANCE: Huxley consistently challenged the status quo, pointing out the dangers of a technologically produced contentment and later advocating mysticism and, in some works, the use of hallucinogenic drugs

After studying literature at Oxford University, Aldous Huxley began writing for the magazine *Athenaeum* in London and also reviewing plays for the *Westminster Gazette* in 1919. By 1921, having already published four volumes of verse, Huxley embarked on a career as a free-lance writer. His early novels *Chrome Yellow* (1921), *Antic Hay* (1923), and *Point Counter Point* (1928), depictions of social decadence, began to establish his reputation; *Brave New World* (1932) confirmed it.

Brave New World has remained his most widely read work. A portrayal of a nightmarish twenty-fifth century dystopia, the novel presents a world in which technology seduces people into becoming willing automatons by providing them with creature comforts and drug-induced happiness. Genetic engineering, meanwhile, produces appropriate numbers of people with appropriate levels of intelligence to fill the requirements of society, thereby eliminating the potential for rebellion as well as such individual virtues as creativity, bravery, and fidelity. It was not, however, the novel's horrific description of technology but its portrayal of sexual freedom and drug use that led to *Brave New World* being banned from some school curricula and many libraries.

Huxley's later work developed these themes while also introducing new ones. *Ape and Essence* (1948) offers a vision of a future dominated by savage individualism, as the survivors of an atomic holocaust struggle to live on; it, too, is a future ravaged by technology. With *Eyeless in Gaza* (1936), Huxley began to advocate a philosophy of mysticism, and he pursued this view for much of the rest of his life. Following his move to California in 1937 for reasons of health, he wrote *Gray Eminence* (1941), a study of a sixteenth century priest who had to choose between a life of reclusive meditation and calls to serve the political interests of the French crown. Huxley later suggested in *The Doors of Perception* (1954) that the use of psychoactive drugs might be a shortcut to mystical experience. His advocacy of drugs made him a favorite of the youth culture of the 1960's and won for him a place among those pictured on the cover of the Beatles' album *Sgt. Pepper's Lonely Hearts Club Band* (1967). During the 1960's, *The Doors of Perception* was banned from some school districts' reading lists.

See also Drug education; Orwell, George.

Hyde Park Speakers Corner

Description: Part of London's Hyde Park

Significance: Since the late nineteenth century, this area has been a center for unrestrained and uncensored speech

Located at the northeast corner of London's Hyde Park, Speakers Corner (which should not be confused with "Hyde Park Corner" at the park's southeast corner) is situated near Marble Arch and Cumberland Gate, close to the site of the notorious Tyburn executions of the eighteenth century. Here, "soap box" orators have long gathered—especially on Sundays—and held forth on numerous, often controversial, topics of public interest. This practice has spread to at least one of Great Britain's former colonies, as a similar site developed in Australia, at Sydney's Domain, a park in the center of Sydney. Speakers may say virtually anything at Speakers Corner; however, three kinds of restrictions are enforced: no microphones, no obscenity, and no "breaches of the peace." The latter restriction essentially means that neither "fighting words" nor fighting itself is allowed.

The free-wheeling free speech traditions of Speakers Corner go back to the growth of democratic workers' protest meetings during the nineteenth century, when Hyde Park was the site of numerous political demonstrations, including the "Reform Riot" of 1866, which was staged by protesters demanding an extension of Britain's franchise. The name "Speakers Corner" itself, however, was not generally used until after World War I. In 1872 the area was officially set aside as a haven for speaking and political demonstrations. By the early twentieth century, the appearance of Sunday "lecturers" of all varieties was well established. Some orators have brought placards and ladders or other portable platforms to increase their visibility. Heckling speakers is an accepted practice, and, among experienced speakers, answering hecklers has become a fine art.

See also Australia; Fighting words; Free speech; Street oratory; United Kingdom.

Speakers supporting every imaginable view on politics, religion, and other subjects roll makeshift lecterns into Hyde Park on Sundays and hold forth without fear of government restraints. (R. Kent Rasmussen)

Hypocrisy

Definition: Advocating one form of behavior while practicing another

Significance: Because political leaders can practice hypocrisy only under secrecy, hypocritical politicians support excessive censorship for their own self-protection

Although hypocritical behavior can exist in many people and circumstances, it is especially likely to arise under conditions of censorship and secrecy. It feeds on secrecy because it is impossible to pretend to be virtuous when one's vices are in public view. Censorship, in turn, reinforces secrecy by protecting hypocrites, even when secrecy breaks down. Hypocrisy can occur in the secret areas of the hypocrites' lives even in open societies, but in closed societies, the secret lives of top officials are protected by censorship as well.

Censorship and secrecy combine to allow governmental or societal leaders to be hypocrites. Historically, censors have often pretended to uphold virtuous ideals and enforced them on others, while secretly violating those standards. Some medieval popes, for example, decried sex outside monogamous marriage, while fathering illegitimate children themselves.

Although Marxist theory espoused personal liberation (favoring easy divorce and free love), the Soviet Union's sponsored Marxist-Leninist regimes imposed highly puritanical rules on citizens. The regimes insisted that building a new socialist world required everyone's energy and thus condemned sexual activity outside monogamous marriage. These regimes enforced extensive censorship in culture and the arts as well as in politics and education. While Puritanism was imposed on the people, top Communist Party officials often used censorship to hide their own libertine sexual lives from public view. The Soviet Union's long-term dictator Joseph Stalin, China's Communist Party chairman Mao Zedong, and Cuba's Fidel Castro all married many times or had numerous extramarital affairs in violation of their own regimes' espoused monogamous ideals.

Some of these leaders' high-level subordinates were even worse. Stalin's long-term secret police chief, Lavrenti Beria, was the final enforcer of censorship on everyone, but became notorious for driving around in government limousines, picking up underage females, and demanding sexual favors from them under the threat that their families would be secretly killed or sent to labor camps if they did not comply. One of Mao Zedong's principal cultural and sexual censors, Kang Sheng, amassed a large collection of Chinese erotica. With the help of the secret police, Kang Sheng confiscated any erotica he could find in China, sorted through it, and kept the "best" for himself. Communist regimes' censorship of sexual materials was only part of a broader governmental censorship banning many political or social ideas, even if those ideas were secretly advocated by top officials in secret conversations of their own.

Even open societies, such as the United States, have some secrecy and censorship enabling some leaders to advocate strict censorship of sexually explicit materials, while using such materials themselves. Throughout the 1980's and 1990's, some conservative religious leaders sought to impose puritanical sexual standards on society while engaging in the very behavior they decried. Evangelist Jimmy Swaggart, for example, decried prostitution and pornography while engaging in those activities.

See also China; Cuba; Mao Zedong; Soviet Union; Stalin, Joseph.

I

I Am Curious—Yellow

Type of work: Film
Released: 1967
Director: Vilgot Sjöman (1924-   )
Subject matter: Exploration of the intimate relationship of a young Swedish couple
Significance: This pioneering treatment of explicit sex on the screen became the focus of several court cases that helped reinterpret the legal definition of obscenity in the United States

This Swedish film, directed by Vilgot Sjöman, a protégé of Ingmar Bergman, is widely considered one of the most sexually explicit films ever intended for a general audience. This was Sjöman's second battle with American censors, the first being his film *491* (1964), which an appellate court had finally permitted to enter the country. The importer and distributor was Grove Press, which had also published Henry Miller's novel *Tropic of Cancer.*

Although only ten minutes of the two-hour film contain sex scenes, they include full-frontal male and female nudity, sexual intercourse, fellatio, and cunnilingus. The director had consciously tried to produce a film that would break previous boundaries; he testified that he had wanted to portray Swedish society of the 1960's and show a woman asking for "the same freedom" as men. The film, therefore, attempted a certain amount of social commentary; Lena, the female lead, demonstrates against the Vietnam War outside the American embassy, interviewing Swedish citizens about their opinions on the war. Some judges saw this social commentary as a patently strained and contrived ploy to provide legitimacy for the sexual scenes.

Scene from the Swedish film I Am Curious—Yellow. (Museum of Modern Art/Film Stills Archive)

The standards for obscenity had been established in *Roth v. United States* (1957): If the dominant theme of the material taken as a whole appeals to a prurient interest in sex, and the material is patently offensive because it affronts contemporary community standards relating to the description or representation of sexual matters, and the material is utterly without redeeming social value, then the book or film is obscene.

I Am Curious—Yellow was banned from entry into the United States by the U.S. Customs Service. A jury in New York State declared it obscene, but the Court of Appeals for the Second Circuit, by a vote of two to one, reversed the decision and permitted the film into the country. Much litigation followed, the most significant case being *Grove Press v. Maryland State Board of Censors* (1971), which relied heavily on the dissenting opinion in the earlier case to find the film obscene. The lawyer representing the film appealed the case to the U.S. Supreme Court. Because Justice William O. Douglas had been published by Evergreen Press, which was owned by Grove Press, he excused himself from the case. The Court split four to four, which therefore affirmed the state court's finding of obscenity. Since then, *I Am Curious—Yellow* has been available in some communities and not in others.

See also Customs laws, U.S.; Film censorship; Grove Press; Obscenity: legal definitions; Sex in the arts; Sweden; *Tropic of Cancer.*

I Dream of Jeannie

Type of work: Television program
Broadcast: 1965-1970
Creator and executive producer: Sidney Sheldon (1917-   )
Subject matter: Sitcom about an astronaut who becomes the reluctant master of an attractive female genie
Significance: Although the sitcom was designed to exploit the physical beauty of its star, network censors would not allow her navel to be exposed

This sitcom began with an American astronaut (Larry Hagman) finding an old bottle on a deserted beach. When he opens it, an attractive two-thousand-year-old female genie (Barbara Eden) pops out. Grateful for being freed, she rewards the astronaut by making him her master. The astronaut is flabbergasted by what has transpired. The genie—who is named Jeannie—is determined to make life wonderful for her newfound master, whether he likes it or not.

Although *I Dream of Jeannie* was never anything more than a male wish-fulfillment fantasy, censors of the National

Broadcasting Company (NBC) were adamant about covering Eden's body as much as possible. The first costume presented to the censors was too revealing: Eden's outfit was to consist of a bolero jacket top, an Asian dancer's belt, and Arabian pantaloons. It was such a titillating and sexy outfit that the network censors were outraged. They insisted that Eden wear lined pantaloons in order to hide her legs. They also insisted that her navel could not be exposed. When newspaper reporters learned of the furor, they wrote editorials ridiculing the network, which refused to back down. Through the five years that the series was produced, Eden never exposed her navel to audiences; instead, she hid it under wide belts or plugs that matched her skin tone.

In 1985 the cast of the original series reprised their roles in a television film entitled *I Dream of Jeannie: Fifteen Years Later*. For the first time in her Jeannie role, Eden was allowed to expose her navel.

See also Nudity; Television; Television networks.

I Know Why the Caged Bird Sings

Type of work: Book
Published: 1970
Author: Maya Angelou (Marguerite Johnson; 1928-   )
Subject matter: Memoir of Angelou's childhood and adolescence, and the troubles she experienced growing up as a poor African American during the 1930's
Significance: Although honored as a modern African American classic, this book ranks as one of the most frequently challenged books of the late twentieth century

The American Library Association repeatedly included Maya Angelou's *I Know Why the Caged Bird Sings* on its lists of the most frequently challenged books during the 1980's and 1990's. People for the American Way reported it as the ninth-most challenged book in American public schools. Angelou's steamy autobiography of her early years has offended many parents and pressure groups who want the book banned from schools and libraries. They have objected to the book's grimly graphic descriptions of child molestation, its explicit sex scenes, its coarse language, its irreverent attitude toward institutional religions, and its pervading bitterness toward whites and the racism of the 1930's. They have particularly objected to a key scene of an incestuous rape and to Angelou's account of her own out-of-wedlock teen pregnancy. In attacking the autobiography as indecent and religiously offensive, challengers have overlooked Angelou's purpose: to inspire others by showing how she overcame poverty, abuse, social barriers, and low self-esteem to reach artistic success, acclaim, and a sense of personal dignity.

See also African Americans; American Library Association; Banned Books Week; Books, young adult; Libraries, school; Offensive language; People for the American Way; Race; Sex in the arts.

Ibsen, Henrik

Born: March 20, 1828, Skien, Norway
Died: May 23, 1906, Christiania, Norway
Identification: Norwegian playwright and poet

Kate Mulgrew and Dakin Matthews in a 1986 production of Henrik Ibsen's Hedda Gabler *adapted by Christopher Hampton.* (Jay Thompson, Mark Taper Forum)

Significance: Ibsen's plays advocating social reform were frequently attacked for their sharp criticisms of social ills, such as subjection of women, hypocrisy, political fraud, and corrupt journalism

Ibsen's work in the theater can be divided into three periods. The first phase, emphasizing historical dramas, featured such works as *Peer Gynt* (1867). His last phase, focusing on symbolist introspection, featured such plays as *The Master Builder* (1892). It was Ibsen's middle phase, however, focusing on realistic social drama, that witnessed his most famous—and most widely censored—works for the stage. In particular, the male-dominated society of the later nineteenth century objected to his portrayals of strong women characters. His work was sharply scrutinized and criticized in efforts to suppress socially objectionable aggressive female protagonists. Bourgeois society was scandalized by such characters as Ibsen's notorious Nora of *A Doll's House* (1879), who abandons family in order to "find herself," and the wicked heroine of *Hedda Gabler* (1890), who provokes her lover into shooting himself and then commits suicide, rather than be trapped in a loveless marriage of convenience. Ibsen himself noted that "a woman cannot be herself in the society of the present day, which is an exclusively masculine society, with laws framed by men and a judicial system that judges feminine conduct from a masculine point of view." By late twentieth century standards, however, Ibsen's plays seemed almost tame, at least in their treatment of women's rights.

The barrage of negative criticism and attempts to restrain Ibsen from creating femmes fatales is demonstrated by the comments of many critics during the waning years of the

Victorian era. For example, his women were perceived as "an unlovable, unlovely and detestable crew," or, even worse, as "a lot of crazed, hysterical geese." His fictional women did not fit the mold of societal propriety, virtue, and family dedication. Critics could not appreciate Ibsen's truthful portrayals of women who were multifaceted and torn by emotional and spiritual conflicts, much as were their male counterparts. Owing in part to Ibsen's plays, European countries began enacting legislation that supported women's rights—such as their right to account for their own money.

See also Drama and theater; Feminism; Shaw, George Bernard; Women.

Immigration laws

DEFINITION: Laws regarding entry of aliens into sovereign nations

SIGNIFICANCE: Governments can use their immigration law as a censoring tool to exclude certain aliens

The People's Republic of China is a typical authoritarian government that practices censorship severely. The Chinese government often refuses to give visas to aliens based on their political views, and expels aliens whose political speeches are not welcome by the Chinese government. Chinese political dissidents who have become nationals of other countries have been kept from going back to China. The laws and practices of censorship of aliens based on their political views have been more lenient in the Western democratic countries, such as Canada and the United States. Under Canadian immigration law, however, aliens who have engaged in or who there are reasonable grounds to believe will engage in acts of espionage, subversion, or violence, and aliens who are members of or are likely to participate in the unlawful activities of a violent organization are inadmissible to Canada. Since the 1970's, Canadian immigration officials have deported many aliens who were members of terrorist organizations. These deportations were confirmed by the Canadian Federal Court.

U.S. Immigration Laws. Generally, immigrants were officially welcomed to the United States for about one hundred years after independence. In 1798, however, Congress passed the Alien and Sedition Acts of 1798, authorizing the president to deport anyone who was dangerous to the peace and safety of the country. After the official ending of the slave trade, immigrants were imported for specific jobs in response to an expanding economy. For instance, Irish workers were brought to the East Coast regions of the United States for manufacturing industries and Chinese to the West Coast for construction of railroads. Despite the contribution of these immigrants, they were exposed to violent attacks. Under the influence of anti-immigrant hysteria, the federal government passed regulations controlling the entry of foreign workers and limited their right to settle.

From 1882 to 1952 Congress enacted several laws to restrict immigration from southern and eastern Europe and to exclude most Asians, particularly Chinese, from coming to the United States. These laws gave most immigrant quotas to northern and western European countries in order to preserve the northern and western European majority of the United States population. The racial exclusion and national origin quota systems were abolished in 1965, when Congress established a preference system for immigration worldwide. This system was intended to facilitate the entry of relatives of United States citizens and those persons possessing certain professional qualifications or special skills. In 1986 Congress adopted the Immigration Reform and Control Act. The act focused on discouraging illegal immigration by penalizing employers for illegally hiring aliens who have no employment authorization. In 1990 Congress passed a series of amendments to the Immigration and Nationality Act, collectively referred to as the Immigration Act of 1990. The most notable change was in overall increase in immigration quotas.

Censorship of Aliens. The Alien and Sedition Acts of 1798 were the first American legislation allowing exclusion of aliens if they were considered dangerous to the peace. In September, 1901, the assassination of President William McKinley by anarchist Leon Czolgosz marked a turning point in U.S. immigration history. President Theodore Roosevelt, McKinley's successor, urged Congress to exclude aliens who acted on anarchistic principles, those who believed in or espoused such principles, and those who belonged to anarchist societies. Congress responded to Roosevelt's call by enacting the Immigration Act of 1903; the first immigration act to exclude persons on the basis of their ideology or affiliation.

The U.S. Supreme Court, in the 1904 case of *Turner v. Williams*, affirmed the power of Congress to exclude aliens because of their beliefs or opinions. In this case, Turner, an English labor organizer, was arrested by immigration officers. Based on his speech and a list of proposed lectures found in his pocket, an administrative board determined that Turner was an anarchist and ordered him deported. Turner's attorney used the First Amendment as a defense and lost. The court held that aliens, unlike citizens, could not assert the Bill of Rights or other provisions of the Constitution. This proposition was affirmed and reinforced by the decision of the Supreme Court in *Knauff v. Shaughnessy* in 1950. In these two cases of excluding aliens based on their opinions, the court saw the issue as one of sovereignty, rather than civil liberty.

During World War I, due to the fear of political unrest, a provision allowing expulsion of aliens who believed in or advocated overthrowing the government of the United States was included in the Immigration Act of 1917. In the 1930's and 1940's the rise of fascism and communism created a heightened feeling of distrust and insecurity toward aliens. In 1940 Congress passed the Alien Registration Act. Under this act, any person who printed, published, or distributed any material advocating the overthrow of any government, or who was a member of a questionable organization, could be excluded or deported.

During the McCarthy era, Congress enacted the Immigration and Nationality Act (also called the McCarran-Walter Act) of 1952. This act provided that individuals entering the United States, either temporarily or permanently, who were anarchists or who advocated or were affiliated with the Communist Party or any other totalitarian group were excludable at the port of entry or deportable if already residing in the United States. The act promoted the unconstitutional censorship of aliens within U.S. borders and the anticipatory exclusion of aliens seeking entry.

In the early 1960's President John F. Kennedy tried to reform the McCarran-Walter Act. He pointed out that the United States was acting like a closed society by excluding visitors because of their political views. In 1963 America lost its most powerful advocate for reform of the McCarran-Walter Act with Kennedy's assassination. As a result of the McCarran-Walter Act, many aliens, including some distinguished intellectuals, were denied permission to visit the United States from the 1950's to the 1970's. In 1972 the Supreme Court reaffirmed the ideological exclusion of the McCarran-Walter Act in *Kleindienst v. Mandel*. In this case, Ernest Mandel, a Belgian journalist and Marxist, was invited to speak at several prestigious universities in the United States. Mandel's visa was denied because of his political views. Mandel and the American citizens who had invited him to speak challenged the constitutionality of the McCarran-Walter Act by arguing that the act had also violated the American citizens' First Amendment right to receive information and ideas. Many other intellectuals were kept from entering the United States by enforcement of the McCarran-Walter Act.

In 1975 the United States entered the Helsinki Accords (the Final Acts of the Conference on Security and Cooperation in Europe), in which the United States agreed to the free flow of ideas and people across its borders. The Helsinki Accords pushed Congress to reform the ideological exclusion of aliens under the McCarran-Walter Act. In 1977 Congress enacted an immigration amendment, the McGovern Amendment. It required the State Department to waive exclusions on grounds such as membership in, or affiliation with, one of the groups prohibited from entry into the United States under the McCarran-Walter Act for short-term visits, unless the alien's admission would be contrary to the security interests of the United States. However, this amendment did not provide protection to those aliens seeking to reside in the United States on a permanent basis. In addition, the federal courts began to scrutinize more carefully the statutory basis for visa denials under the ideological exclusion provisions. In 1986 the court of appeals for the District of Columbia in *Abourezk v. Reagan* held that aliens invited to impart information and ideas to American citizens may not be excluded solely on account of the content of their proposed messages.

In 1987 Congress enacted section 901 of the Foreign Relations Authorization Act to protect aliens within the United States from exclusion and deportation based solely on ideologies that would otherwise be protected under the U.S. Constitution if espoused by U.S. citizens. Congress also preserved, however, in section 901 the U.S. government's power to exclude and deport aliens engaged in, or likely to engage in, terrorist activities, or whose entry is adverse to foreign policy. In 1990 Congress promulgated the Immigration Act of 1990, which eliminated many of the ideological exclusion provisions of the McCarran-Walter Act. However, the 1990 Act retained the provisions of exclusion or deportation of aliens enacted in section 901 of the Foreign Relations Authorization Act of 1987. Under the new act, an alien could be deported or excluded based on the six grounds. One of these is to "act in a way that threatens national security." This broad definition is limited by the fact that an alien can only be deported through certain deportation processes and can be represented (although not at government expense) by legal counsel to seek relief from deportation. Aliens could be considered for immigration to the U.S. under refugee or asylum status if they had been persecuted or had a well-founded fear of persecution in their home countries because of race, religion, nationality, or membership in particular social or political groups. Qualified refugee aliens could seek refugee status outside the United States or apply for asylum status if already present in the United States or at its borders.

The World Trade Center Bombing. On January 25, 1993, two employees of the Central Intelligence Agency (CIA) were shot and killed by a gunman outside CIA headquarters in Langley, Virginia. The accused perpetrator was Mir Aimal Kansi, a member of Pakistan's elite who had entered the United States with a business visa and then applied for asylum as a political refugee, claiming he was fleeing political persecution in Pakistan. One month later, on February 26, 1993, the World Trade Center in New York City suffered an explosion. After investigations and a trial, a group of Muslim Fundamentalists headed by Sheik Omar Abdel-Rahman, a blind Egyptian cleric, was convicted for conspiring to levy a war of urban terrorism against the United States. These two terrorist incidents made Americans feel vulnerable to foreign terrorist attacks.

In response to this renewed fear of foreign terrorism, lawmakers in Congress introduced many bills related to immigration reform. Most bills proposed to sharply curtail immigration to the United States. Some sought to exclude persons from the United States based on their ideological beliefs, associations, or affiliations with alleged terrorist organizations. These proposals, if passed, could revive the ideological exclusions that many Americans consider contrary to the spirit and perhaps the letter of the Constitution. Although ideological exclusion provisions and guilt by association were repealed in the Immigration Act of 1990, proponents of these bills believe that excluding aliens on associational and ideological grounds can stop future terrorist incidents. *—Wei Luo*

See also Customs laws, U.S.; Lennon, John; Race; Terrorism.

BIBLIOGRAPHY

The following law review articles discuss thoroughly U.S. immigration laws related to the issue of ideological exclusion of aliens: Susan M. Schreck's "The Accidental Terrorists: Excludable Aliens Who Slip Across U.S. Borders" in *Georgia Journal of International and Comparative Law* 23 (Fall, 1993), Edward F. Sherman's "The Immigration Laws and the 'Right to Hear' Protected by Academic Freedom" in *Texas Law Review* 66 (June, 1988), and Steven R. Shapiro's "Ideological Exclusions: Closing the Border to Political Dissidents" in *Harvard Law Review* 100 (February, 1987). Milton Ridvas Konvitz's *Civil Rights in Immigration* (Ithaca, N.Y.: Cornell University Press, 1953) discusses the issue of discrimination on account of race, color, creed, political opinion, or national origin in U.S. immigration laws, particularly in the McCarran-Walter Act. David S. Weissbrodt's *Immigration Law and Procedure in a Nutshell* (3d ed. St. Paul, Minn.: West, 1992) gives a succinct general picture of the U.S. immigration laws.

Impressions reading series

TYPE OF WORK: Books
FIRST PUBLISHED: 1987
PUBLISHER: Holt, Rinehart and Winston (1987-1990); Harcourt Brace Jovanovich (1990-)
SUBJECT MATTER: Language arts texts designed for kindergarten through sixth grade classes
SIGNIFICANCE: The most frequently banned (and litigated) books of the 1990's were the Impressions textbook readers

Language arts texts in schools traditionally harkened back to the days of "Dick and Jane" readers. Such material was greatly simplified, repetitious, and—many educators felt—dull and boring. Modern reading texts are meant to inspire and encourage reading by providing beginning readers with creative literature chosen from classic and modern children's writers. Impressions series, for example, has used works by C. S. Lewis, Laura Ingalls Wilder, Martin Luther King, Jr., Rudyard Kipling, A. A. Milne, Dr. Seuss, Jan Slepian, Katherine Paterson, and other classic and award-winning authors and illustrators. The series, which was created in Canada, has taught reading and writing through exposure to poetry, myth, folklore, song, fiction, and nonfiction stories.

Impressions has been a popular series among both teachers and students. After years of close evaluation, the set was adopted by fifteen hundred schools in thirty-four states and most of Canada's provinces. Teachers who have used the series have called Impressions a great advance over the many instructional texts that had been systematically "dumbed down" for many years, thereby causing children not to care about reading.

Despite the praise and popularity received by Impressions, protests against its use began to be made as early as 1987. These attacks spread and escalated without abatement. During the 1987-1988 school year, parents in several small communities in Washington and Oregon protested that the Impressions books contained traces of witchcraft, mysticism, and fantasy, as well as themes encouraging rebellion against parents and authority figures. Some American parents objected to the books' occasional use of Canadian spellings. Parents in Oak Harbor, Washington, claimed that the texts were filled with morbid and frightening imagery, and that the books promote Eastern and other religions to the exclusion of Christianity. The protests began on the West Coast, but quickly spread east. At the Talent Elementary School in Phoenix, Arizona, a national organization called Citizens for Excellence in Education reportedly accused the series of promoting secular humanism and witchcraft. In Coeur d'Alene, Idaho, parents claimed that there were too many halloween-type themes in the series. In Fairbanks, Alaska, a parent read from an article in the *Citizen*, a newsletter published by the Christian group Focus on the Family, which stated that "nightmarish textbooks await your kids—concerned parents says Impressions' violent and occult content torments even happy, well-adjusted children." In an Atlanta, Georgia, elementary school, parents used an article by the Reverend James Dobson in the *Citizen* to give point-by-point guidelines on how to fight the series.

During 1989-1990 alone more than two dozen challenges were made against the series. This increased to forty-five school districts during the following school year. A member of the Parent Teacher Association in Winters, California, replied to a challenge there by criticizing those who wanted to ban the materials, commenting that, "this is not a group of local parents, but a nationwide group seeking censorship." In fact, there have been a number of national groups involved. The American Family Association, for example, brought suit against Impressions in California. Other groups such as the Christian Educators Association International, Citizens for Excellence in Education, the Traditional Values Coalition, and a Canadian group, Parents for Quality Education, also joined in the attack.

In most cases, district school boards reviewed the series and decided to keep the books. However, so much time, energy, and expense went into defending the books that there was little doubt that some districts were discouraged from using the books because of the controversy. In other cases Impressions was removed from the schools after originally being approved in some districts. Lawsuits were filed over the use of Impressions in districts in California, Ohio, Illinois, and Nevada after they had responded to challenges by retaining the series. None of these suits was successful, however, and the courts have not been inclined toward the views of the censors. One judge said that there was no evidence that the Impressions books had been adopted or retained because of "hostility toward Christianity or fealty to any Wiccan or Neo-Paganist credo . . . far from preferring one religion over another, Impressions materials were chosen in part to reflect the cultural diversity of North American society." Meanwhile, organized attacks on Impressions continued.

See also Gabler, Mel, and Norma Gabler; Kanawha County book-banning controversy; King, Martin Luther, Jr.; Kipling, Rudyard; Libraries, school; *Little House on the Prairie*; Parent Teacher Association; Pressure groups; Secular humanism; Textbooks.

Index Librorum Prohibitorum

TYPE OF WORK: Catalog
PERIOD ENFORCED: 1559-1966
PUBLISHERS: The Vatican and other agencies of the church
SUBJECT MATTER: Catalogs of books banned by the Roman Catholic church
SIGNIFICANCE: These catalogs of "forbidden books" were historically the most significant manifestations of official Roman Catholic censorship

Instances of Roman Catholic book censorship can be traced back to the church's early first centuries. From the fourth century C.E. into the sixteenth century church leaders periodically compiled lists of banned books; however, the church did not establish its official index of prohibited books, the *Index Librorum Prohibitorum*, until the Council of Trent in 1559. The Vatican and other Roman Catholic authorities issued many variations of this list until 1966, when it was discontinued. By then the Index had reached a total of more than four thousand titles.

These indexes were alphabetical listings of works that lay Catholics were forbidden to read without permission of church authorities. Their purpose was not to be systematic listings of all possible banned books, but rather cumulative listings of individual church decisions. During the Reformation the church took extensive measures to condemn Martin Luther's writings and other works considered heretical. Bishops, provincial councils, and universities issued catalogs of forbidden books, whose bannings often were enforced by civil authorities in consultation with the clergy. England's King Henry VIII, for example, had a strict policy of prohibiting books which he deemed objectionable. In an effort to preserve a theological and moral code among its followers, the church took measures to protect its members from being exposed to material it considered heretical. The Index contained general guidelines for restricted reading; most of the books it listed were theological, philosophical, and scientific treatises and literary works.

Historical Perspective. According to its canonical law, the Roman Catholic church has the right of censorship by virtue of natural law and its supernatural mission. Competent ecclesiastical authorities have a responsibility to protect membership in matters of religion and morals, as the church is seen as an effective instrument for the salvation of the human race. The church's concern for striking a balance between freedom of inquiry and purity of doctrine is documented in the *Index Librorum Prohibitorum*. Early allusions to censorship can be traced back to apostolic times. Acts of the Apostles and Paul's Epistle to Titus contain references to writings that Christians should not read. The church's policy on book censorship began around 170 C.E. with the Muratorian Canon. In 325 C.E. the First Council of Nicaea condemned the Greek ecclesiastic Arius' book, *Thalia*. The first formal listing of forbidden books was made by Pope Innocent I in 405. Ninety-three years later a council in Rome published an index of forbidden books known as the Gelasian Decree. It included lists of authentic scriptural books, recommended readings, and heretical books. Between the fifth and sixteenth centuries there were many specific laws against reading certain books considered heretical by the church.

Examples of book censorship through that millennium included the *Three Chapters*, which was condemned in 548 by Pope Vigilius. Forty-one years later the Council of Toledo forbade books on Arianism. The writings of Monothelites were condemned in 649 by Pope Martin I. The works of Adalbertus and Clement were forbidden in 745 by Pope Zacharias. In 869 Pope Adrian II burned the books written by Photius. Also condemned were works by the Abbot Joachim in the thirteenth century, Peter Jean Olivi in the fourteenth century, and John Wyclif and Jan Hus in the fifteenth century. In 1469 Pope Innocent III decreed that all books were to be submitted to local bishops for examination before being issued for general reading—an edict repeated by Pope Leo X in 1515. Book bannings became more frequent after the Council of Trent in 1559. Revised indexes were issued through the succeeding centuries, the last in 1948. Eighteen years later, in 1966, the church declared the Index to be a historical document that would not be reissued again.

Rules of the Index. It was unlawful for Catholics to read, translate, own, or print a forbidden book. General decrees prohibited books defending heresies; books that were considered obscene; books on spiritualism, sorcery, or superstitions; books defending divorce, suicide, or socialism; and newspapers and magazines that regularly attacked religion, morality, or Roman Catholicism. Certain types of publications had to be approved by bishops. Publications requiring their formal approval, or imprimatur, included theological works; books and pamphlets on devotion, religious instruction, and piety; and books, pamphlets, and leaflets on apparitions, visions, or miracles. Noncompliance with the rules was considered a mortal sin, but exemptions were granted to those engaged in theological, historical, or philosophical studies. Permission in writing was required.

The *Index Expurgatorius*, which is often confused with the *Index Librorum Prohibitorum*, was a list of passages deleted from certain books, which could be read only after they were expurgated by church officials.

The Council of Trent. This council, which met in 1545-1563, codified church regulations on book censorship. At one of its sessions, the church leaders authorized use of the Vulgate version of the Bible for sermons and public discussions and ruled that no books on religion could be issued without prior approval of the church. In 1557 Pope Paul IV asked the Congregation of the Inquisition to compile a list of forbidden books which was published in 1559. This became the first official *Index Librorum Prohibitorum*. The Council of Trent undertook to revise the Index because of dissatisfaction among Catholic leaders. The project was too complex to be finished by the council, however, and was left to be completed by the Holy See.

In 1564, after the Council of Trent, Pope Paul IV introduced his *Tridentine Index*, which included a list of forbidden books and ten rules regulating censorship and reading of future books. Its first nine rules concerned works that were to be automatically forbidden because they were thought to be heretical or against church teachings. The last rule required examination and censorship of works prior to authorization of publication. An amended Index was ordered by Pope Pius V. Two editions of the Index were ordered by popes Clement III and Alexander VII in 1664. Jansenistic works were added to the list. In 1753 Pope Benedict XIV issued a bull, *Sollicita ac Provida*, which remained the basic church document on forbidden works until 1897, with new titles being added each year.

The Modern Index. During the First Vatican Council, church fathers asked for a revision of the Index. However, the council adjourned before the issue could be resolved. In 1897 Pope Leo XIII gave the church a new Index, along with new regulations; his revised *Index Librorum Prohibitorum* was officially published in 1900. Little change took place under the general legislation of the Code of Canon Law (1917), which

Authors Listed in the Index Librorum Prohibitorum

Among the thousands of authors whose works, in whole or in part, have been listed in the Index Librorum Prohibitorum, *are the following—all of whom are discussed under their own headings in this reference set:*

Bacon, Francis	Goldsmith, Oliver
Balzac, Honoré de	Hobbes, Thomas
Boccaccio, Giovanni	Hugo, Victor
Bruno, Giordano	Hume, David
Casanova, Giovanni Giacomo	James I
	Kant, Immanuel
Copernicus, Nicolaus	Locke, John
D'Annunzio, Gabriele	Luther, Martin
Dante Alighieri	Machiavelli, Niccolò
Darwin, Charles	Mill, John Stuart
Defoe, Daniel	Montaigne, Michel de
Descartes, René	Montesquieu
Diderot, Denis	Pascal, Blaise
Dumas, Alexandre, *père*	Rousseau, Jean-Jacques
	Sand, George
Erasmus, Desiderius	Spinoza, Baruch
Flaubert, Gustave	Stendhal
France, Anatole	Sterne, Laurence
Galileo Galilei	Swedenborg, Emanuel
Gibbon, Edward	Swift, Jonathan
Gide, André	Voltaire

described the general classes of restricted writings: editions of the Bible lacking ecclesiastic license (Imprimatur) to be printed; books on Catholicism lacking an Imprimatur; books attacking religion, morals, Catholic dogma, divine worship, church discipline, bishops, or the clerical or religious state; books that defend divorce, suicide, heresy, schism, or superstitious practices; and books that are deliberately obscene. Popes, through the Holy Office (Sacrum Officium) have exercised the right to condemn books considered offensive to the church. In 1948 the last edition of *Index Librorum Prohibitorum* was issued.

During the Second Vatican Council in the early 1960's, Pope John XXIII proposed a revision of all church laws, including the Index, which was declared primarily a historical document in 1966. The new regulations emphasized the positive value of books. Bishops became responsible for cooperating with authors and publishers to ensure that the church remained the custodian of divine revelation and the interpreter of the teachings of Christ. Restrictions on reading became more liberal; however, permission was still required for some publications for purposes of accuracy; for example, portions of the Latin Bible, vernacular translations of the Bible, catechisms, and Catholic decrees. Members of religious communities still needed special authorization to publish commercial books on morals and religion. Although many changes have taken place regarding the *Index Librorum Prohibitorum* in order to keep it in tune with modern society, the church reserved the right to censor materials that are deliberately against Catholic theology, dogma, or moral teachings. The main body of church regulation was detailed in codes that are exhortative rather than obligatory. Individual authors and publishers were asked to exercise proper moral judgment over the works they published. *—Maria A. Pacino*

See also Christianity; Henry VIII; Heresy; Hus, Jan; Lateran Council, Fourth; Legion of Decency; Luther, Martin; Paul IV, Pope; Reformation, the; Savonarola, Girolamo; Spanish Empire; Spanish Inquisition; Vatican.

Bibliography

Francis S. Betten's *The Roman Index of Forbidden Books* (St. Louis, Mo.: B. Herder, 1909) is a brief but informed commentary on the history of the Index, with an explanation of its ten rules and a list of forbidden books. R. A. Burke's *What Is the Index?* (Milwaukee, Wis.: Bruce Publishing, 1952) is written by a librarian who explains the meaning of the Index, its uses throughout centuries of Roman Catholic history, and its implication for librarians. Walter M. Daniels' *The Censorship of Books* (New York: H. W. Wilson, 1954) includes a chapter on the Index with an essay by Redmund A. Burke explaining the church's concern for books that threaten faith or attack morality, religion, or divine worship generally. Harold C. Gardiner's *Catholic Viewpoint on Censorship* (Garden City, N.Y.: Hanover House, 1958) provides an informed perspective on how the Catholic church regards censorship. The second part of the book discusses controversies within the United States. Richard P. McBrien's *Catholicism* (2 vols. Minneapolis, Minn.: Winston Press, 1980) provides a balanced and comprehensive historical perspective on the Catholic church. John L. McKenzie's *The Roman Catholic Church* (Garden City, N.Y.: Image Books, 1971) is a comprehensive historical survey of the global expansion of the Catholic church.

Index on Censorship

Type of work: Magazine
First published: 1972
Founder: Stephen Spender (1909-   )
Subject matter: A forum for discussion of censorship issues
Significance: This magazine focuses on occurrences of censorship around the world and publishes articles on the subject by well-known writers

Founded by the British poet Stephen Spender, the *Index on Censorship* is a bimonthly magazine published in London. It has devoted itself to defending freedom of expression around the world by providing news coverage of censorship incidents, and by serving as a forum for discussions of censorship issues. The periodical was founded partially in response to an open letter sent in 1969 by a group of Russian dissidents requesting support from the West. Since its beginning the magazine has featured articles on freedom of expression from writers such as Václav Havel, Salman Rushdie, Doris Lessing, Arthur Miller, Noam Chomsky, Nadine Gordimer, Aung San Suu Kyi, Julian Barnes, Dubravka Ugresic, Jack Mapanje, Naguib

Mahfouz, and Umberto Eco. In addition to publishing articles discussing various censorship issues, the *Index on Censorship* has regularly surveyed abuses of free speech from around the world and has occasionally published works from writers that have been banned in particular venues.

To assist in the advocacy of freedom of expression in places where this freedom most needs advocates, the magazine provides an assisted subscription program which allows readers in South America, Africa, Asia, and the former Communist Bloc countries to receive the publication free of charge.

See also Chomsky, Noam; Havel, Václav; Intellectual freedom; Mahfouz, Naguib; Rushdie, Salman; United Kingdom.

India

Description: Independent south Asian republic whose territory included modern Pakistan and Bangladesh when it was under British colonial rule before 1947

Significance: Although India has a long and complex history of censorship, it has allowed one of the freest presses among third world nations

Within India—which is the world's largest democracy—the diversity of ethnic groups speaking sixteen hundred languages and a rancorous relationship between the country's majority Hindu and minority Muslim populations have helped to make censorship a constant threat. From ancient times to the Mughal dynasty, Indian rulers ruthlessly suppressed all dissension. After Great Britain began colonizing India, its regime also found censorship a useful tool for governing. Since India won its independence in 1947, its central government, its various state governments, and diverse pressure groups have invoked censorship on the media, fine arts, and films.

The British Period. During Britain's long period of rule, it hardly mattered whether newspapers were published by Indians or British nationals. Colonial authorities never hesitated to punish publications criticizing British rule. One of the earliest censorship incidents occurred in 1780, after India's first officially recognized modern newspaper, the *Bengal Gazette* (also known as the *Calcutta General Advertiser* or *Hicky's Gazette*) published an article attacking the wife of Governor General Warren Hastings. The government had the press's types confiscated and the newspaper's postal privileges removed, and James Hicky, the paper's publisher, was fined and jailed. Thereafter, the British regime embarked on regulating the press. The first of a number of censorship laws, enacted in 1799, required preapproval of publication from the government's secretariat. Licenses for publishing newspapers were mandated by the Regulation of the Press Ordinance of 1823, promulgated by Acting Governor General John Adam. The first law regulating the establishment of printing presses was popularly known as the "Gagging Act of 1857." It came in the wake of the great mutiny of Indian soldiers that year.

The law that had the most far-reaching consequences for the Indian subcontinent was the Press and Registration of Books Act of 1867, which helped to shape the modern press laws of independent India, Pakistan, and Bangladesh. This law mandated printing press owners and newspaper publishers to secure declarations from magistrates. As demands for self-rule became vocal, the colonial regime cracked down on the vernacular papers with the Vernacular Press Act of 1878. Unable to stop the ever-growing anti-British sentiments, Viceroy Lord Minto attempted to buy good relations with some vernacular newspapers by paying them subsidies. Many other press and press-related laws followed. Under provisions of these acts, publications deemed objectionable had their declarations revoked, they were forced to pay security deposits, and their journalists were jailed. Despite strict government controls over newspapers in the last years of British rule in the mid-twentieth century, a number of underground publications appeared that reported details of the independence struggle and the performance of British troops on the World War II battlefields.

Modern India. On attaining independence in 1947, many Indian leaders—including Prime Minister Jawaharlal Nehru, called for press freedom. Unlike the First Amendment of the U.S. Constitution, India's new constitution of 1950 guaranteed freedom of the press within the larger provision of free speech and expression that was accompanied by a number of restrictions, including the disallowing of speech undermining the security of the state. A constitutional amendment was subsequently passed to disallow free speech that could hurt friendly relations with foreign countries.

After independence the Indian press vigorously covered the political scene. The national government's Press (Objectionable Matters) Act of 1951 rescinded a British law of 1931 and the press acts of thirteen states. The new law empowered the government to demand forfeitable security deposits from newspapers, to seize unauthorized printing presses for printing unauthorized newssheets, to confiscate certain newspapers, and to deny privileges to offensive publications. Other laws restricting the press followed, such as the Press and Registration of Books (Amendment) Act of 1955, the Defense of India Act of 1962, the Sixteenth Amendment to the constitution, and the Maintenance of Internal Security Act. States also adopted their own versions of the Special Powers (Press) Act. Between October, 1962, and November, 1965, the state governments censored eighty-two newspapers.

Wartime Measures. During India's 1965 and 1971 wars with Pakistan, the Defence of India Rules was used to censor the press. Prime Minister Indira Gandhi invoked the law to impose a state of national emergency that lasted from June 26, 1975, to March 20, 1977. A major facet of this emergency declaration was its blanket imposition of censorship on the press. The measure was enforced by cutting off electrical power to certain newspapers, by arresting journalists, by forcing foreign journalists to leave—or not enter—the country, and by subjecting sixty newspapers to precensorship. Also, the Press Council was dissolved, and new restrictive laws were passed. Most of the new restrictions were lifted after Gandhi was defeated in the 1977 elections, allowing the press to renew its watchdog role. The press then exposed a scandal in which government officials were involved in a bribery scheme to purchase weapons from a Swedish firm.

After Indira Gandhi was assassinated in 1984, government economic and political pressures on Indian newspapers con-

Indian riot police confront supporters of a Hindu splinter party at a Delhi train station in February, 1993. (AP/Wide World Photos)

tinued. The government has supported friendly newspapers through such means as favorable allocations of scarce newsprint and government advertising. As part of an effort to fight terrorism in rebellious Indian states, the government passed the Terrorist and Disruptive Acts in 1985. This law has been widely used against the press, especially in states with centers of antigovernment rebels, such as Punjab, Jammu, and Kashmir. Antigovernment separatists in those states have also imposed a form of censorship by murdering journalists and physically stopping the printing and distribution of publications.

The Broadcast Media and Films. In contrast to the press, radio and television have remained under the direct control of the national Ministry of Information and Broadcasting. Neither medium has been allowed to air critical news or commentaries about the government. A change came in the 1990's, when as many as seventy channels of uncensored satellite television programming became available, including limited broadcasting of the U.S.-based Cable News Network.

The government's film censor board, another British legacy, certifies every film exhibited in India. Cultural reservations about public displays of sexuality have kept even displays of kissing off the screen. Nevertheless, Indian films have a long tradition of showing scantily clad women performing sexually suggestive dances.

During the 1990's Indian print advertising started using models in erotic poses and positions for products such as "Kama Sutra" condoms and MR Coffee to the ire of law enforcement authorities. Censorship of books has not been uncommon. The most famous case was the 1989 banning of Salman Rushdie's novel *The Satanic Verses*. International publications containing critical articles about India have been seized or kept out of the country. However, sexually explicit magazines, such as *Debonair* and *Fantasy*, have been openly circulated. —*Niaz Ahmed Khan*

See also Bhopal disaster; Cable News Network; Islam; Journalists, violence against; *Kama Sutra*; Kipling, Rudyard; Language laws; *Little Black Sambo*; Pressure group.

BIBLIOGRAPHY

Since 1986 the Committee to Protect Journalists has published a survey, *Attacks on the Press*, in which the year-by-year censorship activities of the world's nations, including India, have been detailed. Marcus F. Franda focuses on the press restraints of the late 1970's India emergency in "Curbing the Indian Press," *American University Field Services Report* 20, nos. 12, 13, and 14 (1977). Since 1952 the International Press Institute has provided monthly and annual roundups of censorship in India, along with the rest of the world, in the *IPI Report*. Censorship of the Indian media is highlighted in John Luter and Jim Richstad's survey of Asian and Pacific nations in *Global Journalism: A Survey of the World's Mass Media*, edited by John C. Merrill (New York: Longman, 1983). Useful glimpses of restraints on Indian media can be found in *India: A Country Study*, edited by Richard F. Nyrop (Washington, D.C.: U.S. Government Printing Office, 1986). The Scholars and Writers Institute has kept thorough records of censorship in India since 1972 in the periodical *Index on Censorship.*

Indonesia

DESCRIPTION: Southeast Asian archipelago that was the Dutch East Indies until 1949

SIGNIFICANCE: Government leaders have often employed strict censorship of mass media outlets to maintain political stability and suppress dissent

After several centuries of Dutch rule, Indonesia was occupied by Japan in 1940. At the end of World War II, Indonesian nationalists declared the country's independence. After independence was recognized in 1949, the country struggled through a politically unsettled period. Martial law was imposed in 1957. In 1965 under the leadership of anticommunist president Suharto and his New Order, the government was more strongly centralized and new organizations were formed to crush subversive groups. The following year a military agency called the Operational Command for the Restoration of Security and Order (Kopkamtib) began moving against underground antigovernment movements. Many arrested persons thought to be Muslim extremists never received trials.

Kopkamtib functioned as media censors and implemented new restrictions on the press. Economic sanctions further limited small presses. A government agency called SARA listed topics that could not be covered by the press and the information ministry used blackouts to keep unwanted topics out of the press. In 1985 Kopkamtib's functions were reorganized within a body called the Coordinating Agency for National Stability (Bakorstanas).

In 1945 leaders seeking an egalitarian society had instituted a set of principles, known as Pancasila, that promoted belief in one God, humanitarianism, nationalist unity, consultative democracy, and social justice. In 1978 President Suharto sought to impose these principles on all citizens, especially children and civil servants, and an indoctrination program commenced. Looking to promote unity, stability, and development, the New Order monitored the press to guarantee that no issues would be raised to alter this process and a government press council set rules for what the press could and could not do.

A 1982 press law acknowledged minimal press freedoms, while outlawing communist, Marxist, and Leninist publications. It stated that the duty of the press was to strengthen the country by maintaining the ideology of Pancasila. Violators were sanctioned, beaten, or jailed. Bans were also placed on membership in the extremist Muslim and communist parties. Tight controls were placed on foreign publications, and two antigovernment university newspapers had their licenses revoked when they disregarded the rules.

Censorship was practiced in other media as well. Motion picture content, which had been curbed in colonial times, was also regulated under the Suharto Administration. During the 1970's only a single, government-controlled, television station existed. By early 1990's there were eighteen government-owned stations and eight privately owned commercial television stations.

The government permitted several independent radio stations to broadcast programs, but screened them before airing and would not permit the stations to broadcast news. Instead, stations had to read fifteen-minute government-written news bulletins six times a day. Failure to comply would result in their being shut down. Books were censored prior to publication and could be banned after printing. All theatrical productions, public story readings, and films had to be cleared before presentation to Indonesian audiences.

See also Broadcast media; Colonialism; News media censorship; Philippines; Vietnam.

Inside the Company: CIA Diary

TYPE OF WORK: Book

PUBLISHED: 1975

AUTHOR: Philip Agee (1935-)

SUBJECT MATTER: The experiences of a former agent in the Central Intelligence Agency (CIA)

SIGNIFICANCE: CIA opposition to the book's publication provoked a major legal struggle

After a decade of service as an officer of the CIA, Philip Agee resigned in disillusionment in 1968. He then began work on a book that would expose the agency's operations in Latin America and name many of its agents. He moved to Europe to write the book and also visited Cuba to do research. The CIA did not initially take legal action against Agee, but kept him under close surveillance. After the book was published in Great Britain in 1975, it became a best-seller and the CIA tried to discourage American publishers from handling it. This proved unsuccessful, however, and an American edition came out later in 1975.

After the publication of an article by Agee in a magazine that specialized in naming CIA personnel abroad, the CIA's chief of station in Athens, Greece, was murdered. Agee was subsequently accused of contributing to the murder and of being a Soviet agent. Waging a long legal campaign, the U.S. government revoked Agee's passport, an action resisted by Agee but eventually upheld by the U.S. Supreme Court, and applied pressure that resulted in his expulsion from five European countries. However, he was able to remain abroad on passports issued by Nicaragua and Grenada, and continued writing books and giving speeches critical of the CIA.

See also Central Intelligence Agency; *CIA and the Cult of Intelligence, The*; Espionage; Intelligence Identities Protection Act; National security; National Security Decision Directive 84; *Spycatcher.*

Intellectual freedom

DEFINITION: The right to hold or research any thought, belief, or speculation and to express it in any way the holder or researcher considers appropriate

SIGNIFICANCE: Intellectual freedom is considered to be the foundation of Western thought and the cornerstone of academic research

The concept of intellectual freedom originated with nineteenth century German thinkers as the right of scholars and scientists to engage in research and speculation without interference from church or state. This notion, however, has evolved to that of academic freedom, with ramifications for scientific, speculative, literary, and even artistic pursuits, including freedom to express or communicate the results in any medium. Without ability and freedom of expression, intellectual freedom is meaningless. Intellectual freedom is arguably the indispensable foundation of Western civilization.

The Greeks were the first to consider the nature and limits of intellectual freedom seriously. It began with their discovery of the powers of reason. They regarded the intellect as divine. True freedom, they believed, emanates from reason and philosophy. A true slave was one who could not or would not think for himself. In their excitement over their discovery, the ancient Greeks applied reason even to aesthetics and ethics. That meant freedom to question and criticize Greek religion and national and mythological heroes.

Socrates' trial in 399 B.C.E. is a quintessential example of intellectual freedom and its repression. His student Plato believed that the best ruler was one who was intellectually liberated—a philosopher king. The Greeks could not imagine that one who experienced the joys of intellectual freedom would want to return to a life of superstition, narrow-mindedness, and censorship.

When Arabs, Jews, and Christians of the Middle Ages took hold of Greek ideas and tasted the fruits of intellectual and critical freedom, they created imaginative theological and scientific theories that still dazzle the mind. Saint Thomas Aquinas, for example, synthesized Aristotelian metaphysics with Christian theological doctrine. His *Summa theologiae* (1266-1273), longer than the entire works of Aristotle, is only one of some sixty books Aquinas wrote.

In one way or another, the success of intellectual freedom has always been connected with institutions of higher learning. Aquinas, for example, was a professor of theology. Universities have been breeding grounds for intellectual activities based on the assumption that members must be free to think, deliberate, speculate, and experiment.

Intellectual freedom is at the root of Western liberal, democratic institutions. The First Amendment to the U.S. Constitution is testimony to this aspect of intellectual freedom. Any concept of freedom incorporates freedom of thought and expression. The most eloquent arguments for freedom of thought and expression come from John Locke's *Letters Concerning Toleration* (1689) and John Stuart Mill's *On Liberty* (1859). Both English philosophers knew that true intellectual freedom can only be experienced by those who can tolerate cognitive and intellectual conflict. People unaccustomed to such challenges tend to resist intellectual analysis.

Intellectual Freedom and Censorship. Seeking truth is said to be inherently subversive. Truth may undermine established religion, aristocracy, political power, and other received ideas, such as the scientific intellectual hierarchy. According to Thomas Kuhne in his *Structure of Scientific Revolution* (1970), scientists too become intellectually lazy. Kuhne contends that gaining acceptance by a well-established circle in the scientific community is difficult, even if a new discovery or theory is valuable. The history of science is replete with battles between old and new scientific communities. The new wants acceptance; the old wants to retain authority.

In the case of Socrates, some Athenian politicians feared having their prestige and authority undermined by the intellectual gadfly. Socrates was condemned to death for insisting on freedom of thought and freedom of expression. The Athenian politicians condemned him in the name of the common good, a cause that would be cited repeatedly in persecutions, as would national security and the good of the country. Similar rationales were offered by Romans for regulation of morality and by Christian inquisitors for saving souls.

Intellectual freedom, according to many historians, suffered some of its greatest setbacks in the name of Christianity. For example, the *Index Librorum Prohibitorum*, published by the Roman Catholic church from 1559 until discontinued in 1966, eventually contained a list of more than four thousand books forbidden to Catholics around the world. Saving souls and regulating morality are still used as excuses for censorship.

In modern Western societies, however, few constraints are imposed on intellectual freedom. This is also true in some non-Western countries such as India. In most Islamic and communist societies, however, poets, novelists, journalists, artists, and scientists are monitored. Media and academic pursuits in Cuba and China, for example, are entirely government-run.

In a series of landmark decisions in the 1950's and 1960's, the Supreme Court restricted the ways in which public and private censorship organizations could prosecute publishers and filmmakers, as had been common prior to the 1950's. In *Abrams v. United States* (1919) Justice Oliver Wendell Holmes, in a dissenting opinion, wrote that the U.S. Constitution justifies the notion that "the ultimate good desired is better reached by free trade in ideas." The Abrams case involved street-level intellectual freedom: distribution of antiwar pamphlets during wartime. Holmes's famous dissent was the beginning of a series of deliberations that progressively explicated the connection between an open society and intellectual freedom. Justice Louis Brandeis in a minority opinion in *Whitney v. California* (1927) wrote: "Those who won our independence . . . knew that order cannot be secured merely through fear of punishment for its infraction; that it is hazardous to discourage thought, hope, and imagination; that repression breeds hate."

One certitude of intellectual freedom is that there will always be those who oppose it, usually for a common good. During the 1986-1987 academic year there was a 21 percent jump in intellectual censorship incidents and a 168 percent increase since 1982. According to many analysts, this was attributable to Ronald Reagan's and George Bush's conservative administrations and greater activism of Fundamentalist religious groups headed by such televangelists as Pat Robertson, Jerry Falwell, and Jimmy Swaggart.

The 1980's produced another debate over censorship and intellectual freedom called the battle of canons. The debate began with Allan Bloom's influential book, *The Closing of the*

American Mind (1987), followed by E. D. Hirsch's *Cultural Literacy* (1987). The canon advocates, such as Bloom and Hirsch, believe that there is a list that contains the universally proven intellectual and artistic masterpieces by such geniuses as William Shakespeare, Michelangelo, Plato, and Wolfgang Amadeus Mozart. Critics of the canon see no special value for the classics other than that they have withstood the test of time among Europeans. —*Chogollah Maroufi*

See also American Civil Liberties Union; American Library Association; Censorship; Free speech; Political correctness.

Bibliography

Two influential books in the canon debate are Allan Bloom's *The Closing of the American Mind: How Higher Education Has Failed Democracy and Impoverished the Souls of Today's Students* (New York: Simon & Schuster, 1987), and E. D. Hirsch, *Cultural Literacy: What Every American Needs to Know* (Boston: Houghton Mifflin, 1987). Richard Curry's edited collection, *Freedom at Risk: Secrecy, Censorship, and Repression in the 1980's* (Philadelphia: Temple University Press, 1988), covers a wide variety of topics. The *Newsletter on Intellectual Freedom by the Intellectual Freedom Committee of the American Library Association* (1952-) deals with the relationship between intellectual freedom and censorship. Evelyn Fox Keller's "Science and Its Critics," in *Academe* 81, no. 5 (September, 1995), analyzes intellectual freedom within the scientific framework.

Intelligence Identities Protection Act (IIPA)

Enacted: June 23, 1982

Place: United States (national)

Significance: This federal law made it a crime to publish the names of Central Intelligence Agency (CIA) agents

Congress' passage of the IIPA in 1982 outlawed publication of the names of covert government agents. The law was drafted as a response to former CIA employee Philip Agee's publication of *Dirty Work: The CIA in Western Europe* (1978) and *Dirty Work Two: The CIA in Africa* (1980), books that revealed the names of more than a thousand alleged CIA officers. Congress was also reacting to the work of Louis Wolf, coeditor of the *Covert Action Information Bulletin*, a magazine containing a section devoted to identifying CIA operatives. According to the congressional report accompanying the IIPA, Agee's practice of "naming names" had led directly to the assassination of CIA station chief Richard Welch in Athens, Greece, in 1975, and to other violent attacks on persons Agee identified as CIA officers.

The IIPA made it a crime intentionally to disclose the identities of CIA agents, establishing various penalties based on the accused's degree of access to classified information. The harshest penalties were reserved for "insiders"—persons holding authorized access to classified information. Any person with access to information identifying CIA agents who purposely disclosed an agent's identity could be jailed for up to ten years and fined as much as fifty thousand dollars. Any person who intentionally revealed the identity of a CIA agent after having had access to classified information in general could face up to five years in jail and a fine of twenty-five thousand dollars. Those penalties applied primarily to current and former government employees.

"Outsiders"—persons who did not have authorized access to classified information—were to be treated differently. Any such person who intentionally disclosed an agent's identity while knowing that such disclosure might harm U.S. foreign intelligence operations could be imprisoned for up to three years and fined up to fifteen thousand dollars.

A survey of news stories written before the IIPA was passed in 1982 turned up more than eighty major books and news articles whose authors could arguably have been indicted under the law. A representative sample would include revelations that former CIA agents were involved in the Watergate break-in, accounts of illegal domestic spying by the CIA, and disclosures that a CIA employee tried to infiltrate the House and Senate intelligence committees in 1980 at the direction of the Soviet State Security Committee (KGB).

See also *CIA and the Cult of Intelligence, The*; Espionage; *Inside the Company: CIA Diary.*

Internet

Definition: Two-way computer communications methods of indeterminate size and boundaries

Significance: The Internet has provided new opportunities for freedom of speech; its advocates have argued that the same principles that apply to print or broadcast media should apply to other electronic communications

The Internet is a collection of free-standing computer networks, not a physical entity. In the 1960's, the U.S. Department of Defense began the Advanced Research Projects Agency (ARPA), which is credited with creating a way to interconnect various computer sites through what is known as "packet switching." This is approximately the same as dropping a message in an envelope (or a packet), addressing the packet, and dropping it in the mail, with a computer acting as the postal service. This original "ARPAnet" connected four university campuses: Stanford University, the University of California at Los Angeles, the University of California at Santa Barbara, and the University of Utah at Salt Lake City.

Following the 1972 International Conference on Computer Communications, a new agency, the Defense Advanced Research Projects Agency (DARPA), began a program called the Internetting Project to study how to link packet-switching networks together. In 1974, the Internet Protocol (IP) and the Transmission Control Protocol (TCP) were released and would continue to serve the Internet community into the 1990's. Researchers also created a multitasking operating system (UNIX) that understood networking. The wide distribution of minicomputers running the UNIX operating system created a large network of computers running over the public telephone systems—the epitome of a decentralized, ungoverned network.

Toward the end of the 1970's, computer networks were popping up everywhere. In the mid 1980's, service providers linked to the Internet such as Prodigy, America Online, and Compuserve began to emerge. In 1993, U.S. president Bill Clinton charged U.S. vice president Al Gore, Jr., with running the newly created U.S. Advisory Council on the National Information Infrastructure (NII), which was created to integrate hardware, software, and skills in order to make it convenient for people to use computers to acquire large amounts of information.

Concerns over Government Intrusion. Most Internet users have had little privacy, since most e-mail (electronic mail that can be exchanged with others on the Internet) is in plain text and can be read by nearly anybody along the route. There are a number of techniques available to encode messages and data for secure delivery; however, some Internet users fear that the government will require that the NII use a method called two-key encryption, in which one key would be a public number that could be known to anyone and the other key would be a private number known only to the user. A message could be sent in the public key number but could only be decoded in the private key number. Users fear that the government would issue both keys, keeping key numbers on file in order to have the ability to decrypt any data.

University of Pennsylvania students registered their protests against the new Communications Decency Act—which threatened censorship on the Internet—when Vice President Al Gore visited the campus in February, 1994. (AP/Wide World Photos)

While some users fear government interference in this electronic highway, there are others who would welcome the intervention and who have argued that major communications bills should be adopted. One way to access the Internet is through what is known as a local bulletin board system (BBS), which can be run by anyone. Most BBSs provide facilities for chatting among users, and most offer computer files that can be accessed by users. In addition to its many socially acceptable uses, however, this technology offers a new way of distributing pornography, communicating threats, or defaming people. Many parents, schools, and industries have refused to defend the status quo on the Internet, arguing that it provides too-easy access to pornography and obscenity. Internet connections are achieved either through telephone or cable-television services, both of which regulate free expression.

Decisions Concerning Obscenity. Constitutional questions of First Amendment free-speech and free-expression rights have been addressed by the Supreme Court in cases such as *Roth v. United States* (1957), *Alberts v. California* (1957), *Manual Enterprises v. Day* (1962), and *Jacobellis v. Ohio* (1964); in most of these and other such cases, the Court has recognized few restrictions on rights to expression. The Court has, however, continued to recognize the need for legislative flexibility in regulating expression in cases such as *Ginsberg v. New York* (1968), *New York v. Ferber* (1982), and *Sable Communications v. Federal Communications Commission* (1989).

A May, 1995, article in *The New York Times* reported the arrest of a man on charges of possessing child pornography that prosecutors said he obtained from the Internet. In July, 1995, *Time* magazine issued the results of a report on Internet pornography by a Carnegie Mellon University research team; the report stated 83.5 percent of the images stores on certain Internet facilities were pornographic. The article stated that the images included nude photography of children as well as numerous images of bondage, sadomasochism, urination, defecation, and sex acts with animals. In a June, 1995, article, *The New York Times* reported that a University of Michigan student had been arrested for publishing a violent fantasy about another student on a computer bulletin board, leading to summary suspension from the university and criminal charges of transmitting threats across state lines; however, the criminal charges were eventually dismissed.

In response to the charges against the University of Michigan student, a November 3, 1995, article in *The Chronicle of Higher Education* stated that "Electronic communication does seem to inspire excess, hyperbole, and incivility among users to a degree seldom found in print," evoking a degree of fear caused by the anonymity of the sender. The article noted, however, that Internet threats may be less likely to create the incendiary conditions that in real life would permit the arrest of a person for hurling slurs and insults; moreover, the article noted that the recipient of a digital message is less likely to be a "captive audience" unable to escape verbal assaults.

Defenders of efforts to regulate electronic communication often claim that anticensorship activists often miss a critical point: The First Amendment guarantees only that federal and state governments will not interfere with freedom of speech.

Such observers note that if a private provider of online or network services wants to interfere with a user's public message, there is no law preventing it from doing so; according to this line of argument, freedom of the press means freedom of the owner of the press.

The rapid evolution of the Internet and other computer networks makes it inevitable that such issues will continue to be debated. Freedom of speech may take on a whole new meaning in the computer network environment; precedent-setting cases no doubt rest on the horizon. Courts and legislatures may apply standard First Amendment principles just as to a work in print, or they may create a whole new set of principles. Regardless, the final level of control will lie with the sender and the receiver. —*Dana Lesley-Draper*

See also American Booksellers Foundation for Free Expression; Communications Decency Act; Computers; Copyright law; Technology; Video games.

BIBLIOGRAPHY

Edmund L. Andrews presents a brief overview of the case involving the University of Michigan student in "Internet Case Is Dismissed" (*The New York Times*, June 29, 1995). Philip Elmer Dewitt provides some interesting results of a Carnegie Mellon study of pornography on the Internet in "On a Screen Near You: Cyberporn" (*Time*, July 3, 1995). *The Internet Unleashed* (Indianapolis, Ind.: Sams Publishing, 1994), by Martin Moore and Lance Rose, is an excellent general reference book giving the history of the Internet and an excellent overview of First Amendment issues. Robert M. O'Neill's "Free Speech on the Electronic Frontier" addresses freedom of speech as it applies to threats on the Internet (*The Chronicle of Higher Education*, November 3, 1995).

Iran

DESCRIPTION: Middle Eastern nation with predominantly conservative Muslim population

SIGNIFICANCE: Censorship, long a part of authoritarian Iranian governments, reached new levels after the establishment of a fundamentalist Islamic government in 1979

Two major social revolutions during the twentieth century have significantly changed the political fabric of Iranian society. Both were public uprisings against dictatorship and censorship, but each failed to establish a democratic system. The Constitutional Revolution of 1906 was a secular movement. It marginalized the Islamic clergy (known as Ulama) forcing them to subsist on their own. The clergy became independent of the state but remained influential in the social and political life of the people. The 1979 revolution, on the other hand, empowered the clergy by legitimizing their control over all social and political institutions.

The Constitutional Monarchy. The 1906 revolution brought a compromise between secular nationalists seeking Western-style democracy and Ulama, who wanted to make the state accountable for Islamic law and morality. Five eminent Ulama were seated in the parliament as guardians of Islamic law, ready to veto legislation contradicting Islamic principles or morality. Lack of strong leadership after the establishment of the constitutional monarchy in 1907 caused chaos and power struggles among several groups. This led to a 1925 coup by Reza Khan, the founder of the Pahlavi Dynasty. The new regime brought stability and order, along with government control and censorship.

Reza Shah and his son, Muhammad Reza Shah, created a modern army and police force to maintain internal security. They also established secular education along Western lines, and initiated other social reforms. At the same time they undermined the constitution, weakened the role of Ulama in the parliament, and attempted to eliminate all opposition. In 1961 the shah launched the "White Revolution," which extended state control into all areas of Iranian public life. SAVAK, the shah's secret service, ensured that individual citizens, members of the mass media, and organizations critical of the shah's regime were crushed. In 1975 the government closed down 95 percent of all publications by requiring that they all must have circulations of at least three thousand. Book publishers faced an additional obstacle, in that the censorship authorities only passed books after they were printed. The film industry started under similar adverse conditions. However, despite the repression of official censorship, a generally critical cinema was developed under the Pahlavi Dynasty.

State control pervaded other institutions. State-run trade unions operated to enforce labor codes and to mobilize support for the regime. In the rural tribal areas, the regime recruited chiefs into the government apparatus, executing them if they did not collaborate. The intelligentsia were also forced to follow the regime's policies, and the state subsidized magazines and journals published by collaborating writers. In 1975 the shah founded a monolithic party system in which the entire society was supposed to participate. Those who refused to join the new party were, in the shah's view, communists or traitors, for whom there was no place other than jail or exile.

The Islamic Republic. The 1979 Iranian Revolution was launched against the shah's dictatorship by a coalition of social groups including the intelligentsia and Ulama. The core of the uprising was to end dictatorship and censorship by establishing a democratic state. Initially, the Ayatollah Ruhollah Khomeini was one of the shah's opponents who condemned his dictatorship and asked for social and political freedom. However, after Khomeini's leadership was confirmed in several mass demonstrations, his own ideas of Islamic government—though radical innovations in Shiite history—were promoted as the alternative to the monarchy. Contrary to Khomeini's promises and early behavior, he could not abide criticism. As the supreme leader, "the Vallee-e-Faqih," he considered himself above both the law and constitution.

In 1979 Khomeini established the Supreme Council of Cultural Revolution. Its first duty was to close all schools and universities so that the entire educational system could be revised. It then tried to check all textbooks and remove all traces of un-Islamic opinion and illustration. In the first instance, this meant covering up pictures of women and rewriting Iranian history to glorify the Muslim invaders as national liberators. Rewriting of the textbooks extended to biology textbooks, in which scientific theories of evolution were replaced by Islamic interpretations of creation.

Iranians gather outside the U.S. embassy in Tehran in December, 1979—a month after it was seized by students. (Library of Congress)

Although media censorship began during the first days of the Islamic Republic, it was codified by a 1985 law that banned all challenging views and adverse political interpretations of Islam as slanderous to "pure Islam" or Ulama. The press was not allowed to publish "immoral" pictures, which meant that unveiled women could never be shown at all. As one result, heavy black lines were drawn across unveiled women in Western magazines that were imported. In August, 1988, the new council reiterated the ban on publications criticizing the government and charged them with being anti-Islamic. Material supporting "corrupt Western values" were labeled "Westoxification" and banned. Dish antennas capable of receiving satellite television signals were outlawed, and the interior minister deputed special law enforcement officers to enforce the law. Finally, advocacy of sexual freedom or feminism was also strictly restricted.

The Islamic Republic has relegated women to second-class status. A month after Khomeini returned to Iran in March, 1979, he dismissed all female judges and ordered the compulsory veiling of all women. Within months co-education was banned, married women were barred from attending school, and the government began to close down workplace nurseries. Sea resorts were sexually segregated and women were publicly lashed for violating these rules. Morality codes were declared and for the first time women were stoned and executed on charges of prostitution or moral degradation. The revised legal code followed the Koran in equating the evidence of two women to that of one man; and then took this one step further by ruling that any evidence given by women that was uncorroborated by men would not be accepted by the courts.

Suppression of government opposition went beyond censorship of the press. Amnesty International reported that more than five thousand people were executed in Iran during 1987-1990, and that more than 50 percent of them were political prisoners. Iran ranked first in the world in holding and torturing political prisoners. Political and religious terrorism of the Islamic Republic has expanded out of Iran. According to a *Time* magazine report in early 1994, more than sixty Iranian dissidents had been murdered abroad since 1979. Salman Rushdie, the British author of the novel *The Satanic Verses*, was placed under a death sentence in 1989 that was later reconfirmed. Khomeini's regime grew so repressive that Ayatollah Montazeri, his one-time successor, protested that his regime's crimes had become far worse than those of the shah. Montazeri also criticized press censorship and said that the revolution brought more slogan than action and the regime had been guilty of injustice and denial of people's rights.

—*Max Kashefi*

See also Evolution; Ghazzali, al-; Iran-Contra scandal; Iraq; Islam; Koran; Muhammad; Rushdie, Salman; Terrorism.

Bibliography

Ervand Abrahamian's *Iran Between Two Revolutions* (Princeton, N.J.: Princeton University Press, 1982) and Fred

Halliday's *Iran: Dictatorship and Development* (2d ed. New York: Penguin Books, 1979) discuss dictatorship in twentieth century Iran before the 1979 Revolution. Shaul Bakhash's *The Reign of the Ayatollahs* (rev. ed. New York: Basic Books, 1990) is a good source on dictatorship and censorship in the Islamic Republic. For an overview of the status of women under the Islamic Republic, see Homa Omid's *Islam and the Post-revolutionary State in Iran* (New York: St. Martin's Press, 1994). Shireen T. Hunter's *Iran After Khomeini* (New York: Praeger, 1992) examines the religious basis of censorship in Iran.

Iran-Contra scandal

DATE: November 3, 1986-January 25, 1988

PLACE: Iran, Nicaragua, and the United States

SIGNIFICANCE: In an example of what may be called American censorship, public attention to this presidential scandal was diverted and distracted by various means

The Iran-Contra scandal began in early November, 1986, when *Al Shiraa*, a Beirut magazine, reported that American officials had made covert contacts with leaders in the Iranian capital, Teheran, that resulted in the release of David Jacobsen, who had been held hostage. The next day Iranian leader Hashemi Rafsanjani disclosed on Teheran radio that Robert McFarlane and several security advisors to President Ronald Reagan had visited Iran and offered military equipment in exchange for cooperation in curbing terrorism. In early November the *Washington Post* reported: "If the McFarlane visits to Teheran were linked to allowing even indirect arms or spare parts shipments to Iran, it would represent a reversal of what had been Reagan administration policy."

As this story developed, several accusations emerged: that the Reagan Administration-elect had negotiated with the Iranian government in late 1980 to have American hostages held until after Reagan took office in early 1981 (the Iranians, not trusting Reagan, released the embassy hostages on the day of Reagan's inauguration), that the administration sold arms to what Reagan publicly acknowledged was a terrorist government, that the sales occurred after the administration initiated Operation Staunch, an effort to cut off arms shipments to Iran, and that profits from the arms sale financed the Contra revolution in Nicaragua, in violation of the law, specifically the Boland Amendment.

In his first public response on November 13, 1986, Reagan denied all charges. In subsequent news conferences reporters raised issues of credibility and competence. Polls showed Reagan's approval rating in decline; comparisons were made to Watergate. Reagan's next response, a national address on December 2, 1986, began a strategic shift from denying the accusations to promising to investigate them. In a December 6 radio address, he said he would reveal all the facts. Reagan's 1987 State of the Union address defended his policy but admitted "serious mistakes were made." He promised to investigate the actions of his staff and take appropriate action. Meanwhile, discrepancies in administration accounts were revealed, and McFarlane attempted suicide. On March 2, *Newsweek* used the word "cover-up" on a page-one story.

On February 26, 1987, the Tower Commission Report charged Reagan with "failure in responsibility." The bipartisan group appointed by Reagan had fulfilled his promise to investigate. On March 4, 1987, Reagan took full responsibility, promising to make changes in staff, policy, and processes. Assuming the role of accuser and investigator, he assumed—or made a show of assuming—the news media's investigative responsibilities and neutralized the significant charge of a cover-up. As Reagan neared retirement, attention turned to the possible involvement of presidential candidate George Bush.

In January, 1988, journalists and presidential candidates became increasingly curious about Bush's involvement. Bush brought matters to a head on January 25 in a highly publicized live CBS interview with Dan Rather on the evening news. Immediately, Bush began to question the news broadcast. He rejected Rather's questions, arguing he had already addressed all Iran-Contra issues. Rather repeated his questions, but Bush talked over him. Eventually Rather was forced to end the broadcast. Bush had countered scrutiny of the candidate with scrutiny of the reporter.

Bush's rejection of reporter authority over the news gathering process was evidenced most dramatically not in what he said but in the way he said it. The interviewer and the interviewee were talking simultaneously. Aside from Bush's two long soliloquies, almost every question and answer overlapped. Significantly, Bush's comments interrupted Rather's comments two to one. Bush also undermined Rather's authority by raising an issue that preceded the interview: "Would you like it if I judge your career by those seven minutes when you walked off the set in New York?" Subsequent surveys revealed a divided response from the public.

See also Bush, George; Iran; Reagan, Ronald; Terrorism; Watergate scandal.

Iraq

DESCRIPTION: Oil-rich Middle Eastern country that occupies most of what was once Mesopotamia

SIGNIFICANCE: Under the authority of a single party Iraq has tightly controlled press and other communication media

The control of Iraq fell under the dictates of the Ba'ath Party in 1963 and followed the dictates of a provisional constitution established in 1968. For brief periods sanctions were lifted, as when Kurdish and communist parties were allowed to form in the 1970's, only to be suppressed again in 1978. Although President Saddam Hussein—who came to power in 1979—authorized other parties to exist in 1991, the country basically remained a one-party state. Hussein himself held positions of chairman of the Revolutionary Command Council, prime minister, and commander of the armed forces.

An article of the provisional constitution of 1968 called for freedom of the press, but with the qualification that publications must be inside "the limits of the law." A press code promulgated that same year prohibited publication of adverse remarks about the government, its agencies, or Iraq's economy. Praise for President Hussein and condemnation of his enemies—particularly Iran—later became an instrumental part of the news coverage. In 1981 Iraq's Ministry of Culture and Information Act required all news media to deliver, to promote, and to support the ruling Ba'ath Party's ideology. Foreign news reporters, who had been banned from 1970 to 1981, were again allowed to publish, but with government approval and editing. Government officials accompanied reporters on their assignments and during their news transmissions. All equipment had to be registered and licensed. While the Ministry of Guidance screened printed materials, the Ministry of Culture and Information possessed the authority to suppress all media who did not adhere to the standards of the government.

A 1973 law banned imported films. In 1980 a government-controlled body called the General Federation of the Literate and Writers superseded all other Iraqi cultural and literary organizations, and required all writers and artists to join it. Those who refused to join who had been in their professions longer than fifteen years had to repay the government for their educational costs. Those who resisted the new regulations were jailed and sometimes tortured or killed. Under these new rules four hundred persons fled the country.

In order to ensure loyalty throughout the country, party members were kept under watch by the Amn al-Hizb (Party Security), Amn al-Amm (State Internal Security), Estikhbarat (Military Intelligence), and Mukhabarat (Party Intelligence). The national penal code set the death penalty for Ba'ath Party members who joined other political parties. Those suspected of opposing the government were executed; especially targeted were members of the outlawed Da'wa Party.

By 1988 only six daily national newspapers remained in the country; all of them were published in the national capital, Baghdad. Other media outlets were also based in Baghdad such as radio which reached 2.5 million listeners and Baghdad Television, which aired government-supplied news on two channels. Imprisonment, confiscation of property, and death could be inflicted upon those who did not adhere to the censorship regulations.

See also Iran; Islam; News media censorship; Persian Gulf War; Police states.

Ireland

DESCRIPTION: Independent Western European nation with a predominantly Roman Catholic population

SIGNIFICANCE: Ireland's moral conservatism and resistance to foreign influences are reflected in government efforts to suppress the serious literature of modern world writers

The moral ethics of Ireland's Roman Catholic government are most effectively demonstrated in the Censorship of Films Act of 1926 and the Censorship of Publications Act of 1929. The Irish theater was not rigorously subjected to censorship before the establishment of the Irish Free State in 1922. Although cases of unofficial censorship of the theater took place before the Censorship of Films Act was passed, official censorship of the theater had not existed and did not become a significant political issue in the Irish Free State.

The purpose of the Censorship of Publications Act that became law in 1929 was to ban publications considered to be without literary merit: those deemed indecent or obscene, that focused on crime, or that advocated birth control. The most distinctive feature of the law was its provision for a censorship board of five members appointed by the minister of justice. Their duty was to assess the suitability of publications circulating in the nation. Once a publication was banned, its publication, importation, or distribution were prohibited in Ireland.

The Censorship of Publications Act was modified twice after 1929. Provision for an appeal board was incorporated in 1946. Although this legislation liberalized the act, it had little real impact because of the small number of appeals brought before the board. In 1967 the length of a ban was limited to twelve years. However, the impact of this modification was also limited because provision for rebanning publications was also incorporated into the act. The greatest impact of the 1967 legislation was the automatic removal of several thousand publications from the government's Register of Prohibited Publications. The Censorship of Publications Act was further modified in 1979 when the Irish Parliament passed the Health Act. This act removed the Censorship Board's authority to ban literature advocating birth control.

Proponents and Opponents of Censorship. After World War I several nations advocated government regulation of obscene publications. Formation of the Committee of Inquiry on Evil Literature in Ireland in 1926 was a response to a global trend in censorship of indecent publications. Ireland's censorship law, however, represented more than a government's effort to restrict pornography. Before Ireland achieved its independence in 1922, British Statutes regulated publication of literature in Ireland. Establishment of the Irish Free State that year generated a Gaelic cultural revival in which Irish national identity was defined around the Roman Catholic religion and the country's early Gaelic culture. This was evident in the "Irish Ireland" movement, which advocated government-sponsored protection from foreign influences. This movement's philosophy was rooted in the assumption that Ireland could retain its unique qualities only through cultural isolation. Ireland's Catholic government accepted responsibility for protecting the public from external influences, particularly those from England.

Public support for censorship was generated by Irish vigilante societies. Catholic activists, particularly the Catholic Truth Society, campaigned for censorship. Several Irish journals, including *The Catholic Bulletin* and *The Irish Rosary*, published articles condoning censorship. In addition, the Roman Catholic church itself lobbied the government to regulate literature. Many Irish politicians advocated censorship. Eamon de Valera, who was Taoiseach of the Free State in 1932, considered censorship a necessary tool to achieve national purity.

Opposition to the Censorship of Publications Act began before the bill even became law. Several writers objected to it out of fear that it would stifle intellectual life. Authors William B. Yeats, George Bernard Shaw, and George Russell—whose work was latter censored—opposed the act because they believed it was part of an effort to restrict individual freedom. Opposition to the act culminated in the establishment of the Irish Academy of Letters in 1932. Founded to protect Irish writers from censorship, the academy was largely unsuccessful in its efforts.

Censorship in Action. The Censorship of Publications Act legitimized the unofficial censorship that existed before it became law in Ireland. The xenophobia and cultural puritanism evident in unofficial censorship was apparent in the actions of the Censorship Board. Books containing references to sexual activity and birth control were banned. Novels by European and American writers also were prohibited. In addition, foreign periodicals and the work of many modern Irish writers were barred. Nude images were deemed indecent, and removed from public display in locations such as the National Gallery.

The Censorship Board was aided by Catholic societies and custom officials. The board banned literature based on the recommendations of Catholic activists, and relied on custom officials to seize banned books published in foreign countries upon their arrival in Ireland. Writers whose work was censored became stigmatized. A moralism dominated Irish society so much between the 1930's and the 1950's that anyone objecting to censorship risked both public and private persecution. The supplies of libraries and bookstores shrank until only literature relating to religion and Irish culture was available to the Irish reading public.

The rigor of censorship began to lessen in the 1940's. Controversy over the banning of *Tailor and Antsy* (1942) by the English scientist Eric Cross escalated into a serious debate on censorship policy, and resulted in the establishment of an Appeal Board in 1946. However, the work of Irish, American, and European writers continued to be banned in the post war period. Approximately 1,034 publications were banned by 1954.

The 1950's and 1960's were a period of political change in Ireland. This is demonstrated by the changing attitudes toward censorship. An investigation of the Censorship Board in 1956 resulted in the appointment of two new members to the board. The new Fianna Fail minister of justice appointed three additional new members to the board a short time later. The changing social values of Ireland were evident in the new board's attempts to limit their duties to the regulation of offensive literature. As Ireland modernized, censorship and authoritarian control could not fight foreign influences.

Although a growing part Ireland's modern reading public has become familiar with modern literature, a restrictive mentality has remained in the country. The government's Register of Prohibited Publications contained four thousand titles in 1970. The Censorship of Publications Act remains law, and additional literature continues to be banned in Ireland more than in any other Western European nation.

—Diane L McNulty

See also Birth control education; Christianity; Drama and theater; Fear; Irish Republican Army; Joyce, James; Northern Ireland; O'Connor, Sinead; Shaw, George Bernard; Swift, Jonathan; United Kingdom.

BIBLIOGRAPHY

Michael Adams, *Censorship: The Irish Experience* (University: University of Alabama Press, 1968), provides a detailed analysis of censorship in Ireland from a legal and cultural perspective. Terence Brown's *Ireland: A Social and Cultural History* (Ithaca, N.Y.: Cornell University Press, 1985) examines the cultural and social changes in Ireland from 1923 to 1983. Julia Carlson, ed., *Banned in Ireland* (Athens: University of Georgia Press, 1990), discusses the intellectual and social effects of censorship in Ireland from the viewpoints of censored writers. For a narrative history of Irish political, economic, and social events from earliest times through 1988, Thomas E. Hachey, Joseph M. Hernon, Jr., and Lawrence J. McCaffrey, *The Irish Experience* (Englewood Cliffs, N.J.: Prentice Hall, 1989), is useful. Kieran Woodman's *Media Control in Ireland: 1923-1983* (Carbondale: Southern Illinois University Press, 1985) provides a detailed account of the progress of media censorship in Ireland.

Irish Republican Army (IRA)

FOUNDED: 1919

TYPE OF ORGANIZATION: Nationalistic, ethnic, illegal revolutionary force committed to the expulsion of British forces from Northern Ireland and the creation of a unified Irish Republic

SIGNIFICANCE: The Irish Republican Army (IRA) has employed various forms of censorship and has often been the target of numerous state efforts to suppress it and its political message

The IRA has a long tradition of suppression, which has typically involved violence. The IRA has used violence to quiet its enemies and has been suppressed with violence. In the 1920's, the IRA began to target British intelligence operatives and the most effective police officers. In doing so, the IRA reduced the efficiency of counterterrorist organizations. The IRA also intimidated prison wardens, court witnesses, and jurors. The Provisional Irish Republican Army (PIRA), which was formed in 1969, continued these practices and escalated the level of violence. After 1969 assassinations, involving snipers or bombs, became a modus operandi. In addition, the IRA has acted aggressively to suppress and punish informants. Informants have been crippled or executed to stop their testifying and to act as warnings to other potential informers. The PIRA also censors its publications: for example, the forced resignation of an editor of a PIRA newspaper in 1974.

Throughout their existence the IRA and later the PIRA have faced extensive censorship. Their terrorist tactics have three main goals: to intimidate their enemies; to blackmail the three governments involved (Britain, the Irish Republic, and Northern Ireland) into cooperation; and to generate propaganda. The governments involved have used censorship to attempt to destroy the IRA and PIRA and to reduce the illegal organizations' access to media coverage.

In 1919 the IRA was banned. In 1922 Northern Ireland passed the Civil Authorities Act, which granted the government the authority to arrest without warrant, intern without trial, ban any organization or meeting, prohibit coroner's inquest, and to execute suspected terrorists. In 1925 the Roman Catholic church, influential in Ireland, was persuaded to condemn the IRA and to refuse them the administration of sacraments. In 1931 the Irish Republic outlawed the IRA and banned its newspaper. In 1939 and 1940 the Irish Republic passed legislation that allowed internment without trial and execution for terrorist acts. In 1957 the Republic passed the Offenses Against the State Act, which created military tribunals to try IRA suspects. In 1971 Great Britain allowed internment without trial. By 1976 all three governments allowed nonjury trials for terrorists. They also limited access through trials to the media. In 1971 the Irish Republic prohibited any interviews with representatives of the IRA, PIRA, or Sinn Fein, the political wing. In 1974 Great Britain and the Irish Republic banned terrorists from speaking on television. In 1988 Great Britain banned the broadcasting or televising of any pro-Irish terrorist statements. Television shows have been censored even of IRA references. Despite these efforts, the IRA and PIRA remain functional, and the use of sensational terrorist attacks—such as attacks on the prime minister and mortar attacks on Heathrow airport in the 1990's—ensure continuing media exposure for the IRA.

See also Criminal trials; Fear; Propaganda; Terrorism; United Kingdom.

Islam

DEFINITION: Predominantly Middle Eastern religion founded on the words of the Prophet Muhammad

SIGNIFICANCE: Like most religions, Islam has been a party to stringent censorship

Censorship in Islam is prompted by the conviction that speech, writing, and other expressions of thought that are harmful to the Islamic community should be suppressed by the use of legal and other forms of sanctions as provided for in the Koran and in Islamic law. To understand censorship in Islam, a clear distinction must be drawn between religiously inspired censorship and politically inspired censorship imposed by the rulers of Islamic countries.

Foundations of Islamic Censorship. There are three main sources of Islamic censorship: the Islamic law against heresy and blasphemy, rejection of modernity and its values, and the rise of fundamentalism. Islamic law springs from the two primary sources of the Islamic faith: the Koran, Islam's founding scripture, and the Sunna, which is a compilation of tradition, laws, and practices. Muslims are expected to regulate their behavior according to the rules suggested or specified in these sources. The Koran is believed to be God's final revelation given to the Prophet Muhammad, the last of God's prophets. Muslims believe that there can be no new revelation and the Koran is not subject to revision or alteration.

Islam, perhaps more than any other contemporary religion, discourages religious disagreements and independent thinking. It does not permit questioning of what the Koran and the tradition teach. In Islamic nations, openly challenging the official teachings of Islam is typically a heresy punishable by law. Similarly, blasphemy, the use of profanity and contemptuous language in referring to God or Muhammad, is a serious crime punishable by imprisonment or even by death. The Koran explicitly condemns blasphemers to hell with the verse: "Is there not in hell an abode for blasphemers?"

Islam is generally antimodernist and antisecularist in outlook. It rejects the modern Western ideas concerning the separation of church and state, inalienable rights of human beings,

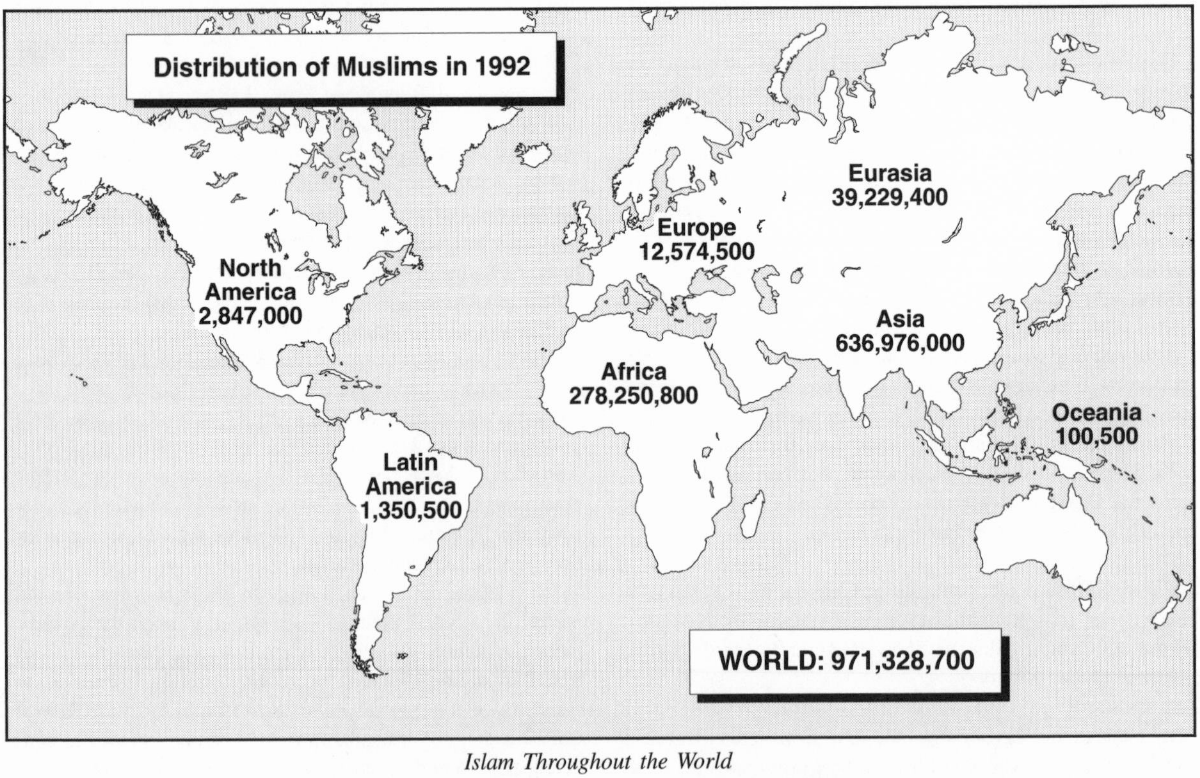

Islam Throughout the World

freedom of expression, the Western understanding of human rights, the secular purpose of law, and the need for democratic procedures. The separation of religion and government is unacceptable to Islam because of the example that Muhammad set. Muhammad assumed the role of a spiritual as well as a temporal leader. By the time of his death, through numerous wars, negotiations, and tactics, he had become the ruler of virtually all of Arabia. In a unique manner he combined the earthly with the heavenly, the political with the spiritual, and the social with the familial.

Following Muhammad's example, in a true Islamic state there can be no sharp distinction between the laws of the state and the laws of Islam. An offense against God is simultaneously an offense against the state. Nor can there be a division between the private and the public. The principles that guide the lives of individuals and families cannot be different from those that guide the state and the community at large. The values and assumptions that support the notion of individualism, such as freedom of thought and expression, belief that laws must not prohibit behaviors that are private and affect no one, and the assumption that individuals have inalienable rights are alien to Islam. Censorship is a natural consequence of the rejection of individualism and the modernist ideas that support it. Pluralism and democratic procedures are also alien to Islam because of the belief that laws and practices of Islam are not open to change through popular consensus. A true Islamic state is necessarily a theocracy, not a democracy.

The devotion of Egyptian Muslims to their religion is evident as thousands perform their morning prayers in Cairo during the holy month of Ramadan in 1992. (AP/Wide World Photos)

The firm belief in the finality of God's revelation as given to Muhammad fosters a fundamentalist attitude in Muslims. Additionally, the contemporary resurgence of fundamentalism in Islam and the stringent control of thought and expression that it advocates is to be understood as a reaction to the spread of modern secular values through Western colonialism. During colonialism in the nineteenth century the liberal ideas of the West were introduced to the Arab world through Western education. They were accepted by the Islamic elites, many of whom achieved positions of leadership after their Islamic nations became independent. These leaders promoted Western education in the belief that science and technology would help bring progress and plenty to their nations. Some of these countries, such as Algeria, Egypt, Morocco, and Turkey, officially and openly embraced the secular ideology in politics and social life.

The espousal of Western ideas and the introduction of Western lifestyles gradually caused widespread resentment among the masses, creating a crisis of leadership. Traditionalists blamed the moral and social decline of their societies on the importation of foreign values and ideas. After decolonization, resentment against the West fomented into mass movements that found a common basis in traditional Islamic values. Under the influence of fundamentalism several Islamic states were forced to pass laws to reestablish traditional social institutions and social practices. Much of the contemporary censorship in Islam is an expression of this protest against the invasion of Western culture that has threatened the basic character of Islamic states.

Book Banning. Banning books, articles, and cartoons and punishing their authors for heresy or blasphemy are forms of censorship found in many Islamic countries. Perhaps the most celebrated instance of book banning in recent times and pronouncing death sentence on a writer for the crime of blasphemy is the case of an English writer Salman Rushdie, who in 1988 published a novel titled *The Satanic Verses*. This fictional work makes derogatory references to the Koran, portrays Muhammad as an impostor, Muhammad's wives as prostitutes, and his followers as deranged. The book triggered protest riots in India and Pakistan that resulted in the death of six persons and caused injuries to more than a hundred. The governments in many countries, including India, Pakistan, the Sudan, South Africa, Iran, Tanzania, Singapore, Indonesia, and Sri Lanka almost immediately banned the book. Bookstores in the United States and United Kingdom that carried copies of this book were threatened. Shortly after the book's publication the then leader of Iran, the Ayatollah Ruhollah Khomeini, issued a fatwa (a finding, a religious declaration, a death sentence) that stated: "I inform the proud Muslim people of the world that the author of *The Satanic Verses* book, which is against Islam, the prophet, and the Koran, and all involved in its publication who were aware of its content, are sentenced to death." A cash reward for Rushdie's assassination and promise of martyrdom for anyone who would assassinate him were also issued by the Iranian government. The death threat forced the author into hiding.

A similar incident involved a physician and writer from Bangladesh, Taslima Nasrin. In 1993 she published a novel titled *Lajja* (shame). Muslim fundamentalists in that country accused her of blasphemy and conspiracy against Islam and issued a fatwa. Fearing public unrest, the Bangladesh government quickly moved to ban the book. Nasrin was eventually forced to leave the country and live in exile and in hiding.

The Arts. Islamic tradition prohibits painting, sculpture, or other representations of humans or any living being. This prohibition against representative art is based on two assumptions: Those who represent creatures in art are attempting to compete with God, who alone is the creator of life. Artistic representation of anything may contribute to the sin of idolatry. Although the traditional injunction against representational art has never been completely obeyed by every Islamic country, the spirit of the prohibition has been faithfully preserved by emphasizing the ornamental and symbolic value of paintings and sculptures, rather than their representational value. A positive outcome of this discouragement of representational art is the development of calligraphy.

During the formative years orthodox Islam severely discouraged the development of music, poetry, and dance. Music was restricted to the recitation of the Koran. In the course of time, however, Muslim princely courts as well as unorthodox sects such as the Sufis introduced and cultivated vocal as well as instrumental music. The koranic criticism of poetry as reckless wandering of the imagination and free indulgence of emotions has had an inhibiting influence upon the development of poetry in Islam. Poetry is also viewed with suspicion due to its tendency to celebrate worldly pleasures, erotic love, and other human passions. Although the original orthodox suspicion of poetry, literature, and music have diminished with time, these creative expressions of the human imagination have often been required to conform to Islamic doctrine. Other forms of the fine arts, such as dance and drama, were also for centuries discouraged in Islam because of the belief that God is the only free actor who can do whatever he pleases, whereas human beings are no more than puppets. Dance and dramatic expression have been seen as implicitly contrary to this view.

Fundamentalist, anticolonial rejection of Western culture in Islamic nations has renewed the vigor of censorship in all its forms in many Islamic countries. In countries such as Iran, writers, poets, artists, and other cultural leaders who do not conform to fundamentalist norms are routinely imprisoned or executed after summary trials. In countries such as Iran, millions of library books have been burned, thousands of publications have been banned, many monuments have been smashed, and museum pieces have been destroyed. Certain forms of folk music, dancing, theater, and paintings have been prohibited; and mass media have been brought under strict state censorship.

Censorship in Education. Early Islamic education consisted of systematizing and disseminating the teachings of the Koran and the Sunna. In the Middle Ages, when Arab philosophers introduced Greek philosophy to the Islamic world, opposition was fierce. This confrontation between rationalists and traditionalists led to the final settlement of doctrinal conflicts and the exclusion of secular knowledge from school curriculum. Rote learning and conformity to tradition rather than independent and critical thinking was emphasized. This is not to deny that dissenting Islamic sects and thinkers continued to foster independence and scientific thinking.

In the contemporary Arab world the resurgence of Islamic fundamentalism has led to very stringent control of educational institutions. In Iran, the epicenter of Islamic fundamentalism, for example, the notion of academic freedom is rejected as a Western ploy to weaken religious belief, the content of school textbooks must pass government censorship, research must be preapproved by authorities, the teaching of Islam is made a large part of the school curricula, private schools have been closed, students are separated by gender, and schoolteachers and university instructors whose religious orthodoxy was suspect have been dismissed.

Suppression of Women's Voice. Another form of censorship concerns the silencing of women in society and the suppression of reports of crimes against them. In the wake of Islamic fundamentalism in many countries, women's social and political rights have been severely restricted. Muslim leaders and theologians have undertaken a revision of earlier Islamic history to argue that at the beginning of Islam women played no leadership role in public life. Within the sphere of the family the leadership of the husband has been legally reaffirmed by such legislative efforts as, for example, the Moroccan Code of Personal Status. In countries such as Saudi Arabia and Pakistan, the testimony of a man is accorded a higher value than the testimony of a woman in a court of law. Although mistreatment of women and young girls—violence, sexual molestation, enforced prostitution, buying and selling of women in exchange for what is called the bride price—

occur rather frequently in many Islamic countries, reporting and open criticism of these and similar crimes are often suppressed under the pretext of avoiding public scandal.

—*Mathew J. Kanjirathinkal*

See also Buddhism; Christianity; Ghazzali, al-; India; Iran; Iraq; Judaism; Koran; Muhammad; Nasrin, Taslima; Pakistan; Rushdie, Salman; Turkey.

BIBLIOGRAPHY

Syed Ameer Ali's *The Spirit of Islam: A History of the Evolution and Ideals of Islam* (New York: Humanities Press, 1972) provides a highly readable history of Islam as a world religion. Fazlur Rahman's *Islam* (Chicago: University of Chicago Press, 1976) is an informative and coherent presentation of the essential message of Islam. *The Struggle Within Islam: The Conflict Between Religion and Politics* (New York: Penguin Books, 1989) by Rafiq Zakaria examines the conflict between faith and power among believers. In *Islam and Democracy* (Reading, Mass.: Addison-Wesley, 1992, translated by Mary Jo Lakeland) Fatimah Mernissi explores, in highly personalized terms, Islam's fear of coping with the process of political, social, and cultural modernization. The thin but highly stimulating book, *Rethinking Islam: Common Questions, Uncommon Answers*, by Mohammed Arkoun (Boulder, Colo.: Westview Press, 1994, translated and edited by Robert D. Lee) is an attempt to demonstrate to Western audience the dynamic and evolving nature of Islamic thought.

Israel

DESCRIPTION: Predominantly Jewish nation established in 1948 in the Middle East's historical Palestine region

SIGNIFICANCE: Israel's existence has been opposed by its neighbors, and large numbers of non-Jewish Arab people live in this Jewish state and in territories occupied by it; national security problems have therefore led to censorship

From the end of World War I until 1948 most of the region that became modern Israel was ruled by the British as Palestine. In 1933 the British Mandate of Palestine passed the Press Ordinance, which provided for the licensing and regulation of the press. When Israel became independent, it retained the Press Ordinance. The Ministry of the Interior supervised the press and granted licenses, and the Israeli Defense Forces (IDF), Israel's military, enforced censorship regulations. In 1953 cooperation between the Israeli military and the press was institutionalized with the formation of the Editors' Committee. Under an agreement between this committee and the government, newspapers were allowed to exercise self-censorship. Only articles that touched directly on national security had to be submitted to the military censor.

The Israel Broadcasting Authority (IBA) was set up in 1965. This organization operated under the Ministry of Education and Culture and it controlled the nation's radio and television networks. The IBA, however, is under its own board of directors and, for the most part, radio and television programming have suffered little government interference.

Censorship has been most strongly enforced in the Palestinian areas occupied by Israel. In a war waged in June, 1967, Israel seized territory from Egypt, Syria, and Jordan that more than doubled Israel's size. This brought under Israeli occupation large numbers of Palestinians, Arab inhabitants of the region. In contrast to the Palestinian people living in pre-1967 Israel, those in the occupied territories did not hold the rights of citizens. Palestinian publications in the occupied territories did not enjoy the power of self-censorship exercised elsewhere. Editors of newspapers in the West Bank and in the

Thousands of Israelis celebrate the anniversary of their nation's independence in the streets of Tel Aviv around the late 1950's. (National Archives)

Gaza Strip had to submit all articles to the military censors each night. Newspapers that did not cooperate with these regulations could be summarily shut down. In 1987 discontent with Israeli rule erupted in the *intifadeh*, an uprising of Palestinians in the occupied territories. The government of Israel, suspecting Arab journalists of involvement in the uprising, began to shut down many Arab publications, and many Arab journalists were arrested.

In 1995 Israel allowed the establishment of Palestinian self-rule in the occupied territories of the West Bank and the Gaza Strip in an attempt to achieve internal peace and peace with Israel's Arab neighbors. Censorship by the new Palestinian National Authority, headed by Yasir Arafat, almost immediately became an issue. In January, 1996, Bassem Eid, a Palestinian critic of human rights violations, was detained for twenty-four hours by Palestinian security forces. In that same month, a Palestinian newspaper editor, Maher al-Alami, was held six days for refusing to publish a favorable article about Yasir Arafat. Al-Alami accused Arafat of violating press freedoms and claimed that the Palestinian media were being coerced into following Arafat's instructions.

See also Dead Sea Scrolls; Holocaust, Jewish; Islam; Judaism; National security.

Italy

Description: Southern European peninsular country in the Mediterranean Sea

Significance: Italy has a history of censorship extending from its ancient Roman Empire to its modern Fascist and post-World War II eras

Italian censorship began at least as early as the time of the ancient Roman Empire; however, no period better represents the dangers and problems of Italian censorship than the Fascist era of the early to mid-twentieth century. After Benito Mussolini led the Fascist Party to power in 1922, he imprisoned most of his political opponents, including the leader of the Italian Communist Party, for expressing views contrary to the interest of the government. The Fascists closed or nationalized all newspapers and other media organizations that expressed any opposition to their policies. During the twenty-three years that Mussolini remained in power, he was thus able to control almost all information disseminated to citizens of Italy, thereby enhancing his personal power and ensuring his continued rule. Nevertheless, his government collapsed after he led Italy into a disastrous alliance with Nazi Germany in World War II.

After the war a modern democracy was established. Italy's postwar constitution guaranteed the right of all citizens freely to express their thoughts, by any and all means of communication. The constitution unburdened the press from having to obtain government authorization to publish stories. At the same time, however, it forbade publication or display of anything that offended public decency.

Despite Italy's constitutional protections of free expression, powerful censorship forces remained. The country's highly organized criminal confederation—popularly known as the "Mafia"—assumed many of the censorship functions previously performed by government. During the 1980's, for example, organized crime was alleged to be responsible for killing nine journalists who were working to expose its activities. In early 1984, Giuseppe Fava, director of the anti-Mafia publication *I Siciliani* was assassinated.

See also Censorship; Dante Alighieri; Germany; Machiavelli, Niccolò; Newspapers; Newspapers, underground; Opera; Roman Empire; Vatican; World War II.

J

Jackson, Michael

Born: August 29, 1958, Gary, Indiana

Identification: American pop music performer

Significance: One of history's most successful recording stars, Jackson has been criticized for his songs emphasizing violence, sex, and racism, and accusations that he molested a child moved some radio stations not to air his recordings

Reared in a large family of talented musicians, Jackson began singing with his older brothers when he was five. He was only eleven when he and his brothers started recording professionally as the Jackson 5. He became the group's lead singer and also began performing as a solo act before he turned twenty-one. The brothers' repertoire comprised mostly upbeat and innocent love songs; in 1972 both houses of Congress formally commended them for their wholesome contributions to American youth.

After Jackson began writing, arranging, and performing his own material, he rose to the highest levels of success and popularity as a solo performer during the 1980's. Named "Entertainer of the Decade," he was congratulated by President George Bush at a White House reception. Although his musical genius was rarely challenged, unconventional aspects of his lifestyle—such as having his physical appearance altered—attracted criticism and some condemnation. During the 1990's several widely publicized incidents raised calls to censor his work.

Public controversies surrounding Michael Jackson in the United States moved him to devote more time to performing abroad. Here he opens a concert in Japan during his December, 1996, "HIStory" tour. (AP/Wide World Photos)

On November 14, 1991, Jackson's music video, "Black or White," premiered simultaneously on Fox Television, MTV, and the Black Entertainment Network, as well as in twenty-six other countries. It was seen by more than fourteen million people on Fox alone. Part of a publicity campaign for Jackson's *Dangerous* album, the eleven-minute video cost four million dollars to produce. It has been seen as a serious and complex evocation of the contradictions in racial identity in the United States, but its final four minutes provoked a storm of controversy. In the final sequence a black panther turns into Jackson himself. After taking several steps, Jackson finds himself under a surveillance light, reaches for a gun, and is pelted with bullets. He then explodes into an energetic dance, at times grabbing and rubbing his groin. When he sees a parked car defaced with racist slogans, he jumps on it and wrecks it with a tire iron. Finally, he stops to zip up the fly on his pants.

Immediately after the video's broadcast, Fox affiliates received calls from irate viewers objecting to its violence and simulated masturbation. They were particularly upset that the video aired when many young children were watching. Both Fox and Jackson issued apologies, and his recording company announced that the eleven-minute version of the video cassette would be replaced by a new six-minute version.

In 1993 Jackson was accused of sexually molesting a thirteen-year-old boy. Shortly afterward, a St. Louis radio station announced that it would drop his records from its playlist. Other stations either quietly stopped airing Jackson's recordings, reduced their airplay, or said they would make no changes until formal charges were filed against Jackson. Meanwhile, the National Broadcasting Company had scheduled a two-hour awards special, "Jackson Family Honors," for February, 1994. Prior to its airing, some advertising executives stated they would not recommend that their clients buy time on the special for fear of negative viewer reactions stemming from the sex-abuse allegations.

In early 1995 Jackson released a song titled "They Don't Care About Us" on his *HIStory* album. He was soon criticized by leaders of the Anti-Defamation League of B'nai B'rith and the Simon Wiesenthal Center for Holocaust Studies because of the song's ostensibly anti-Semitic lyrics, such as "Jew me" and "kike me." Explaining that his song dealt with the pain of prejudice, Jackson angrily claimed that he was being misinterpreted. Later, however, he issued an apology and announced that he would rerecord the song and replace the offending phrases with "do me" and "strike me."

See also Anti-Defamation League; Beatles, the; Federal Communications Commission; Madonna; Pornography, child; Presley, Elvis; Radio; Recording industry; Rock 'n' roll music; Rolling Stones, the; 2 Live Crew.

James I

Born: June 19, 1566, Edinburgh, Scotland

Died: March 27, 1625, Theobalds, Hertfordshire, England

Identification: King of England (1603-1625)

Significance: An exponent of moderate royal absolutism, James warned Parliament against public criticism of his politics

The son of Mary, Queen of Scots, King James VI of Scotland succeeded Queen Elizabeth I as monarch of England in 1603 and became England's King James I. He brought with him a strong belief in the divine rights of kings, Old Testament morality, and Scottish law. Although his mother had been a Roman Catholic, he himself had been raised as a rigid Calvinist and did not easily accept criticism. As a firm exponent of a moderate royal absolutism in his many written works, James argued that kings possessed a monopoly of political power, which they derived from God, and that active resistance to the will of kings was sinful.

No friend of the free public discussion of ideas, James exploited the power of the Church of England to issue government policy statements from the pulpit, and he empowered the church's high commission to enforce censorship and to restrain "heretical, schismatical and seditious" books. In one of his frequent addresses to Parliament, in 1610, he warned its members that they could not tell him how to govern, and forbade them to criticize either the high commission or his own royal prerogative. His most famous written work, *Basilicon Doron* (1598), asserts the power of the king to make all decisions on foreign and domestic policy and insisted on his right to dictate church policy. His autocratic notions ill served his son, King Charles I, who inherited his father's inflexibility and was executed by Parliament

See also *Areopagitica*; Bible; Calvin, John; Henry VIII; Latimer, Hugh; Milton, John; *Utopia*.

Japan

Description: Far East Asian island nation

Significance: Government censorship policies have shifted over the centuries to meet the needs of Japan's changing government systems

When the Tokugawa clan consolidated power in Japan in 1603 and gained control over the emperor, it set up a military dictatorship known as the shogunate. Europeans at this time were not unknown in Japan, having been able to come and go freely since about 1542. One of the fears of the early shogunate was the detrimental effect that foreign influences might have had on the Japanese people. The most dangerous of these influences was Christianity, so the religion was banned in the late 1620's. Although the majority of Japanese people were illiterate, the shogun issued an edict outlawing "books intended to propagate Christianity" in 1630.

By 1640 it was evident that Europeans were interfering with internal Japanese politics by lending their support to various factions vying for power. In order to protect itself and its grip on power, the Tokugawa shogunate took the drastic step of expelling all Europeans from Japan in 1640. This removal was an early and dramatic example of Japanese censorship.

In 1853 U.S. Navy commodore Matthew Perry sailed a squadron of warships into Yedo (Tokyo) Bay and insisted, under threat of force, that the Japanese open the country to trade with the West. This embarrassment of the shogun helped trigger an uprising against him; in 1868 the emperor was restored to full power. Subsequent American and European pressure on Japan contributed to the decision to modernize the country. To supplement economic, political, and military modernization, the traditional religion of Buddhism was suppressed and Buddhist property was confiscated. To replace it, the Japanese government encouraged Shinto, a religion that combined nationalism with a worship of the imperial family. The suppression of Buddhism was another example of early censorship by the Japanese government.

During the modernization period, Japanese leaders promoted education as the key to industrialization. The government faced the problem of reconciling the spirit of free thought necessary to technological advancement with the need to maintain respect for the absolute authority of the emperor. The answer was found in the 1870's and 1880's, when a dual system of education was established. The primary, compulsory school organization focused on indoctrinating Japanese youth with the values of traditional respect and reverence toward the emperor and a nationalism bordering on the fanatic. The secondary, noncompulsory university system was based on the Western ideal of free thinking. To ensure that university students did not question national authority, a system of middle schools was set up to train graduates of the primary schools in national and traditional Japanese values. Thus it was assured that "free" academic thinking would never spill over into the political venue.

Modern Japanese Censorship. One result of the Japanese modernization movement was a period of imperial expansion between 1890 and 1945. In the early twentieth century, Russian and Japanese economic interests in East Asia came into conflict that broke into open war in 1904. The Russo-Japanese War was widely supported in Japan, but a small number of socialists opposed it on the grounds that war was essentially evil and a danger to the working classes. The Japanese socialists published their objections to the war in their *Commoner's Newspaper*. In the face of increasing antipathy from the government, the socialists continued their opposition to the war until late January, 1905, when the government officially suppressed their newspaper and ordered the Socialist Party to disband.

Japan's entry into World War I assured her attainment of great power status. Economically, the war triggered a surge of industrial growth, and a commensurate surge in socialism. After the war, an economic downturn stirred labor unrest, and the socialist movement gained strength. In December of 1920, the socialists whose party had been disbanded in 1905 organized the Japan Socialist Federation. To maintain domestic peace, the Japanese government officially dissolved the Socialist Federation in May, 1921, in a move similar to the American suppression.

After Japan's entry into World War II, the Japanese were subjected to the same type of news censorship that all of the major participants in that war experienced. Newspaper articles, films, and newsreels attempted to engender nationalistic support for the war effort, while casting a poor light on "slackers" and other opponents of the war. Factory workers, school children, and other nonmilitary members of Japanese society were mobilized through literature, music, plays, and artwork designed to elicit patriotic responses aimed at higher arms production and other tangible support of the war effort.

Early Japanese military successes were reported to the Japanese people in exaggerated terms, and when the war effort began to turn sour, the government imposed a strict news blackout on reports of military reverses. In several cases, outright Japanese defeats—such as the Battle of Midway and Guadalcanal—were reported as stunning victories or, at worst, highly successful strategic withdrawals. This use of censorship again compares with the practice of American censors suppressing graphic film coverage of actual combat, as well as the suppression of the true casualty rates in battles until well after the fact. This was done so that American public opinion would not be turned away from support of the war as a result of a revulsion to the carnage.

As a consequence of Japan's defeat in the war, the government was forced to adopt a constitutional democracy with the emperor as figurehead. Included in the constitution was an article which declared that military forces would never again be maintained. In the early 1990's, a school textbook claimed that the "interpretation and application of Article Nine of the Constitution have changed significantly" since the fall of the Soviet Union. Japanese censors demanded that the textbook publisher alter the language of the phrase to indicate that Japan was adhering to the constraints of the article. Censorship of this type seemed to be an attempt to cover the fact that Japan was spending $11.5 billion per year to support its self-defense forces in the 1990's. —*Tim Palmer*

See also Buddhism; China; Historiography; *Mikado, The*; Military censorship; United States; World War I; World War II.

BIBLIOGRAPHY

The historical context of Japanese censorship is covered in *Imperial Japan: 1800-1945* (New York: Pantheon, 1973) and *Post-War Japan: 1945 to the Present* (New York: Pantheon, 1973), edited by Jon Livington, Joe Moore, and Felicia Oldfeather. Ian Buruma's *Behind the Mask* (New York: Pantheon, 1984) discusses censorship in modern Japan. G. B. Sansom's *The Western World and Japan* (New York: Knopf, 1968) explains Japan's reaction to Western influence. In "Japan Re-Arms Its School Books" in *Nation* 233 (December 19, 1981), Donald Kirk explains Japanese behavior since the Soviet Union's demise.

Jefferson, Thomas

BORN: April 13, 1743, Shadwell, Goochland (later Albermarle) County, Virginia

DIED: July 4, 1826, Monticello, Albermarle County, Virginia

IDENTIFICATION: Primary author of the Declaration of Independence, governor of Virginia, and third president of the United States

SIGNIFICANCE: Jefferson advocated freedom of expression, without censorship, as a fundamental cornerstone of democracy

Jefferson's advocacy of free expression without censorship was intimately linked to his conceptions of personal life, liberty, and happiness. Writing to Edward Carrington in 1787, he associated freedom of expression with public opinion, as well as happiness. "The basis of our government," he wrote, "being the opinion of the people, our very first object should be to keep that right." He then added, "were it left to me to decide whether we should have a government without newspapers or newspapers without a government, I should not hesitate for a moment to prefer the latter." From there he cited Native Americans as examples of people living happily without government.

Jefferson's phrase "without government" could not have meant without social order to him. He knew Native American societies too well to argue that they functioned totally without social cohesion, in the classic Noble Savage image as autonomous wild men of the woods. They did it, instead, with a non-European conception of government, one which utilized "natural law" and "natural rights," including uncensored personal expression. Jefferson regarded free expression without censorship as one of the primary "natural rights"—those granted not by government, but by nature itself.

Like his mentor Benjamin Franklin, Jefferson sought to create a society that operated as much as possible on consensus and public opinion, the result of uncensored public debate. Both men described the American Indian passion for liberty while making it a patriotic rallying cry. Jefferson once raised the question of which was the greater evil: "no law, as among the savage Americans, or too much law, as among the civilized Europeans." He concluded that anyone who has seen both would pronounce too much law to be the greater evil.

Throughout his life Jefferson opposed censorship on principle. After the Articles of Confederation was superseded by the U.S. Constitution in 1789, he helped lead a movement to add the Bill of Rights, which included First Amendment guarantees of free expression. Later he led opposition to the Sedition Act of 1798 and other government attempts at censorship. His opposition was credited in helping to propel him into the presidency in 1801. During his two terms as president, Jefferson often suffered severe criticism from the Federalist Party press, and he sometimes reacted in anger. Never, however, did he support censorship as ideologically justifiable.

See also Congress, U.S.; Constitution, U.S.; Federalist Party; First Amendment; Paine, Thomas; Presidency, U.S.; Sedition Act of 1798.

Dr. Leonard Jeffries, Jr., being interviewed on Phil Donahue's television show in September, 1991. (AP/Wide World Photos)

Jeffries, Leonard, Jr.

Born: January 19, 1937, Newark, New Jersey

Identification: American college professor

Significance: The U.S. Supreme Court ruled City College of New York did not violate Jeffries' First Amendment rights when it removed him from chairmanship of his department after he made a controversial speech

Jeffries became a tenured professor and chairman of the black studies department at the City College of New York (CCNY) in 1972. Over the ensuing years, he angered many people on and off campus with his controversial theory that black people, because they have more melanin than whites, are intellectually superior. In July, 1991, he gave a speech in Albany, New York, that many considered antiwhite and, especially, anti-Semitic. City University of New York (CUNY), the system of which CCNY is part, responded by reducing Jeffries' term as chairman of CCNY's black studies department from three years to one in March, 1992, while allowing Jeffries to stay on as a tenured professor. Jeffries then sued CUNY, arguing that it had removed him as chairman in response to the speech he had given in Albany and had therefore violated his First Amendment rights and was, in effect, censoring him. In May, 1993, a federal jury agreed with Jeffries; it ordered CUNY to reinstate him as chairman and pay him $400,000 in punitive damages. The trial judge ordered CUNY to reinstate Jeffries as chairman. CUNY appealed the case to the U.S. Court of Appeals, Second Circuit, which also decided in Jeffries' favor as to the constitutional violation, but ruled that CUNY did not have to pay him punitive damages. CUNY then appealed the case to the U.S. Supreme Court.

In November, 1994, the Supreme Court ordered the appeals court to reconsider its decision concerning Jeffries in light of its own recent *Waters v. Churchill* decision, which placed less stringent requirements on public employers seeking to prove that employee speeches are disruptive than had previously been in effect. The appeals court then reversed its earlier decision, finding that CUNY had acted properly, after all, in limiting Jeffries' term as chairman. In October, 1995, the Supreme Court refused to hear Jeffries' own appeal, thereby ending the matter's lengthy journey through the courts.

See also Courts and censorship law; First Amendment; Intellectual freedom; Multiculturalism; Race; Universities.

Jehovah's Witnesses

Founded: 1881

Type of organization: Church

Significance: Jehovah's Witnesses worked for over a century to secure for its members full freedom of worship, speech, and press

Organized in Pittsburgh, Pennsylvania, by Charles Taze Russell, the Jehovah's Witnesses, in pursuit of the right to proselytize, engaged in a century-long advocacy of the constitutional rights of freedom of worship, speech, and press. In 1891, the society became active on the international level. Initially through the distribution of print materials, especially *The Watchtower*, and later radio and electronic devices, Witnesses pioneers conducted religious activities that were severely censored by other religious groups, fraternal organizations, and governments.

Reaction against the Jehovah's Witnesses was especially pronounced during years of global conflict and economic depression. In 1918, in Canada and the United States, various groups demanded that governmental action be taken against the society for what were called its seditious activities. On February 12, 1918, the Canadian government placed a ban on the society and imposed press censorship regulations on its publications. That same year government officials in the United States invaded the Brooklyn, New York, and Los Angeles, California, headquarters and halls of the Jehovah's Witnesses. Eight leaders, including the church's president, J. F.

Rutherford, were convicted and imprisoned on conspiracy charges against the U.S. government. An attempt was made to try Rutherford under the Espionage Act of 1917, but such action failed. Other Witnesses were tarred and feathered, beaten, forced to relocate, and imprisoned for refusing to be inducted into military service. Persecution lessened during the next decade; meanwhile, in May, 1920, Rutherford and his colleagues were cleared of any judgment against them.

During the 1930's persecution of Jehovah's Witnesses again intensified in the Western Hemisphere, Asia, and Europe. Italian and German Witness headquarters and halls were closed, printing presses seized, and distribution of literature banned. In 1933 nearly six thousand Witnesses in Nazi Germany were arrested and sent to concentration camps, where two thousand were executed. In the United States, clergy and special interest groups employed boycotts and intimidation to prevent the society from having access to the air waves. Appeals for assistance from the newly created Federal Communications Commission were ineffective. The Witnesses again entered the legal arena to obtain their full civil liberties.

Witness refusals to salute the flag, accept service in the military, and—by the 1950's—accept blood transfusions as a therapeutic measure, were among the issues that led to censorship and litigation in the United States. Using the First and Fourteenth amendments as the baseline of their legal defense, the Witnesses turned to the Supreme Court to redress their grievances. On the international level after World War II, Jehovah's Witnesses went before the European Commission of Human Rights and the European Court of Human Rights to obtain civil and human rights.

See also American Civil Liberties Union; Leafletting; Pledge of Allegiance; Press-radio war; Sedition; Street oratory.

Jeremiah's Book of Prophecies, burning of

Date: 605 B.C.E.

Place: Jerusalem, Kingdom of Judah

Significance: Book burnings and an attempted assassination challenged the message of a religious leader

Chapter thirty-six of the book of Jeremiah in the Old Testament relates that after the death of king Josiah of Judah in 609 B.C.E., Egypt dominated the kingdom of Judah. Egypt's pharaoh appointed Eliakim, a son of Josiah, to rule Judah. The pharaoh gave Eliakim a new name, Jehoiakim, and required him to impose stiff taxes upon the people, which were then paid to Egypt. Four years later, King Nebuchadnezzar of Babylon subdued the region but permitted Jehoiakim to continue to rule.

Jeremiah, a prophet of Judah's God, had been urging the king and people to trust in their God and not resist Babylon, or the kingdom would perish. The words of this prophecy were recorded in a scroll that Jeremiah's scribe, Baruch, read to those who assembled for worship at the temple in Jerusalem. When the princes of Judah heard about this, they urged Jeremiah and Baruch to hide themselves. The princes then had the scroll read to Jehoiakim, who attempted to silence the words by periodically cutting from the scroll those portions already read, whereupon they fell into the hearth and were consumed by the fire. Protests of his actions by some of the courtiers went unheeded. Subsequently, the king unsuccessfully sent agents to search for Jeremiah and Baruch, presumably to silence them permanently. Rebellions against Babylon began occurring, during which time Jeremiah and Baruch rewrote the scroll. Jehoiakim died within a few years, and in 587-586 B.C.E. the prophecy was fulfilled as the Babylonians destroyed the city of Jerusalem and brought the kingdom of Judah to an end.

See also Bible; Book burning; Israel; Judaism; Sedition.

Joan of Arc

Born: c. 1412, Domremy, France

Died: May 30, 1431, Royen, France

Identification: French peasant burned at the stake for heresy after leading French armies against the English

Significance: Joan's reports of "voices" and "visions" made her the target of persecution

Joan of Arc began seeing visions when she was about thirteen. She claimed that Saint Michael gave her instructions on how she was to live her life. Later, Saint Catherine and Saint Margaret ordered Joan to help France's uncrowned king, or dauphin, to claim his throne. When Joan told her father, he refused to let her go. Joan's visions and voices continued. Some of her friends believed that she was truly inspired and decided to help her. They disguised her as a boy and helped her reach the dauphin. He was not convinced. There was a long wait while Joan was questioned, but finally an army was gathered to fight against the English, who controlled most of France.

Although Joan was not allowed to lead the troops, she was given a special banner and traveled with the men to provide inspiration. When the army reached the besieged city of Orleans, Joan expressed disapproval of the plan of attack. The dauphin followed her suggestion and the city was taken. Joan later led the army to other victories, guided by her "voices." Later Joan became separated from her troops and was captured and sold to the English. The English wanted her dead but did not want the responsibility. They turned her over to a church court and Joan's visions were declared diabolical. When she was tried for heresy she was tricked into an admission of heresy and witchcraft. Joan was burned at the stake on May 30, 1431, forever silencing her "voices."

See also Death; France; Heresy; Hus, Jan; Hutchinson, Anne; Shaw, George Bernard.

Jonson, Ben

Born: June 11, 1573, London, England

Died: August 6, 1637, London, England

Identification: English playwright

Significance: Although one of England's leading writers, Jonson was constantly harassed by censors during his early career, when he was jailed and tried on charges as flimsy as that of being a playwright

Of humble Scottish origins, Jonson was fortunate in receiving a sponsorship to the Westminster School, one of England's best. After apprenticing to a bricklayer, he joined the English army. Later, he entered what proved to be an equally dangerous profession by becoming an actor at the Rose Theatre. At that time, actors were continually under suspicion for personal immorality, slander, and political subversion.

Shifting from acting to writing, Jonson helped Thomas Nashe complete a play, *The Isle of the Dogs*, which the Privy Council decided was lewd in 1597. Its authors and lead actors were ordered arrested. Jonson spent over two months in prison before it was decided that no major offense had taken place. By that time Jonson had decided to write his own plays.

Jonson's first major play, *Every Man in His Humour* (1598), was a success, but its sequel, *Every Man Out of His Humour* (1599), got him into difficulty, since it was produced shortly after verse satire was prohibited by church decree. After seeing the satirical works of his acquaintances publicly burned, he saved himself further trouble by revising the ending of his play.

Jonson then turned to tragedy and wrote *Sejanus* (1603), a new type of tragedy which led to his being called before the Privy Council for possible sedition, popery, and treason. He was found innocent, however, and his life took a turn for the better as he gained royal favor of England's new king, James I—like Jonson, a Scot.

Jonson's fortunes soon tumbled again after he coauthored *Eastward Ho!* (1605), a comedy lightly satirizing Scotland and the king's practice of selling offices. Jonson's plea that his words were misconstrued and the support mustered by influential friends ultimately got him released. However, a year later, in the midst of the hysteria produced by the Guy Fawkes's Gunpowder Plot to blow up Parliament, Jonson was arrested and charged with complicity. In his trial in April, 1606, the evidence was very slim. He was accused of being "a poet, and by fame a seducer of youth to the Popish religion." In six court appearances, the strongest evidence brought against him was his poor church attendance record and the failure of him and his wife to take Anglican communion. While the court refused to make a final decision, Jonson regained the royal favor of King James.

Jonson continued to fall in and out of royal favor in the succeeding years, tweaking royal and aristocratic sensitivities in plays such as *The Devil Is an Ass* (1616), which satirized corrupt business practices in land reclamation projects. However, he did not again run into serious censorship problems. In February, 1616, he received a royal pension, becoming, in effect, England's first poet laureate. He continued to gain royal favor for staging spectacular masques, short dramatic extravaganzas with elaborate scenery and costumes.

See also Drama and theater; James I; Leighton, Alexander; Master of the Revels; Molière; Prynne, William.

Journalism reviews

DEFINITION: Periodicals specializing in coverage of journalism issues

SIGNIFICANCE: As watchdogs of journalism, these reviews have historically been a minor force for and against subtle forms of censorship

If there is a censorship continuum running from complete suppression to absolute freedom, the experience of journalism reviews as forces for—and victims of—censorship probably falls in the middle, according to insiders and observers. Journalism reviews as press-criticism publications began around 1900. At that time they were a slight censorship factor as a result of their influencing or chilling press performance, and a censorship casualty as a result of suffering limited access to sources and pressures from the trade they covered.

According to Staci Kramer, a member of the advisory board of the *St. Louis Journalism Review*, censorship issues that journalism reviews deal with are self-censorship and editing. Kramer has pointed out that contributors to journals censor themselves because they think certain information or points of view may offend someone or because they anticipate cuts by an editor. Editors, as every contributor discovers, do make cuts, for all sorts of reasons—style, content, taste, and substance—and that can anger contributors. It is debatable whether such edits are overt censorship. More troubling, according to Kramer, is the occasional practice of newspapers' telling journalists that they cannot contribute articles to a journalism review, or of newspapers' prohibiting a source from talking to a review reporter.

Commerce also can be a force for censorship, according to the head of a self-described anticensorship organization, the media watchdog group, Fairness and Accuracy in Reporting (FAIR), which publishes the journalism review *Extra!* According to FAIR member Jeff Cohen, the main culprits of censorship in North American society are the corporations that own the media. According to Cohen, censorship in the media is caused less by government or religion than by business interests.

The market for criticism by journalism reviews is limited. Tom Goldstein's *Killing the Messenger: 100 Years of Media Criticism* (1989) argues that the media respond about as positively to criticism as any other large institution. George Seldes, who from 1940 to 1950 published the respected journalism review *In fact*, said that press critics can hold the news media accountable, but that it is not easy. According to Seldes, the critic can help keep the press honest. Newspapers, he argues, "like kings, pretend they can do no wrong."

Journalism reviews and press critics have included series of magazine articles and books by Will Irwin and Upton Sinclair in the early twentieth century and the *New Yorker* column "The Wayward Press," launched in 1927 by editor Robert Benchley. According to H. Eugene Goodwin in *Groping For Ethics in Journalism* (1983), journalists have resisted critical appraisals out of concern that such appraisals might diminish press freedom. In the United States, there is no systematic audit of the performance of the press or of its fulfillment of its duty to keep the public informed about vital national issues.

A list of late twentieth century U.S. journalism reviews include *Accuracy in Media Report*, *American Journalism Review*, *Columbia Journalism Review*, *Extra!*, *Forbes MediaCritic*, *Lies of Our Times*, *Media Culture Review* and *St. Louis Journalism Review*. Although some fear that a review organization of the news media would be the first step toward censorship, Kramer, the *St. Louis Journalism Review* reporter and editor, has argued that censorship by or upon journalism reviews is rare. Rather, reviews have functioned as a conscience upon the news industry.

See also Advertisers as advocates of censorship; FAIR; News media censorship; Newspapers; Newspapers, underground; Project Censored; Project Censored Canada; Seldes, George; Sinclair, Upton.

Journalists, violence against

DEFINITION: Physical assaults on news reporters

SIGNIFICANCE: Assassination is the ultimate form of censorship; every week at least one journalist is killed somewhere in the world

Every year throughout the world hundreds of journalists are assaulted, kidnapped, harassed, falsely imprisoned, illegally detained, or threatened with physical harm. Murders of journalists are rare in the most repressive societies, but this is because journalists themselves are rare in such societies. Between 1985 and 1996 no killings of reporters were confirmed in North Korea, Saudi Arabia, Cuba, Libya, Syria, or Burma (Myanmar). However, although working journalists are rarely killed in such countries as China, Ethiopia, and Kuwait, many are routinely imprisoned, often for life terms.

JOURNALISTS KILLED THROUGHOUT THE WORLD, 1986-1995

Region	*Number*	*Percent of total*
Western Hemisphere	**125**	**27%**
Colombia	43	
Peru	19	
Mexico	13	
Brazil	10	
El Salvador	10	
United States	7	
Haiti	5	
Chile	3	
Guatemala	3	
Canada	2	
Honduras	2	
Venezuela	2	
Argentina	1	
Dominican Republic	1	
Ecuador	1	
Nicaragua	1	
Panama	1	
Paraguay	1	
Europe (incl. former Soviet Union)	**114**	**25%**
Tajikistan	29	
Croatia	25	
Bosnia and Herzegovina	20	
Russia	22	
Azerbaijan	5	
Georgia	3	
Latvia	2	
Romania	2	
Slovenia	2	
Belgium	1	
Lithuania	1	
Ukraine	1	
United Kingdom	1	
Middle East and North Africa	**85**	**19%**
Algeria	53	
Turkey	19	
Lebanon	6	
Iraq	5	
Egypt	2	
Asia	**79**	**17%**
Philippines	29	
India	15	
Sri Lanka	9	
Afghanistan	8	
Pakistan	8	
Cambodia	3	
Indonesia	2	
China	1	
Japan	1	
Papua New Guinea	1	
Thailand	1	
Vietnam	1	
Africa	**53**	**12%**
Rwanda	15	
Somalia	9	
Angola	6	
South Africa	6	
Chad	4	
Ethiopia	3	
Burundi	2	
Liberia	2	
Zaïre	2	
Nigeria	1	
Sudan	1	
Uganda	1	
Zambia	1	
Total	**456**	**100%**

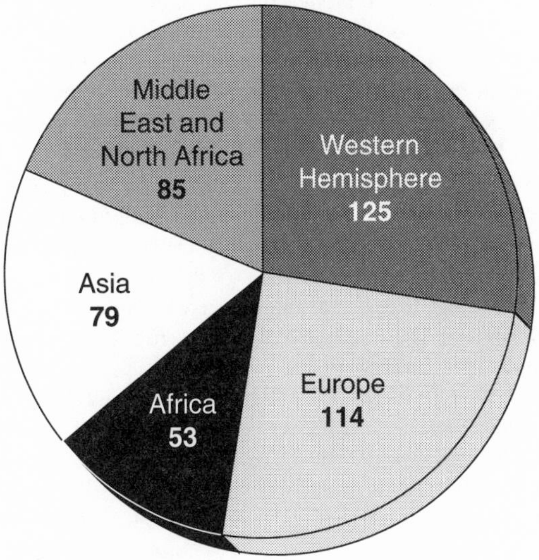

Source: Attacks on the Press in 1995. New York: Committee to Protect Journalists, 1996.

The most widespread violence directed against journalists tends to occur in countries that have recently escaped autocratic rule and are beginning to allow publication of independent newspapers, magazines, and journals. In such societies, officially instigated violence is combined with a systematic failure of government authorities to investigate, let alone prosecute, criminal acts against journalists.

The extent of violence against journalists reached such a shocking level in 1981 that the Committee to Protect Journalists (CPJ) was formed by American foreign correspondents in response to the often brutal treatment of their colleagues by authoritarian governments and other enemies of free and independent journalism. Since then CPJ has monitored abuses against the press and promoted freedom of expression around the world. It accomplishes this through fact-finding missions, independent research, annual reports, and the International Freedom of Expression Exchange—a global electronic mail network. Walter Cronkite, formerly of CBS News, has served as CPJ's honorary chairperson.

Between 1986 and 1995 CPJ reported that 456 journalists were killed in the line of duty, including 125 in the Western Hemisphere, 114 in Europe and the former Soviet Union, 85 in the Middle East and North Africa, 79 in Asia, and 53 in Africa. In 1995 alone, fifty-one journalists were killed, most by political assassins. The single largest group were twenty-four Algerian reporters and editors.

In 1995 CPJ reported that there were at least 720 incidents of violence against journalists throughout the world, outside of industrial democracies. By the end of that year, 182 journalists were imprisoned in twenty-two different countries, often on charges of sedition, or on no charges at all. Most of the imprisoned reporters, eighty-six, were in the Middle East and North Africa, more than half of these in Turkey.

Violence against journalists knows no ideological or religious limitations. Extreme right-wing and left-wing governments have harassed, beaten, imprisoned, and assassinated journalists in order to censor dissent and suppress information at odds with their official propaganda. Both governments and their opponents kill journalists: During the 1970's, Argentina's military government killed nearly a hundred journalists in an effort to impose Christian values; during the 1990's Algerian rebels murdered more than fifty reporters and editors in a campaign for Islamic rule.

Beyond political persecutions, journalists covering organized crime and drug trafficking have been singled out as targets of physical violence. Colombia claimed the third-largest number of confirmed deaths between 1985 and 1995: forty-three journalists, most victims of drug-cartel contract murders. Unsolved and uninvestigated disappearances would probably increase this figure immensely. Similar threats exist in Central America, Peru, Venezuela, Russia, Central Europe, Central Asia, and Indochina. Even in the United States, a symbol of press freedom around the world, journalists have been murdered in Arizona, California, Colorado, Florida, New York, Texas, Virginia, and Washington, D.C.

See also Bolles, Donald F., Jr.; Death; News media censorship; Walker, David.

Joy of Sex, The

Type of work: Book
Published: 1972
Author: Alex Comfort (1920-   )
Subject matter: Illustrated manual on human sexual behavior
Significance: Sexual-behavior research became an object of censorship or prior restraint in many communities when it became popularized with verbal or visual explicitness, or when accompanied with nonorthodox attitudes toward contraception, homosexual behavior, or casual sex

The prelude to the modern sexual revolution may be said to have begun with the sexual-behavior researches conducted by Alfred Kinsey during the 1940's and 1950's. He was followed by the revolutionary work of William H. Masters and Virginia E. Johnson in the 1960's. Their work and other research culminated in the 1970's, with the rise of what has been called the American sexual revolution—with its accompanying mass-media presentations and visual depictions showing precisely what the researchers were talking about. Open discussion of normal sexual behavior and debates about "proper" sexual techniques became increasingly popular.

The Joy of Sex appeared on the scene at the height of the so-called sexual revolution. This book described and illustrated—in clearly drawn and explicit detail—virtually every aspect of heterosexual physical activity. Its author, Alex Comfort, a British gerontologist, biochemist, novelist, and sexologist, saw the book make the best-seller list of *The New York Times* and remain there for more than a decade. Eventually it sold more than eight million copies, including later editions and variations such as *More Joy of Sex* (1973). Other titles that followed included *The New Joy of Sex* (1991) and *The Compact Joy of Sex* (1994); related books by other authors are Edmund White and Charles Silverstein's *The Joy of Gay Sex* (1978) and *The New Joy of Gay Sex* (1992) and Emily L. Sisley and Bertha Harris' *The Joy of Lesbian Sex* (1977).

Despite the anticensorship stance of the American Library Association, public libraries did not acquire books such as *The Joy of Sex* that might potentially disrupt their services, provoke community controversies, or invite theft by young patrons or by people opposed to such publications.

Despite the resurfacing of opposition to books such as *The Joy of Sex* during the 1980's and 1990's, renewed efforts to promote intelligent sex education programs in schools, more open tolerance of homosexual rights, and the proliferation of X-rated videos and television cable services led to the publication of more books like *The Joy of Sex.* In 1995, more than a half-century after publication of *The Kinsey Report*, Comfort's *The Joy of Sex* went on the market in CD-ROM format—complete with parent access codes, adults-only warnings, and a pocket-sized book, *The New Joy of Sex.*

See also Homosexuality; Kinsey Report; Sex education; Sex manuals.

Joyce, James

Born: February 2, 1882, Dublin, Ireland
Died: January 13, 1941, Zurich, Switzerland

IDENTIFICATION: Irish author

SIGNIFICANCE: Joyce's books have been attacked and censored for their language and subject matter

Joyce was born into a Roman Catholic Irish family. His early life was molded by the conservative religious and moral values of late Victorian Ireland as well as the nationalistic passions that led to Ireland's independence from Great Britain in 1922. He left the church in his late teens and exiled himself from Ireland after 1904, only rarely to return. Nevertheless, he never escaped his Irish and his Catholic background, which formed the core of the subject matter in his short stories and novels.

At his preparatory school Joyce was incensed when books were locked up and restricted. While at the university in Dublin he wrote an essay criticizing the parochialism of Irish-language drama that was censured by the university authorities because it mentioned an author listed in the church's *Index Librorum Prohibitorum.* Refusing to accept the censure, Joyce published the essay privately.

While living in Italy with his future wife, Nora Barnacle, Joyce wrote a series of short stories about Dublin life. *Dubliners* was later recognized as a brilliant work, but Joyce faced considerable difficulties in getting it published. The first English printer he approached objected that his book contained immoral passages contravening English law. In contrast to Ireland after independence, England had no censorship board to pass judgement on literary works before their publication, but offending works could be prosecuted after publication. Although Joyce reluctantly made changes, his book continued to be rejected. It was not until 1914, after the passage of almost ten years and only with the public intervention of Ezra Pound, that he found an English publisher willing to risk prosecution.

James Joyce, author of Ulysses*—perhaps the single most-censored book written in the twentieth century.* (Library of Congress)

Pound was also essential in the publication of Joyce's second major work, the autobiographical novel of his youth, *Portrait of the Artist as a Young Man*, which began appearing in the London literary journal *The Egoist* in late 1914. During this work's serial run, however, the printer edited or censored numerous portions relating to sexual matters. Afterward Joyce had difficulty getting the work published in book form because D. H. Lawrence's book *The Rainbow* (1915) had recently been successfully prosecuted for obscenity. *Portrait of the Artist as a Young Man* was finally published in the United States in late 1916. An edition of only 750 copies was issued in England early the following year.

Joyce's *Ulysses*, possibly the greatest of modern novels, was published privately in Paris but it faced prosecution in Britain and the United States, where it was initially banned. His last work, *Finnegans Wake* (1939), was not subject to such censorship, possibly because few readers could fully understand the difficult novel's language and plot.

Joyce was a controversial writer because of the elements of sexuality and other social behavior that did not meet the professed public standards of the early twentieth century. In Ireland, it was not only elements of sexuality that generated controversy, but also his often antagonistic position toward the Roman Catholic church and the parochial Irish nationalism of the times.

See also Adultery; Book publishing; Cerf, Bennett; Girodias, Maurice; Ireland; Lawrence, D. H.; *Little Review, The*; *Ulysses*.

Judaism

DEFINITION: A religion developed among the ancient Hebrews before the rise of Christianity; its modern adherents are known as Jews

SIGNIFICANCE: The persecution of Jews has usually involved censorship, and Jews have censored other Jews

Censorship of Jewish works has taken various forms: erasure or revision of objectional expressions from manuscripts; suppressing circulation of scriptural books written in the vernacular; incineration, confiscation, or mutilation of individual books and libraries; excommunication of authors; injunction against reading printed texts; cessation of printing press privileges; punishment of booksellers; and expulsion or extermination of authors and readers.

Gentile Censorship. Toward the end of the twelfth century, physician and Jewish scholar Moses Maimonides (also known as Moses ben Maimon) produced a code of Jewish law, *The Code of Maimonides* (1168), and a work on the philosophic principles of Judaism, *Guide of the Perplexed* (1190). Some of his coreligionists, inflamed by Maimonides' scientific approach to religious issues, views on immortality of the soul, explication of Haggadah (homiletic passages), and focus on study beyond the Hebrew Bible and the Talmud, turned to the Roman Catholic church for inspiration and support.

Solomon ben Abraham of Montpelier, with the aid of Joshua ben Abraham Ferundi and David ben Saul, issued a ban against those who read Maimonides. As the struggle between Maimonists and anti-Maimonists escalated in the early years of the thirteenth century, ben Abraham asked the Dominican and Franciscan friars for help against those led astray by the Jewish heretic. The zealous defenders of the Church searched Jewish homes in Montepelier for Maimonist writings, confiscated found copies, and in December of 1233, engaged in the first public and official burning of Hebrew books, setting the standard for subsequent search and destroy missions throughout France. In the aftermath, less than a month after the initial fires, other Hebrew books became the targets of the Church and any incensed mob.

About this time, the French rabbis excommunicated a Talmudic scholar named Donin who had expressed doubts about the authority and teachings of the Talmud. Unlike Maimonides, who had protested against accusations that he was trying to alienate Jews from tradition and who had anguished about the schism that his ideas generated, Donin converted to Catholicism and decided to punish the Jews for his perceived mistreatment. As the newly baptized Nicholas de Rupella, Donin met with Pope Gregory IX and maintained that the Talmud subordinated the Bible, distorted biblical passages, used derogatory language in speaking of Jesus and Mary, and kept the Jews resolute about their religion. Gregory, incited by these and other inflammatory complaints by de Rupella, confiscated and gave all copies of the Talmud to the Dominicans and Franciscans for evaluation, sanctioned death threats against those who preserved their copies, and proclaimed a public burning in 1239 if de Rupella's attacks were proven to be true.

France collected Talmudic tomes and formed a tribunal to study the works and to question several rabbis on the indictments. The commission, consisting of men who could not read or understand Hebrew or Aramaic (the primary languages of the Talmud), found the Talmud guilty on all counts and condemned all copies to the flames. For about the next eighty years, while subsequent popes—at the behest of tribunals who found the Talmud to be anti-Christian and antimorality—continued to order the destruction of the Talmud, Jews bribed Church officials, prayed, asked for stays, concealed editions of the Talmud in wells, buried volumes under trees, and snatched them from bonfires.

In Spain, King James invited Rabbi Moses ben Nachman to hold a disputation about the messiahship of Jesus with Dominican Brother Paul Christian. The July, 1263, debate ended with the king honoring the rabbi. Unhappy with the results, Brother Paul appeared before Pope Clement IV, reciting the same charges de Rupella had used in France. In August of that same year, the king—at the behest of the pope—ordered the Jews of Aragon to submit their books for examination, authorized the removal of objectionable passages by blackening the words with ink, and returned the expurgated books to their owners.

In England, King Edward, faced with the expensive annoyance of adhering to Pope Honorius IV's decree of preventing anyone from reading the Talmud, simply rid himself of the problem by expelling the Jews from England in 1290. In 1516 Pope Leo X issued a bull that all books before publication had to be submitted to censors for examination; following his lead, the General Synod of Italian Jewish Congregations in 1554 required three ordained rabbis to examine before publication all subsequent Hebrew books and to sign their names at the beginning of each book.

In the 1559 edition of the *Index Librorum Prohibitorum*, Pope Paul IV subjected the Talmud to continued disputations, charges, and burnings. In 1595 a list (*Sefer ha-Zikkuk*) appeared that contained the names of Hebrew books that could not be read unless certain passages or terms were deleted, clipped, or altered before publication. The list included a prayer book by a famous mystical scholar, Rabbi Isaac Luria; a cabalistic work; haggadic collections; Latin books written or translated by Jews; books about the immortality of the soul and resurrection; books by apostate Jews and Jewish renegades; histories of the Jewish people; occasional anti-Semitic diatribes; some books about the life of Jesus; and a book on the trial of Jesus from a Jewish perspective.

Occasionally, revisers (also known as expurgators or cleansers), often apostate Jews appointed by the Church, tore out whole pages in their zeal to do a good job. The Church was fearful of moral lapses, so Hebrew books went through successive revisions. Objectionable terms included the words "Talmud" and "goy." The last edition of the *Index Librorum Prohibitorum*, published in 1948, still included works produced by and about Jews. Contemporary scholars assert that many textual errors seen in current editions of the Talmud and Hebrew Bible are a result of revisers' modifications and repeated editing.

In addition to the *Index Liborum Prohibitorum* and other lists and acts by the Church to censor Judaica, the Inquisitions of Spain and Portugal produced indices of their own. Hebrew books not listed on any of these lists still faced repression by the Church. By the 1800's, Jewish censorship extended to political and economic arenas. Poland burned or destroyed Hasidic literature. Polish censors would not permit Hebrew books to be read unless they were printed in Poland, and government examiners made rounds to enforce this regulation.

In Prague, for about two hundred years a special decree enabled the Jesuits to revise all Hebrew books brought to the city. At the end of the eighteenth century, censorship authority transferred to the state government known as the *Landesgubernium* who hired a Jewish *Vorcensor*, a preliminary censor who was usually a rabbi, to read a book before the official censor examined it with the assistance of Jews or apostates who understood Hebrew. The state, however, added restrictions: It did not permit the printing or reprinting of books dealing with superstition; it refused to permit epitaphs on tombstones without permission of a censor; and it proscribed importing books from outside Prague.

In 1781 Austrian censors marked printed works with *admittitur* (may be printed without reservations), *permittitur* (may be printed if some references to moral, politics, and religion were edited), and *toleratur* (may be printed despite some harsh expressions about religion and the state). Reprints required the correction of the offensive passages. By 1810 the classifications changed: *admittitur* (may be sold in public and advertised in newspapers), *transeat* (may not be advertised), *erga schedam* (may be owned only by scholarly people), and *damnatur* (may be used with permission of the police). As the century progressed, because censors suppressed all writings and Jewish writings in particular, Jewish playwrights, poets, and authors who feared prison either fled the country or converted to Christianity.

In 1919 amid growing anti-Semitism, Hungary created its own list of undesirable authors and deprived writers and scientists of the freedom of speech. Hungary banned the works of Jews and of those who objected to fascism or to the law limiting the number of Jewish students in universities. On February 28, 1933, Paul von Hindenburg's *Verordnung des Reichspresidenten zum Schutze von Volk und Staat* was published, listing the works of more than 2,293 authors who were considered poison to Germany. The Gestapo's *Polizeiindex* and the Ministry of Propaganda's *Staatindex* together listed more than 12,000 book titles deemed unsafe. The Nazi's *Verzeichnis jüdischer Authoren* listed further items dangerous to the German people. Listed prominently on all of these lists were Jewish playwrights, poets, journalists, artists, and scholars. Germans students, ordered by the government to liberate their cultural life from Jewish intellectualism, began cleaning libraries and bookstores of works by Franz Kafka, Sigmund Freud, Sholom Asch, Karl Marx, and other Jews. For the glory of Germany, these students threw books into large public bonfires in cities across the nation.

The Nazis banned works by Jewish writers and persecuted or murdered Jews and their protectors. They confiscated from Jews, and transferred to German hands, valuable works of art, including those created by Jewish artists such as Marc Chagall and Amedeo Modigliani. After Hungarian Jews had been sent to concentration camps to be exterminated, more than 500,000 of their works, written in various European languages, were collected and ground to pulp in mills.

In exile during this period, Jewish German poet Heinrich Heine, a convert to Christianity, mocked religion (even his adopted one) and insulted the German monarchy. In Prussia, Bavaria, and Denmark he faced repercussions. His works were banned, confiscated, and forbidden to be published or sold; his patriotic songs became forbidden to be sung.

Jewish Censorship. After the translation of the Pentateuch into Greek was completed, the rabbis who had permitted whole passages of Greek literature to be cited in the Talmud insisted that the Septuagint be kept in storage places, hidden from the general public; some rabbis imposed a ban on it.

In the years following 150 C.E., rabbis opposed Jews owning any Roman emperors' statues or fragments from them, statuary of any kind, flags, engraved images, or any artistic object that were seen by the public as cult objects. In this era, rabbis also prohibited the illumination in gold ink of the five books of Moses because it made the Bible accessible only to the wealthy.

A millennium later, while some rabbis opposed wall paintings and stained glass windows in synagogues, Maimonides and others permitted Jewish ornamentation largely in the form of birds, fish, and floral depictions. As guilds developed in Europe, Jewish and Catholic clergy forbade Jews to manufacture or trade sacramental objects with the name of Jesus or Mary on it.

Rabbi Akiva and Maimonides, among others, mocked or criticized apocryphal writings (books not in the biblical canon and sectarian works) but did not impose sanctions against them. Some argued that apocryphal works could be read only in private, not in public. Rabbis criticized and sometimes banned books by authors who—such as Rabbi Ephraim Solomon ben Aaron of Luntschits—neglected to cite their sources. Rabbi Samson of Sens even found fault with Maimonides for this lapse. Rabbi Raphael Cohen's eighteenth century code of laws, published in Berlin, was banned and publicly burned in the courtyard of a synagogue for egregious errors. Other legal books were condemned because authors promoted changes in tradition, printers were apostates, or Jewish producers were not Sabbath observers.

In the seventeenth through nineteenth centuries, while rabbis permitted verbal parodies of people, institutions, and sacred texts on the festive holiday Purim, some rabbis banned, burned, or hid written parodies. From the twelfth through the eighteenth centuries, Jewish authorities either expurgated offensive passages or prohibited the printing (although permitting the manuscript form to survive) of books containing questions and critiques by Jewish authors about Christian beliefs.

To protect the economic welfare of authors, the Council of the Four Lands (the supreme communal authority for Jews in Western Europe from 1594 to 1764) threatened a ban or excommunicated plagiarists and forgers. In 1745 Jewish leaders in Amsterdam asked printers not to commemorate or publicize the rescinding of orders against Jews. Throughout the next 150 years, because of fear of reprisals within and without their communities, Zionistic and politically motivated Jewish writers published their works under pen names, in limited runs, or in cities other than their own. Often, found copies were burned, torn to pieces, or trampled upon.

In the twentieth century, Maimonides' works came to be considered mainstream; art was no longer affiliated with idolatry or worship of foreign deities; the vernacular became critical for transmission of traditional ideas; an explosion of religious and secular works—old and new, serious and frivolous, printed and calligraphed, challenging and embracing—lined walls of Jewish homes. In the world at large, now that Jewish authors are part of the intelligentsia, religious authority no

KOSHER SURFING

In late 1996 a new Internet service in Israel announced creation of "Torah Net." This service was linked to fifteen hundred other web sites certified as "kosher"—that is, sites containing no pornography or material violating the Jewish faith.

Source: Christian Science Monitor. October 22, 1996.

longer retains the same control on creative works, and democracy affords freedom of speech, the history of Jewish censorship offers insight into the anxiety and terrors that change engenders. —*Mareleyn Schneider*

See also *Amerika*; Anti-Defamation League; Bible; Blasphemy laws; Book burning; Christianity; France; Germany; Holocaust, Jewish; Literature; Poland; Simon Wiesenthal Center; Talmud.

Bibliography

Censorship imposed by the Church on Jews is the focus of William Popper's *The Censorship of Hebrew Books* (New York: Ktav Publishing House, 1969). Moshe Carmilly-Weinsberger's *Censorship and Freedom of Expression in Jewish History* (New York: Sepher-Hermon Press, 1977) and *Sepher va-sayif* (New York: Sura Institute, 1966) provide detailed information regarding the history, consequences, and reasons for Jewish internal censorship. Carmilly-Weinsberger's *Fear of Art: Censorship and Freedom of Expression in Art* (New York: R. R. Bowker, 1986) extends understanding of the regulating of paintings and sculpture by religious and secular authorities. Isaiah Sonne's essay "Expurgation of Hebrew Books: The Work of Jewish Scholars" in Charles Berlin's *Hebrew Printing and Bibliography* (New York: New York Public Library and Ktav Publishing House, 1976) concentrates on censorship of Hebrew books in Italy during the sixteenth century.

Judicial publication bans (Canadian)

Definition: Court-ordered bans on the publication, broadcast, or other dissemination of news about criminal trials

Significance: Publication bans have demonstrated that certain press freedoms are more limited in Canada than in the United States

In the 1980's and 1990's Canadian courts occasionally imposed publication bans prohibiting the publication of details related to criminal cases. These bans, usually imposed during preliminary hearings, reflected the fear that widespread media coverage of particularly sensational cases might prevent defendants from receiving fair trials by making it impossible to find impartial juries.

The most famous case of a publication ban occurred in the province of Ontario in 1994-1995. The case involved a married couple, Paul Bernardo and Karla Homolka, who were charged with the brutal murder of two teenage girls. Homolka was permitted to plead guilty to a lesser charge in return for agreeing to testify against her former husband. The court then imposed a complete publication ban surrounding Homolka's trial out of concern that any public revelations of what occurred during her trial might imperil Bernardo's own right to a fair trial. Ironically, it was not the defendant but the prosecution, fearing the potential grounds for either a mistrial or an appeal, that applied for the ban.

Unprecedented measures were undertaken to ensure that the publication ban worked in Homolka's trial. All members of the American news media were barred from attending her trial because a Canadian court order could not be enforced in the United States if reporters chose to publish stories there. Within Canada the publication ban was applied throughout the country; at its height Canadian cable television companies were required to black out segments of American programs they carried that might have violated the ban. Universities blocked access to Internet discussion groups that might be discussing the trial. Travelers returning to Canada from the United States with copies of newspapers carrying material on the trial were limited to no more than one newspaper each.

All of these measures prompted cries of censorship, especially from the Canadian media. The case actually received more attention from the news media in the United States because of the censorship issues that it raised, and because O. J. Simpson's murder trial, with its extensive media coverage, was taking place at the same time. In only one case, however, was a person charged with violating the publication ban. A retired police officer was arrested after he tried to mail material on the trial.

In 1994 the chief justice of the Supreme Court of Canada issued several suggested guidelines for lower court decisions respecting demands for publication bans. These guidelines included allowing the media legal standing while a proposed ban is under consideration; requiring those seeking a ban to justify it; ensuring that a ban is the last available option, and finding ways to limit the ban's extent as much as possible.

See also Canada; Courtrooms; Courts and censorship law; Criminal trials; Free speech; Gag order; Intellectual freedom; Simpson, O. J., case.

Junk food news

Definition: News that resembles "junk food" in being empty of useful content

Significance: Junk food news often takes the place of more substantive news, thereby effectively censoring it

"Junk food news" is a term coined by Carl Jensen, the founder of Project Censored, to identify the sensationalized trivia reported by the media in the guise of news and at the expense of serious news. Jensen first used the term in an article titled "Pandering to the Public" that appeared in *Penthouse* in March, 1983. According to Jensen, the journalistic phenomenon of junk food news tends to focus on sensationalized, personalized, and homogenized trivia, often belonging to one of the several categories, such as "name-brand news" (for example, stories about O. J. Simpson, the British royal family, Michael Jackson, or Madonna), "yo-yo news" (reports on the up-and-down trends of the stock market, unemployment rates, crime rates, interest rates, or commodities prices), "crazed news" (stories about new diet fads, changing fashions, dance fads, sports, video games, music recordings, or the always newsworthy crazed killer), "anniversary news" (anniversaries of major wars, celebrity birthdays, heinous crimes such as the 1932 Lindbergh baby kidnapping, natural disasters such as the 1906 San Francisco earthquake, or outstanding sporting events such as Hank Aaron's career home-run record).

In the late 1980's and early 1990's the amount of junk food news in the mainstream media increased greatly, leading to what was dubbed the tabloidization of the news. In 1984 Jensen started compiling lists of the top junk food news stories of the year; he later enlisted the aid of the national Organiza-

Events such as people demonstrating in support of Lorena Bobbitt during her early 1994 trial for emasculating her husband exemplify "junk food" news. (AP/Wide World Photos)

tion of News Ombudsmen in selecting the ten most sensationalized news stories of each year. Some classic junk food news stories over the years have included Clara Peller's "Where's the beef?" hamburger commercials, which were covered as a craze; the tribulations of television evangelists Jim Bakker and Tammy Fay Bakker; the marital woes of billionaire Donald Trump; Vice President Dan Quayle's misspelling of "potato"; John Wayne Bobbitt's severed penis; Michael Jackson's wedding to Lisa Marie Presley; and O. J. Simpson's criminal murder trial.

Various reasons are given for the abundance of such trivia in the news: junk food news is easier and cheaper to produce; the pervasive influence of pseudonews television programs such as *Hard Copy* and *A Current Affair* and publications such as *People* and *The National Enquirer*; evidence that junk food news increases ratings and circulation; and junk food news offers both journalists and the public a welcome diversion from the political and complex side of life. The concept of junk food news refutes the argument by news managers that there is no such thing as news media self-censorship, but rather only differences of opinion on what is most important to publish or broadcast.

See also News broadcasting; News media censorship; Project Censored.

K

Kama Sutra

Type of work: Book
Written: Between the first and fifth centuries C.E.
Compiler: Mallanga Vatsyayana(?)
Subject matter: Hindu advice on love and sensual pleasure
Significance: U.S. Customs' seizure of sexually graphic illustrations intended for publication in the *Kama Sutra* led to a court case challenging the constitutionality of banning importation of obscene materials

Mallanga Vatsyayana is credited with compiling the classic collection of Hindu aphorisms on love known as the *Kama Sutra* early in the first millennium C.E. Nothing is known about him beyond the fact that he was a student of ancient Hindu works, from which he adapted his own book. The texts of the *Kama Sutra* taught that human life should be directed toward three goals: *dharma*, or doing good works to gain religious merit; *artha*, acquiring wealth and fame; and *kama*, achieving pleasure. *Sutra* are aphorisms—brief instructive statements—so *Kama Sutra* can be translated as "aphorisms on pleasure." The *Kama Sutra* contains explicit descriptions of various forms of human sexual activity, but much of it is taken up with more prosaic advice on matters such as finding a spouse, making oneself more attractive, and how spouses should treat each other. It carries the underlying message that people in love should do whatever brings them pleasure.

In 1883 the English explorer and linguist Richard Francis Burton privately published his own translation of the *Kama Sutra*. The public at large could not buy an unexpurgated edition of the book until 1963, when it appeared in lavishly illustrated editions in Great Britain and the United States (early editions were not illustrated). No one tried to censor the work at this time. In 1969, however, Milton Luros, an American book publisher, tried to bring sexually graphic Indian illustrations into the United States for a new edition of the *Kama Sutra*. U.S. Customs agents confiscated thirty-seven of his illustrations from his suitcase and charged him with violating the Tariff Act of 1930, which prohibited importation of obscene material. Luros sued, claiming that the law violated his First Amendment rights. A federal district court in California ruled in his favor, declaring the 1930 law unconstitutional.

In 1971 the U.S. Supreme Court overturned the lower court's decision, in *United States v. Thirty-Seven Photographs*. The majority opinion, written by Justice Byron White, rejected Luros' argument that Americans had a right to possess obscene material in the privacy of their homes and that his suitcase was an extension of his home. Earlier, in *Stanley v. Georgia* (1969), the Court had proclaimed citizens' right to such privacy; however, White ruled that because a suitcase was not part of a person's home, it was not protected from searches. Moreover, since Luros had clearly intended to make his pictures available to the public, he was not bringing them into the country solely for his private viewing. Congress thus had the power to prohibit any commerce, including obscene material, from entering the country. Justice Hugo Black dissented, defending a "zone of privacy" for citizens that included their luggage. In his view, Congress had no power to act as censor, and he asserted the right of citizens to read and view whatever they pleased.

See also Black, Hugo; Books and obscenity law; Burton, Richard Francis; Customs laws, U.S.; First Amendment; India; Obscenity: sale and possession; Roth, Samuel; *Roth v. United States*; Sex manuals.

Kanawha County book-banning controversy

Date: April, 1974-December, 1975
Place: Kanawha County, West Virginia
Significance: Demands by conservatives that 325 titles be banned from the schools led to a sympathy strike, high absenteeism, the resignations of the superintendent and president of the school board, and charges of censorship

Charleston, the capital of West Virginia, lies within nine-hundred-square-mile Kanawha County. The controversy began when a five-member faculty panel of Kanawha County language arts teachers recommended the adoption of 330 basic texts, supplementary materials, and hardbound and softbound texts to replace old grammar, reading, English, and literature books. Such actions are typical of public school book-buying methods, in which old books are periodically discarded and new ones selected for purchase. The term used for the selection of books is "adoption."

Christian Fundamentalists and Others. Alice Moore, a school board member and the wife of a Fundamentalist baptist minister, objected to the books selected and to the manner of selection. Moore claimed the books contained material that was disrespectful of authority and religion, destructive of social and cultural values, obscene and pornographic, unpatriotic, and in violation of individual and family rights of privacy. The textbook series under attack included Heath's *Communicating* and *Dynamics of Language* series, McDougal-Littell's *Man* series, Houghton Mifflin Company's *Interaction*, Ginn's *Responding* series, and Scott Foresman's *Man in Literature* and *Galaxy* programs. Moore extended her attack to include the writings of e. e. cummings, Sigmund Freud, Eldridge Cleaver, Malcolm X, Dick Gregory, Gwendolyn Brooks, and Allen Ginsberg. Specific titles to be banned from library shelves included the *Iliad*, Plato's *Republic*, John Milton's *Paradise Lost* (1667) and *Paradise Regained* (1671), James Fenimore Cooper's *The Deerslayer* (1841), Herman Melville's *Moby Dick* (1851), Ernest Hemingway's *Old Man and the Sea* (1952), other classic works, and a children's book of jump rope rhymes. In all, 325 titles and 96,095 volumes were considered offensive and, under conservative protest, temporarily removed to a warehouse.

The objections of Moore won quick support from Fundamentalist churches, parents, and the executive committee of the county Parent Teacher Association. However, the National Association for the Advancement of Colored People, the Episcopal church, and the state Human Rights Commission endorsed the committee's selection. On June 27, at a three-hour hearing, eight of the supplementary paperbacks were dropped, but the school board adopted the other offending titles by a vote of 3-2.

Over the summer of 1974 antitextbook committees organized in rural Kanawha County and called for a boycott of the schools on opening day. In early September 20 percent of the school system's 45,000 students were absent on the first day of classes. The next day 3,500 coal miners staged a wildcat strike in sympathy with the book protesters. School book protesters picketed businesses and industrial plants, successfully closing the warehouse of a supermarket chain and a trucking terminal.

The pressure of court injunctions, arrests, and school shutdowns forced Superintendent Kenneth E. Underwood to close all the schools and negotiate a truce between the opposing factions. When the schools reopened and a thousand preacher-led antitextbook demonstrators still picketed the schools making new demands, Superintendent Underwood resigned.

During the month of October two men were shot, eleven men were arrested, three schools were vandalized, more than three thousand miners remained out of work in a sympathy strike, an empty school was dynamited, school attendance dropped to 70 percent, and the school board president, Albert Anson, Jr., resigned. On October 21, a conservative delegation from Kanawha County visited the White House and met with presidential adviser Roger Semerad. The White House agreed to look into the matter.

On November 8, the school board voted 4-1 to return all the controversial books to the schools. The board also decided that any parent objecting to a textbook on moral or religious grounds could have their child excused from using it. The board stated that no teacher was authorized to indoctrinate a student to follow either moral or religious values which were objectionable to either student or parents. A new committee of five teachers and fifteen parents was created by the board to select textbooks. The American Library Association and the Association of American Publishers claimed the board's actions represented censorship.

The school system appeared to be the only institution connecting the diverse populations of Charleston's urban, industrial, middle-class with the rural, Fundamentalist miners of Kanawha County. The rift between Charleston and Kanawha County parents began over the issue of teaching sex education in the public schools, widened when Kanawha County's rural schools were consolidated in 1973, and erupted over the issue of language arts textbook selection for classrooms in grades kindergarten through twelve.

Outside Intervention. The National Education Association (NEA) sent an eight-member panel to Kanawha County to investigate the issues and actions undertaken by the school board. The NEA concluded their investigation in March, 1975, and published the NEA Report, *Kanawha County, West Virginia: A Textbook Study in Cultural Conflict*. The NEA chastised the school board for placating the opposition when the book selection committee's composition was changed to give the community more decision making authority than educators had. The NEA did not examine the textbooks in dispute but did hold hearings and interviews with educators, parents, students, and others concerned with this issue. Only one member of the board refused to meet with the panel. The NEA backed the embattled school board "in principle" but criticized the board for its failure either to foresee or to respond quickly to the crisis. The school board's most serious transgression was its failure to communicate with Kanawha County's more tradition-bound rural communities. The NEA report urged that Kanawha County consider establishing alternative schools or classes where both controversial books and textbooks could be included in the curriculum along with schools offering a more traditional educational format. The report deplored the exploitation and prolongation of the dispute by right-wing elements but expected the school board to be more attuned to the community's needs.

In December, 1975, the U.S. Court of Appeals for the Fourth Circuit upheld a federal district court's order dismissing the action of parents of two school-age children to restrain the board of education of Kanawha County from adopting textbooks. The appeals court decision was consistent with earlier Supreme Court rulings that guaranteed First Amendment protection of speech, inquiry, and belief in the schools. The Court found nothing wrong with the school board's procedures, actions, or conduct incident to the placing of the books in the schools that abrogated the rights to privacy by parents or children. At the time the appeals court ruled, students in Kanawha County were given a choice from among several language arts textbooks. Superintendent John Santrock noted that parents had stopped complaining about the curriculum. Even school board member Moore was satisfied that her book banning demands had achieved a greater level of parental involvement in Kanawha County's public schools. Ironically, Kanawha County received the 1975 national award for outstanding community education. —*William A. Paquette*

See also Banned Books Week; Censorship; Education; First Amendment; Free speech; Gabler, Mel, and Norma Gabler; Parent Teacher Association; Textbooks.

BIBLIOGRAPHY

The Teacher Rights group of the National Education Association, *Kanawha County, West Virginia: A Textbook Study in Cultural Conflict* (Washington, D.C.: National Education Association, 1975) provides background, analysis, and recommendations for the textbook controversy in Kanawha County. Informative contemporary magazine accounts offering a variety of political and regional views about the Kanawha County textbook controversy and censorship include John Mathews' "Access Right to Children's Minds: Texts for Our Times: Problems in Kanawha County" in *The New Republic* (January 4, 1975), John Egerton's "Battle of the Books: Kanawha County" in *The Progressive* (June, 1975), Russell W. Gibbons'

"Textbooks in the Hollows" in *Commonweal* (December 6, 1974), Calvin Trillin's "U.S. Journal: Kanawha County, West Virginia: Anti-textbook Controversy" in *The New Yorker* (September 30, 1974), and Curtis Seltzer's article "West Virginia Book War: A Confusion of Goals: Controversy in Kanawha County" in *Nation* (November 2, 1974).

Kant, Immanuel

BORN: April 22, 1724, Königsberg, Prussia
DIED: February 12, 1804, Königsberg, Prussia
IDENTIFICATION: German philosopher
SIGNIFICANCE: Kant was a leading figure in the German Enlightenment whose writings on religion got him into difficulties with the Prussian monarchy

The first philosopher to write his principal works in German, Kant spent his entire life in Königsberg, East Prussia, and he taught at the university there. Under Frederick the Great Prussia was governed by a form of enlightened absolutism that allowed Kant to write freely on whatever he pleased. Indeed, his essay *What Is Enlightenment?* (1784) defended absolutism as a means of reconciling the potentially conflicting demands of political stability and free inquiry. He suggested that the watchword of Prussia should be: "Argue as much as you like and about whatever you like, but obey!"

Frederick's successor, Frederick Wilhelm II sought to impose religious orthodoxy. In 1788 his minister of justice and head of the state department of church and schools, Johann Christoph Wöllner, issued edicts on religion and censorship that effectively prohibited publication of unorthodox writings on religion. Three years later Kant and his publisher, J. E. Biester, sought permission to publish the four parts of his *Religion Within the Limits of Reason Alone*. The first part received the censor's imprimatur, but the other parts did not. Kant then submitted the entire manuscript to the theological faculty of the University of Königsberg, which affirmed that it was principally a philosophical, not a theological, work. Under laws governing publication of books, Kant was entitled to seek approval from the philosophy faculty of another university, which he did. With the imprimatur of J. C. Hennings, dean of the philosophy faculty of the University of Jena, he published his book in Königsberg in 1793.

Kant's publication of this book moved Frederick Wilhelm personally to admonish him and to threaten "unpleasant consequences," should he continue to defy royal wishes on the subject of religion in October, 1794. (A year later the government forbade professors at the University of Königsberg to lecture on Kant's book.) Kant responded to this admonition by insisting that because his work was intended for a scholarly audience, it could not corrupt the general public. He also asserted that his work was devoted to an examination of the essentially rational core of revealed religion, not to revelation itself. He concluded by promising, as a loyal subject, to abstain from pubic lectures and publications on religious topics.

Kant scrupulously adhered to his promise until after the king's death. In 1798 he published an essay on conflict between philosophy and theology faculties, as part of *The Conflict of the Faculties*, defending the right of scholars, as scholars, to write whatever they please. In so doing, he returned to the distinction he had made in *What Is Enlightenment?* between the need for scholars to conform to the wishes of the government while pursuing the truth wherever it leads them. Kant thus remained consistent in arguing that political health requires publicly enforced and supported orthodoxy and freedom of inquiry for scholars.

See also Germany; Hume, David; Locke, John; Religion; Schiller, Friedrich von; Spinoza, Baruch.

Kennedy, John F., assassination of

DATE: November 22, 1963
PLACE: Dallas, Texas
SIGNIFICANCE: After the possibility of a conspiracy was rejected by a presidential commission, efforts were made to suppress unofficial inquiries and withhold evidence from public view

The assassination of President John F. Kennedy created an atmosphere of doubt, largely because the accused assassin, Lee Harvey Oswald, was himself murdered before he could stand trial. A commission was appointed by Kennedy's successor, President Lyndon Johnson, to investigate and report on the circumstances surrounding Kennedy's assassination. Chaired by Chief Justice Earl Warren, the commission concluded that Oswald and his own killer, Jack Ruby, had both acted alone. Public opinion polls, however, showed that many Americans questioned the lone-assassin thesis, and numerous books were written advancing various conspiracy theories. Although the Warren Commission published twenty-six volumes of material from its hearings and evidence, most of its files were declared sealed for seventy-five years.

One of the Warren Commission's severest critics, attorney Mark Lane, wrote the best-selling book *Rush to Judgment* in 1966. Lane's public activities were closely monitored by the Federal Bureau of Investigation (FBI), and the Central Intelligence Agency (CIA) instructed its overseas posts to employ their propaganda assets to refute this book, and Lane himself complained of having his radio and television appearances canceled. He also found his motives questioned and his arguments misrepresented by the press and, especially, by those defenders of the Warren Commission who opposed dissent. His experience was shared, at least to some extent, by other critics who sought to be a voice independent of the mainstream press.

The most important piece of evidence related to the assassination, an eight-millimeter motion picture taken by a man named Abraham Zapruder, was purchased by *Life* magazine for more than $150,000. *Life* placed the film under lock and key. The magazine occasionally published single frames, but the film was not seen by the American public until Geraldo Rivera showed it on ABC's *Goodnight America* in 1975. The Warren Commission had concluded that Oswald alone shot Kennedy from a building behind the president's motorcade. The film's vivid depiction of President Kennedy's backward movement after the head shot in Dallas—a movement interpreted by many viewers as evidence of a bullet coming from the so-called Grassy Knoll in front of the president's car—made the showing of the film a key event in initiating a new

PUBLIC OPINION ON ASSASSINATION THEORIES

In November, 1993, thirty years after President John F. Kennedy was assassinated in Dallas, Texas, a CNN/*USA Today*/Gallup Poll asked a cross section of Americans to express their opinions on who killed the president. Of those polled, 75 percent said they believed that more than one person was involved in the assassination. Only 15 percent believed that one man was responsible; the remaining 10 percent expressed no opinion.

investigation of the assassination in 1976-1979 by the U.S. House of Representatives.

Official control of assassination evidence proved to be an even greater obstacle to public disclosure than private ownership. The Warren Commission relaxed its initial seventy-five year ban on disclosure, and passage of the Freedom of Information Act in 1966 gave private researchers an important tool in securing the release of documents, but many were still being withheld decades later. Following the publication of twelve volumes of hearings on the Kennedy assassination, the U.S. House of Representatives in 1979 ordered the remaining files of its Select Committee on Assassinations sealed for fifty years. Later, Oliver Stone's 1991 film *JFK* prompted a debate over this secrecy policy that led to creation of a federal Assassination Records Review Board, which in 1994 began the process of reviewing and releasing withheld assassination files, including those of the Warren Commission, the House Select Committee, the FBI, and the CIA.

See also Central Intelligence Agency; Classification of information; Congress, U.S.; *Death of a President, The*; Federal Bureau of Investigation; Freedom of Information Act; Presidency, U.S.; Warren, Earl.

Kent, Rockwell

BORN: June 21, 1882, Tarrytown Heights, New York
DIED: March 13, 1971, Plattsburgh, New York
IDENTIFICATION: American artist, illustrator, and writer
SIGNIFICANCE: Accused of having communist sympathies, Kent was harassed by the U.S. House Committee on Un-American Activities

Born into an established middle-class family, Kent began studying art at sixteen and later took evening art lessons while learning architecture at Columbia University. His first jobs were in drafting, but art soon took over. He held his first exhibition in 1905 at the National Academy of Design in New York City. In 1910, he helped organize the first Exhibition of Independent Artists in New York.

Kent's travels influenced his art and writing. He emigrated to Newfoundland in 1914, but was charged with pro-German activities and deported a year later. To fund a trip to Alaska, he incorporated himself and sold shares to friends. *Wilderness* (1920), his book about his Alaskan experience, increased his popularity. He described his 1922-1923 trip to Tierra del Fuego in *Voyaging Southward from the Strait of Magellan* (1924). *N by E* (1930), about his first journey to Greenland, became a Literary Guild selection. Meanwhile, Kent also worked as a commercial artist, sold drawings and cartoons to magazines, and illustrated books. In addition to his own writings, he illustrated new editions of such classics as *The Decameron*, *Beowulf*, *The Canterbury Tales*, William Shakespeare's plays, *Leaves of Grass*, and *Moby Dick*. Under the pseudonym "Hogarth, Jr.," he published drawings in *Vanity Fair*. He was also a contributing editor of *Colophon* and editor of the modernist publication *Creative Art*.

Kent fought openly against all forms of fascism. A champion of independent art, he resisted domination by conservative artists, tried to organize an artists' union for the Congress of Industrial Organizations, and served as president of the International Workers Order, an allegedly communist group dissolved by court order in 1950. When he painted a mural at the U.S. Post Office Building in Washington, D.C., in 1937, he included a message in Eskimo calling for Puerto Rican independence. In 1939, he was charged as a communist before the House Committee on Un-American Activities (HUAC), and ten years later HUAC linked him to eighty left-wing groups. Kent denied being a communist but was a Socialist Party member. In 1949 he helped write the Stockholm Appeal, a document calling for a complete ban of atomic weapons. In 1953, he evoked his Fifth Amendment rights when called to testify before Senator Joseph McCarthy. Although these accusations tarnished his reputation in the United States, they earned little attention elsewhere. In 1960 he gave the Soviet Union eighty landscapes and eight hundred other drawings, which were installed at the Pushkin Museum and the Hermitage. When the Soviet Union awarded him the Lenin Peace Prize in 1967, Kent donated the money to North Vietnam. Sympathetic to the U.S. Civil Rights movement, he also supported the National Association for the Advancement of Colored People. A life-long nonconformist who yearned to retain youthful values, Kent believed that art is a by-product of enthusiasm for life. He was not concerned with the principles of art, which for him came naturally. He painted rugged scenes of mountains and seascapes, in which humans played insignificant roles. His erotic book illustrations suggest his enjoyment of life and sex.

See also Art; Mural art; Rivera, Diego; Socialist Realism.

Kent State shootings

DATE: May 4, 1970
PLACE: Kent State University, Kent, Ohio
SIGNIFICANCE: In shooting students on a college campus and then trying to cover it up, the Ohio National Guard denied students their right to free speech and assembly and denied the public at large the right to know

Two days after the burning of the Kent Sate University ROTC building by bikers from out of town, the adjutant general of the Ohio National Guard, Sylvester Del Corso, mobilized and deployed troops in the center of campus, demanding that students scatter and leave, even though three groups had obtained permission from the university president to meet there.

Kent State University campus on May 5, 1970: The burned-out Reserve Officer Training Corps building is in the middle; the area in which National Guard troops shot four students to death is behind the building at the upper left. (AP/Wide World Photos)

One of the groups had planned to discuss President Richard Nixon's military invasion of Cambodia, but those who did show up for that purpose were peaceful, even according to National Guardsmen later interviewed by the Scranton Commission, the president's official commission to investigate the shooting of the students.

When the students would not disperse, one platoon fired bullets at them; the troops later claimed they had been out of tear gas—a claim found to be untrue by the Federal Bureau of Investigation. Four students as far away as a parking lot were killed and one was paralyzed.

In the cover-up that followed, Del Corso spoke for the guardsmen to the media, constantly contradicting himself. Though the Scranton Commission damned the shooting, no grand jury ever indicted anyone.

See also Federal Bureau of Investigation; Military censorship; My Lai massacre; Nixon, Richard M.; Vietnam War.

Khachaturian, Aram

Born: June 6, 1903, Tiflis, Russian Empire (now Tbilisi, Georgia)

Died: May 1, 1978, Moscow, Soviet Union

Identification: Russian composer

Significance: One of the most popular Soviet composers, Khachaturian was admonished in Joseph Stalin's clampdown on Soviet artists in the late 1940's

Like other leading Soviet composers of the post-World War II era, Khachaturian fell victim to Stalin's brutal efforts to impose ideological control over the arts, under the supervision of his arts commissar, Andrei Zhdanov. Late in discovering his musical gifts, Khachaturian became a student of Miaskovsky at the Moscow Conservatory. He became quickly established as the composer of such popular works as the *Violin Concerto* (1940) and the ballet *Gayane* (1942), with its universally popular "Sabre Dance."

Khachaturian was named one of the offenders when the Central Committee published its report on the dire state of Soviet music in February, 1948. Although the main targets were the most famous names, Dmitri Shostakovich and Sergei Prokofiev, Khachaturian was included in the complaint against "formalism," which meant individualistic experimentation. This was an odd charge, since the composer's music was generally cheerful, accessible, and flavored with local color. Like the other composers called to account, Khachaturian was forced to confess his alleged errors; he nervously blamed bad advice from critics and a preoccupation with technique. He survived the era of "Zhdanovschina," however, and after Stalin's death in 1953 was quick to argue for greater creative freedom for Soviet artists. By Zhdanov's own bizarre logic, Khachaturian should have been commended for his successful use of regional and folkloric elements within the great tradition of Russian music.

See also Music; Prokofiev, Sergei; Shostakovich, Dmitri; Soviet Union; Stalin, Joseph; Zhdanov, Andrei.

King, Martin Luther, Jr.

BORN: January 15, 1929, Atlanta, Georgia
DIED: April 4, 1968, Memphis, Tennessee
IDENTIFICATION: American civil rights leader
SIGNIFICANCE: King's doctrine of nonviolent resistance added a new dimension to the struggle of African Americans for their civil rights, including their right to freely express themselves at the ballot box

The oldest son of a Baptist minister, King graduated from Atlanta's Morehouse College at nineteen, received a divinity degree from a theological seminary, and earned a doctorate at Boston University in 1955. During his student years, he searched for ways to emancipate African Americans from the bondage of segregation and became interested in the potential of Christian love to effect social change. King's search ended when he attended a lecture on Mohandas Gandhi, who led India's nationalist movement against British rule. Gandhi was not interested in defeating the British, but in redeeming them through love.

The reconciliation of power and love, which Gandhi called satyagraha, provided a philosophical basis for his strategy of nonviolent resistance to unjust laws. King equated Gandhi's concept of satyagraha with *agape*, the Greek word for Christian love. He left the lecture convinced that the liberation of African Americans could be achieved through nonviolent resistance predicated upon the power of brotherly love.

The Civil Rights Movement. In 1954 King settled in Montgomery, Alabama, where he had accepted an appointment as pastor of Dexter Avenue Baptist Church. The following year he was able to put his theory of nonviolent resistance to the test. In December, 1955, Rosa Parks, a middle-aged, African American seamstress, was arrested when she refused to give up her seat on a city bus to a white man. The next evening leaders of the African American community met in King's church. Under his leadership they organized a boycott of the bus system that lasted more than a year. Before it ended, King's home was firebombed, and he was jailed for the first of many times. Ultimately, however, the boycott was successful and King emerged as a national figure in the Civil Rights movement, which mobilized millions of people to break down the barriers to racial equality.

Shortly after the boycott, African American clergymen organized the Southern Christian Leadership Conference (SCLC) and made King its president. King used the SCLC to organize high-visibility, nonviolent campaigns against discriminatory practices, hoping that exposing the evils of racism would arouse national consciousness against its debilitating effects. One of the most famous of his campaigns was a march from Selma, Alabama, to Montgomery, in which his supporters faced powerful opposition while exercising their right to protest their grievances and express their determination to vote.

The Vote. The Fifteenth Amendment to the U.S. Constitution had been ratified in 1870 to prohibit states from denying male African American citizens their right to vote. For nearly a century, however, African Americans in the South who attempted to register to vote had encountered state election laws designed to disfranchise them. In 1958 King led a voter registration drive in the South in order to increase the numbers of African American voters for the 1960 presidential elections. Seeing the right to vote as the key to lasting change in race relations, King chastised African Americans for their political apathy. He warned that they would remain voiceless victims of the political system unless they exercised the fundamental right to express their political preferences at the ballot box.

The effect of King's registration drive was minimal. The voting booth remained off-limits for most African Americans in the South, until March 7, 1965. On that day—which historians have dubbed "Bloody Sunday"—approximately seven hundred Selma African Americans, with King's support, began a fifty-four mile trek to Montgomery to dramatize their challenge to Alabama's discriminatory election laws. Shortly after starting out, they met state troopers who ordered them to return. Instead, with heads bowed in prayer, they continued. Television cameras captured images of state troopers attacking marchers with billy clubs, whips, and rubber tubing wrapped in barbed wire. The next day television audiences watched in horror as defenseless men and women fell to the ground covered with blood.

The response to "Bloody Sunday" was immediate and overwhelming. Thousands of Americans abruptly converged on Selma to support the marchers. Members of Congress from both political parties were deluged with mail and telephone calls condemning the violence, and demonstrators converged on the White House demanding that President Lyndon B. Johnson send federal troops to Selma. On Monday evening, March 15, the president made an impassioned appeal for civil rights legislation that would guarantee that no one would be denied the right to vote because of race. Two days later a federal district judge lifted an injunction against another planned march from Selma to Montgomery. Then the president, after nationalizing the Alabama National Guard, sent military police and other federal officials to Selma. The following Sunday, more than three thousand people resumed the march to Montgomery.

They arrived on March 24. The following day, King led what had swollen into a jubilant procession of twenty-five thousand people through Montgomery to the capitol. As expected, Governor George Wallace, refused their pleas. However, in August President Johnson signed into law the Voting Rights Act of 1965. This legislation outlawed the use of literary tests, which had been used to prevent African Americans from registering to vote, and authorized federal marshals to register voters in states where 50 percent of the voting-age population had registered for or failed to vote in the 1964 national election. Today, the millions of African Americans able to express their political preferences by voting owe a great deal to King.

In 1964 King was accorded a Nobel Peace Prize for his work in the Civil Rights movement. But on April 4, 1968, his life was ended by an assassin. —*Thomas J. Mortillaro*

See also African Americans; Alabama; Civil Rights movement; Malcolm X; *New York Times Co. v. Sullivan.*

BIBLIOGRAPHY

For King's own discussion of his beliefs see his *Why We Can't Wait* (New York: Harper & Row, 1964). Taylor Branch's *Parting the Waters: America in the King Years, 1954-63* (New York: Simon & Schuster, 1988) is a Pulitzer Prize-winning account of the Civil Rights movement with close attention to King's life. For a treatment of the influences that shaped King's personality and philosophy see *To Make the Wounded Whole: The Cultural Legacy of Martin Luther King Jr.*, Lewis V. Baldwin (Minneapolis, Minn.: Fortress Press, 1992). David J. Garrow's *Protest at Selma* (New Haven, Conn: Yale University Press, 1978) is a detailed study of the Montgomery march; a shorter, rivetting version can be found in *Freedom Bound: A History of America's Civil Rights Movement* (New York: Norton, 1990) by Robert Weisbrot.

King, Stephen

BORN: September 21, 1947, Portland, Maine

IDENTIFICATION: Popular American author of horror fiction

SIGNIFICANCE: King's books have frequently been challenged, and attacked, as well as banned from public school and community libraries

King began writing in high school and sold two short stories before finishing college. In 1974 he published his first novel, *Carrie*, about an outcast teenager with telekinetic powers, her religious fanatic mother, and her humiliation at the hands of fellow teens. Over the next twenty years, King published twenty-five novels under his own name, eight collections of short stories, five novels under the pen name Richard Bachman, and three works of nonfiction. Almost all of King's books involve supernatural forces and violent action; many have been best-sellers.

King's books have been challenged since 1975, when *Carrie* was criticized by officials at Clark High School in Las Vegas, Nevada. By 1988 the report *Attacks on Freedom to Learn* listed King as the third-most censored author in the United States (after Judy Blume and John Steinbeck). According to the American Library Association, in 1994 King and V. C. Andrews were challenged more often than any other authors. The most common charges against King's books are his use of profanity, violent subject matter, ridicule of religion, and celebration of the occult. King's novels have often been taken from public school libraries or placed on restricted shelves.

See also Banned Books Week; Horror series controversy; Libraries, school; Library Bill of Rights; Violence.

King Kong

TYPE OF WORK: Film

RELEASED: 1933

DIRECTORS: Merian C. Cooper (1893-1973) and Ernest B. Schoedsack (1893-1979)

SUBJECT MATTER: Fantasy about a giant ape found on a remote island that is brought to New York, where it escapes and wreaks havoc

SIGNIFICANCE: Made during a comparatively lenient period of American film censorship, this film was extensively cut and altered when it was re-released in 1938, reflecting increasingly strict censorship of sex and violence

When *King Kong* was produced in 1933, it was a relatively straightforward, if technically revolutionary, action-adventure/fantasy. Explorers led by Carl Denham visit Skull Island, where prehistoric creatures still live. Among these is Kong, a giant ape worshipped as a god by islanders. Denham and his crew trap Kong and take him to New York for exhibition; however, disaster ensues when he breaks free. Ultimately, his

Scenes of the giant ape fondling actress Fay Wray, eating people, and pitilessly killing others disappeared from King Kong *shortly after the film's release in 1933.* (Museum of Modern Art/Film Stills Archive)

affection for Ann Darrow (Fay Wray) leads to his destruction.

Changes made when the film was rereleased in 1938 clearly reflect the toughening of Hays Code standards during the 1930's. Shots of Kong eating and crushing people were deleted, along with a scene of the ape dropping a woman to her death from a New York skyscraper. Remaining action scenes were darkened to soften their impact. A scene of Kong toying with Ann Darrow, removing part of her clothing, was also cut. (These scenes were fully restored on video in the 1980's.)

A 1976 remake of *King Kong* received a PG rating and stirred no controversy, although its violence and nudity exceeded that of the 1933 film.

See also Film censorship; Hays Code; Nudity; Violence.

Kinsey Report

Type of work: Books

Published: 1948 (*Sexual Behavior in the Human Male*); 1953 (*Sexual Behavior in the Human Female*)

Author: Alfred Charles Kinsey (1894-1956)

Subject matter: Scientific surveys of human sexual behavior

Significance: These surveys of sexual behavior sparked a national controversy about what topics should be open to public discussion and helped to ignite a sexual revolution in the United States

Following the publication of European studies and the development of the new profession of psychoanalysis, American colleges during the 1930's began to move with the times and offer courses in sex education and marriage. Indiana University introduced a noncredit course on marriage in 1938. To teach the course the university tapped a middle-aged biologist of unquestioned moral standing.

Alfred C. Kinsey was an unlikely point man for a sexual revolution. Raised in a strict Methodist family and trained as a scientist, he was a crew-cut, bow-tied paragon of Midwestern virtue. He had earned a doctorate in entomology from Harvard University in 1920. His two-volume study of gall wasps marked him as a leading geneticist of his day and proved that he excelled in collecting and interpreting statistical data. For his sex and marriage course, Kinsey used interviews to quantify American sexual behavior through sex histories scientifically. A public controversy over his work arose almost immediately.

In 1940 the president of Indiana University, who was sympathetic to Kinsey's work, responded to complaints from local clerics by advising Kinsey that he could either teach his course or record his histories, but not both. Kinsey chose the latter. By 1948 he was ready to begin publishing his findings.

Kinsey's first book, *Sexual Behavior in the Human Male* (1948), was an immediate best-seller. Its findings supported the idea that healthy sexual activity made for healthy marriages; it also suggested rates of extramarital sex and homosexuality were higher than previously suspected and said that virtually all young males masturbated. Church groups united in accusing Kinsey of trying to lower moral standards. One well-known minister summed up this sentiment by raging that it was "impossible to estimate the damage this book will do to the already deteriorating morals of America."

Kinsey defended his research methods and worried about his funding for ongoing research. His second book, *Sexual Behavior in the Human Female* (1953) also became a best-seller. His revolutionary findings included observations of great variety in female sexual activity and a lack of frigidity among women. In short, the book established that there was little that could be called "normal" in sexual behavior. An Indianapolis minister labeled Kinsey "a cheap charlatan." A New York rabbi called Kinsey's book "a libel on all womankind." McCarthyism, which was then sweeping the country, led Roman Catholic publications to suggest that Kinsey was helping Americans to "act like Communists" and moved a New York congressman to demand that the postmaster general ban Kinsey's book from the mails because it was "the insult of the century against our mothers, wives, daughters, and sisters." The Rockefeller Foundation dropped its support for Kinsey's research.

See also Ellis, Henry Havelock; *Joy of Sex, The*; *Our Bodies, Ourselves*; *Playboy*; Sex education; Sex in the arts; Sex manuals; Stopes, Marie.

Kipling, Rudyard

Born: December 30, 1865, Bombay, India

Died: January 18, 1936, Hampstead, London, England

Identification: British writer best known for stories and verse set in India

Significance: Closely associated with the British Empire, Kipling's writings have often been attacked for being racist and violent

The writings of Rudyard Kipling have long been controversial. As an author unafraid to expose his personal political and social beliefs to his readers, Kipling voiced his views not only through the actions of his characters, but also through public meetings, the courts, and the press. Censorship of his work goes back to 1898, when his new book *A Fleet in Being: Notes of Two Trips with the Channel Squadron* was suppressed by the British Government because it allegedly revealed Royal Navy secrets. (Copies of the book are now rare.)

Kipling's *Just So Stories for Little Children* (1902) have been attacked as part of Canada's *Impressions* reading series. One story, for example, has been singled out for its use of the word "nigger." Even Kipling's widely known poem "Gunga Din" has been removed from some Canadian libraries as a result of pressure from groups claiming that the poem is "violent and racist and unsuitable for a multicultural society."

See also Books, children's; Colonialism; India; Military censorship; Poetry; Political correctness; Pressure groups; Race.

Kiss, The

Type of work: Film

Released: 1896

Director: Thomas Edison (1847-1931)

Subject matter: A man and woman discreetly embrace and kiss

Significance: One of the first motion pictures seen by public audiences, this short film was also one of the first to raise cries for censorship

The first motion picture screen kiss. (Museum of Modern Art/Film Stills Archive)

Filmed from a scene of the play *The Widow Jones*, this forty-two-foot-long film runs for less than a minute on screen. It simply depicts a middle-aged couple, May Irwin and John C. Rice, together in a romantic scene taken from the popular Broadway play in which they were then performing. Although the scene of the couple kissing was discreet and brief, members of various morality and religious groups in New York City were horrified by what they regarded as an act of public indecency. Under their relentless urging, city public officials banned the film out of concern that its flagrant display of sexuality might incite people to act similarly in public.

See also Hays Code; Legion of Decency; Pressure groups.

Kneeland, Abner

Born: April 7, 1774, Gardner, Massachusetts

Died: August 27, 1844, Salubria, Iowa

Identification: American Universalist clergyman and Rationalist

Significance: Kneeland's conviction for blasphemy made him a martyr and hero to believers in freedom of religion

After attending the common schools and spending one term in an academy, Kneeland joined the Baptist church in Putney, Vermont. In 1803 he moved to the Universalist church and the following year became a licensed preacher in that denomination. In succeeding years he held ministerial positions in Universalist churches in Langdon, New Hampshire; Charlestown, Massachusetts; Whitestown, New York; Philadelphia; and New York City. While in Philadelphia in the early 1820's Kneeland edited the *Christian Messenger*, the *Philadelphia Universal Magazine and Christian Messenger*, and the *Gazetteer*. In New York City he began, in 1827, to publish the *Olive Branch and Christian Inquirer*. All his journals advanced liberal religious views and championed free inquiry and rational Christianity.

By 1829 Kneeland's increasingly radical views had estranged him from his fellow Universalists, and he resigned from the denomination and his ministerial posts. He then went to Boston, where he established the First Society of Free Enquirers and began, in 1831, to publish the *Boston Investigator*, a journal devoted to the exploration of religious rationalism in which he could present his increasingly pantheistic views.

The *Investigator* issue of December 20, 1833, in which Kneeland quoted from Voltaire's *Philosophical Dictionary* on the Virgin Birth and declared his disbelief in Christ, in miracles, and in immortality, led to his indictment for publishing an "impious, obscene, blasphemous and profane libel of and concerning God." He was convicted in January, 1834, but appealed and had the verdict set aside. Two further trials ended in hung juries, but the Massachusetts authorities grimly persisted and secured a second conviction at a fourth trial in 1835. Kneeland again appealed, but his case was postponed until 1838, when the Massachusetts Supreme Court confirmed his conviction and upheld the sentence of sixty days in jail.

The long drawn-out court battles secured more attention to Kneeland and his views than he had achieved with any of his short-lived magazines. News of the sentence caused an outpouring of support for him from believers in religious freedom. Within a few days a petition for his pardon, protesting his prosecution as a violation of liberty of conscience and freedom of the press, arrived before the Massachusetts Governor's Council, signed by 168 leading Transcendentalists, Unitarian, and Universalist ministers, and some eminent ministers of Boston Baptist churches. However, the Council refused to act and Kneeland served his sixty days in jail. Kneeland had lost his personal battle, but his principles prevailed; his was the last conviction in Massachusetts on the charge of blasphemy.

In the spring of 1839, shortly after his release from jail, Kneeland moved to Iowa, where his First Society of Free Enquirers planned to found a settlement on the Des Moines River, near Farmington, Iowa. Kneeland named the chosen site Salubria and lived there until his death five years later.

See also Blasphemy laws; Intellectual freedom; Religion; Voltaire.

Knox, John

Born: c. 1514, Giffordgate, near Haddington, East Lothian, Scotland

Died: November 24, 1572, Edinburgh, Scotland

Identification: Scottish Protestant reformer

Significance: A prominent and controversial Protestant who often found his views and writings proscribed, Knox was the leading force in establishing Protestantism in Scotland after the overthrow of Roman Catholicism

One of Scotland's greatest figures, Knox was probably educated at St. Andrews University before he became a minister and Protestant reformer under the influence of George Wishart, who was martyred in March, 1546. This event had a profound effect on Knox, who developed a hatred for the Roman Catholic church and Cardinal David Beaton, the archbishop responsible for Wishart's execution. After Beaton himself was murdered by Wishart's friends in May, 1546, Knox joined the murderers at St. Andrews Castle. There he was captured by Scotland's allies, the French, and spent time as a galley slave.

After his release Knox served as a royal chaplain to England's King Edward VI. He became an influential figure in England's acceptance of Protestantism, and it was at his insistence that the Black Rubric was added to the Second Book of Common Prayer (1552) stating that kneeling during communion did not imply adoration, only respect. Upon the accession of the Catholic queen Mary I in 1553, Knox fled to the Continent to escape persecution. Under the influence of John Calvin in Geneva, Knox became firmly convinced of the correctness of the more forward Protestant views—views that would characterize Puritans. As pastor of the English congregation at Frankfurt in 1554, Knox demonstrated such views when he adopted a form of worship closer in practice to continental Protestants. This caused a rift with a faction of the congregation which insisted on usage of the Book of Common Prayer.

While in exile Knox wrote *The First Blast of the Trumpet Against the Monstrous Regiment of Women* (1558), which argued that it was unnatural and unbiblical for a woman to rule. His book was aimed at the Catholic rulers Mary of Guise, the regent of Scotland, whose daughter Mary Stuart, Queen of Scots, was married to French king Francis II, and Queen Mary of England, but its misogynist tone angered England's Queen Elizabeth I, so Knox was not welcome in England. Returning to his native Scotland, Knox led the quick, drastic overthrow of Catholicism and its replacement by a partial Presbyterian system. This was done with English assistance while Mary, Queen of Scots, by then a widow, was still in France. The Catholic church, which had established the *Index Librorum Prohibitorum*, placed the complete works of Knox on the list. These included the *Book of Discipline* (1559), *Confession of Faith* (1560), and the *Book of Common Order* (1564). When Mary, Queen of Scots, returned to Scotland in 1561, she and Knox had memorable audiences during which he tried unsuccessfully to convert her to Protestantism. After Mary's overthrow and flight to England, Knox preached at the coronation of her infant son, James VI, who later became England's King James I. Knox recorded his role in the Reformation in several historical works, the *Treatise on Reformation* (1560) and *History of the Reformation in Scotland*, published in 1584 after his death. In 1572 he died of a stroke shortly after receiving news of the St. Bartholomew's Day Massacre, the organized attack on French Protestants known as Huguenots.

See also Calvin, John; Christianity; *Index Librorum Prohibitorum*; James I; Puritans; Reformation, the; United Kingdom.

Koran

TYPE OF WORK: Book
RECORDED: c. 644-656 C.E.
MESSENGER: Muhammad (570-632)
SUBJECT MATTER: Followers of Islam believe this holy book to be God's last message to humanity
SIGNIFICANCE: The Koran has been both a force for and a target of censorship

The Arabic word *qur'ân* means "recitation," specifically a recitation that was given to the Prophet Muhammad by the angel Gabriel as the final message of God (Allah) to humanity. Unlike Judeo-Christian scriptures, the Koran is not a collection of works written by multiple authors compiled over a long period of time. Believed to have been revealed to Muhammad over a period of about two decades, the Koran is neither a book of history, nor a memoir of Muhammad, nor a philosophical treatise. Advocating uncompromising monotheism, its purpose is to proclaim the sovereignty of God, his coming judgment, and humanity's need to submit to him.

Muhammad had the text of the Koran recorded on materials such as tablets, palm leaves and hides. During the rule of Othman, the third successor after Muhammad, its 114 chapters, or suras, were assembled and standardized in their modern form; their total length is close to that of the New Testament. The suras are arranged in approximately descending order of their size, thereby disrupting the message's chronological and thematic sequence. If the suras are separated so that those revealed in Mecca, when Muhammad was a prophet opposing the established order, and those revealed in Medina after he became the leader of the Arabs, the Koran's tone and contents would differ profoundly. The former suras are more individualistic and mystical, while the latter are clearly more collective and political.

Muslims believe that the Koran is God's simplest, clearest and most comprehensive message to humanity. Its language, eloquence, rhythm, and rhetoric are said to reveal something of how God thinks and feels. The Koran is said to be untranslatable and many regard only the Arabic original as authentic; however it was translated into English in 1734.

Illiterate according to tradition, Muhammad is recognized as merely the Messenger of God. Indeed, in many Muslim cultures to say that Muhammad, rather than God, was the author of the Koran is regarded as criminally blasphemous. Piety is also expressed through the avoidance of idolatry, including representational art in almost any form. Both official and self-censorship have been common to avoid blasphemy and idolatry.

The Koran divides humanity into the Abode of Islam and the Abode of War, implying that salvation and peace cannot be realized without being part of Islam. No other religion's scriptures devote so much space to characterizing and condemning unbelievers. Twenty-three suras detail the fate of unbelievers, who are depicted as arrogant and worldly. Three others extol believers to refuse aid, compassion, and friendship to non-Muslims. The rights of non-Muslims are minimized and the Muslim world has never experienced a period of reappraising its often violent historical victories.

Later Islamic traditions have added numerous restrictions on the behavior of believers and non-believers alike. Often judgmental and punitive, many Muslim societies have promoted political systems that have used the Koran to control every aspect of human existence, sometimes through violence and violations of human rights. As Islam had continued to exercise an unusually powerful hold over its faithful, the unscrupulous and selfish use of religion to silence opposition and maintain power has also been common.

The Koran itself has been the subject of censorship. Banned in some parts of medieval Europe, it was restricted in the

Soviet Union, China and other communist countries in the twentieth century.

See also Islam; *Mohammed, Messenger of God*; Muhammad; Rushdie, Salman.

Korean War

Date: 1950-1953

Place: Korean peninsula

Significance: During this U.S.-led war against North Korea's invasion of South Korea, U.S. government efforts to constrain negative media coverage contrasted sharply with World War II censorship policies, foreshadowing an even more adversarial government-media relationship during the later Vietnam War

North Korea's invasion of South Korea in June, 1950, triggered a renewal of American military operations barely five years after the end of World War II. American press coverage of the Korean War represented a sharp departure from the role the media had played in the earlier conflict. Whereas the media generally accepted the need to support the Allied effort against the Axis powers, American involvement in the Korean War was controversial and less generally accepted.

General Douglas MacArthur, the supreme commander in Korea, initially instituted a system of voluntary censorship resembling the system used in the world war. However, as it became evident that journalists were less willing to toe Washington's official line, MacArthur instituted a system of formal, prepublication review for all dispatches from the war zone. As a consequence, many press reports were heavily censored, fostering resentment among members of the press corps. This further weakened the shared sense of mission that had characterized military-press relations in the previous war. Moreover, the increasingly critical perspective of press reports in turn fostered the belief among military leaders that the press was handicapping the war effort.

More than practicing simple censorship, MacArthur's headquarters has been accused of deliberately disseminating misinformation during the Korean War. Press conferences, communiqués, and other official statements from the military headquarters in Tokyo, Japan, were frequently challenged by journalists and columnists in the United States and Britain. The official exaggerations of foreign threats and the downplaying of national casualties might partly be explained as owing to the Cold War climate that permeated virtually all aspects of international relations. However, some critics attributed the high command's thoroughgoing control and manipulation of war information to be a function of the supreme commander's personal hubris. Against this interpretation, the fact that press censorship and media manipulation did not significantly ease after President Harry S Truman's dismissal of MacArthur in April, 1951, suggests that there was a driving force larger than MacArthur's ego behind military censorship. Indeed, censorship was significantly strengthened after the United States began committing troops to the Vietnam War during the 1960's.

Meanwhile, as late as 1996 investigations were continuing into charges that the U.S. government had deliberately hidden embarrassing information about the Korean War effort. U.S. Senate hearings and Pentagon investigations uncovered documents revealing that up to a thousand American prisoners of war (POWs) remained in North Korea after the July, 1953, armistice and prisoner exchange. The possibility that POWs had been left behind has often been raised, but it has repeatedly been discounted by U.S. authorities. Recently discovered evidence indicates, however, that President Dwight D. Eisenhower himself may have been aware that some POWs remained behind in North Korea.

See also Military censorship; Vietnam War; War; World War II.

Kropotkin, Peter

Born: December 21, 1842, Moscow, Russia

Died: February 8, 1921, Dmitrov, Soviet Union

Identification: Russian anarchist philosopher

Significance: Established governments sought to suppress the anarchistic ideas of Kropotkin as dangerous to all authority

Kropotkin was born into an ancient aristocratic family of Russia. His father valued his membership in the Russian ruling class, but Kropotkin rejected it wholly. Volunteering for military service in Siberia, he established for himself a high reputation as a professional geographer.

Kropotkin's alienation from the feudal system into which he was born grew until, by the time of his thirtieth birthday, he had rejected all forms of government that rested on authority. He put his faith in what he called "mutualism," a belief that the natural self-interest of the individual dictated cooperation with one's fellows to solve the problems of social living. Because these views challenged the legitimacy of existing authority, he was imprisoned in 1874. Transferred to a military hospital in 1876, he managed a spectacular escape. After fleeing to western Europe, Kropotkin spent most of the rest of his life in exile. There he published a number of books in which he explained his anarchist theories. He returned to Russia after the 1917 revolution. At the time of his death his previously banned books were being published in Russia for the first time.

See also Bakunin, Mikhail Aleksandrovich; Goldman, Emma; Intellectual freedom; Russia; Sedition.

Ku Klux Klan (KKK)

Founded: 1866

Type of organization: American white supremacist organization

Significance: One of the oldest of white power organizations, the Klan has occasionally had to struggle for the right to speak or demonstrate in public

The Ku Klux Klan, also known as the Invisible Empire of the South, was founded in Pulaski, Tennessee, in 1866 by former Confederate general Nathan Bedford Forrest. Ostensibly created as a social group for Southern Civil War veterans, the Klan soon was busy terrorizing former slaves to discourage them from exercising their new rights as American citizens. The Klan has ever afterward been known for its racist attitudes. Moreover, its members have on occasion had their own

Members of the National Knights of the Ku Klux Klan burn crosses and speak out against Jews and African Americans at a Stone Mountain, Georgia, rally in September, 1966. (AP/Wide World Photos)

views stifled from public discourse by law.

One attempt to silence the Klan came in 1969 when Ohio prosecuted a Klan organizer under a state criminal syndicalism law. The Ohio law made it an offense to advocate using criminal or violent means to achieve political reform, or to organize a group in order to teach such activities. In the case of *Brandenburg v. Ohio* (1969), the U.S. Supreme Court ruled Ohio's statute unconstitutional on the grounds that the First Amendment's free speech guarantees prevented states from forbidding advocacy of violence unless such advocacy was "directed to inciting or producing imminent lawless action and is likely to incite and produce such action." This ruling helped pave the way for future rulings expanding free speech

Another First Amendment incident involving the Klan developed in 1990 in Georgia when Shade Miller, Jr., a Klan member, defied a 1952 state law forbidding the wearing of masks or hoods in public. The Georgia law was initially struck down by the Gwinnett County State Court, only later to be upheld on appeal by the state's supreme court. The law was then sent back to the trial court and Miller was acquitted despite the higher court's ruling.

See also Abolitionist movement; African Americans; *Birth of a Nation, The*; Civil War, U.S.; Criminal syndicalism laws; Hate laws; Race; Skokie, Illinois, Nazi march.

L

Labor unions

Definition: Workers' organizations formed for purposes of collective bargaining and mutual aid and protection

Significance: News coverage of this mass constituency has tended to be minimal and slanted, resulting in censorship by omission

Censorship and control of labor news, information, and imagery is subtle—through omissions and errors, generalizations and stereotypes, misrepresentation and prejudice, and a double standard on commercial access to media, according to media observers. Censorship of labor is real, several studies have confirmed.

Oddly, labor and the press may pursue different agendas but share a heritage, according to Albert Zack, former public relations director for the American Federation of labor-Congress of Industrial Organizations (AFL-CIO). Zack pointed out in 1977 that the free trade union movement and the free press in the United States have the First Amendment to the Constitution in common.

In the 1800's and early 1900's, newspapermen such as Benjamin Day, Horace Greeley, John Swinton, William Allen White, E. W. Scripps, and yellow journalists Joseph Pulitzer and William Randolph Hearst all courted working people in their coverage and crusades. The labor movement benefited from exposés about bad working conditions, child labor, and robber barons, all written by muckrakers and mainstream journalists alike. In the later twentieth century, labor began to be overwhelmingly portrayed as powerful, greedy, corrupt, and unnecessary.

Reporting about working people and organized labor declined from the early 1960's to the late 1980's according to reporter Jonathan Tasini, who authored "Lost in the Margins: Labor and the Media," a 1990 study by the media watchdog group Fairness and Accuracy in Reporting (FAIR).

Left Out. News about labor is censored in several ways, not the least of which is the absence of such news. The near-invisibility of labor news may stem in part from instructions from supervisors. According to *Chicago Tribune* reporter James Warren, however, most journalists stopped doing labor stories because labor means unions and unions are seen in decline. Warren, who wrote many labor stories, has argued that fewer stories mean less interest, creating a steady decrease in coverage that major newspapers, themselves large businesses, have not sought to halt. For example, the *Tribune*, at his prodding, put in a one-paragraph news story in the Saturday business section about a major local labor story.

In 1989 nightly newscasts during an eight-day period devoted thirty-six minutes in stories about a miners' strike in the Soviet Union, but stories on the United Mine Workers' strike against Pittston Coal in the United States totaled half that amount for that whole year.

Television news segments rarely mention unions unless there is a story about wage demands, a possible strike, or internal corruption. When a strike is covered, the emphasis tends to be on the fact that the workers want more money, for example, rather than on the fact that management refused to give the workers a raise. Texas AFL-CIO communications director Christopher Cook has also pointed out that instead of covering legitimate union concerns in a labor-management dispute, reporters almost always focus on the potential negative economic impact that the conflict may have. Environmental reporter Karl Grossman, who also teaches at the State University of New York, has summed up media coverage thusly: "Censorship in the United States really functions as a sin of omission."

Labor's view is even omitted from mediated discourse. The press fails to seek and use labor's perspective on national questions, whether the story is on the stock market or a debate over the North American Free Trade Agreement, according to scholars such as authors Michael Parenti and William Puette.

Generalizations and Stereotypes. Several analysts have outlined patterns relevant to the censoring and shaping of news about labor. Author Robert Cirino has cataloged thirteen types of bias, from sourcing, selection, and interviewing to placement, images, and the hidden editorial. Parenti has made a list of seven generalizations: labor struggles as avoidable disputes arising from unreasonable unions; company offers as uniformly positive; no comparison of executive compensation or company wealth with the sought-for worker concessions; emphasis on impact of strikes (for example, whether the flow of goods will continue despite the strike), not their causes; failure to consider harm to workers if strikes fail; few stories of workers solidarity and support; portrayal of the government as a neutral arbiter instead of a business ally.

Puette has described eight "lenses," or judgments, that color coverage: labor protects lazy, insubordinate workers; powerful unions inhibit U.S. competitiveness; unions fail to represent members' interests; union leaders are likely to be corrupt; unions and their membership dues should be voluntary; enlightened employers and benevolent laws make unions obsolete; unions institutionalize conflict; and unions are all alike and therefore share in the guilt or shame of any other union or labor leader.

Parenti has cited typical terminology as an example. The label "special interests" is commonly applied to unions, while "national interest" is applied to military and economic forces.

A *Los Angeles Times* survey found 54 percent of newspaper editors favored business over labor, while 7 percent sided with labor, Parenti reports. In their book *Unreliable Sources: A Guide to Detecting Bias in News Media* (1990), Norman Solomon and Martin Lee write that "News coverage provides little affirmation for working people. It's routine for employers to receive much more respectful treatment than employees do. Rather than focus on the well-being of workers, mass media are busy doting on the fortunes of corporations."

Limited Access. Sometimes censorship occurs as a result of limiting access to media. Public broadcasting, for instance, is reluctant to accept underwriting grants from labor unions because they are considered advocacy groups, while corporations are regularly featured and even solicited for contributions. Unions even have trouble getting newspapers and broadcast stations to take advertising, according to Morton Bahr, president of the Communications Workers of America.

Labor has gained a negative image, which discourages workers from unionizing and leaves them suspicious of labor groups. Working-class culture has been pushed out of existence by the motion picture and television industries, according to Parenti, who also points out that labor history is seldom taught in the schools. Working people have no sense, for example, of the origins of the minimum wage or the eight-hour day.

No Conspiracy. People who believe labor is being censored or tainted by media treatment agree on some reasons: the notion that labor, with dwindling membership and power, no longer matters; that there is a class bias by corporate media owners and publishers; and that labor promotes itself poorly. It is also generally agreed that there is no conspiracy in the media not to cover organized labor. The media are not so well organized as to be able to conspire; on the other hand, the media are sensitive to such general and pervasive influences as advertising money, the money that pays reporters' salaries, and the corporate environment of newspapers and broadcasters.

Janine Jackson, a FAIR staffer, has argued: "A CEO doesn't walk into a newsroom and announce a decision to kill labor stories. It doesn't have to be so direct." Reporters know, or quickly learn, which stories to write and which not to write: Reporters answer to editors, who answer to corporate managers. Readers of newspapers should not expect, according to Jackson, corporate-owned media to develop concern for workers' issues.

Despite a need for better media coverage, unions often fail to create the type of excitement that attracts the press. Some unions have admitted that at least part of their problem with the media has been their fault, according to Sam Pizzigati and Fred Solowey, who wrote *The New Labor Press* (1992).

—Bill Knight

See also Criminal syndicalism laws; Debs, Eugene; Demonstrations; *Grapes of Wrath, The*; Picketing; Seldes, George; Sinclair, Upton.

Bibliography

Martin A. Lee and Norman Solomon's *Unreliable Sources: A Guide to Detecting Bias in News Media* (New York: Carol Publishing Group, 1990) is a well-documented guide to defining and detecting reporting that is subjective, slanted, or even false. It also features six valuable appendices listing or breaking down media business, journalism groups, and resources to analyze the press. Michael Parenti has written two exceptional titles that deconstruct media into information and entertainment, *Make-Believe Media: The Politics of Entertainment* (New York: St. Martin's Press, 1992) and *Inventing Reality: The Politics of News Media* (2d ed. New York: St. Martin's Press, 1993). The former is a detailed overview of familiar images in mass communications and their meanings and alternatives. The latter—with its handy guide to alternative media—narrows the topic to the press. Similarly, William J. Puette's *Through Jaundiced Eyes: How the Media View Organized Labor* (Ithaca, N.Y.: ILR Press, 1992) focuses on labor itself. Puette surveys media treatment of unions from the subject's perspective, extending as far as public attitudes and back to entertainment imagery. Finally, *The New Labor Press: Journalism for a Changing Union Movement* (Ithaca, N.Y.: ILR Press, 1992), edited by Sam Pizzigati and Fred J. Solowey, settles on coverage of labor by labor and its publications, and touches on future possibilities as well as past performances.

Lady Chatterley's Lover

Type of work: Book
Published: 1928
Author: D. H. Lawrence (1885-1930)
Subject matter: Novel about the adulterous relationship between an aristocratic Englishwoman and the gamekeeper on her paralyzed husband's estate
Significance: Legal battles to lift bans on this book in Great Britain and the United States contributed to refining the conditions under which allegedly obscene works can be suppressed

In this story Constance Chatterley is married to Sir Clifford Chatterley, a wealthy older man whose paralysis from war wounds has left him sexually impotent. As Lady Chatterley enters into a passionate affair with the gamekeeper, the novel focuses on their passionate couplings, often describing them in graphic detail, and using language considered taboo in literature when the book was published.

Opponents of this novel have identified four aspects of the book that they regard as "obscene": its portrayal of a woman as a sexually aggressive being; its depiction of an interclass relationship in which an aristocratic woman couples with a man "beneath her station"; its coarse language, which includes words such as "fuck" and "cunt"; and its depiction of "unnatural" (anal) intercourse.

In defending his book, Lawrence called attention to industrial England's negative and paralyzing influence on people. He argued that his novel contrasted the cold anti-intellectual bent of his fictional Sir Clifford and his friends with the warm passion of Lady Chatterley and her lover, describing their acts not in moral, scientific, or judicial terms, but in sincere and "accurate" ways.

Lady Chatterley's Lover was first published in Florence, Italy, in 1928 by Guiseppe Orioli. It was banned almost immediately in Great Britain, whose home secretary, Sir William Joynson-Hicks, declared it obscene. This banning overlooked a British law permitting books with tendencies to "deprave and corrupt" to be reconsidered if they could be shown to serve some "public good," such as a contribution to literature or learning. The British banning was imitated in the United

States, where the book did not publicly surface until 1957, when the U.S. Supreme Court's *Roth v. United States* ruling, defending "obscene" publications with "redeeming social importance," was made.

Grove Press published the first unexpurgated edition of *Lady Chatterley's Lover* in 1959. It was quickly seized by federal postal authorities under the Comstock Act and was declared obscene by U.S. postmaster general Arthur Summerfield. Grove immediately filed a countersuit to restrain the post office ban. A district court judge ruled that the postmaster general had "no special competence or technical knowledge on this subject which qualifies him to render an informed judgment." The court ordered the ban to be lifted because no book should be "judged by excerpts or individual passages but must be judged as a whole." In 1960 an appeals court upheld the lower court's decision. Buoyed by Grove's legal success in the United States, Penguin Books challenged the ban in Britain that same year in *Regina v. Penguin Books Ltd.*, citing the Obscene Publications Act of 1959, which permitted literary experts to testify in behalf of books' "literary merit."

A British film adaptation of *Lady Chatterley's Lover* that was released in 1957 passed through U.S. Customs, but was banned in the state of New York under a provision of a state education law. The state's board of regents refused to license any film that presented adultery "as being right and desirable for certain people under certain circumstances." Barring presentations of "sexual immorality, perversion or lewdness" as "desirable, acceptable or proper," the state board ignored the fact that the film contained neither taboo language nor "obscene" scenes. The resulting legal case, *Kingsley International Pictures Corporation v. Regents of the University of the State of New York* reached the U. S. Supreme Court in 1959. There, in a 5-2 decision, the Court found the film's banning to be unconstitutional under the First Amendment. Writing for the majority, Justice Potter Stewart maintained that the film could not be banned simply because it condoned an idea that "adultery under certain circumstances might be proper." Stewart also argued that "judges possess no special expertise [in] providing exceptional competency to set standards and to supervise the private morals of the Nation."

See also Adultery; Comstock Act of 1873; Customs laws, U.S.; Film adaptation; Grove Press; Lawrence, D. H.; Literature; Morality; Obscene Publications Acts; Postal regulations; *Regina v. Penguin Books Ltd.*; Roth, Samuel.

Language laws

DEFINITION: Laws that make the use of particular languages a matter of official policy

SIGNIFICANCE: Laws regulating language use take many forms, some of which may be characterized as varieties of censorship

The regulation of language use by law is a common feature of multiethnic societies. The most frequently encountered examples of language regulation are those establishing an official language or national language. In the eyes of ethnic groups whose languages do not garner the designation of official or national language, such laws may be seen as a censorship of an ethnic identity in favor of a melting-pot concept of national identity. Less commonly, language policies may seek not to assimilate particular ethnic groups within a national culture but to isolate such groups by depriving them of fluency in a national tongue. The apartheid educational policies of South Africa in the twentieth century illustrate the use of language policies as a tool of cultural marginalization and subordination in this latter sense.

Language Designations. Whether for the purpose of enhancing national unity or fostering national pride, numerous countries have designated one or more official languages or national languages. The distinction between an official language and a national language is not always articulated precisely. Generally, however, an official language is one in which a government conducts its business—its legislative, executive, administrative, and judicial functions. A national language is one considered an essential expression of a nation's culture or society.

Approximately half of the constitutions of the world make provision for one or more official languages or national languages. For example, Jordan's constitution declares Arabic to be the official language, as does Algeria's. Switzerland's constitution, however, designates German, French, and Italian as official languages. The national language of Malaysia is Malay, while the Republic of Seychelles designates French, English, and Creole as national languages.

The impetus behind language designations takes various forms. Official language policies—having to do generally with the language or languages in which a government conducts its various operations—typically find their justification in the asserted need for a common language to facilitate the business of government. National language debates, concentrating as they typically do on the effects of language on cultural unity, turn more frequently on the perceived cultural fragmentation of a civil society occupied by multiple ethnic and linguistic subgroups. Against the threat of such fragmentation, advocates of a national language assert the necessity of an increased cultural homogenization and view a common language as a key resource in achieving this homogenization. A quotation attributed to President Theodore Roosevelt captures the essence of this sentiment as it has found expression in the United States: "We have room for but one language here and that is the English language, for we intend to see that the crucible turns our people out as Americans, of American nationality, and not as dwellers in a polyglot boarding house." Attempts to coerce cultural assimilation by discouraging ethnic languages in favor of one or more official or national languages may be labeled a form of censorship. Such attempts seek to suppress or at least partially diminish ethnic loyalty and identity for the sake of national unity.

The United States has never adopted an official language, but it has not escaped the tensions created by the presence of numerous linguistic minorities. During the late twentieth century American opposition to multiculturalism has expressed itself in an English-only movement. This movement seeks to make English the official language of the United States. It has successfully elevated English to this official position in a

Thousands of supporters of Canadian unity march in Montreal before a referendum on French-speaking Quebec's independence in October, 1995. (AP/Wide World Photos)

number of states and has sought to do so at the federal level by amending the U.S. Constitution to make English the nation's official language. This movement has itself attracted opposition in the form of suggestions that the Constitution be amended not to elevate English to an official status but rather to guarantee the cultural and language rights of all citizens.

In contrast with the United States, Canadian language policy reflects a more deliberate form of bilingualism—embracing English and French speakers. This policy has not been without its tensions. Canada's Official Languages Act of 1969 made English and French official languages and was enacted at least partially in an attempt to defuse separatist sentiments of the French-speaking majority of Quebec. Quebec separatists replied to this gesture, however, by attempting to make French the only official language of Quebec. A 1977 law refused to provide English-speaking immigrants with an English language education unless at least one of the immigrants' parents had studied in one of Quebec's English-language schools. Furthermore, in provisions later declared unconstitutional by the Canadian Supreme Court, the 1977 law ceased publication of certain official documents in English. In spite of—or perhaps even because of—the volatile political issues raised by Quebec's separatist elements, Canada has continued to forge bilingual language policies. Its 1982 constitutional Charter of Rights and Freedoms again declares English and French the nation's official languages and provides equality of status and privileges for both English and French speakers in Canada's government institutions.

Language Laws and Education Policy. The designation of official or national languages sometimes has consequences for a nation's educational policy. Chad, for example, whose official language is French, mandates that public education be in that language. Similarly, the constitution of Honduras, whose official language is Spanish, specifies that the government must protect the purity of and increase learning in Spanish. The Portuguese constitution lacks this mandatory provision for education in the nation's official language, but nevertheless the state requires to provide education in the Portuguese language and exposure to Portuguese culture to immigrant children.

Numerous modern constitutions are solicitous to the rights of ethnic minorities and acknowledge the interest of linguistic minorities in preserving their indigenous languages. India's constitution of 1949, for example, secured to religious and linguistic minorities the right to establish education institutions of their choice and to provide facilities for the education of minority children in their native tongue in the primary stages of education. Often, national constitutions protect particular indigenous languages by safeguarding their place within the educational process. Thus, the 1967 constitution of

Paraguay provides that the Guarani language will be safeguarded by promoting teaching in this indigenous tongue. Similarly, the constitutions of Ecuador and Peru provide for instruction in Quechua or other relevant indigenous languages in addition to Spanish in areas of Indian population.

Although bilingual education remains a matter of serious dispute in the United States, attempts to proscribe education in languages other than English have not survived constitutional challenge. In the first decades of the twentieth century, anti-German sentiments produced statutes in Nebraska, Iowa, and Ohio prohibiting the teaching of the German language. The statute passed in Nebraska in 1919, which prohibited teaching subjects in any language but English and prohibited foreign language altogether for students who had not completed the eighth grade. A challenge to this law ultimately reached the Supreme Court. The purpose of the statute was to assure that English became the favored language of immigrant children by prohibiting their parents from sending them to schools in which they might be educated in their indigenous languages.

In *Meyer v. Nebraska* (1923), the Supreme Court held that the Nebraska law violated the Constitution. The Court relied upon the Fourteenth Amendment, which provides that no state may deprive any person of life, liberty, or property without due process of law. Among the liberties protected by this provision were, according to the Court, the liberty of parents to have their children receive instruction in a foreign language and of teachers to teach such a language. The Nebraska statute arbitrarily infringed on these liberties, in the view of the Supreme Court, and thus violated due process. In effect, the Court found that the state of Nebraska had no legitimate reason to adopt an English-only policy for the younger children of its residents.

In addition to *Meyer v. Nebraska*'s constitutional barrier against English-only language policies in the schools, a number of federal and state laws and regulations secure important rights to a bilingual education on the part of minority language children in the United States. At the federal level, the Bilingual Education Act of 1968 provided grants to promote research and experimentation in bilingual education. Moreover, in 1970 the Department of Health, Education, and Welfare issued a regulation requiring schools receiving federal aid to take affirmative steps to allow minority language students to participate in educational programs. Slightly more than a decade later, Congress elevated this regulation to the level of statute by including in its Equal Educational Opportunity Act of 1982 a provision requiring schools to take such action as necessary to overcome language barriers that might prevent minority language students from having access to an equal educational opportunity. These federal provisions for bilingual education have been mirrored by numerous state laws that provide for the bilingual education of non-English-speaking students.

Language and Apartheid. Some language policies evidence a clear purpose of frustrating the communication of particular ideas. For example, the South African regime of apartheid used language policy to maintain the political supremacy of the white minority prior to the democratic revolution of the early 1990's. In 1953 the South African National Party, committed to the policy of apartheid, enacted the Bantu Education Act. This act established the policy of educating blacks in the Homeland reserves primarily in their various African languages. Black students had rudimentary instruction in English and Afrikaans, the two official languages of South Africa. This limited instruction was intended to equip black students for the relatively unskilled employment opportunities thought appropriate to them and their limited contacts with government.

The Bantu Education Act's more significant focus on the various indigenous languages of the black students had two important benefits for the regime of apartheid. First, it tended to relegate black students to lesser employment opportunities by denying them concentrated training in English and Afrikaans. This relegation was altogether consistent with the aims of apartheid in sustaining the supremacy of whites and continuing the subordination of blacks. Second, the focus on education in the vernacular had the effect of isolating students from various tribal backgrounds and hindering the formation of political protest across language lines. The latter effect of the Bantu Education Act, in curtailing cross-tribal protest of apartheid, had the effect of censoring such protests. It aimed to retribalize black Africans and thus frustrate the formation of black nationalist sentiments that might threaten white supremacy. —*Timothy L. Hall*

See also Colonialism; Education; Ethnic studies; Fourteenth Amendment; Multiculturalism; South Africa; Torquemada, Tomás de.

BIBLIOGRAPHY

For a thorough collection of constitutional provisions relating to language policies, see Albert P. Blaustein and Dana Blaustein Epstein's *Resolving Language Conflicts: A Study of the World's Constitutions* (Washington, D.C.: U.S. English, 1986), published by an organization that seeks to establish the primacy of English in American life, contains little commentary concerning the various constitutional provisions but helpfully reproduces the substance of the provisions and organizes them under relevant topical headings. Bill Piatt's *¿Only English?: Law and Language Policy in the United States* (Albuquerque: University of New Mexico Press, 1990) discusses the historical context of and present controversy relating to the English-only movement in the United States. *Apartheid and Education* (Johannesburg, South Africa: Raven Press, 1984), edited by Peter Kallaway, includes information on the place of language policies in the regime of apartheid. For collections of essays treating language rights in a variety of national contexts, see *Ethnic Groups and Language Rights* (New York: New York University Press, 1993), edited by Sergij Vilfan, and *Ethnicity in Eastern Europe: Questions of Migration, Language Rights and Education* (Clevedon, England: Multilingual Matters, 1994), edited by Sue Wright with Helen Kelly.

Lardner, Ring, Jr.

BORN: August 19, 1915, Chicago, Illinois

IDENTIFICATION: American film writer

SIGNIFICANCE: Though Lardner has been one of the most honored screenwriters in the film industry, his career was interrupted for many years when he was blacklisted for political reasons

The son of humorist Ring Lardner, Ring Lardner, Jr., began his own career as a reporter for the *Daily Mirror* in New York but later became a Hollywood screenwriter. He received his first Academy Award for his screenplay for the 1942 film *Woman of the Year*, starring Spencer Tracy and Katharine Hepburn, and received a second Oscar for his screenplay of Robert Altman's 1970 screen version of M*A*S*H. For a long interval between these two awards, however, Lardner was blacklisted in Hollywood as a member of the "Hollywood Ten."

In 1947 Lardner earned the ire of the House Committee on Un-American Activities by refusing, along with nine other Hollywood figures, to respond to the committee's inquiries as to whether he had ever been a member of the Communist Party. To this question Lardner reportedly stated: "I could answer that the way you want, but I'd hate myself in the morning." All of the Hollywood Ten served jail sentences for contempt. Lardner served nine and a half months in Danbury Federal Correctional Institute. After leaving jail, Lardner found himself blacklisted in Hollywood and was forced to sell his work under assumed names. In 1964, his ostracism finally ended when he was hired to write the screenplay for *The Cincinnati Kid*, which starred Ann-Margret and Steve McQueen.

See also Blacklisting; Communist Party of the U.S.A.; *Front, The*; Hollywood Ten; House Committee on Un-American Activities; Sedition.

Last Exit to Brooklyn

TYPE OF WORK: Book
PUBLISHED: 1964
AUTHOR: Hubert Selby, Jr. (1928-)
SUBJECT MATTER: A collection of stories about Brooklyn degenerates, homosexuality, prostitution, and sexual violence
SIGNIFICANCE: Attempts to ban this book as obscene in Great Britain failed

When Grove Press published *Last Exit to Brooklyn* in 1964, the firm encountered relatively few censorship efforts, despite the book's violence, graphic sexual activities, and vulgar language. An effort was made in Massachusetts to get an injunction against the book, but the state attorney general directed the local district attorney to dismiss the charges. In Connecticut, however, a district court issued a temporary injunction prohibiting the sale and distribution of the book, which it ruled obscene and pornographic. A similar injunction was granted in British Columbia, Canada.

In Great Britain, however, Selby's book encountered more serious problems. Although the British government did not officially rule the book obscene, Sir Cyril Black, a Conservative member of Parliament, took it to court. A London magistrate then ruled that the book, taken as a whole, would tend to "deprave and corrupt" readers. This ruling applied only to the magistrate's own Marlborough Street area; however, Selby's problems were compounded when a later jury trial, in 1967, found that his book violated Britain's Obscene Publications Act of 1959. American publishers who had planned to publish books in Great Britain either postponed their plans or edited their books to avoid similar censorship problems. In August, 1968, Selby's case was taken to a British appeals court, which reversed the lower court's decision on a technicality.

The Last Exit to Brooklyn case was almost as important and controversial as an earlier case involving D. H. Lawrence's *Lady Chatterley's Lover*. A 1988 film adaptation of Selby's book by Neue Constantin Film Productions was graphic but encountered no censorship problems.

See also Grove Press; Homosexuality; *Lady Chatterley's Lover*; Obscene Publications Acts; Pornography; Southern, Terry; Women, violence against.

Last P.O.W.?: Bobby Garwood Story, The

TYPE OF WORK: Television film
BROADCAST: June 28, 1993
DIRECTOR: Georg Stanford Brown (1943-)
SUBJECT MATTER: Dramatization of the real-life story of a U.S. Marine who was accused of collaborating with the enemy after being released by his communist captors during the Vietnam War
SIGNIFICANCE: Broadcast of this film was delayed by fears that its airing would harm the U.S. military effort in the Persian Gulf War

Captured by Vietcong guerrillas in 1965, Robert R. Garwood was not allowed to leave Vietnam until 1979. Upon his return to the United States, he was immediately charged with several military crimes. Court-martialed in February, 1981, for collaborating with the enemy, he was reduced in rank to private, forced to forfeit pay, and dishonorably discharged from the U.S. Marines. Public reactions to Garwood's sentence were mixed. Some people wanted to see him punished more severely; others claimed that he had been selectively punished as the only U.S. soldier charged with collaborating with the enemy during the Vietnam War. Meanwhile, Garwood himself claimed that other missing-in-action (MIA) personnel might still be held in Vietnam, and he became involved with that sensitive issue.

In 1990 the American Broadcasting Company (ABC) made a television film of Garwood's version of his story. Its broadcast was scheduled for December, 1990, but was delayed until June 28, 1993. ABC said the broadcast was delayed to prevent raising questions about patriotism during the Persian Gulf crisis. Ralph Macchio, who played Garwood in the film, stated that Garwood's involvement with MIA's also delayed the film's release.

See also *Amerika*; Persian Gulf War; Television; Vietnam War; War.

Last Tango in Paris

TYPE OF WORK: Film
RELEASED: 1972
DIRECTOR: Bernardo Bertolucci (1940-)
SUBJECT MATTER: An American living in Paris who is devastated by his wife's suicide takes up with a young French woman, who eventually betrays him

Marlon Brando and Maria Schneider cavort in a staid dance hall in Last Tango in Paris. (Museum of Modern Art/Film Stills Archive)

Significance: A landmark in the depiction of sex in film, this film also led to two court decisions overturning attempts at prior restraint

Marlin Brando plays a character named Paul, who is deeply disturbed by his wife's recent suicide. While inspecting a vacant apartment, he meets a young woman (Maria Schneider) with whom he almost immediately engages in sexual intercourse. Afterward, they agree to meet in the apartment each day and to keep their full identities secret from one another. Their relationship develops until Paul decides to tell the woman who he is and he asks her to marry him. Meanwhile, however, she has already agreed to marry her young French boyfriend, a movie director. Outraged and bitter at her betrayal, Paul follows the woman to her mother's home and forces his way into the house, where she finds her father's gun and shoots him.

Lawsuits based on prior restraint were brought against the film in Montgomery, Alabama, and Shreveport, Louisiana. The Alabama case claimed that, since the film had been rated X by the Motion Picture Association of America, there was reason to believe that it violated obscenity laws, and that, therefore, a judicial declaration should be sought. In *United Artists v. Wright*, the Alabama law was declared unconstitutional. In the Shreveport case, a district court found the film obscene and issued an order barring it from being shown. However, in 1974 this judgment was reversed by the Louisiana Supreme Court in *Gulf State Theaters of Louisiana v. Richardson*.

See also Courts and censorship law; Film censorship; Motion Picture Association of America; *Nova Scotia Board of Censors v. McNeil*; Obscenity: legal definitions; Prior restraint; Sex in the arts.

Last Temptation of Christ, The

Type of work: Book
Published: 1955
Author: Nikos Kazantzakis (1883-1957)
Subject matter: Fictional portrayal of Jesus as a man of strong emotions, torn between his calling to be the Christ and his desire to be an ordinary mortal
Significance: The Greek Orthodox church denounced the book's author as a heretic, and the Roman Catholic church placed the book on its index of forbidden books

Nikos Kazantzakis has been called the most outrageous, most important, and most controversial writer in twentieth century Greek literature. *The Last Temptation of Christ*—his personal and literary quest for self, reality, and understanding of the myths of religion—made him famous for starting a major theological controversy: Could Jesus Christ have actually slept with Mary Magdalene? Could he have had children by her and other women? Did all these things really happen in Kazantzakis' story, or were they merely a dream? The novel challenged the legitimacy of sacred Scripture for readers throughout the world. Many readers could not accept the idea of Christ's facing the same temptations of the flesh as mortal men. To them, the book was blasphemous.

In 1988 film director Martin Scorsese revived interest in Kazantzakis and his novel with his adaptation of *The Last Temptation of Christ*. Some American critics called Scorsese's film the best of 1988, and Scorsese was nominated for an Academy Award. From the pulpit, through the press, and by pressures imposed upon local film distributors, Scorsese received the wrath of many Christians of different traditions with his interpretation of Kazantzakis' novel. In addition, many American communities opposed public screenings of the film, which was often seen in private showings arranged and attended by local ministers, parents, rabbis, and school administrators, to determine whether it conformed to community standards. In many communities, the film was available only on videocassette. Some Christians expressed disappointment in the artistic merits of the film, while others were drawn to the original novel by the author who had also written *Zorba the Greek*, whose sales also increased.

See also Film censorship; Heresy; *Index Librorum Prohibitorum*; Moral Majority.

Lateran Council, Fourth

Date: November 11-30, 1215
Place: Rome, Italy
Significance: Along with decrees dealing with Roman Catholic doctrinal matters, this council established procedures for dealing with heretics and granted crusading privileges to those who would wage military campaigns against heretics

The Church of Saint John Lateran in Rome served as a meeting for general councils of the Roman Catholic church during the Middle Ages. Those held in the years 1123, 1139, 1179, 1215, and 1512 to 1517 are collectively known as the Lateran Councils. Of these, the Fourth Lateran Council, in 1215—which is also called the Great Council because it was

Self-described members of the Sisters of Perpetual Indulgence demonstrate against censorship in front of a San Francisco theater showing The Last Temptation of Christ *in August, 1988.* (UPI/Corbis-Bettmann)

the largest such gathering—is most famous. The cleric behind this council was Pope Innocent III. Convinced that secular powers should be subordinate to the Church, Innocent envisioned a relationship between the papacy and kings similar to that which existed between feudal lords and their vassals. Whereas the Church received its authority directly from God, emperors and kings received their authority from the Church as so-called fiefs, which could be revoked for noncompliance with certain obligations to the Church. Through a combination of consummate diplomatic skill and political shrewdness, Innocent translated this vision of papal power into reality.

Nothing illustrates the degree of papal hegemony over medieval Christendom better than the list of 1,383 dignitaries who answered Innocent's summons to the Fourth Lateran Council. The assemblage included more than a thousand bishops, archbishops, abbots, and other church leaders from all over Europe, as well as the emperor of the Holy Roman Empire, the Latin emperor of Constantinople, and the kings of Aragon, Bohemia, Cyprus, England, Estonia, France, Hungary, Lithuania, and Sicily. The purpose of the gathering was formally to approve Innocent's religious and political programs—which the council did with dispatch.

Among the decrees proclaimed by the council, none more clearly demonstrated Innocent's intent to enhance the papacy's power than the disciplinary measures adopted by the council to combat heresy. Declared a crime of high treason against the Divine Will, heresy was defined as any aberration of faith that contradicted Church doctrine as defined by the papacy. Convicted heretics were excommunicated from the Church and their property and the property of their descendants—even unborn descendants—was confiscated. Moreover, the council declared it the duty of the king to exterminate heretics from their kingdoms. Should a king be remiss in this duty, he himself was to be declared a heretic; his subjects were to be released from their obligations to him; and the king himself was to be replaced by a person loyal to the teachings of the Church.

The decrees of the Fourth Lateran Council regarding papal hegemony were not idle threats. Before Innocent's pontificate ended, he established the papacy as the major political force of the times. He had returned Constantinople to papal obedience, forced King Philip Augustus of France to take back the wife he had disavowed, and humbled England's King John into adding his realm to the list of European countries that recognized the Church's overlordship.

See also Heresy; Spanish Inquisition; Vatican.

Latimer, Hugh

Born: Between 1485 and 1492, Thurcaston, Leicestershire, England

Died: October 16, 1555, Oxford, England

Identification: English Protestant cleric

Significance: A prominent Protestant bishop, Latimer was burned at the stake for refusing to accept the reestablishment of Roman Catholicism during the reign of Mary Tudor (1553-1558)

Latimer, who took his degrees at Cambridge University, initially attacked Lutheran doctrines but later became a Protestant himself whose criticism of Roman Catholic teachings would lead to his death. During the turbulence of the English Reformation, Latimer's views were censored; however, his support of King Henry VIII's divorce from Catherine of Aragon won for him royal favor and a chaplaincy, which he used to criticize indulgences, or the purchase of forgiveness for sins. The appointment of Thomas Cranmer as archbishop of Canterbury gave Latimer greater influence and earned for him the bishopric of Worcester. He resigned in protest against the Six Acts (1539) because they upheld the doctrine of transubstantiation; this led to a one-year term in prison. In 1546 his connection with an unpopular preacher resulted in another incarceration, this time in the Tower of London. The death of Henry VIII in 1547 and the accession to the throne of Edward VI brought his release and the gradual establishment of Protestantism in England.

Under Queen Mary I, however, who reigned from 1553 to 1558, the country would return to Catholicism, occasioning Latimer's final, fatal conflict with established authority. Along with Thomas Cranmer and Nicholas Ridley, he was ordered to defend his Protestant views at Oxford University. After Parliament revived heresy laws in December, 1554, the three men were condemned to death. Latimer and Ridley were burned at the stake on October 16, 1555; Cranmer suffered a similar fate the following year.

See also Death; Henry VIII; Heresy; Reformation, the; United Kingdom.

Laurence, Margaret

Born: July 18, 1926, Neepawa, Manitoba, Canada

Died: January, 1987, Lakefield, Ontario, Canada

Identification: Canadian novelist

Significance: Throughout her career Laurence was attacked by critics claiming that her work was blasphemous and pornographic

From her own experience, Laurence created a story cycle consisting of five books, each of which features a strong female protagonist. Of the five, *The Stone Angel* (1964), *A Jest of God* (1966), and *The Diviners* (1974) were all denounced as immoral. Published during a time of rising Canadian conservatism, *The Diviners* was subjected to particularly vicious attacks. Although it won Canada's prestigious Governor General's Medal for Fiction and the coveted Molson Prize, the novel became the focus of a 1976 effort by right-wing Protestant churches to remove it from the grade thirteen curriculum in Peterborough, Ontario. Two years later the book was subjected to yet another attempt to remove it—along with J. D. Salinger's *The Catcher in the Rye* (1951) and John Steinbeck's *Of Mice and Men* (1937)—from grade thirteen English in southeastern Ontario.

The Diviners is a coming-of-age story that includes—like many of Laurence's other novels—earthy language and moderately explicit depictions of sexuality. Nonetheless, many critics believe that Laurence suffered at the hand of censors primarily for her attempts to portray the development of female independence.

See also Blasphemy laws; Books, young adult; Canadian Library Association Statement on Intellectual Freedom; *Catcher in the Rye, The*; Steinbeck, John.

Lawrence, D. H.

BORN: September 11, 1885, Eastwood, Nottinghamshire, England

DIED: March 2, 1930, Vence, France

IDENTIFICATION: British novelist and poet

SIGNIFICANCE: Several of Lawrence's books were banned, suppressed, and attacked for obscenity

Lawrence's battle with what he called "the censor-morons" began in 1915 with his publication of the novel *The Rainbow*. Amid a storm of accusations of indecency from critics, police seized more than a thousand copies from the publisher and the printer. When the case came to court in London, the prosecuting attorney, representing the police, called the book "a mass of obscenity of thought, idea, and action throughout." The magistrate, Sir John Dickinson, ordered the novel destroyed. Lawrence was not alone in his belief that the real reason for this attack was that Britain was at war: His book denounced war, and the British government feared that it would hamper recruitment. Philip Morrell raised questions in Parliament as to the legality of the ban. Home Secretary Sir John Simon explained that the action against the novel had been taken under the Obscene Publications Act of 1857.

After Lawrence published *Women in Love* in 1920, this novel was attacked in *John Bull* magazine as "a loathsome study of sex depravity leading youth to unspeakable disaster." The following year saw an unsuccessful attempt in the United States to suppress the novel, led by John W. Sumner, acting for the Society for the Suppression of Vice. Lawrence's last novel, *Lady Chatterley's Lover*, was banned in 1928 because of its graphic depictions of adulterous sex and coarse language.

D. H. Lawrence in the late 1920's, around the time he was finishing Lady Chatterley's Lover. (D.C. Public Library)

In 1929 Lawrence sent a package containing the manuscripts of his collection of poems, *Pansies*, to his agents in London. They never reached their destination. The postmaster-general opened the package and sent the manuscripts to Home Secretary Sir William Joynson-Hicks, who seized them. Questions were raised in Parliament as to the legality of the postmaster-general's action. Later that year the publisher Secker brought out a bowdlerized version of *Pansies*, without the fourteen poems that had upset the home secretary. Unexpurgated editions of the collected poems were printed in Australia and Europe. Thanks to the publicity generated by the manuscript seizure, these editions sold exceptionally well.

The same year, police confiscated Lawrence's paintings from an exhibition in a London gallery. Another court case followed. Herbert G. Muskett, the attorney who had helped crush *The Rainbow*, branded the pictures obscene. The defense protested government censorship of art, but agreed that the paintings would not be shown again.

Lawrence was dismissive of the "censor-morons" who banned his works. In an essay titled "Pornography and Obscenity," he wrote that much so-called obscenity was simply a "mob-habit of condemning any form of sex" in spite of our natural individual inclination to enjoy sexual arousal. But he was not against censorship in principle: "Even I would censor genuine pornography, rigorously. . . . Pornography is the attempt to insult sex, to do dirt on it. This is unpardonable."

See also Grove Press; *Lady Chatterley's Lover*; Obscene Publications Acts; Obscenity: legal definitions; Sex in the arts; Society for the Suppression of Vice, New York; World War I.

Leafletting

DEFINITION: Distribution of leaflets, tracts, or other materials to passers-by in public places

SIGNIFICANCE: In the United States the right to distribute leaflets is not absolute; it depends on content, time, place, and manner of distribution

American citizens generally have the right to distribute leaflets on public property, provided they do so at reasonable times and in a reasonable manner. An exception exists if the distributed material is pornographic. In most cases leaflets may be distributed on sidewalks, which are usually public property, even if distribution results in a sidewalk's becoming littered with discarded materials. However, distribution must not unduly hamper the flow of traffic or the public safety. Public parks and other public property are also acceptable locations. Leaflets may also be distributed on the streets themselves under certain circumstances, such as during parades or demonstrations, or at other times, so long as normal traffic flow is not disrupted. However, the First Amendment right to free speech does not guarantee access to property merely because it is owned or controlled by a government agency. A government may regulate or restrict access, so long as such restrictions are formulated in a neutral manner.

Public Property. Although individual persons and groups have a First Amendment right to distribute leaflets on public property, it is not always clear just what constitutes "public" property for purposes of leaflet distribution. Government-owned properties are generally considered to be public property; however, government property that allows restricted public access—such as military installations, the federal White House, prisons, or the headquarters of the Central Intelligence Agency—may be off limits. Religious groups have been prevented from distributing their literature on state fairgrounds unless they have permits to operate booths. A government may not deny issuance of such permits for discriminatory reasons; however, it may legitimately limit the number of permits issued because of space constraints.

Leaflets may not be placed in private letter boxes unless they are stamped and posted because letter boxes are not considered to be public forums, even though they are considered to be government-owned or government-controlled property. Laws that require the leaflets to have the names and addresses of the persons or groups who have printed, written, compiled, or otherwise prepared the messages printed on the leaflets have been struck down as placing a chilling effect on free speech.

Jury Nullification. An exception to the general right to distribute leaflets on public property exists in the case of jury nullification—the right of a jury to disregard a law and hold a defendant innocent, even though a law has been broken. Jury nullification was prevalent in the American colonies in cases in which the British government tried to prosecute colonists for smuggling. Juries would find their fellow colonists not guilty even when evidence of their guilt was overwhelming because of the general and widespread feeling that the laws themselves were repugnant. In modern times juries occasionally find defendants not guilty in cases in which the police have resorted to repulsive tactics, such as planting evidence or lying on the witness stand, or in cases in which a jury feels that the law in question should not be applied.

Although jury nullification is a basic right that is enshrined in many state constitutions, anyone who distributes leaflets that discuss jury nullification on or near courthouse property can be arrested for jury tampering. Individuals accused of jury tampering may not assert their free speech rights and may not even be able to exercise their right to a jury trial.

Distributing Leaflets on Private Property. As a general rule in the United States, there is no right to distribute leaflets on private property. There are two basic and diametrically opposed views on this point. One view holds that the rights of private property owners can never conflict with the free speech rights of those who would distribute leaflets because no one may exercise free speech rights on private property without the owner's consent. The other view holds that there must be a balancing of rights between property owners and those who distribute leaflets. This balancing of interests approach gained prominence in the twentieth century but has been criticized as being a flawed doctrine. Furthermore, although the U.S. Constitution prohibits only the abridgement of free speech by government, some state constitutions go further and prohibit private individuals from abridging free speech in certain circumstances—a principle that the U.S. Supreme Court has held is a constitutional exercise of state prerogative.

New Jersey's state constitution allows individuals to distribute political literature at private universities, such as Princeton, whose own regulations state that free speech is a necessary element in the search for knowledge. However, individuals do not have the right in New Jersey to distribute antiabortion literature in medical complex parking lots, where no space is provided for the public to congregate, where there is no general invitation to the public at large, and where the expressive activity is incompatible with the services provided by the facility.

The U.S. Supreme Court has held that religious groups may distribute religious literature in a company-owned town. Although the town in question was privately owned, all normally public functions were performed by a private entity, and the town was otherwise indistinguishable from other towns.

While a few courts have held that groups may distribute literature in private shopping malls under certain conditions, the majority view has been that shopping mall owners can exclude such groups on property rights grounds. The majority of courts have either rejected the balancing of rights argument when applied to shopping mall cases, or have held that the balancing should be in favor of shopping mall owners. The U.S. Supreme Court has refused to resolve this issue, which has left courts split. However, the Supreme Court has held that a shopping center is not the functional equivalent of a municipality, and that the First Amendment does not protect the right to expression in a shopping center.

At issue in the shopping mall cases is whether the shopping mall has taken the place of the town square or public business district as a public forum. Where courts have held that shopping malls have become the new town square, individuals and groups have been allowed to distribute leaflets. However, most courts do not regard shopping malls as being the equivalent of a town square or other public forum. Some commentators have argued that allowing individuals or groups to distribute leaflets on private property against the owner's wishes constitutes a "taking" of property, which requires compensation under the Fifth Amendment. *—Robert W. McGee*

See also Chilling effect; Courtrooms; First Amendment; Marching and parading; Picketing; Political campaigning; Street oratory; Symbolic speech.

BIBLIOGRAPHY

Most books on U.S. constitutional law have sections on the right to distribute leaflets. Several law reviews have also published articles on this topic. One of the leading Supreme Court cases is *Pruneyard Shopping Center v. Robins* (1980), which examined the right of individuals to gather petitions in a privately owned shopping mall. Articles discussing the conflict between the right to distribute literature and the right of property owners to exclude such distribution include Curtis J. Berger, "Pruneyard Revisited: Political Activity on Private

Lands," *New York University Law Review* 66 (1991); Frederick W. Schoepflin, "Speech Activists in Shopping Centers: Must Property Rights Give Way to Free Expression?" *Washington Law Review* 64 (1989); and Robert W. McGee, "Free Speech in Shopping Malls: What Are the Limits?" *Policy Analysis* 96, no. 12 (1996).

Lear, Norman

BORN: July 27, 1922, New Haven, Connecticut

IDENTIFICATION: American television producer, writer, and social activist

SIGNIFICANCE: Lear has fought for the right to air socially relevant television programs

By 1970 Norman Lear had secured the American rights to the popular British television series *Till Death Do Us Part*. The British series was a satirical comedy whose central character was a working-class bigot. Working with Bud Yorkin, Lear wrote a pilot script for an American adaptation in which the central character would be a working-class New York bigot by the name of Archie Bunker. Lear not only got his inspiration for Bunker from the British series, but also from his memories of his own father's intolerant attitudes. The completed pilot was presented to the American Broadcasting Company (ABC). ABC executives who viewed the pilot found it to be too profane for their tastes, so they canceled the project. Not to be deterred, Lear presented the pilot to the Columbia Broadcasting System (CBS). With some reservations, CBS approved the project. CBS executives attempted to convince Lear that the program should be toned down before it could be aired, but Lear stood firm. On January 12, 1971, *All in the Family* premiered. Its cast included Carroll O'Connor as Archie Bunker, Jean Stapleton as his wife, Sally Struthers as their daughter, and Rob Reiner as the liberal future son-in-law.

CBS braced itself for complaints from viewers and conservative groups. There were outraged segments of the population, but *All in the Family* quickly became a top-rated program. During its tenure on television, it tackled such sensitive topics as male impotence, racial prejudice, homosexuality, rape, and female menopause. For its time, *All in the Family* was a revolutionary show. It broke many traditional situation comedy rules. Although Lear had to fight with network executives over issues such as blue-collar dialogue and potentially divisive subject matter, the viewing public made *All in the Family* the number-one show from 1971 to 1976.

With the success of *All in the Family*, Lear and Yorkin's company Tandem Productions developed a number of other top-rated shows for network television, including *Maude*, *Good Times*, *The Jeffersons*, and *Sanford and Son*. One of Lear's 1970's projects, *Mary Hartman, Mary Hartman*, was turned down by the networks. It was sold to independent stations and began airing in 1976. *Mary Hartman, Mary Hartman* was a parody of afternoon soap operas and included a number of eccentric characters.

In 1970, Lear founded the People for the American Way. The organization became a strong voice against censorship that has involved itself in disseminating educational material and in leading research programs. Throughout his professional life, Lear has fought against network censors and repressive organizations. It is his belief that America becomes stronger when a diversity of ideas may flourish.

See also *Lou Grant*; *Murphy Brown* controversy; People for the American Way; Propaganda; Television; Television networks.

Leary, Timothy

BORN: October 22, 1920, Springfield, Massachusetts

DIED: May 31, 1996, Beverly Hills, California

IDENTIFICATION: American psychologist, educator, and advocate of recreational drug use

SIGNIFICANCE: After Leary was fired from Harvard University for conducting drug experiments, his advocacy of using psychedelic drugs to experience mystical states led to the first legal challenges concerning the religious use of psychoactive substances

Leary first tested the effects of mind-altering drugs in the summer of 1960 while in Mexico with friends and other scholars. He concluded that sacred mushrooms, containing the active ingredient psilocybin, might have profound implications for the study of religion and human consciousness. As a lecturer in clinical psychology in Harvard's Department of Social Relations, he was well positioned to conduct drug experiments with student volunteers. As a result of the publicity and contro-

Timothy Leary (left) and conservative talk show host G. Gordy Liddy before they broadcast a debate in July, 1982. (AP/Wide World Photos)

versy surrounding the famed Good Friday Experiment in the basement of Boston University chapel, he was dismissed from Harvard on April 30, 1963.

In August, 1963, Leary moved his operations into a large mansion in Millbrook, New York. There he formed the Castelia Foundation to experiment with lysergic acid diethylamide (LSD). After a trip to India, he returned as a Hindu convert and established the League for Spiritual Discovery. He argued in the U.S. Senate in May, 1966, that the LSD session was a "religious pilgrimage." Constantly harassed by authorities, he was eventually sentenced to thirty years in prison for possession of a small amount of marijuana. The verdict was overturned, however, by the U.S. Supreme Court in May, 1969.

See also Ginsberg, Allen; Huxley, Aldous; *Naked Lunch*; Native Americans; Pharmaceutical industry.

Lee, Dennis

BORN: August 31, 1939, Toronto, Ontario, Canada

IDENTIFICATION: Canadian poet and author of children's books

SIGNIFICANCE: Although Lee is one of Canada's most popular poets for children, two of his works have been challenged for the violence they depict

Lee's collection of poems *Alligator Pie* (1974) vaulted him to prominence as a poet whose work spoke to children. Despite the popular response to this work, as well as another poetry collection, *Garbage Delight* (1977), and a picture book, *Lizzy's Lion* (1984), all have been challenged for containing material considered too violent for their intended audiences. Of *Garbage Delight*'s forty-two poems, four have been singled out: "Suzy Grew a Moustache," "The Big Molice Pan and the Bertie Dumb," "Bloody Bill," and "The Bratty Brother (Sister)." While these poems contain much humor, those seeking the book's removal have based their objections on a literal reading of the poems.

A study of challenges to materials in Canadian public libraries identified *Lizzy's Lion* as Canada's most frequently challenged book from 1985 to 1987. For his illustrations which accompanied the book's fourteen four-line stanzas, Marie-Louise Gay received Canada's most prestigious illustration award, the Canada Council's Children's Literature Prize. The story describes how a burglar breaks into a little girl's bedroom to steal her piggy-bank but is thwarted by her guardian lion. Gay's bloodless illustrations require readers to draw inferences about the burglar's fate. As Gay explained, "It is clear that the lion has devoured the robber, but the violence is never graphically detailed." While the book encountered frequent opposition, it has continued to be widely available.

See also Books, children's; Books, young adult; Canada; Libraries, Canadian; Libraries, school; Poetry; Violence.

Legion of Decency

FOUNDED: April, 1934

TYPE OF ORGANIZATION: Film-monitoring body

SIGNIFICANCE: This Roman Catholic organization's film-rating system influenced content standards in American cinema for forty-five years

With the introduction of sound in the late 1920's, films were perceived as a threat to moral values that the Roman Catholic church could no longer neglect. In April, 1934, Catholic film reformers formed the Legion of Decency, to condemn "vile and unwholesome moving pictures." An estimated ten million lay Catholics signed a voluntary pledge promising to boycott films that offended decency and Christian morality. At the urging of local bishops, protesters publicly demonstrated against theaters showing films that had been condemned in church newspapers. Young Catholics checked the lists of Legion-approved motion pictures posted at Roman Catholic churches before attending Saturday afternoon shows with their friends, as attendance at such nonapproved films constituted a venial sin. By February, 1936, the Legion had instituted its own rating system: Class A included films that were morally unobjectionable (with several subcategories); Class B, those that were morally objectionable in part for all; and Class C, films that were condemned.

Unlike fundamentalist Christian groups, the Catholic church did not desire to shut down the film industry; however, it did wish to exercise its power in the marketplace. In Philadelphia, box-office receipts decreased by 40 percent following a boycott of picture houses by Catholics who were aided by several Protestant and Jewish groups. To stave off an all-out war against the industry, the Hays Office created an internal regulatory office, the Production Code Administration (PCA) to levy heavy fines against members of the Motion Picture Producers and Distributors Association of America (MPPDA) that released films without PCA seals of approval. Hays expressed his welcome for the Legion of Decency "with open arms," stating that his own office and the Legion together "created a mutual defense pact that finally made the Code a working reality."

By 1938 not a single film made by a major Hollywood producer had been condemned since the PCA was formed. However, many people felt that the combination of government censorship and industry self-regulation suffocated American film creativity, as local censorship boards throughout the country were independently cutting film scenes of kissing,

THE LEGION OF DECENCY PLEDGE

The estimated ten million Roman Catholics who joined the Legion of Decency signed this pledge:

"I wish to join the Legion of Decency, which condemns vile and unwholesome moving pictures. I unite with all who protest against them as a grave menace to youth, to home life, to country, and to religion.... Considering these evils, I hereby promise to remain away from all motion pictures except those which do not offend decency and Christian morality. I promise further to secure as many members as possible for the Legion of Decency. I make this protest in a spirit of self-respect, and with the conviction that the American public does not demand filthy pictures, but clean entertainment and educational features."

Legion of Decency Film-Rating System

Class	Description	Examples
A-1	morally unobjectionable for general patronage	*The Old Man and the Sea* (1958), *No Time for Sergeants* (1958), *The Bridge on the River Kwai* (1957)
A-2	morally unobjectionable for adults and adolescents	*Witness for the Prosecution* (1957), *The Return of Dracula* (1958)
A-3 (1958)	morally objectionable only for adults	*South Pacific* (1958), *Cat on a Hot Tin Roof* (1958), *Desire Under the Elms* (1958)
A-4 (1963)	morally unobjectionable for adults, with reservations	*Who's Afraid of Virginia Woolf* (1966), *Midnight Cowboy* (1969), *Saturday Night Fever* (1977)
B	morally objectionable in part for everyone	*A Farewell to Arms* (1957), *A Streetcar Named Desire* (1951), *God's Little Acre* (1958), *The Sun Also Rises* (1957)
C	condemned for all	*And God Created Woman* (1957), *The Outlaw* (1941), *The Miracle* (1951), *The Moon Is Blue* (1953), *Lolita* (1962), *Blow-Up* (1966), *The Valley of the Dolls* (1967), *Friday the 13th* (1980)

hand-holding, and anything they thought might exert unwholesome influence in their communities.

Among the films sanctioned by the Legion were *Gone with the Wind* (1939), which earned a B rating because of its alleged "low moral character and suggestive implications," and Elia Kazan's *Baby Doll* (1956), the tale of a Southern bigot with a child bride. Due to the Legion's threatened crusade against Mae West for sexually suggestive performances on Edgar Bergen's radio show, the National Broadcasting Company banned reference to her name on all its stations. Kazan was again singled out as twelve cuts (comprising three minutes of footage) from *A Streetcar Named Desire* were approved by its producer without Kazan's knowledge. Despite these cuts, the film earned a B rating.

By the mid-1960's, the film industry was in a state of turbulence, compounded by the fact that nearly half of its audience was between the ages of sixteen and twenty-four. The brief papacy of the moderate John XXIII combined with the election of Roman Catholic John F. Kennedy to the American presidency helped to bring Catholics into the mainstream of American life—a development that paradoxically weakened the Legion. In 1963, the Legion instituted a liberalized category to notify Catholics of films dealing maturely with "serious themes": A-4, films that were morally unobjectionable for adults, with reservations.

In 1965, the Legion renamed itself the National Catholic Office of Motion Pictures. Increasingly, both foreign and national films were shown without approval by either this office or the MPPDA; Michelangelo Antonioni's *Blow-Up* (1966) was an artistic and financial success despite its nude scenes and C rating. In October, 1980, the National Catholic Office closed its offices for good, citing financial reasons. In truth, it had became irrelevant. The Catholic church continued to classify films, but it moved from the role of censor to adviser, and it merged the old B and C ratings into a single category: O, morally offensive.

See also Film censorship; Hays Code; Pressure groups; Vatican; West, Mae; Williams, Tennessee.

Leighton, Alexander

Born: 1568

Died: 1649

Identification: English Puritan divine and physician

Significance: A harsh critic of English bishops, Leighton was punished with bodily mutilation and imprisonment

A Puritan trained as both a physician and a clergyman, Leighton argued for the removal of the bishops from the Church of England in *An Appeal to the Parliament: Or, Sions Plea Against the Prelacie* (1628). Arguing that "the Lord Bishops, and their appurtenances are manifestlie proved, both by divine and humane Lawes, to be intruders upon the Priviledges of Christ, of the King, and of the Common-weal," Leighton denounced the bishops for their irrelevance and anti-Christian administration. They should, he argued, "have no place in God's house."

In 1630 Leighton was seized under a warrant from the Court of High Commission, charged with encouraging anarchy. He was tried and convicted by the Star Chamber court and sentenced to be whipped, have an ear cut off, his nose slit, and his face branded "SS," for "sower of sedition." He escaped from prison briefly but suffered the mutilation prescribed by his sentence in November, 1630. He then spent eleven years in jail before being released at the beginning of the English Puritan Revolution.

The ferocity of Leighton's punishment for publishing *Sions Plea*—more than the book's actual arguments—contributed to the erosion of popular support for the bishops and the discrediting of the Star Chamber. Leighton himself continued his crusade against the bishops in two further books, *A Decade of Grievances . . . Against the Bishops* (1641) and *An Epitome or Brief Discoverie* (1646). Early in the reign of King Charles I, Leighton anticipated the arguments of John Milton in his anti-episcopal tracts of the 1640's.

See also *Areopagitica*; Crop-ears; English Commonwealth; James I; Latimer, Hugh; Milton, John; Stubbs, John; United Kingdom; *Utopia*.

Lenin, Vladimir Ilich

BORN: April 22, 1870, Simbirsk, Russia

DIED: January 21, 1924, Gorki, near Moscow, Soviet Union

IDENTIFICATION: Russian revolutionist and first leader of the Soviet Union

SIGNIFICANCE: Lenin used strong government censorship to silence opponents to his new Soviet state

Born into an upper-middle-class Russian family, Lenin expected to pursue a respectable career as a lawyer, but his plans were was rudely shattered at age seventeen, when his brother was executed for plotting to kill the czar. Lenin himself then became a revolutionary disciple of German communist philosopher Karl Marx. The government of Czar Alexander III was a repressive one, with ambitious censorship of publications and the educational system. Lenin's efforts to evade censorship in 1895 led him to use a false-bottomed trunk to sneak forbidden publications from Western Europe into Russia. Police detected them, however, and placed him under surveillance while he was trying to establish a radical newspaper. Before his paper appeared, the police arrested him and his associates. Lenin then spent a year in prison and three years in exile. While in prison he composed *The Development of Capitalism in Russia*. So that it would pass prison censors, he held his Marxist rhetoric in check.

Upon his release, Lenin left Russia for Western Europe in order to publish a radical newspaper without czarist censorship. Called *Iskra* ("The Spark"), his new paper became a leading influence among revolutionaries. From 1900 to 1917 he was active in the new Social Democratic Labor Party, and helped to shape its Bolshevist wing into a small, highly disciplined centralized conspiratorial organization. World War I provided Lenin—then living in Switzerland—with an opportunity for action.

In reaction to devastating wartime casualties and hardships in Russia, a liberal-democratic revolution that erupted in March, 1917, forced the czar to abdicate and led to a provisional government. Germany sought to weaken Russian resistance by helping Lenin return home. Capitalizing on Russian opposition to the war and on peasant antipathy toward wealthy landowners, his Bolshevist followers mounted a second revolution in October, 1917, that brought Lenin to supreme power in the country.

Still facing violent opposition in Russia and the unfinished war with Germany, and trying to launch radical economic changes, Lenin and his followers extended their power through all sectors of the society. Direct opposition to the domination of the Bolshevist Party—restyled the Communist Party—was not tolerated. In July, 1918, Lenin had all other political parties suppressed. Communist Party leaders and government officials used their control over the communication media to emphasize Marxist ideology and suppress competing views. The newspaper *Pravda* ("Truth"), which the Bolsheviks had established before coming to power, became their chief mouthpiece. However, many competing publications continued to appear in the early 1920's.

Outside the realm of political and economic policies, the new Soviet state permitted substantial freedom for cultural, artistic, and literary expression. Government subsidies were given to promote favored forms, but the scope of freedom was limited. In 1920 Lenin expressed hostility to the Proletkult, a modernist literary organization. At that time, it continued to operate and receive state aid, but in 1923 it was forcibly abolished.

V. I. Lenin speaking into a recording device some time around the early 1920's. (AP/Wide World Photos)

Lenin's physical disability and death in early 1924 brought on a relatively liberal atmosphere. However, this ended abruptly when Joseph Stalin established himself as the supreme power in 1927. Under Stalin, media control and censorship went even beyond what Lenin had carried out.

See also Communism; Marx, Karl; Mayakovsky, Vladimir; Stalin, Joseph; Trotsky, Leon.

Lennon, John

BORN: October 9, 1940, Liverpool, England

DIED: December 8, 1980, New York, New York

IDENTIFICATION: English popular music recording artist

SIGNIFICANCE: As a member of the Beatles and as a solo performer, Lennon was attacked for his political and religious views, as well his as alleged use of obscenity

Lennon's first encounter with U.S. censorship resulted from a 1966 remark he made to a British journalist, expressing his view that the Beatles "were more popular than Jesus." The casual remark caused little stir in Great Britain, but in the United States it led to public burnings of Beatles records and calls for banning the group's music, particularly in the religiously conservative South. Lennon made a public apology for his comment, but after the Beatles received numerous death threats during their 1966 tour of the United States, the group stopped touring.

Another controversy arose from the Beatles 1969 single, "The Ballad of John and Yoko." In that song Lennon lamented, "Christ, you know it ain't easy/ You know how hard it can be./ The way things are going,/ they're gonna crucify me." A number of U.S. radio stations banned the song outright, but others simply bleeped the offending word "Christ."

With his very public liaison and marriage to Japanese conceptual artist Yoko Ono in 1969, Lennon seemed to court controversy on both sides of the Atlantic. Before their marriage, the pair privately released the album *Two Virgins* (1968), whose cover included front and back photographs of them standing in the nude. U.S. Customs officials in Newark, New Jersey, seized a shipment of thirty thousand copies of the album. Lennon's erotic lithographs of Ono, part of a London show titled *Bag One*, were confiscated by Scotland Yard on January 16, 1970.

As a solo recording artist, Lennon ran afoul of radio censors with "Working Class Hero," a cut from *Plastic Ono Band* (1970). That song combines a Marxist message with the word "fucking." Though banned from commercial stations, the song became one of the first hits of underground radio. Meanwhile, Lennon continued to dabble with radical politics, recording *Some Time in New York City* (1972), whose album cover included a doctored portrait of President Richard Nixon and Chinese leader Mao Zedong dancing naked. The album itself contained protest songs for a galaxy of radical causes—most notably, calls for the release of "political prisoners" Angela Davis and White Panther John Sinclair. However, the only song on the album banned by commercial radio was a feminist paean, which was censored not for its political message, but for its inflammatory language: "Woman Is the Nigger of the World."

Lennon's radical politics earned him a spot on President Nixon's infamous enemies list, and instigated deportation proceedings by the U.S. Justice Department. Citing Lennon's prior drug convictions, the Justice Department sought to revoke his U.S. visa. The Watergate scandal interrupted the government's action, and Lennon was awarded a green card in 1976. Four years later he was assassinated by a religious fanatic and obsessed fan named Mark David Chapman. Chapman numbered among his reasons for shooting Lennon the latter's earlier claim that the Beatles were more popular than Jesus.

See also Beatles, the; Blasphemy laws; Immigration laws; Nixon, Richard M.; Nudity; Offensive language; Protest music; Recording industry; Rock 'n' roll music.

Letters to editors

DEFINITION: Letters that readers send to newspapers for possible publication

SIGNIFICANCE: Letters to the editor are a means of public participation in democracy; charges of censorship have been made when some letters have not been published

Letters to the editor were once a mainstay of Western newspaper content. With the modern development of the role of journalists as professional providers of public information and argumentation, letters have been relegated to a lesser role. This trend has restricted access to mediated public debate. From the beginning of the eighteenth century, early newspapers in Europe were seen as an extension of the public forum that had developed mainly with the proliferation of coffeehouses. Publications in Great Britain such as the *Tattler*, the *Guardian*, and the *Spectator* devoted themselves to soliciting and printing letters intended to be read aloud in these coffeehouse debates. Even in this early stage of journalism, letters to the editor were subject to the prejudices of editors. Joseph Addison, an editor of the *Spectator*, for example, saw himself as an arbiter of manners and morals. Thus, letters to the editor were censored or published according to the decision of the editor.

American Newspapers. During the period of the partisan press (the first of three phases in the development of American journalism), when newspapers were dedicated to particular parties or ideas, letters to the editor sometimes constituted most of the editorial content of a newspaper. From roughly 1750 to 1850, even editors would publish their personal comments as letters, a practice that continued into the twentieth century. Usually such a letter was anonymous or signed with a pseudonym. Social critics from Karl Marx to Alexis de Tocqueville recognized the essential role these early publications of letters played in the development of modern democracies. Newspapers were the essential bearers and leaders of public opinion at a time when public opinion was dissolving, creating, and legitimizing governments.

In principle, individual partisan newspapers openly reflected the bias of the particular political parties that sponsored them. It was the partisan press collectively that created an open public forum that affirmed or denied civic arguments. Thus, while individual publishers selected and composed letters reflecting narrow, subjective points of view, a subscriber to several newspapers surveyed the broad scope of public debate. Consequently the meaning of censorship in this period is inverted. By exercising prejudice in selecting letters for publication, editors simultaneously participated in an overall process that provided the widest possible representation of ideas.

In the next phase of professional journalism in America, the period of the penny press, both the range of opinion and the amount of space allocated to letters were greatly restricted. The period of the penny press is named for the machines that made mass production of newspapers possible. The large, inexpensive daily newspapers put the smaller, more expensive partisan publications out of business. While on the one hand a kind of censorship of the marketplace thus occurred—as the few voices of the big city dailies replaced the many voices of small publishers—on the other hand, as newspapers became more affordable, more readers potentially gained access to public debate.

Public access was more apparent than real, however. Newspapers in the late nineteenth century developed the roles of reporters and editors as spokespersons for the public. They selected issues, conducted interviews with newsmakers, and provided analysis. The results were fewer publications and fewer voices speaking through those publications. The effects could be seen in a drastic reduction in the amount of space allocated to letters to the editor.

The period of the "objective" press began around 1900. Where newspapers primarily made up of letters were a conduit for public debate, professionally guided publications stood above the fray, synthesizing and critiquing the arguments of others and producing a kind of narrative of public debate. One of the effects of the growing dominance of this writing style was that letters to the editor, opinion columns, and editorials became the only places in newspapers in which opinions could be frankly expressed. Thus, in the twentieth century press, the style of objective news writing was to filter out opinions, and letters to the editor became one of the few outlets for opinion. Furthermore, since in the post-penny press environment letters pages were the only places where those who were not newspaper employees expressed themselves, letters to the editor became one of the last bastions of public opinion in the newspaper.

Letters to the editor pages expanded in the 1930's. *Time* magazine first published volumes of correspondence from readers in 1934. These publications included letters that, because of space limitations, were never published in the magazine itself. There is no indication that reader mail has fallen off since the 1930's. In the 1970's *The New York Times* received approximately forty thousand letters a year. *Time* magazine had its letters double to approximately eighty thousand, as a result of the Watergate scandal, in 1973. In the 1990's *USA Today* reported receiving more than twenty thousand letters annually. However, *The National Enquirer* apparently held the record, with a million letters a year.

Selection and Editing of Letters. The guiding principle of objectivity in twentieth century newspapers pervades even the letters to the editor page. Editors do not expect letter writers to be objective, although catering to the objectivity standard may make a letter more attractive to the editorial staff. Nowhere, however, is it practice to edit a letter to make it objective. The significant manifestation of the objectivity principle in publishing letters to the editor is in the attempt on the part of editors to tell what is commonly referred to as both sides of the story. Thus reporters interview people with opposing views, and letters page editors tend to select letters with opposing arguments to those found in news stories, editorials, or other letters.

While this dichotomous paradigm of mediating public debate would seem to ensure inclusion of opposing opinion, it also biases the process against opinions that do not fit the point-counterpoint narrative of a particular news theme. For example, if a newspaper were following a story about a bill before Congress to grant thirty million dollars to a group of armed rebels in a foreign country, and the debate were about whether the amount should be thirty million dollars, as the Republicans wish, or twenty million dollars—with guarantees that the money would be spent only on tents and uniforms instead of mines or guns—which is what the Democrats want, letters to the editor decrying any participation in another country's affairs, or documenting the group's atrocities, or arguing that the foreign country in question should be subjected to nuclear attack, might be judged too extreme to be published. Paradoxically, the objectivity principle, which arguably promotes access to public debate, restricts debate by biasing letters to antithetical positions. *—Thomas J. Roach*

See also FAIR; *New York Times, The*; News media censorship; Newspapers; Obituaries; Printing.

Bibliography

Michael Schudson's *Discovering the News: A Social History of American Newspapers* (New York: Basic Books, 1978) shows how the objectivity principle governs the selection and editing of newspaper copy. Herbert J. Gans's *Deciding What's News: A Study of "CBS Evening News," "NBC Nightly News," "Newsweek," and "Time"* (New York: Vintage Books, 1979) provides statistics on letters received by news magazines and television news broadcasts. In *The News at Any Cost* (New York: Simon and Schuster, 1985) Tom Goldstein gives a journalist's account of how letters are processed by writers and editors. Daniel C. Hallin's "The American News Media: A Critical Perspective," in *Critical Theory and Public Life*, edited by J. Forester (Cambridge, Mass.: MIT Press, 1985) discusses the significance of the transition form newspapers as collections of opinions in the eighteenth century to newspapers governed by the scientific principles of objectivity. Jürgen Habermas' *The Structural Transformation of the Public Sphere: An Inquiry into a Category of Bourgeois Society*, translated by Thomas Burger (Cambridge, Mass.: MIT Press, 1989), deals with the development of modern public deliberation and gives a detailed account of letters to the editor in the earliest newspapers and their integral relationship to public debate. While the above authors focus on letters to the editor only to the extent that they represent the early stages in the evolution of the newspaper profession, Thomas C. Leonard includes later data in *News for All: America's Coming-of-Age with the Press* (New York: Oxford University Press, 1995). Statistics and discussion of letters to the editor are incorporated into this scholarly history of newspapers.

Lewis, Jerry Lee

Born: September 29, 1935, Ferriday, Louisiana

Identification: American popular music performer

Significance: Known for his flamboyant and rowdy rock 'n' roll performances, Lewis won stardom during the mid-1950's, but ruined his career by marrying his young cousin

In 1956 Lewis auditioned successfully for Sun Records in Memphis, Tennessee, where Elvis Presley had begun his recording career several years earlier. Within a year Lewis was recording his first hit records: "Whole Lot of Shakin' Going On" and "Great Balls of Fire." These were quickly followed by "Breathless," "High School Confidential," and others.

By 1958 Lewis was a national star in the new field of rock 'n' roll. The year began promisingly: Presley's induction into the Army left Lewis poised to succeed him as the number one rock 'n' roll star. That same year Lewis began a concert tour of Great Britain. He took with him thirteen-year-old Myra Gale Brown, a cousin whom he had secretly married the previous

December. He presented Myra Lewis to the British press as his younger sister, but the truth was soon out and he had to cancel his tour. The public outcry against him in the United States was strong, especially among church leaders, who denounced his marriage as immoral. Radio stations refused to play his records, so Sun stopped promoting them. The negative publicity surrounding his marriage essentially halted his career as a recording star.

Through the ensuing years Lewis persevered by performing at small venues and county fairs. His marriage to his cousin lasted thirteen years, but other problems in his personal life further tarnished his reputation. Nevertheless, he continued to perform and record and gradually regained some of his earlier stature over the next four decades.

See also Jackson, Michael; Morality; Presley, Elvis; Recording industry; Rock 'n' roll music; United Kingdom.

Lewis, Sinclair

Born: February 7, 1885, Sauk Centre, Minnesota

Died: January 10, 1951, Rome, Italy

Identification: Prominent American writer of fiction and nonfiction

Significance: The first American author to be awarded the Nobel Prize in Literature, in 1930, Lewis wrote satirical and controversial novels that attacked social complacency and hypocrisy, several of which have been banned in Europe and the United States

A prolific and provocative writer of newspaper editorials, magazine articles, and novels, Sinclair Lewis joined such literary contemporaries as H. L. Mencken and Sherwood Anderson in condemning the "village virus" affecting small towns throughout America. Lewis' novel *Main Street* (1920) established his reputation as a social satirist with its meticulous depiction of a stifling and reactionary small town in Minnesota. His cynical dissatisfaction with post-World War I American life seemed even stronger in *Babbitt* (1922), a portrait of a corrupt real estate agent which exposes the pomposity, materialism, and vulgarity beneath the pretenses of American business.

Lewis' persistent assaults on American values and institutions drew attention from literary critics and the general public, many of whom found his indictments mean-spirited and excessively harsh. Public outrage reached international proportions with his publication of *Elmer Gantry* (1927), which features an unscrupulous preacher consumed not with religious fervor but with ambitions for personal glory and power. The novel's suggestion that religious faith in modern America had been tainted by morally weak and calculating evangelical leaders provoked widespread condemnation, including threats of lynching the author himself. In 1927 the novel was banned in Boston, Massachusetts; Camden, New Jersey; and Glasgow, Scotland. In 1931 it was banned in Ireland, and the same year the U.S. Post Office prohibited any catalog from listing the title.

Many of Lewis' later works are less effective, although *It Can't Happen Here* (1935) stirred considerable debate about the possible takeover of the United States by a totalitarian dictatorship. A 1935 film based on the novel was abandoned after news circulated that film censor Will Hays would ban the film. Nearly ten years later, Lewis' novel *Cass Timberlane* (1945) renewed calls for censorship because of its emphasis on extramarital sexuality; the book was banned in Ireland in 1953 and in East Berlin in 1954.

Lewis succinctly conveyed his own views on censorship in an article in the *New York World* on August 20, 1922. "Any committee which sets itself up to judge the morality of any branch of art is . . . an absurdity," he wrote. "Art should be, must be and is creative and original. In order to bloom with those qualities it must be unhampered. Any artist who works with the tapeworm of censorship gnawing at his vitals . . . would be stifled from the onset."

See also American Booksellers Foundation for Free Expression; *Elmer Gantry*; Film adaptation; Hays Code; Literature; Mencken, H. L.; Postal regulations.

Libel

Definition: Defaming a person's reputation or character by writing, printing, or drawing

Significance: Libel law can be used to discourage those who criticize public or private figures

Cases of libel fall into two classes. In the first class there is the written or printed defamation of a private citizen, usually defined as someone who is not a public official. In the second class, known as seditious libel, the attacks made are upon the reputation of the government itself or else upon the government's representative. Both classes have excited great controversy, and legal scholars in North America have debated, since the inception of North American libel law, key questions on libel law.

Historical Background. In English law those who made printed attacks on government or its officers met vigorous prosecution and draconian punishment. In 1663, for example, William Twyn published a book advocating the right of the people to revolt against the Crown. Found guilty of seditious libel, Twyn was hanged, disemboweled, castrated, and beheaded. The noted authority William Blackstone wrote that in English common law, freedom of the press guaranteed the government would make no prior restraint of the press. On the other hand, once publication was made the freedom of the press did not protect the writer or printer from punishment for illegal or improper publications.

In the British colonies of North America prosecutions for libel were much less common than in the mother country. The most noted case was that of Peter Zenger, who published one of New York City's two newspapers. When Zenger published an attack on the royal governor of New York in 1734, he was arrested for seditious libel and incarcerated. Zenger was also denied access to pen and ink. The royal judges ruled that the jury should only decide the fact of whether Zenger actually published the attack in question while the judges decided whether the material was libelous. The jurors, however, did not take the judges' suggestion. Instead, the jury returned the verdict that Zenger was not guilty because the material published was not libelous. The Zenger case contributed to a reluctance of colonial officials to bring libel cases.

Constitutional Foundations. The foundation of U.S. libel law is the First Amendment, with its guarantees of freedom of the press. Legal scholars agreed early on that the First Amendment was a limitation on Congress' power to regulate the press, but that states still held considerable powers to move against libel. One question that remained open, however, was whether the First Amendment, built on the tradition of freedom of the press, did not protect writers and printers from punishment for improper attacks, or whether the amendment marked a break with the English common law in this area. Some of the earliest libel cases under the new Constitution arose when Congress passed the Alien and Sedition Acts of 1798, aiming to punish publications that brought contempt upon the nation's government and its officers. Federal attorneys brought many successful prosecutions, but the model of the Zenger case was followed and juries were permitted to rule both on the question of whether the defendant actually wrote or published the words in question and whether the words were libelous.

Congress and the Supreme Court held largely aloof from the area of libel until the second half of the twentieth century. Congress' passage of the Espionage and Sedition Acts in the World War I era were an important exception. Libel was considered to be chiefly a state matter. Typically, state law permits the defendant to offer proof of the truth of his statements as one defense against charges of libel.

Modern cases of the U.S. Supreme Court. The landmark decision on libel in modern times was *New York Times Co. v. Sullivan*, handed down by the U.S. Supreme Court in 1964. A New York group supporting the Civil Rights movement published an advertisement in *The New York Times* charging state and local officers in Alabama with a number of abuses of power against Martin Luther King, Jr., and his followers. The advertisement alleged, for example, that officers had arrested King seven times on dubious charges and had assaulted him and bombed his home. A city commissioner of Montgomery, Alabama, named L. B. Sullivan sued *The New York Times* and four Alabama residents who had signed the ad for libel. As someone responsible for police activities, Sullivan argued that his reputation had been unfairly damaged by the untrue or exaggerated charges in the ad. Under common law as generally interpreted in Alabama, *The New York Times* would have difficulty in winning its case. Sullivan would not need to prove actual damages; he would only need to prove the ad had hurt his official reputation. The defendants could not defend themselves solely by the truth of the charges since the ad did make some accusations that turned out to be incorrect. As expected, the Alabama jury found for Sullivan; damages were set at $500,000.

In reversing the Alabama verdict, the Supreme Court laid down a new rule for libel. Public officials could recover damages for attacks on their official actions only if it could be shown that the defendants made the charges while knowing them to be false, or else that the publication was made with reckless disregard of whether the statements were true or not. The Court found no evidence *The New York Times* or the advertisement's sponsors had known the charges to be false or had exhibited reckless disregard for the truth. The Sullivan rule has become the standard in libel law, while the Court placed certain limitations on its rule in a number of subsequent cases.

In *Gertz v. Robert I. Welch, Incorporated* (1974), the U.S. Supreme Court ruled that to recover actual damages, private individuals bringing libel cases need not meet the strict tests set down in *New York Times v. Sullivan*, since private individuals had less opportunity to correct the record via the media than did public figures. In *Herbert v. Lando* (1979) the Court denied that writers, editors, and publishers had a First Amendment right to draw a veil over their editorial states of mind and actions. Under the rule laid down in the *Sullivan* case, the plaintiffs in libel cases had the right to probe for any reckless disregard of the truth. The Court's decision in *Milkovich v. Lorain Journal Co.* (1990) held that a writer or publisher could not defend against libel action simply by arguing that the writing in question was a statement of opinion. The Court held that a statement of opinion could still constitute libel if the statement could be proven false. Prefacing a libelous false statement with "I believe" would not bar a libel case from moving forward.

The *Sullivan* case and subsequent libel decisions of the U.S. Supreme Court have had the effect of federalizing libel law within the U.S. While libel cases are tried in state courts and under state law, there is now a national set of rules and norms that are applied in cases of libel. The degree of freedom of speech—or of censorship—allowed in libel cases has become largely the same in all jurisdictions in the United States.

—Stephen Cresswell

See also Defamation; First Amendment; Howe, Joseph; *Hustler*; *New York Times Co. v. Sullivan*; Sedition; Sedition Act of 1798; Zenger, John Peter.

Bibliography

On early American libel cases, see Leonard W. Levy's *Emergence of a Free Press* (New York: Oxford University Press, 1985). On the colonial period in particular, see Harold L. Nelson, "Seditious Libel in Colonial America," *American Journal of Legal History* 3 (1959). An excellent contemporary study of the *Sullivan* decision is Karry Kalven, Jr., "*The New York Times* Case," in *Supreme Court Review* 191 (1964). A journalists' historical overview of libel cases of the U.S. Supreme Court is provided by Clifton O. Lawhorne and Howard R. Long's *The Supreme Court and Libel* (Carbondale: Southern Illinois University Press, 1981). To place libel law in the context of the whole of legal history, the best book to consult is Kermit Hall's *The Magic Mirror: The Law in American History* (New York: Oxford University Press, 1989).

Libraries

Definition: Collections of books and other written and recorded materials for puposes of research and reading

Significance: As disseminators of information and knowledge throughout the world, libraries have traditionally been prime targets of censorship

A library is an organized (using a classification system) collection of books and other print and nonprint materials. Library contents and materials vary according to the patrons or clientele being served. Library searches used to be done through the card catalog, a record of the collection's materials. Most libraries, in the late twentieth century, switched their records (under the same classification systems) to computers, so that users can access information in various databases. Libraries' vast collections of materials can be obtained by such methods as going to the shelf and finding a desired book, requesting a book (many libraries do not allow patrons to access books directly), making a computer printout, or asking for a book through interlibrary loan. Libraries are vital organizations in modern global societies. They house not only books but also other resources, including periodicals, newspapers, audiovisual materials and various other print and nonprint information. Librarians provide a variety of services to a clientele used to a service oriented, computer-age society. The Internet has enabled individuals to reach libraries across nations and to acquire information instantaneously. The roles of libraries and librarians have become more complex and challenging, especially in issues of selection and censorship.

Historical Perspective. The earliest known libraries (of clay tablets) date back to Mesopotamia of 3500 B.C.E. The ancient library (of papyrus documents) in Alexandria (305-283 B.C.E.) was destroyed in various fires. Scholars at this Egyptian library copied, revised, and collated works of classical Greek writers. Libraries flourished for centuries and held about 500,000 rolls. The Roman Empire had many libraries, but during the Middle Ages the Roman Catholic church kept the library traditions in Europe. Libraries in the Middle Ages were primarily in monasteries, cathedrals, and universities. Books were laboriously made by hand, by monks, thus limiting the size and number of libraries. Additionally, books that the Church thought immoral were destroyed. The great libraries of Damascus and Baghdad were destroyed by the thirteenth century. The first libraries in China appeared with the Ch'in Dynasty. A copy of every book was stored in the imperial library.

During the Renaissance more libraries emerged, including the Vatican Library. The invention of the printing press further increased the number of libraries, and more books became available, primarily for elites with private libraries. Public libraries started in the seventeenth century and their number multiplied throughout Europe and America. As illiteracy rates decreased, the use of public libraries increased in the eighteenth century. National libraries appeared—La Bibliotheque National in Paris in the seventeenth century, the British Museum in London and Italy's National Library in Florence in the eighteenth century, Russia's Saltikov-Shchdrin Library in Saint Petersburg, and the Library of Congress in Washington, D.C., which started with purchases from Thomas Jefferson's personal library.

Most countries have national libraries, as well as other scholarly libraries—Charles University in Prague, the Jewish National and University Library in Jerusalem, the Egyptian National Library in Cairo, and others. In some countries, public libraries are not as abundant as in the United States and Canada. Canada maintains government libraries in Ottawa—the Library of Parliament, the National Library of Canada, and the Canadian Institute for Scientific and Technical Information. The Internet allows easy access to these libraries and others throughout the world. Several organizations work to improve libraries across the world, including UNESCO (United Nations Educational, Scientific, and Cultural Organization), AID (the Agency for International Development), IFLA (International Federation of Library Associations), IASL (International Association of School Librarianship), and others.

Types of Libraries, Organization, and Services. There are various types of libraries: private, public, academic, school, and specialized. The first libraries were private collections of rulers, aristocrats, and those who could afford to build collections. With the advent of the printing press, more books became available and public libraries were organized. Most private and public libraries benefited from donor generosity, and many private collections are available to the public for research (such as Huntington Library in San Marino, California, or the Ambrosian Library in Milan, Italy). Andrew Carnegie helped establish two thousand public libraries in the United States. Private libraries may limit access to their collections, and use is often based on the research needs of clients. Public libraries have a responsibility to maintain a collection that reflects the needs of the community and that is accessible to all users.

Public libraries often work cooperatively with other libraries, especially school libraries. In some cases, public libraries may lend collections to schools for a period of time. Public libraries are actively involved in providing services for children and young adults. Story hour and literacy programs are popular, along with writer group meetings and other community activities. Services for special groups are also available, for example materials for the visually impaired. More and more public (and school) libraries are purchasing materials in many different languages to accommodate the needs of culturally diverse communities. Public libraries often provide literacy and immigrant services, as well as provide programs that enrich the community. Special libraries (medicine, law, and other fields) can be located in private companies and large academic libraries.

Academic libraries are associated with universities and colleges. The content of academic libraries varies according to the size and goals of the university. Large research libraries have specialized content in addition to the range of subjects available in other libraries. Original manuscripts, some historical documents, and rare books are usually housed in the special collections area of academic libraries. Academic libraries require large, specialized staffs to meet the needs of the campus population in supporting and facilitating research for students and faculty.

School libraries are run by school districts and serve students in elementary, middle school, and high school settings. The contents of school libraries usually support the curriculum and encourage students to become library users of public and academic libraries. School libraries often work cooperatively with public libraries for additional resources and information. Librarians are also certified teachers who must not only provide resources to support curricula but also must also work cooperatively with other faculty members to provide a variety of library curricular and extracurricular programs.

The American Library Association (ALA), founded in 1876, is devoted to the advancement of library and information

BOOKS IN U.S. LIBRARIES IN 1991

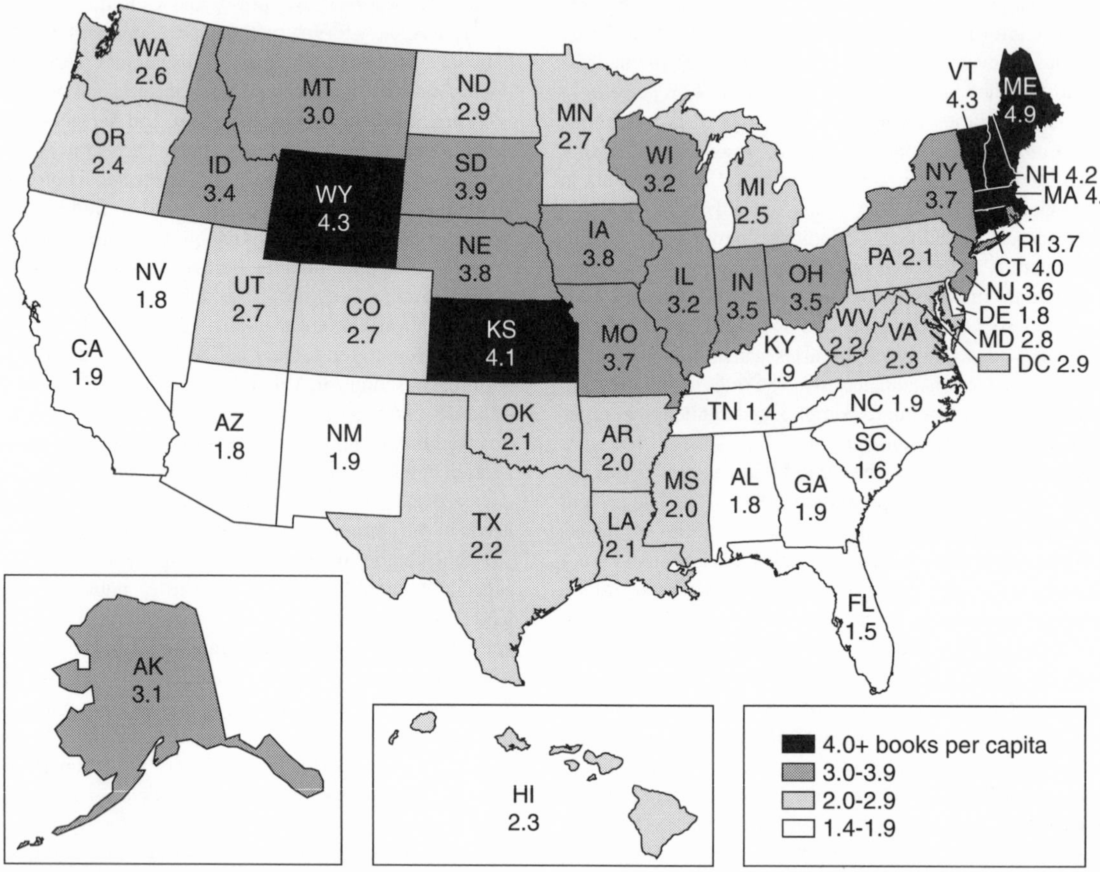

Source: Kathleen O'Leary Morgan, Scott Morgan, and Neal Quitno, eds., *State Rankings 1994: A Statistical View of the 50 United States.* Lawrence, Kans.: Morgan Quitno Corp., 1994.

science and to the provision of library services and materials to all users. This association is active in many library related issues—library education, library publications, and the establishment of standards for all types of libraries. It encourages open access to library stacks, the increase of special services for children and young adults, the disabled, linguistically diverse populations, and other cultural groups. The ALA seeks to improve standards for library schools and ensure that professionals are updated on electronic databases, the Internet, and other challenges of the information highway. The Intellectual Freedom Committee of the ALA works diligently to preserve the users' right to read and to assist librarians with censorship issues. United States public libraries and especially school libraries have always been targets of censorship. Library censorship includes other materials besides books—films, videotapes, photographs, and other nonprint information.

Censorship and Selection. Acquisition of library materials is usually delegated to a committee (of professional librarians and community members) decision and is based on a written selection policy. Ultimate control over those controversial decisions that cannot be handled by librarians are determined by library governing boards for public libraries and school boards for school library media centers. Librarians and selection committees choose materials for the whole community, especially in public libraries.

School libraries select materials to support the curriculum; public libraries must meet the needs of a variety of patrons. Adult materials often fall victim to censorship complaints. The Intellectual Freedom Committee of the ALA provides counsel and legal support to librarians embattled by censorship issues. School libraries report the highest incidence of censorship complaints, followed by public libraries. Academic libraries appear to have few censorship incidents, perhaps because of the academic freedom afforded university libraries. Private, religious colleges, however, may actually practice censorship through the selection process. Authors such as Judy Blume and Kurt Vonnegut, along with publisher associations, are stout defenders of libraries and the freedom to read.

The ALA is concerned about attempts to suppress individuals' rights of access to library materials. The association believes that free communication is necessary for the preservation of creativity in a free society. The ALA has publicly affirmed its stance against censorship and on behalf of free debate. It argues that it is in the public interest for publishers and librarians to make available the widest diversity of views and expressions, including those which are unorthodox or unpopular with the majority. The association's Library Bill of Rights specifically addresses censorship concerns and affirms that all libraries are forums for information and ideas. The ALA recognizes the educational level and program of school libraries; however, it encourages librarians to follow the principles of the Library Bill of Rights, specifically recommending that school librarians take the lead in promoting the freedom to read.

Among the many forms that censorship has taken, there have been efforts to get librarians to reveal users' names and borrowing patterns. To prevent censors from acquiring information on library users, the ALA has developed a policy that clearly states that records of users and usage are confidential. Whether or not specific legislation exists to enforce this confidentiality, librarians are urged to respect the rights of all users, including children. Despite efforts to protect individuals' rights to read, libraries still face censorship. One way to address censorship problems is to have a written selection policy with a censorship clause and a form in which would-be censors may express, in writing, their specific concern regarding the material in question.

Censorship concerns date back to Plato, who reasoned that fiction could be potentially disturbing to young people. Subjects deemed worthy of censorship are boundless. They include: profanity, blasphemy, and un-Christian thought; indecency (sexual language, nude pictures, explicit sex descriptions, and discussion of human sexuality); drug use; politics; sexist or racist ideas and language; racial stereotypes and derogatory descriptions of culturally diverse groups; ideas undermining the family, society, human relationships, and traditional values; description of extramarital affairs; expressions of unpatriotic ideas; lack of educational value; vulgarity; secular humanism; cultural diversity; ethnic studies; multicultural education; critical thinking; and ecology.

There is very little, perhaps nothing, in a library that will not offend someone. Examples of works that have been censored, and, at times, removed from libraries include: the Bible (certain passages seen as violent), dictionaries (for containing vulgar words), works by Shakespeare (fond of the dirty pun, plus his tragedies have sad endings), and textbooks. *Bury My Heart at Wounded Knee* (1970) has been censored for being slanted (presumably, when it comes to a massacre, only a balanced view of both sides of the issue is allowable). Dr. Seuss's *The Lorax* (1971) has been attacked in Oregon for encouraging saving trees. *The Diary of Anne Frank* (1947) has been censored for being a "downer." Maya Angelou's autobiographical *I Know Why the Caged Bird Sings* (1970) has been censored for "preaching hatred and bitterness against whites" and for Angelou's description of her being raped as a child, which one censor said was pornographic. Henrik Ibsen's *A Doll's House* (1879) has been called feminist propaganda, which to some means that it should be censored. Examples, unfortunately, abound. Censorship organizations such as the National Legion for Decency, along with governing boards of public libraries and schools, often act to remove materials from classrooms and library shelves. —*Maria A. Pacino*

See also Alexandria library; American Library Association; Banned Books Week; Book publishing; *Fanny Hill, The Memoirs of*; Grove Press; *Index Librorum Prohibitorum*; Index on Censorship; Libraries, Canadian; Libraries, school; Library Bill of Rights.

BIBLIOGRAPHY

Walter M. Daniels' *The Censorship of Books* (New York: H. W. Wilson, 1954) provides a comprehensive historical perspective on book censorship. Grant S. McClellan's *Censorship in the United States* (New York: H. W. Wilson, 1967) presents a historical perspective. Mary Duncan Carter, Wallace John Bonk, and Rose Mary Magrill's *Building Library Collections* (Metuchen, N.J.: Scarecrow Press, 1974) provides information and guidelines for developing library collections. Eli M. Oboler's *Censorship and Education* (New York: H. W. Wilson, 1981) focuses on issues of censorship in educational settings. The *Newsletter on Intellectual Freedom*, published serially by the American Library Association, gives examples of censorship, along with the court cases involved. Jean Key Gates's *Guide to the Use of Books and Libraries* (New York: McGraw-Hill, 1983) presents a historical perspective on books and libraries, organization and management, including censorship. *Information Power: Guidelines for School Library Media Programs* (Chicago: American Library Association, 1988) gives standards for developing, organizing, and managing school library media programs, along with policy statements for dealing with censorship. Henry Reichman's *Censorship and Selection: Issues and Answers for Schools* (Chicago: American Library Association, 1993) is a useful resource for school media specialists offering suggestions for dealing with censorship problems. Daniel F. Ring's "Has the American Public Library Lost Its Purpose?" in *Public Libraries* (July-August, 1994) is an insightful article on many aspects of public librarianship. Phyllis J. Van Orden's *The Collection Program in Schools: Concepts, Practices, and Information Sources* (2d ed. Englewood, Colo.: Libraries Unlimited, 1995) includes policies, guidelines, and procedures for selecting library materials for schools.

Libraries, Canadian

DEFINITION: Public libraries throughout Canada

SIGNIFICANCE: Studies of Canadian public libraries have shown Canada to be a nation of quiet censors

In 1984 Canada's Book and Periodical Council announced that it was sponsoring a new initiative, Freedom to Read Week. It declared: "While there have not been any public book burnings, a quieter form of censorship exists in Canada. Often the suppression of a book is done so quickly the public is not even aware it has happened. Censorship is becoming an acceptable way of dealing with social issues of concern to Canadians."

By the late 1980's there were almost exactly a thousand public libraries and library systems throughout Canada, with more than three thousand service points. In 1988 the Canadian Library Association undertook a survey of Canadian library censorship of incomparable scope, depth, and geographic coverage. That study found that 70 percent of public libraries had some or all of the basic institutional access policies that relate to intellectual freedom. These include policies relating to selection of materials, patron objections, and donations of materials; objections forms; and support of the Canadian Library Association's Statement on Intellectual Freedom. Some 60 percent of the libraries also reported that they did not restrict the access of children and young adults to materials. Nevertheless, the study found that between 1985 and 1987 an average of one direct challenge a day to materials occurred throughout the country.

Almost as many different titles were challenged between 1985 and 1987 as there were challengers: more than 500 titles by fewer than 600 persons. The most common grounds for these challenges were sexual content, violence, and unsuitability for particular age groups. Three out of four complainants wanted the challenged materials removed from the shelves. In 86 percent of the cases, however, public library staff did not remove the offending items. The study also found that at least 10 percent of public libraries experienced incidents of covert censorship—theft, defacement, alteration, mutilation, or destruction of materials. Twenty percent of the public libraries were pressured unduly to acquire or accept materials for their collections. The only empirical study done in the academic library sector was limited to the three prairie provinces. Among school libraries there have been a small number of province-wide and state-wide studies.

Professional library publications in Canada contain many exhortations, especially to public librarians, to uphold the principles of intellectual freedom. These statements of principle include the formal statements on intellectual freedom of various local, regional, and national associations. Much of Canadian public library philosophy and practice with respect to intellectual freedom emanates from the United States. Although there have been many exhortations, there have been few empirical investigations assessing the relevance of statements of principle to professional practices. Much of the censorship research that has been done has concentrated on librarians and their practices of self-censorship.

See also Canada; Canadian Library Association Statement on Intellectual Freedom; Freedom to Read Week; Libraries; Libraries, school.

Libraries, school

DEFINITION: Library facilities designed to support the needs of students

SIGNIFICANCE: More than any other kind of library, school libraries have been targets of censorship

Attempts to censor in classrooms and school libraries have grown steadily, and the success rate of censors in having materials removed from school libraries is disturbingly high. Of the fifty most-banned books in the United States during the 1990's, forty-eight were banned in school libraries.

In Loco Parentis. No librarians are more vulnerable to censorship attack than school librarians. The reasons for this are best seen by comparing school and public libraries. Public libraries are fairly well understood as places holding all sorts of materials for all sorts of readers, including adults, children, and teenagers. Their broad mandate gives them some degree of protection. In addition, many public libraries have strengthened their position by adopting an open-access policy. Open access makes all materials in the library available to everyone regardless of age. This means that the librarians do not interfere with patrons choosing and borrowing any materials that they desire. Such policy declares that librarians will not assume responsibility for a child's selection and use of library materials. This burden is placed back on the parents, who are generally required to sign a child's borrower's card acknowledging this arrangement.

Although this approach has been effective in discouraging censorship challenges in public libraries, it cannot be used by school libraries. Most school librarians sign teaching contracts when they are hired. Such contracts contain clauses specifying that all teachers act *in loco parentis*, that is, in the place of the parents. In the case of school librarians, this principle is taken to mean that librarians must assume responsibility for all the library materials that students borrow or read.

Censorship and Selection. Censors sometimes point out that every time that librarians make decisions to include materials in a library, they are also deciding to reject other materials. In other words, what librarians call selection may be seen by others as censorship. In particular, librarians have been criticized for excluding materials that may present traditional viewpoints on, for example, the role of women in the family. There is a rebuttal to this argument. The approach of those who select is positive, that of censors is negative. Selectors look for reasons to buy or keep a book; the values, virtues, and strengths of a book overcome negative objections. Censors find reasons to reject a book, looking for any objection. There is, arguably, no flawless work, and even the Bible has been censored not for having flaws but because of the possibility that its readers might err in interpreting it. The censor's approach is to discard, the selector's to keep. If all imperfect works were discarded; there would be no libraries.

School library censorship cases occur when the interests and rights of parents, teachers, students, and school boards come into conflict. The school resource center, unlike the public library, is seen as specifically intended for the use and instruction of children and young adults. There are differing views, however, about the nature of the educational process and the role of the school library in it. Some parents regard education as a process in which young people, like empty vessels, are filled to the brim with good things. The resource center, according to this model, ought to consist solely of exemplary materials. To include books in a school library is to endorse and sanctify them, according to this philosophy.

The alternative argument, that education is a process in which children are taught to think critically for themselves, and that this is best accomplished by exposing them to a wide range of materials, is often paid lip service but seldom embraced when political pressure comes. Parents often think that children should be protected from books that are seen as harmful, and that schools should transmit traditional societal values by bringing the best in classic literature to the students.

Teachers, however, may wish to use novels and texts that are current, engaging, and sometimes controversial. School boards, for their part, must answer to diverse community concerns, and as a result, are frequently sensitive to complaints and are quick to remove offending materials. Students, caught up in the resulting controversies, may be offended by the way in which their freedom to read has been abruptly abridged by adults who ban library or classroom materials. In the center of such cases is the school librarian, who is apt to be attacked for having chosen the item being challenged, and who must defend the principles of intellectual freedom.

Defending intellectual freedom has grown increasingly difficult to do as the variety of materials used in the schools has grown, and the challenges have multiplied. The growth of the whole language approach to teaching reading, with its employment of popular children's books, as opposed to standard textbooks, for example, has resulted in a much wider variety of books being used in the schools. These new materials have become the targets of special interest groups, as well as those traditionally opposed to innovation in the schools. Most censorship in the past was attributed to the conservative right. Liberal groups who formerly may have fought alongside the librarian against censorship have begun to take issue with materials that they label as sexist, racist, violent, or environmentally incorrect.

Vulnerability of School Libraries. School librarians are also made vulnerable because of their professional isolation. Public librarians generally work as part of a team of professionals who can be turned to for support, understanding, and encouragement in times of trouble. The school librarian, however, is often the sole library professional in a school, outnumbered by classroom teachers, who may or may not have thought through the issues concerning the library and intellectual freedom, and the principal, who may prefer to run a quiet ship than to face political heat for doing what is right.

Most complaints come from parents and guardians, and most of these complaints are made individually, rather than by groups. Well-organized procensorship groups do exist, and may be consulted by parents who are not satisfied with the initial results of their complaints. Most of these groups are based in the United States, but they have been quite effective in using electronic methods of communicating their messages over the fax wires or the Internet. As a result, chapters of American organizations have been formed abroad, particularly in Canada.

Organizations concerned with limiting materials available in school libraries include Parents for Quality Curriculum, who have as their goal "to express concern about the perceived negative implications and anti-Christian slant in certain poetry, short stories, and plays that can be or are currently being taught to secondary school students." Another group, Citizens for Excellence in Education (CEE), has published a manual titled *How to Elect Christians to Public Office* as a means of placing members on school boards. The CEE and other similar organizations, such as the Rutherford Institute, the Blackstone Society, Christian Advocates Serving Evangelism, and the Western Center for Law and Religious Freedom, have gone to court in their attempt to control school curricula and the use of some reading materials. The American Family Association (AFA) filed suit against the Impressions reading series in Ohio and California. The AFA complained that the series promoted "the religion of witchcraft" or "neo-Paganism," and circulated this complaint to other states. As a result, other organizations joined the attack.

It should be noted, however, that in addition to external challenges from parents and procensorship groups, another strong source of censorship is from within the schools. Studies have shown that the classroom teachers, school staff, administrators, and volunteers, when grouped together, account for nearly half the challenges made. The combined complaints of teachers and principals practically equaled those of parents. In other words, the pressures to censor are as likely to be felt within the school as to be imposed from outside. Principals, for example, have been known to remove books from the library overnight during the absence of the librarian.

Self-censorship. School librarians sometimes hope to avoid censorship problems by sagaciously anticipating what may be objected to, and carefully excluding such materials from their purchase list. This strategy is unlikely to succeed. The variety of materials attacked in school libraries is truly bewildering. An A-B-C book was removed from a school library in Alberta because a parent complained that the reference for the letter *N*, a nudist eating noodles in Naples, was not appropriate for kindergarten students. Two volumes of an encyclopedia were removed from a rural school because they dealt with human reproduction, which the complainant saw as explicit sex. Bad language—quite often a matter of one or two words in the entire book, and words that are presented in a context of disapproval for their use—is the reason given for attempts to censor many children's and young adult classics.

Paul Zindel's novel *The Pigman* (1968) has been attacked for profanity, although there is no profanity in the book; the characters are shown using such typographical symbols as "#@%&" to represent cursing, and this was enough to draw a challenge.

Another traditional reason for complaints has been sex. Two romance novels were declared pornographic by the parent of a Texas high school student. The parent demanded that all romance novels be removed from the library. Other titles attacked for sexual content include many literary classics and many sex education books. Sex education books were removed after complaints that they contained material that dealt with such topics as alien to adolescent experience as masturbation, homosexuality, and premarital sex.

Violence is also a source of concern. Traditional fairy tales require that villains be punished, and realistic young adult novels sometimes record the violent nature of society. Some parents seek to censor such books in order to protect young readers. C. S. Lewis' *The Lion, the Witch and the Wardrobe* (1950) was criticized by a parent in Howard County, Maryland, for its "graphic violence, mysticism, and gore."

Religious Challenges. During the 1990's a new concern took over as the most common reason for censoring school materials. Books were attacked for being anti-Christian, satanic, or "New Age." There has been a strong concern with witchcraft and the supernatural. For example, Madeleine L'Engle, a Christian writer, had her award-winning book *A Wrinkle in Time* (1962) withdrawn from a Winnipeg school following complaints from parents that the book was anti-Christian and too fanciful. The Impressions reading series has been said to advocate occult and satanic topics. Any title containing the word "witch" has been apt to draw attacks, a fact that has made nearly every book in the fantasy genre a target. The materials which were chosen to serve as fuel for the bonfires lit by a Dayton, Ohio, minister of the Victory Bible Church provide an inventory of the latest targets of censors: books and materials considered satanic or pornographic, horoscopes, tarot cards, rock albums, materials related to Islam, Buddhism, Hinduism, Mormonism, Jehovah's Witnesses, Christian Science, and New Age religions.

A growing area of concern among those of the liberal left are books accused of being racist, sexist, or otherwise objectionable. *Babar* (1966) was banned in a Massachusetts school because the elephant "extols the virtues of a European middle-class lifestyle and disparages the animals and people who have remained in the jungle." Rudyard Kipling's story "How the Leopard Got His Spots" and Mark Twain's novel *Adventures of Huckleberry Finn* (1884) have been opposed because of their use of the word "nigger." *Little House on the Prairie* (1935) has been banned in Alberta because of the book's "negative stereotypes about native people." William Shakespeare's *The Merchant of Venice* (c. 1596-1597) has been banned in a large Ontario school district in response to parents' complaints that the play is anti-Semitic.

Defenses Against Censorship. The first line of defense against censorship is a clearly written collection policy. The first section of this document indicates who is responsible for selecting materials. This is generally the school board, which delegates this responsibility to the school librarian. This fact should be made clear in the policy. Also included in the first section are the criteria and procedures used in selecting materials.

The second section of the collection policy describes the procedures implemented when someone complains about a book. At the initial level, the complainant is urged to meet with the librarian or teacher and the principal to discuss the complaint. Most often the problem is solved at this point. The complaint may be withdrawn on the basis of the explanation given, or the offending book may be replaced by another for the complainant's child.

If an agreement is not reached, a more formal challenge is made. A form, which is included in the collection policy, is filled out by the complainant, and the book is reconsidered by a special committee. If this decision is also rejected, the process moves on to the school board. It is extremely important that every school jurisdiction have a carefully written collection policy. Research has demonstrated that those schools which have a policy have a better record of retaining challenged materials than those that do not have a policy.

The other important preparations which school librarians can make are to keep informed about trends in censorship; make allies of local, state, or provincial organizations that oppose censorship and defend intellectual freedom; and stay in close touch with parents, teachers, and principals. Explaining what the library does in the education system, and the importance of intellectual freedom is a vital task for the school librarian. —*Larry Amey*

See also Impressions reading series; Libraries; Libraries, Canadian; Library Bill of Rights.

Bibliography

Herbert N. Foerstel's *Banned in the USA: A Reference Guide to Book Censorship in Schools and Public Libraries* (Westport, Conn.: Greenwood Press, 1994) analyzes several major book banning incidents in American schools and libraries from 1976 through 1992; it also summarizes challenges to the fifty most banned books during the 1990's. The American Library Association *Newsletter on Intellectual Freedom* (Chicago: American Library Association, 1986-) provides a registry and description of censorship challenges and a running bibliography of intellectual freedom. Dave Jenkinson's "Censorship and Canadian Schools" in *Contemporary Educational Issues: The Canadian Mosaic*, edited by Leonard Stewin and Stewart McCann (rev. ed. Toronto: Copp Clark Pittman, 1993) is a survey. A resource for ways to deal effectively with censorship is Henry Reichman's *Censorship and Selection: Issues and Answers for Schools* (rev. ed. Chicago: American Library Association, 1993).

Library Bill of Rights

Type of work: Tract

Adopted: 1948; revised 1961, 1967, and 1980

Authors: Members of the American Library Association (ALA)

Subject matter: Statement denouncing censorship

Significance: The ALA adopted this declaration to foster the free exchange of ideas through the unrestricted use of library materials

An articulation of the basic rights of library patrons, the Library Bill of Rights asserts that the resources of any library should be for use of all members of the community that it serves; that no material should be excluded because of the origin or background of the creator; that all points of view should be represented; that libraries should challenge censorship and cooperate with individuals and groups concerned with opposing restriction of free speech; that no persons should be denied the use of a library because of their origin, age, background, or views; and that library exhibit rooms and meeting spaces should be available on an equitable basis, regardless of the views of individuals or groups requesting their use. The bill pertains not only to books, but to nonbook materials and access to electronic services.

Prior to its revision in 1967 the bill permitted librarians to remove materials they regarded as not being "of sound factual authority." Because the bill defined no standards for "factual authority," it left librarians free to remove books that they found personally objectionable, or that they believed did not serve the public's best interests. The language justifying such behavior has since been removed from the bill.

LIBRARY BILL OF RIGHTS

The American Library Association affirms that all libraries are forums for information and ideas, and that the following basic policies should guide their services.

1. Books and other library resources should be provided for the interest, information, and enlightenment of all people of the community the library serves. Materials should not be excluded because of the origin, background, or views of those contributing to their creation.
2. Libraries should provide materials and information presenting all points of view on current and historical issues. Materials should not be proscribed or removed because of partisan or doctrinal disapproval.
3. Libraries should challenge censorship in the fulfillment of their responsibility to provide information and enlightenment.
4. Libraries should cooperate with all persons and groups concerned with resisting abridgment of free expression and free access to ideas.
5. A person's right to use a library should not be denied or abridged because of origin, age, background, or views.
6. Libraries which make exhibit spaces and meeting rooms available to the public they serve should make such facilities available on an equitable basis, regardless of the beliefs or affiliations of individuals or groups requesting their use.

Adopted June 18,1948.
Amended February 2, 1961, June 27, 1967,
and January 23, 1980,
by the ALA Council.

The bill's 1980 revision broadened its encouragement of having libraries provide the widest possible range of ideas on all topics. The ALA's Office of Intellectual Freedom has condemned as unwarranted censorship such behavior as the removal of materials meeting the standards of the library's collection policy; restricting access to materials to certain groups or persons for any reason other than physical protection of the materials (such as rare books and special collections); labeling of materials that some may find "objectionable"; and restricting access of minors to certain materials, instead of relying on parents to guide their own children.

Many American libraries have adopted all or part of the Library Bill of Rights into their own internal policies. This has occasionally led to controversy over the bill's interpretation—particularly in the question of having to provide the same services to all people regardless of age.

See also American Library Association; Banned Books Week; Canadian Library Association Statement on Intellectual Freedom; Intellectual freedom; Libraries; Libraries, school.

License plates, customized

DEFINITION: Vehicular license plates with letters and numbers in arrangements requested by the licensees

SIGNIFICANCE: States censor obscene language in custom license plates

For most of the twentieth century the customization of license plates in the United States consisted solely of low-number license plates issued to political figures within a state. Such low-number plates have often been prized, and in countries that have a cultural tradition of lucky numbers, the coveting of such numbers reaches unusual heights. In Hong Kong, for example, the number nine was auctioned in 1994 for $1.7 million (U.S.). Around the early 1970's American states began issuing customized license plates to raise revenue. These states have typically restricted the combinations of letters and numbers that can be used. The criteria for disapproval have usually been taste and offensiveness, although the number of disapproved combinations has varied widely from state to state. California has fifty thousand officially forbidden combinations, Mississippi only two. Approval decisions have generally been left up to each state's motor vehicle agency. Indiana's law, which is typical, states that its motor vehicle bureau may refuse to issue any plate that "carries a connotation offensive to good taste or decency."

This governmental oversight is clearly censorship, although whether this censorship is unconstitutional is debatable. The answer depends on whether states have created a government-sponsored public forum by permitting citizens to express themselves on their license plates. The U.S. Supreme Court has consistently ruled that governments that create a public forum are constitutionally permitted to regulate only the time, place, and manner of expression occurring in that forum, not the content.

In *Wooley v. Maynard* (1977), the Supreme Court took up the question of whether First Amendment rights of expression extended to vehicle license plates. George Maynard had obscured the state motto "Live Free or Die" on his New Hampshire license plates because of philosophical objections. Convicted of a misdemeanor, Maynard appealed to the federal courts, where his conviction was overturned. The Supreme Court affirmed this reversal on First Amendment grounds, ruling that Maynard's "right of freedom of thought protected by the First Amendment against state action includes both the right to speak freely and the right to refrain from speaking at all."

This ruling did not, however, deal with customized license plates. In 1994 U.S. district judge Albert V. Bryan, Jr., extended the First Amendment protection of speech into this arena. A Virginia resident, Mark Steckbeck, had requested and received license plates bearing the expression "GOVT SUX." After receiving a complaint, Virginia Department of Motor Vehicles officials revoked the license plates. Steckbeck sued in federal court, where Judge Bryan agreed that Steckbeck's First Amendment rights to free speech had been violated by the department's action. The ruling did not attempt to set out a general principle of First Amendment protection for customized license plates, however, and it remained to be seen whether higher courts would recognize a First Amendment issue in this area.

See also Armbands and buttons; Billboards; Bumper stickers; Symbolic speech.

Licensing Act of 1662

ENFORCED: 1662-1679, 1685-1694

PLACE: England

SIGNIFICANCE: Enacted shortly after the restoration of the English monarchy, this law was designed to control unlicensed publications; it set the pattern for later prior restraint laws in the United Kingdom and the United States

England's 1662 Licensing Act indicates how powerful printing had become as a threat to established authority by the mid-seventeenth century. The immediate context for the law was the publishing of millenarian pamphlets by opponents of the religious settlement that accompanied the restoration of the monarchy after the Commonwealth period. In 1660 the English government appointed Sir John Berkenhead as licenser, and the Stationers' Company was empowered to seize unauthorized publications. In 1661 a parliamentary bill was introduced that resembled a 1637 decree from the Court of Star Chamber. This had support from King Charles II and was passed in 1662 with a two-year time limit. Control of printed matter was placed under parliamentary authority rather than royal prerogative. The act provided that nothing could be printed that opposed Christianity or the Church of England, or which would cause scandal. Various officials were designated to approve different areas of subject matter; the number of master printers in the Stationers' Company was limited to twenty and new appointments had to be approved by the archbishop of Canterbury, and the chancellors or vice chancellors of the universities were to license books. Searches for illegal presses were authorized. The act was renewed until it lapsed in 1679.

In February, 1662, Roger L'Estrange was appointed surveyor of the press; he was empowered to search for and seize all seditious material, and to arrest authors, printers, and publishers—which he did in extensive raids in early 1662. L'Estrange acted as sole licenser and had a monopoly to publish narratives and advertisements. Ejections of nonconformist clergy in 1662 caused an increase in radical publications. In June, 1663, L'Estrange published a strong attack on the radical press, which he accused of inciting people to rebel. He proposed reducing the number of presses and master printers and offering rewards. In August he was named Surveyor of the Imprimery and Printing Press.

Under L'Estrange's direction England's government maintained effective control over the press. In October, 1663, its arrest of a prominent radical publisher, John Twyn, was a major victory for the government. As an example to others Twyn was hanged and drawn and quartered for treason; his offense was publishing material maintaining that government should be accountable to the people, who have the right to revolt and take government in their hands. Twyn was one of two printers executed during the Stuart Dynasty.

When the Licensing Act lapsed in 1679 during England's Exclusion Crisis, attempts to exclude James, Duke of York, from the monarchical succession unleashed a flood of pamphlets. Whigs, who wanted to exclude James, and Tories, who sought to protect his rights to the throne, developed as political parties and produced pamphlets to defend their own positions and to attack those of their rivals. Such activities heightened tensions and raised political awareness. The Licensing Act was renewed in 1685, but lapsed again in 1694, when the House of Commons refused to renew it because of the difficulties in administering it and because of the monopolies it created.

See also English Commonwealth; Libel; Printing; Prior restraint; Slander; United Kingdom.

Licensing Act of 1737

ENACTED: June 24, 1737

PLACE: Great Britain (national)

SIGNIFICANCE: This act of Parliament gave the Lord Chamberlain control of Britain's theaters, as well as power to precensor stage production manuscripts, thereby retarding development of English drama

Although entertainment censorship by Britain goes back at least as far as the fourteenth century, formal censorship of the theater was not sanctioned by an act of Parliament until 1737. Political circumstances ushered in the Licensing Act that year. Dramatists had been finding in political controversies opportunities for renewed vitality on the stage. Prime Minister Robert Walpole, members of his cabinet, and his policies had become the subjects of many playwrights' satires and caricatures. Henry Fielding was foremost among them. In 1736 his play attacking Walpole, *Pasquin: Or, A Dramatic Satire on the Times*, opened at London's Haymarket Theater. It was a great success, and audiences cheered its vigorous attack on Walpole. The next year, Walpole successfully secured the legislation that he believed would give him some relief, while effectively ending Fielding's career as a playwright.

The Licensing Act of 1737 gave the office of the Lord Chamberlain statutory power to license both plays and theaters. It required that new plays be submitted to the Lord Chamberlain for his inspection at least fourteen days before their first scheduled performances. The Lord Chamberlain was empowered to prohibit any play from being performed throughout Great Britain. Penalties could be imposed on those performing plays in unlicensed theaters, or who did not obtain the sanction of the Lord Chamberlain. These were extensive powers, but the stage was then regarded as an influential social and political force that required government control. The pertinent criticisms of the day against stage censorship were voiced by Lord Chesterfield in his speech to the House of Lords in June, 1737, when he questioned a system that gave absolute control of the drama to one officer, while allowing no appeal against that officer's decisions.

There was no organized effort to oppose theatrical censorship in Britain until 1909, when a joint committee of Parliament investigated the issue. Precensorship of the drama in Britain was finally abolished by the Theatres Act of 1968.

See also Abridgment; Drama and theater; Fielding, Henry; Licensing Act of 1662; Lord Chamberlain; Sedition; United Kingdom.

Although The Life and Death of Colonel Blimp *had nothing to do with the buffoonish cartoon character created by David Low, the film greatly offended British prime minister Winston Churchill.* (Museum of Modern Art/Film Stills Archive)

Life and Death of Colonel Blimp, The

TYPE OF WORK: Film
RELEASED: 1943
DIRECTOR: Michael Powell (1905-1990)
SUBJECT MATTER: The career of a twentieth century British military officer
SIGNIFICANCE: Made during World War II, this satire provoked the opposition of Great Britain's top political leadership

During South Africa's Boer War Clive Candy (played by Roger Livesey) is a dashing British army officer. As the years pass, he becomes a stuffy reactionary who loses touch with modern military thinking. As Britain is drawn in to the horrors of World War II, he is forced to retire to make way for younger and more aggressive military leadership. By then, Candy is little more than a caricature of "Colonel Blimp"—a cartoon character created by David Low. At the time of the film's release, "Blimp" was a popular British slang term used to ridicule the archaic leadership in the British military establishment.

Prime Minister Winston S. Churchill, apparently believing that this film was designed to ridicule him, campaigned against its production and asked the British Board of Film Censors to reject its script. Unable to halt the film's production, Churchill tried to have it censored, arguing that its ridiculing of the military during wartime made it a "threat to the morale and discipline of the army." This effort, too, failed. Churchill's war cabinet passed the film for export to the United States—on a day when he was absent. However, more than sixty minutes were cut from the film's 163-minute length for its American distribution. Whether this was done to appease Churchill is not known, but the editing clearly weakened the film's satirical thrust. Meanwhile, the British press condemned the film as "disastrously bad propaganda."

See also British Board of Film Censors; Film censorship; Military censorship; United Kingdom; World War II.

Limbaugh, Rush

BORN: January, 1951, Cape Girardeau, Missouri
IDENTIFICATION: American radio talk-show host, television commentator, and author
SIGNIFICANCE: Limbaugh helped to reinvent talk radio by creating a national network and vigorously opposing the government's fairness doctrine

In 1988 Limbaugh launched a conservative nationwide call-in radio show which by 1996 was heard by more than twenty million Americans on more than six hundred stations. Meanwhile, he expanded his media empire to include a daily syndicated television show, a political newsletter, and two best-selling books, *The Way Things Ought to Be* (1992) and *See, I Told You So* (1993). His radio programs have been built around topical discussions of political, social, and cultural issues in which he has espoused a philosophy of self-reliance, traditional morality, and individual desire to improve one's life. He has freely attacked government spending programs, cultural policies, and social programs, combining his own interpretations of facts and events with a biting wit.

Limbaugh's popularity alarmed people in the liberal political, communications, and education communities; many people attempted to fight his influence by advocating censorship through consumer boycotts, letter-writing campaigns, and efforts to reinstate the former fairness doctrine of the Federal

Rush Limbaugh (right) interviews President George Bush on his radio program during the 1992 presidential election campaign. (AP/Wide World Photos)

Communications Commission (FCC). These efforts were discussed in many articles and editorials that tied the fairness doctrine directly to Limbaugh, causing the proposed legislation to be nicknamed "The Hush Rush Law."

Limbaugh discusses the fairness doctrine in his book *See, I Told You So*. He shows how freedom of the press has been denied the electronic press by the 1964 Supreme Court decision in the *Red Lion v. Federal Communications Commission* case, which effectively ruled that broadcasters did not have the same First Amendment protections as the print media. Through the FCC, both Republican and Democratic administrations have overtly and covertly censored electronic programming through broadcast station licensing and the fairness doctrine. In 1987, when the FCC discovered that the doctrine actually inhibited its intended goals, the doctrine was abolished. Limbaugh concludes by showing that the intended goals of political diversity have been achieved through deregulation. When his critics have demanded equal time, Limbaugh has pointed to the predominantly liberal mainstream press and said, "I am equal time."

See also Call-in programs; Fairness doctrine; Federal Communications Commission; First Amendment; News media censorship; Stern, Howard; Talk shows.

Literature

DEFINITION: General term for imaginative writing of poetry, fiction, and drama

SIGNIFICANCE: Legal decisions about a written work's obscenity often depend on whether the work is defined as literature or pornography.

The word "literature" holds a respected place in human thought and is usually being reserved for written works that artistically reflect human concerns. If a written work focuses, however, on the human concern of sexuality, and if a work includes sexual acts described in graphic detail, and if a work is not considered artistic (serious or well-written), the work may be denied the honorific term "literature" and called pornography or obscenity instead. Such written works have often been characterized by lawmakers, courts, and law enforcement agencies as a threat to the common good.

A basic reason for legal decisions to prohibit the distribution of a book that focuses on sexuality in graphic detail is the assumption that "literature" and "pornography" are mutually exclusive terms. Literature is thought to be born of detachment and some sort of truth to observable reality; pornography is thought to create obsessive involvement and to appeal to unrestrained fantasy. The view of many psychologists and literary critics is that literature aims at the contemplation of experience and the revelation of its significance, but that the purpose of pornography is to give the reader a vicarious sexual experience. The basic presumption is that if a work of literature arouses one physically, it cannot also appeal to the intellect, the emotions, the spirit—all of which are required for the aesthetic and intellectual response generated by true literature. Underlying the *Roth v. United States* decision of 1957, which argues that all "ideas having the slightest redeeming social importance" have First Amendment protection, is the assumption that pornography does not contain or embody ideas; therefore, it cannot be literature.

Erotica and Obscenity. The only literature to focus on sexuality that critics have found acceptable is usually termed erotica and distinguished from pornography by being thought to be a serious treatment of sexuality, or at least a well-written treatment. Feminist author Erica Jong has said that whereas erotica is literature that celebrates the erotic nature of human beings, probing what is erotic in the human soul and mind artfully and dramatically, pornography has no artistic value, no artistic pretensions, and serves only as an aid to masturbation.

The problem is, however, that not all readers agree on how to distinguish between literature, which probes sexuality in an artful and dramatic way, and pornography, which exists merely to arouse one sexually.

To classify a work as pornography is, by the definition, to suggest that the work's only purpose is to arouse one to sexual excitement, not to encourage one to contemplate and understand the nature of the universal human experience of sexuality. The original function of such writing (and pictures) on the walls of houses of prostitution in ancient Greece was to put clients in the mood for sexual activity. Thus, pornography has always been a genre of effect rather than one of contemplation. The problem that the courts have always had with such distinctions is how to determine what the author intended and how to identify what reader might be sexually aroused by the work. The most basic fear of the courts is that once a reader is sexually aroused by a written work, he (and it is usually assumed that only males are susceptible to such arousal) will be driven to assault someone sexually.

The word "obscenity," from the Greek, means "off the scene" and originally referred to an action in classical drama that was presented offstage because of its shocking nature. Oedipus' blinding himself with the broaches of his wife and mother Jocasta is such an act. The word has taken on a strictly legal meaning, reserved for a work that is, by law, forbidden to be published, distributed, or presented in public. Such banning is primarily typically the result of graphic sexual content. Thus, a written work might be classified as pornography because it may arouse someone sexually, but not obscene because it does not fit the current legal definition of that term. Although some readers may find graphic descriptions of violence obscene, the courts have not usually been concerned with such matters unless the violence involves sex. Depending on one's point of view, erotica may be serious literature, well-written pornography, or trashy obscenity. The slippery nature of these terms explains why disagreement over what written works deserve First Amendment protection and what ones do not has a tortuous history.

History of Legal Definitions of Literature. Since the beginning of the law's interest in literature, court cases that have established the legal definition of obscenity have involved written works about which the definition of "literature" has been strenuously debated. The first case in an English-speaking country in which obscenity law was used to restrain the publication of a written work that many critics defined as serious and significant literature occurred in 1868, when a court in

England convicted a respected publisher for the publication of a translation of French naturalist Émile Zola's novel *Germinal* (1885). The case made clear the danger of the so-called Hicklin test (based on the Obscene Publications Act of 1857 and set out by Chief Justice Cockburn), which allowed law enforcement agencies to prevent the publication of a book if its tendency was "to deprave and corrupt those whose minds are open to such immoral influences" regardless of whether the work in question had any literary or artistic merit. The problem this test created for writers and publishers was that it had the tendency to reduce the subject matter of permissible literature to a child's level.

Forbidding the publication of any written work that might conceivably influence a child badly was the law of the land in Great Britain and the United States until it was challenged in 1933 by another novel that many critics had praised as a work of serious literature—James Joyce's *Ulysses* (1922). In this case, Judge John M. Woolsey dismissed the Hicklin criterion that an obscene work might arouse lust in a child and made a judgment instead on the work's effect on the "average person." By determining that *Ulysses* did not arouse him or two of his friends sexually, Woolsey determined that it could not be banned. Although Woolsey's decision permitted the publication of Joyce's great novel in the United States and thus liberated literature from its being restricted to the level of children, it still allowed the courts to prohibit the publication of a work, even though it might be serious literature, if its effect was to arouse someone sexually. An appeal decision that upheld Woolsey's new test of the average person's response did significantly add that a written work could only be defined as obscene if "taken as a whole" its "dominant effect" was to arouse the reader sexually; it could not be banned based on objectionable isolated scenes. Judges ruled that they had read *Ulysses* and determined that the objectionable parts were relevant to the theme of the work—an important new judgment based on criteria applied to the work rather than to its possible effect on the reader.

The first banned work defined by many critics as literature to be challenged in the United States after the *Roth* decision of 1957—in which the courts ruled that whereas literature was protected by the First Amendment, obscenity was not—was D. H. Lawrence's *Lady Chatterley's Lover* (1928), which the New York Postmaster tried to prohibit Grove Press from distributing through the U.S. mail. The questions posed to literary critics Malcolm Cowley and Alfred Kazin in *Grove Press v. Christenberry* focused on whether Lawrence's novel contained serious ideas and whether the description of sexual encounters in the book were relevant to the expressions of those ideas. Based on Judge Woolsey's decision in favor of *Ulysses*, the court ruled that *Lady Chatterley's Lover* was an honest, serious book with literary merit and charged that the Postmaster General was doing precisely what the courts in the *Ulysses* and the *Roth* cases said should not be done: Lifting from the novel individual passages that he found in isolation to be obscene, while disregarding the basic theme and effect of the book. Thus firmly establishing the dominant effect criterion in addition to the average reader and the redeeming social value criteria already grounded as law, the courts were carefully trying to distinguish the word "literature" from the word "obscenity."

The distinction was further clarified by the courts in the case involving Grove Press's publication and distribution of Henry Miller's *Tropic of Cancer* (1934) in 1964. The respected scholar Richard Ellmann testified in the Chicago *Tropic of Cancer* case as an expert witness for the defense, claiming that Miller's controversial novel was "definitely a work of literary merit and importance." It was a Florida case, however, that was heard by the Supreme Court in 1964. Justice William J. Brennan, Jr., reiterated the decision in the *Roth* case that obscenity is excluded from constitutional protection but reemphasized that the portrayal of sex in art and literature was not sufficient reason to restrict it, regardless of whether it might arouse one sexually or whether it was offensive to someone, so long as the work in question was serious literature with social value.

The Court's careful effort to distinguish between literature and pornography was challenged by a novel that had always been classified as pornography, John Cleland's *The Memoirs of Fanny Hill*, a book that had been suppressed since its original publication in 1749. Literary experts in court cases in England in 1964 and America in 1966 testified that while *Fanny Hill* was not a major work of literature, such as Joyce's *Ulysses* or Lawrence's *Lady Chatterley's Lover*, it did have literary merit and was an important contribution to social history. In the English trial, literary critic Ian Watt said: "It has its place in the history of literature and not in the history of smut."

In America, the defense in a *Fanny Hill* case attempted to make the argument that if a work is well written it cannot be pornography, for it has literary value and thus has constitutional protection. Although the attorney for the prosecution argued that *Fanny Hill* was nothing but a series of sexual scenes and therefore had no value except as pornography, Charles Rembar, attorney for the defense, bolstered by the opinion of a number of literary critics, argued that the book had "elements of literary value" such as "good writing, observation of human nature, the drawing of character, psychological insight," and that it involved real people rather than mere fantasy projections. The Court's ruling that *Fanny Hill* was not obscene had the effect of removing the previous rigid distinction between pornography and literature. It now seemed that pornography could be literature rather than obscenity if it were well written and thus had some literary merit.

As a result of these important cases, the courts gradually abandoned efforts to try to define the obscene as that which had no literary worth, thus freeing themselves from the responsibility of being the national arbiters of what was good literature. The next series of legal cases that attempted to define and thus prohibit the publication of written works as obscene was not based on making a distinction between literature and pornography but rather on defining the subject matter of pornography as being one that posed a danger to a certain segment of the public—mainly women.

The Feminist Debate on Pornography. In the 1970's sexually explicit writing was condemned and its censorship urged by influential feminist critics on the argument that pornography encourages mistreatment of women. Although this gender-specific characterization of pornography had been established earlier by literary critics, it was not until the feminist movement argued that the subject matter of pornography encouraged the abuse of women that it began to take on legal implications. Literary critic Norman Holland, in a study of pornography for the Commission on Obscenity and Pornography in 1968, argued that pornography embodies only two fantasies: male sexual pleasure and male sexual domination. In a well-known study, *The Other Victorians* (1966), Steven Marcus affirms what has historically always been thought to be the case—that pornography, which Marcus defines as the fantasy world of "pornotopia," is a male world.

Based on this definition of the genre as gender-specific, feminist objections to pornography ranged from those who wished only to ban works that depict violence against women, to those who suggested that all sex actions between men and women, by nature, are degrading to women. The most vocal spokespersons for the extreme antiporn feminists have been novelist Andrea Dworkin and law professor Catharine MacKinnon, who have argued that pornography should be suppressed even if it does have serious literary or artistic value because of its focus on male domination of women. Dworkin and MacKinnon helped draft ordinances that defined pornography as "the graphic sexually explicit subordination of women." However, the U.S. Supreme Court held an ordinance that the two feminists drafted as unconstitutional. Richard Posner, an appellate judge, argued that much of the world's great literature portrays the subordination, often by force, of women by men, citing examples from the Bible, the *Iliad* (c. 800 B.C.), *Paradise Lost* (1667), and William Shakespeare's *The Taming of the Shrew* (c. 1593-1594). Posner argued that since literature is writing that survives over time, older literature may present values that modern readers may find offensive. Although the values in some works of literature may become so repulsive that the works will disappear from the body of literature, Posner argued, such a process should be left to the literary marketplace, not politicians, prosecutors, judges, and jurors. Posner concluded that if the only expression that the First Amendment protects is the expression of ideas and opinion, then much of literature would be left unprotected—a state of affairs that would be "a shocking contradiction of the First Amendment as it has come to be understood."

Literature and Ideas and Feelings. The effect on a reader of a so-called obscene passage is no different in its mechanism than the effect of a sublime or a sentimental passage. All three have the ability to break down critical detachment and directly involve the reader. Approval of one and disapproval of the other is based on a cultural distinction between those manifestations of desire that are given cultural approval and those that are not—not on an aesthetic distinction. Moreover, as Judge Posner reminded his readers in striking down the feminist-inspired ordinance against pornography, literature exists for other purposes than the expression of an opinion. It expresses hopes, fears, dreams, wishes, anxieties—in short, all that the human mind is capable of thinking and the human heart is capable of feeling.

—Charles May

See also Abridgment; Art; Book burning; Book publishing; Books, children's; Books, young adult; Books and obscenity law; Copyright law; Dworkin, Andrea; *Fanny Hill, The Memoirs of*; *Index Librorum Prohibitorum*; *Lady Chatterley's Lover*; Libraries; MacKinnon, Catharine A.; Obscene Publications Acts; Obscenity: legal definitions; Pornography; *Roth v. United States*; *Tropic of Cancer*; *Ulysses*.

Bibliography

Books that focus on the aesthetic issue of the relationship between literature and pornography include Peter Michelson, *The Aesthetics of Pornography* (New York: Herder and Herder, 1971); Albert Mordell, *The Erotic Motive in Literature* (rev. ed. New York: Collier Books, 1962); John Atkins, *Sex in Literature* (4 vols. London: Calder and Boyars, Ltd., 1970-1982); Steven Marcus, *The Other Victorians* (New York: Basic Books, 1966); Michael Perkins, *The Secret Record: Modern Erotic Literature* (New York: William Morrow, 1976); *The Perverse Imagination: Sexuality and Literary Culture*, edited by Irving Buchen (New York: New York University Press, 1970); and Morse Peckham, *Art and Pornography: An Experiment in Explanation* (New York: Basic Books, 1969). Books that deal with the relationship between literature and the law include Felice Flanery Lewis, *Literature, Obscenity, and Law* (Carbondale: Southern Illinois University Press, 1976); Edward de Grazia, *Girls Lean Back Everywhere: The Law of Obscenity and the Assault on Genius* (New York: Random House, 1992); Richard Posner, *Law and Literature: A Misunderstood Relation* (Cambridge, Mass.: Harvard University Press, 1988); and Charles Rembar, *The End of Obscenity* (New York: Random House, 1968). Books that deal with women and pornography include Angela Carter, *The Sadeian Woman: And the Ideology of Pornography* (New York: Pantheon Books, 1978); Susan Griffin, *Pornography and Silence* (New York: Harper & Row, 1981); Susanne Kappeler, *The Pornography of Representation* (Minneapolis: University of Minnesota Press, 1986); Carol Avedon, *Nudes, Prudes, and Attitudes: Pornography and Censorship* (Cheltenham, England: New Clarion Press, 1994); Andrea Dworkin, *Pornography: Men Possessing Women* (New York: Perigee Books, 1981); Catharine MacKinnon, *Only Words* (Cambridge, Mass.: Harvard University Press, 1993); Donald Alexander Downs, *The New Politics of Pornography* (Chicago: University of Chicago Press, 1989); Betty-Carol Sellen and Patricia A. Young, *Feminists, Pornography, and the Law: An Annotated Bibliography of Conflict, 1970-1986* (Hamden, Conn.: Library Professional Publications, 1987); Marcia Pally, *Sex and Sensibility: Reflections on Forbidden Mirrors and the Will to Censor* (Hopewell, N.J.: Ecco Press, 1994).

Little Black Sambo

Type of work: Book
Published: 1899
Author: Helen Bannerman (1862-1946)
Subject matter: Children's story about an Indian boy who outwits tigers that wish to eat him
Significance: Although this story is set in India (where its author lived when she wrote it) and has nothing to do with

Americans, its title's ostensible allusion to a negative African American stereotype has offended many Americans and helped to drive the book out of libraries and bookstores

The Story of Little Black Sambo is a simple, illustrated children's story about a young Indian boy who outsmarts four tigers that threaten to eat him. After Sambo saves himself by giving each tiger an article of his gaudy outfit, the tigers argue among themselves over which of them is the grandest. Eventually, the tigers chase each other around a tree so fast that they simply blur into butter, which Sambo takes home and uses on 169 pancakes that his mother, Black Mumbo, makes for him.

Long widely popular among children, this book came under attack in the United States during the 1960's for what many people claimed were its racist illustrations and generally negative portrayals of black people. In late 1964 a Nebraska school superintendent removed *Little Black Sambo* from the open shelves of libraries in his school system, on the grounds that it was inherently racist. After the book was placed on reserve and made available only as optional material, it faded from circulation.

In 1972, shortly after Bannerman's book was republished in England, *The London Times* published an essay discussing censorship of children's books that were charged with fostering undesirable viewpoints. The Central Committee of Teachers Against Racism complained that Sambo depicted a stereotypical image of African American gluttony because of a scene in which Sambo eats 169 pancakes. Right-wing activists insisted that the book did not patronize or degrade blacks despite stereotypical illustrations of flashy multicolored clothing, bare feet, and grossly exaggerated physical features.

By the 1970's Bannerman's book had disappeared from public and school library shelves. Many of the arguments for and against *Little Black Sambo* formed the basis of guidelines for determining racism and sexism in children's books. These guidelines generally included examination of the illustrations, storyline, lifestyles portrayed, relationships described, and racial or ethnic identity of the heroes and heroines.

During the era of slavery in the United States, "Sambo" was a pejorative term for a slave who was satisfied with his servitude. Since then the word has had negative connotations among African Americans. Popular opposition to the word resurfaced during the 1980's when the Sambo's restaurant chain was forced to change its name.

See also Books, children's; Libraries; Libraries, school; Political correctness; Race.

Little House on the Prairie

Type of work: Book

Published: 1935

Author: Laura Ingalls Wilder (1867-1957)

Subject matter: Novel about a family leaving its Wisconsin home in order to homestead on the Kansas prairie

Significance: This 1935 children's classic has often been banned from schools and libraries because of its stereotyped views of Native Americans

Little House on the Prairie is one of a series of books that Laura Ingalls Wilder wrote about her own experiences as a child growing up on the Kansas prairie in the late nineteenth century. The family settles there in 1870 and proceeds to build a homestead, break sod, and plant crops, only to learn that their new, hard-earned home is actually on land belonging to the Osage tribe. The Ingalls return to Wisconsin before they are removed from their land by force.

This children's classic continues to appear on banned book lists because of Native American objections to its themes and language. It focuses on the hardships endured by the pioneer family and ignores the sufferings of Native Americans. In addition, it contains such expressions as "The only good Indian is a dead Indian."

A television series of the same name was broadcast from 1974 to 1983. Its characters and plots were adapted from Wilder's books. The book regained popularity because of the television series; not surprisingly, its resurgence caused renewed complaints. In 1993, for example, *Little House on the Prairie* was banned in Thibodaux, Louisiana, and in 1994 it made the banned-book list in Sturgis, South Dakota.

See also Books, children's; Books, young adult; Libraries, school; Native Americans; Race.

Little Review, The

Type of work: Magazine

Published: 1914-1925

Founder: Margaret Anderson (1893?-1973)

Subject matter: Literary reviews and essays

Significance: U.S. postal authorities suppressed five numbers of this journal, and a state court fined its editors for publishing obscene material

Margaret Anderson, former literary editor of *The Dial*, founded *The Little Review* in Chicago in March, 1914. In the fall of 1916 Jane Heap became Anderson's coeditor; Ezra Pound was enlisted as foreign correspondent, subscription salesman, and shadow editor, eliciting contributions from his friends James Joyce and Wyndham Lewis. Pound's tenure at the magazine, from 1917-1921, coincided both with its golden age and with its problems of censorship.

The magazine first ran into difficulties when it published Lewis' graphic portrait of trench warfare: "Cantleman's Spring-Mate" (October, 1917). The New York post office stopped delivery of the issue, declaring it in violation of the Comstock Act of 1873. The magazine next encountered trouble during the publication of Joyce's *Ulysses*, which appeared in twenty-three monthly installments from March, 1918, to December, 1920. The novel's "Lestrygonians" episode (January, 1919) featured the hero Leopold Bloom's scatological ruminations on a lunchtime crowd. The New York post office banned the mailing of any further copies of the issue—a tactic repeated, on similar charges of indecency, with the publication of the "Scylla and Charybis" (May, 1919) and the "Cyclops" (January, 1920) episodes. The matter came to a head with the "Nausicaa" episode (July-August, 1920), in which Bloom is sexually aroused by a teenage girl. New York City vice officers removed the issue from the Washington Square Bookstore, and all subscriptions were confiscated by the post office. In February, 1921, despite a vigorous defense by John Quinn, a special sessions court found Anderson and Heap guilty of violating the Comstock Act and fined each fifty dollars; in addition, *The Little Review* was banned from publishing any further installments of *Ulysses*.

See also Comstock Act of 1873; Joyce, James; *New Worlds*; Postal regulations; Society for the Suppression of Vice, New York; *Ulysses*.

Liveright, Horace

Born: December 10, 1886, Osceola Mills, Pennsylvania
Died: September 24, 1933, New York, New York
Identification: American book publisher
Significance: The publishing firm of Boni and Liveright was at the center of censorship controversy during the 1920's

The founders of one of several new American publishing firms willing to gamble on controversial writers, Horace Liveright and Albert Boni began working together in 1916. Their Modern Library series reprinted great literary works, drawing acclaim from such literary figures as H. L. Mencken, but scorn from the censors. The first Modern Library selection to be censored was Andreas Latzko's pacifist novel *Men in War* (1918). Hutchins Hapgood's *The Story of a Lover* was seized in 1920, and T. R. Smith's translation of Petronius Arbiter's *The Satyricon* was attacked in 1922. The Clean Books League increased pressure on Liveright in 1923, but in 1925, he published several daring works: Anita Loos's *Gentlemen Prefer Blondes*, Sherwood Anderson's *Dark Laughter*, Eugene O'Neill's *Desire Under the Elms*, Maxwell Bodenheim's *Replenishing Jessica*, and Theodore Dreiser's *An American Tragedy*. The latter two were tried as obscene, and Clarence Darrow defended Dreiser.

Major figures in censorship and publishing history, Dreiser and Liveright worked together from 1917 through the 1920's. Although Dreiser's *Sister Carrie* (1900), *Jennie Gerhardt* (1911), and *The Genius* (1915) had previously been censored, Liveright gambled on Dreiser's popularity by reprinting *Sister Carrie* and by publishing his new works, including the play *The Hand of the Potter* (1918).

See also Book publishing; Boston Watch and Ward Society; cummings, e. e.; Dreiser, Theodore; Literature; Mencken, H. L.; O'Neill, Eugene; *Satyricon, The*; Society for the Suppression of Vice, New York; Sumner, John.

Locke, John

Born: August 28, 1632, Wrington, Somerset, England
Died: October 28, 1704, Oates, Essex, England
Identification: English political philosopher
Significance: An advocate of classical liberal ideals, Locke had a strong influence on Western ideas about freedom of expression

Locke's political philosophy offers a sustained defense of individual liberty against violation by other individuals and governments. Individual liberty, for Locke, includes freedom to believe, speak, and act as one's own judgment dictates, and the freedom to use the products of one's actions. In other words, individual liberty includes the freedoms of conscience, speech, action, and property. But since different individuals have different beliefs, respect for liberty requires tolerance for those whose views differ.

In Locke's time religious intolerance was a major social and political problem. Church and state were intimately connected, and recent English history had provided many examples of religions' using political power to suppress other religions. Locke himself was affected by the use of political power for religious purposes. He was a "Dissenter" friend of Lord Shaftsbury, a prominent politician involved deeply in religious and constitutional events of his day. Shaftsbury tried to have King James II excluded from the succession: Shaftsbury argued that James's Roman Catholicism would be incompatible with England's basic Protestantism. Shaftsbury lost, was dismissed from his position, and fled to Holland. Because of his association with Shaftsbury, Locke too was under suspicion; in 1683 he, too, fled. While in Holland Locke became acquainted with Prince William and Princess Mary of Orange, who together assumed the English throne in 1688. Locke was thus in a good position to argue his ideas for political liberty, especially those on religious toleration and a free press.

Locke's most extended discussion of freedom of conscience and speech appears in his *A Letter Concerning Toleration*, published anonymously in 1689. In the *Letter*, Locke advanced four major arguments against government suppression of beliefs, focused particularly on the issue of religious beliefs. He argued, first, that the power and responsibility to decide what to believe and how to live lies with each individual. That power and responsibility cannot be delegated to another. Second, Locke argued that because government should be the servant of the individuals and not their master, its power should be limited to protecting individuals' rights to life, liberty, and property, and that governments should be impartial with respect to what individuals believe and how they choose to live. Third, Locke argued that especially in the case of religious differences, no group can prove that its beliefs are correct, so no government is justified in forcing a particular set of beliefs on anyone.

Finally, Locke argued that government attempts to suppress some beliefs and force acceptance of others are futile: Suppression causes resentment and drives opposition underground where political rebellion is fostered, and force cannot actually cause citizens to change their minds—only evidence and argument can do that.

Locke's arguments have been historically influential. The constitutional separation of church and state in the United States is one prominent example.

See also *Aeropagitica*; Constitution, U.S.; Descartes, René; Free speech; Hume, David; Intellectual freedom; Jefferson, Thomas; Religion.

Lolita

Type of work: Book
Published: 1955
Author: Vladimir Nabokov (1899-1977)
Subject matter: Novel about a European émigré who falls in love with and seduces a twelve-year-old American girl nicknamed Lolita; when her mother dies, he takes Lolita on a cross-country jaunt, from which she finally escapes

Significance: This complex, stylish, and widely misunderstood novel survived the outrage that greeted its publication to become considered one of the great American novels of the twentieth century

Vladimir Nabokov was already a widely respected Russian American novelist when his third novel in English, *Lolita*, was published by Olympia Press in Paris in 1955. It had been rejected by five American publishers and was not published in America until 1958. Although *Lolita* is now widely regarded as a classic, in the 1950's it was regularly denounced, even generating calls for the deportation of its author. Although the novel became a best-seller, many libraries refused to keep it on the shelves. The 1962 film version, directed by Stanley Kubrick, retreated from the novel's most disturbing aspects. Later adaptations—a musical comedy by Alan Jay Lerner and John Barry and a dramatic version by Edward Albee—failed promptly.

The elegant first-person narrative of an émigré professor writing under the pseudonym Humbert Humbert is still often mistaken for an endorsement of pedophilia, particularly by those who have not actually read it. In the book, Nabokov mocks the moralizing smugness and pretensions to family values of the 1950's United States, and parodies his own difficulties in coming to terms with American culture. *Lolita* is comic, tragic, and, ultimately, highly moral, not because it carries a simplistic message, but because it painfully evokes, as Humbert notes, that "the moral sense is the duty mortals have to pay, on the mortal sense of beauty."

See also Film adaptation; Literature; Pornography, child; Sex in the arts.

London, Jack

Born: January 12, 1876, San Francisco, California

Died: November 22, 1916, Glen Ellen, California

Identification: American writer

Significance: London's radical political views and often gruesomely realistic portrayals of violence have caused his works to be frequently censored and banned

From the publication of his first story just before the turn of the century to his death less than two decades later, London rose to become one of America's most popular novelists. At various times in his career he was a believer in socialism, Social Darwinism, and racism. Most of his many writings were controversial, and many were censored. Moreover, London's constant need for money and public exposure led him to practice self-censorship and tone down his writings to placate publishers. This behavior contrasted sharply to his public utterances about the inviolability of his work, and his open contempt for censorship—which he called the tool of capitalists.

London's diverse writings were censored for a variety of reasons. For example, his early Yukon fiction, most notably *The Call of the Wild* (1903), was often censored because its raw depiction of violence upset the sensibility of polite society. The book was banned in Fascist Italy in 1929, and the Yugoslavian government followed suit by banning all of London's writings the same year. Even in countries in which his work was not outlawed, such as the United States, it was often edited almost beyond recognition. His violent and dramatic stories of the struggle to survive in the wilderness have often been reduced to harmless children's stories. In the film adaptations of his adventure stories, the rawness and intensity of his original words have usually been lost—replaced by sanitized family-film fare. Hollywood transformed *The Call of the Wild* from a brutal Social Darwinist struggle for survival into a conventional adventure story with a predictable happy ending.

London's political works were often banned by conservative governments that feared his class-warfare message. His volume of revolutionary essays and lectures, *The War of the Classes* (1905) was a modest commercial success, but it caused many bookstores to refuse to stock London's books. This book, along with *The Iron Heel*—which predicted a future struggle against fascism—caused Nazi Germany to burn all of London's writings in 1932. Although he became a favorite American author among Russians after the Russian Revolution of 1917, London's socialist views caused his work to be banned repeatedly by right-wing military dictatorships such as the Greek junta which came to power in 1967. Even when not outlawed, the message of his socialist writings has caused these works to be excluded from many anthologies of his writings published in English as well as in translation.

See also Books, young adult; Greek junta; Italy; Literature; National Socialism; Police states; Russia; Violence.

Lord Chamberlain

Definition: British office established in the eighteenth century to oversee theaters

Significance: Through their power to license theaters, holders of this office were the chief forces of censorship over the British stage for more than two centuries

The Lord Chamberlain, a court official, had among his duties to oversee, with the Master of Revels, royal entertainments. In 1737 he was additionally given wide powers of censorship over the British stage. At that time, antigovernment dramatic satires by Henry Fielding and others bothered the government of Robert Walpole, moving it to take action against entertainments it considered seditious and dangerous. Parliament passed the Licensing Act of 1737, which required the Lord Chamberlain and his Examiner of Plays to license all theaters in Britain and granted them sweeping powers to suppress any dramatic performance. An 1843 revision of the act cleared up inconsistencies in the law and made the office less subject to the bribery and corruption that by then had become common.

According to the law, the scripts for all new plays had to be submitted to the Examiner of Plays for approval at least seven days before the opening performance. The Lord Chamberlain's office could require that changes be made or could ban performance of a play outright. Once a script was approved, the actors were to perform the play exactly as written. There was no mechanism to appeal the Lord Chamberlain's decisions, and the office was not responsible to Parliament. Over the years, plays were censored in part or in their entirety for religious, political, and moral reasons. Each historical period and each individual Lord Chamberlain redefined what was considered offensive or unacceptable. Among the most commonly censored items, however, were antigovernment or antiroyal sentiments, violence, indecency (including nudity, obscene language, and references to sexual acts), and such themes as atheism and homosexuality. After public sentiment turned quite sharply against this form of censorship, the Lord Chamberlain's powers over the theater were ended by the Theatres Act of 1968.

See also Drama and theater; Fielding, Henry; Licensing Act of 1737; Master of the Revels; Theatres Act of 1968.

Lord of the Flies

TYPE OF WORK: Book

PUBLISHED: 1954

AUTHOR: William Golding (1911-1993)

SUBJECT MATTER: Novel set in the near future, when an airliner carrying schoolboys away from a war zone goes down in the sea by an uninhabited island, where the unsupervised boys revert to savagery

SIGNIFICANCE: Frequently taught in American high school and college literature classes, this book has been frequently challenged because of its apparent implication that evil is inherent in human nature

Lord of the Flies is a kind of parody of Robert Michael Ballantyne's *The Coral Island* (1858), a Robinson Crusoe-type story that was once popular with English boys. Nobel Prize-winning author William Golding's modern characters are schoolboys marooned on an island while fleeing the horrors of an unspecified nuclear war. In the absence of adult rules and institutions, their behavior grows increasingly uncivilized, until the dominant band actually begins killing boys. The novel concludes at the moment that the band is about to capture Ralph, the last civilized boy. The bloodthirsty chase is interrupted by the sudden appearance on the beach of a British naval officer, who thinks the boys are merely playing. An unspoken irony is the fact that the warship of the ostensibly civilized officer is itself in the midst of a deadly manhunt.

First published in 1954, *The Lord of the Flies* became an American campus favorite during the 1960's. Since that time it has been challenged in many school districts because of its graphic violence and occasionally profane language—but particularly because of its pessimistic view of human nature.

Many scenes in the 1962 film adaptation of William Golding's Lord of the Flies *depict the savagery to which the marooned British schoolboys revert in the novel.* (Museum of Modern Art/Film Stills Archive)

The novel has been adapted to film twice. In 1963 a black and white film version was made in Britain. A color version filmed in 1990 updated the story's setting and replaced the British public-school boys with young American military cadets.

See also Books, young adult; Film adaptation; Literature; Morality; Secular humanism; Textbooks.

Lotteries

Definition: Form of legalized gambling in which people buy chances to win money on randomly drawn numbers

Significance: Questions about whether gambling should be legalized, and if legalized, whether it should be promoted through advertising, have promoted considerable public debate

Most conservatives consider lotteries a form of gambling, and therefore immoral; most liberals consider participation in games of chance an exercise of individual freedom. The 1934 Communications Act included prohibitions on the importing and transporting of lottery tickets, post office employees becoming de facto lottery agents, broadcasting lottery information, financial institutions participating in lotteries, and states conducting lotteries. Since 1948, however, amendments to the prohibitions of the 1934 Communications Act have all but ended the original law's effectiveness.

On a worldwide scale, laws regulating lotteries vary from country to country. The United States, despite frequent discussion of the concept, had no national lottery in 1996. This is not true of other countries, in which lottery tickets have long been sold on street corners. In Spain, for example, a major national lottery organization provides charity and employment for the blind. In the United States, the citizens of each state decide by referendum and the passing of state laws whether to legalize or prohibit lotteries in that state.

Arguments in favor of lotteries include their widespread popularity—referendums on state lotteries almost always pass. States frequently emphasize their need for revenue—lotteries are called the "painless tax," which is usually earmarked for education. Lobbying by firms that market computer systems and other lottery paraphernalia has been instrumental in advancing lottery legislation.

Opposition to lotteries has come from civic leaders who see lotteries as inconsistent with the principles of good government and who have cited the inappropriateness of a government's encouraging addictive behavior such as gambling. Religious groups that view gambling as immoral have also strongly opposed lotteries.

See also Advertising as the target of censorship; Communications Act of 1934; Morality; Political correctness.

Lou Grant

Type of work: Television series

Broadcast: September 20, 1977, to September 13, 1982

Creators: James L. Brooks, Allan Burns, and Gene Reynolds

Subject matter: The staff of a metropolitan daily newspaper work under the direction of editor Lou Grant

Significance: This award-winning series was canceled during a national debate over the politics of its star, Edward Asner, and pressure against its sponsors and network

The winner of a Peabody Award and thirteen Emmy Awards, including outstanding drama of 1978 and 1979, *Lou Grant* was one of the most acclaimed television series of its era. Its realistic and thoughtful treatment of important issues set it apart from other programs; however, its liberal tone eventually fell out of step with the conservative national swing begun by the election of President Ronald Reagan in 1980.

In February, 1982, actor and liberal activist Edward Asner appeared in Washington, D.C., as part of a group raising funds for medical aid for El Salvador. Contending that people in rural areas of the Central American nation were suffering from its civil war, the group donated twenty-five-thousand dollars for relief efforts by antigovernment rebels. Right-wing critics and pressure groups charged Asner with supporting procommunist forces opposing U.S. policies and called for boycotts against the Columbia Broadcasting System (CBS) and the sponsors of his show, *Lou Grant*. Several advertisers dropped their sponsorship. Whether the political beliefs of a celebrity should have an impact on his or her craft and livelihood was debated for months. That spring *Lou Grant* began a steep slide in viewership. When CBS canceled the series in May, 1982, it cited poor ratings rather than the political controversy. Critics of the cancellation, however, contended that pressure on CBS and its sponsors had effectively censored Asner and could have a chilling effect on actors who might publicly support unpopular causes. Asner, a television star for twelve years and a seven-time Emmy winner, did not work in series television for the next three years. He blamed industry blacklisting.

See also Advertisers as advocates of censorship; Blacklisting; Central America; Chilling effect; Communism; Pressure groups; Reagan, Ronald; Television; Television networks.

"Louie Louie"

Type of work: Song

Released on record: 1956

Original artist: Richard Berry (1935-1997)

Subject matter: A boy's longing for a girlfriend across the sea in Jamaica

Significance: Although early recordings of the song are almost incomprehensible, many people believed that its lyrics were "dirty" and campaigned to have the song banned

Whatever made "Louie Louie" a target of censors is one of the classic mysteries in broadcast music history. Readily available in record stores from the time that Richard Berry first recorded the song, "Louie Louie" was denounced by school principals; it eventually attracted the scrutiny of a number of censoring agencies, including the Federal Bureau of Investigation. Many people believed that playing recordings of the song at slower speeds made it possible to hear obscene allusions to the singer's sexual exploits. The fact that a popular new recording released by the Kingsmen in 1963 was virtually undecipherable failed to dampen such popular perceptions. Later that year, the Kingsmen's recording was banned from Boston radio stations.

Although a Federal Communications Commission investigation into the song concluded that its lyrics were indecipherable and therefore not obscene, the song's banning contributed to its becoming a cult favorite. The song's fame was revived in 1978, when it was featured in the raucous film *National Lampoon's Animal House*.

Over the years many singers have covered "Louie Louie." Some of these artists have contributed new lyrics that have nothing to do with the original song.

See also Federal Communications Commission; Radio; Rock 'n' roll music; 2 Live Crew.

Lovejoy, Elijah Parish

Born: November 9, 1802, Albion, Maine
Died: November 7, 1837, Alton, Illinois
Identification: American newspaper publisher
Significance: Lovejoy's outspoken opposition to slavery led to his murder by a mob

The eldest son of a Congregational clergyman, Lovejoy taught school in St. Louis, Missouri, until he found the occupation unchallenging. He then bought a half-interest in the *St. Louis Times*, a political paper of which he became editor. Lovejoy was considered fairly "straitlaced," the influence of a strong New England Christian home. "Converted" in 1831 during a religious revival sweeping the country, he sold his interest in the newspaper in order to study theology at Princeton so that he could become a Presbyterian minister.

After completing his theological training in thirteen months he returned to St. Louis in 1833 and launched a new newspaper, the *St. Louis Observer*, for a group of Christian business leaders. Intolerant of those not sharing his Presbyterian beliefs and growing disdain for slavery, he soon had many enemies in the slave state of Missouri. Lovejoy tried to explain in his editorials that he was not an abolitionist, and that he favored a gradual solution to the problem of slavery. Nevertheless, proslavery advocates circulated handbills denouncing Lovejoy as an advocate of miscegenation and advising him to leave St. Louis. Threats of mob violence led him to move his newspaper across the Mississippi River to Alton, in the free state of Illinois.

Even in Illinois, however, Lovejoy's belief in "liberty to speak, to write, and to publish" won him new enemies as he took an increasingly strong antislavery stand and finally identified himself as an "abolitionist" in late July, 1837. Four months later a mob killed Lovejoy while he was protecting the warehouse where his press was stored.

See also Abolitionist movement; Bolles, Donald F., Jr.; Death; Douglass, Frederick; Journalists, violence against; Newspapers; Newspapers, African American; Smith, Joseph.

Loyalty oaths

Definition: Sworn promises not to be disloyal to the government
Significance: During the 1940's, 1950's, and 1960's loyalty oaths served as a form of censorship to suppress "subversive" speech by public employees, teachers, and union leaders

In the late 1940's, when many U.S. government officials and other public employees were suspected of harboring communist sympathies, the federal government and many state governments began requiring loyalty oaths to be administered to those working on the public payroll. These oaths were first used by the administration of President Harry S Truman, who issued Executive Order 9835 on March 21, 1947, creating the Loyalty Review Board to coordinate loyalty policies. The board was empowered to dismiss workers or refuse to hire anyone who might be disloyal to the government.

Initially, Congress allowed only dismissals from limited numbers of executive departments, such as State and Defense (and, later, Treasury, Commerce, and Justice). Under Truman's successor, President Dwight D. Eisenhower, the policy extended to all executive branch departments. Eisenhower also tightened the loyalty program through Executive Order 10540, under which anyone suspected of disloyalty was required to prove otherwise.

Decisions Upholding Loyalty Oaths. The first instance in which such an oath was challenged in court occurred in 1950 in *American Communications Association v. Douds*. The challenge arose from a section of the Labor Management Relations Act of 1947 mandating that in order for a labor union to benefit from national labor laws, all officers had to sign affidavits stating that they were not Communist Party members and did not believe in the party's goals. The U.S. Supreme Court, in an opinion written by Chief Justice Fred M. Vinson, ruled 5-1 that the law was in the purview of Congress through its power to regulate interstate commerce. Only Justice Hugo L. Black dissented, stating that the law violated the First Amendment's bans on regulation of speech and assembly.

The next year three more cases came before the Court challenging loyalty oaths. In April, in *Joint Anti-Fascist Refugee Committee v. McGrath* (1951), the authority of the U.S. attorney general to list organizations that were deemed subversive was declared constitutional. The Court, however, also decided that the attorney general had exceeded his bounds in including three groups, the Joint Anti-Fascist Refugee Committee, the National Council of American-Soviet Friendship, and the International Workers Order, on the list without allowing them a hearing. The Court recognized this as a due-process case and avoided ruling on any First Amendment issue.

The Court also rendered 1951 decisions in *Gerende v. Board of Supervisors of Elections* and *Garner v. Public Works of the City of Los Angeles*. The former concerned a Maryland law that required candidates running for public office to sign affidavits affirming that they had no intention of plotting a government overthrow. The law was upheld by the Court in a 7-2 decision, with only Black and William O. Douglas dissenting. In the majority opinion, Justice Tom C. Clark wrote that the law did not constitute a bill of attainder, as had been charged by the plaintiffs, but was merely a qualification for running.

Clark also spoke for the majority in *Garner*, again concluding that the loyalty oath required of public employees did not constitute a bill of attainder; nor was it an *ex post facto* law, since it involved a type of activity that had been previously proscribed for public employees. Black and Douglas, this time joined by Felix Frankfurter and Harold H. Burton, again dissented, holding that the law did indeed constitute a bill of attainder. Again, there was no discussion of First Amendment rights of speech or assembly in either case.

In 1952 the Court again upheld a state loyalty requirement. Unlike in previous instances, however, the case addressed First Amendment concerns of free speech and assembly. A teacher had been fired under New York State's Feinberg Law, which stated that membership in any organization that advocated overthrow of the government was grounds for dismissal of anyone employed by the public. A list of such organizations was kept by the New York Board of Regents. The Supreme Court decided, 6-3, in *Adler v. Board of Education, City of New York*, that it was the duty of the state to screen its employees in order to ensure that they maintained the integrity of public office. In the majority opinion, Justice Sherman Minton also held that freedom of speech and assembly were not violated because it was the prerogative of the individual to choose between public employment and organization membership. Two of the dissenters, Black and Douglas, disagreed vigorously, arguing that the law amounted to little more than guilt by association, thereby violating the First Amendment.

Decisions Striking Down Loyalty Oaths. In 1952 the Court for the first time struck down a loyalty oath. In *Wieman v. Updegraff*, the Court considered an Oklahoma law that required all public officials to take a loyalty oath and that also stated that anyone involved either knowingly or unknowingly in a subversive organization would be dismissed or denied employment. Justice Clark wrote that association alone could not be used as grounds for dismissal; rather, such association had to be coupled with a complicity in an organization's beliefs and goals.

By the mid-1960's, the Court began to look at loyalty oaths less favorably. In *United States v. Brown* (1965), it ruled the provision of the Labor Management Relations Act upheld in *Douds* to be unconstitutional. In 1959 Congress had eliminated the affidavit requirement and replaced it with a provision forbidding Communist Party members from holding union offices. The law was challenged by Communist Party member Archie Brown, who had been denied a seat on the executive board of a local branch of the International Longshoremen's and Warehousemen's Union. The Court, in an opinion by Chief Justice Earl Warren, ruled in Brown's favor. Stating that while Congress does have the authority under the Constitution's commerce clause to regulate the activities of unions and to weed out dangerous members of the labor movement, Congress must do so in a more general way. According to Warren, the revised law did not meet that requirement, thus violating the Constitutional prohibition of bills of attainder.

In 1966 another loyalty-oath statute was struck down. In *Elfbrandt v. Russell*, an Arizona law requiring state employees to take an oath that they had no affiliation with the Communist Party or any other organization with intent to overthrow the government was ruled unconstitutional. In contrast to the law struck down in *Wieman*, the Arizona law stated that only those who were knowingly involved in such an organization could be prosecuted; however, such individuals could still be punished even if they did not agree with the organization's subversive beliefs. In his opinion for the Court, Justice Douglas concluded that the oath was in violation of the First Amendment's right of association.

Archie Brown (with picture frame) leaves San Francisco's courthouse with his attorney, Richard Gladstein, after being convicted in 1962 of violating a law against Communist Party members holding office in a union. His case led to a 1965 Supreme Court decision against loyalty oaths. (AP/Wide World Photos)

The *Adler* decision was the next to be reversed. In *Keyishian v. Board of Regents of the University of the State of New York* (1967), Justice William J. Brennan, Jr., declared the New York law that had been upheld in *Adler* unconstitutionally vague and overbroad, an issue that had not been considered in the earlier case. Brennan reasoned that it would prove impossible for a teacher, for example, always to know if all statements made about abstract doctrines could be considered either treasonable or seditious. —*John B. Peoples*

See also Assembly, right of; Civil service; Communist Party of the U.S.A.; Labor unions; National security; Prior restraint; Slander.

BIBLIOGRAPHY

Ralph S. Brown's *Loyalty and Security: Employment Tests in the United States* (New Haven: Yale University Press, 1958) gives an account of the early court cases involving loyalty oaths, as does Milton R. Konvitz's *Fundamental Liberties of a Free People: Religion, Speech, Press, Assembly* (Ithaca, N.Y.: Cornell University Press, 1957). Information on the origins of the federal loyalty-oath program can be found in Richard M. Freeland's *The Truman Doctrine and the Origins of McCar-*

thyism: Foreign Policy, Domestic Politics, and Internal Security (New York: Alfred A. Knopf, 1972), and Alan D. Harper's *The Politics of Loyalty: The White House and the Communist Issue, 1946-1952* (Westport, Conn.: Greenwood, 1969). A section on loyalty oaths can also be found in Henry J. Abraham's *Freedom and the Court: Civil Rights and Liberties in the United States* (4th ed. New York: Oxford University Press, 1982).

Luther, Martin

Born: November 10, 1483, Eisleben, Saxony
Died: February 18, 1546, Eisleben, Saxony
Identification: German priest and religious reformer
Significance: The leading figure in the Protestant Reformation, Luther attacked the Roman Catholic practice of indulgences; as a result, his personal freedom was threatened and his books were burned

On October 31, 1517, Martin Luther, an Augustinian monk and university professor, posted ninety-five theses protesting the sale of indulgences by the Roman Catholic church on the door of a church in Wittenberg, Germany. Objecting to the use of German money to help build St. Peter's basilica in Rome, he maintained that Pope Leo X should divest the church of all its riches and distribute the money to the poor in the spirit of the Gospel. He also protested that the pope, who justified the sale of indulgences by claiming that he had the spiritual authority to release souls from Purgatory, had no such power. Finally, Luther pointed out that because indulgences relieved Christians of having to perform their duties according to the Gospel, there would be no incentive for them to live according to Christ's teachings.

Luther Versus the Church. Luther's objections challenged the spiritual and temporal authority of the Church. Instead of focusing on the ethical question of indulgences, the issue became who would decide the true content of Christianity—the Church or the individual believer. When Luther posted his theses, he never intended that anyone but scholars should see and discuss them. However, the theses were translated by others from Latin to German and hundreds of copies were printed and distributed. Suddenly the battle was waged in the public square outside the walls of the cloister and the university. The authority of the Church was subverted as individuals could review for themselves the points of debate and come to their own conclusions.

Shortly after Pope Leo received a copy of Luther's theses, he imposed a ban on Luther, who soon defied the ban by speaking boldly in one of his sermons. In October, 1518, Luther was summoned to Ausburg by Cardinal Cajetan, who tried to persuade him to recant his views. After Luther refused, he believed his arrest was imminent and fled from Ausburg.

For two years, Luther enjoyed a respite from Church persecution. The pope was in a difficult position. Thanks to publication of his writings, Luther enjoyed strong public support because his views concerning the social oppression and the questionable theology of the Church were popular among the people. The public perceived him as the advocate of German nationalism because he asserted that the Church was fleecing the German poor. Finally, in October, 1520, the pope issued a bull excommunicating Luther. At the same time, Luther's books were burned in Rome. After the bull was published in Germany, Luther's books were burned by Church officials in Mainz, Cologne, and Leipzig. Luther retaliated in Wittenberg. In December, 1520, he and his supporters at the university burned the papal constitution, canon law, and the works of scholastic theologians. Luther added the papal bull for good measure, stating that because "they have burned my books, I will burn theirs."

Luther Versus Holy Roman Empire. From the Church's point of view, publication of the bull settled the matter. However, Luther still had to confront civil authority. The Holy Roman Emperor Charles V was a loyal, devout Catholic. However, since the movement supporting Luther rapidly developed political as well as religious overtones, Charles was in an awkward position. Many saw Luther's rebellion against the Church as an opportunity to force the government to break ties with Rome and to keep German economic resources within Germany. Yet Charles's own political authority depended on that of the Church.

Charles ordered Luther to appear before the Diet of Worms on April 17, 1521. When Luther was ushered into the imperial court, most of his books were piled on the floor. Johann von der Ecken, the imperial spokesman, asked Luther if any of the books were his. When Luther assented, von der Ecken asked him to recant his views. Luther asked for twenty-four hours to think about the matter. The next day he repeated his refusal, asserting that his "conscience is bound by the Word of God so that I cannot and will not recant. . . . I can do nought else; here I stand, God help me, amen." The day after Luther made this famous statement, Emperor Charles denounced him as "a notorious heretic."

A week later Luther repeated his refusal to recant before the archbishop of Trier. While he was being taken from Worms, he was kidnapped by sympathizers and was taken secretly to Wartburg Castle, where he remained safe but in exile.

The Edict of Worms. Soon after Luther disappeared, Charles issued the Edict of Worms, which forbade anyone to aid or comfort him in any way. Distribution of his works was forbidden and punishable. No one could distribute his picture or teach his doctrines. All writing, including Luther's, was subject to strict censorship. All those loyal to the emperor were instructed to arrest Luther or even encouraged to kill him. Although Luther remained under an imperial ban for the rest of his life, the ban was not enforced by local princes, who were afraid of inciting trouble after the Peasant Wars had begun. Luther thus remained free for the rest of his life and the Reformation he started flourished. —*Pegge Bochynski*

See also Book burning; Christianity; Erasmus, Desiderius; France, Anatole; Henry VIII; Heresy; Hus, Jan; Latimer, Hugh; Reformation, the; Vatican; Worms, Edict of.

Bibliography

Roland H. Bainton's *Here I Stand: A Life of Martin Luther* (New York: Abingdon Press, 1950) is considered the definitive biography of Luther. Gerhard Brendler's *Martin Luther: Theology and Revolution*, translated by Claude R. Foster, Jr. (New

York: Oxford University Press, 1991) is a Marxist view of the positive social change brought about by the Reformation. *Martin Luther* (Garden City, N.Y.: Doubleday, 1961), edited by John Dillenberger, is a collection of Luther's writings from 1517-1525. *Luther and the False Brethren* (Stanford: Stanford University Press, 1975), by Mark U. Edwards, Jr., explores Luther's fiery relationship with other Protestant reformers and how he advocated censoring their books. Edwards' *Printing, Propaganda, and Martin Luther* (Berkeley: University of California Press, 1994) examines the effect of the printing press on the rapid spread of Lutheran theology.

Lyon, Matthew

BORN: July 14, 1750, County Wicklow, Ireland
DIED: August 1, 1822, Spadra Bluff, Arkansas
IDENTIFICATION: American politician
SIGNIFICANCE: Lyon was convicted of criticizing President John Adams under the terms of the Sedition Act of 1798

Matthew "Ragged Matt the Democrat" Lyon, a Revolutionary War veteran who had immigrated to America from Ireland, was elected to Congress to represent Vermont in 1797. In several published letters, he criticized President John Adams, claiming that Adams was engaged "in a continual grasp for power" and "an unbounded thirst for ridiculous pomp." Lyon's letters landed him in federal court. He became the first person tried under the Sedition Act of 1798, which made it a crime to criticize the president, Congress, or the U.S. government "with the intent to defame them or bring them into disrepute."

Lyon later wrote that his defense "consisted of an appeal to the jury of the unconstitutionality of the law," and "the innocence of the passage in my letter." However, Supreme Court justice William Paterson, presiding as a circuit judge, rejected Lyon's constitutional defense, instructing the jury to follow the law, which he declared to be constitutional. After the jury convicted Lyon, Paterson sentenced him to four months in jail and a one-thousand dollar fine.

Afterward members of Adams' Federalist Party expected Lyon to lose his re-election bid because of his conviction; however, Vermont voters returned him to office with almost twice the number of votes of his closest rival. In the 1880 presidential election, Adams lost to Thomas Jefferson, in part because of the unpopularity of the Sedition Act.

See also Courts and censorship law; Federalist Party; Jefferson, Thomas; Sedition; Sedition Act of 1798.

M

M

Type of work: Film

Released: 1951

Director: Joseph Losey (1909-1984)

Subject matter: A psychopathic killer of young girls is pursued by both police and other criminals

Significance: Ohio's banning of *M* in 1952 led to a U.S. Supreme Court decision forbidding states to censor films based on vague and indefinite criteria

M was a remake of a 1932 Fritz Lang film that had been based upon a real incident in Düsseldorf, Germany. The harrowing story of a psychopathic murderer of little girls was judged by critics to be a strong, exciting melodrama, but it was often recommended as strictly adult entertainment. Although Norman Reilly Raine and Leo Katcher's script made it clear that the girls in the story were not actually molested, the killer was depicted as a paranoid schizophrenic. In 1952 the Ohio censorship board banned the film, stating that the film demonstrated and created sympathy for complete perversion that "could lead to a serious increase in immorality and crime."

Almost simultaneously with this action against *M*, in a case against Roberto Rossellini's *The Miracle* (1948), the U.S. Supreme Court reversed its 1915 decision that films were not "organs of opinion," and instead declared them to be "a significant medium for the communication of ideas." On appeal, Ohio's state supreme court excluded *M* from *The Miracle* decision and upheld the state's ban because the film was not of a "moral, educational, or amusing or harmless character." However, in 1954 the U.S. Supreme Court cited the precedent of *The Miracle* case and reversed the decision against *M*. This reinforced the status of films, protecting them from censorship based on vague and indefinite criteria. *The Miracle* and *M* decisions determined that states could not "vest such unlimited restraining control over motion pictures in a censor."

See also Film censorship; First Amendment; Fourth Amendment; Free speech; *Miracle, The.*

The psychopath in the 1951 film adaptation of M *abducts a young girl.* (Museum of Modern Art/Film Stills Archive)

MacBird

Type of work: Play
Staged: 1967
Author: Barbara Garson
Subject matter: Political satire suggesting parallels between William Shakespeare's tragedy *Macbeth* and Lyndon B. Johnson's rise to the U.S. presidency on the death of John F. Kennedy
Significance: Because of its political content, Garson had trouble getting her play printed, staged, and advertised

Originally written as a skit to be staged at anti-Vietnam War demonstrations in the 1960's, *MacBird* evolved into a full-length play using *Macbeth* as a means of commenting on 1960's politics. When Barbara Garson was unable to find a publisher, her husband, Marvin Garson, had five thousand copies printed at his own expense. After the book sold more than 100,000 copies, Grove Press—which had earlier turned it down—became its publisher. The play had similar problems with television: WCBS-TV had planned to screen a segment of the play, but canceled the broadcast without explanation.

Staging the play was also difficult. Roy Levine, the original director, withdrew for "personal reasons" and was replaced by Gerald Freedman, postponing opening night from February 8 to February 22, 1967. There were also problems with overzealous city inspectors regarding building and fire regulations. With a cast of characters including MacBird (modeled on President Lyndon B. Johnson), Ken O'Dunc (assassinated president John F. Kennedy), and the Earl of Warren (Chief Justice Earl Warren), the play was regarded as political dynamite, dividing audiences along ideological lines. *The New Yorker*, which had never before turned down a drama advertisement, refused to advertise *MacBird*; the magazine feared offending readers. Although no violent incidents occurred in the theater, the play's audiences were vocal during its performances and in print.

President Johnson was reportedly furious about Garson's play; however, Attorney General Robert F. Kennedy—who was depicted in the play as Ken O'Dunc's younger brother, who deposes MacBird—liked it. *MacBird* enjoyed sell-out crowds; by early May its backers recouped their thirty-thousand-dollar investment. The lack of real political harassment reflected the liberalism of the late 1960's.

The title of *MacBird* was a wordplay on *MacBeth*, Lady MacBeth and the names of Lyndon Baines Johnson and his wife, Lady Bird Johnson.

See also Advertisers as advocates of censorship; Drama and theater; Grove Press; Kennedy, John F., assassination of; Presidency, U.S.; Shakespeare, William; Vietnam War; Warren, Earl.

McGuffey Readers

Type of work: Books
Published: 1836-1920
Author: William Holmes McGuffey (1800-1873)
Subject matter: Graded reading material for use in American primary schools
Significance: Although these books are believed to have been second only to the Bible in overall sales and influence on popular standards of morality and conduct, they were attacked for their heavy use of religious material, their negative images of women and minorities, and their inattention to real-world social problems

From the late 1830's until the early 1900's William Holmes McGuffey's "Eclectic Readers" were the most widely used school textbooks in the United States. To reach that position, however, they had to overcome a rocky start. Their original publisher was sued for copyright infringement by another publisher, Samuel Worcester, who claimed that McGuffey had plagiarized extensively from his own set of textbooks. McGuffey responded by removing every offending passage and adding new material. (During the Civil War, a Nashville, Tennessee, company that published the McGuffey Readers under its own imprint avoided copyright concerns because it was under the jurisdiction of the Confederate States of America.)

The McGuffey Readers became enormously popular for several reasons. Their publication coincided with the development of free public schools, and the books reflected the values and tastes of the age. The intended audience—conservative, white, middle-class Protestants—embraced the books eagerly. Chief features of the books included controlled word repetition and sentence length; phonics and penmanship exercises; selections from great writers; short factual essays on a wide range of subjects; and an emphasis on moral obedience and self-reliance.

The readers were not universally welcomed, however. They were denounced by some for their religiosity; for perpetuating sexual stereotypes and traditional roles; for ignoring, or showing obvious prejudice against, African Americans, Jews, Roman Catholics, Spaniards, East Coast intellectuals, and others; and for their seeming neglect of real social issues, such as slavery. The publishers responded to these accusations by self-censorship—-quietly removing certain passages and adding new text in later editions. What had read like theology textbooks in 1836, promoting values of salvation, righteousness and patriotic piety, evolved into secularized and somewhat sentimental children's elementary schoolbooks reflecting homogenized small-town morality.

The McGuffey Readers lost their dominance in the textbook field as society's needs and values changed after World War I. Seen as antiquated, sexist, and racist, they were gradually replaced as the demands of school curricula changed. However, in the late twentieth century the books came to be regarded with reverent nostalgia. Concern over modern illiteracy, the back-to-basics movement, and a desire on the part of some parents and educators to inculcate moral behavior in the young helped spur grass-roots enthusiasm for the readers and widespread sales. A reaction to values-neutral textbooks containing insufficient patriotism, little respect for religion, and less challenging lessons also contributed to the renewed popularity of the Readers, which were in use in schools in the Midwest and South, usually as adjuncts to other primary-level reading texts.

See also Books, children's; Copyright law; Education; Morality; Multiculturalism; Religious education; Textbooks.

Machiavelli, Niccolò

BORN: May 3, 1469, Florence, Italy
DIED: June 21, 1527, Florence, Italy
IDENTIFICATION: Italian politician and political theorist
SIGNIFICANCE: Publication of Machiavelli's writings was banned by those who regarded them as contrary to standards of ethical conduct

Machiavelli became a political figure in Florence at a young age. He became secretary to the second chancellory at twenty-nine, then spent his political career managing the day-to-day operations of the Florentine government. After losing his position in 1513, he turned to writing, often advancing arguments of a controversial nature. Although Machiavelli is most noted for his books *The Prince* (1532) and *The Discourses* (1517), he also wrote several other works and plays with the encouragement of several popes. He wrote his *History of Florence* (1525) with the benefit of a financial stipend from the Roman Catholic church, and his play *Mandragola* (1518), a story about romance and sexuality, won praise and support from Pope Leo X.

In 1559 Pope Paul IV created the *Index Librorum Prohibitorum*, a list of "unholy and dangerous books." While the pope's edict did not explicitly prohibit the reading of Machiavelli's works, it did describe *The Prince* as "unwholesome." The church reiterated its negative appraisal of *The Prince* when the Council of Trent issued its own index in 1664. However, the publication of the indexes did not prevent the spread of Machiavelli's writings. *The Prince* was republished in French and Latin. Interestingly, Cardinal Richelieu of France encouraged Louis Machon to prepare a volume analyzing Machiavelli in positive terms. Machon's thesis was that Machiavelli's writings had been misunderstood, and that *The Prince* was based on Christian concepts. However, the controversial nature of Machon's claim prevented the book from being published, despite Richelieu's backing. English translations of *The Prince* did not appear until the seventeenth century.

With the lack of an English translation of *The Prince*, Machiavelli's political theory was introduced to England through secondary writings. Failing to portray Machiavelli's thought accurately, these writings tended to dismiss Machiavelli's arguments as atheistic. Innocent Gentillet's *Against Nicolas Machiavelli, Florentine*, published in 1576, was a major influence on the English understanding of Machiavelli. Gentillet's work was an attack on the policies of Catherine de Medici, with Gentillet arguing that Catherine relied on Machiavelli's advice in carrying out violent internal policies. Reginald Pole also played a role in shaping the English view of Machiavelli's thought by claiming that Machiavelli's ideas represented the embodiment of the Antichrist.

See also Atheism; Paul IV, Pope; Richelieu, Cardinal; Savonarola, Girolamo.

MacKinnon, Catharine A.

BORN: October 7, 1946, Minneapolis, Minnesota
IDENTIFICATION: American feminist legal scholar and political activist
SIGNIFICANCE: A strong advocate of women's rights, MacKinnon has been at the forefront of the movement opposing pornography on the grounds that it is a form of sexual discrimination against women

A law professor at the University of Michigan since 1990, MacKinnon has claimed in books such as *Pornography and Civil Rights: A New Day for Women's Equality* (co-authored with Andrea Dworkin 1988), and *Towards a Feminist Theory of the State* (1989) that the law ought to treat pornography as a civil rights issue. In sharp contrast to the liberal view that pornography deserves constitutional protection under the First Amendment as a form of free speech, MacKinnon has argued that pornography is better identified as discriminatory action, the "graphic, sexually explicit subordination of women," than as obscene words or images. On this basis, she has fought to pass antipornography ordinances in several U.S. cities designed to enable women to file sexual discrimination lawsuits against those involved in the distribution or production of pornographic materials. Some feminists, most notably those involved in the Feminist Anti-Censorship Task Force, have opposed these efforts out of concern that they have the potential to lead to the censorship of feminist speech. MacKinnon's efforts did not meet with success in the United States, but they were influential in the 1992 Canadian court decision *Butler v. The Queen*, which extended the definition of "obscenity" to pornography portraying women in a degrading or dehumanizing manner.

See also *American Booksellers Association, Inc. v. Hudnut*; *Butler v. The Queen*; Dworkin, Andrea; Feminism; Obscenity: legal definitions; Pornography; Women, violence against.

MAD magazine

TYPE OF WORK: Periodical
FOUNDED: October, 1952
CREATORS: William Gaines (1922-1992) and Harvey Kurtzman (1924-1993)
SUBJECT MATTER: Satirical cartoons and features and mock advertisements
SIGNIFICANCE: By defying the censorial efforts of the Comics Code Authority, *MAD* has broached a variety of controversial topics rarely available to average comic book readers

MAD magazine was founded in 1952 by William Gaines and Harvey Kurtzman as a satirical comic book. The next year a doctor named Fredric Wertham wrote a book entitled *Seduction of the Innocent*, excerpts of which appeared in *Ladies Home Journal*, claiming that horror and pulp comics contributed to juvenile delinquency. In 1954 a Senate subcommittee led by Estes Kefauver came to a similar conclusion, leading to the formation of the Comics Code Authority (CCA). William Gaines, who at that time published such comic books as *The Vault of Horror* and *Tales from the Crypt* as well as *MAD*, testified before the subcommittee, opposing efforts to censor comic books. However, the CCA immediately began to censor the comic book industry, banning words such as "horror" from the comic book format. The CCA seal of approval was required by all the major comic book distributors of the day. In 1955 Gaines and Kurtzman responded to the CCA by transforming the comic book *MAD* into *MAD* magazine, thereby allowing the publication to escape the CCA's authority.

In the decades since, *MAD* has made a name for itself in the world of satirical literature. By depicting comic scenes that satirize the hypocrisies of the adult world, the publication created an outlet for the repressed, natural hostilities of children toward their parents. Topics satirized within the pages of *MAD* range from sophomoric depictions of vomit and mucus to such highly charged issues as racism, divorce, drug and alcohol abuse, and sexual experimentation among college students. The teenagers who read *MAD* in the 1950's and 1960's were being exposed to the same issues that faced their parents and elder siblings. According to Maria Riedelbach, author of the book *Completely Mad*, a history of the magazine, *MAD* was "the only semi-sanctioned place where kids could read about sex, divorce, alcoholism, drugs, corruption, other religions, and lifestyles then considered over the head of and therefore off-limits to healthy children."

While the magazine's format has changed little since the mid-1950's, its continued satire of adult hypocrisies has led to many attempts to ban the publication from school libraries and campuses throughout the United States. A child of censorship, born from the efforts of the CCA, *MAD* magazine has continued to challenge the boundaries of socially acceptable satirical expression.

See also Caricature; Comic books; Crumb, Robert; *Doonesbury*; Drug education; *Far Side, The*; Hypocrisy; Libraries, school.

Madison, James

BORN: March 16, 1751, Port Conway, Virginia
DIED: June 28, 1826, Montpelier, Virginia
IDENTIFICATION: Fourth president of the United States
SIGNIFICANCE: A strong advocate of free speech, Madison was among the first to propose amending the U.S. Constitution to guarantee freedom of religion, speech, and press

After helping to frame the U.S. Constitution and get it ratified, Madison served in the First Congress, in which he proposed that the Constitution be amended to include protections for the liberties of religion, speech, and press. The Bill of Rights that emerged from his proposals protected these liberties only from incursions by the federal government, but Madison would have gone further. He proposed an additional amendment that would have restrained the states from violating these rights; however, other members of the First Congress declined to recommend this amendment for ratification by the states.

After ratification of the Bill of Rights, Madison continued to be an ardent opponent of government censorship. With the failure of the Whiskey Rebellion in 1794, many government officials, including President George Washington, wished to censure the various Democratic Societies that had expressed support for the rebels. Madison vigorously opposed a congressional move to do so, arguing that "the censorial power is in the people over the Government, and not in the Government over the people." He also criticized the Sedition Act of 1798 for its inconsistency with principles of free speech.

See also Congress, U.S.; Constitution, U.S.; Federalist Party; First Amendment; First Amendment Congress; Jefferson, Thomas; Sedition Act of 1798; War of 1812.

Madonna (Madonna Louise Veronica Ciccone)

BORN: August 16, 1958, Bay City, Michigan
IDENTIFICATION: American singer, dancer, and film star
SIGNIFICANCE: In the 1980's pop singer Madonna became a role model for teenagers, but over the next decade the increasingly sexually explicit nature of her work subjected her to widespread criticism

Born into a working-class family, Madonna proved to be so talented a dancer that she won a scholarship to the University of Michigan. She stayed only a short while, opting instead to try for stardom in New York. After working as a backup singer, she landed a recording contract and released her first album, *Madonna*, in 1983. Videos accompanying this album depicted her as the controversial—but certainly not threatening—"material girl." Her next album, *Like a Virgin* (1984), however, gave a strong indication of the direction her career would take. The 1985 video accompanying the song "Like a Prayer," shows Madonna with stigmata, as she makes love to an animated statue of a black saint and dances in a slip before a field of burning crosses. This video cost her a lucrative endorsement contract with Pepsi-Cola. It is difficult to say which the

Madonna sings "Express Yourself" during her first Blond Ambition concert in Los Angeles in May, 1990. (AP/Wide World Photos)

company found most offensive: Madonna's distortion of religious symbols or the racial implications of her performance.

In the early 1990's Madonna became even more provocative, releasing the video "Justify My Love" (1990), which included sadomasochistic images, and an explicit picture book simply entitled *Sex* (1992). *Sex* sold briskly, but Madonna was accused of having crossed the line from titillation to vulgarity.

See also Advertisers as advocates of censorship; Junk food news; Morissette, Alanis; Music TeleVision; National Federation for Decency; Recording industry; Right of reply; Rock 'n' roll music; Sex in the arts.

Magazines

DEFINITION: Periodicals, often illustrated, that contain written material such as factual articles, short stories, poetry, or essays

SIGNIFICANCE: Magazines have long been the target of censors on a variety of grounds, ranging from the depiction of sexuality to criticism of political leaders

Magazines play an important role in the media of many nations. They provide a medium of expression for pieces often too long or specialized for newspapers, yet not long enough to warrant the expense of publishing a separate book. Most magazines appear regularly, usually weekly, biweekly, monthly, or quarterly. Some contain material encompassing a diverse array of subjects, such as *Reader's Digest* and *Harper's*. Often, however, magazines seek to address particular segments of society. These may include magazines written primarily for one sex (*Playboy*, *Woman's Day*), members of particular organizations (such as the American Association of Retired Persons' *Modern Maturity*), particular age groups (*Highlights for Children*), particular ethnic groups (*Ebony*), or members of particular professions (*Police*). Also, magazines may target enthusiasts of certain hobbies (*Beckett Baseball Card Monthly*), individuals who practice certain religions (*The Lutheran*), adherents of certain political philosophies (*The Progressive*), or residents of certain areas (*New York Magazine*). Though many are privately published for profit, magazines may also be produced by government agencies, colleges and universities, foundations, religious organizations, and associations.

History of Magazine Publishing. Although the precursor of the modern magazine may be traced back as far as the circulation of handwritten manuscripts in ancient China, magazines in their current forms surfaced only after Germany's Johannes Gutenberg developed the movable-type printing press in the fifteenth century. Numerous magazines appeared throughout Europe in the late seventeenth century. Among these earliest magazines were the *Erbauliche Monaths-Unterredungen*, which began in Germany in 1663, and the French *Journal de Scavans*, which was introduced in 1665.

Most early magazines were scholarly in nature and short-lived. Magazine publishers were faced with the constant obstacles of censorship, lack of funds, and small circulations. The monarchs of Europe had little tolerance for articles that criticized their governments or allies. France's *Journal de Dames*, a monthly reformist periodical published by women, was suspended twice by French censors for its attempt at fostering social and political consciousness among France's female population. In 1848 Karl Marx, having already been expelled from several countries for his controversial publications, founded the *New Rhenish Gazette* in Germany. The magazine's antiestablishment views, however, led to his arrest for inciting rebellion, though he was later acquitted. To combat this censorship, many publications were published in exile in Holland, then known for its relatively tolerant publishing laws.

Not until the late nineteenth century did magazines gain a more stable ground in Europe. Increased literacy meant increased circulation and, therefore, rising revenues. Also, the Industrial Revolution sparked an increase in the number of corporations willing to spend money to advertise in such publications.

Throughout the early twentieth century, censors continued to restrict numerous magazines that portrayed nations or their leaders in a negative light. This was particularly true of foreign publications in military dictatorships and states with one-party rule. In 1939 *Time* was banned in both Italy and Germany by the regimes of Benito Mussolini and Adolf Hitler. Later in the century, Argentine dictator Juan Peron banned a number of American magazines from being mailed through the Argentine postal service.

The first magazines distributed in the North American colonies were the *American Magazine* and Benjamin Franklin's *General Magazine*, both founded in Philadelphia in 1741. By 1800 the number of magazines had reached nearly one hundred. Notable early American magazines included *New York Magazine* and Thomas Paine's revolutionary *Pennsylvania Magazine*. In 1798 Congress passed the Sedition Act, a measure aimed at curtailing attacks on President John Adams. Although aimed primarily at newspapers that acted in support of Adams' chief rival, Thomas Jefferson, the act was also used to intimidate some magazine publishers.

As it had in Europe, the latter part of the nineteenth century brought new stability to the magazine publishing industry in America. Some of the titles started in the mid-to-latter part of the century survive today—among them *Harper's* (1850), *The Atlantic Monthly* (1857), and *National Geographic* (1888).

By the beginning of the twentieth century, the American magazine industry had come under increasing attack. This was brought about by the rise of organizations devoted to moral causes, among them advocates of temperance, and an increase in the number and influence of magazines. Numerous magazine editors and writers were accused of promoting communism during the Red Scare. *The Masses*, a socialist magazine, was banned by the U.S. Postal Office in 1917 for its antiwar themes, and a 1938 issue of *Life* magazine was banned from thirty-three cities because it contained graphic photographs of a childbirth. During World War II, antiwar magazines were continually harassed, and magazines were prohibited from showing photographs of dead American soldiers.

Magazine Publishing Throughout the World. In nearly all countries, publishers of magazines face certain restrictions. The question is not whether or not censorship exists, but rather the degree to which it exists. In several communist countries, such as China, North Korea, and Cuba, magazines are seen not as outlets of free expression but rather as organs of official propaganda. Writers are allowed to reveal their thoughts, providing that those thoughts are consistent with official policies. Before its collapse, the Soviet Union, too, used the magazine for state purposes. In the late 1980's, however, numerous independent periodicals sprang up in Russia and the other Soviet republics; often, those periodicals featured writing banned by the communist regime.

The Middle East, with its deep Islamic roots, continues to be one of the most heavily censored regions in the world. In states ranging from Algeria to the nations of the Persian Gulf, there is little tolerance for criticism of the political and religious leadership. In Saudi Arabia, for example, it is expected that magazine editors understand this; those who choose to criticize the ruling family or deviate from the teachings of Islam can face stiff punishment. Although Kuwait dropped some restrictions after its 1991 liberation from Iraq, heavy controls remained in place.

In many parts of Asia governments also exercise a high degree of power over the press. In Singapore foreign magazines including *Time* and *The Far East Economic Review* have been sanctioned for their analyses of Singaporean affairs. In South Korea, despite movement toward an increasingly free press, magazine writers and editors must be sure not to upset the military and intelligence establishments, which still exercise substantial influence over the media.

Magazine Publishing in Modern America. In modern America censorship has remained significant. In the landmark 1957 ruling *Roth v. United States*, the U.S. Supreme Court ruled that obscenity is not protected by the First Amendment. Several states also have antiobscenity legislation making it a crime to distribute certain types of material on newsstands, and most states limit the sale of publications to minors.

The U.S. Postal Service has also acted as an agent for censorship. As nearly all magazines require the second-class rate to remain profitable, the Postal Service has at times sought to revoke second-class mailing privileges. In other cases, magazines have been barred from the mail outright. Magazines such as *Esquire*, *Grecian Guild Pictorial*, *The Chicago Review*, and *Trim* have seen their postal status challenged.

During the late twentieth century, moreover, many magazine publishers increased the percentage of copy devoted to advertising to increase revenues. This has led to charges by some writers that editors practice censorship by rejecting articles that may upset their advertising clients.

—*Paul E. Tanner, Jr.*

See also Comstock, Anthony; Men's magazines; News media censorship; Obscenity: legal definitions; *Playboy*; Postal regulations; Steffens, Lincoln.

Bibliography

The Magazine in America: 1741-1990, by John Tebbel and Mary Allen Zuckerman (New York: Oxford University Press, 1991), provides a thorough history of the magazine publishing industry in the United States. Edward de Grazia's *Girls Lean Back Everywhere: The Law of Obscenity and the Assault on Genius* (New York: Random House, 1992) discusses how obscenity legislation has affected magazines. L.A. Scot Powe's *The Fourth Estate and the Constitution: Freedom of the Press in America* (Berkeley: University of California Press, 1991) gives an overview of the constitutional issues involved in both historic and modern magazine censorship. *Free Speech for Me—But Not for Thee: How the American Left and Right Relentlessly Censor Each Other* (New York: HarperCollins, 1992), by Nat Hentoff, places some of the issues of magazine censorship in the context of competing political ideologies. For an in-depth look at important Supreme Court decisions affecting freedom of the press, see *Freedom of the Press from Hamilton to the Warren Court* (New York: Macmillan, 1967), edited by Harold N. Nelson. Leonard Levy's *Emergence of a Free Press* (New York: Oxford University Press, 1987) provides information on some of the historical challenges presented to free expression in various publications.

Maggie: A Girl of the Streets

Type of work: Book
Published: 1893
Author: Stephen Crane (1871-1900)
Subject matter: Novel about the disgrace, downfall, and suicide of a young American woman named Maggie Johnson
Significance: Considered shocking in its day, Crane's novel is an early example of American naturalism

Maggie: A Girl of the Streets was among the early American novels to break from British literary antecedents and move toward the kind of naturalism that Émile Zola was then writing in France. *Maggie*'s plot is thought to have been suggested by Zola's novel about alcoholism, *L'Assommoir* (1877). In 1893, when Crane paid $869 to have eleven hundred copies of *Maggie* privately printed, most American readers of novels were innocent of many aspects of the real world. The moral priggishness and hypocrisy that pervade Crane's novel afflicted not only the common, slum-dwelling people about whom he wrote, but characterized East Coast society generally.

Despite the power of Crane's writing, *Maggie* shocked the small audience it reached partly because of Maggie Johnson's fall into prostitution and partly because of the level of language that Crane employed to depict his characters convincingly. Hamlin Garland praised the book, as did William Dean Howells, who compared Crane to Leo Tolstoy. Reviewers recognized *Maggie* as a powerful book; however, as E. J. Edwards wrote in the *Press*, the novel was notable for its "cold, awful, brutal realism." Edwards urged Crane to tell his story in a less shocking manner.

A warehouse fire destroyed most of the 1893 edition of *Maggie*. Had Crane not gained the recognition that *The Red Badge of Courage* (1895) brought him, it is doubtful he would have ever published a revised edition of *Maggie*. His 1896 edition of the book contains less profanity than the original and was toned down to meet some of the earlier objections to the book.

See also Abridgment; Literature; Prostitution; Tolstoy, Leo; Zola, Émile.

Magruder's American Government

Type of work: Book

Published: 1917-

Authors: Frank Abbott Magruder (1882-1949) and William A. McClenaghan (1927-   )

Subject matter: Civics and political science

Significance: The leading high school textbook in its field, Magruder's *American Government* became the target of attacks by anticommunist crusaders during the late 1940's

The Boston-based firm Allyn & Bacon began publishing Frank Abbott Magruder's civics textbook *American Government* in 1917. Revised annually, the book became a fixture in U.S. high schools, where it was long regarded as a straightforward explication of the American political system. During the Joseph McCarthy era after World War II, however, a number of conservative critics, notably Lucille Cardin Crain and Allen Zoll, called for the book's removal from schools because of its allegedly procommunist stance. Crain's attacks appeared in the *Educational Reviewer*, a quarterly newsletter published by the Conference of American Small Business Organizations. Zoll assailed the book in privately issued pamphlets. The criticisms of Crain, Zoll, and others included charges that the textbook promoted communism by endorsing the United Nations Charter and by referring to the U.S. post office as a practical example of socialist policy. As a result, the book was removed from schools in Georgia, Texas, and Arkansas and was the target of pressure in several other states.

After Magruder died in 1949 authorship of *American Government* was assumed by his protégé, William A. McClenaghan. Attacks on the book did not, however, stop. During the 1950's the John Birch Society, the Texas Daughters of the American Revolution, and the Minutewomen (a Connecticut group of McCarthy devotees) also began to campaign against the book. With the waning of the Red Scare, such criticisms gradually abated. During the 1960's, however, Christian Fundamentalists Norma Gabler and Mel Gabler renewed attacks on *American Government*, this time on religious grounds. They periodically managed to impede adoption of new editions of the book by Texas schools well into the 1990's.

See also Communism; Daughters of the American Revolution; Gabler, Mel, and Norma Gabler; Textbooks.

Mahfouz, Naguib

Born: December 11, 1911, Cairo, Egypt

Identification: Egyptian writer

Significance: Attacked by the Egyptian government, its internal opponents, and other Arab regimes, Mahfouz exemplifies the difficult position that politically moderate intellectuals occupy in Muslim nations

Until the 1960's Naguib Mahfouz was considered a talented but uncontroversial author and public servant. He was a member of Egypt's ruling elite whose initial enthusiasm for Gamal Abdel Nasser's revolutionary government led to his 1954 appointment as director of censorship in the Egyptian government's department of art. His reputation as a loyalist was enhanced by his publication of the "Cairo Trilogy"—*Palace Walk* (1956), *Palace of Desire* (1957), and *Sugar Street* (1957). These works (which later brought him a Nobel Prize in Literature) celebrated Egyptian modernization, winning Mahfouz widespread acclaim throughout the Arab world and further promotion in the civil service.

Meanwhile, however, Mahfouz was becoming disillusioned by the failure of Nasser's government to improve the lives of the common people. In a series of sharply critical works that included *The Thief and the Dogs* (1961), *Conversations on the Nile* (1966), and *Miramir* (1967), he traced the demoralizing effects of authoritarian government and stressed the negative consequences of modernization. In 1967 he overstepped the boundaries of governmental tolerance with *Children of Gebelawi*, a pessimistic religious allegory satirizing self-proclaimed prophets—and, by implication, Nasser. It was first printed in Lebanon and did not appear in Egypt until 1969, when it was serialized by the Cairo daily newspaper *Al Ahram*. It was immediately condemned by state officials and declared heretical by clergy at the prestigious Al Azhar University. In the ensuing furor, the novel's publication in book form was prohibited and Mahfouz was demoted to a consulting position in the culture ministry.

The Egyptian government's official reaction to Mahfouz's novel was relatively mild; however, Muslim fundamentalists and pan-Arab nationalists were permanently alienated by its liberal, humanistic values. Mahfouz was expelled from Arab writers groups, many of his works were proscribed in neighboring countries, and he was widely castigated for his support of Egypt's 1979 peace treaty with Israel and for his later defense of Salman Rushdie's writings.

Mahfouz's outspoken criticism of the coercive tactics of Muslim fundamentalists provoked further hostility. In 1989 radical Egyptian cleric Sheik Omar Abdel Rahman called him a Westernizing heretic, and some Islamic militants vowed to assassinate him. In 1994 Mahfouz was attacked and seriously wounded by a member of the Islamic Group, an extremist organization connected to Sheik Rahman. In an attempt to use this assassination attempt in its campaign against Muslim radicalism, the Egyptian government praised Mahfouz and lifted its twenty-five-year prohibition against *Children of Gebelawi*. Unwilling to be manipulated by his former censors, Mahfouz protected his reputation for intellectual independence by publishing *Arabian Nights and Days* (1995), a harsh allegorical indictment of corruption in President Hosni Mubarak's regime.

See also Death; Intellectual freedom; Islam; Rushdie, Salman.

Malcolm X

Born: May 19, 1925, Omaha, Nebraska

Died: February 21, 1965, New York, New York

Identification: American political activist and religious leader

Significance: Largely because Malcolm has been popularly regarded as violently antiwhite, his autobiography has been banned from many public schools

Born Malcolm Little to parents who were followers of the Jamaican black nationalist leader Marcus Garvey, Malcolm learned early about the tribulations of being an outspoken black man. His father, an ardent opponent of white racism, was killed in 1931 by—his family believed—the Ku Klux Klan. The death of his father precipitated the breakup of his family, and Malcolm grew up with relatives and in foster homes. In his early twenties he was arrested for burglary and sent to prison, where he discovered the teachings of Elijah Muhammad, leader of the Nation of Islam. During the 1950's he became a minister of the sect and began speaking out publicly in favor of black separatism.

Many people consider that the Federal Bureau of Investigation's (FBI) activities amounted to an abridgment of Malcolm's First Amendment rights and that they helped to "demonize" him via mass media. A special FBI Counter Intelligence Program (COINTELPRO) was established in order to disrupt black nationalist organizations. As a leading spokesperson of the Nation of Islam (NOI), Malcolm was a prime target of FBI attempts to destroy African American leadership. Most vocal African American groups and individuals had come under FBI scrutiny and harassment long before the establishment of COINTELPRO, and mass media were often used by the FBI to carry out its activities.

One element of censorship was that the mass media often focused on Malcolm's self-defense rhetoric, obscuring his broader message of black self-determination and self-reliance, thereby depicting him as a hatemonger. He was fully aware of this, asserting in his posthumously published autobiography that he would be used, dead or alive, as a symbol of hatred so that white Americans could avoid accepting responsibility for racial discrimination. An editorial commenting on Malcolm's 1965 assassination in a Wisconsin newspaper illustrated his point in declaring that Malcolm was one of the "most violent of racist leaders" of an "ultra-racist Organization of Afro-American Unity" and that "he died as he lived, in violence and bloodshed."

Undoubtedly, Malcolm recognized the power of the media in forming public opinion. Throughout his public career, he used the podium, rallies, television, radio, and the press to spread the Nation of Islam's message and—after his break with the NOI—the messages of his own Muslim Mosque and Organization of Afro-American Unity. In 1957 he founded *Muhammad Speaks*, a newspaper which was to be the positive voice of the Nation of Islam and a tribute to its spiritual leader, Elijah Muhammad. The paper's circulation outside of NOI membership helped to gain support for the organization, and Malcolm, in the larger African American community.

Ironically, the newspaper was to be used later to censor Malcolm and, some suspect, lead to his death, the ultimate silencing. He learned in 1962 that orders had been given by NOI leadership that as little as possible about him and his activities be printed in the paper. By this time, most of the African American and mainstream white press had begun to cover Malcolm's speeches and activities, inciting jealousy within the NOI hierarchy. When Malcolm's break with the Nation of Islam occurred and he was given a ninety-day silencing, he was not able to tell his side of the events through the newspaper that he had established. However, it was in *Muhammad Speaks* that calls for Malcolm's death were made; in 1965 he was silenced forever by Nation of Islam zealots.

Censorship can also be seen in the different treatments afforded Malcolm in the white and black presses. Because the white media had few reporters, black or white, covering the African American community on a regular basis, their coverage of Malcolm was sometimes skewed. They simply reported on what they saw as sensational news. For example, "The Hate That Hate Produced," a television program produced by Mike Wallace in 1959, captured and promoted the negative white reaction to Malcolm that was to plague him for the rest of his life and beyond.

The African American press tended to give a more balanced report of Malcolm and his activities, often reporting on human interest stories, such as information about his family. Nevertheless, most of the African American press, at first, self-censored by refusing to cover the Nation of Islam. Art Sears, an African American journalist, recalled how the newspaper he was working for and other African American media censored information about Malcolm and the Nation of Islam by excluding references to them and by refusing to carry a column written by Malcolm.

By censoring themselves, the African American media were responding to the climate of intimidation prevalent in the United States. The FBI had long monitored the black press for signs of disloyalty. African American newspapers and journals, such as *The Crisis* and *The Messenger*, were sometimes censored or suppressed by government order and editors were visited by agents who threatened them with treason charges.

Self-censorship can also be seen in the lack of coverage or negative treatment given Malcolm in many African American history texts published during his public ministry or shortly after his death. Years later, such texts had to include Malcolm in order to present a valid picture of the African American experience.

Civil rights leaders and organizations initially ignored Malcolm and the Nation of Islam or used them to show an antithetical position between the nonviolence preached by the civil rights movement spokespersons and the self-defense advocated by some black nationalists. In his famous "Letter from Birmingham Jail," Martin Luther King, Jr., said that he stood "in the middle of two opposing forces" in the African American community: complacency and violence. He used the NOI as an example of a violent organization. Inevitably, civil rights leaders acknowledged the strength of Malcolm's message; even the Student Nonviolent Coordinating Committee (SNCC), the youth arm of the Southern Christian Leadership Conference (SCLC), broke with the SCLC and adopted a more militant position. On the other hand, grassroots civil rights workers such as Fannie Lou Hamer embraced Malcolm, the man, even if she could not accept his methods. Paradoxically, the FBI also targeted pacifist civil rights groups and people such as King and Hamer.

In the end, Malcolm's appeal to the African American masses was too great for the media to dismiss. Actor Ossie Davis summed up the difference in perspectives between blacks and whites concerning Malcolm—a difference that was apparent in media coverage—in an interview of him by a white journalist in which he was asked the question, "Why did you eulogize Malcolm X?" He says that "no Negro has yet asked me that question. . . . Every one of the many letters I got from my own people lauded Malcolm as a man, and commended me for having spoken at his funeral."

The media's negative image caused Malcolm's autobiography to be banned in some public schools. For example, it was challenged in the Duval County, Florida, schools in 1993, and it was restricted in the Jacksonville, Florida, middle school libraries in 1994. The reasons given included charges that the book is "anti-white," "promotes violence," and is "racist."

—*Ella Forbes*

See also African Americans; Civil Rights movement; Death; Farrakhan, Louis Abdoul; Fear; Federal Bureau of Investigation; Garvey, Marcus; King, Martin Luther, Jr.; Libraries, school; Newspapers, African American.

Bibliography

The Autobiography of Malcolm X (New York: Ballantine Books, 1965) is a candid account of Malcolm's life, as told to Alex Haley. It contains Ossie Davis' remarks about his eulogy of Malcolm. Kenneth O'Reilly covers FBI surveillance of African American leaders, including Malcolm X, in *Black Americans: The FBI Files* (New York: Carroll & Graf, 1994). O'Reilly's book also discusses censorship of the African American press. *Malcolm X: The Man and His Times*, edited by John Henrik Clarke (Trenton, N.J.: Africa World Press, 1990), is a collection of wide-ranging essays, including one by Art Sears. Martin Luther King, Jr.'s "Letter from Birmingham Jail" can be found in *Why We Can't Wait* (New York: New American Library, 1964).

Man with the Golden Arm, The

Type of work: Film
Released: 1955
Director: Otto Preminger (1905-1986)
Subject matter: A drug-addicted poker dealer struggles to escape from narcotics and create a new life for himself
Significance: The production company's release of the film without an industry seal of approval led to revision of the production code

Nelson Algren's *The Man with the Golden Arm*, a novel describing the drug addiction of Frankie Machine, appeared in 1949. Proposals to film it were vetoed because the film industry's voluntary production code banned depictions of narcotics traffic. The code even banned bringing the existence of narcotics traffic to the attention of film audiences. Filmmakers also feared negative reactions from the Legion of De-

Frank Sinatra, playing a drug addict, threatens Kim Novak with a chair in The Man with the Golden Arm. (Museum of Modern Art/Film Stills Archive)

cency and the U.S. Treasury's Bureau of Narcotics.

Having successfully defied the production code with *The Moon Is Blue* in 1953, Otto Preminger filmed *The Man with the Golden Arm* in 1955. It starred Frank Sinatra and was released through United Artists without a production code seal of approval. In protest, United Artists resigned from the Motion Picture Association of America and, with Preminger, demanded changes in the code.

When state censors in Maryland demanded cuts in the film, United Artists took the matter to court. The Baltimore city court upheld the censors' decision, but it was overturned by the Maryland Board of Appeals, which ruled that the movie described—but did not advocate—drug addiction and thus could not be seen to corrupt public morals or incite the public to crime. Denial of simple discussions of ideas or practices, it indicated, would violate constitutionally protected freedom of expression.

After the success of the court challenge, the willingness of theater owners to show the film without a seal of approval, the B rating granted by the Legion of Decency, and the film's box office success, production code authorities approved changes to the code in 1956 that permitted portrayals of addiction, as well as other previously forbidden subjects, such as prostitution and miscegenation. When United Artists resubmitted the film in 1961, it was given a seal of approval.

See also Drug education; First Amendment; Legion of Decency; Miscegenation; *Moon Is Blue, The*; Motion Picture Association of America; Prostitution.

Mandela, Nelson

BORN: July 18, 1918, Mdhashe, Transkei, South Africa
IDENTIFICATION: President of the Republic of South Africa
SIGNIFICANCE: Mandela emerged from decades of imprisonment and government-imposed silence to lead South Africa to true democracy

Born into a royal African family in rural South Africa, Mandela was the hereditary successor to a chieftainship, but he renounced it in order to pursue a legal career. He attended South Africa's leading nonwhite educational institution, Fort Hare College, but was expelled after two years for leading a student strike. He then worked as a policeman in the country's rich mining industry, while studying law by correspondence. In 1942 he earned his law degree. Two years later he joined the African National Congress (ANC) and helped to found its Youth League, which soon came to dominate the ANC.

When South Africa's all-white electorate voted the Afrikaner-dominated National Party into power in 1948, Mandela was among the country's most important African nationalist leaders. Over the next decade the National Party government began developing the rigid system of racial segregation known as apartheid. It instituted such repressive measures as the Prohibition of Mixed Marriage Act (1949), the Population Registration Act (1951), the Group Areas Act (1950), and other laws designed to limit the freedom of nonwhite peoples. As a high-ranking ANC officer Mandela played a leading role in mobilizing African resistance to these laws. In 1952 he helped lead the national Defiance Campaign.

Nelson Mandela casts his vote in South Africa's first all-race elections in April, 1994; by an overwhelming majority the former political prisoner was elected the country's first nonwhite president. (AP/Wide World Photos)

To silence Mandela, the government officially banned him in 1953 under provisions of the Suppression of Communism Act of 1950. "Banning" not only prohibited banned persons from speaking out publicly, it also prohibited others from even mentioning their names publicly. It thus had the effect of censoring opponents of the government by making them disappear from public notice. Mandela's banning was lifted in 1955, but the following year he was among more than 150 Africans charged with treason and subjected to a prolonged mass trial. He and others finally were acquitted in 1961—the same year that the government declared itself a republic and left the British Commonwealth. That year Mandela led a nationwide work stoppage to protest the republic. After the ANC was banned, he went underground.

In August, 1962, Mandela was arrested after returning home from an illegal trip out of the country. A year later he was tried yet again, on charges of sabotage and treason. In June, 1964, he was sentenced to life imprisonment. He spent the next twenty-seven years in prison. Through his long incarceration his quiet courage and refusal to compromise on his convictions increased his stature, both within South Africa's nonwhite communities, and in the world at large. He became a symbol of resistance to the government and pressures for his release steadily mounted. By the late 1980's the government was prepared to let Mandela go in order to reduce tensions within the country. It offered him freedom on the condition that he publicly renounce the use of violence to oppose the government, but he refused to accept anything but an unconditional release. In February, 1990, the government finally released him unconditionally.

After resuming leadership of the ANC, Mandela spoke out strongly in favor of universal democracy and racial conciliation and led the ANC to a sweeping victory in South Africa's first fully democratic election in early 1994. The new nonracial parliament then unanimously elected him president of the country. In this position he worked to expand freedom of expression, full democracy, and human rights, and he condemned tribalism, racism, and authoritarian rule at home and abroad.

See also Havel, Václav; Prisons; South Africa; Music.

Manet, Édouard

Born: January 23, 1832, Paris, France
Died: April 30, 1883, Paris, France
Identification: French Impressionist painter
Significance: Although Manet's work was never overtly censored, constant public scorn and rejection by the government-controlled Official Salon hampered his career

Manet was a pioneering French Impressionist painter whose most famous works simultaneously undermined the dominant academic conventions of the day in both form and content. During Manet's lifetime, his work was never confiscated and he was never arrested for his artistic endeavors. Nevertheless, he endured vitriolic scorn from the public and continual rejection by the Official Salon—virtually the sole vehicle through which artists of his time could achieve financial solvency and reputation. Rejection by the Salon guaranteed loss of artistic livelihood. During most of Manet's working life, the Salon was run by the cultural ministry of the authoritarian regime of Napoleon III. Manet was known as an anti-Napoleonic sympathizer, and police files were kept on him.

In 1863 his painting *Luncheon on the Grass* was exhibited at the Salon des Refuses. The painting provoked cruel insults from press and public alike. His *Olympia* was exhibited at the Official Salon in 1865. The humiliating controversy that followed led many to view Manet as a freak. Although the artist continued to exhibit on his own—by setting up booths outside of the Salon—his career was marked by a rejection that deeply distressed him.

The fact that less than thirty years after his death, Manet was publicly celebrated as the most challenging and leading artist of his generation continues to inform the issue of political control over major cultural venues for artistic expression.

See also Art; Daumier, Honoré; Degenerate Art Exhibition; France; National Endowment for the Arts.

Mani

Born: April 14, 216 C.E., near Ctesiphon, Babylonia
Died: c. February, 277 C.E., Gundeshapur, Susiana
Identification: Persian religious visionary and founder of Manichaeism
Significance: Mani and his new "world faith" enjoyed early success under the protection of the Persian monarchy, but were later persecuted

The radically dualistic faith founded by Mani had its closest parallels in such competing religious systems as Christianity, Judaism, Zoroastrianism, and Buddhism. In the year 240 C.E., according to Manichaean tradition, Mani was instructed by angelic command to begin his public proclamation of the true faith. From the beginning he relied upon written materials (including pictorial books and translations), as well as oral communication, in the missionary process as a way of spreading more quickly the tenets of the faith and of ensuring the continuing accuracy of his message. Manichaeism spread rapidly to all parts of the Persian realm during his lifetime, thanks in part to the encouragement of the Persian royal family. However, following the death of Shapur I in 272 C.E., the still dominant Zoroastrian clergy was successful in curtailing Manichaean proselytizing. Mani himself was ultimately summoned to stand trial before Bahram I on the charge of converting a Persian notable. Upon his conviction, Mani was imprisoned and tortured.

Although Manichaeism was to spread from the Near East to Western Europe, India, Central Asia, and China during subsequent centuries, its writings and adherents were often the objects of polemic, persecution, and destruction at the hands of Zoroastrians, Christians, and Muslims.

See also Buddhism; Christianity; Islam; Judaism; Religion.

Mann, Sally

Born: 1951, Lexington, Virginia
Identification: American photographer
Significance: Mann's photographs of her own nude children contain hints of violence and sexual precocity that have inspired calls for their censorship

Mann's photographs of her preadolescent children have inspired critical interest and gained notoriety because of their disturbing suggestions of precocious sexuality. Although children have always been her preferred subjects for her photography, their nudity and implied eroticism have frequently caused concern. In published collections of her photographs, such as *Immediate Family* (1992) and *Still Time* (1994), Mann has shown her children dressing, swimming, sleeping, and lounging—often in tattered clothes or completely nude. In her best-known photograph, *Emmett, Jessie, and Virginia* (1989), the three children stare defiantly at the viewer, with an intense awareness that suggests intelligence, belligerence, and sexual provocation. Mann's photographs have generally been taken in isolated regions of Appalachia, where the presence of aged people and languid pets combine with backdrops of broken toys and rusty cars to hint at a stereotypical view of the Appalachian experience. The presence of blood and bruises on the children imply violence and sexual activity that many viewers find upsetting. Other people, however, admire her photographs for their formal elegance.

Mann's earliest published photographs seem indebted to

Georgia O'Keeffe's paintings and Diane Arbus' photographs of grotesques, but her eye for elegant composition and unique version of "family values" in her children's photographs make her artistry distinctive. Their content, however, has inspired calls for their censorship. Conservative critics have demanded an end to National Endowment for the Arts funding of artists such as Mann, whom they link unreflectively with artists such as Robert Mapplethorpe and Jeff Koons.

Mann has also been attacked by those feminists who argue that pornography objectifies women as sexual objects and thus inspires men to commit rape. By this argument, Mann has contributed to the commodification of her children and the general imperilment of women. Although Mann has never been prosecuted for her work, a local district attorney once itemized for her the photographs for which he felt he could legitimately prosecute her.

See also *Alice's Adventures in Wonderland*; *Lolita*; Mapplethorpe, Robert; National Endowment for the Arts; Nudity; Photographic film processing; Pornography, child.

Mao Zedong

Born: December 26, 1893, Changsha, rural Hunan province, Empire of China

Died: September 9, 1976, Beijing, Peoples' Republic of China

Identification: Chinese revolutionary leader and chairman of China's Communist Party

Significance: As the long-term leader of China's communist revolution, Mao was a staunch supporter of censorship in almost all areas of Chinese political, social, economic, and cultural life

A founding member of the Chinese Communist Party in 1921, and its principal leader from 1935 until his death in 1976, Mao was an uncompromising supporter of censorship and control of ideas throughout his period of control of the party and the Chinese government. In 1927 he penned his famous revolutionary slogan, "A single spark can start a prairie fire," by which he meant that ideas have the capacity to cause political and social upheaval. Acting on this belief, Mao resolutely promoted censorship of the government under his control so that there would be little or no danger of any upheaval against him or his regime.

Chinese society has long been governed by authorities who exercised tight control over any expression of ideas that dissented from either the Confucian or communist orthodoxies. Although Mao was the leader of a party motivated by a revolutionary ideology, he opposed censorship only when it was applied to him, and never hesitated to impose it on others whenever he could. Despite the communist state's revolutionary pretensions, most scholars have come to recognize the cultural continuity between the post-1949 communist regime and the earlier Chinese imperial society. Thus, the continuity of censorship under Mao might well have been expected.

Censorship also played a large role in Mao's communist ideology. As early as the 1940's, while many in the West were praising Mao's communist followers as democratic heroes in the war against the Japanese, it was already clear that Mao was exercising censorship over anyone who came within his jurisdiction. The 1942 Yenan rectification campaign made it clear that censorship was a key part of their program of thought control. The censorship of all ideas continued after the communists gained control of the mainland government and manifested itself in a particularly puritanical censorship of any sexual expression—despite Mao's own behavior to the contrary. Even with relaxation of controls after the 1970's, censorship remained a critical part of the Chinese policy through the 1990's.

At one point in the early 1960's, Mao was politically eclipsed by Communist Party associates who used the governmental censorship apparatus to prevent him from publishing his views. Ironically, it was Mao who overcame the censorship apparatus he had created by encouraging the use of wall posters during the Cultural Revolution of the 1960's. Mao was clearly a master both at censoring and evading censorship. Once he displaced his opponents, he quickly returned to his own tight control over the publication and expression of ideas throughout China.

See also China; Communism; Confucius; Cultural Revolution, Chinese; Hypocrisy; Stalin, Joseph; Tiananmen Square; Wall posters.

Mao Zedong uses national radio to proclaim the People's Republic of China on October 1, 1949. (AP/Wide World Photos)

Supported by young children, antipornography demonstrators protest the Robert Mapplethorpe photograph exhibition in Cincinnati, Ohio, in April, 1990. (UPI/Corbis-Bettmann)

Mapplethorpe, Robert

Born: November 4, 1946, New York, New York
Died: March 9, 1989, Boston, Massachusetts
Identification: American photographer
Significance: Controversy surrounding a traveling exhibition of Mapplethorpe's work spurred debate about the use of government funds to support art and led to changes in the granting process of the National Endowment for the Arts (NEA)

Mapplethorpe gained notoriety during the 1970's for his homoerotic photographs exploring New York's gay subculture. Some critics charged that his most explicit images, particularly those showing sadomasochistic sexual activity, crossed the line between "fine art" and "pornography." Nevertheless, by the end of the decade Mapplethorpe's photographs found their way into museums and uptown galleries; by the early 1980's, he was considered a mainstream photographer. His images included portraits and still-life work—particularly flower studies, in addition to homoerotic work. Some critics considered him to be the finest studio photographer of his generation. As he matured, his work became more formal and classical, and less sexual in content.

In 1988 two major Mapplethorpe retrospectives were organized, one by the Whitney Museum of American Art in New York; the other by the Institute of Contemporary Art in Philadelphia. Supported in part by an NEA grant, the Philadelphia exhibit opened in December, 1988, and was scheduled to travel to six other cities later.

Conservative politicians led by Republican senator Jesse Helms of North Carolina and civic and religious leaders decried NEA use of taxpayer money to support the exhibit. The American Family Association, the Traditional Values Coalition, the 700 Club, the Eagle Forum, and Concerned Women for America were involved in the campaign. The NEA became the focus of the debate, and the Mapplethorpe show and an exhibit of work by photographer Andres Serrano, organized by Winston-Salem's Southeastern Center for Contemporary Art, were singled out to "represent" the kinds of objectionable exhibits receiving grants.

Controversy over the Mapplethorpe show reached a fever pitch in June when the exhibit's third venue, the Corcoran Gallery of Art in Washington, D.C., abruptly canceled the show. (It was instead exhibited by the Washington Project for the Arts.) Other artists boycotted the Corcoran and pulled out of their own forthcoming exhibitions; memberships were terminated, donations canceled, and several key employees resigned.

The timing of the Mapplethorpe and Serrano exhibitions coincided with congressional hearings to reauthorize NEA funding. Senator Helms sought to attach content restrictions to grants by raising the specter of "offensive art" promoting "deviant sexuality." He called for Congress to cut NEA funding significantly and for the two institutions behind the Mapplethorpe and Serrano exhibitions to be banned from receiving further NEA grants for five years.

Helms's amendment was ultimately replaced by a compromise bill that removed the harshest penalties, requiring the NEA merely to observe bans on obscenity—as defined in the U.S. Supreme Court's 1973 *Miller v. California* ruling. The NEA budget was cut by $45,000—the exact amount that it had granted to the two offending shows. A commission was appointed to study NEA standards and peer-review procedures. Grant recipients were asked to sign agreements to abide by the terms of the new law, and review panels were asked to consider whether works of art were obscene. The law thus encouraged self-censorship by artists, institutions, and review panels.

In April, 1990, just as the Mapplethorpe show was scheduled to open at the Contemporary Arts Center in Cincinnati, the museum and its director, Dennis Barrie, were charged with two obscenity counts each: pandering and use of a minor in pornography. The latter charge was associated with the photograph "Honey," a portrait of a little girl revealing her genitals. In anticipation of legal challenges, Barrie had taken several preemptive steps. No NEA funds were used to support the Cincinnati venue, and all explicit photographs of homosexual activity were displayed in a separate room, outside of which a sign warned that persons under eighteen could not enter unless accompanied by an adult. In addition, the museum had filed a suit on March 27, 1990, in Hamilton County Municipal Court asking a jury to determine whether the images in question were legally obscene. On April 6, one day before a Cincinnati grand jury indicted the museum on charges of obscenity, a municipal judge dismissed its suit. Two days later a federal judge ruled that local police could not further interfere with the exhibit, and the museum and Barrie were ultimately acquitted of the obscenity charges.

After Mapplethorpe died of AIDS in early 1989, his photographs came to symbolize the battle for artistic freedom in America.

See also Art; Eagle Forum; Helms, Jesse Alexander; Homosexuality; Mann, Sally; *Miller v. California*; National Endowment for the Arts; Obscenity: legal definitions; Serrano, Andres.

Marching and parading

DEFINITION: Organized movements of large numbers of people who demonstrate support for a cause

SIGNIFICANCE: Marching is an old form of political advocacy that has been the target of government suppression and censorship

Marches and parades are two of the more dramatic methods that disenchanted groups employ in the exercise of free speech. Yet, despite widespread legal protections for such activities, most democracies have a long and undistinguished history of attempts to suppress marching and parading by people expressing unorthodox viewpoints and demanding policy changes. In the United States, the First Amendment explicitly protects the freedoms of speech and "the right of the people peaceably to assemble, and to petition the Government for a redress of grievances." Despite the First Amendment's inarguable clarity, the amendment has functioned less as an unquestioned guarantee against censorship of expression than as the starting point of an enduring struggle between government officials, ever anxious about their authority, and those agitating for social change and unpopular causes.

Examples of Government Suppression. Governments assert, and courts routinely recognize, that the government has a legitimate interest in maintaining public peace and order, and in the protection of the rights of citizens from unreasonable interference. These objectives have served on occasion as pretexts for government suppression of marches and parades. The history of the U.S. labor and civil rights movements provide some telling examples. The largest labor demonstration in New York City's history took place in January, 1874, when a parade of unemployed marched on City Hall demanding a relief program. Forbidden by authorities to remain there, the paraders moved to Tompkins Square. Without warning, the police violently dispersed the demonstrators. Women and children were among the hundreds injured; several men were given prison sentences for allegedly attacking the police. In March, 1930, more than one hundred thousand unemployed people gathered in New York's Union Square, and in an attack reminiscent of Tompkins Square fifty-six years earlier, the police, twenty-five thousand strong, mounted a full-scale attack on the marchers. This was a time when authorities reflexively viewed any mass movement of unemployed as a communist-inspired step toward overthrow of the government.

In what became known as the Bonus Army March of 1932, twenty-five thousand veterans of World War I, in economic distress and frustrated at their inability to get the U.S. government to pay them a cash bonus promised in 1923, marched on Washington, D.C. Carrying signs ("Heroes in 1917—Bums in 1932") and accompanied by wives and children, the veterans camped on public grounds near the Capitol building, where they remained for several weeks while their leaders actively lobbied Congress to meet their demands. After two veterans were shot and killed by local police for refusing to leave the Capitol building, President Herbert Hoover ordered the U.S. Army to evict the veterans from their encampments. On July 28, 1932, Army troops led by General Douglas MacArthur drove the veterans from their shantytown.

In the 1960's, the Civil Rights movement was in full swing, and the federal government was called upon to protect blacks from Southern state and local authorities who sought to maintain their segregated way of life. In short, the threat to peace and order came not from those leading peaceful marches but from the local and state authorities who were violently breaking up those marches or who were allowing hooligans to use violence against the marchers. The federal government was faced with the choice of helping people in their cause or of supporting, through omission, violations of the First Amendment by state and local governments.

For example, learning of planned mass demonstrations by blacks, city officials in Birmingham, Alabama, obtained a court injunction against marching. The marches went on without permission. City police responded with violence as thousands were arrested in marches that continued from April through May. Only after the threat of federal troop intervention on behalf of the marchers did civic leaders consent to desegregate downtown stores. Martin Luther King, Jr., led two of the most famous political marches in American history from Selma to Montgomery, Alabama, to press the government for equal voting rights for blacks. The first of these voting rights marches saw about five hundred marchers attacked by mounted state troopers using tear gas and nightsticks. The second, three weeks later, drew thirty thousand marchers, national media attention, and the protection of federal troops. Five months later the Voting Rights Act became law.

Constitutional Protections of Marches and Parades. Beginning with *Hague v. Congress of Industrial Organizations* in 1939, when the Supreme Court first declared that public streets and parks were "public forums" that must accommodate free speech activities, the Supreme Court has repeatedly affirmed that marching and parading to express viewpoints enjoys broad constitutional protection. Authorities may impose reasonable regulations affecting the use of public parks, streets, and sidewalks, but they may not deny the use of these forums to some groups while allowing it for others. For example, the Supreme Court allowed a city to forbid noisy marches near schools when classes were in session. When black students marching to the State House in Columbia, South Carolina, in March of 1961 to protest nonviolently against race discrimination were charged with breach of peace, however, the Supreme Court overturned their convictions in *Edwards v. South Carolina* (1963), saying that the marchers were exercising "basic constitutional rights in their most pristine and classic form." Another mass protest against race segregation led to an important Supreme Court ruling in *Cox v. Louisiana* (1965). In the *Cox* case, Baton Rouge police, using tear gas, broke up a peaceful march of civil rights demonstrators near the city's courthouse. Mr. Cox was charged with breach of peace, and at his trial the judge ruled that the mere presence of fifteen hundred blacks in the downtown business district constituted "an inherent breach of the peace." The Supreme Court overturned his conviction in part because city officials enjoyed "unfettered discretion" in the "regulation of the use of the streets for peaceful parades and meetings."

To avoid charges of "unfettered" discretion, local authorities began to require a permit before allowing a public march or parade. Such regulation shows that authorities' discretion is not unfettered, because the regulations do not allow parades and demonstrations by default and disallow them only when authorities are displeased by the nature of the parade or demonstration. Permits may regulate the use of public space, but the Court struck down permit procedures used as a pretext for government censorship of unpopular groups in *Forsyth County, Ga. v. Nationalist Movement* in 1992.

Constitutional problems arise when marchers express controversial or offensive political views that may incite violence, directly interfere with the rights of others, or disrupt important operations of government. The Supreme Court must in such cases balance freedom of speech against valid state interests in maintaining public safety. In *Adderly v. Florida* (1966) the Supreme Court let stand the trespass convictions of several college students who marched from campus to the county jail to protest the arrest of their classmates the night before. The Court ruled that the students' First Amendment rights did not allow them to directly interfere with the operation of the jail by blocking the entrances. Generally, however, the Court has protected even extremely offensive speech, as in *Brandenburg v. Ohio* (1969). Even the American Nazi Party won the right to parade through Skokie, Illinois, a community with a large number of Jewish people, several of whom had survived Nazi concentration camps in World War II.

Parades are a kind of march. Celebratory in nature, parades typically are not designed to press particular political demands upon government. Nevertheless, insofar as they have a theme, parades are constitutionally protected forms of expression. The Supreme Court ruled in *Hurley et al. v. Irish-American Gay, Lesbian and Bisexual Group of Boston et al.* (1995) that the private organizers of the St. Patrick's Day Parade could not be forced by the state of Massachusetts to include a group whose message the organizers deemed antithetical to the theme of their parade. The First Amendment, they said, protects paraders from government interference with the message they seek to communicate by means of the parade.

—Philip Zampini

See also Assembly, right of; First Amendment; Skokie, Illinois, Nazi march; Street oratory.

Bibliography

William Cohen and David Danelski's *Constitutional Law* (3d ed. Westbury, N.Y.: Foundation Press, 1994) discusses court cases. Madeleine Adamson and Seth Borgos' *This Mighty Dream* (Boston: Routledge and Kegan Paul, 1984) offers accounts of governmental repression of labor and civil rights protests. Richard O. Boyer and Herbert Morris' *Labor's Untold Story* (New York: E. P. Dutton, 1973) also tells of the labor movement's thwarted attempts to assemble peaceably. Arthur I. Waskow compares the effectiveness of marches to other forms of nonviolent protest in *From Race Riot to Sit-In* (New York: Doubleday, 1966).

Marcuse, Herbert

Born: July 19, 1898, Berlin, Germany

Died: July 29, 1979, Starnberg, West Germany

Identification: German American political philosopher and leading New Left spokesperson

Significance: Because Marcuse criticized the United States as repressive and defended the disruption of establishment spokesmen, a campaign was launched to dislodge him from his university teaching position

Marcuse's political philosophy was essentially a synthesis of the ideas of Karl Marx, Sigmund Freud, and G. W. F. Hegel. From this position he took his stand against fascism—as it appeared in Europe from the 1920's until the end of World War II, and later in the allegedly fascist aspects of modern industrial society. In several works, including *Eros and Civilization* (1955) and *One-Dimensional Man* (1964), Marcuse attacked advanced industrial society as repressive. In *Soviet Marxism* (1958) he was equally hostile to bureaucratic communism.

In 1965 Marcuse joined the faculty of the University of California at San Diego and published his controversial essay "Repressive Tolerance." It criticized as repressive a United States that neither heard dissenting voices nor considered alternatives to the establishment view. The correct response to this oppression, argued Marcuse, was to disrupt and obstruct establishment persons.

Marcuse came under attack during the 1960's for allegedly influencing campus rebellions. In 1968 he briefly disappeared from his home after receiving a threatening letter from the Ku Klux Klan, and an unsuccessful movement was begun to dislodge him from his teaching position. The following year he dedicated *An Essay on Liberation* (1969) to the student militants who he hoped would effect the revolution that he deemed justifiable against an oppressive society.

See also Communism; Davis, Angela; Intellectual freedom; Ku Klux Klan; Marx, Karl; Universities.

Martí, José Julián

BORN: January 28, 1853, Havana, Cuba
DIED: May 19, 1895, Dos Ríos, Cuba
IDENTIFICATION: Cuban nationalist leader
SIGNIFICANCE: Deported from Cuba because of his political views, Martí used the press and periodicals to champion his vision of a free Cuba and an international Spanish American culture

Cuban patriot hero José Martí. (Library of Congress)

As a boy growing up in Havana, Martí came under the influence of the revolutionary poet Rafael María de Mendive. By the age of seventeen he was imprisoned for writing a treasonous letter to a friend. After being deported to Spain, he began a career of publicizing the call for Cuban liberty. He wrote and taught in Spain, Mexico, and Guatemala before returning to Cuba with his wife in 1878.

Deported again (for conspiracy) in 1879, Martí settled in New York City in 1880, where he translated, taught, and wrote newspaper articles for both Spanish-language and English-language presses throughout the Americas. He taught that liberty was the right of every man to think and speak honestly. He envisioned not only a free Cuba but a united culture of all the Americas based on peaceful coexistence and mutual respect. He cautioned against allowing the United States to dominate its southern neighbors. After returning to his homeland again to fight for a free Cuba in 1895, he died in battle. He was later generally hailed to be Cuba's most important national hero of the nineteenth century.

See also Colonialism; Cuba; Radio Martí; Spanish-American War; Spanish Empire.

Marx, Karl

BORN: May 5, 1818, Trier, Germany
DIED: March 14, 1883, London, England
IDENTIFICATION: German economic philosopher
SIGNIFICANCE: Marx's revolutionary political and economic theories, which formed the basis for modern communism, caused many different government regimes to ban his writings

Marx asserted that real freedom of expression could only be realized in a future society in which economic power would no longer destroy the essence of formal freedoms. He thus believed that formal freedom of the press, though clearly preferable to censorship, was seriously undermined by the concentration of economic power within society. There was, therefore, limited value in having the right to express ideas without the practical means to do so. Marx argued that those who owned the material means of production also owned the means of producing ideas. The fate of his own writings during his lifetime confirmed this belief, for he often found the production and distribution of his ideas restricted by his lack of money. In addition, he often found his writings suppressed by hostile governments.

Censorship During Marx's Lifetime. On October 15, 1842, the young Marx took over editorship of the newspaper *Rheinische Zeitung*. It had been the liberal democratic publication of a group of young merchants, bankers, and industrialists. Under his editorship, it began printing fierce criticisms of German governments. After Marx's year as editor, the paper was suppressed and Marx himself had to go to Paris. In 1845 he contributed articles to the Paris based radical magazine *Vorwarts*. After pressure from the Prussian foreign office, this publication was outlawed and Marx was expelled from France.

Along with Frederick Engels, Marx was commissioned by the Communist League, a small organization of German revolutionaries, to write *The Communist Manifesto.* Completed in early 1848, this was to become one of the most widely read political pamphlets in world history—as well as one of the most-often suppressed tracts in history. It was, for example, outlawed in many German states upon its appearance; it was later banned from Prussia by Otto von Bismarck, and was prohibited from Nazi Germany by Adolf Hitler.

With the outbreak of revolutions throughout Europe in 1848, Marx returned to Germany and assumed editorship of the renamed *Neue Rheinische Zeitung*, which called itself "an organ of democracy." The paper called for tax resistance and advocated armed self-defense against Prussian emperor Frederick William. In response, the government suppressed the publication and tried Marx for treason. Though acquitted by a jury, he was expelled from the country.

While spending most of the remainder of his life in England, Marx continued to expand on his early ideas. Although he faced almost no censorship in his adopted homeland, his writings were frequently censored abroad. For example, in his native Germany, Bismarck pressured the parliament to prohibit socialist literature and activity in 1878. Marx's work then became available there only through the socialist underground. In czarist Russia, *The Communist Manifesto* and most of Marx's other writings were prohibited. Oddly, however, the censors allowed his massive work *The Capital* to enter uncut—on the grounds that the huge book was too complex to be of any practical political danger.

In addition to direct government suppression, Marx's work was often subject to self-censorship by fearful European social democrats. Since many of his ideas and political proposals ran the risk of bringing government repression down on those who distributed them, many editions of his work were edited to remove provocative passages. In Prussia, for example, where calls for a republic could be easily interpreted as insults to the kaiser, the German Social Democratic Party issued Marx's work in carefully prepared editions that could pass government censors.

Even when his works were not suppressed, Marx found that they often were not readily available. Plagued by financial problems throughout his life, Marx had difficulty funding his writing work. Once his works were published, they often met with what he saw as a conspiracy of silence. His first volume of *The Capital*, for example, was so little noticed that his collaborator, Engels, wrote a number of positive reviews under pseudonyms to generate publicity.

Censorship After Marx's Death. Marx's death in 1883 did nothing to reduce the hostility many governments felt toward his work. His writings were later banned in Fascist Italy and burned in Nazi Germany. Many right-wing governments in Eastern Europe, such as that of Romania, followed suit during World War I. Access to his writings was severely limited in Spain from 1939 until the end of Francisco Franco's dictatorship in the 1970's. After Joseph Stalin established his dictatorship in the Soviet Union, Marx's unpublished writings were often purchased and kept from publication if their contents were seen as deviating from the Soviet Union's current Communist Party policies. Even outside of Europe, Marx's writings were often regarded as threatening. In 1929 the Chinese government sent armies into the countryside to fight communist insurgents and prevented, whenever possible, the reading of *The Communist Manifesto* and *The Capital.*

During the Red Scare period of the early 1950's in the United States, Marx's writings were attacked as subversive. Many book stores refused to carry his books. Trustees of the Boston Public Library, under attack by the *Boston Post*, came within one vote of removing his works from their shelves. Professors who assigned *The Communist Manifesto* or others of Marx's writings to their classes, were often attacked as communists, and some lost their teaching positions. Suspected subversives called before government investigatory committees were often asked if they had read Marx; affirmative answers were seen as admissions of disloyalty to the United States.

In numerous other countries, Marx's books were associated with subversion and suffered various degrees of censorship. Marx was banned in Indonesia after a 1965 military coup liquidated the nation's Communist Party. Likewise, in Greece when a military junta took power in 1967, the writings of Marx were outlawed. Throughout Latin America right-wing military regimes frequently outlawed *The Communist Manifesto* and others of Marx's writings as subversive. For example, after a coup assassinated the popularly elected socialist president Salvador Allende in Chile in 1973, the leaders of the Chilean military junta proscribed Marx's works for "sake of the public good."

When not banned outright, Marx's writings have often been heavily edited—often by hostile editors who sought to discredit his work. Many editions of his writings have been published with antagonistic introductions written to demonstrate Marx's errors or prejudices. For example, one volume of excerpts of his writings on religion was issued with the provocative title, *A World Without Jews*, in order to portray Marx—who was himself of Jewish ancestry—as anti-Semitic. At times, anticommunist regimes have even issued books and pamphlets containing completely fictitious passages attributed to Marx. —*William A. Pelz*

See also Bakunin, Mikhail Aleksandrovich; Boston; Chile; Communism; Germany; Greek junta; Soviet Union.

Bibliography

The fifty volumes of *Karl Marx and Frederick Engels: Collected Works*, trans. by Richard Dixon et al. (New York: International Publishers, 1965-), constitute the most complete and definitive English language collection of Marx's work available. Robert Tucker, ed., *Marx-Engels Reader* (New York: W. W. Norton, 1973), contains a representative selection of his basic writings. For detailed discussions of Marx's political views and bibliographical references to specialized studies, consult Tom Bottomore's *A Dictionary of Marxist Thought* (2d ed. Oxford: Basil Blackwell Reference, 1991). A useful and sympathetic—yet critical—assessment of Marx is Hal Draper's four-volume *Karl Marx's Theory of Revolution* (New York: Monthly Review Press, 1977-1990). Marx's economic thought is discussed from the same viewpoint in Ernest Mandel, *The Formation of the Economic Thought of Karl Marx, 1843 to Capital* (New York: Monthly Review Press, 1987.

Masonry

DEFINITION: Semisecret fraternal organization

SIGNIFICANCE: Masons have applied self-censorship to protect their secret rituals, and have been the target of efforts to restrain their activities and political influence

Masonry is an international fraternal organization engaged in a broad range of charitable causes; it also serves as a mutual assistance network for its members. Not a religion, masonry is not formally associated with any single denomination, although it places emphasis on Christian values and precepts. Masons operate through local lodges, and use secret signs and ceremonies that draw loosely upon Oriental mysticism. Upon initiation, Masons pledge to preserve the secrecy of the order and to maintain loyalty to their brethren. This pledge of secrecy might be construed as a form of self-censorship. In addition, the combination of secrecy and a reputation for political influence has periodically made Masons a target for political opponents and a source of public vituperation.

Censorship by Masons. Maintaining Masonry's secrets is a basic requirement for membership. When disaffected members have sought to reveal those secrets, the organization has taken efforts to suppress them. The most celebrated case in this regard concerns the kidnapping of William Morgan in 1826. Morgan had written a manuscript, published in 1826 as *Illustrations of Masonry, By One of the Fraternity Who Has Devoted Thirty Years to the Subject*. The book's title aside, it has never been conclusively established that Morgan was formally initiated as a Blue Lodge Mason—the primary order among the amorphous collection of organizations associated with Masonry. He did, however, possess knowledge of the secrets of Blue Lodge Masonry, as the accuracy of his manuscript's descriptions has generally been affirmed.

Morgan, a former stonemason, had taken up residence in the village of Batavia in New York. There he developed a reputation for drinking and fighting, and was constantly burdened by debt. After being denied membership in a Masonic lodge being formed in Batavia and, perhaps more important, sensing the potential to make money, Morgan undertook to write his book. In March, 1826, he formed a partnership with three other individuals to publish the book. One of these, David C. Miller, was a newspaper publisher and a Mason who had taken the first of three Blue Lodge degrees. When word of the manuscript's impending publication got out, Masons from the northern region of New York made various attempts to suppress it. Morgan was enjoined to abort his effort. All four of the partners were harassed and received personal threats. Miller's print shop was set on fire on two occasions. Finally, a prominent Mason from Ontario obtained a warrant for Morgan's arrest, charging that he had stolen clothes from a tavern. Morgan was arrested on September 11, 1826, but released for lack of evidence. He was immediately rearrested on new charges, however, this time that he had failed to pay a $2.69 debt. Morgan admitted to this charge and was jailed.

The next day Morgan was removed from jail by several Masons who paid his debt. Morgan gave several shouts of "murder!" as he was taken away. He was never seen again. Subsequent trials and investigations failed to prove that a murder had indeed occurred, but Morgan's Masonic abductors admitted to charges of conspiracy to kidnap. In the end, some fifty-four Masons were indicted in connection with the alleged conspiracy.

The Morgan case is among the most famous cases of Masonic efforts to protect their secrets, but there are numerous others. Stories range from the relatively friendly admonitions to mind one's words, to dramatic theories of conspiracy.

Efforts to Censor Masons. Because of the mystery surrounding their meetings and the extent of their political influence, Masons have periodically come under attack by outside groups, including religious organizations and governments. The Roman Catholic church, for example, historically opposed Masonry as an institution promoting atheism and revolution. Masonry was specifically denounced by Pope Clement XII in 1738 for imposing upon its members obligations that could not be revealed at confessional. Subsequent popes continued the denunciation of Masonry into the nineteenth century. As an organization, Masonry was outlawed by the fascist regimes of Italy, Germany, and Spain. Masons as a group (as well as various other noncommunist organizations) were persecuted virtually to the point of extermination in the Soviet Union. After World War II, the practice of Masonry was forbidden in most communist countries.

Masonry has come under attack in the United States as well. In the late eighteenth century Protestant groups charged the Masons with being under the secret control variously of Catholics, antireligious groups, and the French. Efforts were initiated to disband Masonic lodges and to ban their publications. It was the Morgan affair, however, that began one of the most focused attacks against Masonry: the so-called Anti-Masonic movement.

The Anti-Masonic movement responded to the perception that Masonry had acquired undue power in American society. It was not so much Morgan's abduction that drove the movement (although this was a rallying point) but rather the perception that a Masonic conspiracy, involving well-placed Masons throughout the government and judiciary, managed to prevent the official determination that Morgan had been murdered. In addition, Morgan's confessed kidnappers were perceived to have received unduly light sentences. Out of these events grew a widespread movement that sought not only to reduce the political influence of Masons but also to expose the alleged immoral, irreligious, and even evil aspects of Masonry. The movement was characterized by anti-elitism and moralism, as well as bigotry and opportunism. Books, newspaper accounts, gossip, and other tools were employed against suspected Masons and Masonry in general. More than one hundred specifically anti-Masonic newspapers were established. Political weapons were also employed, particularly elections.

Before long, the Anti-Masonic movement developed into the Anti-Masonic Party, the United States' first national third political party, which held its first national convention in 1830. The Anti-Masonic Party nominated a candidate, William Wirt, to run against Andrew Jackson (the Democratic candidate) and Henry Clay (the National Republican candidate), both of whom were Masons. Jackson won handily. The Anti-Masonic Party was disbanded after its candidate for president in 1836, William Henry Harrison, was also defeated.

The Anti-Masonic movement illustrates the potential for American anxiety about secrecy to manifest itself in illiberal intolerance. The ideals of American pluralism and freedom of association and privacy were put aside, and elements of the Anti-Masonic movement sought to deny Masons these rights.

—*Steve D. Boilard*

See also Fear; Morgan, William; Privacy, right to.

Bibliography

For a general discussion of Masonry, see Michael Baigent and Richard Leigh's *The Temple and the Lodge* (1989). On the Morgan affair and the Anti-Masonic movement, see William Preston Vaughn's *The Antimasonic Party in the United States, 1826-1843* (1983); Lorman Ratner's *Antimasonry: The Crusade and the Party* (1969); and Ronald P. Formisano and Kathleen Smith Kutolowski's "Antimasonry and Masonry: The Genesis of Protest, 1826-1827," in *American Quarterly* 29 (1977). A fictional account of one of Sherlock Holmes's cases, Arthur Conan Doyle's *The Valley of Fear* (1915) provides a good example of the dark side of Masonry as it might have been conceived by the Anti-Masonic movement.

Master of the Revels

Definition: British government office created by King Henry VIII in 1545

Significance: Holders of this office acted as censors by reviewing the content of all plays performed in public

In 1545 King Henry VIII of England established the office of Master of the Revels, with responsibility for all theatrical entertainment provided for the court. Although the office holder was essentially a minor functionary, his responsibilities included reviewing theme and content of all plays presented before a royal audience. Those responsibilities were expanded in 1574 when Queen Elizabeth I placed the Master of the Revels in charge of the Earl of Leicester's players, a company of actors licensed by decree to perform both in London and the provinces. The master's control of all performances in the realm was confirmed by royal patent in 1579, although nothing in the patent referred specifically to censorship. In 1589 the covert circulation of the infamous Martin Marprelate tracts—pamphlets generated by Puritan extremists virulently attacking the episcopacy of the Church of England—created the controversy that established the Master of the Revels as a censor. In an attempt to placate both the growing Puritan political powers of London and the Church of England, with whom the playwrights and theater companies generally sympathized, the privy council gave the Master of the Revels unlimited censorship responsibilities and absolute licensing power. He was to be advised by, but not responsible to, representatives of both factions.

Through a variety of abuses, including extortion of "fees" from theaters and bribes from those wanting certain plays suppressed, the office fell gradually into disrepute. After the fall of the House of Stuart in 1688, the censorship duties of the Master of the Revels were taken over by the Lord Chamberlain.

See also Drama and theater; Examiner of plays; Henry VIII; Lord Chamberlain.

Maupassant, Guy de

Born: August 5, 1850, Château de Miromesnil, near Dieppe, France

Died: July 6, 1893, Paris, France

Identification: French short-story writer and novelist

Significance: Maupassant's fiction was implicated in the campaign against obscene literature directed at Émile Zola and naturalist writers in England in 1888

Maupassant's contributions to literature have often been overshadowed by the facts of his life. His sexual promiscuity, profligate Parisian lifestyle, and tragic death from syphilis (which was later frequently cited as an example of the dangers of sex) have often received more attention than his work.

Maupassant began his literary career with the publication of "Boule de Suif," a touching story of a prostitute who reluctantly beds a Prussian officer in order to secure release of her traveling companions, who then scorn her. His first full volume of short fiction appeared in 1881 under the title of his second important story, "La Maison Tellier"—a comic piece about a group of prostitutes who attend a Holy Communion. After this book's success, Maupassant published numerous stories in newspapers and periodicals that were reprinted in books that appeared at a rate of about two volumes a year. Many of his stories created considerable of controversy among the French critics of the time because he dared to focus on the experiences of so-called lowlife characters.

Maupassant's first brush with censorship law occurred in 1879 with the publication of his poem "La Mur," which was attacked as an "outrage on public morality." Maupassant asked his most important mentor, Gustave Flaubert, to write what became a famous letter defending another of his poems, "Au bord de l'eau," that had been accused of being obscene. The case was dropped, but not before Maupassant exploited the publicity to promote his career.

Maupassant's first novel, *Une Vie* (1883), about the frustrations of a young wife in Normandy, faced private censorship when Hachette, a publishing and book-selling company that supplied books for the stalls in French railway stations, refused to stock it. Maupassant wrote a petition to the authorities that was published and widely discussed. The case created abundant publicity, which only succeeded in bolstering the book's sales and furthering Maupassant's career.

Une Vie and Maupassant's second novel *Bel Ami* (1885), which focused on Parisian life, were involved in an even more famous censorship case in England in 1888. It centered on the respectable publisher Henry Vizetelly, who was charged with obscene libel for publishing works by Maupassant, Zola, and Paul Bourget. Zolaism, or naturalism, a school with which Maupassant was identified, was called a "study of the putrid" by the courts, and Vizetelly was sentenced to three months in prison.

Many decades later Maupassant's story "La Maison Tellier" appeared in an issue of *Eros* magazine that the U.S. government prosecuted in 1966. Maupassant was thus indirectly involved in publisher Ralph Ginzburg's obscenity case in 1966.

See also Flaubert, Gustave; France; Ginzburg, Ralph; Zola, Émile.

Maya books, destruction of

Date: 1562

Place: Mani, Yucatán, Mexico

Significance: The Spanish burning of Maya books in public bonfires destroyed most of the writings of the only indigenous Americans with a true writing system

In 1562, at the town of Mani in the Yucatán peninsula, the Spanish friar Diego de Landa burned twenty-seven Maya books in a public bonfire. The *auto-da-fé*, or show of faith, was a persecution by clergy who represented the Spanish Inquisition. De Landa judged the books to contain "superstitions and falsehoods of the devil"; he also burned corpses and five thousand statues. This *auto-da-fé* was one incident in a conversion effort that included whippings, water torture, enslavement, amputations, hangings, and suppression of Mayan religious practices. De Landa's bonfire encouraged other Spanish clergy to destroy most of the remaining books, along with "idols" and any vestiges of the Mayan religion. Only four glyphic books are known to have survived into the twentieth century; they are held in museums of Dresden, Madrid, Paris, and Mexico City. Others were sent to Europe during Spanish colonial times, but their fragile bark paper did not last.

De Landa was censured and sent back to Spain in 1563, but he was cleared and returned to the Yucatán as bishop from 1573 to 1579. Meanwhile, he wrote a book, *Yucatan Before and After the Conquest*, that described Mayan culture and bark books.

The pre-contact Maya of Mexico, Guatemala, and El Salvador had a fully developed written language, with about eight hundred glyphs used to represent phonetic syllables and whole words. Their bark books, or codices, contained works on astronomy, prophecies, narratives, and histories. Readings from these books were central to some ceremonies. At the celebration *Pocam*, or the Washing, for example, Mayan priests purified a book with water and then read its predictions for the coming year. The books were made from lengths of beaten fig-bark paper, folded continuously like accordions. Bark was prepared with a white glaze background, and then scribes painted illustrations and text with red and black paint. Covers were made of jaguar skin.

The Spanish suppressed the Maya writing system because its glyphic elements embodied Mayan gods. Illustrations and glyphs in bark books connoted complex religious concepts, correlated with the calendar, the stars and planets, and mathematics. Numerals corresponded to gods as well as abstractions such as zero. The sacred nature of the glyphs resembles the original roman alphabet, whose letter *A*, inverted, once represented the horned bull god of the Phoenicians.

Because only the Mayan upper classes were literate, knowledge of glyphs was lost quickly. Spanish clergy taught the Christianized Maya the European alphabet for Maya dialects. A number of seventeenth century manuscripts appear to be transcriptions of glyphic texts. Among these are the creation account, the *Popol Vuh*, and town chronicles from the Yucatán called *The Sacred Books of Chilam Balam.*

The Maya written language also survives in stone monuments, vase paintings, and cave paintings. In the late twentieth century epigraphers decoded most of the Mayan glyphs, though they have not yet determined the exact sounds.

See also Book burning; Mexico; Native Americans; Spanish Empire; Spanish Inquisition.

Mayakovsky, Vladimir

Born: July 19, 1893, Bagdadi (now Mayakovsky), Georgia, Russian Empire

Died: April 14, 1930, Moscow, Soviet Union

Identification: Russian poet

Significance: A significant writer who supported the Bolsheviks through the Russian Revolution, Mayakovsky grew disillusioned with the authoritarian Soviet system and committed suicide

Of an independent and rebellious nature, the youthful Mayakovsky joined the Bolshevik Party in 1908 and was arrested several times as a result. He spent nearly one year in prison. He also embarked on a writing career, associating himself briefly with the Futurist School. His first poems were published in 1912. He enthusiastically supported the Bolshevik revolution in 1917, and later assisted in preparing textual and visual party propaganda during Russian's civil war. In 1923 he helped found LEF ("Left Front"), a circle of like-minded writers organized to promote literary and cultural experimentation.

Although much of his output is considered propagandistic and didactic, serving the communist cause, Mayakovsky nonetheless also is recognized for the freshness of his literary imagery. His poetry is stark and challenging, confronting readers with the dramatic forces of change, energy, and movement. Metaphors represent the "leap" of modern society and civilization into the future, leaving behind a tired and anachronistic past. His lengthy poem *150,000,000* (1919-1920) speaks for the aspirations of the Russian people as they emerge from their backwardness. Although political in its purpose, his literary skill is evident. His verse is irregular in meter, deliberately uneven, so as to create a jarring mood. His poetry, to be effective rather than tendentious and posturing, is especially dramatic when read aloud with fervor and varied inflection. Hyperbole characterizes his work.

Mayakovsky's poetry could serve the state's communist ideology, as in *All Right!* (1927) or *Vladimir Ilich Lenin* (1924). But his writing also give free reign to his creative spirit. His later work became increasingly independent, and periodically evoked official criticism. Two plays are noteworthy for their satirical portrayal of life under the communist regime. *The Bedbug* (1928-1929) ridiculed the materialistic drive of the Soviet economy and the Party hacks in the 1920's, while *The Bathhouse* (1929-1930) was a fantasy about the inventor of a time machine facing the deadening bureaucratic system of the one-party state.

From the mid-1920's Mayakovsky had growing personal and emotional problems complicated by an unsuccessful love affair. He also became more acutely aware of the intellectual and creative restrictions imposed on Soviet culture. In one of the last poems he wrote before shooting himself, Mayakovsky criticized the narrow ideological tasks that intellectuals had to serve: "I subdued myself, setting my heel on the throat of my own song."

Mayakovsky's suicide in 1930 posed a problem for the authorities, who did not wish to admit that one of their famous intellectual supporters had become disillusioned with the communist cause. Public explanations of his death therefore emphasized his unbalanced psychological state and other personal difficulties.

See also Akhmatova, Anna; Communism; Intellectual freedom; Lenin, Vladimir Ilich; Poetry; Soviet Union; Stalin, Joseph.

Mead, Margaret

BORN: December 16, 1901, Philadelphia, Pennsylvania
DIED: November 15, 1978, New York, New York
IDENTIFICATION: American anthropologist and writer
SIGNIFICANCE: Mead's writings were sometimes censored because of her liberal views on sexual morality as well as her frank descriptions of sexual practices in preliterate cultures

One of the pioneers of modern American anthropology, Mead was known as a tireless field investigator and a skillful writer with a popular appeal. Conducting most of her ethnographic work in Samoa and other islands of Oceania, she emphasized the determining influences of culture on the individual personality, and she focused on cultural differences in child rearing, gender roles, sexual rules, and sexual practices. In addition to descriptions of life in "primitive" societies, Mead's writings included strong criticisms of gender roles and conventional sexual morality in the United States.

The most controversial of her twenty-three books included *Coming of Age in Samoa* (1928), *Sex and Temperament in Three Primitive Societies* (1935), and *Male and Female* (1949). Although governmental agents rarely censored her books, conservative critics often tried, and sometimes were able, to keep these books out of local libraries, and from time to time high school teachers were criticized for including her works in reading lists. In 1961, for example, the Mothers United for Decency of Oklahoma City operated a "smutmobile" which prominently displayed a paperback edition of *Male and Female*.

See also Libraries, school; Morality; Sex education; Sex in the arts.

Medical malpractice

DEFINITION: The failure of physicians or other medical professionals to meet professional standards of care, thereby making them subject under civil law to claims for compensation by injured patients
SIGNIFICANCE: Fear of malpractice lawsuits often restrains communications among patients and health care providers or inhibits professionals from divulging information about negligent colleagues

Medical malpractice is patient care that fails to satisfy the professional standards of a nation's doctors, or other health professionals, such as nurses or dentists. It becomes a social and legal problem when a medical professional's mistakes or substandard care injures a patient. When physicians are deemed negligent according to civil law, their patients may sue for damages to pay for further medical treatment, or to compensate for pain and suffering.

Although valuable tools for policing medical practices, malpractice suits are complicated, expensive, time-consuming, adversarial, and often anguishing for patient-plaintiffs and physician-defendants alike. Medical malpractice does not always involve censorship; however, health care providers, lawyers, and consumer advocates have complained that fear of malpractice suits discourages doctors from reporting negligent colleagues, prompts self-censorship over medical treatments, and hinders doctor-patient communications.

In the United States only about 10 percent of malpractice complaints lead to law suits, and only about 20 percent of such suits result in damages being paid to plaintiffs. Most often, patient complaints of inadequate care arise because of misunderstandings that conferences among doctors and patients can clear up. Unsatisfied patients can complain to local medical boards, which in the United States are state government panels staffed by doctors who judge whether doctors have in fact failed to meet professional standards of care.

If a patient is still unsatisfied, and can prove that an injury has resulted from inadequate medical care, the patient can retain a lawyer and initiate a law suit. The doctor is notified, and there follows a period of evidence gathering, called "discovery," during which sworn statements and documentary evidence, such as medical records, are collected. At the ensuing civil trial lawyers for the each side argue whether the evidence presented does or does not establish harmful negligence. Meanwhile, lawyers elicit further evidence in question-and-answer sessions called examination and cross-examination. Finally, a jury decides whether the plaintiff or defendant has the stronger case and dismisses the suit or awards damages accordingly.

Fear of Malpractice and Self-Censorship. All health care providers dread malpractice suits. Win or lose, such legal actions cost money and time, and are likely to leave defendants feeling compromised or humiliated. With the rapid rise in malpractice suits filed in the United States since the 1960's, this concern has assumed ever greater importance. It can induce three types of self-censorship.

In the first type, doctors overrule their own medical judgment. All medical treatments entail some risk, but the greater the risk, the less defensible is a particular procedure or drug if it turns out, for any reason, to harm rather than help a patient. Consequently, some doctors who perform major, technology-dependent procedures—such as obstetricians and surgeons—have admitted being unwilling to offer radical or experimental operations, even when such procedures hold a great promise of benefiting a patient. Similarly, doctors may order medical tests that they know are unnecessary—and thereby censor their best advice—so that, in case of a law suit, they can demonstrate that they did everything possible for their patient. Furthermore, doctors may feel constrained in how they report treatments in patients' medical records, knowing that patients, lawyers, and review boards may eventually scrutinize those records. Doctors call such constraints upon their practice "defensive medicine." The extent and effects of defensive medicine, although generally acknowledged, are controversial.

In the second type of self-censorship, doctors' fear of malpractice claims inhibits their communications with their patients. Doctors who believe that some patients are eager to press malpractice claims speak warily, fearing that such patients may seize upon simple slips of the tongue, or poorly explained remarks, to make legal trouble for them. The fear of making damaging misstatements can affect the communications between a doctor and any patient. Psychiatrists and psychoanalysts in particular have remarked that such self-censorship limits the types of questions they can use during interviews with patients. Doctors have been known to refuse to reveal that they are doctors when they come upon victims of automobile accidents—especially if a victim is unconscious—because many law suits have been filed against doctors whose emergency care—however well intended—has failed to prevent serious disability.

The third type of self-censorship strains relations among doctors. When one physician observes another give a patient substandard care, the first may feel pressured to say nothing. Doctors inclined to be whistle-blowers worry that they will only earn reputations as troublemakers and that other physicians will shun them. Furthermore, physicians who recognize their own capacity for error and its attendant dangers hesitate to criticize others publicly. An incorrect accusation of malpractice, especially if it encourages a patient to sue, harms both the accuser and the accused, while doing nothing to help the patient.

Legal Action and Censorship. During malpractice suits, censorship becomes more direct. In forty states in the United States doctors named as defendants in such suits may not discuss the cases with the plaintiffs' other health care providers after the discovery phase begins. These *ex parte* communications can only occur after a plaintiff's approval.

To strengthen arguments concerning alleged malpractice, lawyers for both defendants and plaintiffs may ask expert witnesses to comment upon a defendant's medical treatment of a plaintiff. Some doctors called as expert witnesses have reported pressure from other doctors not to testify. The pressure, they claimed, might be as simple as overt displeasure from colleagues, or involve threats to the careers of the witnesses, who might suddenly find, for example, that their colleagues no longer refer patients to them. The extent of such peer-pressure censorship is difficult to assess; however, the "conspiracy of silence" that popular writers have evoked gives a mistaken impression of doctors unified against the rest of society. Some doctors do encourage injured patients to sue negligent colleagues, and others do testify in court for plaintiffs.

Health care providers understandably do not want to become stigmatized by claims of malpractice, which can happen even if the claims lack justification. For this reason, fear of malpractice claims has subtly changed doctor-patient relationships by introducing into it a strong undercurrent of wariness. Where doctors once saw themselves first of all as advocates for patients' physical well-being, they have come to watch themselves carefully in order to avoid legal complications.

—Roger Smith

See also Courtrooms; Courts and censorship law; Pharmaceutical industry.

BIBLIOGRAPHY

Medical Malpractice (Durham, N.C.: Duke University Press, 1987), edited by Duncan Yaggy and Patricia Hodgson, presents reactions to legal constraints. Harvey F. Wachsman's *Lethal Medicine: The Epidemic of Medical Malpractice in America* (New York: Holt, 1993) accuses the medical establishment for suppressing disclosures of malpractice. Margaret Davidson explains the legal trouble doctors face in "Why It's Dangerous to Talk About a Malpractice Suit," in *Medical Economics* 72, no. 21 (November 13, 1995). For a general discussion of malpractice, see *Law and Ethics: A Guide for the Health Professional*, edited by Nathan T. Sidley (New York: Human Sciences Press, 1985), and Frank John Edwards' *Medical Malpractice: Solving the Crisis* (New York: Holt, 1989).

Medical research

DEFINITION: The collection of data concerning diseases or clinical tests of drugs, surgical procedures, or other methods examined in order to improve human health care

SIGNIFICANCE: Some medical research requires temporary censorship to ensure objectivity; however, private and government organizations have often tried to suppress research findings out of self-interest or for moral reasons

Most medical research seeks to gather data establishing that a particular treatment, such as a drug, surgical procedure, or diet, is more effective and safer than other treatments for the same malady. Direct tests of treatments, called clinical trials, usually divide the test subjects into two groups in order to compare the treatment's effects: One group receives the new treatment; the other, called the control group, receives either a standard treatment or, in the case of a drug test, a placebo (a harmless inert substance). Directors of experiments randomly assign test subjects to groups without revealing the full nature of the test to them, or, often, to the medical personnel administering the treatments in a technique called blinding. Since participants do not know who is receiving the experimental therapy, this form of censorship minimizes the influence of bias on data gathering, such as a researcher's expectations about the treatment or a subject's hopes or fears about it. Moreover, when studying diseases and disorders in the general population, researchers normally withhold their findings until enough information accumulates to form statistically significant data bases.

Scientists deem such temporary censorship proper and routine. However, research findings can pose problems for both government bodies and private organizations. For example, when collected data expose the cause of an existing or potential public health problem, the responsible party faces political and financial damage from liability claims. When the data show a new treatment to be effective, the profits from marketing it can be enormous. Moreover, new ideas that appear to contravene cultural mores may cause public hostility for research and development of practical applications. In all these cases, medical research may sustain extended censorship.

Government Censorship. Governments frequently cite national security to justify suppressing experimental results, especially those obtained by their military. Research conducted to develop biological weapons or defenses against biological agents provide a prime example. However, since World War II veterans groups have also claimed that the U.S. Department of Defense and, later, the Department of Energy have hidden or destroyed data establishing that radiation from atomic bomb tests caused cancer in military personnel, an issue in which national security is not clearly at risk.

Furthermore, most governments try to control information in nonmilitary departments, usually to prevent leaks by employees or to avoid criticism and misuse of data. The Soviet Union frequently banned publication of cancer research and restricted the kinds of data epidemiologists gathered, according to investigations undertaken since the breakup of the Soviet Union. Great Britain's National Health Service has been accused of withholding information about research on azidothymidine (AZT), a treatment for acquired immunodeficiency syndrome (AIDS), and about the hospitals participating in drug trials.

To control information from publicly funded studies, the National Institutes of Health (NIH) in the United States has usually prohibited participating research institutions from publishing results individually unless first receiving permission. In 1990 Stanford University sued the NIH over this restriction, calling it censorship. When in 1993 the NIH reassigned two researchers, Walter Stewart and Ned Feder, who had called attention to fraudulent medical research, other scientists denounced the action. They saw it as an attempt to gag whistle-blowers and squelch embarrassing disclosures about government projects. Similarly, in 1990 government-employed doctors in Denmark and the Netherlands tried to halt publication of studies that revealed medical researchers were not recruiting test subjects ethically.

Censorship by Private Organizations. Not surprisingly, universities and private laboratories may refuse to share information from research projects until securing a patent in order to assure royalties from practical applications of the research. In the United States, federal law permits universities to retain certain rights to research that has been supported by government grants; nevertheless, some commentators believe that censorship of data for any reason contradicts the spirit of science, especially censorship by an educational institution.

More commonly, private organizations delay publication or conceal information from studies when the data may establish negligence and legal liability. During the 1990's, for example, both legislators and consumer advocate groups accused tobacco companies of censoring their own research that linked smoking and lung cancer or that showed nicotine to be addictive. According to their critics, the tobacco companies feared their research would be used against them as evidence during law suits by smokers seeking damages for the health problems that smoking had fostered.

When research results reach professional journals for publication, censoring forces may still slant the information. According to a 1993 article by A. J. Gelenberg in the *Psychopharmacological Bulletin*, journal editors hesitate to publish observations by practicing doctors that reveal harmful side effects of new drugs because drug companies—their major advertisers—pressure them to publish only positive information.

Morality and Censorship. Occasionally, citizen groups find a type of medical research morally abhorrent. In the United States, moral conflict occurs most readily when sexuality is the target of research. Those concerned that sexual mores would degenerate have condemned the development of contraceptive devices and drugs, experimental transsexual operations, and studies of homosexuality; in some cases they demanded that public funding stop for the research and its results be suppressed, at least in popular media. Simple fear of the unknown can cause similar reactions when radical new types of medical therapies have unclear consequences, as has been the case with medical research involving genetic engineering. Critics tried to halt the research because they worried that scientists might create deadly new organisms or alter the genome in some unforeseen way. —*Roger Smith*

See also Birth control education; Human Genome Project; Intellectual freedom; Nuclear research and testing; Pharmaceutical industry; Sex education; Smoking; Universities; Vesalius, Andreas.

BIBLIOGRAPHY

Tom L. Beauchamp and James F. Childress' *Principles of Biomedical Ethics* (4th ed. New York: Oxford University Press, 1994) lucidly explains the ethics that govern medical research. The technical aspects are described in *Designing Clinical Research*, edited by Stephen B. Hulley and Steven R. Cummings (Baltimore, Md.: Williams and Wilkins, 1988) and Robert J. Levine's *Ethics and Regulation of Clinical Research* (2d ed. Baltimore, Md.: Urban and Schwarzenberg, 1986). About governmental censorship, see Sandra K. Marlow's "Nuclear Radiation Information: Suppressed and Distorted," *Library Journal* 111, no. 12 (July 1986).

Meese, Edwin, III

BORN: December 3, 1931, Oakland, California

IDENTIFICATION: American government official

SIGNIFICANCE: As presidential counselor and attorney general in President Ronald Reagan's cabinet, Meese provided justification of expanding government secrecy and strengthening enforcement of obscenity laws

Meese was the oldest of four sons of Edwin Meese, Jr., a tax collector in Alameda County, California. He graduated from Yale in 1953 and the University of California at Berkeley Law School in 1958. For the next eight years he was deputy district attorney in Alameda County, where he took an active role in opposing antidraft and free speech protests in Oakland and Berkeley, where the Free Speech Movement convulsed the University of California campus in 1964.

After serving as Ronald Reagan's secretary and executive assistant when Reagan was governor of California, Meese accompanied Reagan to Washington as counselor to the president from 1981 to 1985, and as attorney general from 1985 to 1988. Meese was infuriated when secret discussions and activities of the Reagan Administration were published in the daily press. He strongly supported administration moves to increase the number of categories of government documents classified as secret and to require all government personnel with access to classified material to sign lifetime secrecy pledges.

When the 1986 Attorney General's Commission on Pornography urged greater enforcement of obscenity laws by federal prosecutors, Meese hailed the report and ordered the establishment of a special team of federal prosecutors to engage in an all-out campaign against obscene material. He also urged citizens to use picketing and boycotts to pressure stores into removing obscene material, such as *Playboy* magazine, from their shelves.

See also Attorney General's Commission on Pornography; Classification of information; Free Speech Movement; *Playboy*; Reagan, Ronald.

Meiklejohn, Alexander

BORN: February 3, 1872, Rochdale, England
DIED: September 16, 1964, Berkeley, California
IDENTIFICATION: American educator and legal philosopher
SIGNIFICANCE: Meiklejohn developed a two-level theory of free speech that would guarantee absolute protection to "public" speech but not to "private" speech

A professor at the University of Wisconsin, president of Amherst College, and founding director of the San Francisco School of Social Studies, Meiklejohn is best known for his book *Free Speech and Its Relationship to Self-Government* (1948) and its theory of freedom of speech. Meiklejohn believed the most important function of free speech was to guarantee democratic self-government, and that this could be accomplished only through free and open debate over public issues and the actions of public officials. Political discussion was, therefore, meant by the drafters of the First Amendment to be absolutely protected from government limitation. Private speech, speech of concern only in private matters such as television and literature, was given only minimal protection under the due process clause and could be regulated since it had no implications for government.

Although Meiklejohn's theory is credited with contributing to the U.S. Supreme Court's decision in *New York Times Co. v. Sullivan* (1964), it was also criticized because of the inherent difficulty in distinguishing between "public" and "private" speech, as in the case of a literary piece that also contained political elements.

See also First Amendment; Free speech; Hume, David; Locke, John; Marcuse, Herbert; *New York Times Co. v. Sullivan*.

Mein Kampf

TYPE OF WORK: Book
PUBLISHED: 1925-1927
AUTHOR: Adolf Hitler (1889-1945)
SUBJECT MATTER: This rambling memoir summarizes Hitler's worldviews and reveals plans he made for Germany's racial reconstruction and expansion well before he came to power
SIGNIFICANCE: An abridged English translation became available in 1933, but Jewish organizations and several countries attempted to ban the book because of its vicious racism and Social Darwinism

Adolf Hitler, the dictator of Nazi Germany from 1933 to 1945, wrote the first volume of *Mein Kampf* ("My Struggle") while imprisoned Bavaria after his failed attempt to seize power in Munich in November, 1923. Published in the summer of 1925, it was followed by the second volume in December, 1926. The book presents Hitler's Social Darwinist worldview and reveals his hatred of Jews and bolshevists. The German government did not restrict the publication or sale of *Mein Kampf*, but the book did not become a best-seller until 1930.

In 1933 an abridged English translation was published in Great Britain and the United States. This version retained Hitler's remarks on his main goals, but it omitted many of his crude comments about Jews and nonwhite peoples and his belligerent references to France. This censorship was the work

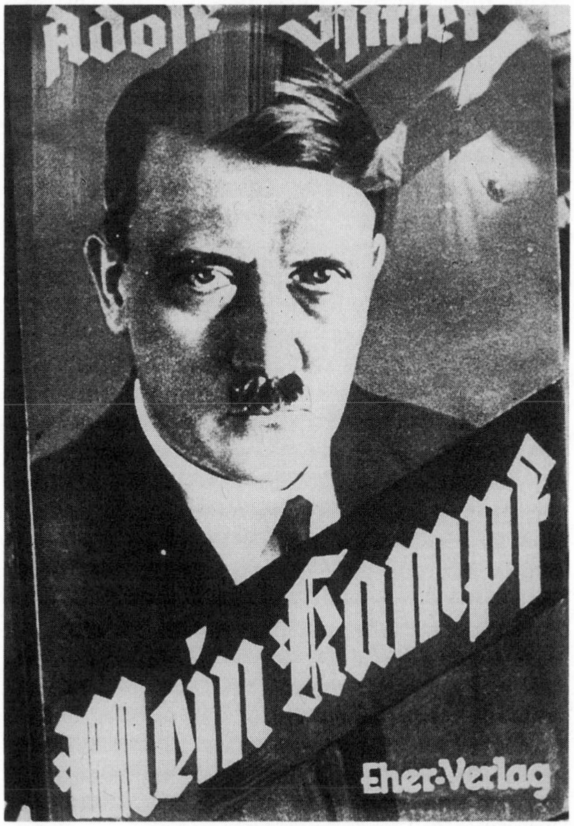

Adolf Hitler's blueprint for a fascist dictatorship was banned in some liberal democracies. (National Archives)

of Nazi government officers who had to approve the translation before permitting it to be published abroad.

Jewish interests in the United States and Britain attempted unsuccessfully to suppress the book's publication and distribution. An August, 1933, article entitled "Greed Conquers American Decency" in *The Jewish Ledger* of New Orleans denounced *Mein Kampf*'s American publisher, Houghton Mifflin. The publisher of the *Chicago Israelite*, sent a letter to President Franklin D. Roosevelt, asking "Is there not some way that publication of this book can be suppressed?" Wall Street broker Louis Lober even urged New York City's board of education to boycott textbooks published by Houghton Mifflin.

In 1939 a complete and unabridged English translation of *Mein Kampf* by Ralph Manheim that included scholarly notes was published. It became the book's standard English translation in the United States both before and after World War II. After 1945—when Hitler's "Thousand-year Reich" was in ashes—Germany's Bavarian state, which acted as legal executor of Nazi property, refused permission to publish *Mein Kampf* in Germany. German booksellers who attempted to sell copies of the book were charged with unconstitutional acts. Not until 1979 did Germany's highest court rule that the book could be publicly sold. Literary critic Fritz J. Raddatz opposed this ruling because he thought the book too dangerous.

Hutchinson Publishing, the British publishing house that held the British copyright to *Mein Kampf*, also faced massive opposition to its decision to reissue the book in 1969. The firm's chairman, Sir Robert Lusty, was opposed by his board, the West German government, and the Board of Deputies of British Jews. However, the Council of Christians and Jews supported the publication of the new edition. This organization, like many scholars, contended that making *Mein Kampf* freely available would help to expose Hitler's brutal racist philosophy.

See also Abridgment; Book publishing; Boycotts; Germany; Holocaust, Jewish; National Socialism; Propaganda; Race.

Memoirs of Hecate County

TYPE OF WORK: Book
PUBLISHED: 1946
AUTHOR: Edmund Wilson (1895-1972)
SUBJECT MATTER: Upper-middle-class life in suburban New York
SIGNIFICANCE: Although a serious literary work by an established writer, this collection of stories was found obscene and unprotected by constitutional rights of free expression

Memoirs of Hecate County is a collection of five short stories and a novella dealing with well-to-do New York suburban life. One of Edmund Wilson's few attempts at fiction, the book was not a critical success, as were his earlier works of literary criticism. Its novella, "The Princess with the Golden Hair," intimately describes sexual intercourse during two love affairs conducted by its male protagonist. These erotic passages provoked attack.

The New York Society for the Suppression of Vice instigated prosecution of Wilson's publisher, Doubleday and Company, for publishing obscene material under the New York Penal Code. Without presenting a full written opinion, the court found the book obscene and unprotected by the First Amendment to the U.S. Constitution in *People v. Doubleday* (1947). After Doubleday appealed the ruling, the U.S. Supreme Court, in the absence of Justice Frankfurter, ruled four to four that the book was obscene, thus sustaining the lower court's ruling.

See also Comstock Act of 1873; Literature; Sex in the arts; Society for the Suppression of Vice, New York.

Mencken, H. L.

BORN: September 12, 1880, Baltimore, Maryland
DIED: January 29, 1956, Baltimore, Maryland
IDENTIFICATION: American journalist and author
SIGNIFICANCE: Mencken's critiques of literary, political, and social conservatism—what he labeled "The New Puritanism"—dominated American anticensorship discourse during the 1920's

Mencken was a lifelong resident of Baltimore. His formal education ended in 1896, when he graduated as the valedictorian from Baltimore Polytechnic Institute. Three years later he became a cub reporter for the Baltimore *Morning Herald* and *Sunpapers*. He was named city editor in 1903 and managing editor in 1905. In 1914 he began coediting *The Smart Set* with his friend George Jean Nathan, with whom he also founded and coedited *The American Mercury*, beginning in 1924. Mencken became the latter journal's sole editor in 1925, the same year that he covered the Scopes trial for *Sunpapers*.

Along with satirical novelist Sinclair Lewis, Mencken dominated the American literary world of the 1920's. His essays took two forms: literary criticism and social and political criticism. His ideas appealed to the younger generation because he railed against religious fundamentalism. Particularly opposed to Southern conservatism, he coined the term "Bible Belt" to describe the South. Mencken was a complete religious skeptic, whose primary targets were the Puritan traditions that influenced literary conservatism, censorship, and prohibition. His satire was not subtle, and critics labeled his style "Menckenese."

Mencken championed such writers as Joseph Conrad and Theodore Dreiser, and praised daring new publishers such as Boni and Liveright. He intentionally antagonized censorship groups, including the Boston Watch and Ward Society and the New York Society for the Suppression of Vice. The most notorious instance began in September, 1925, when *The American Mercury* published his essay "Keeping the Puritans Pure," which attacked the Boston Watch and Ward Society and its new leader Henry Chase and the Boston Booksellers Committee. When Boston banned the April, 1926, issue of *The American Mercury* containing Herbert Asbury's "Hatrack," a story about a prostitute in a small Midwestern town, Mencken went to Boston with his lawyer, Arthur Garfield Hays, and publicly sold Chase a copy. After Mencken's immediate arrest, national attention harassed Chase's organization, and the dispute resulted in a lengthy court battle. Mencken's comprehensive records of the dispute were later published by Carl Bode

H. L. Mencken as a young man. (Library of Congress)

as *The Editor, the Bluenose, and the Prostitute: H. L. Mencken's History of the "Hatrack" Censorship Case* (1988).

Perhaps Mencken's most influential work is his philological study *The American Language* (1919). Others include *George Bernard Shaw—His Plays* (1905), *Philosophy of Frederich Nietzsche* (1908), *A Book of Prefaces* (1917), *In Defence of Women* (1918), *Prejudices* (six series, 1919-1927), and three volumes of memoirs (1940-1943). After suffering a stroke in 1948, Mencken stopped writing. He died in 1956.

See also Books and obscenity law; Boston; Boston Watch and Ward Society; Dreiser, Theodore; Lewis, Sinclair; Liveright, Horace; Magazines; Scopes trial; Society for the Suppression of Vice, New York.

Mendelssohn, Felix

Born: February 3, 1809, Hamburg

Died: November 4, 1847, Leipzig, Saxony

Identification: German composer

Significance: Because of Mendelssohn's Jewish background, his music was suppressed and later banned by Germany's Nazi regime

Mendelssohn and other composers of Jewish background came under attack when the National Socialists began eliminating Jewish influences from the concert platforms and opera stages of Germany and her satellite countries during the 1930's. The fact that Mendelssohn's family had converted to Christianity and that he had been baptized did not spare him from being included in these purges. His music was a target of Nazi criticism because it had received great acclaim and was still affectionately regarded by the public. In fact, after 1879 composition and performance prizes named in his honor were given in Germany.

Anti-Semitic propaganda appearing in Germany in the 1920's and 1930's characterized Jewish musical compositions as not contributing to the good of the German state; at the same time a move began on the part of Nazi officials to effect the "Aryanization" of the musical repertoire. This program sought new scores to replace the incidental music that Mendelssohn had written for William Shakespeare's *A Midsummer Night's Dream*, removed his name from catalogs of available printed music and recordings, and, in 1936, destroyed a memorial to him that had stood in Leipzig since 1892.

See also Germany; Judaism; Music; National Socialism; Wagner, Richard.

Men's magazines

Definition: Periodicals intended for a male audience

Significance: Men's magazines have often been the target of censorship, typically as a result of their depictions of nude or seminude women

Before 1953 many men's magazines published articles about sex and photographs of women exposing considerable flesh, but those articles and photographs were not the magazines' primary fare and their editors were scrupulous about staying on the good side of the U.S. Post Office.

The Post Office could, and did, prohibit the use of the U.S. mail to publications that violated the standards of decency it established, and thus for decades was a key American censorship unit. As late as 1943, editor Arnold Gingrich of *Esquire* took each issue's copy and art for the magazine to Washington, D.C., to get it approved by the Post Office before it was printed, much less mailed. The magazine's mailing rights were nevertheless pulled in 1943. *Esquire* fought the Post Office, first in hearings before postal officials and then in court, and won a Supreme Court ruling restoring its mailing privileges and limiting the censorship powers of the Post Office. After that the Post Office still occasionally attempted to assert its censorship powers over men's magazines, but without notable success.

In 1953 *Playboy* magazine, followed by some copycats and some raunchier publications, made sex a primary item of content.

Such content found critics and opponents in many communities. In Riverton, Wyoming, for example, a grocer in 1968 removed *Playboy* from his shelves and said he would remove any other magazine that customers found offensive. (The promise was not kept when some customers said they were offended by *Guns & Ammo* magazine; it was not removed.)

It appears that attempts to censor men's magazines in the United States have been limited mostly to such efforts, although Congress prohibited the publication of *Playboy* in braille for a time in the mid-1980's, and the federal government, in the wake of the report of the Attorney General's

Commission on Pornography in 1986, attempted to lend its support to local efforts to remove the magazines from newsstands. In 1996, a bill was introduced in Congress that would prohibit military base exchanges from selling *Playboy*, *Penthouse*, and *Hustler*. It has not been uncommon to hear *Playboy*, *Penthouse*, or *Hustler* attacked because of their emphasis on the sexual aspects of women that appeal to men. Many groups have attacked the magazines as purveyors of the offensive custom of viewing women as objects rather than as people.

See also Attorney General's Commission on Pornography; *Hustler*; Magazines; Nudity; *Penthouse*; *Playboy*; Postal regulations; Prior restraint.

Mercator, Gerardus

BORN: March 5, 1512, Rupelmonde, Flanders

DIED: December 2, 1594, Duisburg, Duchy of Cleves (today Germany)

IDENTIFICATION: Cartographer, geographer, and mathematician

SIGNIFICANCE: Mercator was imprisoned for heresy, but was later released and allowed to continue his scientific studies

Caught in the turmoil of the Reformation and Counter-Reformation, Mercator is perhaps best known for the Mercator projection, a method of drawing the spherical surface of the earth on a flat map. While a student at the University of Louvain in his native Flanders (now part of Belgium), Mercator is said to have expressed religious doubts brought on by his study of Aristotle and the Bible. Although his exact religious beliefs are unknown, he seems to have been sympathetic to the emerging Protestant Reformation.

While working as a cartographer in Louvain, Mercator was viewed with suspicion by zealots of the Catholic Counter-Reformation because of his doubts as a student, his inclination to Protestantism, and his frequent absences from Louvain to gather information for his maps. He was arrested for heresy in 1544 and imprisoned for seven months. Although the charges brought against him were not directly related to his scientific work, it is possible that some of the details of his world maps may have conflicted with the teachings of the Church. University officials managed to secure his release, and he was allowed to continue his work. In 1552 Mercator moved to more tolerant surroundings in the Duchy of Cleves, where he spent the rest of his long and productive life.

See also Exploration, Age of; Heresy; Reformation, the.

Metzger, Tom

BORN: 1938

IDENTIFICATION: Founder of the American white supremacist group White Aryan Resistance

SIGNIFICANCE: Debarred from mainstream media because of his racist ideology, Metzger pioneered the use of cable-access television as a propaganda tool

About five hundred demonstrators gathered to protest Tom Metzger's white-only "Aryan Woodstock" rally near Napa, California, in March, 1989. (AP/Wide World Photos)

Metzger's White Aryan Resistance, based in Fallbrook, California, became a significant white supremacist movement by using cable television and by recruiting members of Skinhead groups. His programs first appeared on community access channels in San Diego, California, and Austin, Texas, in 1984. However, because of his extremist views there have been attempts to limit his exposure. In 1988, for example, Metzger engaged in a month-long battle in Kansas City, Missouri, to broadcast his *Race and Reason* program on a cable service. Rather than give Metzger air time, the city council voted to eliminate the public access channel. In 1989 Metzger's plans for an "Aryan Woodstock" concert featuring rock 'n' roll music by neo-Nazi bands was thwarted by a Napa County, California, judge because he lacked a permit for a concert.

In 1990 Metzger, his son John, and his organization were sued by the Southern Poverty Law Center and the Anti-Defamation League for inciting Oregon Skinheads who murdered an Ethiopian immigrant. Metzger claimed that the suit was an attempt to persecute them for exercising their right of free speech. The Oregon chapter of the American Civil Liberties Union, in a friend-of-the-court brief, argued that certain aspects of the suit could have violated First Amendment rights of the defendants; however, in October, 1990, a jury ruled against Metzger and awarded the victim's family $12.5 million.

See also American Civil Liberties Union; Anti-Defamation League; Cable television; Hate laws; Ku Klux Klan; Race.

Mexican-American War

DATE: 1846-1848

PLACE: Mexico

SIGNIFICANCE: Issues arising from the lack of censorship during the Mexican-American War influenced later U.S. government wartime censorship

The Mexican-American War was the first American war reported daily in newspapers across the country. The American public followed the conflict with great interest and anticipation. Newspaper reports did more to influence American attitudes toward the war than any other medium. They also molded American perceptions of the war, its causes, and its effects on the United States. Remarkably, government and military censorship of newspaper reports did not exist.

Newspapers used war correspondents for the first time to report from the front lines in Mexico and the Southwest. These reporters followed the campaigning American armies and occasionally participated in the fighting. Instead of rehashing often late and nondescript military dispatches, reporters wrote firsthand accounts that fed the American public's desire to know more about the war. War correspondents rapidly and efficiently wrote their stories and sent them off to press. Their

General Winfield Scott leads the American occupation of Mexico City at the conclusion of the Mexican-American War. (Library of Congress)

stories proved not only more plentiful but also more accurate than their military counterparts. No military or government authority censored their stories. Although some in military and government circles complained about the lack of censorship, the large audience reached by the newspapers had a positive effect. The journalistic freedom exercised by newspapers provided Americans more information about this war than previous ones. Thus, the American people may have been better able to form informed, intelligent opinions about the conflict.

Dissident opinion against the war also enjoyed widespread freedom. The government did not attempt to silence those who spoke out against "Mr. Polk's war"—namely, radical Whigs. President James K. Polk publicly complained about opposition to the war, but charges of treason for opposing the war rarely occurred. Authorities did not constrain civil liberties. The Polk Administration worried that dissident opinion might affect the prosecution of the war, but not to the point of taking drastic measures to curb opposition. While the war was not without controversy over which side started the conflict and what motivated the United States in the war, censorship had yet to become standard practice. War correspondents informed the American public. Sketch artists, so prevalent in the American Civil War, provided uncensored visual depictions of battles to American readers. This freedom caused concern, notably among the military, who worried that reporters might unintentionally leak secret information to the enemy, and that negative reporting might turn public opinion against military action. Journalistic freedom and dissident opinion did not enjoy such freedom in later conflicts.

See also Civil War, U.S.; Presidency, U.S.; Thoreau, Henry David.

Mexico

DESCRIPTION: Federal republic bordering the United States to the south

SIGNIFICANCE: Essentially a one-party state since 1917, Mexico has a history of superficially free speech with subtle—and not so subtle—restrictions on actual expression

As was typical in Spanish colonial America, early Mexican society was dominated by small, powerful, elite groups, including the Spanish military, administrators, and the Roman Catholic church. Catholicism was the official religion of Spain. As the only permitted religion, the Catholic church was responsible for education, which enabled it—and the elite in general—to isolate Mexico from the modern ideas of the Renaissance (which would later have considerable influence on the British colonies that became the United States of America). In addition, in order to limit access to nonacceptable information, ports were closed and trade was only allowed with Spain. The legacy of this system was a fundamental lack of tolerance of diverse views that affected Mexican society for decades after its independence from Spain.

Besides this power, the Catholic church also controlled nearly half of the arable land in Mexico by the early nineteenth century. This enabled the church, and the Spanish colonists, forcefully to integrate the native population. As was common throughout Latin America, this power structure left a legacy of a divided society, in which a small number of powerholders oppressed the vast majority.

Mexican independence, declared in 1810, was followed by years of civil war, violently crushed rebellions, and oppression of Indians and others. After Porfirio Díaz became dictator of Mexico in 1876, he established many of the patterns of behavior that would characterize Mexican politics for the next century. He forcefully recruited labor into government-controlled organizations, while at the same time violently repressing strikes. Díaz's position was secured by government censorship of virtually all forms of expression. He was driven from office in May of 1911 at the beginning of what Mexicans have since called their revolution.

The Mexican Revolution, after several years of back and forth fighting, produced the institution that would dominate the Mexican landscape for the rest of the century, the Institutional Revolutionary Party (PRI). Although there were no formal censorship laws, PRI and the interests of its leadership shaped all forms of expression allowed and outlawed over the next several decades through various mechanisms and the party's control of the most powerful institution in Mexican society, the federal presidency.

Mass Media. One of the most important areas in society for an authoritarian government to control is the press. PRI developed several mechanisms for controlling what newspapers, television, and radio could present to citizens. Reporters have been expected to respect the privacy of individual leaders (a tradition that has protected politicians against investigation of possible crimes or abuses of power), and not to disturb the public peace or morals (which has resulted in control of artistic forms of expression and latitude in rejecting stories). The most severe tool has been violence. Between 1984 and 1986, for example, 152 journalists were attacked physically, and from 1971 to 1986 forty-two journalists lost their lives for pursuing stories that the government did not want publicized, or for being overly critical of leaders or policies. Many of them were victims of death squads with suspected links to the military.

Although most of the press and broadcast media have been privately owned, they have operated under strict governmental supervision by several different agencies. The government and the PRI have also used bribery to prevent reporters from developing stories counter to elite interests. Salaries for journalists have been small, and their unions have been weak. Some estimates suggest that up to 90 percent of reporters have accepted pay-offs. Newspapers and magazines have also frequently published, without attribution, materials prepared by government officials.

The entertainment industries have been subject to moral laws under the Organic Law of Public Education (1951), which provided for the regulation of films—the one constitutionally acceptable form of censorship in Mexico.

Labor. Mexican labor unions were organized under the guidance and direction of the state. This represents another typical pattern of PRI control, co-optation. Union leaders, through bribery or intimidation, have been forced to subordinate the interests and views of union members to those of the party. The state has also had the power to decide if strikes were legal or not. It has incarcerated leaders of wildcat strikes as political prisoners, as was done in 1958-1959 to the leaders of a railway strike. Whenever the rank-and-file members of these groups have begun to demand union democracy, the state has violently repressed these movements. During the 1950's and 1960's, peasants and workers launched numerous protest actions, which were either repressed or co-opted.

Political Opposition. Some degree of political dissent has always been allowed in Mexico, but its level and tone have been controlled by the government. During the Díaz administration, for example, special police forces were established to patrol the countryside to control radical dissent. When opposition expressions were seen by elites to be threatening to society or social order, the military stepped in. The military in Mexico has defined its role as "maintaining national security," which has often meant breaking up strikes and controlling mass protests, which have often been seen by the military as insurrection attempts. According to some, the elite counterinsurgency group, "White Brigade," based in Mexico City's Military Camp 1, was responsible for torturing and killing many of the five hundred "disappeared" persons in Mexico, almost all from the left-wing opposition. Private forces have also put down demands by peasants for radical reform, such as redistribution of the land. Twenty-six peasants were killed in one such dispute in 1992, for example.

The government and PRI have also used the allure of political power and money to co-opt and disarm dissident peasant leaders, lawyers, labor leaders, and intellectuals. Many of the best minds of academia—both students and faculty—regardless of their ideological orientations, have worked for the state, because that is where the best opportunities have been.

In the political arena, until the 1980's, Mexicans rarely had the chance to vote for leftist opposition candidates. For many years the only opposition party allowed was conservative. Even when more parties were allowed to participate in the system, mechanisms were put in place to limit their influence, such as limiting the numbers of seats in legislatures open to them, or invoking claims of electoral fraud to prevent them from taking office. Many Mexicans believed, for example, that the 1988 presidential election was actually won by opposition candidate Cuauhtémoc Cárdenas, and not PRI candidate Carlos Salinas de Gortari.

The Roman Catholic Church. After its initial period of dominance, the church was subjected to discrimination from a liberal, anticlerical movement that developed soon after independence. The 1857 constitution, which confiscated church property, began this process. The revolutionary constitution of 1917 went further. Religious education was made illegal, political groups were forbidden from bearing names referring to religious denominations, and religious publications were prohibited from discussing political matters. In fact, the church had no legal standing in Mexico until 1982. Despite these legal provisions, because of the church's traditional heritage and role in society, religious schools continued to exist, and the church continued to have a strong influence on society.

Late Twentieth Century Developments. Freedom of expression was guaranteed under two articles of the 1917 constitution, which states, "the expression of ideas will not be the subject of any judicial or administrative inquisitions" and "the freedom to write and publish on any matter cannot be violated. No law or authority can establish prior censorship." However, the letter of this law has frequently been undermined by the spirit in which it has been enforced. However, after the mid-1980's there were some improvements. In late 1982, for example, legislation was passed outlawing the practice of office-holders' providing payments to reporters.

One mechanism that the government once used to control the press was its monopoly over the production and distribution of newsprint. The government could withhold shipments of paper from newspapers that it wanted to punish, and provide extra paper—which could be sold at a profit—to those it wanted to reward. Mexican membership in the General Agreement on Trade and Tariffs and the North American Free Trade Agreement in the 1990's has reduced this power somewhat, as newspapers have gained access to other sources of newsprint.

In the 1980's and 1990's opposition parties made significant gains at the municipal and gubernatorial levels, sometimes even defeating PRI candidates. At the federal level, opposition seats in the legislature were expanded from 100 to 150 in 1986. Even the Mexican Communist Party was legalized. In 1987 student demonstrations with more than 150,000 participants were met with negotiations rather than troops, as in the past. In 1991 Mexican bishops openly expressed their concerns about torture, political persecution, corruption, and electoral fraud, and no action was taken against them.

Nevertheless, the state and PRI still maintained important controls on the expression of opinions. Sixty-eight percent of the revenue that newspapers and magazines received came from government sources, directly and indirectly (as through government-owned businesses.) This fact has led many publications to engage in self-censorship to avoid the possibility of losing these revenues. Bank loans, electricity, telephone service, and health code inspections can also be manipulated by the state to punish the publication of criticism beyond acceptable levels.

Monopoly ownership has also been an obstacle to freedom in the broadcast industry. Of the country's 118 television stations, 100 have been owned by a single conglomerate. The Ministry of the Interior has retained wide-ranging powers to ensure that "information meets the established norms" in this area. The ministry has also controlled much of the production and content of films as well. In the book-publishing business, while generally open, many publishers continued to engage in self-censorship because of the punishment tools available to the government.

While there have been improvements in the treatment of opposition opinions, discrimination against Indians has endured. As late as 1993 there were still paramilitary bands and local police controlled by political bosses or landowners, who routinely threatened or killed peasant activists. While the number of minority seats in the national legislature was increased, PRI still controlled three hundred seats reserved for its members. Because so many people continued to depend on the largesse of the state for survival, it remained likely that the diversity of expression would remain limited in Mexico.

—Eduardo Magãlhaes III

See also Central America; Exploration, Age of; Fear; Japan; Journalists, violence against; News media censorship; South America; Spanish Empire.

BIBLIOGRAPHY

James D. Cockcroft's *Mexico* (New York: Monthly Review Press, 1990) provides a glimpse at Mexican political and popular history, with references to repression of various groups and institutions. Joe Foweraker and Ann L. Craig, eds., *Popular Movements and Political Change in Mexico* (Boulder, Colo.: Lynne Rienner Publishers, 1990), focus on various social movements, from the perspective of these groups with special emphasis on the restriction and co-opting of these groups by the state. With an extensive bibliography, Neil Harvey, ed., *Mexico: Dilemmas of Transition* (New York: St. Martin's Press, 1993), focuses on recent social and political reforms, as well as general state-society relations. These reforms and the lack of genuine improvement in freedom they have produced are the subject of Dan LaBotz's *Mask of Democracy: Labor Suppression in Mexico Today* (Boston: South End Press, 1992). Carlos B. Gil edits a volume that looks at the process of liberalization from the perspectives of the opposition in *Hope and Frustration: Interviews with Leaders of Mexico's Political Opposition* (Wilmington, Del.: SR books, 1992). A pair of resources that examine repression of speech in the past are Paul J. Vanderwood's *Disorder and Progress: Bandits, Police and Mexican Development* (Wilmington, Del.: SR books, 1992), which looks at the rural police and their suppression of peasant movements in the Díaz era, and José Vasconcelos' *A Mexican Ulysses: An Autobiography* (translated by William Rex Crawford; Bloomington: Indiana University Press, 1963), which provides a moving account of Mexican intellectuals' collisions with the realities of Mexican society, and the role of the Mexican state.

Meyer, Russ

BORN: March 21, 1922, Oakland, California

IDENTIFICATION: Creator of sexually explicit films satirizing pornography

SIGNIFICANCE: Meyer's films have been subjected to official and unofficial censorship in the United States and condemned as exploitative of women

Russ Meyer's first film, *The Immoral Mr. Teas* (1959), was historic in that it was the first soft-core pornographic film actually to make a great amount of money. That success launched Meyer's career and immediately made him the target of censors.

Even though all of Meyer's films have been criticized, the film *The Vixen* (1969) was perhaps the most widely censored. Vice officers in Hamilton County, Ohio, confiscated the film in September, 1969, and a judge ruled that it was obscene, thus prohibiting it from being shown in the county. This ruling was upheld by the Ohio Supreme Court. A major player in this case was Charles H. Keating, founder of Citizens for Decent Literature, and a member of the President's Commission on Obscenity and Pornography. (To Meyer's great delight, Keating was years later sentenced to federal prison for his role in a savings and loan fraud scheme). In 1984 a student group at the University of Cincinnati planned a campus screening of the film, but the Hamilton County prosecutor's office informed the university that showing the film would still violate the law.

In the 1960's, the film *Mudhoney* was seized by deputy sheriffs in Texas who had vowed to shut down any film that showed women's breasts. The confiscated print has never been returned, and authorities have said that it will be returned only when Meyer apologizes for having made it. Strongly opposed to censorship, Meyer makes no apologies for his films, which he calls "sexual cartoons in the same realm of satire as Al Capp's cartoons."

Meyer contends that America's leading censor is Jack Valenti, president of the Motion Picture Association of America (MPAA). This, he believes, is because of MPAA censorship, done for economic reasons through its system of film ratings. A film with a rating of NC-17, for example, cannot be advertised in many newspapers. Filmmakers are forced to alter their films, to avoid the NC-17 stamp, which can be fatal to a film's commercial viability.

Although still banned in some places, Meyer's films have come to be widely accepted in many communities. He and his work have attained cult status, with frequent showings on campuses and at film festivals. Even feminists have reevaluated Meyer's films and softened some of their criticisms.

See also Citizens for Decent Literature; Film censorship; Motion Picture Association of America; Nudity; President's Commission on Obscenity and Pornography; Sex in the arts.

Michelangelo

BORN: March 6, 1475, Caprese, Tucscany, Italy

DIED: February 18, 1564, Rome, Italy

IDENTIFICATION: Italian sculptor, painter, and poet

SIGNIFICANCE: Although Michelangelo was one of the greatest artists of the Italian Renaissance, his works have frequently been censored as obscene

Michelangelo, widely regarded as one of the greatest sculptors and painters of all time, has nevertheless been subject to censorship. Although his works are regarded as examples of what lifts the fine arts above the prurient and humdrum interests of the everyday, Michelangelo's major works—in particular, the *David* statue and *The Last Judgment* mural in the Sistine Chapel— were attacked as obscene in both the sixteenth and the twentieth centuries. Most scholars dismiss such episodes without comment, while others treat them as attempts by prudish minds to stifle creative genius. Michelangelo's exalted status, however, illuminates the complex relationship between censorship and the changing mores of society.

Michelangelo's Life. Michelangelo's life presents perhaps for the first time, the notion of the "modern" artist, the creative individual constrained neither by the traditions and rules of art nor by social and legal restrictions that apply to others.

Born near Florence, Michelangelo became an artist over the objections of his family. At about fourteen, he was apprenticed to a Florentine painter, but after a brief period, he left that workshop to continue his education in the household of Lorenzo de' Medici. Influenced by the Neoplatonic philosophy of the Renaissance, the young artist was also affected by the austere views of the Dominican preacher, Girolamo Savonarola. By 1500 Michelangelo was producing commissions in both Florence and Rome. His patrons included the city of Florence (for which he produced the *David*), the Medici family, and the Vatican. For Pope Julius II, he did the frescoes of the Sistine Chapel ceiling (1508-1512) and numerous tomb statues; for Pope Paul III, his work included the Sistine Chapel's *The Last Judgment* (1534-1541) and the frescoes of the Vatican's Pauline Chapel. In addition to painting, sculpture, and architecture, Michelangelo also composed about two hundred poems during the course of his life that gained recognition throughout Europe.

Early Censorship of His Work. Michelangelo worked for patrons imbued with the classical, Neoplatonic attitudes characteristic of the educated classes of the Italian Renaissance. To these people, the human being was the highest of God's creations, and nudity suggested the ideal of beauty, as it had during the ancient world. To the common man, however, uneducated in the classics, nudity smacked of the lascivious. While there has been occasional opposition to Michelangelo's works on theological grounds, his critics have usually objected to his prominent use of the unclothed figure.

In the marble statue *David*, artist and patrons agreed on the philosophical and political importance of depicting the hero nude. The populace, however, was incensed. As the finished statue was being moved into its position in a Florence city square, people stoned it, breaking it in several places. The statue was made more modest by the addition of gilded leaves covering the figure's genitals.

Similar but more intense debates surrounded Michelangelo's frescoes in the Sistine Chapel, especially those of *The Last Judgment*. In this case, the arguments were not between erudite patrons and an uneducated laity but between two generations of patrons. To Pope Julius II and, to a lesser extent, Pope Paul III, the nudes in these frescoes reflected the classical leanings of the papal court and were seen as a nonsexual celebration of the male spirit. But even while Michelangelo was completing the fresco of *The Last Judgment*, attitudes about what was appropriate in religious art were changing, largely in response to pressures brought by the Reformation in Germany. The Council of Trent (1545-1563) set specific standards for artists to follow, including the avoidance of all nudity in religious art.

What had been the quintessential representation of the human spirit to one generation was offensive to Roman Catholic morals in the next. In 1540, even before *The Last Judgment* was completed, it was criticized by papal officials. Michelangelo treated these criticisms with disdain, and the pope supported the artist. By 1558, however, Paul IV hired another artist to overpaint the fresco, adding loincloths to many of the naked figures. Pope Paul IV's successor, Pius V, had further sections repainted, and Clement VIII actually considered having the entire composition destroyed.

Modern Censorship of Michelangelo's Work. Just as Church leaders of the sixteenth century censured Michelangelo's works to protect public morals, officials in the following centuries have also occasionally condemned his work. In the twentieth century, there has been scattered opposition worldwide. In the United States, the Tariff Act of 1842 provides for the seizure of pictorial materials of an obscene or sexual nature which are being imported into the country. On several occasions in the 1930's, it was invoked against importers of postcards and books depicting Michelangelo's works. In February, 1933, a U.S. customs officer seized books illustrating the frescoes of the Sistine Chapel, calling them obscene. Reported in the newspapers, the case came to the attention of the customs assistant solicitor, and the books were immediately released, with apologizes offered.

The great *David* statue has also met with opposition in the twentieth century. When Los Angeles' Forest Lawn cemetery exhibited a replica of the statue in 1939, it did so with fig leaves placed over the genitals. In the 1960's and 1970's, when replicas and posters of the *David* were put on sale without the fig leaves, they were seized by police in Australia, Brazil, and the United States. Such cases indicate that even the works of an artist universally considered among the greatest of all time can be suppressed by authorities following the social mores of the time. —*Jean Owens Schaefer*

See also Art; Customs laws, U.S.; Italy; Nudity; Vatican.

BIBLIOGRAPHY

On art and censorship, see Jane Clapp, *Art Censorship: A Chronology of Proscribed and Prescribed Art* (Metuchen, N.J.: Scarecrow Press, 1972) and John Henry Merryman and Albert E. Elsen, *Law, Ethics and the Visual Arts* (Philadelphia: University of Pennsylvania Press, 1987). On Michelangelo, see Howard Hibbard, *Michelangelo* (Cambridge: Harper & Row, 1985) and Charles Seymour, *Michelangelo's David: A Search for Identity* (Pittsburgh: University of Pittsburgh Press, 1967). On the developing status of the artist in society, see Arnold Hauser, *The Social History of Art*, vol. 2, *Renaissance, Mannerism, Baroque* (New York: Vintage Books, 1957).

Mighty Morphin Power Rangers

TYPE OF WORK: Television series

FIRST BROADCAST: 1993

SUBJECT MATTER: High school students "morph" into "Power Rangers," who use karate to fight improbable monsters and evil characters

SIGNIFICANCE: This program has been heavily criticized for its violence, and a case of copycat violence led to its being taken off the air in Norway and Sweden

The children's television program *Mighty Morphin Power Rangers* received front-page coverage on American newspapers in October, 1994, when it was implicated in the death of a five-year-old girl in Norway. Three young boys, who were apparently imitating the Power Rangers' karate kicks, repeatedly kicked their young playmate to the point of unconsciousness on a playground, leaving her in the snow, where she froze to death. The Swedish satellite television network TV-3 then immediately suspended all broadcasts of *Power Rangers*.

American educators have also expressed concern over the impact of *Power Rangers* on children, charging that the show provokes violence by giving young children the message that kicking, shoving, and punching are acceptable behaviors because they are merely forms of play. Some educators have charged that *Power Rangers* has turned school playgrounds into "war zones" in which children transform all their free play time into "Power Ranger" games. To counter this tendency, many teachers have replaced free play with structured play at recess. Some schools have gone even further. For example, students at a Wilmington, Delaware, school were not allowed to wear clothes portraying *Power Rangers* characters or to bring any *Power Rangers* toys to school.

In December, 1995, *Power Rangers* was taken off the air in Malaysia—not because of its violence, but because the Malaysian government feared that children would associate the word "Morphin" with "morphine," and parents would think that the program encouraged drug abuse.

See also *Beavis and Butt-head*; *Man with the Golden Arm, The*; Television, children's; Violence.

Mikado, The

TYPE OF WORK: Operetta

PREMIERE: March 14, 1885, Savoy Theatre, London, England

LYRICIST: William S. Gilbert (1836-1911)

COMPOSER: Arthur S. Sullivan (1842-1900)

SUBJECT MATTER: Fictitious story about the son of a Japanese emperor who disguises himself as a minstrel in order to woo the Lord High Executioner's ward

SIGNIFICANCE: Out of fear of offending the Japanese people, the operetta was banned in both Great Britain and Japan at various times, from its creation until after World War II

During the visit of Japan's Crown Prince Fushimi to England in 1907, Gilbert and Sullivan's *The Mikado* was banned for six weeks by the Lord Chamberlain, who was concerned that its frivolous portrayal of the emperor would offend the Japanese—who had recently entered an alliance with the British. At the same time, British military bands were instructed not to play arrangements from the operetta although Japanese bands on Japanese ships in the Medway River were doing so.

The operetta had been presented once in Yokohama, Japan, under a different title, but was then banned in Japan until 1946, when it was produced by American occupation forces. Japanese reactions to the operetta had been mixed from its premiere; some Japanese dignitaries found the material grossly insulting, while others were not offended. Gilbert's sources for his libretto included a Japanese exhibition held in London during 1884-1885, but he created a mythical Japan merely based on the concept of emperor worship, not intended to denigrate a revered being or his surrounding culture.

See also Drama and theater; Japan; Lord Chamberlain; Music; Opera; United Kingdom.

Military censorship

DEFINITION: Censorship exercised by military authorities

SIGNIFICANCE: The rights of military personnel are almost always more restricted than those of other citizens, and the speech and writings of civilians are often censored by military authorities

During the 1500's and 1600's almost all European nations developed Articles of War, formal codes of law governing the behavior of soldiers and sailors. One of the key principles of these codes was the concept of subordination: Those in armed forces were subject to the power of their superiors and those below had to show respect for their superiors. Another principle was loyalty: Those serving in the armed forces were expected show much greater loyalty to the armed forces and to the nation than were civilians. These two principles gave military authorities a greater claim on the expression of those in the services than civilian authorities had on citizens.

The American Articles of War, which were adopted in 1806, were based on the British articles and carry the same principles of subordination and loyalty generally found in military codes. The Articles of War were in force in the United States until 1950, when the Uniform Code of Military Justice was adopted as the legal system of the Army, Air Force, Navy, Marine Corps, and Coast Guard. The 1950 code incorporated most of the old Articles of War.

Many of the passages in the American military code, and in the military codes of almost all other nations, restrict the rights of those in the military to engage in free expression of views in speech or writing. Article 82, for example, forbids anyone in any of the services to advise others to desert. The principle of subordination, as a limitation on freedom of speech, may be found in articles 88 and 89. Article 88 states that members of the military who speak or write contemptuously of U.S. government officials may be court-martialed. Article 89 states that those in the services may be court-martialed for showing disrespect toward their superiors.

Since the Uniform Code of Military Justice established a separate legal system for those in the armed forces, and since those who have served have been subject to constant oversight by their superiors, military bases have frequently been heavily censored places. The 1969 military publication *Guidance on Dissent* states that commanders cannot suppress publications that are critical of the U.S. government. Under Army Regulation 381-135, soldiers do have the right to receive written matter through the mail and to keep one copy of any book, newspaper, or pamphlet. If they have more than one copy of material that their superiors feel is objectionable for political or other reasons, however, this can be seen as reflecting an intent to distribute this material, and the soldiers can be prosecuted in a court-martial.

Just how heavily censored a military base should be remains a matter of debate. During World War II, a soldier who referred to President Franklin D. Roosevelt as a "gangster" was court-martialed and sentenced to a year in the stockade. In 1969 at Fort Ord, California, Ken Stolte and Daniel Amick created leaflets protesting the Vietnam War and encouraging their fellow soldiers to form a union to express grievance. Stolte and Amick were court-martialed for conspiracy and for advising others to engage in mutinous behavior. They each received three years in military prison and were dishonorably discharged. If Stolte and Amick had been civilians, handing out such leaflets would have been seen as an expression of their constitutionally guaranteed right to free speech. Indeed, their defenders argued that the two men did not lose their constitutional rights when they were drafted.

The U.S. Civil War and Military Censorship of Civilians. Organized military censorship of civilians in North America dates from the period of the U.S. Civil War. At that time, the federal War Department, under Secretary of War Edwin Stanton, established its power of censorship over all telegraph lines. The military also exercised censorship over newspapers to an extent never before seen in American history. In March, 1862, Stanton ordered the military governor of the District of Columbia to seize the offices of *The Sunday Chronicle*, which had been printing news about troop movements. In Missouri, where Union troops had been placed because of the large number of Confederate sympathizers in that state, a newspaper editor was court-martialed and his office, press, and furniture were taken over by the army and sold. In Illinois, General A. E. Burnside seized the office of the *Chicago Times* and prevented the publication of an issue of the paper.

In several of these cases of military censorship during the Civil War, the censors were opposed by civilian authorities. In the case of the *Chicago Times*, for example, a federal judge issued an injunction to keep Burnside's soldiers from carrying out his orders. This injunction was ignored, but civilian powers were often able to hamper the exercise of military censorship. The military enjoyed a freer hand in the conquered territories of the Confederacy, which were under the Union Army during the war and which were occupied by Union troops during the period known as Reconstruction, which lasted until 1877.

The Turn of the Century and World War I. In 1898 the United States went to war with Spain, and invaded the Spanish colonies of Cuba, Puerto Rico, and the Philippines. In order to limit the publishing of strategic information about the war, General A. W. Greeley of the U.S. Signal Corps convinced the Western Union Telegraph Company in Florida to allow him to station military censors at telegraph offices in Tampa, Miami, and Jacksonville.

After the war, the United States continued to occupy all of the former Spanish colonies, and purchased the Philippines from Spain. Many of the Filipinos, who had been engaged in a war of independence against Spain, were displeased at this change of colonial masters, and guerrilla war in the Philippines followed. General E. S. Otis, the commander of American forces in the Philippines, began to censor dispatches to American newspapers. Otis' censorship was heavily criticized because, it was claimed, he showed favoritism in allowing some press representatives to cable dispatches and did not allow others. Under the American military governor of the Philippines, military censorship was established over the telegraph system in that country.

In the years leading up to World War I, the War Department, the army, and the navy began pushing for legislation to control the press. The army chief of staff ordered a study of the methods of press control used by the English. In 1916 the secretary of war established the Bureau of Information, under the command of Major Douglas MacArthur. This agency was the only source of information from the War Department to the press. It was simultaneously a censorship of civilians by the military and a censorship of military personnel, since military personnel could only communicate with the press through the Bureau of Information. When a formal means of censoring media of communication during World War I was created, in the form of the Committee on Public Information (also known as the Creel Committee), it was headed by a civilian, but it contained representatives of the secretary of war and the secretary of the navy.

Occupied Germany and Japan. At the end of World War II Germany was occupied by the allied armies (the British, French, U.S., and Russian armies), and Japan was occupied by the armed forces of the United States. The British, French, and U.S. zones in Germany were combined into a single zone in 1947, which became West Germany. The American military government in Germany found itself caught between the ideal of a free press and the program of de-Nazification. Freedom of the press was to be granted to Germans only after Nazi influences had been largely eliminated.

The Information Control Division (ICD) was the agency of U.S. military government charged with controlling the German press in the first years of occupation. By the time of Germany's surrender, newspapers, radio stations, theaters, and cinemas had been shut down by the invading allied armies. In June, 1945, the first German papers were licensed. These were subject to strict prepublication censorship by the U.S. military.

The ICD was especially interested in the censorship of German books, since Germans read at least four times as much as Americans, and books were therefore a critical means of communication in Germany. The American military wanted to avoid any burning of books, however, because this would recall Nazi book-burning activities. Therefore, pro-Nazi materials were taken out of bookstores and libraries and quietly turned into pulp. All authors of books had to submit their manuscripts to the ICD for clearance. Cinemas were encouraged to show American films, but some American films, such as gangster movies, were forbidden because they might seem to confirm the negative image of American society portrayed by Nazi propaganda. Exchange of views between American soldiers and German civilians was limited by strict regulations forbidding "fraternization" between the two.

In Japan the American military was the sole power, under the command of General Douglas MacArthur, by then a general. During the first month of occupation, a code of censorship was put into place. American military officials, sensitive to the charge that they might be inhibiting freedom of expression, proclaimed the ideal of freedom of the press at the same time that the code was issued. All newspaper stories had to be submitted to American officers, who would decide whether the stories could be printed.

Modern Military Censorship. Compared to earlier wars, reporting on the Vietnam War was relatively free of censorship on the part of military authorities, but the American forces and their allies did try to exercise some control over the flow of information. The military did not forget what greater press freedom had wrought in Vietnam. When U.S. forces invaded the Caribbean island of Grenada in 1983, the military imposed a news blackout on events on the island and barred reporters from accompanying the invading soldiers. This created dissatisfaction and complaints among representatives of the news media, but generally the media's portrayal of the invasion of Grenada garnered favorable responses about the invasion from the public. To respond to the complaints of members of the media, after the Grenada invasion U.S. military leaders attempted to develop a more sophisticated method of military censorship by creating the National Media Pool of rotating news organizations.

The pool system was first used during the American invasion of Panama at the end of 1989. The military chose which reporters it wanted to be part of the pool, and it provided "guides" to reporters once the reporters arrived in the invaded country, thus effectively censoring the news without resorting to direct censorship. The pool system continued to be used as a method of military censorship during the 1991 Persian Gulf War. Reporters received news and videotapes from public information officers, and the authorities attempted to limit and control contacts between ordinary soldiers and the press.

—Carl L. Bankston III

See also Civil War, U.S.; Constitution, U.S.; Draft resistance; Free speech; Grenada, U.S. invasion of; Leafletting; Spanish-American War; Vietnam War; War; World War I; World War II.

Bibliography

Readers may find a description of the development of the Articles of War and of the Uniform Code of Military justice, and a summary of how military law limits the rights to free speech of military personnel in William B. Aycock and Seymour W. Wurfel's *Military Law Under the Uniform Code of Military Justice* (Chapel Hill: University of North Carolina Press, 1955). For a critique of military limitation of the constitutional rights of military personnel, readers may examine Peter Barnes's *Pawns: The Plight of the Citizen Soldier* (New York: Alfred A. Knopf, 1972). Military censorship in occupied Germany is described in John Gimbel's *The American Occupation of Germany: Politics and the Military, 1945-1949* (Stanford, Calif.: Stanford University Press, 1968). Russell Brines provides a description of occupied Japan under MacArthur, including a section on U.S. military censorship, in *MacArthur's Japan* (Philadelphia: J. P. Lippincott, 1948). John Schaller's *The American Occupation of Japan* (New York: Oxford University Press, 1985) is a general history of the American military occupation of Japan.

Mill, John Stuart

Born: May 20, 1806, Pentonville, London, England

Died: May 8, 1873, Avignon, France

Identification: British philosopher and economist

Significance: Mill formulated classical arguments for freedom of expression that have strongly influenced modern Western democracies

The son of a Scottish economist, Mill was a godson and sometime pupil of Jeremy Bentham—a bitter opponent of press censorship. Mill's own most systematic defense of freedom of expression appears in *On Liberty* (1859). In that renowned essay he observes that in liberal democracies—which he calls "constitutional countries"—governments do not often try to censor expression of opinion, except when they express the intolerance of the general public. Mill asserts, however, that even when government and people unite in wishing to suppress an opinion, neither has the right to do so. He regards the power to silence opinion of any kind as illegitimate.

Mill regards it as even worse for governments to censor when the people agree than when they do not. All of humanity has no more right to silence a lone dissenter than the dissenter has the right to silence all of humanity. Here, as elsewhere in his essay, Mill echoes John Milton's *Areopagitica* (1644) by arguing that in suppressing opinion government deprives not only contemporary society of its possible benefit, but posterity as well.

To support this wholesale condemnation of censorship in any form, Mill makes four basic arguments. His first is that if an opinion is silenced, the silenced opinion may be true for all anyone can know. Those who deny that the silenced view may be true are asserting their own infallibility—which is clearly unjustifiable. To help make his case, Mill points out that Marcus Aurelius, a second century C.E. Roman emperor known for his sagacity as a Stoic philosopher, persecuted Christianity.

Mill's second argument is that although an opinion that is silenced may be erroneous, it may—and often will—contain a partial truth. Since opinions on many subjects are only partly correct, the only chance for them to move toward full truth is to let them clash openly with opposing views. This cannot happen to opinions that are silenced. Mill's third argument is related: Even if an opinion in question is the entire truth, unless it is thoroughly tested against contrary opinions, those who hold it will do so merely as a prejudice. Without having to defend their true opinions, people cannot understand the rational basis behind them. Their minds are worse off if they need not be exercised in defending the truth.

Mill's final argument is that the meaning of any doctrine that people defend by censoring opposing views is in danger of being wholly or largely lost. Such a doctrine will lack vitality if it need not be defended; if it lacks vitality, it will not have the desired effect on the character of those who believe it.

For Mill, the very hallmark of a developed civilization is its willingness to tolerate opinions that it opposes or finds noxious, and its willingness to subject its beliefs and what it considers to be knowledge to the rough-and-tumble of open debate.

See also *Areopagitica*; Bentham, Jeremy; Democracy; Morality.

Miller, Henry

Born: December 26, 1891, New York, New York

Died: June 7, 1980, Pacific Palisades, California

Identification: American author

Significance: Miller wrote sexually explicit works that were long banned in English-speaking countries

Miller was an unsuccessful writer until his experiences as a penniless expatriate in Paris galvanized his imagination. The result was *Tropic of Cancer* (1934), a loosely organized account of his life in Paris as well as an ecstatic record of self-discovery. The sexually explicit book establishes a distinction between Miller's often romantic yearnings and the mechanical lustful adventures of his male friends. The novel was published by Obelisk Press, a French publisher specializing in experimental literature, and was followed by *Tropic of Capricorn* (1939), a savage evocation of Miller's earlier years in Brooklyn. Both books drew critical praise, but were routinely seized by U.S. Customs agents because of their allegedly obscene content when tourists attempted to bring them home. As a result, Miller's public reputation was distorted and his income remained negligible.

Obelisk Press went on to publish an even more sexually graphic Miller novel, *Sexus*, in 1949. The firm's successor, Olympia Press, published this book's sequel, *Plexus* (1953), as well as *Quiet Days in Clichy* (1956), an early work that represents one of Miller's few attempts at turning out sexually explicit material for pay. Like most of Miller's other writings, these books were inaccessible to those who might otherwise have made up Miller's natural readership.

Miller returned to the United States in 1940, but it was more than two decades before an American publisher, Barney Rosset's Grove Press, attempted to publish his major works openly. *Tropic of Cancer* appeared in 1961 to generally positive reviews and excellent sales, but was legally challenged in numerous states and localities throughout the country. Grove defended the book in case after case, triumphing in 1964 when the Supreme Court found the book not obscene.

Meanwhile, Grove reprinted *Tropic of Capricorn* in 1962 and an early collection of stories and essays, *Black Spring* (1936), the following year. *Sexus*, *Plexus*, and *Nexus* (1960)—the final volume of the trilogy that Miller called *The Rosy Crucifixion*—appeared in 1965. Because of the manner in which Miller's works had been published abroad, their copyright status was cloudy, and Grove Press rushed the trilogy into print to forestall sales of unauthorized editions. By then most of Miller's books were freely available in the United States, but their aging author suspected that the numerous censorship battles had merely fueled his reputation as a "pornographer" and had obscured the spiritual dimensions of his work.

Among the writers whom Miller influenced were Lawrence Durrell, whose novel *The Black Book* (1938) could not be published in the United States or the United Kingdom for decades, and Erica Jong, whose novel *Fear of Flying* (1973) was hailed by some as a female version of *Tropic of Cancer*.

See also France; Girodias, Maurice; Grove Press; Lawrence, D. H.; Sex in the arts; *Tropic of Cancer*; United States.

Miller et al. v. Civil City of South Bend

COURT: U.S. Court of Appeals for the Seventh Circuit

DECIDED: May 25, 1990

SIGNIFICANCE: This decision held that nonobscene barroom nude dancing constituted "expressive activity," as opposed to "mere conduct," and thus deserved First Amendment protection

This case represents an attempt to navigate the First Amendment's often elusive boundary between expression and conduct. The suit was originally brought in 1985 by several adult-entertainment entrepreneurs and dancers in an effort to prevent the state of Indiana from enforcing its public indecency law, which banned nudity in public places, against them. The plaintiffs challenged the statute as an unconstitutional infringement on their First Amendment rights of expression. In rebuttal, the state justified its law as an attempt to protect the public morality and family structure.

In an earlier case, the same statute had been challenged before the Indiana Supreme Court on overbreadth grounds. In that 1979 suit, the plaintiffs claimed that in addition to its permissible restrictions, Indiana's statute restricted constitutionally protected rights of free speech and expression. The Indiana Supreme Court had rejected this contention and interpreted the statute to apply to conduct alone and not to forms of expressive activity. Moreover, the court held that barroom dancing was "mere conduct," which could be constitutionally prohibited by the state.

In this later case, the district court for the Northern District of Indiana was asked to consider the statute as applied to nonobscene nude dancing. The court was able to skirt the definition of "obscenity" because the state conceded that the activity in question was not obscene. Instead, the state argued that the activity in question was "mere conduct," outside the realm of First Amendment protection. After viewing a videotape of the challenged activity, the district court agreed and held that nude barroom dancing was not expressive activity and thus could be prohibited by the State. *Miller et al. v. Civil City of South Bend* marked an appeal from that ruling.

The U.S. Court of Appeals for the Seventh Circuit reversed the Indiana district court to find that nude barroom dancing, when performed for entertainment, was a form of expression deserving of First Amendment protection. The appeals court reached this result by relying on several strands of U.S. Supreme Court precedent. Most important, in its 1981 decision, *Schad v. Mt. Ephraim*, the Supreme Court had invalidated a zoning ordinance that prohibited all live entertainment and confirmed the First Amendment's protection of live entertainment. The Supreme Court clarified that nudity, or sexual content, does not automatically remove an activity or material from the ambit of First Amendment protection, although nudity alone, when not combined with some form of expressive conduct, was not protected.

In its invalidation of Indiana's public nudity statute as applied to nude barroom dancing, the appeals court rejected the dissent's suggestion that courts should distinguish between "high" and "low" art, on the grounds that such a determination risks affording unpopular forms of expression no constitutional protection at all. Instead, the court reiterated the principles at the heart of First Amendment protection: All expression is presumptively protected against government interference and restraint, and the government cannot prohibit the expression of an idea simply because the idea is offensive or distasteful.

See also Books and obscenity law; Free speech; Nude dancing; Nudity; Obscenity: legal definitions; Symbolic speech; Unprotected speech.

Miller v. California

Court: U.S. Supreme Court

Decided: June 21, 1973

Significance: In reaffirming the principle that obscene material is not protected by the First Amendment, this decision provided a new standard for defining obscenity

In *Memoirs v. Massachusetts* (1966), a state court had banned the novel *The Memoirs of Fanny Hill* as obscene, although the court acknowledged that it might have some "minimal literary value." The U.S. Supreme Court, however, held that a book could be banned only if the dominant theme of its material, when considered as a whole, appeals to a prurient interest in sex; when the material patently offends contemporary community standards; and when the material is utterly without redeeming social value. The Supreme Court reversed the state court on the ground that, although *Fanny Hill* may have been offensive, it was not "utterly without redeeming social value."

The 1973 *Miller* case involved a defendant who had mailed sexually explicit materials to persons who had neither requested them nor expressed interest in receiving such material. After some recipients complained to police, the defendant was convicted in a jury trial of violating a California law making it a misdemeanor knowingly to distribute obscene matter. On appeal a superior court in Orange Country affirmed the decision. However, the U.S. Supreme Court vacated the decision by a 5-4 vote and remanded the case.

Chief Justice Warren Burger, joined by justices Byron White, Harry Blackmun, Lewis F. Powell, and William H. Rehnquist, wrote the majority opinion. Burger cited the Court's earlier holding in *Roth v. United States* (1957), that obscene materials are not protected by the First Amendment. He claimed that in the *Memoirs* case the Court had "veered sharply away from *Roth*" and produced a "drastically altered test." According to Burger, *Roth* presumed that obscene material is, by definition, "utterly without social value," while *Memoirs* required the prosecution to prove that challenged material is utterly valueless—a burden "virtually impossible to discharge under our criminal standards of proof." Burger announced that the Court was returning to *Roth* and abandoning as "unworkable" the "utterly without redeeming social value" test of *Memoirs*.

Accordingly, Burger concluded that material is "obscene" and can be restricted if an average person applying local community standards—rather than uniform national standards—would find that it appeals to prurient interests; if the work is patently offensive; and if it lacks "serious literary, artistic, political, or scientific value."

Justice William O. Douglas dissented, as did Justice William J. Brennan, Jr., joined by Potter Stewart and Thurgood Marshall. While Burger claimed to be returning to the *Roth* test, these other justices argued that "ideas having even the slightest redeeming social importance" should have full protection of the First Amendment. In their opinion, Burger's more restrictive test extended First Amendment protection only to works of "serious value."

See also Community standards; *Fanny Hill, The Memoirs of*; Obscenity: legal definitions; Obscenity: sale and possession; Redeeming social value; *Roth v. United States.*

Milton, John

Born: December 9, 1608, London, England

Died: November 8, 1674, London, England

Identification: English poet, scholar, and pamphleteer

Significance: Considered one of the greatest poets in the English language, Milton wrote prose defending Puritanism that resulted in several of his books being burned and his works being listed in the *Index Librorum Prohibitorum*

Milton grew up in a prosperous home that was strongly Protestant and moderately Puritan. A studious and gifted young man, he was given every educational advantage, including private tutoring and enrollment in St. Paul's School and Christ's College, Cambridge. At Cambridge, Milton pursued classical studies and wrote poems in Latin, English, and Italian. His schooling was expected to lead him to a career as a clergyman, but he disliked the direction of religious and civil affairs in England, so he did not take holy orders. From 1632 to 1638, he lived with his family as he continued his private study of European and classical literature and writings about church leaders. During this period he wrote the masque *Comus* (1634) and the elegy *Lycidas* (1637).

From about 1640 to 1660 Milton was preoccupied with public controversies and wrote prose treatises defending the

John Milton, author of Areopagitica, *one of the most forceful statements against censorship ever written.* (Library of Congress)

Puritan cause that expressed his concerns about religious, civil, and domestic liberties. In works such as *Of Reformation Touching Church Discipline in England* (1641) and *The Reason of Church-Government Urg'd Against Prealty* (1642), Milton attacked the Episcopacy and the demand for a Presbyterian church. In 1643 and 1644, he published *The Doctrine and Discipline of Divorce*, four pamphlets arguing for legitimizing divorce on grounds of incompatibility. These pamphlets, which earned him notoriety from his Presbyterian allies and gained him a reputation as a radical, seem to have originated from difficulties in his own marriage. Further, feeling hampered by censorship of the press, he wrote his most famous prose work, *Areopagitica* (1644), a powerful plea for unlicensed printing, occasioned by a severe parliamentary ordinance for the control of printing.

After the execution of King Charles I in 1649, Milton's public role in helping to create the English Commonwealth was reinforced by his pamphlets against continental critics of Oliver Cromwell's regime and in support of the execution of the king. Despite failing eyesight, Milton continued to write political pamphlets during the 1650's. After the restoration of Charles II to the throne in 1660, Milton was in danger of execution, so he went into hiding; he was arrested, but was soon released. His works, *Eikonoklastes* (1649) and *Defensio Populi Anglicani* (1650), were both called in by royal proclamation and burned in 1660, and *Eikonoklastes* was listed in the Roman Catholic church's *Index Librorum Prohibitorum*.

In the last fourteen years of his life, Milton returned to writing poetry, publishing his three major poems *Paradise Lost* (1667), *Paradise Regained* (1671), and *Samson Agonistes* (1671).

See also *Areopagitica*; Book burning; Censorship; English Commonwealth; *Index Librorum Prohibitorum*; Leighton, Alexander.

Mindszenty, József

BORN: March 29, 1892, Csehimindszenti, Austro-Hungarian Empire

DIED: May 6, 1975, Vienna, Austria

IDENTIFICATION: Hungarian cardinal and prince primate

SIGNIFICANCE: A Roman Catholic church leader who did not disdain political activism, Mindszenty was harassed and imprisoned by both right-wing and communist regimes in Hungary

Mindszenty was born in the western Hungarian village of Csehimindszenti, from which he took his own surname. The son of a German or Austrian farmer, he was ordained a priest in 1915 and rose through the ranks to become bishop of Veszprém in 1944, shortly before German troops occupied his country. The following year, after Hungary had been liberated from the Germans, he was appointed cardinal and prince primate of Hungary—titles that he retained until 1973, when Pope Paul VI deprived him of these offices.

During much of his church career Mindszenty was politically active. As a professor of theology, he helped lead the Christian-National movement that fought against the progressive Karolyi regime in late 1918 and the proletarian dictatorship of Béla Kun in 1919. During the 1930's and early 1940's he was among the advocates of restoring Hungary's monarchy. In late 1944 he was imprisoned for intervening against the extreme right-wing Arrow-Cross regime, and was not released until the time of the liberation of western Hungary by the Soviet army. In December, 1948, he was arrested again, this time accused of plotting against the people's republic. Although he was freed during Hungary's 1956 revolution, his freedom lasted but four days, during which he again attempted to assume a leadership role, more political than spiritual. As Soviet troops put down the Hungarian revolution, he was granted asylum inside Budapest's U.S. embassy building, where he remained for fifteen years.

Mindszenty was a clearly political prisoner on two occasions, the victim of two contrasting regimes. Moreover, he was forced into exile within his own country. These censorship measures backfired, however, serving only to enhance his prestige and propagate his message. Although it was Pope Paul and the government of the United States that negotiated amnesty for Mindszenty in 1971, it was also the pope's intervention two years later that silenced Mindszenty effectively.

See also Communism; National Socialism; Soviet Union; Vatican.

Miracle, The

TYPE OF WORK: Film

RELEASED: 1948

DIRECTOR: Roberto Rossellini (1906-1977)

SCRIPT: Federico Fellini (1920-1993)

SUBJECT MATTER: A peasant woman believes that the stranger who impregnates her is Saint Joseph and that her infant son is Jesus Christ

SIGNIFICANCE: Controversy over this film in the United States led to a U.S. Supreme Court ruling that granted constitutional free expression protection to films for the first time

When *The Miracle* first appeared in Italy in 1948, the Roman Catholic church created a furor over its contents although it did not try to stop its exhibition. Adapted from a book written by Federico Fellini, the film was directed by Roberto Rossellini and starred Anna Magnani as the peasant woman whose drunken sexual encounter with a drifter (played by Fellini) resulted in her pregnancy. Believing the drifter to be Saint Joseph, the woman determines that a miracle has occurred and that she has given birth to Jesus Christ.

In 1949 the film passed U.S. Customs and a New York censorship official licensed it. Its distributor, a Jewish Polish immigrant named Joseph Burstyn, did not show the film until 1950, when it played at New York City's Paris Theatre. After the Roman Catholic Legion of Decency called the film a "sacrilegious and blasphemous mockery," the New York City commissioner of licenses stopped the film's exhibition. Burstyn then went to the state court, which ruled that the commissioner had no right to censor films in that way.

The Catholic church's Cardinal Francis Spellman initiated a new attack on the film in January, 1951, with a condemnation that he ordered a statement to be read at masses in New York

Federico Fellini's The Miracle *was attacked for being sacrilegious; legal challenges to the film led to a U.S. Supreme Court ruling extending First Amendment protections to films for the first time.* (Museum of Modern Art/Film Stills Archive)

City's churches. Calling the film a "vile and harmful" ridicule of the belief in miracles, Spellman requested all citizens to boycott, especially by economic means, all immoral films. Catholic organizations reacted by picketing the theater and threatening to bomb the building. The New York Board of Regents chairman, stating that the film had received hundreds of protests, appointed a review of *The Miracle*. Three regents deemed it "sacrilegious." After closing the film, Burstyn went to court backed by a leading anticensorship lawyer, Ephraim London.

After a New York appeals court decided against Burstyn, the case of *Joseph Burstyn, Inc. v. Wilson* reached the U.S. Supreme Court in April, 1952. Using the concept that censorship by local authorities was not constitutional under the First Amendment, London argued that interference by the church altered church and state divisions. Within a month Associate Justice Tom C. Clark handed down the Court's decision, stating that since films were an important means used in "the communication of ideas" they were protected by the Constitution's free speech guarantees. Clark wrote that states could not "ban a film on the basis of a censor's conclusion that it is 'sacrilegious.'" Justice Clark declared that the government had no right to decide what material was relevant nor to "suppress real or imagined attacks upon a religious doctrine" in any form of available media.

See also Boycotts; Film censorship; Fourteenth Amendment; *Garden of Eden, The*; *Last Temptation of Christ, The;* Legion of Decency; *M*; Spellman, Cardinal Francis Joseph.

Miscegenation

Definition: Intermixing of members of different racial groups in marriage or sexual relationships

Significance: In most states of the United States and in the Republic of South Africa, miscegenation and intermarriage between races were once forbidden by law

Fear of miscegenation has historical roots. In most of the thirteen North American colonies, and later in most of the United States, taboos against exogamy, especially against marriage between black and white partners, were maintained by law. Early in the twentieth century thirty U.S. states had statutes banning marriage between African Americans and European Americans. In 1967, when the Supreme Court finally declared a Virginia antimiscegenation law unconstitutional, racial intermarriage was still banned in nineteen states, not all of which were in the South.

The Film Industry. Popular attitudes and laws against interracial partnerships have been reflected in the arts and in the cinema in particular. Some films and producers thrived on controversy, but generally political and economic pressures led to censorship of films. In 1916 film producers and directors formed the National Association of the Motion Picture Industry (NAMPI). It was resolved that many things would not appear in pictures, and the list included miscegenation. In 1929 this code was superseded by the Motion Picture Production Code. This elaborate code dealt with depictions of criminal and sexual acts, and specified, under "particular applications" of "general principles," that "miscegenation (sex relationship between the white and black races) is forbidden."

Various groups sought to ensure that the code was enforced. The Legion of Decency was one. An organization sponsored by the Roman Catholic church, which boycotted pictures it deemed objectionable, the Legion of Decency did not object to the banning of certain depictions of love and marriage. The Legion set up its own rating system in 1936, and occasionally publicized violations of the Motion Picture Code, but there is no hint in its reports of attempts at portraying miscegenation. This aspect of the code went unchallenged for a long time; since African Americans were either ignored or relegated to farce, musicals, and films specifically for black audiences, there was no difficulty in enforcing this aspect of the code. In the few early films that included black roles other than domestic employees, white actors were made up to play black characters.

In 1956 the Production Code Administration, or board of censorship, amended the code to permit a wider range of subjects, including miscegenation. This liberalization, however, made little immediate difference in the products of the film industry.

The taboo on depicting relations between Asians and white persons was the first to dissolve. *The King and I* was released in 1956, with the European American Yul Brynner in the title role as the Siamese king in love with an English woman. There were a few films, such as *The Quiet American* of 1957, which hinted at interracial relationships. Miscegenation is the theme of *The World of Suzie Wong*, released in 1960.

Miscegenation as a subject of films increased in the 1960's. Roughly forty-eight North American films produced in the decade of 1961 to 1970 dealt with or involved scenes of miscegenation. Many of these were about relations between whites and Asians or Native Americans, rather than whites and blacks, while other films on the subject were produced abroad. The sensitive and subtle film *One Potato, Two Potato* of 1964, the story of a black and white couple, caused a minor sensation, even though it was a low-budget, independent production from Ohio; realistically enough, the couple is penalized at the end of the story for defying conventions.

Television. A television code was drafted in 1951, but its terms were not universally followed. In any case, all major networks followed, by and large, the prescriptions of the Motion Picture Production Code. Regarding miscegenation, some situation comedies, beginning in the 1970's (especially *All in the Family*, *The Jeffersons*, and some serials imported from the United Kingdom), challenged bigotry by portraying or implying relationships between white men and black women. Earlier, producers of the series *Star Trek* had resisted, successfully, network attempts to censor a kiss between the white Captain Kirk and the black Lieutenant Uhura. Although marriages between black men and white women outnumber marriages between black women and white men almost four to one in the United States, this relationship has proven a far touchier issue, and has yet to be consistently portrayed on television.

Literature and Other Arts. Literature and works of art were seldom censored for depicting miscegenation, partly because the topic itself has seldom been addressed. Various English-language translations of the ancient stories from the Middle East, known as *The Arabian Nights Entertainments*, or *The Thousand and One Nights*, have been among the works most often censored or attacked in the courts, but it is not clear that these attacks resulted from the stories' depiction of miscegenation or from the stories' eroticism. In the case of *United States v. Levine* (1936), Levine was convicted of sending obscene materials through the mails, one of which was a book about an Englishwoman kept in a Sudanese harem. As a result of a series of photographs in the 1962 volume of the magazine *Eros*, published and distributed by Ralph Ginzburg, depicting interracial sex, the publisher was charged with the crime of sending obscene materials through the mails, the attorney general's justification being that these pictures might exacerbate feelings of racial hatred in the South. Eldridge Cleaver's *Soul*

CHANGING AMERICAN VIEWS ON MARRIAGE BETWEEN WHITES AND BLACKS

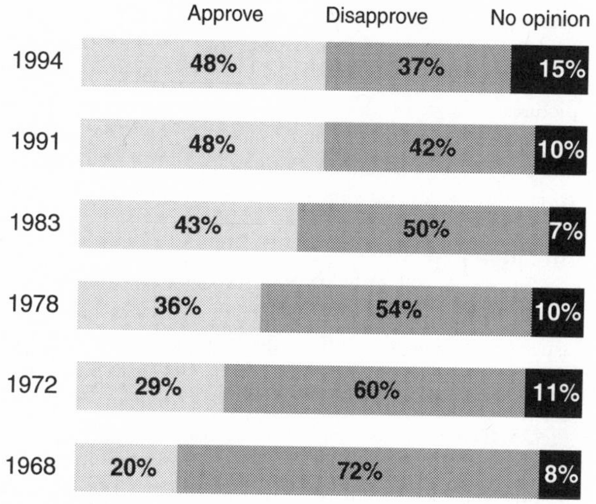

Source: The Gallup Poll: Public Opinion 1994. Wilmington, Del.: Scholarly Resources, 1995.

on Ice (1968) has been banned from certain school libraries because of its references to miscegenation.

In 1967, with the repeal of state laws against miscegenation and intermarriage following the Supreme Court decision, the attitudes of some film producers began to change. In 1967 the film *In the Heat of the Night* appeared, dealing with the topic of racism. Directed by Norman Jewison, the film won the Academy Award for best picture. This was also the year of Stanley Kramer's *Guess Who's Coming to Dinner*, depicting an interracial relationship, starring Sydney Poitier, Katherine Hepburn, and Spencer Tracy. Miscegenation was clearly no longer a topic that was to be censored in film.

Public attitudes among the white population also underwent change, although it is not clear whether this was a result of the portrayal of miscegenation in the media or, what seems more likely, that the media were gradually reflecting changes in attitudes, including greater tolerance in racial matters. Although a large percentage of the white population in the United States continued to object to racial intermarriage, the number of racially mixed marriages has increased more than fourfold after the 1960's.

Artistic productions, including novels and films, have occasionally emphasized interracial relations, without creating a furor. The film *The Bodyguard* (1992), for example, with its interracial affair, was originally conceived in the 1970's (for Diana Ross and Steve McQueen), but had to wait until 1992 to be made (with Whitney Houston and Kevin Costner). Spike Lee's *Jungle Fever* (1991), focussing on interracial sexual and romantic relations, was well received. The film *Showgirls* (1995) was panned by practically all critics, but the interracial sexual relationships portrayed in it were hardly mentioned. The film *Jefferson in Paris* (1995) took for granted that Thomas Jefferson had an intimate relationship with his black slave Sally Hemmings, although many historians argue that there is little evidence that they had such a relationship. Pornographic films depicting interracial sex have been common and appear to have sold well, judging from their marketing, which has tended to emphasize interracial themes over sex. Such films have not, however, been subjected to greater censorship than other categories of X-rated pictures. —*Mario D. Fenyo*

See also African Americans; *Arabian Nights, The*; Attorney General's Commission on Pornography; Film censorship; *Hair*; Hays Code; Motion Picture Association of America; *Pinky*; *Miss Saigon*; Race.

Bibliography

Censorship, edited by Robert Emmet Long (New York: H. W. Wilson, 1990), is a collection of essays on various aspects of censorship. Ruth A. Inglis' *Freedom of the Movies* (Chicago: University of Chicago Press, 1947) advocates self-censorship rather than freedom. The two-volume *The Motion Picture Guide*, edited by Jay R. Nash and Stanley Ralph Ross (Chicago: Cinebooks, 1985-1987), is a compendium of films by title, category, country of origin, and so on. *War of Words: The Censorship Debate*, edited by George Beahm (Kansas City, Mo.: Andrews and McMeel, 1993) contains essays arguing for and against censorship.

Miss Saigon

Type of work: Musical play

Produced: 1989 (London); 1991 (New York City)

Producer: Cameron Mackintosh

Subject matter: A Vietnamese woman sacrifices everything to give her Eurasian son the opportunity to grow up in America

Significance: The play's Broadway production was almost canceled because of protests against its casting of a white actor in the role of a Eurasian

From the 1989 opening night of *Miss Saigon* in London, producer Cameron Mackintosh knew that he wanted the central role of the Eurasian pimp to be played on Broadway by British actor Jonathan Pryce. He believed that the production's success hinged on the performance of this character, which Pryce had originated and helped to develop in London. Following the rules of the American Equity Association (AEA), permission for Pryce to play the role would normally have been a mere formality. However, a small group of militant Asian AEA members led a well-orchestrated protest against Pryce's casting in what they regarded as an Asian role. Calling the decision to cast Pryce racist, the protesters claimed that *Miss Saigon* was being debased to the level of a yellow-face "minstrel show." Their protest moved the AEA's ruling council to go against their own rules by denying Pryce permission to play the role on August 7, 1990.

Feeling personally maligned, Mackintosh, who had gone to extraordinary lengths to ensure appropriate Asian casting for the play's other parts, decided to cancel the Broadway production, although advance ticket sales exceeded twenty-five million dollars. He felt that this introduction of "racial privilege" masquerading as "multi-racial equality" would not only disrupt the rehearsal process, but would establish a dangerous precedent by setting the rights of creative production teams against efforts of minorities to advance their own causes.

Worldwide public and press response to these actions was immediate, passionate, and almost entirely in support of Mackintosh. "When is censorship not censorship?" asked former New York mayor Ed Koch in the *New York Post*, "When it's being exercised by Actors' Equity." Letters and phone calls from AEA constituents poured in condemning the action and prominent members threatened to resign if the ban was not lifted. The AEA council members then reversed their decision. Mackintosh was grateful, but refused to proceed without full AEA support. After several weeks an agreement was reached and on October 7, 1990, tickets went back on sale, thus ending one of the most serious crises in modern American theater.

See also Asian Americans; Charlie Chan films; Drama and theater; Miscegenation; Political correctness; Pressure groups; Vietnam War.

Mitford, Jessica

Born: September 11, 1917, Batsford, Gloucestershire, England

Died: July 23, 1996, Oakland, California

IDENTIFICATION: American author and muckraking journalist

SIGNIFICANCE: Noted for her devastating exposés of corruption and deceit, Mitford was harassed by a congressional committee for her politics and was fired by a university for refusing to be fingerprinted and sign a loyalty oath

Born into one of Britain's most renowned families, Mitford forsook the traditional perquisites of upper-class life in order to fight fascism and government corruption. During the Spanish Civil War, she ran away to Loyalist Spain and married Esmond Romilly, a communist sympathizer who was later killed in World War II. In 1943, after moving to the United States, she met her second husband, Robert Treuhaft, a labor lawyer. They settled in Oakland, California. During the McCarthy era, Mitford was subpoenaed by the House Committee on Un-American Activities (HUAC).

During the mid-1950's, she unsheathed her poison pen and launched her career as a muckraker. After she published *The American Way of Death* (1963), a powerful exposé of the funeral industry, the resulting public outcry forced the industry to restructure itself almost overnight. Her other investigative books included *The Trial of Dr. Spock* (1969), *Kind and Usual Punishment: The American Prison Business* (1973), *Poison Penmanship: The Gentle Art of Muckraking* (1979), and *The American Way of Birth* (1992).

In a series of investigative articles, Mitford single-handedly exposed a variety of society's cherished institutions, including Bennett Cerf and other "faculty" members at the Famous Writers' School, Elizabeth Arden's Maine Chance spa, National Broadcasting Company (NBC) censorship, a restaurant in New York City, and personnel procedures at California's San Jose State University. Censors were among her favorite targets. In September, 1965, she published an article titled "Don't Call It Syphilis" in *McCall's* magazine. The hard-hitting exposé publicly embarrassed NBC for cancelling a two-part segment on the dangers of syphilis.

Meanwhile, Mitford herself was the subject of an attempt at censorship when she was hired to teach at San Jose State University as a distinguished professor in 1973. The trouble began when the university ordered her to sign a loyalty oath, tried to fingerprint her, and deleted the word "muckraking" from her course descriptions. When she resisted these measures, the administration fired her and canceled her classes. However, she ignored both actions and continued teaching her classes without pay. Eventually she signed the oath under duress, but forced the fingerprint issue into court. Finally, an embarrassed university paid her; after the fall semester ended, a court ruled that the fingerprint requirement was not enforceable.

Mitford's long struggle against censorship won her respect as one of the nation's foremost investigative journalists. *The New York Times* conceded that "Mitford's pen is mightier than the sword," and *Time* magazine dubbed her "Queen of the Muckrakers"—a title that she cherished.

See also Cerf, Bennett; *Greer v. Spock*; House Committee on Un-American Activities; Loyalty oaths; Obituaries; Prisons; Seldes, George; Sinclair, Upton; Steffens, Lincoln; Television networks.

Mohammed, Messenger of God

TYPE OF WORK: Film

RELEASED: 1976

DIRECTOR: Moustapha Akkad (1933?-)

SUBJECT MATTER: The Prophet Muhammad's role in establishing and spreading Islam

SIGNIFICANCE: Although made in Libya and Morocco, this film was banned throughout the Middle East and had limited runs elsewhere, in part because of Muslim protests

Moustapha Akkad, a Syrian American producer and director, made *Mohammed, Messenger of God* to inform non-Muslims about Muhammad's role in founding the major world religion of Islam. Aware of the Koranic injunction against pictorial representations of Muhammad, screenwriter H. A. L. Craig permitted neither vocal nor physical representations of the prophet himself within the film, which tells the prophet's story through his eyes. In anticipation of controversy, the film's producers submitted its script to Islamic scholars at Cairo's Al-Azhar University.

Despite these precautions, mistaken rumors that the film contained physical depictions of Muhammad and concerns about the film's religious content led to bomb threats and protests from various Islamic organizations. The word "Mohammed" was dropped from the film's title prior to its London opening in July, 1976. The English-language version ran briefly in London, Germany, and the United States, but its Arabic version was banned everywhere in the Middle East but Libya.

In March, 1977, the film opened in New York and Los Angeles, but it was quickly withdrawn after a local Muslim organization, the Hanifi sect, staged protests, which included takeovers of the offices of the city government, B'nai B'rith, and the Islamic Center in Washington, D.C. A decade later, the film reopened quietly in New York City and other American cities. Its backers' limited financial resources and a lack of audience interest in the three-hour religious epic were ultimately more responsible for the film's limited American distribution than Muslim protests.

See also Islam; Koran; Muhammad; Pressure groups; Religion; Rushdie, Salman.

Molière

BORN: January, 1622, Paris, France

DIED: February 17, 1673, Paris, France

IDENTIFICATION: Comic playwright, actor, and director of a theatrical troupe

SIGNIFICANCE: Molière's plays satirizing religious hypocrisy were censored during his lifetime

Molière, the creator of high French comedy, led a theatrical troupe that, after thirteen years touring the provinces, was brought to Paris in 1659 and placed under the patronage of King Louis XIV. Molière soon learned, however, that influential members of the royal court and even Louis himself would not tolerate performances of any play that dealt overtly with religious hypocrisy.

Two of his comic masterpieces, *Tartuffe* (1664), which was not performed until 1669, and *Don Juan* (1665), which was not published during Molière's lifetime, both provoked strongly negative reactions from influential people, including the archbishop of Paris and the head of the Paris Court of Appeals. The play's opponents believed that any portrayal of religious hypocrisy might diminish public respect for true spirituality.

In a royal edict announced in May, 1664, King Louis condemned *Tartuffe* as "absolutely injurious to religion and capable of producing very dangerous results." In order to persuade the king to reverse this edict, Molière made significant revisions, portraying the title character not only as a religious hypocrite but also as a violent criminal who attempts to rape a woman. The 1669 version of *Tartuffe* points out that the king himself ordered the arrest of this reprehensible criminal, who escaped punishment for many years. In addition to praising the king's sense of justice, Molière also stressed in a lengthy preface that nothing in this comedy should be interpreted as criticism of true piety.

While Molière was finally successful in obtaining permission to perform and publish *Tartuffe*, the same cannot be said about *Don Juan*. The title character in this comedy is not just a seducer of women but also a religious hypocrite. In one scene, he explains that the latter is a "privileged vice," since people do not dare criticize religious hypocrisy because they might be accused of not showing proper respect for religion. *Don Juan* was banned after just fifteen performances in early 1665. In 1682 members of Molière's troupe attempted to publish *Don Juan*, but the royal censor demanded that all references to religious hypocrisy be eliminated from the published edition. By extraordinary luck, three uncensored copies of the 1682 edition of *Don Juan* were discovered in the 1830's, and readers can now appreciate this play for themselves. Molière's plays have long since come to be regarded as cornerstones of French classical theater.

See also Bulgakov, Mikhail Afanasyevich; Chilling effect; Drama and theater; France; Hypocrisy; Pressure groups; Religion.

Montaigne, Michel de

Born: February 28, 1533, Château de Montaigne, near Bordeaux, Périgord, France

Died: September 13, 1592, Château de Montaigne

Identification: French essayist and skeptical philosopher

Significance: Montaigne's *Essays* was placed on the Roman Catholic church's *Index Librorum Prohibitorum* because it encouraged freethinking

In 1580, while he was in Rome, Montaigne was invited by the papal censor to respond to a report on his *Essays* prepared by several theologians. This report charged him with using the word "fortune," referring to heretical poets, arguing against the use of torture to extract confessions from suspected wrongdoers, and defending the emperor Julian. The censor judged these charges as minor imperfections that need not be corrected, and urged Montaigne to continue in "the devotion he had always borne to the Church." Montaigne did not, however, make the changes suggested in the report. During the years of the Counter-Reformation, the ruling argument of his *Essays*, that trust in individual reason and conscience is at once destructive of civil order and conducive to atheism, was used by many Catholic apologists, including Jean-Pierre Camus and Pierre Charron.

A thoroughgoing skeptic who was never convinced of humankind's capacity to find ethical guidance through individual reasoning, Montaigne was a staunch conservative throughout his adult life. "A private fantasy can have but a private jurisdiction," he emphasized in his influential, long, sustained attack on deism, the "Apology for Raymond Sebond." In accordance with that principle, Montaigne repeatedly maintained the Church's authority as the only valid interpreter of Scripture. His belief that a divinely sanctioned teaching from faith, rather than a humanistic reliance on reason, is the basis of trustworthy knowledge and ethical judgment informs the whole of his essays. His attacks on the vanity of human understanding were taken up by leading Catholic intellectuals from the early 1580's to the late 1660's, during which period the *Essays* went through many editions.

Montaigne's reputation as an artist and thinker fell into sharp decline with the waning of the Counter-Reformation and the rise of French neoclassicism. More than fifty years separated the last edition of the *Essays* in seventeenth-century France from its 1724 edition—which had been prepared and printed in England. The disposition of French neoclassicists to prize close craftsmanship and decorous language favored neither Montaigne's loose essay style, nor his earthy diction. A wide range of seventeenth-century French thinkers found his radical separation of faith from reason damaging to both the value of human understanding and the truth of divine revelation. As orthodox Catholic theologians and philosophers alike came to emphasize, Montaigne's writings made no reference to the New Testament.

Montaigne's *Essays* was placed on the Roman Catholic church's *Index Librorum Prohibitorum* in 1676 as a book of secular humanism. Since the late seventeenth century freethinking readers of Montaigne have tended to interpret his expression of fidelity to the Church as a strategy for circumventing the thought police. When the Catholic church canonized Montaigne's niece Jeanne de Lestonnac in 1949, Pope Pius XII expressed his hope that Montaigne's *Essays* would soon be removed from the *Index*. That hope was not fulfilled, but the *Index* itself was abolished in 1966

See also *Index Librorum Prohibitorum*; Reformation, the; Richelieu, Cardinal; Secular humanism; Vatican.

Montesquieu

Born: January 18, 1689, La Brède, near Bordeaux, France

Died: February 10, 1755, Paris, France

Identification: French nobleman, political philosopher, and writer

Significance: Montesquieu avoided French authorities' repeated attempts at censorship and became one of the leading political theorists of the Enlightenment

Montesquieu was born and educated during the repressive monarchy of King Louis XIV. After the monarch's death in 1715, France became increasingly burdened with governmental and ecclesiastical abuses. Disputes between the monarch, the legislature, and the Church broke down the efficiency of the machinery of suppression. In this atmosphere, Montesquieu began his criticism of French politics, society, and religion. In 1721 he anonymously published the *Persian Letters*, easily avoiding French restrictions by publishing the volume in Amsterdam. During the 1720's, he attended the Club de L'Entresol, a salon famous for open discussions on political reforms, until it was closed by the government. In 1748, after twenty years of work, he published *The Spirit of the Laws* in Geneva. This popular volume attacked the monarchy, promoting the separation of powers into equally powerful branches to ensure the defense of liberty. It undermined the Church by arguing that morality was dependent on geography and climate and was not fixed by God. The Sorbonne retaliated by twice drafting detailed censures of the work, but it failed to publish either condemnation. Both Jesuits and Jansenists censured numerous passages; despite Montesquieu's efforts in 1751 the work was placed on the Vatican's index of prohibited books. However, it continued to sell throughout Europe and would eventually become regarded as a classic work in political theory.

See also Diderot, Denis; France; *Index Librorum Prohibitorum*; Intellectual freedom; Rousseau, Jean-Jacques; Vatican.

Moon Is Blue, The

TYPE OF WORK: Film
RELEASED: 1953
DIRECTOR: Otto Preminger (1905-1986)
SUBJECT MATTER: Light comedy about a young woman who marries a man only twenty-four hours after meeting him in New York City
SIGNIFICANCE: After failing to receive a production code seal of approval, the producers of this film upset the system by releasing the film anyway

For three decades the Production Code Administration (PCA), often working with the Catholic Legion of Decency, controlled what American filmgoers could see. Before 1953 no U.S. film company belonging to the Motion Picture Production Association had ever released a movie without its formal seal of approval. Even Jane Russell's sensational film *The Outlaw* (1946) had won PCA approval (though in a revised edition). In 1953 Otto Preminger and United Artists defied the PCA by releasing *The Moon Is Blue* without its approval. The film's resulting notoriety helped it to earn four million dollars—a large sum at the time.

Scripted by the play's original author, F. Hugh Herbert, *The Moon Is Blue* was one of many 1950's Broadway plays to be adapted for the screen. It tells the story of a young architect (David Niven) and free-spirited young woman (Maggie McNamara) who meet and engage in a racy and witty conversation over dinner at the man's apartment. Little else happens in the film. Film reviewer Bosley Crowther, who saw the controversial film in a packed theater, told his readers that "the pit didn't yawn or the heavens fall." In fact, he found *The Moon Is Blue* slow and talky. That talk, however, was exactly what judges, censors, and clerics disliked: Laced with such taboo words as "pregnant," "seduce," and "virgin," the script

William Holden attempts to seduce Maggie McNamara in The Moon Is Blue, *a film whose open ridiculing of virginity helped bring an end to the Hays Code.* (Museum of Modern Art/Film Stills Archive)

provoked censorship efforts throughout the United States. The Legion of Decency condemned it, and Cardinal Francis Spellman of New York urged the faithful to boycott it. Maryland, Ohio, and Kansas, in addition to countless local jurisdictions, banned the film. In 1955 a censorship case originating in Kansas reached the U.S. Supreme Court; in *Holmby Productions, Inc. v. Vaughan* the court struck down the ruling of a local censor board that *The Moon Is Blue* was "obscene, indecent, and immoral," thereby permitting the film to be shown in theaters nationwide.

See also Film adaptation; Hays Code; Legion of Decency; *Miracle, The*; Motion Picture Association of America; Obscenity: legal definitions; *Outlaw, The*; *Ronde, La*; Spellman, Cardinal Francis Joseph.

Moore, George

BORN: February 24, 1852, County Mayo, Ireland
DIED: January 21, 1933, London, England
IDENTIFICATION: Irish novelist
SIGNIFICANCE: Moore's novels were banned from libraries and bookstores; seizure of one of his books by U.S. Customs raised questions about legal definitions of obscenity

Upon the death of his father in 1870, Moore inherited substantial estates in Ireland and a sizable annual income that permitted him to pursue his artistic interests. When he was twenty-one years old he went to Paris to study painting, but soon turned to literature, writing novels strongly influenced by the naturalism of Émile Zola. His first, *A Modern Lover* (1883), which dealt with contemporary bohemian society, embroiled him in a censorship controversy. The powerful commercial libraries removed it from circulation as being immoral after "two ladies living in the country" objected to a scene in which a girl poses nude for an artist painting Venus. Most novels of the time were published in expensive three-volume editions that readers preferred to rent rather than to buy. Book publishers were reluctant to issue books that libraries might not purchase in multiple copies, so the censorship powers of these commercial libraries were considerable. Moore's protest against the banning of his novel set off a newspaper debate over the power of the libraries to decide what the British public could read.

When the libraries refused to carry Moore's next novel, *A Mummer's Wife* (1885), he published it in an inexpensive edition. The opportunity to buy a one-volume edition of a book censored by the libraries at one-fifth the cost of most novels proved attractive to many readers. The renewed controversy gave Moore the reputation of being an innovative, iconoclastic author. Moore collected his attacks on the circulating libraries in *Literature at Nurse, or Circulating Morals* (1885), but failed to impress his enemies. Even *Esther Waters* (1894), which many critics hailed as Moore's best novel, was banned by the libraries, once again setting off a newspaper controversy over censorship that aided sales of his book to the public.

Moore's books also faced censorship in the United States. D. Appleton & Company issued several of his novels, but would only publish *Memoirs of My Dead Life* (1907) if he would permit cutting some passages. Moore agreed, providing that the company would print as a foreword his powerful attack on censorship that rejected puritanical morality and condemned all attempts to control other people's minds. In 1919 Moore shifted to the firm of Boni and Liveright when his previous publisher, Brentano's, refused to issue *A Story Teller's Holiday* without cuts. An innovative publisher, Liveright successfully issued uncut versions of Moore's works in limited editions offered by subscription. However, even Liveright's tactics did not protect Moore from all censors. In 1929 the U.S. Customs Service seized a copy of *A Story Teller's Holiday* signed by the author; the inspector particularly objected to one of the book's illustrations, Botticelli's painting, *The Birth of Venus*.

See also Book publishing; Books and obscenity law; Customs laws, U.S.; Ireland; Libraries; Liveright, Horace; Zola, Émile.

Moral Majority

Founded: 1979

Type of organization: American political pressure group

Significance: This organization has lobbied for the censorship of literature and other media to conform to Christian Fundamentalist viewpoints

The Moral Majority was founded in 1979 by the Reverend Jerry Falwell, an evangelist with a television program called *Old Time Gospel Hour*. Falwell was extremely popular, eliciting huge amounts of money on his show. By 1980 his organization was already receiving about fifty million dollars per year in viewer contributions. Although originally formed to combat legalized abortion, drug proliferation, and homosexuality, the Moral Majority soon became involved in attempts to regulate children's education. Foremost among its interests

In November, 1983, Jerry Falwell held a press conference to denounce the American Broadcasting Company's plan to air the nuclear-war film The Day After *at a time that would interfere with deployment of American missiles in Europe and with President Ronald Reagan's expected announcement of his re-election plans.* (AP/Wide World Photos)

was the attempt, shared by other Fundamentalist groups, to foster the teaching of Creationism, the term such groups used for the version of human origins contained in the Bible's Book of Genesis, either in addition to, or instead of, the teaching of evolution.

Additionally, the organization took a strong stand against what it considered pornography, even when such materials were not considered pornographic by other groups. Its members were among the first to use the term "secular humanism" for what they claimed was a religion taught in public schools, which excluded God from their curriculums. The organization's argument was that secular humanism should either be excluded from the public schools, or that Christianity and other religions should be included on an equal basis.

The Moral Majority had some effect on national politics for approximately a decade. In 1990 it was largely superseded by, and included in, the Christian Coalition, a more politically powerful group, headed by Pat Robertson.

See also Christianity; Examiner of plays; Homosexuality; Pressure groups; Secular humanism; Televangelists.

Morality

Definition: The rightness of an act

Significance: The perceived immorality of a work is often the basis of its being censored; what is immoral and whether an immoral work should be censored are subjects of debate

The terms "moral" and "immoral" apply to acts, especially to the judgment received from tradition regarding certain acts, behavior, and (in some cases) thoughts and intentions as wrong. Moral wrong means that individuals who violate relevant norms should feel guilt, be reprimanded, and, in many cases, be punished by religious or secular law.

What tradition declares right and wrong, however, has ever been open to challenge. Thus, a distinction must be made between beliefs by some—even a majority—that certain acts are morally wrong and what nontraditionalists may believe. To many individuals what is "moral" or "immoral" is clear. Usually, though not necessarily, this certitude is grounded upon religious teachings. "Morality" is the basis that leaders of various groups cite in seeking to censor what others seek to see or hear.

Such judgments are not static. As premodern societies gave way to modern ones, the status of traditional morality came into question. From bloody religious conflict arose religious toleration among groups that previously had denied each other's right to worship freely. In time, secular forces gained influence, reducing the authority of traditional norms, as industrialization revolutionized society.

By the late nineteenth century, German philosopher Friedrich Nietzsche had attempted a thorough undermining of Judeo-Christian morality in *The Genealogy of Morals* (1887) and other works. Moral skepticism later began creeping into universities and some quarters of society at large. The assurance that God has decreed what is right and wrong and has revealed the law in sacred writings broke down among many social groups.

In the United States, by the late twentieth century, the constitutional principle separating church and state limited the areas of law in which religious morality could be enforced. Concurrently, however, many religious believers and others demanded that law enforce traditional, especially sexual, morality.

Moral Relativism and Absolutism. Problems for democracy arise when consensus over right and wrong breaks down among substantial numbers of people. Some, perhaps a majority, may demand that traditional norms be legally enforced, although to do so is often contrary to principles of liberal democracy. When dissenters are few, their interests or wishes can be ignored, and what Alexis de Tocqueville called the "tyranny of the majority" occurs. As active dissent increases in numbers and influence, conflict is heightened.

Conflict is heightened during periods of rapid transition in moral standards, when traditional standards break down, and when standards of any kind appear to be absent among significant parts of society. When such conditions occur, traditionalists demand adherence to rigidly applied, unchanging—"absolute"—standards. The appeal to absolutism typically does not go unchallenged. In classical Athens the sophist Protagoras proclaimed, famously, the relativist dictum "man is the measure of all things." Modern critics point out that many acts or practices considered wrong in one culture are viewed differently in others. Moral absolutism and complete relativism are only the extremes of a continuum of belief, not either-or choices.

One of the strengths of the relativist argument is that cultures differ in their perceptions of right and wrong; one of the strengths of the absolutist argument is that almost all cultures condemn such acts as murder, adultery, theft, and lying. Cultures differ, however, regarding how the human body should be pictorially or cinematically displayed. In some places, for example, the exposure of women's ankles is considered immoral. In India, cinematic depiction of kissing is considered immoral. Within cultures, even a relatively brief passage of time can mean dramatic changes in norms. Thus, in the 1960's comedian Lenny Bruce was arrested in San Francisco for uttering words commonplace in entertainment media less than thirty years later. In the West, the understanding of what is proper for a good Christian woman to wear at the beach changed dramatically from the beginning of the twentieth century to the end.

Classical Liberalism and Democracy. Where to draw the line for acceptable expression is deeply controversial. Famously, John Stuart Mill argued in *On Liberty* (1859) that the "only purpose for which power can be rightfully exercised over any member of a civilized community, against his will, is to prevent harm to others." But others have disagreed with this statement, and others have argued that, for example, a man's looking at pornography injures women generally, and that pornography should—even against his will—be banned.

Reasonable people do not disagree that such acts as murder, rape, theft, assault, and the like must be outlawed. All are almost universally considered immoral as well as harmful to society. But in other cases, there may be no agreement about whether "harm" occurs, for example, when pornography is viewed by consenting adults. Even where some intangible harm may be thought to occur, such as viewing certain bizarre sexual practices, those opposing censorship argue that consenting adults should be allowed to please themselves without interference by the state.

Societies characterized by social pluralism such as the United States have special difficulty defining the criteria of public acceptability when standards vary so widely. Political speech receives wide First Amendment protection by American courts, especially after *New York Times Co. v. Sullivan* (1964) and *New York Times Co. v. United States* (1971)—the Pentagon Papers case. But obscenity and pornography are notoriously more difficult to define and have long been subjects of legal controversy.

Obscenity, Pornography, and Morality. The U.S. Supreme Court has struggled for decades to deal with obscenity issues. In *Chaplinsky v. New Hampshire* (1942), the Court laid down the influential rationale that certain forms of expression, such as obscenity, are unprotected because they play no "essential part" in the exposition of ideas and the search for truth and because any benefit from them is "clearly outweighed by the social interest in order and morality."

Later cases made alterations to this formula. In *Roth v. U.S.* (1957), Justice William J. Brennan said that while the First Amendment does not protect obscenity, it does protect "ideas having even the slightest redeeming social importance." *Miller v. California* (1973) included application of "contemporary community standards" by the average person to determine if the expression is "patently offensive," "appeals predominantly to the prurient interest," and, "taken as a whole lacks serious literary, artistic, political, or scientific value." Later refinements only underlined the fact that the United States has been profoundly divided on whether and to what extent law should enforce morality in the absence of clear, substantial harm to individuals.

Besides traditionalist hostility to certain forms of erotica, some feminists have advocated censoring pornography. They point to studies claiming that, under laboratory conditions, some pornography induces some men to excuse violence against women. But there is no consensus among feminists on this issue, let alone society at large. Critics claim there are flaws in these studies, which, they argue, are invalid or inconclusive. To opponents of blanket censorship, the relationship of the individual to erotica is comparable to the relationships of the normal drinker to alcohol and of the alcoholic to alcohol. Detriment to some is insufficient reason to outlaw something for all.

Age and Moral Censorship. A central issue in debate over the enforcement of morals in liberal democracy is state paternalism. The paternal state acts as parent of citizens, not only protecting them from harm, as is the duty of all states, but also from harming themselves.

The classical doctrine of liberalism in the name of liberty denies the legitimacy of the latter form of paternalism, that of protecting citizens from themselves. Normal adults—those not suffering from some physical or mental aberration that limits their use of reason—should be free to choose for themselves. Antiliberal leaders, however, often adhere to the view that "freedom for moral error" is illegitimate. That is, no one should be free to practice what is morally wrong.

Those who take this view typically claim to know what is morally wrong and wish to apply the sanction of the law to stop it. Justification of censorship does not require proof that material to be censored produces substantial harm to the person; once the immorality is shown, only practicality of enforcement stands in the way of legitimizing censorship.

In the United States after the 1950's, increasingly liberal court rulings allowed adults freedom to view materials previously outlawed as immoral. Although this liberty is subject to the community standards test, adults are free to move to—or visit—communities with standards conforming to their own.

The legal and moral situation with minors is different, however. The degree of censorship that the courts tolerate varies with age. Thus, film ratings determine the age at which minors unescorted by adults may enter cinemas. School administrations may bar some forms of minors' self-expression, requiring uniforms, censoring student newspapers, and elsewhere regulating school life. Because minors are in varying degrees immature, they are not considered in full possession of their rational faculties and therefore, it is argued, can rightly be controlled by parents or those acting as parents.

In an illustrative case occurring in 1996, the Salt Lake City Board of Education banned all student clubs in order to eliminate a gay and lesbian high school club. It sought the ban on the grounds that the club would promote immoral behavior. A U.S. senator from Utah said that school boards have a moral obligation to ban such clubs. Thus, the beliefs of majorities provide a basis for enforcing moral norms, in this case, by regulating youth's right of association.

Such cases illustrate the dilemmas and controversies faced by liberal democracy, where at once certain traditional norms are rejected by substantial minorities and are supported by many others. Liberal democracies leave to the individual a range of decisions regarding the morality or immorality of what they see or read, allowing them to judge for themselves what they should do; but whether this is the right policy in particular cases and what limits, if any, should be set to individual discretion are controversial and involve fundamental political principles. —*Charles F. Bahmueller*

See also *Areopagitica*; Democracy; Free speech; *Miller v. California*; Morality in Media; *New York Times Co. v. Sullivan*; *Roth v. United States*.

Bibliography

A classic work about what should be permitted by the state and what outlawed is John Stuart Mill's *On Liberty* (1859). James Fitzjames Stephens' *Liberty, Equality, Fraternity* (1873) is another classic. The censorship debate was reenacted in the 1960's by two eminent British legal minds, one a judge, the other, an Oxford philosopher; see H. L. A. Hart's *Law, Liberty, and Morality* (Stanford, Calif.: Stanford, 1963) and Lord Patrick Devlin's *The Enforcement of Morals* (New York: Oxford University Press, 1965). Excellent articles on this debate are found in P. M. S. Hacker and Joseph Raz, eds., *Law, Morality, and Society: Essays in Honour of H. L. A. Hart* (New York: Oxford University Press, 1977). *The Oxford Companion to the Supreme Court of the United States* (New York: Oxford University Press, 1992), Kermit Hall, editor in chief, has numerous informative articles relevant to democracy and censorship. Also stimulating is Harry M. Clor's *Obscenity and Public Morality* (Chicago: Chicago University Press, 1969) and David A. J. Richards' "Free Speech and Obscenity Law: Toward a Moral Theory of the First Amendment" in *University of Pennsylvania Law Review* 123, no. 99 (1974).

Morality in Media

Founded: 1962

Type of organization: National interdenominational religious group opposed to dissemination of pornography

Significance: This body has worked to inform the public and government officials about the destructive effects of pornography and the extent of the trafficking of obscenity

Founded by Father Morton A. Hill and originally called Operation Yorkville, Morality in Media holds that there is a direct correlation between the use of pornography and violent and sexual crimes. It has worked to eliminate illegal traffic in hardcore pornography by encouraging vigorous enforcement of state and federal obscenity laws. It has also worked to maintain standards of decency on television.

A major project of Morality in Media is the National Obscenity Law Center, a research office of legal information on obscenity cases. The group also sponsors the annual White

Ribbon Against Pornography Campaign (WRAP) and an annual Turn Off TV Day. In addition to the group's bimonthly newsletter, its Law Center publishes the bimonthly *Obscenity Law Bulletin*.

Morality in Media maintains that it does not believe or promote censorship. Censorship is described by the group as prior restraint by government. The organization believes that those who traffic in obscenity should be responsible before the law.

See also Eagle Forum; Moral Majority; Morality; National Federation for Decency; National Organization for Decent Literature; Pornography; Prior restraint.

Morgan, William

Born: August 7, 1774?, probably Culpeper County, Virginia
Died: September 12, 1826?, probably Fort Niagara, New York
Identification: American writer
Significance: Mystery surrounding Morgan's death set off a furor that led to the establishment of a political party that attacked secrecy in politics

Little is known with certainty of Morgan's early life. Neither his parents nor the exact date or place of birth are known. He was apparently apprenticed to a stone-mason in Virginia. By 1823 he was living in western New York State, where he worked as a brick-and-stone mason in Rochester and Batavia. In May, 1825, Morgan was inducted into the Royal Arch Masons at Le Roy, New York. In August, 1826, he registered the title *Illustrations of Masonry, By One of the Fraternity Who Has Devoted Thirty Years to the Subject*, for copyright protection. As rumors spread through upstate New York that his book would reveal the secret rituals of Masonry, Morgan began to experience a number of petty persecutions, such as being sued and imprisoned for small debts several times. In September he was jailed in Canandaigua, New York, over a debt of $2.69. After someone paid this debt, Morgan was released; however, as he stepped into the street he was seized, gagged, and thrust into a carriage. The carriage took Morgan on a wild ride to Fort Niagara, where he was imprisoned. He was never seen again.

Rumors spread that Morgan had been murdered by Masons determined to prevent publication of his book. Despite denials by eminent Masons, town meetings in Batavia and Canandaigua called for an official investigation. But sheriffs and judges, many of them Masons, moved slowly, leading to suspicion of a cover-up. The sheriff who should have tracked down the kidnappers was a Mason; he could find no one to arrest. Had he arrested anyone, the judge hearing the case would also have been a Mason. When the people of Rochester petitioned to the state legislature for an investigation of the kidnapping, they discovered that their representative was a Mason.

Accusations that members of Masonic lodges were abusing their political power by shielding fellow members from prosecution for murder led to the formation of a short-lived political party. In 1827 an Anti-Masonic Party was organized in New York State, dedicated to breaking the hold on politics of an alleged secret, exclusive society whose members assisted each other in business and combined to dominate government.

By 1831 such parties existed in eleven Eastern states and agreed to unite. To demonstrate their opposition to secrecy, the Anti-Masonic Party held an open convention in September, 1831, to select a presidential candidate. This was the first such convention ever held and established a tradition followed by all political parties thereafter. By the middle 1830's interest in anti-Masonry waned and most party members joined the Whigs.

Morgan personally suffered the ultimate in censorship, being silenced forever, but his kidnappers failed to preserve Masonic secrecy. Morgan's printer brought out *Illustrations of Masonry* in late 1826. The book achieved a wide circulation, often in pirated editions, and was translated into several European languages.

See also Death; Masonry.

Morison, Samuel Loring

Born: October 30, 1944, London, England
Identification: American naval intelligence analyst
Significance: Morison is the first American convicted of spying for leaking classified information to the press; his case raised fears that the Espionage Act of 1917 might also be applied to journalists who publish information provided by leakers or "whistle-blowers"

Morison, the grandson of noted naval historian Samuel Eliot Morison, was a Vietnam War veteran who had served sixteen years in the U.S. Navy. In 1984 he was employed by the Navy as a civilian Soviet ship analyst at the Naval Intelligence Support Center in Maryland. With the approval of the Navy, he also held a part-time job as American editor of *Jane's Fighting Ships*. In July Morison sent the British *Jane's Defence Weekly* three classified spy-satellite photographs of the Soviet Union's first nuclear-powered aircraft carrier, which was then under construction.

The pictures appeared in the weekly in August; they were picked up and distributed by the Associated Press, and were printed in the *Washington Post*, among other papers. The Federal Bureau of Investigation and naval intelligence officers traced the leak to Morison and arrested him on October 1. Morison claimed that his motives were patriotic, to publicize the threat to American security posed by the Soviet military buildup and thereby help the Navy obtain bigger appropriations. The Reagan Administration, however, argued that publication of the photographs might help foreign powers learn more about the capabilities of American spy satellites, conveniently ignoring the fact that the operations manual for the satellite had been sold to the Soviet Union by a Central Intelligence Agency operative in 1978.

Brought to trial in October, 1985, charged with spying under the Espionage Act of 1917 and theft of government property under a related hundred-year-old law, Morison was convicted by a federal court jury and sentenced to two years in prison. Morison's conviction aroused fears among news gathering organizations because of the ambiguous language of the espionage statute, which made it a crime to transmit information relating to the national defense to "any person not entitled to receive it." Under the broad interpretation urged by the Reagan Administration and accepted by the court, motive was irrelevant. Whistle-blowers and government officials who leaked classified information could face criminal prosecution; journalists who accepted classified documents might be ordered to turn over their sources to the prosecution and might themselves be prosecuted.

Morison appealed his conviction to the Fourth Circuit Court of Appeals in Richmond, Virginia. Thirty-one leading newspapers, broadcasting companies, and publishing groups joined to submit a friend-of-court brief urging that the conviction be reversed, arguing that leaking of government information to the press was neither espionage nor theft. Although two of the three judges noted in their opinions that there were substantial First Amendment questions about the government position, on April 4, 1988, the court unanimously upheld Morison's conviction.

Morison then appealed to the U.S. Supreme Court, which on October 17, 1988, rejected the appeal without comment or dissent, leaving uncontradicted the government's claim that leaking classified activity was equivalent to spying. Morison served eight months of his sentence before being paroled in 1989.

See also Civil service; Classification of information; Espionage; Espionage Act of 1917; Military censorship; News media censorship; *Pentagon Papers, The*; Reagan, Ronald.

Morissette, Alanis

Born: June 1, 1974, Ottawa, Ontario, Canada

Identification: Canadian alternative rock music performer

Significance: Although some of Morissette's song lyrics have been considered too offensive to broadcast on radio stations or rock video television shows, she has enjoyed great commercial success

Morissette's Hungarian parents settled in Canada after the Soviet Union occupied their country in 1956. As a child Morissette attended Roman Catholic schools. When she was eleven, she appeared in the popular Canadian children's television program *You Can't Do That on Television*. In 1991 she released her first record album in Canada. Her early recordings did not possess the hard-edged lyrics and raw guitar licks that would later bring her notoriety and fame.

In 1995 Morissette released her first American album, *Jagged Little Pill*. Morissette wrote all the album's song lyrics herself. Many of these songs express her bitterness about love lost. She ran into trouble with some of her lyrics to the hit song "You Oughta Know," in which she blurts, "Is she perverted like me/ Would she go down on you in a theatre." Another line in this song bluntly asks, "Are you thinking of me when you fuck her?" Because of these blatant sexual references, the song was censored for mainstream radio airplay and for video viewing on the Music Television Channel (MTV). "You Oughta Know" was a huge hit and was played numerous times daily on the radio and MTV. At the 1996 Grammy Awards ceremonies Morissette won awards for best album of the year (*Jagged Little Pill*), best rock album, best female rock vocal, and best rock song (both "You Oughta Know"). Public controversy over her song lyrics helped her to sell millions of albums.

See also Madonna; Music TeleVision; O'Connor, Sinead; Recording industry; Rock 'n' roll music; Rolling Stones, the.

Mormonism

Definition: Religion of the Church of Jesus Christ of Latter-day Saints, a Utah-based church founded in the nineteenth century

Significance: The Mormon church has tried to control controversies over its history and doctrines through censorship, secrecy, and restriction of access to historical documents

The Mormon church is a unique religious institution of wholly American origin. It was founded at Palmyra, New York, by Joseph Smith, a young man of limited education and means. In 1830 Smith published the Book of Mormon, which purports to be a history of certain tribes of Israel who fled to North America after leaving Palestine around 600 B.C.E. Smith claimed to have been given the book by an angel, who helped him to translate it and to reestablish the true, original church of Jesus Christ. As a modern day prophet, Smith promulgated new Christian doctrines, in revelations that he published. His followers, known as Mormons, accept his prophecies, as well as those issued by his successors, as divinely inspired.

The modern Mormon church has tried to control controversies over its history and unusual doctrines by censorship, secrecy, and restricting access to historical documents. Church doctrines conflicting with societal viewpoints have included polygamy, subordination of women, and partial exclusion of African Americans and Native Americans. Mormons may be admonished, disfellowshipped, or excommunicated for opposing church authority. Disfellowshipped Mormons retain church membership, but are excluded from some church activities, such as participating in temple functions, until they reestablish their faith. Excommunicated Mormons are expelled from the church and must be rebaptized. Such disciplining in predominantly Mormon communities may cause job loss, social ostracism, or business boycotts. In addition, the church has censored, or attempted to censor, repugnant political and social opinions expressed by individuals and organizations within and without the church.

An early example of church censorship occurred when the central body of church members was living in Nauvoo, Illinois, under Joseph Smith's leadership. In 1844 William Law published an independent newspaper in Nauvoo calling for separating church and state, freeing the press, ending Smith's use of the church for private profit, and abandoning polygamy. Smith retaliated by destroying Law's press and burning his newspapers. Smith himself was arrested for this act and was killed by an anti-Mormon mob while awaiting trial.

Controlling Church History. The church has a long tradition of attempting to control its own history. Lucy Mack Smith's *Biographical Sketches of Joseph Smith, the Prophet, and his Progenitors for Many Generations*, was published by Apostle Orson Pratt in 1853. The book, by Joseph Smith's mother, was condemned by the church's new president, Brigham Young, and the council in 1865. They judged it inaccurate: "a tissue of lies from beginning to end." At that time the Smith family asserted that Smith had considered the church's presidency a hereditary office. Young, however, took control, but doctrinal conflict led to establishment of a separate church, the Reorganized Church of Jesus Christ of Latter-Day Saints, under the Smith family.

Publication of Fawn Brodie's *"No Man Knows My History": The Life of Joseph Smith, the Mormon Prophet* (1945) was followed by her excommunication for apostasy in 1946. A member of a prominent Mormon family and a professional academic historian, Brodie based her book on critical evaluation of a multitude of documents, letters, and newspapers.

In 1945 Mormon historian Dale Morgan won a Guggenheim Foundation grant to support a year's research to complete his Mormon history. In 1947 he activated the grant and embarked on a national search of libraries and archives. The following year, however, renewal of his grant was denied. Shortly thereafter, he was denied access to manuscripts in custody of the church historian's office because "people writing . . . books are rarely qualified to appraise accurately what they read and . . . misrepresent what they find." Finally, in 1949, J. Reuben Clark, first counselor and president of the church, urged the Guggenheim Foundation not to fund Morgan's research.

In 1972 Leonard J. Arrington, a Mormon and a respected professional historian, was appointed church historian and began preparing a sixteen-volume church history. After his first two volumes, *The Story of the Latter-day Saints* and *Building the City of God*, appeared, the project was attacked by high church leaders Ezra Taft Benson and Boyd K. Packer as "faith destroying" for, among other things, excessive emphasis on human frailties of church founders. The church then ended the history project. Arrington was removed as church historian in 1980, access to church archives was narrowly restricted, and the historian's office was removed from Salt Lake City to the Brigham Young University campus.

Silencing Critics. Feminists have been censored and disciplined for advocating female priesthood, praying to "Mother in Heaven" and supporting the Equal Rights Amendment. Only members of the priesthood—to which all adult male members of the church may be admitted—can become leaders of congregations, or administrative officers of the church. In 1979 Sonia Johnson became famous following her confrontation with Utah senator Orrin Hatch in a Senate hearing on the Equal Rights Amendment and for her lecturing and media interviews. She was tried on a charge of apostasy in late 1979 and excommunicated. Circulation of an issue of *MS.* magazine carrying an article by Johnson purportedly was restricted in Utah by an unofficial boycott.

George P. Lee, the only Native American ever appointed to the church's General Authority was excommunicated in 1989 for "apostasy and other conduct unbecoming a member of the church." Lee had accused church leaders of distorting doctrine to justify treating Indians as second-class members and denying their status in Mormon theology as literal descendants of the House of Israel. He also asserted that nonagenarian Ezra Taft Benson was too feeble to make the decisions required of the leader of the entire church.

According to Ron Priddy, a board member of the independent publisher Signature Books in Salt Lake City, five Mormon authors were excommunicated for views expressed in their Signature publications and in preliminary papers and articles. Maxine Hanks, author of a book on Mormon women, believes that she was excommunicated for challenging church policies regarding women by referring to sacred writings. Other excommunicated and disfellowshipped authors have made similar charges. Although First Counselor Gordon B. Hinckley asserted in 1994 that excommunications and disfellowshipping were local decisions, church spokesman Don LeFevre previously acknowledged that high-ranking Mormon officials provided local leaders with names of members criticizing church positions. *—Ralph L. Langenheim, Jr.*

See also Christian Science; Christianity; Religion; Scholarships; Smith, Joseph.

Bibliography

Fawn Brodie's *No Man Knows My History: The Life of Joseph Smith the Mormon Prophet* (2d ed. New York: Vintage Books, 1995) documents Smith's efforts to control opinion. James Coates's *In Mormon Circles: Gentiles, Jack Mormons and Latter-day Saints* (Reading, Mass.: Addison-Wesley, 1991) analyzes late twentieth century Mormon life, including attempts to control expression of opinion. Robert Gottlieb and Paul Wiley's *America's Saints: The Rise of Mormon Power* (New York: G. P. Putnam's Sons, 1984) discusses the political and economic power of the church, including censorship both within and without the church. John Heinerman and Anson Shupe's *The Mormon Corporate Empire* (Boston: Beacon Press, 1985) asserts that the church aims to establish a theocracy in the United States, and gives examples of its exercise of political and economic power—including censorship. Sonia Johnson's *From Housewife to Heretic: One Woman's Spiritual Awakening and Her Excommunication from the Mormon Church* (Albuquerque, N.M.: Wildfire Books, 1989) is a partisan account of her fight for the Equal Rights Amendment. *Dale Morgan on Early Mormonism: Correspondence and a New History* (Salt Lake City, Utah: Signature Books, 1986), edited by John Philip Walker, is an important insight into difficulties faced by Mormons attempting to publish on church history. Jan Shipps's *Mormonism: The Story of a New Religious Tradition* (Urbana: University of Illinois, 1985) is a scholarly account of Mormonism's development, including incidents of censorship.

Motion Picture Association of America (MPAA)

Founded: 1922

Type of organization: Film industry support body

Significance: Founded as the Motion Pictures Producers and Distributors of America (MPPDA), the MPAA has worked to improve the film industry's public image, protect it from government censorship, and perform other services for production companies

During the first two decades of the twentieth century, as films increased in popularity, fierce debates arose over the content and control of the new medium. Progressive reformers, civic and religious organizations, and other guardians of morality demanded that the government protect impressionable minds from the sexual license and criminal violence that they claimed dominated films. As early as 1907, the Chicago City Council empowered the police to prevent the showing of indecent films, and between 1911 and 1921 seven states and more than 150 cities established censorship programs. In 1916 representatives of the film industry formed the National Association of the Motion Picture Industry (NAMPI) in an unsuccessful effort to block further censorship legislation.

By 1921 the film industry faced a deepening crisis. A succession of high-profile Hollywood scandals led to a new outburst of legislative activity. Nearly one hundred measures to regulate films were introduced in thirty-seven state legislatures, and pressures for federal censorship were mounting. When the legislature of New York adopted a censorship program late in the year, industry leaders terminated NAMPI and formed a new, more powerful trade association. To head it, they selected U.S. Postmaster General Will H. Hays. A Presbyterian elder from Indiana, Hays had served as chair of the Republican National Committee, guiding the party to triumphs in 1918 and 1920. He offered both the moral authority and political contacts that the hard-pressed industry needed.

Creation of the Hays Office. On March 10, 1922, a charter of incorporation filed in Albany, New York, created the Motion Picture Producers and Distributors of America. With Hays as president, the MPPDA was to be governed by a board representing the major film corporations. Vitagraph, Pathe, Goldwyn, Fox, Universal, Metro, Associated First National, and United Artists were among the charter members, which together accounted for 85 percent of America's films. The MPPDA's charter promised to promote wholesome pictures, but the new president's principal function was to improve the industry's public image and ease the growing pressure for censorship.

The first crisis that Hays faced was a Massachusetts referendum on censorship scheduled for November, 1922. Hays mounted a massive publicity campaign against the measure, which was soundly defeated. Concurrently, he created three working sections within the MPPDA: One concentrated on internal industry matters, such as labor arbitration and contracts; another focused on foreign markets for American pictures; and a third handled public relations. The first of these sections worked toward the establishment of standardized contracts in the industry and developed such innovations as the central casting office in Hollywood. The office focusing on foreign sales sought to develop contacts abroad in an effort to eliminate resistance to American pictures. The public relations department was staffed by professional writers and publicists who generated a continuous stream of press releases favorable to the industry. It issued a monthly magazine, *The Motion Picture*, drafted speeches for friends of the industry, sent free films to schools and churches and sponsored conferences. A newspaper and magazines department collected stories from the local press and authored countless personalized letters to editors and other community leaders to be sent over Hays's signature.

This massive public relations effort was designed to discourage efforts to censor or regulate the film industry. In addition, the MPPDA maintained a corps of lobbyists, led by General Counsel Charles C. Pettijohn, which was mobilized whenever a legislative threat arose. Its efforts were clearly successful. After the establishment of the Hays Office, no new state censorship boards were created.

Self-Regulation. In his efforts to discourage government censorship, Hays consistently relied on one central argument—that the film industry should be allowed to police itself. He repeatedly promised that the MPPDA would establish an effective system of self-regulation capable of removing objectionable content from the films. Toward that end, in 1924 he introduced the "Formula," a requirement that studios forward to the MPPDA copies of every play, book, or story under consideration for film treatment. The Hays Office would then advise the studios as to which projects contained undesirable elements. While this requirement had few teeth and was often circumvented, Hays did ban 125 plays and novels from the screen.

The MPPDA's second effort at self-regulation took the form of a list of eleven items never to be treated on screen and twenty-six subjects that were to be handled only with special care. Endorsed by the MPPDA's board in 1927, the list was compiled by the Studio Relations Office, which Hays had established in Hollywood in 1926. Under Jason Joy, this office collected data on the practices and predilections of the nation's state and municipal censors. The list represented a distillation of his findings and was meant to steer Hollywood producers away from potentially censorable material. In addition, Joy served as an informal studio consultant, reviewing scripts and finished pictures and advising producers as to what material was most likely to be cut by the censors.

Motion Picture Production Code. These solutions failed to satisfy the industry's critics. Since neither required producers to abide by Joy's or Hays's recommendations, the studios continued to produce controversial pictures. Amid mounting pressure for federal control, Hays introduced a third vehicle for self-regulation by the industry in early 1930, the Motion Picture Production Code. This twelve-page document contained a justification for restricting film content along with a detailed list of the types of material that could not appear on the screen. Popularly called the Hays Code, it was launched with much fanfare but, again, lacked effective enforcement. With the Great Depression came a drastic decline in film attendance and the studios turned to even more sensational film content. In 1934, pressured by a mass Catholic boycott directed by the Legion of Decency, the MPPDA created the Production Code Administration (PCA) and provided it with the authority to censor all studio-made films. Under the threat of a twenty-five-thousand-dollar fine, the studios were required to submit all scripts and films for PCA approval, and no film lacking the PCA's seal could be exhibited in any MPPDA theater. In 1935 the board also required that all advertising copy be submitted to the Hays Office before release. Because the MPPDA member companies controlled the largest and most lucrative theaters in the country, even film producers beyond the MPPDA's official control soon complied with the new system. By the end of the 1930's, more than 90 percent of

Rod Steiger won an Academy Award for his portrayal of a concentration camp survivor in The Pawnbroker*—one of the first films released without an MPAA seal of approval.* (Museum of Modern Art/Film Stills Archive)

all films shown in the United States carried a PCA seal. Under the direction of Joseph I. Breen, the PCA eliminated much of the sex and sensationalism that had offended the industry's critics, and the pressure for government censorship subsided.

In 1945 Eric Johnston, formerly president of the U.S. Chamber of Commerce, succeeded Hays as MPPDA president; shortly thereafter the organization's name was changed to Motion Picture Association of America (MPAA). Also in 1945, the MPPDA's foreign department became the Motion Picture Export Association, with Johnston as president and the same board of directors. Under Johnston, the MPAA continued to function much as it had under Hays. During the 1940's Johnston worked to improve labor relations, defended the industry against charges of communist infiltration, and resisted foreign efforts to impose heavy taxes and quotas on American pictures. In 1948 the MPAA's control of the industry was weakened by the U.S. Supreme Court's antitrust ruling in *United States v. Paramount Pictures* which forced the studio corporations to sell their theaters. In the 1950's the rise of independent and foreign production, the freedom of the newly divorced theater chains to select films not approved by the PCA, and the competition of television gradually undermined the MPAA's system of self-censorship. Beginning with Otto Preminger's *The Moon Is Blue* in 1953, theater owners booked pictures not carrying the PCA's seal with increasing frequency. Despite efforts to modernize the Production Code in 1956, the erosion of authority continued into the 1960's.

The Rating System. In May, 1966, the MPAA board selected presidential adviser Jack Valenti to succeed Johnston, who had died three years earlier. In November, 1968, Valenti implemented a new film rating system. This system, based on an agreement between the MPAA, the National Association of Theater Owners (NATO), and the International Film Importers and Distributors of America, replaced the PCA with the MPAA Classification and Rating Administration. A new seven-member Rating Board was empowered to classify films with regard to their suitability for children. Originally, the agency assigned four different ratings: G (general audience); M (suggested for mature audiences); R (restricted—children under sixteen must be accompanied by an adult); and X (no one under sixteen admitted). In 1970 the M rating was changed to GP (parental guidance suggested), and the age limit on R and X-rated films was raised to seventeen. Later, GP became PG, and in 1984 a category called PG-13 was added to warn parents that such films contained violence unsuitable for children under thirteen.

Aside from the association's X rating, all ratings were protected by copyright. Because the producers of pornographic features normally avoided the rating board and often applied the X to their films without approval, confusion resulted. In 1990, to distinguish officially rated pictures containing adult material from hardcore pornography, the MPAA replaced its X rating with the copyrighted NC-17. Advertising for rated films also had to be submitted to the MPAA's Advertising Code Administration for approval. While distributors were not required to submit their features to the Rating Board, most found theaters reluctant to book unrated pictures, and many newspapers and television stations refused to run advertisements for unrated or X-rated films. To ensure the widest possible audience, producers and distributors learned to alter their pictures to gain a favorable rating. Decisions of the Rating Board could be appealed to the Rating Appeals Board, chaired by Valenti and composed of twenty-two representatives from the MPAA member companies, the NATO companies, and four independent film production companies.

Under Valenti, the MPAA continued to perform multiple functions for the American film industry. While supervising the rating system, Valenti emerged as the industry's principal defender against renewed complaints that films undermined traditional values and contributed to the growing violence in American society. As member companies of the MPAA merged with larger entertainment conglomerates, Valenti broadened his defense to include television and cable programming. In addition to its expansive lobbying and public relations efforts, the MPAA also sought to ease international trade restrictions and to crack down on film and video piracy in the United States and abroad. —*Jerold L. Simmons*

See also Film advisory board; Film censorship; Hays Code; Legion of Decency; *Moon Is Blue, The*; *Outlaw, The*.

Bibliography

Raymond Moley's *The Hays Office* (Indianapolis: Bobbs-Merrill, 1945), commissioned by the MPPA, is dated and uncritical but nevertheless affords useful information on the organization's early years. *The Memoirs of Will H. Hays* (Garden City, N.J.: Doubleday, 1955) is similarly self-serving. Garth Jowett's *Film: The Democratic Art* (Boston: Little, Brown, 1976) provides a wealth of material on the larger concerns of the film industry and its trade association. Gregory Black's *Hollywood Censored: Morality Codes, Catholics and the Movies* (New York: Cambridge University Press, 1994) offers a full account of the creation of the MPAA Production Code and its operation through the 1930's. *The Dame in the Kimono: Hollywood, Censorship and the Production Code from the 1920's to the 1960's* (New York: Grove Weidenfeld, 1990) by Leonard J. Leff and Jerold L. Simmons is an episodic history of the Production Code. Stephen Farber's *The Movie Rating Game* (Washington, D.C.: Public Affairs Press, 1972) gives an inside look at the operations of the Rating Board.

Muhammad

BORN: c. 570, Mecca, Arabia

DIED: June 8, 632, Medina, Arabia

IDENTIFICATION: Arab prophet and founder of the Islamic religion

SIGNIFICANCE: As the founder of one of the world's great religions, Muhammad and his beliefs have been both a cause and a subject of censorship

Muhammad was born in Mecca, a trading city on the Arabian peninsula in what is now Saudi Arabia. As the home of shrines to the many gods of Muhammad's time, Mecca drew numerous pilgrims and was considered neutral ground on which the often warring Arab clans could gather in peace. As a youth, Muhammad was employed as a camel driver. Although he was always reflective, his life was little different from that of other Meccans until he was about forty.

Around the year 611, Muhammad began going into the mountains to meditate and had a series of transforming experiences. Mysterious darkness would come over him, and the archangel Gabriel would appear and command him to recite passages, which he later remembered clearly. These messages stressed the unity of God (Allah), God's authority, and his abomination of idolatry and the judgment day. To the end of Muhammad's life, these revelations continued; he eventually collected them in the Koran—which became the principal holy book of Islam. The Koran is viewed as the direct word of God, not that of Muhammad, who is said to have been illiterate. Within Islam, alternative views have been and continue to be regarded as blasphemous and are therefore censored.

For a decade Muhammad implored his fellow Meccans to obey the calls he was receiving. Having little success, he found his position in Mecca untenable, so he fled to nearby Medina on June 15, 622. This journey, known as the hejira, is the starting date of the Islamic calendar and of Muhammad's public mission on a grand scale. Using Medina as his base, Muhammad soon brought all Arabia under his control. In 632, while returning from a triumphal pilgrimage to Mecca, he preached a farewell sermon and died shortly afterward, leaving the question of his succession open. Mourned as a hero, he had united Arabia under Islam through a combination of diplomacy and military force. To his people he was larger than life: a visionary alone in the desert; a general riding into battle; and a charismatic religious leader holding his followers together by the force of his personality. This blending of spiritual and temporal roles would become a hallmark of Islam.

Perhaps because his own beliefs had originally been subjected to ridicule and restriction, Muhammad's tolerance exceeded that of many of his later followers. Muslim cultures have often been quite rigid. Both official and self-censorship have been and continue to be commonplace. To avoid idolatry, Muslims have banned depiction of images of people—depictions of Muhammad and God. An orthodox view of Muhammad's life and strict codes of acceptable expression have developed and those differing from or questioning established interpretations have been persecuted. Like many other belief systems, Islam has been used by the unscrupulous and selfish. Accusations of blasphemy, heresy trials, violence, and other breaches of human rights have been employed to silence opposition.

See also Islam; Koran; Mani; *Mohammed, Messenger of God*; Rushdie, Salman.

Multiculturalism

DEFINITION: Advocacy of diversity of ethnic representation in education

SIGNIFICANCE: Multiculturalism, a challenge to some traditional educational ideas, has drawn criticism from several fronts

The United States and Canada are essentially nations of immigrants. Multiculturalism has its origins in a problem faced by North American teachers since immigration began: what to do with classrooms filled with pupils coming from different countries, speaking different languages, and possessing different cultural assumptions. Responses have varied, although the push toward assimilation has been largely constant. Educators introduced the idea of ethnic awareness in school curricula during the 1920's. By the 1930's the Service Bureau for Intercultural Education provided in-service programs for teaching minority children.

Goals of Multiculturalism in Education. In general, multiculturalism in education has emphasized diverse ethnic and racial representation, although much misunderstanding and controversy result from a lack of consensus concerning multiculturalism's goals. The source of much of the controversy surrounding multiculturalism in education may be summarized as the challenge that multiculturalism mounts to the melting pot metaphor for North American education. The melting pot metaphor recalls the making of alloys of metal, in which various metals are melted into a new alloy, losing their individual characteristics in the process. This view of how assimilation is to take place dominated educational goals in the United States in the early twentieth century. In practical terms, students were to learn only English, to let their native languages lapse, to renounce their old cultures, and to adapt to North American culture, changing it somewhat as they did so. Many have criticized the melting pot theory as a means of enforcing cultural hegemony and of excluding minority views.

Judging such education as too Eurocentric in its focus and lacking in diversity, pluralist educators recommend opening up the curriculum to embrace many cultures, many of which were represented in the American population. Arguing that the canon defines and sets the boundaries of a community's outlooks, progressive educators advocate for equality in representation and exposure via the inclusion of literature written both by and for minorities and women. *A Curriculum of Inclusion*, written by the New York State Commissioner of Education's Task Force on Minorities (1989) offers a curriculum for allowing marginalized groups to voice their perspectives. Statements of equal respect in curriculum include California's "History-Social Science Framework," which lists acceptable textbooks. These textbooks provide different cultural perspectives that accurately reflect the ethnic diversity of contemporary American communities.

Similarly, in the mid-1990's, many educators in culturally diverse communities, such as New York City and Los Angeles, have struggled to offer ethnically inclusive curricula that address the needs of diverse populations by showcasing the cultural identities of various communities. For example, the New York State Social Studies Review and Development Committee declared in 1991 that a group's ethnic status and presence is acknowledged by its inclusion in the curriculum.

Lack of ethnic representation in the curriculum can affect students' self-esteem, so educators argue that teaching students' ethnic heritage will encourage ethnic pride, thereby augmenting their social involvement and academic achievement. Examples of recognizing minority participation in well-known events include the contributions of Native American and Nisei soldiers in World War II or African American cowboys and Japanese railroad builders contributing to the taming of the Old West.

Not only does a multicultural curriculum increase an excluded groups' self-esteem, it sensitizes nonminority students to cultural differences as well as the wrongdoing of ancestors, a way of teaching tolerance for difference as well as not repeating the colonizing behaviors of the past. During the late 1980's and mid-1990's, educators focused, for example, on minority perspectives in history, including the Trail of Tears traveled by the Cherokee in the nineteenth century, the internment of Japanese Americans during World War II, and the perspectives of Mexicans on the annexation of Texas.

Another educational reform related to reducing racial and social inequality is bilingual education, for example as described in the federal Bilingual Education Act of 1968. In the act, minority language rights are not only recognized but also their preservation is emphasized, a departure from melting pot methods of education.

Criticism of Goals of Multiculturalism in Education. Criticized as nourishing separatism, minority representation in education was interpreted during the 1980's and 1990's as intellectual tyranny. Critics of multicultural education have argued that instead of opening up discussions of curriculum change and evaluating the proposed changes by generally accepted institutional principles, pluralists have undermined the foundations of professionalism and objectivity in making changes. One may argue, however, that multiculturalism has merely entered, not created, the volatile political environment surrounding what to teach students.

For example, Stanford University, a highly regarded California institution, implemented a core curriculum called "Cultures, Ideas and Values" (CIV) in 1989 that required study of at least one non-Western culture. Critics have argued that such a focus teaches provincialism and ethnocentrism. The selection of textbooks and course materials based solely on ethnic and gender categories are, critics argue, neither rational nor adequate because this approach prevents the nonbiased examination of precepts underlying Western civilization. In the late 1980's Mount Holyoke College, the University of Wisconsin, and Dartmouth College required students to take ethnic studies courses, but not to take courses on Western civilization. The continued focus on diversity prevents the possibility of discussing the classics without looking through the lenses of gender and race. Pluralists argue that people always are wearing glasses of gender and race; the point is to learn to recognize how the glasses shape what one sees.

Critics of multiculturalism have been derided for overlooking the curriculum that preceded it. Few today would argue in favor of segregation in schools, of punishing students for speaking their native language, of deliberately discounting the contributions of women and minorities, of describing Western imperialism as a grand adventure, or of promoting racism. Debate has not centered on whether the curriculum should return to that of the early twentieth century but whether multiculturalism has gone too far.

In addition, critics have argued that an educational agenda that emphasizes diversity imprisons students within their ethnic or ancestral heritage, defining them merely as representatives of a group, thereby impeding them from full participation within the broader culture. By defining students solely as ethnic beings, there is a social censorship that bolsters ethnic separatism. Issues of race and gender, in such a setting, cannot be examined in a nonpartisan, nonconfrontational manner. While such social limitations on college campuses are neither legislative nor preventive censorship, students are aware of a common expectation that they will be punished if they verbalize unaccepted views on race and gender. For example, in the late 1980's students at the University of Michigan at Ann Arbor who did not toe the multicultural line were required to take sensitivity training workshops.

Although a goal of multiculturalism in education is to promote ethnic tolerance, its censoring effects via institutionalized public intimidation may cause racial segregation. Furthermore, a curriculum that focuses on atonement for past wrongs also encourages a victim mentality and collective guilt; this assignment of blame contributes to the idolizing of non-Western cultures and a demonizing of Western cultures. Thus, current discussions of multiculturalism in the classroom take an either-or structure, forcing students to choose between Eurocentrism or ethnicity.

Critics maintain that the multicultural movement minimizes any form of critique in which uncommendable qualities of minority cultures are highlighted. Acts of hostility, racism, sexism, and elitism within minority cultures are ignored or disregarded. In addition, the definition of Western civilization as a static and monolithic entity, beginning with Homer and ending with Ernest Hemingway, is erroneous. Critics of multiculturalism in education argue that when students are encouraged to make judgments based on ethnicity alone, they are discouraged from bona fide evaluation and critique, skills necessary for thoughtful and responsible citizenship.

—Sue Hum

See also Education; Ethnic studies; Free speech; Intellectual freedom; Language laws; Political correctness.

BIBLIOGRAPHY

Calvin Beisner, "The Double-Edged Sword of Multiculturalism" in *The Freeman* 44 (March, 1994), argues that multiculturalism builds on a victim mentality and is a dogma spawned in ignorance. Dinesh D'Souza's *Illiberal Education: The Politics of Race and Sex on Campus* (New York: Free Press, 1991) criticizes the goals of multiculturalism and identifies the conflicts underlying the ideology for social reform via education. Michael Olneck's "Terms of Inclusion: Has Multiculturalism Redefined Equality in American Education?" in *American Journal of Education* 101 (May, 1993), defines equality in terms of the distribution of resources and rewards within a community, examining whether multiculturalism in education has helped redistribute resources. Mary Louise Pratt's "Humanities for the Future: Reflections on the Western Culture Debate at Stanford," in *The Politics of Liberal Education*, edited by Darryl J. Gless and Barbara Herrnstein Smith (Durham, N.C.: Duke University Press, 1992), surveys the debate surrounding reform of the Western culture requirement at Stanford University. Irene Pyszkowski argues in "Multiculturalism—Education for the Nineties: An Overview" in *Education* 114, no. 1 (1994) that multiculturalism in education plays a major role in including more of America's minorities and ethnic groups. Aminur Rahim's "Multiculturalism or Ethnic Hegemony: A Critique of Multicultural Education in Toronto" in *Journal of Ethnic Studies* 18, no. 3 (1990) explores the curricular development and implementation of multicultural education programs in a Canadian city. Arthur Schlesinger, Jr.'s "A Dissent on Multicultural Education" in *Partisan Review* 58, no. 4 (1991) discusses the New York State Social Studies Syllabus Review Committee's decision to diversify education.

Munsch, Robert N.

BORN: June 11, 1945, Pittsburgh, Pennsylvania

IDENTIFICATION: Children's author and storyteller

SIGNIFICANCE: Canada's best-selling author of picture books for preschoolers and primary school students has seen many of his titles challenged and removed from schools

While Robert Munsch's juvenile audiences certainly enjoy his stories, and adults have made the sentimental *Love You Forever* (1986) a best-seller, a number of Munsch's books have been targeted by Canadian censors. The use of the word "pee," for example, has created problems for *I Have to Go!* (1987) and *Pigs* (1989), while a pig urinating on a school principal's shoes has caused the latter book to be charged with "showing disrespect to adults." Administrators in Lloydminster, Saskatchewan, felt their authority undermined by *Thomas' Snowsuit* (1985), in which a male principal and female teacher accidentally switch clothes. Some parents described *The Paper Bag Princess* (1980) as "antifamily" because, at story's end, the princess refuses to marry the prince. *Giant, or Waiting for the Thursday Boat* (1989), which portrays God as a little girl, cannot be read to children in Ontario's Middlesex County schools "because of the book's religious implications." *Giant* was also labeled "violent," because the central character, Ireland's largest giant, threatens to "pound him [God] til he looks like applesauce." An Inuit cautionary tale, *A Promise Is a Promise* (1988), coauthored with Michael Kusugak, has been incorrectly accused of containing reference to witches. Finally, *Good Families Don't* (1990), the story of a young girl's attempts to remove a "great big purple, green and yellow fart" from her bedroom, has likely been subjected to the silent censorship hidden within the school library selection process.

See also Books, children's; Canada; Libraries, school; Offensive language; Religion.

Mural art

DEFINITION: Paintings on walls, especially walls open to public view

SIGNIFICANCE: Public condemnation of murals has sometimes resulted in the destruction of mural art

The earliest mural paintings were executed on cave walls at least fifteen thousand years ago. Ancient Egypt, Greece, Italy, and the Near and Far East have left murals. The Renaissance in Italy saw the greatest expression of mural art in history. Many of the murals of Michelangelo, Raphael, Giovanni Battista Tiepolo, and others still inspire. Mural painting requires that artist and client collaborate. At times communication fails and controversy arises. This was the case with Michelangelo.

One of the greatest artists of all time, Michelangelo became embroiled in a vehement controversy over his enormous mural *The Last Judgment* in the Sistine Chapel in Rome. The work depicts countless nude human figures meeting their ultimate fate as judged by God. It was described as a "bathing establishment" by Biagio de Cesena, a papal assistant. Another critic, Pietro Aretino, commented that "such things might be painted in a voluptuous bathroom, but not in the choir of the highest chapel." Michelangelo is supposed to have inserted the portraits of both these critics in the mural. Aretino was represented as Bartholomew holding the skin of a flayed martyr. The head and body of the martyr dangle limply from Aretino's hand. The martyr resembles a self-portrait of Michelangelo. He caricatured the assistant, Biagio de Cesena, as Minos, the supreme judge of hell, with ears resembling a donkey's. Biagio complained to the pope, but the pope responded that to rescue de Cesena from hell was outside the pope's power, but had de Cesena been in purgatory, it would have been a different matter. On December 3, 1563, the Council of Trent announced that representation of nudity was forbidden. Under popes Paul IV and Gregory XIII the fresco was in danger of being completely destroyed.

Finally the offending parts on all figures were painted over. Other overpaintings were made in 1632 and again in 1762. In the 1980's and 1990's a massive restoration of the Sistine Chapel was undertaken, and *The Last Judgment* was restored. The loin cloths that had covered the previously offending parts were removed. In his heroic figures Michelangelo was portraying ideal human forms, and nudity in many of the figures supported the concept of that ideal. The censorship actions by the church were to have a negative effect on how much nudity other artists portrayed in their murals from that time on.

Revolutionary Painters. In 1923 a group in Mexico called the syndicate of revolutionary painters, sculptors, and engravers included Diego Rivera, David Alfaro Siqueiros, and José Clemente Orozco. These artists painted murals that promoted communist propaganda. The conservative middle class became enraged at these artists' inflammatory works. Rivera stirred up controversy when he refused to remove a portrait of V. I. Lenin from his Radio City mural in New York City in 1933. The event was covered on the front page of many newspapers across America. Rivera lost the battle. The owners of the building, with the indirect involvement of Nelson Rockefeller, destroyed the mural. Artists leaning toward the communist ideology generally viewed the destruction of the mural as an act of the Rockefeller family. Rivera had a vehement hatred of the capitalist system and all those who symbolized it. In the central areas of the Radio City mural were various technological devices for the production of electrical power, the harnessing of energy, and the exploration of scientific knowledge. On the left side were the oppressors: businessmen, aristocrats, and bayonet-wielding soldiers. On the right were pictured the working masses, children, and a heroically morose figure of Lenin, the leader of the Russian Revolution. Artists and Marxists were incensed at the destruction of the mural.

Diego Rivera's inclusion of Soviet leader V. I. Lenin (upper left) in a mural he painted at Rockefeller Center in 1933 led to his being stripped of his commission and his mural's being covered over. (AP/Wide World Photos)

Thomas Hart Benton. In 1934 the mural painter Thomas Hart Benton gave a speech at the John Reed Club in New York City. He criticized Marxist art, which was characterized by Rivera's mural. Benton held that Marxist art was too idealistic, and not based on life experiences. Benton expressed his indifference to the destruction of the Rivera mural. In conclusion he said: "I respect Rivera as an artist and a great one, but I have no time to enter into affairs concerning him, because I am intensely interested in the development of an art which is of, and adequately represents the United States—my own art." These were incendiary words. One of his lectures during this period resulted in a chair-throwing brawl.

In 1936, Benton completed his social history of Missouri murals in the Missouri State Capitol. Walter Heren reported in the Kansas City *Journal-Post* the results of a poll he had taken. There was no middle ground in the opinions of the murals. "You either like them or you want the wall to be painted a deep black," he observed. Benton had elected to portray Missouri not from an idealized, noble, and refined point of view, but rather he depicted miners, laborers, politicians going about their business, along with the Jesse James gang robbing a bank and a train and black slaves being whipped as they worked the lead mines. Benton showed breweries, shoe factories, and clothing sweatshops of St. Louis, as well as the story of Frankie and Johnnie, where Frankie shoots Johnnie dead because "he done her wrong." The mural aroused the admiration or hostility of lay people and artists alike. In Benton's mind the ugliness of some of the figures had a certain truthfulness and nobility of character not found in the more idealistic paintings, as found in Rivera's work, for example.

Murals accompanied socialism in the former Soviet Union, Mexico, and Chile. Mural painting has seen somewhat of a revival from the 1960's to the 1990's. In the 1960's and 1970's in Chile it was used by communist painting brigades to bring messages to the people during the revolution. In the 1970's and 1990's it has been used to communicate ethnic consciousness and pride, particularly in the inner cities of America.

—Thomas Cappuccio

See also Art; Graffiti; Michelangelo; Propaganda; Rivera, Diego; Socialist Realism; Wall posters; Warhol, Andy.

BIBLIOGRAPHY

Robert Sommer's *Street Art* (New York: Links, 1975) is an introduction to mural paintings created mainly in the inner cities of America by professional and amateur groups. David Goldscheider's *Michelangelo* (New York: Phaidon Publishers, 1973) is a thorough review of all the artist's murals, sculptures, and architecture. John Wilmerding's *The Genius of American*

Painting (New York: William Morrow, 1973) traces the development of American painting from the sixteenth to the twentieth century. Henry Adams' *Thomas Hart Benton: An American Original* (New York: Alfred A. Knopf, 1989) has particular emphasis on his mural paintings. Barbara Rose's *American Art Since 1900* (New York: Praeger, 1975) discusses the social and cultural influences on modern painting in America.

Murphy, Eddie

Born: April 3, 1961, Brooklyn, New York

Identification: American comedian and film actor

Significance: As a stand-up comedian, Murphy has attracted protests for his comments regarding women and gays

Murphy became a stand-up comedian at fifteen; he was on the nightclub circuit at sixteen, and landed a spot on television's *Saturday Night Live* (*SNL*) at nineteen. While starring on *SNL* from November, 1980, to April, 1984, he launched a second career as a film actor. He starred in such blockbuster films as *48 HRS* (1982), *Trading Places* (1983), and *Beverly Hills Cop* (1984) and its sequels. In 1987 he returned to stand-up work in a tour that provided the backdrop for a film titled *Raw* (1987).

During the *Raw* tour, and on other occasions, Murphy earned the ire of gay rights advocates and women because of what they viewed as his homophobic and misogynist humor. In 1985, for example, a militant gay rights group infuriated by Murphy's jokes about homosexuals and AIDS took out full-page advertisements in *Billboard* and *Rolling Stone* denouncing him as a "homophobe."

See also Bruce, Lenny; Carlin, George; Sahl, Mort; *Saturday Night Live*.

Murphy Brown controversy

Date: May 19, 1992

Place: U.S. network television

Significance: The depiction of a television sitcom character having a baby out of wedlock drew attacks from a high government official, which in turn raised fears of government censorship

From the mid-1980's into the late 1990's Candice Bergen played a television news reporter on the network situation comedy *Murphy Brown.* In an episode that aired on May 19, 1992, Bergen's unmarried character—Brown—decided to give birth after becoming pregnant. The episode presented no hint of nudity, sexual activity, or objectionable language, but many viewers perceived its adult theme as condoning unwed parenthood. The show became the subject of serious criticism from religious conservatives, who attacked it for promoting immorality. U.S. vice president Dan Quayle—who was about to run for reelection—joined in these attacks, speaking out for these groups by castigating the show for failing to reinforce "family values" and for endorsing declining morality in America.

Bergen, the show's producers, and the entertainment industry generally, lashed back at Quayle's criticisms as censorship by public pressure. They accused him of fostering a chilling effect on television. Although the U.S. government did not formally try to censor television by classic prior restraint, pressure on the entertainment industry by its high officials has often been considered as having a chilling effect. Quayle defended himself by asserting that he too had a right to exercise his own right of free speech. The furor subsided after a few weeks.

See also Chilling effect; Prior restraint; Television; Television networks.

Public Reaction to the *Murphy Brown* Controversy

After Vice President Quayle criticized the *Murphy Brown* episode in which the lead character bears a child out of wedlock, a CNN/*USA Today*/Gallup Poll surveyed whether the public thought his criticism was justified. These are the results:

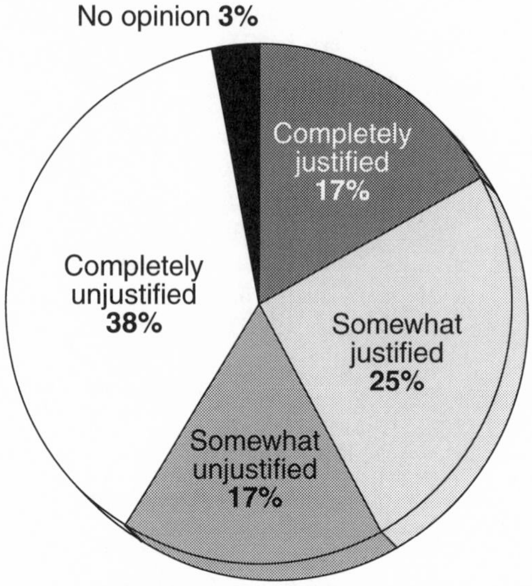

Source: The Gallup Poll: Public Opinion 1994. Wilmington, Del.: Scholarly Resources, 1995.

Music

Definition: Artificially produced sounds arranged to produce aesthetic pleasure

Significance: Music has regularly been subjected to censorship

From the fourth century B.C.E., when Plato envisioned a model state in which music would be closely regulated, to the modern controversy over gangsta rap, music has been a perennial object of censorship. Almost every element of music—from melody and rhythm to instrumentation and lyric—has had its official detractors. Plato objected to particular scale formations and the melodies elaborated upon them, as well as to certain instruments. In 1322 Pope John XXII decreed that counterpoint was forbidden in the church. In colonial America, William Cosby, governor of New York, ordered song sheets disrespectful of the king of England to be burnt and attempted unsuccessfully to ferret out the composers of these lyrics. During the 1930's and 1940's, composers in the Soviet Union were routinely chastised for the excessive formalism of their music and thus accused of an elitism that betrayed the proletariat revolution. In the 1950's, the rhythm of rock and roll scandalized older Americans. Gangsta rap lyrics in the 1980's and 1990's, celebrating violence and misogyny, have reinvigorated attempts to censor popular music.

Plato and the Censorship of Music. When the Greek philosopher Plato imagined his ideal society in the *Republic*, he took care to elaborate the kind of music fitting for that society. Plato realized, as have rulers in every age, that music can be subversive. He believed with many of his contemporaries in late antiquity that different kinds of music wrought different effects upon their hearers, some to be desired, some to be shunned. Plato accordingly envisioned a society that took care in the kinds of music it permitted. Students being prepared for citizenship should be exposed to the courageous Dorian strain and the contemplative Phrygian, but authorities would do well to ban the mixed Lydian harmonies of lamentation and "drinking" harmonies such as the Ionian and pure Lydian. In Plato's state, where each individual occupied a single role, simplicity was the rule of the day. Simplicity in music, he believed, was the parent of "temperance in the soul." Complexity had no place, either in life or in music. Thus, Plato would have banned multistringed and multishaped instruments, as well as complicated rhythms.

Music and Modern Totalitarian Governments. Totalitarian suppression of dissident speech has inevitably included music censorship. Totalitarian governments have suppressed not only outright criticisms, in music, of their regimes, but also music deemed more generally to threaten the political projects of those regimes. For example, in China Mao Zedong believed, as he revealed in 1956, that music should serve the Communist Party's ideological aims. Western music especially was to be shunned as decadent. During the Cultural Revolution in China (from 1966 to 1976, when Mao launched a reign of repression), Western music and traditional Chinese music were discouraged or banned outright as counterrevolutionary. Many music schools and publishing houses were closed and performing groups disbanded. The only music that flourished was officially sanctioned mass music and songs expressing revolutionary ideology. With Mao's death in 1976 this suppression of ideologically threatening music relented in some measure, but music—especially Western music—retained its suspiciousness in the eyes of party officials. During the early 1980's, for example, university students and schoolchildren were required to turn over their tapes and records, or produce lists of them, so that the government could ban the music it thought unfit for these youths. Nevertheless, an underground subculture of rock music began to flourish in China during the 1980's and in fact became a crucial element in the student-led protests that climaxed in the demonstration and massacre at Tiananmen Square in 1989.

The Soviet Union also displayed a ready willingness to make music serve the ideological aims of the state. In 1936 the Stalinist regime attacked Dmitri Shostakovich's *Lady Macbeth of the Mtsensk District* (1934) through the Communist Party newspaper *Pravda* and a notorious editorial titled "Chaos Instead of Music." This opposition by the Party essentially censored further productions of *Lady Macbeth of the Mtsensk District* until nearly a generation later, in 1963. In 1948 the Communist Party's central committee lambasted "formalism" in music, and thereafter denied commissions to composers such as Shostakovich and Sergei Prokofiev unless their works illustrated the simple melodic lines and patriotism favored by the Party.

Political Protest. Music has often been at the forefront of political protest. One can scarcely speak of the Civil Rights movement in the United States during the 1960's and 1970's without making reference to "We Shall Overcome," the spiritual song that accompanied so many of the movement's crucial events. Along with other forms of protest, music has endured its share of official opposition to messages, including musical messages, that have threatened the established political order. The Latin American *nueva canción* (new song) is an example of the role of music in political protest and its frequent censorship. *Nueva canción* is a Spanish-language genre that developed during the 1960's, arising out of the opposition among Latin American youth to domestic political repression and social inequalities and the greater inequality of North American imperialism—including the domination of North American music in the media. In Chile the *nueva canción* came to be aligned with the socialist party of President Salvador Allende after his election in 1970. The music incorporated Andean instruments and reflected a resurgent national pride. However, after a military junta led by Augusto Pinochet overthrew the Allende government in 1973, *nueva canción*—with its overt political messages—was censored. Its principal performers were driven out of Chile or imprisoned, and the musical genre survived—as did those of its performers who were not executed—chiefly in exile.

Before the democratic revolution of the early 1990's in South Africa, the suppression of particular forms of music was of a piece with the South African government's general attempts to censor ideas that threatened the regime's program of apartheid. The state-owned South African Broadcasting Corporation (SABC) governed the airways and used its power to censor political protest. The corporation demanded that it be given translations of all music lyrics performed in an indigenous language and refused to air songs of political protest whether the protest was stated directly or indirectly by mentioning an exiled or imprisoned political protester. Musical dissent in South Africa, like other forms of dissent, frequently brought torture or imprisonment. For example, in the late 1980's the lead singer of a South African reggae group was sentenced to three years in jail for recording a song about apartheid opponent Nelson Mandela. The song, according to South African officials, had been intended to advance the cause of a banned organization. Performers such as Bob Marley, Pete Seeger, and Pink Floyd, whose songs frequently contained overt political messages, were also objects of censorship in South Africa. Pink Floyd's "The Wall" was banned for its line, "We don't need no education," which Soweto youths used in their boycott of public schools in the 1970's. After Stevie Wonder won an Academy Award in 1985 for his song, "I Just Called to Say I Love You," and dedicated it to Nelson Mandela, the SABC banned all of Wonder's songs on its stations.

Censorship in Western Democracies. The felt need to suppress dangerous music has not been confined to totalitarian governments. Democracies have also sought to regulate the availability of particular forms of music. Sometimes these regulations are concerned less with the alleged harmfulness of particular music than with perceived threats to indigenous music. For example, a number of Western democratic governments have imposed restrictions on the amount of broadcast time occupied by nonindigenous music. Music quotas—requiring certain amounts of air time to support indigenous music—have been used in Canada, France, Sweden, and Finland. In other cases, certain music has been treated as threatening the existence of democratic government itself. In December, 1992, for example, the German government banned the sale to individuals under eighteen years of age of neo-Nazi rock music, which advocated violence against foreigners. The German constitution, enacted in the wake of World War II, generally prohibits censorship, but an exception is made for expression relating to the Nazis. The German authorities thus viewed an alarming increase in right-wing violence and a resurgent Nazism as sufficiently dangerous to German democracy to warrant an abridgment of free expression.

Music Censorship in the United States. The U.S. Supreme Court has construed the First Amendment's free speech clause to prohibit most government attempts to censor speech thought to be objectionable. This prohibition applies to music and other forms of entertainment. Thus, while federal, state, or local governments may sometimes regulate when and where and how speech is communicated, they may generally not suppress particular speech simply by virtue of opposition to the content of that speech. The Court has, however, viewed one category of speech—obscenity—as falling outside the First Amendment's umbrella of protection. Governments may censor obscenity, which the Court has defined as being speech that the average person—applying community standards—would find appeals on the whole to prurient interest, that depicts or describes sexual conduct in a patently offensive manner, and that lacks on the whole any serious literary, artistic, political, or scientific value. Governments may also censor speech designed to produce unlawful conduct, but only if such conduct is imminent and is, in fact, likely to be produced by the speech. The normal presumption is in favor of free expression; findings that a particular piece of music is either obscene or likely to produce imminent unlawful conduct have been rare.

Rock 'n' Roll. Popular music has routinely earned the ire of government officials who have feared that it would corrupt impressionable youth. Jazz, blues, and rock 'n' roll were denounced as "jungle rhythms" (sometimes the racist overtones of the denunciation were made direct and explicit) and "the devil's music." In the 1950's Elvis Presley's records were burnt and local governments banned the airing of rock 'n' roll songs. Local communities threatened by the arrival of rock concert tours used zoning laws and ordinances concerning large public gatherings to deny admittance to the tours. Rock 'n' roll eventually penetrated mainstream culture, but in doing so was sometimes pruned of its more objectionable features. Ed Sullivan initially refused to allow Presley to perform on *The Ed Sullivan Show*, suggesting that Presley's music was not fit for American families. When Sullivan relented a few years later and invited Presley to perform, Presley appeared on screens only as an upper torso, television camera operators leaving the gyrations of his lower body off the camera. Later, when Sullivan invited the Rolling Stones to appear on the show, he balked at their singing "Let's Spend the Night Together." Threatened with being replaced by a trained seal act, the Stones—anxious to promote a new tour—compromised by instead singing the line, "Let's spend some time together."

In the decades that followed rock 'n' roll won a grudging acceptance within mainstream culture, although particular lyrics continued to draw political protests. One may argue that the satanic powers of rock 'n' roll were made manifest by such events as the great concert at Woodstock in 1969, at which hundreds of thousands of youths enjoyed music, celebrated peace while their nation was at war, took drugs, and made love. As a result of a complaint by Vice President Spiro Agnew in 1970, the Federal Communications Commission instructed media license holders to acquaint themselves with the content of their broadcasts to determine whether lyrics being presented to the public were "drug oriented." Public concern for the sexual content of rock lyrics replaced earlier concern with drugs. In 1985 the Parents' Music Resource Center, co-founded by Tipper Gore, the wife of then-senator Al Gore, began a campaign against "porn rock," focusing primarily on the music of heavy metal and punk rock groups such as Twisted Sister, Iron Maiden, Black Sabbath, and Judas Priest. The center prompted Senate hearings on the subject and urged a voluntary system of ratings on objectionable albums to alert parents of album content.

Gangsta Rap. Public attempts to censure objectionable rock lyrics reached a new level of fervor when confronted with a new musical style: gangsta rap. Created in the mid-1980's by young black men immersed musically in hip hop culture and familiar with gang life, gangsta rap celebrates violence, drugs, sex, and misogyny. Gangsta rap has drawn protest from an especially varied array of groups: from conservatives who oppose its sexually explicit lyrics, to African American women who criticize the music's misogyny, to law enforcement officials who demonstrate against rap's occasional celebration of violence against the police.

Attempts to suppress gangsta rap have also taken a variety of forms. Police officers who objected to the rapper Ice T's "Cop Killer" or to the group NWA's "Fuck the Police," organized a campaign to frustrate tours by these performers by denying them concert security services. They also coordinated protests made to the Time Warner corporation, which owned an interest in a gangsta rap record label, threatening to have their pension funds divest themselves of the company's stock. These and similar protests ultimately caused Ice T to remove the "Cop Killer" song from his album and caused Time Warner to sever its relationship with Ice T's gangsta rap recording label. More informally, a wide assortment of radio and television stations simply refused to play gangsta rap music, and record store boycotts by critics of gangsta rap induced some stores to remove the genre from their stock.

A more common form of regulation aimed at gangsta rap has been to require—as a matter of state law—that violent and sexually explicit recordings be labeled to alert consumers of their possibly objectionable content. Sometimes, critics of rap music have attempt to suppress the music through judicial action. Prosecutors in an Alabama town brought obscenity charges against a record store in 1988 for carrying *Move Somethin'*, by the Miami rap group 2 Live Crew. Although the Alabama record store was ultimately acquitted of the obscenity charge, a Florida sheriff launched a similar attack on 2 Live Crew's *As Nasty as They Wanna Be* two years later. A federal district judge eventually determined that the album was obscene, but a federal appeals court later overturned this finding.

Copycat Lawsuits. Critics of particular speech have sometimes argued that it should be suppressed or punished because of its tendency to promote harmful conduct. For example, in the early 1990's, heavy metal rock star Ozzy Osbourne found himself the object of a wrongful death lawsuit when a teen-aged boy committed suicide after having listened to the lyrics of Osbourne's song "Suicide Solution." Originally, the parents of the suicide victim alleged that "Suicide Solution" contained the following lyrics which—buttressed by a subliminal message urging listeners to commit suicide—prompted their son to take his life. A federal district court in Georgia summarily rejected the attempt to hold Osbourne legally responsible for the suicide of the young man. Three years previously, Osbourne had been found not liable in a similar suit brought in California as a result of the suicide of a young man who had listened repeatedly to Osbourne's recordings.

The British group Judas Priest was the object of a similar suit in Reno, Nevada, in 1991. Two teen-aged boys attempted suicide after listening repeatedly to lyrics in the song "Better by You, Better than Me." One youth survived the attempt and sued the group, claiming that its song contained a subliminal message to commit suicide. After a seventeen-day trial, a Nevada judge absolved Judas Priest of legal responsibility for the occurrences.

As these cases illustrate, attempts to blame song lyrics for harmful conduct carried out by listeners face a stiff constitutional obstacle. Although the Supreme Court has recognized that some speech might directly incite criminal or other harmful conduct and be suppressed on this basis, it has insisted that the conduct be imminently threatened and likely to be incited by the challenged speech. Opponents of objectionable musical lyrics are not likely to be able to satisfy this rigorous requirement in most cases.

—Timothy L. Hall

See also "Cop Killer"; Copycat crime; Folk music; Morissette, Alanis; Obscenity: legal definitions; Opera; Parents' Music Resource Center; Plato; Presley, Elvis; Protest music; Rap music; Reggae music; Rock 'n' roll music; Rolling Stones, the; Suicide; 2 Live Crew.

Bibliography

For general surveys of contemporary censorship issues in the United States relating to art, music, television, and cinema, Edward de Grazia's *Girls Lean Back Everywhere: The Law of Obscenity and the Assault on Genius* (New York: Random House, 1992) and Marjorie Heins's *Sex, Sin, and Blasphemy: A Guide to America's Censorship Wars* (New York: New Press, 1993) are useful resources. Peter Manuel's *Popular Musics of the Non-Western World* (New York: Oxford University Press, 1988) is a musically sophisticated and politically informed discussion of various indigenous music forms and their encounters with political life throughout the world. It includes chapters on Latin America, Africa, Europe, the Middle East, South Asia, Southeast Asia, China, and the Pacific. Robin Denselow's *When the Music's Over: The Story of Political Pop* (Winchester, Mass.: Faber & Faber, 1989) considers the intersection between popular music and political protest in a variety of social contexts. Andrew F. Jones' essay, "The Politics of Popular Music in Post-Tiananmen China," in *Popular Protest and Political Culture in Modern China*, edited by Jeffrey N. Wasserstrom and Elizabeth J. Perry (Boulder, Colo.: Westview Press, 1994), focuses primarily on Chinese popular music during the 1990's but also includes a brief, useful discussion of popular music in China since communist rule began in the late 1940's.

See also "Cop Killer"; Copycat crime; Folk music; Morissette, Alanis; Obscenity: legal definitions; Opera; Parents' Music Resource Center; Plato; Presley, Elvis; Protest music; Rap music; Reggae music; Rock 'n' roll music; Rolling Stones, the; Suicide; 2 Live Crew.

Music TeleVision (MTV)

Founded: August 1, 1981

Type of organization: American cable television network specializing in rock music videos aimed at a young audience

Significance: MTV censors have occasionally banned videos, but more often they have simply run disclaimers or resorted to bleeping or blurring objectionable content

Robert Pittman founded MTV in 1981 as the world's first all-music video network, gearing its programming primarily at a white suburban audience aged fifteen through twenty-five. The fledgling company refused to show videos by African American artists until Columbia Records threatened to boycott the network if it did not air Michael Jackson's videos. With popular music videos such as "Beat It" and "Thriller," Jackson quickly became the superstar of the new medium. However, only a few other black artists—such as Prince and Whitney Houston—managed to break into MTV's broadcast rotation.

Bending to recording industry pressure and audience demand, MTV eventually created a rap-music segment entitled *Yo! MTV Raps*, which premiered on August 6, 1988. The segment segregated rap from the rest of MTV's play list, but it quickly became one of the network's most popular shows. Critics renewed charges of racial censorship when the network launched *MTV Unplugged*, a series of live acoustic concerts featuring occasional black artists, in 1989.

Individual cable companies have occasionally dropped MTV from their service. A Texas-based company, for example, stopped carrying the network during the summer of 1991 in response to audience protests. More often, however, censorship of MTV has been conducted within the video industry itself. The high cost of production, often underwritten by music companies, usually imposes a form of self-censorship on video artists. Nevertheless, some artists who are successful enough to underwrite their own production expenses have been able to produce videos that MTV censors have suppressed.

MTV censors initially refused to approve Neil Young's song "This Note's for You," alleging that it endorsed a product, but they subsequently rescinded the order. Young's work received MTV's award for best video of 1989. In each of the six following years a video originally censored won this award.

MTV has also censored videos for indecency, or for glamorizing drug use or violence. In perhaps the most notable example, it banned the December 1, 1990, debut of Madonna's sexually explicit "Justify My Love." In 1993 it demanded that the violent ending of Pearl Jam's "Jeremy" be cut. MTV's symbiotic relationship with artists and the music industry makes such bans relatively rare, however. The network has typically relied on bleeping out objectionable words or blurring objectionable images. For example, MTV censors bleeped the line "I wanna fuck you like an animal" in Nine Inch Nails' song "Closer" in 1995. The year before, it blurred images of water pistols in the "Hip Hop Hooray" video of Naughty by Nature. In a number of videos, particularly by rappers, censors have blurred commercial product logos from artists' shoes, shirts, and hats—often at the instigation of the companies themselves, when they have not wanted their products to be associated with rap music.

As the network has grown, it has abandoned its all-music format to include cartoons, situation comedies, documentaries, and even news programs.

An October, 1993, episode of MTV's cartoon program *Beavis and Butt-head* featured the title characters setting fire to household objects. A five year-old viewer in Dayton, Ohio, followed suit, starting a blaze that killed his two-year-old sister. In response, the network afterward began running disclaimers before episodes of the program. A few years later the network's documentary-soap opera titled *Real World* showed a male cast member dragging a female housemate out of bed. Considering this scene a bit too real, MTV censors insisted that the female's bare chest be blurred.

See also Advertisers as advocates of censorship; *Beavis and Butt-head*; Boycotts; Cable television; Jackson, Michael; Madonna; Rap music; Recording industry; Rock 'n' roll music; Television; Violence.

Mutual Broadcasting System scandal

Date: January 30—February 5, 1959

Place: United States and Dominican Republic

Significance: Revelation of a secret agreement between an American radio network and the dictator of a Caribbean republic dealt a serious blow to the credibility of news broadcasting in the United States

In 1959 the Mutual Broadcasting System (MBS), a radio network of more than four hundred stations, and its president, Alexander Guterma, faced financial problems growing out of Guterma's questionable stock dealings. To raise cash in early 1959, Guterma proposed to the Dominican Republic's dictator, Rafael Trujillo, a plan for MBS to broadcast at least seven hours a month of favorable news about Trujillo and his country for eighteen months. In return, Trujillo would pay Guterma $750,000. After Trujillo accepted the proposal in early February, MBS began broadcasting pro-Dominican news. In mid-February Guterma was suddenly arrested for stock manipulation and he resigned as president of MBS.

When the new MBS president, Robert F. Hurleigh, discovered the Guterma-Trujillo agreement during a press trip to the Dominican Republic in May, he reported it to the U.S. Justice Department. In September Guterma was indicted for violating the Foreign Agents Registration Act of 1938, which required Americans dealing with agents from foreign countries to register with the Justice Department. Guterma was sentenced to eight months in jail. Trujillo's suit for repayment of the money he had paid Guterma for nonfulfillment of their agreement was unsuccessful.

See also Foreign Agents Registration Act of 1938; News broadcasting; News media censorship; Press-radio war; Radio.

Mutual Film Corporation v. Industrial Commission of Ohio

Court: U.S. Supreme Court

Date: February 23, 1915

Significance: This Supreme Court decision—and *Mutual Film Corporation v. Kansas*, which the Court decided at the same time—upheld the constitutionality of 1913 Ohio and Kansas laws allowing the states to censor films on the grounds that motion picture films were not protected forms of speech under the First Amendment; these decisions opened the door to decades of government censorship of films

At stake in Mutual's suits against Ohio and Kansas was the right of states to allow public officials to review films for their moral content before permitting them to be shown to the general public. Under Ohio's and Kansas' laws, films found to be "sacrilegious, obscene, indecent, or immoral," or that might "corrupt the morals," could be banned from being shown in public. In appealing an earlier decision against it to the Supreme Court, the Mutual Film Corporation claimed that state review of films was a violation of "the freedom to say, write or publish whatever one will on any subject." In defense of their right to act as censors, the states of Ohio and Kansas argued that film censorship was a legitimate exercise of the authority of the state to protect public morality.

In deciding in the states' favor, the Court reflected for the first time on the question of just what a motion picture was. Possibly influenced by the popular press, which reported on the infant film industry as though it were primarily a source of cheap mass entertainment, the Court determined that films fell into the category of entertainment designed to make a profit. Although films certainly contain ideas, the Court explained, they are not a means of communicating them. With that distinction in mind, the Court decided for Ohio on the grounds that state censorship of films did not violate any personal liberties covered by the First Amendment. Using the same line of reasoning, it also ruled in Kansas' favor.

Coming at a time when films were new, these decisions had a powerful impact. They made film censorship possible, allowing for state and local governments to control what films were shown in theaters. They also opened up a wide latitude for the censorship of films, which could be banned as "immoral" for many different reasons. The decisions enabled private pressure groups, particularly religious-related organizations such as the Legion of Decency, to bring pressure and influence to bear on the decisions of public censorship boards. It took more than thirty-five years for the Supreme Court, ruling on a case relating to the film *The Miracle*, to overturn this decision by ruling that films did indeed communicate ideas and thus were entitled to constitutional protection.

See also *Birth of a Nation, The*; Film censorship; *Miracle, The*; Unprotected speech.

My Lai massacre

Date: March 16, 1968

Place: My Lai, South Vietnam

Significance: U.S. military officers suppressed information about a cold-blooded massacre of Vietnamese civilians by U.S. troops

On March 16, 1968, a battalion of American troops from the Eleventh Brigade, American Division, conducted a search and destroy mission in the Son My district in northeastern Vietnam. The Americans considered Son My an enemy stronghold, but they met no resistance when they entered My Lai, a district village. On the orders of Lieutenant William Calley, the soldiers shot and killed the town's civilians, including the women and children. Participants later estimated that between four and five hundred villagers died. My Lai was in an isolated province, and no civilian newspaper reporters witness the incident. Newspapers accounts were drawn from official military communications, which reported that American troops had killed "128 enemy soldiers Saturday during an assault against a Vietcong stronghold."

After American helicopter pilots who witnessed the event complained to their superiors that a massacre had occurred, American Division headquarters ordered Colonel Oran Henderson of the Eleventh Brigade to conduct an investigation. In his report filed in April, 1968, Henderson claimed that no civilians had been murdered. He reported that the only civilian casualties were twenty villagers who were killed accidentally in the crossfire between American and enemy troops.

The truth about My Lai remained secret until March, 1969. Ronald Ridenhour, a Vietnam veteran who had heard about the massacre, wrote letters about the incident to several U.S. government officials. The letters prompted preliminary investigations into Ridenhour's allegations. In November, 1969, after

Lt. William Calley is besieged by the press at Saigon's airport in October, 1970, during his return to the United States to face a court-martial for the massacre of civilians at My Lai two years earlier. (AP/Wide World Photos)

The New York Times published stories about the My Lai allegations, the army ordered General William R. Peers to head an investigative commission on the My Lai incident.

The final commission report concluded that the U.S. troops had massacred civilians at My Lai. Furthermore, the report noted that "efforts to suppress and withhold information concerning the Son My incident were made at every level in the American Division." The commission condemned Colonel Henderson's report as a falsification intended to mislead division commanders, and blamed division headquarters for accepting Henderson's report without question. In addition, complaints from Vietnamese officials about the massacre had been ignored, and files concerning My Lai had mysteriously disappeared.

Army Chief of Staff William Westmoreland received the commission report in March, 1970. Three days later fourteen officers were charged with covering up the My Lai affair. Although all charges against the fourteen were later dropped, the Army reprimanded several of the officers. Calley was found guilty of murder and given a life sentence, which was later reduced to twenty years confinement. He served three years under house arrest before his release in 1974.

The cover-up of the My Lai massacre served no national security interests. The army officers involved realized that American troops had committed war crimes while under their command, and these officers suppressed information to hide those crimes. My Lai heightened doubts about America's involvement in a war that had become increasingly unpopular by the end of the 1960's.

See also Bay of Pigs invasion; Iran-Contra scandal; Kennedy, John F., assassination of; Kent State shootings; Military censorship; Tonkin Gulf incident; Vietnam War; War.

My Secret Life

Type of work: Book

Published: c. 1890

Author: Anonymous

Subject matter: A British Victorian gentleman's sexual memoirs

Significance: This work's 1930's suppression in New York and later censorship in England set the precedent that "historical significance" cannot protect obscene works from censorship

My Secret Life's eleven volumes contain approximately forty-two hundred pages of an anonymous Victorian Englishman's sexual memoirs, including extensive descriptions of his sexual escapades with more than a thousand women. The author provides elaborate accounts of how he procured women and details about what they did together, including his tastes for flagellation and group sex. His discussions of the broader vice industry in London and throughout Europe create a rich history of sexual life in Victorian England.

An edition of this book was banned in New York because of pressure from the New York Society for the Suppression of Vice in the early 1930's. It was reprinted by Grove Press in 1966, but not without incident. Arthur Dobson, an often-prosecuted British bookseller and publisher, sold 250 copies of the Grove edition in England, but when authorities threatened to raid his shop, Grove rescinded Dobson's distribution rights. Dobson published his own paperback edition combining the first two volumes, but before selling any copies, he was arrested and charged with violating the Obscene Publications Act of 1959. At the ensuing trial, his lawyer unsuccessfully argued that the book should be immune from censorship because of its historical value. Dobson's guilty verdict established the precedent that "historical importance" does not justify producing or distributing obscene works.

See also Books and obscenity law; Casanova, Giovanni Giacomo; *Fanny Hill, The Memoirs of*; Grove Press; Harris, Frank; Obscene Publications Acts; Pornography; Society for the Suppression of Vice, New York; United Kingdom.

Mythology

Definition: "Myth" derives from the Greek word *mythos*, for a fictitious or untrue story

Significance: Many of the cultural taboos that have been used to justify censorship have an underlying basis in myth

In the modern understanding of the concept, myths are imaginative stories of enduring significance that embody the values, beliefs, and the worldview of a given society. True myths are different from philosophical allegories, fables, fairy tales, and parables, although there are similarities among all of them. True myths embody the central beliefs, typically religious beliefs, of a people. Ideologies such as fascism, nationalism, and civil religion are also rooted in myths and derive appeal from mythical context. Myths are found in every society, however primitive or advanced, and are jealously guarded by every society as part of its heritage.

Origin. Most myths originated in the preliterate stages of societies and for centuries were passed on orally before some of them came to be written down as epics by poets and writers. Myths also continue to survive in unwritten or uncodified forms in less literate societies. Comparative studies have uncovered similarities among the myths of all peoples, leading some scholars to hypothesize that myths represent certain archetypes of the collective unconscious that are common to humanity. Others believe that these similarities have resulted from cultural interchanges. Some theorists attribute the origin of myths to the need to create stories in order to give meaning to the ritual practices of primitive tribes. In their view, the rituals predate the myths.

Meaning and Functions. Most myths are highly complex in structure, containing multiple layers of meaning, open to differing interpretations, and are closely tied to a nation's collective experiences, self-image, and identity. Theoretical elaborations of myth result in metaphysics and theology; the enactments of myths in rituals give rise to cultic practices that engender emotionally charged responses in their participants.

Myths serve numerous functions for a given society. They may provide ultimate answers for perennial philosophical problems, such as questions concerning the origin of the universe; the nature of human beings and varieties of life forms; and the meaning of disease, suffering, and death. Myths may also serve as legitimizing ideologies for the existing social and political systems, customs, taboos, and practices. For example, the existence of the fundamental inequality of various castes in India is explained by the myth of the origin of these castes from different parts of the same divine body. Myths also contain explanations for various ritual practices and taboos associated with birth, initiation rites, burial ceremonies, and annual celebrations. Finally, myths embody the cultural ideals of a society insofar as they help to determine what is important, how its members are expected to live their lives, and which historical figures (saints and heroes) exemplify the ideals that are worthy of imitation.

Enduring Significance. In spite of the numerous attempts over the centuries either to discredit myths as lies or to interpret myths as allegorical narratives of ordinary human experiences or to devalue myths as preoperational thought, myths continue to flourish. Myths energize human experience, as Sigmund Freud and Carl Jung have argued; myths help maintain social cohesion through the enactment of cultic practices and rituals, as French sociologist Émile Durkheim has argued; myths definitely form the substance of the arts and literature, as art historians and literary critics know. Some have argued that sciences themselves utilize mythological models to understand the physical world and help create new myths through fictions and conjectures. Myths may serve as the broad framework for explaining—correctly or incorrectly—historical events and political upheavals. while providing the ideological basis for battles between contending groups. It is a reflection of the power of myth in human affairs that in the twentieth century, the efforts at demythologizing religious narratives and the efforts of social and political reformers to secularize their societies have failed, as is evident from the resurgence of fundamentalist movements in virtually every part of the world.

Mythology and Censorship. Myths effect and affect the censorship of ideas in various ways. First, because of their influence upon a society's collective understanding, they set the basic parameters for public discourse and action on social issues, and thus exercise direct and indirect control over the expression of ideas. Careful analysis of a day's news reports—reports on crime, political debates, cultural controversies, ethnic and racial conflicts, sporting events, scientific advances, and so on—reveal wide use of mythical concepts, images, and explanations. Decisions as to what is considered newsworthy, what narrative formats and words are appropriate, what behaviors and actions are to be upheld as exemplary and what conducts deserve public condemnation, who should be elevated to the status of heroes, and who are to be denounced as villains depend upon the underlying mythical beliefs and their preferred interpretations within a particular group.

Second, in the social-political arena, myths express themselves as a society's civil religion that affirms its institutions, history, and cultural practices as sacred and designed to further some ultimate divine plan. The American civil religion—a mixture of Protestantism and nationalism—for example, casts the national symbols, heroes, holidays, and political rituals as sacred and beyond criticism. Desecration of the national flag or other symbols of national identity draw widespread social condemnation and even legal sanction. It is true that some societies have invoked myths to justify a complete overthrow of an existing social order. However, successful revolutions result in the establishment of a new order that may suppress criticism as counterrevolutionary, foreign, and traitorous. The religiously inspired revolution in Iran in 1979 and the subsequent extensive censorship of ideas deemed counterrevolutionary illustrate this point. Even in a relatively more open society such as the United States, media generally tend to legitimize the government's action, especially when it involves a domestic law enforcement situation or foreign military intervention. The mainstream media generally tend to denounce or silence dissenting voices as unpatriotic and harmful to the national interest.

Third, since myths are the source of a society's moral beliefs and practices, creative works in the arts and literature come under censorship to scrutinize their moral rightness and political correctness. Works that contain sexual themes have often been subjected to censorship in the belief that they serve the prurient interest of the public. For this reason, as every art history student knows, artistic depictions of male nudes, for example, tend to be of Jesus on the cross or of Saint Sebastian shot with arrows.

In order to understand the Western cultural opposition to obscenity and pornography, it is important to trace that opposition's origin back to its mythological grounding. The mythologies that exert the heaviest influence on Western culture are Middle Eastern in origin and these have been transmitted through Judaism and Christianity. These mythologies contain the theme of the epic struggle between the forces of good and evil. Good is whatever is associated with the world of the spirit (light), whereas evil has affinities with the flesh (darkness). The monastic and the spiritual tradition within Christianity has reinforced this dualistic metaphysics through its insistence on renouncing worldly pleasures in all its forms. Sins of the flesh or sexual indulgences were particularly condemned because of the belief that Satan, the leader of the forces of evil, utilizes sexual pleasures as a means to deceive and enslave human beings.

Throughout history efforts to suppress sexuality and its expressions have resulted in extreme forms of censorship in art and literature. Because Christianity considers sex a taboo subject, open discussion of related matters such as sexual development, birth control, and sexually transmitted diseases have been discouraged. Several Christian Fundamentalist organizations in the United States in the twentieth century have advanced the cause of censoring sexually oriented materials. Christian Crusade, Citizens for Decency Through Law, Citizens for Decent Literature, Clean Up Television Campaign, Crusade for Decency, Morality in Media, and the National Federation for Decency are a few of these organizations.

Fourth, mythical beliefs may prompt a society to suppress scientific ideas that are perceived as harmful to traditional faith. The Roman Catholic church, for example, established an *Index Librorum Prohibitorum* (index of prohibited books) as its official mechanism to censor books that it considered offensive to faith and morals. The establishment of the *Index* was justified by appealing to the practices of the early church and the Apostles. For example, it is claimed that at Ephesus the Apostle Paul witnessed the burning of a heap of superstitious books (Acts 9:19). The burning of books was a common practice wherever the Church expanded its influence.

Religious groups also vigorously seek to suppress scientific ideas that seem to threaten their religious beliefs. The most celebrated case of a state attempting to suppress the teaching of a scientific theory in the United States was the 1925 Scopes Trial in Tennessee. The teaching of the theory of evolution was outlawed or suppressed in several states. Although the Supreme Court of the United States in 1967 overturned laws prohibiting the teaching of the theory of evolution, the teaching of the theory in public schools continued to draw opposition from Fundamentalist groups. Other areas of study, such as archeology, history, ethnographic studies, anthropology, sociology, and new methods of biblical and literary criticism have also come under fire from Fundamentalist groups.

Censorship and Differences in Worldviews. The desire to censor a set of ideas and expressions is common to Christianity and other messianic and prophetic religions, such as Islam. They view history as the story of an ongoing conflict between the dual forces of good and evil, which is expected to end in a final victory for the forces of good under the leadership of a divine messiah or prophet. This view of history and world events compel the members of these societies to engage in missionary activities, and many of them consider censorship as part of that mission.

The worldview of messianic, militant religions, which seek converts and condemn nonbelievers, is in contrast with the more (but not perfectly) tolerant, pluralistic, and cyclical worldviews of nonmessianic religions, which are generally less concerned with dogma. Censorship in these societies is likely to be for political rather than for moral or religious purposes, although political censorship may take the disguise of religiousness. —*Mathew J. Kanjirathinkal*

See also Bible; Blasphemy laws; Book burning; Buddhism; Citizens for Decent Literature; Clean Up Television Campaign; Evolution; *Index Librorum Prohibitorum*; Moral Majority; National Federation for Decency; Ovid; Poetry; Religion; Sex in the arts.

BIBLIOGRAPHY

G. S. Kirk's *Myth: Its Meaning and Functions in Ancient and Other Cultures* (1970) contains an excellent discussion of the major modern theories of myth. Burton Feldman and Robert D. Richardson's *The Rise of Modern Mythology, 1680-1860* (1972) presents an excellent anthology of scholarly opinions on myths, with commentary and bibliography. Joseph Campbell's *The Masks of God* (New York: Viking Press, 1969) is a multivolume study that sheds light on the relationship between myth and culture. Mircea Eliade's *Myths, Dreams, and Mysteries: The Encounter Between Contemporary Faiths and Archaic Realities* (1957) explores the place of myth in modern society. Campbell's *Myth and Reality* (1963) contains an insightful analysis of the persistence of myths in modern times.

N

Nader, Ralph

Born: February 27, 1934, Winsted, Connecticut
Identification: American consumer advocate
Significance: Automobile industry officials admitted harassing Nader to silence his criticisms of the industry

During his law school studies at Harvard, Ralph Nader's study of automobile injury cases gave him an interest in automobile technology. His research showed that driver error was typically blamed for accidents, while unsafe vehicle design was ignored. This bothered Nader. His first article on the subject, "American Cars: Designed for Death," appeared in the *Harvard Law Record* in 1958. He continued his campaign for improved safety regulations by making speeches throughout Connecticut and Massachusetts. In 1964 he transferred his efforts to Washington, D.C., where Daniel P. Moynihan, the assistant secretary of labor, gave him a position as a consultant to the Labor Department. Nader took this post seriously, generating a two-hundred-page study calling for greater governmental responsibility in promoting automobile safety. Nader also provided information to Connecticut senator Abraham A. Ribicoff, chairman of a Senate committee on executive reorganization. Ribicoff shared Nader's concern over the increasing number of highway deaths.

Ralph Nader testifies before a congressional subcommittee early in his career as a consumer advocate. (Library of Congress)

Although he continued to work with Ribicoff, Nader left the Labor Department in May, 1965, in order to complete his book *Unsafe at Any Speed: The Designed-in Dangers of the American Automobile*. The book criticized the entire automobile industry, but its main thrust was aimed at the subcompact Chevrolet Corvair. It soon became a best seller. Despite the success of his book, Nader increased his efforts in behalf of automobile safety legislation. In February, 1966, he testified before Ribicoff's subcommittee on criticism of the auto industry. Apparently he got someone's attention. On March 6, 1966, newspapers published his account of harassment at the hands of the automobile industry. Around the time of his testimony for Ribicoff, Nader had come under investigation by several private investigators. One of them later stated that he had been instructed by General Motors officials to find information on Nader that would give them leverage to silence him. The investigator also reported that the automobile executives had made false statements to subcommittees. Nader complained of harassing phone calls and of women trying to entice him into compromising situations. During a televised hearing, General Motors president James M. Roche admitted to Ribicoff's subcommittee that there had been some harassment and he apologized to Nader. Ribicoff obtained a complete text of the detectives' reports from General Motors and determined that the investigation had been aimed at smearing Nader's reputation. Instead, it had the opposite effect.

On September 9, 1966, President Lyndon B. Johnson signed the National Traffic and Motor Vehicle Safety Act. Many people gave Nader credit for the law's passage. Nader's efforts to protect consumers continued with Congress' passage of the Wholesome Meat Act in 1967. His college followers, nicknamed "Nader's Raiders," helped him investigate government regulatory agencies. He also aimed his attention at tax reform, health issues, insurance-rate reduction, automobile airbags, natural gas pipeline safety, and radiation hazards control. Nader remained a visible public figure into the 1990's.

See also Advertisers as advocates of censorship; Automobile safety news; Mitford, Jessica; Seldes, George.

Naked Amazon

Type of work: Film
Released: 1954
Director: Zygmunt Sulistrowski
Subject matter: Documentary about life in a Brazilian rain forest that included scenes of naked Camayura Indians

SIGNIFICANCE: Efforts to censor this film raised the issue of whether nudity could be labeled obscene without regard to its context

Naked Amazon was filmed along a remote stretch of the upper Amazon River in the Brazilian state of Mato Grosso. A party of explorers led by director Zygmunt Sulistrowski entered the area to film the exotic environment and its inhabitants. Along with jaguars, boa constrictors, and other forest denizens, the resulting film contained scenes of Camayura Indians hunting and engaging in other activities in their normal state of nudity. After the film was released in the United States in 1957 the Maryland state board of censors demanded that all scenes showing people naked below the waist be excised. The board argued that such scenes were obscene and would stimulate sexual desires among "irresponsible" people. The film's distributors sued in court.

Both a Baltimore city court and a state appeals court disagreed with the censors. In *Maryland State Board of Motion Pictures Censors v. Times Film Corporation* (1957), the appellate court found that only a person with a "prurient imagination" could derive any "unchaste or lustful ideas" from the film. The court enjoined the board to apply community standards, and not to cater to the young, immature, ignorant, or sensually inclined. Seven years later, in *Fanfare Films, Inc. v. Motion Picture Board*, the Maryland Court of Appeals again overruled the censorship board, finding that "nudity is not necessarily obscene or lewd."

See also Brazil; Community standards; Film censorship; Native Americans; Nudity.

Naked Lunch

TYPE OF WORK: Book

PUBLISHED: 1959

AUTHOR: William S. Burroughs (1914-)

SUBJECT MATTER: Fantasy about a hallucinating drug addict's quest for drugs

SIGNIFICANCE: This book had to overcome attempts at censorship by the U.S. Post Office, U.S. Customs Service, and the Commonwealth of Massachusetts before it could be legally published in the United States

Surrealistic in its tone, this novel is narrated by a drug addict traveling through the American South and Mexico in search of drugs. Along the way he sees grotesque scientific experiments on human beings, subhuman monsters, and bizarre sexual activity. His largely formless narrative ends in violence, with him killing narcotics officers as he struggles through a nightmarish withdrawal from drugs.

When the manuscript of *Naked Lunch* was almost complete in 1958, Allen Ginsberg sent a copy to French publisher Maurice Girodias, whose Olympia Press had produced many books that were banned in the United States and Great Britain. After Girodias dismissed the book as "uncommercial," Ginsberg sent it to Irving Rosenthal, the editor of *The Chicago Review*. Rosenthal tried to publish eighty pages of the manuscript in the journal, but the administrators of the University of Chicago suppressed the entire issue. Rosenthal then founded a new journal, *Big Table*, which was published with ten episodes from *Naked Lunch* in the spring of 1959.

Hoping to capitalize on this publicity, Girodias requested the entire manuscript and published it in Paris in 1959. The book was not legally available in the United States until Barney Rosset of Grove Press, which published Henry Miller's *Tropic of Cancer* in 1961, decided to release an American edition in 1962. Burroughs added an introduction in which he compared the book to Jonathan Swift's satirical *A Modest Proposal*, a response to reviews like those by John Willett in the *Times Literary Supplement* which called for "the book world" to "clean up the mess"—an obvious invitation to censor the novel.

The book was prosecuted as obscene by the Commonwealth of Massachusetts, an action following what scholar Michael Goodman cited as the last step in the publishing history of a book "censored by the academy, the U.S. Post Office, the U.S. Customs Service, and the state and local government." After an illustrious group of artists, including Norman Mailer, John Ciardi, and Ginsberg were called as expert witnesses to testify to the book's artistic objectives and values, the Massachusetts Supreme Court declared the work not obscene based on national criteria in 1966.

See also Books and obscenity law; Ginsberg, Allen; Girodias, Maurice; Grove Press; Obscenity: legal definitions; Redeeming social value.

Nasrin, Taslima

BORN: August 25, 1962, Mymensingh, East Pakistan (now Bangladesh)

IDENTIFICATION: Bangladeshi author

SIGNIFICANCE: Nasrin's strong views on women's rights have provoked charges of blasphemy and calls for her death by Muslim fundamentalists

In poems, novels, and newspaper columns Nasrin has advocated equal rights for women and attacked male chauvinism in a country dominated by conservative Islam. In September, 1993, for example, members of an obscure religious group called the Soldiers of Islam met in the northeastern town of Sylhet and demanded Nasrin's execution, posting a reward for her death.

Nasrin's 1993 novel, *Lajja*, or *Shame*, containing scenes in which Muslim men rape Hindu women, sparked a campaign against her that escalated in Bangladesh into riots and increases in the amounts offered for her murder. Her case became an international *cause célèbre* when the Bangladeshi government banned her novel and decided to prosecute her under an nineteenth century statute outlawing acts that flouted religion.

After seeking refuge in Sweden, Nasrin responded to her persecution by attacking not only Islamic fundamentalists but reformers in her own country for doing too little to oppose religious and political tyranny. Her literary merit, her judgment in bluntly attacking her enemies, and some of her self-serving statements have been questioned even by those sympathetic to her cause. An avowed atheist, she argues for a modern, secular state as the only way to protect women's rights. Meanwhile, Her openly rebellious lifestyle has attracted a cult following among the young in Bangladesh. Married and divorced three times, she flouts Islamic tradition by smoking and wearing her hair in Western styles.

See also Islam; Pakistan; Rushdie, Salman; Women.

National Association for the Advancement of Colored People (NAACP)

Founded: 1909

Type of organization: Nonracial civil rights organization dedicated to improving the political and social condition of African Americans

Significance: During its long struggle against racial discrimination and prejudice, the NAACP has also been an important censorship force

The NAACP was organized in the early twentieth century by a group of white and black Americans concerned about the continuing racial discrimination directed against African Americans and the lack of employment opportunities for blacks. By the end of the century the organization had grown to encompass more than fifteen hundred local branches with more than 400,000 members. Through its legal arm the NAACP played a major role in breaking down legal segregation and it was a major supporter of the Civil Rights movement of the 1960's.

In its role as a defender of the public image and the rights of African Americans, the NAACP has constantly monitored publications, films, and other materials that might contain racist ideas or stereotypes. Its national board has encouraged members of every branch to protest any local offenses that they observe, bringing to the attention of the central offices only those matters meriting national concern. For example, Mark Twain's novel *Adventures of Huckleberry Finn* (1884) provoked many local NAACP branches to object to its assignment in classrooms. Protests focused on perceptions that the novel stereotypes the fleeing slave Jim as a stupid and accommodating black man.

The NAACP has also been a major force in changing stereotypes of African Americans on a national level. In 1914 the organization achieved its first national prominence when its members demonstrated against D. W. Griffith's film *The Birth of a Nation*, which chronicles the South during Reconstruction, when African Americans used their newly won franchise to elect many black officeholders throughout the South. Depicting African Americans as evil and sex-crazed, the film made heroes of members of the Ku Klux Klan, which arose to protect white women and Southern civilization.

Along with other African American rights organizations, the NAACP objected to the making of Margaret Mitchell's Civil War novel, *Gone with the Wind*, into a film because of the book's negative black stereotypes. NAACP protests were so strong during the film's production that many scenes were cut from the film or softened. During the 1940's the NAACP led protests against Rand McNally's use of the "Little Black Sambo" character in its publications. During the 1950's it protested Hallmark's sales of greeting cards with stereotypical and negative depictions of African Americans. The popular radio comedy *Amos 'n' Andy* was transferred to television and began airing in 1951. It was canceled after only one season largely because of NAACP protests over the show's portrayal of African Americans as charlatans and tricksters.

See also *Adventures of Huckleberry Finn*; *Amos 'n' Andy*; *Birth of a Nation, The*; Civil Rights movement; *Little Black Sambo*; Race.

National Association of Broadcasters (NAB)

Founded: 1922

Type of organization: Trade organization for American television and radio station owners

Significance: NAB originally promoted self-regulation among its members, but later turned to lobby Congress for government help

Since its founding NAB has been the primary trade association for U.S. radio and television stations. It was organized in 1923 to combat demands that radio stations pay royalties for on-the-air use of music. Although NAB failed to prevent stations from having to pay royalties, the organization remained a powerful industry voice.

Signal interference among early radio stations led broadcasters to call for government regulation in the 1920's and 1930's. The government regulation came, and later, NAB began to lobby Congress for repeal of government regulation. Broadcasting regulation has been based on a trusteeship model—a station was not merely a for-profit business, it operated as a public trustee. NAB championed the trusteeship model through its code of ethics and standards of commercial practice.

Where threat of government regulation exists, NAB has reacted by advocating self-regulation. In the 1970's NAB television members adopted a family viewing time policy rather than have Congress impose television programming rules. Though self-regulation may be preferred to government regulation, either action can prohibit broadcasters from airing programming they wish to carry.

The voluntary NAB code was abolished after a federal district court ruled that the code's advertising time limits constituted a restraint of trade, a form of economic censorship. NAB typically opposes proposals to increase media competition through creation of more radio or television stations or expanding cable television services. NAB has supported regulations that expand the ownership rights of existing station owners. Obligatory censorship results from NAB opposition to communications proposals that increase the number of broadcast stations.

NAB has increased its lobbying to protect broadcasters from cable, direct broadcast satellites (DBS), and telephone competition. Such lobbying protects the economic interests of broadcasters but seldom promotes better programming for viewers or more programming choices.

See also Blue Book of 1946; Canadian Radio-Television and Telecommunications Commission; Federal Communications Commission; Television, children's.

National Coalition Against Censorship (NCAC)

Founded: 1974

Type of organization: Federation of American anticensorship organizations

SIGNIFICANCE: The NCAC has promoted and defended First Amendment rights on both national and local levels

The NCAC is a loose association of more than forty national, nonprofit organizations that have a stake in First Amendment rights. Some of the participating organizations are the American Jewish Congress, the American Library Association, Planned Parenthood of America, and the Screen Actors Guild. The NCAC works for this wide array of organizations as their anticensorship program. The organizations involved either do not have an anticensorship program of their own or they work with and contribute to the NCAC as part of their First Amendment activities.

The NCAC works toward disseminating information about current censorship practices in the United States. It runs education programs for its participating organizations on how to deal with censorship. It publishes a quarterly newsletter, *Censorship News*, as well as *Books in Trouble*, a summary of book banning controversies, which is published as a part of NCAC's special program on countering censorship in schools and libraries. The NCAC helps to organize state and local coalitions against censorship and sponsors meetings and conferences for discussion of current First Amendment issues. It monitors legislation with First Amendment ramifications. The NCAC compiles information packets on First Amendment issues including creationism, feminism, women and pornography, government secrecy, black literature, and educational material selection guidelines.

See also American Booksellers Foundation for Free Expression; First Amendment.

National Endowment for the Arts (NEA)

FOUNDED: 1965

TYPE OF ORGANIZATION: Federal agency created to support the fine arts through the distribution of grant money

SIGNIFICANCE: Controversies surrounding NEA activities have raised questions about First Amendment protections of the arts, while illuminating conflicting visions of the proper role of government in culture

The National Endowment for the Arts, the National Endowment for the Humanities (NEH), and the Federal Council on the Arts and Humanities were collectively created when the U.S. Congress passed the National Foundation on the Arts and Humanities Act on September 29, 1965. That law's purpose was to provide federal grant support for the fine arts and the humanities. The law specified that support should go only to artistic projects that were not for profit, that were undertaken professionally, and that were recognized as of high quality by professionals in their fields.

Government and the Arts. Establishment of the NEA authorized the federal government to be a continuous sponsor of fine art. Since its creation the NEA has stimulated debate on the nature of government-subsidized art that has highlighted contrasting assumptions about government's proper role in the arts. The two fundamental positions on government sponsorship of the arts divide on the question of whether government should act impartially or as an advocate. Each position is associated with a particular political vision. When those visions conflict, questions of whether the NEA censors art arise.

The Modernist-Postmodernist Paradigm. Critics who have viewed the NEA as an impartial agent have seen it ideally as an unbiased nurturer of the cultural life of America. The law that established the endowment forbade it from exercising any direction, supervision, or control over the operations of its grantees. It was merely to distribute funding impartially, following the advice of art professionals. Applications for endowment funds were to be reviewed by rotating panels of recognized experts. The experts who decided which submissions should be funded were to do so by utilizing rare insight and judgment that would advance public culture and art. From this point of view, any interference in the charge given to the NEA by Congress would constitute a philistine or censorious blocking of the advancement of the cultural life of America. This viewpoint assumes the modernist position that art is the product of genius—that it can be recognized by experts, that it is intrinsically serious, and that it is subject to disinterested contemplation, in other words: art for art's sake.

This same viewpoint informed attempts by Supreme Court Justice William J. Brennan, Jr., and Chief Justice Warren Burger, to distinguish art from obscenity in the Court's 1973 *Miller v. California* decision. For those who maintain a modernist position, any interference in the exercising of that advocacy or interference in the activities of the artists who benefit from its largess would constitute an act of censorship.

There have been those, however, who have doubted that art can ever be truly "for its own sake," or that the NEA can, or should be, an impartial sponsor of the cultural life of America. The modernist position that art is for art's sake and that it must be serious has been challenged by postmodernism. This is a challenge that neither the NEA nor the courts were prepared to meet. At the time of the *Miller* decision, a critic pointed out that the Court articulated its test for "serious artistic value" at precisely the moment that modernism itself was dying. *Miller*, the critic further argued, was based on outmoded modernist ideas that some art is not good or serious enough to be worthy of First Amendment protection, and that clear distinctions can be drawn between good and bad art. The decision further accepted the ideas that the value of art can be verified objectively and that art can be distinguished from obscenity.

A case in point is the example of the "NEA Four"—artists whom the NEA refused to fund. Performance artists Holly Hughes, Tim Miller, Karen Finley, and John Fleck gained national attention when their applications for NEA grants were rejected. Their work involved such elements as smearing a nude body with chocolate and with bean sprouts symbolizing sperm, urinating into a toilet bowl containing a picture of Jesus, urinating into the audience, and performing explicit sexual activities. NEA chairman John Frohnmayer recalled in his memoirs that "one could not glean, from reading the transcript, why specific performers were recommended or what artistic ability distinguished them from other applicants." What should he say, he asked, "when one of our critics says that we funded a guy who whizzes on the stage?

The work of the NEA Four is characteristic of postmodernism, which holds that art should not be grounded in genius or expert opinion, but that it should serve as the expression of—or attempts to deconstruct—oppressive power structures. By this view, art is never for its own sake, but must be for the sake of the political; judgments of quality, obscenity, or seriousness are seen as intrinsically arbitrary and therefore necessarily oppressive and censorious. From this perspective the failure of the NEA Four to obtain NEA funding resulted from government censorship. That perceived censorship is seen as an improper interference with the congressionally authorized duty of the endowment, and with freedom of expression and the exercise of First Amendment rights.

More broadly, the controversy surrounding the NEA Four reflects a clash of distinct cultural visions. The modernist definition of art as something that is aesthetic and intrinsically serious conflicted with the postmodernist assertion that such criteria—indeed any criteria for judging art or obscenity—are arbitrary, oppressive, and censorious. There is, however, another cultural vision to consider, a vision that subscribes to neither modernist nor postmodernist positions. That vision is conservative.

The Conservative Paradigm. It is mainly political conservatives who have viewed with skepticism both the modernist notion of art for its own sake and the postmodernist notion that the quality of art, and of human actions, is indiscernible, unqualifiable, and therefore arbitrary and oppressive. They maintain that fine art properly entails the expression of positive values, and that those values are better grounded in free conviction than in legislative decree. While defending free speech as a positive cultural value, they have hesitated to equate it with artistic expression. In this respect they have found common ground with postmodernist feminists who have argued that pornography is unworthy of First Amendment protection.

Conservatives have generally regarded with skepticism the possibility of impartially subsidizing the arts, and they have questioned whether any form of governmentally subsidized free speech can truly be free. If, however, such subsidies must be offered, conservatives have argued that their purpose should be to advance the highest ideals and aspirations of American culture. To conservatives, therefore, the NEA's proper role is not to act impartially or as a liberator from tradition and values, but rather to be a steward of American culture. Furthermore, if—as the modernists claim—governmental funding even can be impartial, conservatives would maintain that it should not be, and that governmental largess should not be distributed to suit the judgment of particular art experts or of their favorites.

Thus there are those who believe that as a governmental agency the NEA can and should be impartial, those who believe that it should reflect a liberation from tradition and values, and those who believe that it should reflect a living heritage of national values. Within a political, cultural, or

Protesters interrupt an NEA committee meeting in 1990 to demand that the agency support homoerotic art. (Donna Binder/ Impact Visuals)

academic context, these views are not easily, if at all, compatible, and result in charges and countercharges of censorship. Those holding that the NEA ought to be impartial will resist a perceived politicizing of art. Those who believe in advocacy via the arts will resist art that is perceived to be reactionary, or alternatively, nihilistic or obscene.

The NEA and Connoisseurship. As a governmental agency the NEA has been asked both to subsidize art impartially and to act as an advocate. Any subsidizing of art implies connoisseurship—a practice that involves recognizing what constitutes works of art and evaluating their quality. Modernists, postmodernists, and conservatives tend to view the phenomenon of a governmental agency dedicated to funding the arts differently. Postmodernists would see the interaction of connoisseurship and politics as inescapable; modernists would insist that qualitative determinations be justified; conservatives would want the ideals advocated by government-funded art to be those of the American people as a whole.

The responsibility of being a connoisseur of fine art entails a reckoning with two distinct visions of art. One vision is modernist: art for its own sake, unencumbered by dogma. Another is that of art in the service of belief. That vision can be either postmodernist or conservative. However, whereas the postmodernist argues that liberating art should be funded, the conservative argues that if art is to be governmentally funded, it should represent the positive core values of American culture. These distinct visions of art correspond with differing assumptions about the proper role of government in art. In addition to the examples of the NEA Four, these differing assumptions came to the surface when the NEA funded exhibitions of work by Robert Mapplethorpe and Andres Serrano.

Mapplethorpe has been widely recognized as a technically brilliant photographer whose work included subject matter regarded as sadomasochistic. Serrano is also a photographer, whose *Piss Christ* depicted a plastic crucifix submerged in a urine-filled container.

Those dedicated to a modernist approach to sponsoring fine art reject evaluating art in political and social terms. They view the issue of connoisseurship neutrally and see the proper role of the NEA as impartially subsidizing the cultural life of America. In this context, professionals in the fields who evaluate potential grantees are expected to judge artistic quality without regard to partisan politics or content bias. In seeking to be especially neutral concerning the content of works of art, they adopt a bureaucratic view of funding for the arts: Efficiency and formal excellence, rather than substantive quality, become paramount. From this perspective, the technical and aesthetic qualities of the work of Mapplethorpe and Serrano would warrant serious consideration for NEA funding, despite their provocative subject matter.

Those who hold that art should not be funded impartially are those who assume that art is connected with advocacy. The postmodernists advocate a liberation from oppressive power structures, from societal norms that are held to limit both the imagination and life. In seeking to be an advocate of liberation from values and tradition, the postmodernist perspective adopts an exhilarating but arguably nihilistic vision of the fine arts. From this perspective the content of these works by Mapplethorpe and Serrano warranted subsidization by the NEA.

In contrast, from a conservative perspective *Piss Christ*, regardless of its technical brilliance or the intentions of the artist, is an offensive exercise in public bigotry, and Mapplethorpe's art depicting sadomasochism is judged to be advocating behavior that undermines basic human dignity. Therefore, from a conservative perspective neither Serrano's nor Mapplethorpe's art warrant NEA funding. *—Arthur Pontynen*

See also Art; Brennan, William J., Jr.; De Grazia, Edward; Feminism; First Amendment; Helms, Jesse Alexander; Mapplethorpe, Robert; *Miller v. California*; Obscenity: legal definitions; Performance art; Serrano, Andres.

Bibliography

Livingston Biddle's *Our Government and the Arts: A Perspective from the Inside* (New York: American Council for the Arts, 1988) and Michael Straight's *Nancy Hanks: An Intimate Portrait: The Creation of a National Commitment to the Arts* (Durham, N.C.: Duke University Press, 1988) provide thorough accounts of the NEA's founding. A modernist-postmodernist analysis of the controversies surrounding the NEA can be found in Edward de Grazia's *Girls Lean Back Everywhere: The Law of Obscenity and the Assault on Genius* (New York: Random House, 1992). Also in this mode is John Frohnmayer's *Leaving Town Alive: Confessions of an Arts Warrior* (Boston: Houghton Mifflin, 1993). Hilton Kramer's *The Revenge of the Philistines* (New York: Free Press, 1985) provides a modernist critique of postmodernist influence in the NEA. A conservative analysis can be found in a volume edited by Laurence Jarvik and others, *The National Endowments: A Critical Symposium* (Los Angeles: Second Thoughts Books, 1995). Dick Netzer attempts to weigh both sides of the argument in *Subsidized Muse: Public Support for the Arts in the United States* (Cambridge, England: Cambridge University Press, 1978).

National Endowment for the Humanities (NEH)

Founded: 1965

Type of organization: Independent agency of the U.S. government

Significance: The NEH has been regularly attacked by conservatives for funding projects that they have contended oppose values held by most Americans, and by liberals who have objected to traditional American cultural values

The NEH is an independent executive agency of the U.S. government dedicated to the preservation of, and research into, the humanities. It has provided financial support to individual scholars, not-for-profit groups, colleges and universities, museums, libraries, publications, and schools. The NEH has also supported such diverse projects as publishing the papers of notable historical and literary figures, sponsoring symposia on important academic issues, financing documentary films, and organizing forums on multicultural issues. The NEH was founded by an act of Congress in 1965 on the recommendation of President John F. Kennedy. Along with the National Endowment for the Arts (NEA), The Institute of

Museum Services, and the Federal Council on the Arts and the Humanities, it helps to make up the National Foundation on the Arts and Humanities. Both the chairperson of the NEH and twenty-six other members of the foundation's governing council are appointed by the president with Senate confirmation.

Despite extensive criticism from both the Right and the Left, the NEH survived with strong support from presidents Kennedy, Lyndon B. Johnson, and Richard Nixon. The NEH came under increased scrutiny, however, after President Ronald Reagan called for its elimination. In the 1980's and 1990's, the NEH came under further attack, particularly by conservatives. In 1990, for example, Congress passed legislation making all grants awarded by the NEH and the NEA subject to an obscenity clause. North Carolina senator Jesse Helms proposed the bill that required grant recipients to sign pledges stating that any government funds they received would not be used to produce obscene material. The measure was, however, later ruled unconstitutional.

Lynne Cheney, the NEH chairperson under President George Bush, was often accused by liberals of using her position to promote her own conservative ideologies. When the Senate rejected Cheney's nomination of Carol Iannone to the NEH Advisory Council in 1991, she contended that the decision was based on Iannone's opinions published in the right-leaning *Commentary* magazine. Senate members who voted against the nominee insisted that they rejected Iannone because of her weak academic credentials. Cheney also joined Kansas senator Robert Dole and former NEH chairperson William Bennett in condemning the National History Standards. Though they were co-sponsored by the NEH at the time Cheney was chairperson, she claimed to have no knowledge of its specifics.

With both the House and the Senate gaining Republican majorities in the 1994 election, some congressional leaders called for the elimination of the NEH. In 1995 funding for the endowment was barred from being used to support projects that "promote, disseminate, sponsor, or produce materials or performances that depict or describe in a patently offensive way, sexual or excretory activities or organs" and "which denigrate the objects or beliefs of the adherents of a particular religion."

See also Dole, Robert; Helms, Jesse Alexander; National Endowment for the Arts; Political correctness; Scholarships.

National Federation for Decency (NFD)

FOUNDED: 1977

TYPE OF ORGANIZATION: Christian pressure group

SIGNIFICANCE: The NFD has had a significant influence on sponsors of television programs and in leading protests against films

The NFD was founded in Tupelo, Mississippi, by United Methodist minister Donald E. Wildmon. His intentions in founding the NFD were to pressure the entertainment industry to be more responsible about what they produced. The NFD wished to hold accountable the companies that sponsor programs that the NFD perceived as attacking traditional family values. The NFD's protest started with a "Turn Off the TV Week" in 1977 that brought the group to the forefront of the entertainment industry's attention. Since then the NFD has expanded its group to a nationwide network of more than 450 local affiliates.

In 1988 the National Federation for Decency changed its name to the American Family Association (AFA). It has broadened its organizational views by extending its values to other areas besides the entertainment industry. The AFA has a nonprofit law center for defending the civil rights of Christians. It operates a radio station with the intention of creating a nationwide network of radio stations.

The AFA has been effective in its work by achieving the removal of pornography magazines from the federal prisons, pressuring the Pepsi-Cola company into removing Madonna as their spokesperson, and causing ABC a loss of nearly one million dollars in advertising revenues per episode for its drama *NYPD Blue*. In 1988 Wildmon was an outspoken figure in the protests against Martin Scorsese's film *The Last Temptation of Christ*.

See also Coalition for Better Television; *Last Temptation of Christ, The*; Madonna; *NYPD Blue*; Pressure groups.

National Organization for Decent Literature (NODL)

FOUNDED: 1938

TYPE OF ORGANIZATION: Roman Catholic body opposed to offensive magazines

SIGNIFICANCE: The NODL has organized effective campaigns against the publication and sale of lewd magazines and brochure literature

During the mid-twentieth century the NODL was a strikingly successful group. The NODL was organized by the Roman Catholic church in America as a parallel organization to the film-oriented Legion of Decency. The goals of this group were to arouse public awareness, more rigorously enforce preexisting laws, promote more strict legislation, distribute monthly lists of objectionable material prepared by the group, and to visit newsstands to guarantee the removal of blacklisted publications.

The standards used by the NODL for their objections were those publications that glorified crime, that had content of a sexual nature, that had illustrations considered indecent, that published articles on immoral relations, and that carried disreputable advertising. Many popular authors, including James A. Michener, Mickey Spillane, and James M. Cain, fell under the indecent category of the NODL. The NODL was successful while it was in operation, getting publishers to alter their materials in order to be removed from the NODL blacklist.

See also Citizens for Decent Literature; Legion of Decency; Magazines; Men's magazines.

National Organization for Women (NOW)

FOUNDED: 1966

TYPE OF ORGANIZATION: Women's advocacy

SIGNIFICANCE: The National Organization for Women (NOW) has campaigned against censorship of birth control information and has urged boycotts

Gloria Steinem (left) and Mary Chung of the National Asian Women's Health Organization participate in a NOW rights march in San Francisco in April, 1996. (AP/Wide World Photos)

NOW was created by a group of educated, politically active American women to protest discrimination against women. Its organization has been largely federally oriented, with a national center in Washington, D.C., but much effective decision making reserved to local and state chapters. Over the years, NOW has focused on many issues, including equality in hiring and in the workplace, improving the media portrayal of women, increasing women's political presence, passing the Equal Rights Amendment, guarding women's reproductive rights, and antirape programs.

Because of the leadership's personal backgrounds (education and activism) and a historical tendency for government and private institutions (especially the church) to exclude and censor women, NOW has opposed formal legal censorship. In opposing government and private practices, NOW has resorted—often effectively—to dissemination of information, typically through the media and public forums, but also through public demonstrations. NOW has infrequently employed boycotts and more usually the threat thereof.

NOW actively opposed the abortion gag rule, whereby federally funded family clinics were prevented from presenting information about abortion as an alternative to unwanted pregnancies. NOW has consistently supported abortion as a woman's right of free choice and has strenuously opposed attempts to limit access to information about abortion or to limit legal abortion.

The area where NOW has come closest to restricting free speech involves violence against women and degrading sexual material. National conventions have passed several resolutions encouraging the study of the relationship between pornography and crime, supporting the rights of those victimized by sexual crimes, and compensation for these victims. The strongest resolution (1991) decried the publication of patently offensive material, partly a response to Bret Ellis' violently misogynist novel, *American Psycho* (1991), but the resolution never developed into a boycott.

Public protests at the local level have effected some change. For example, in November, 1992, the Los Angeles NOW chapter threatened a boycott against E! Entertainment Television for hiring Howard Stern. E! then agreed to consult with NOW regarding programming ideas dealing with women's issues. Nationally, NOW participated successfully in a boycott against Rush Limbaugh's reappointment to the Florida Citrus Commission.

The concern with the power of mass media was incorporated into NOW's original statement of purpose: the "endeavor to change the false image of women now prevalent in the mass media." One of the earliest task forces, formed in 1967 and called Image of Women in the Mass Media, recommended speaking out publicly and writing letters. In addition, NOW pushed for inclusion of women as part of the team that prepared material in the mass media—for reasons of content as well as equality in the work place. In a number of cities, NOW led campaigns to negotiate with local media, with some measure of success.

See also Abortion gag rule; *American Psycho*; Feminism; Women; Women, violence against; Women Against Pornography; Women Against Violence in Pornography and Media.

National Public Radio (NPR)

Founded: 1970

Type of organization: U.S. network of publicly supported radio stations

Significance: Criticized by both the Left and the Right, NPR has faced persistent threats of losing its main sources of financing

In 1967 Congress established the Corporation for Public Broadcasting (CPB) with a commitment for its funding. The CPB, in turn, created National Public Radio, a network with studios developing national programming and a system of affiliates. Public radio serves about one million listeners across the nation—a small audience compared to commercial networks.

Almost from the beginning, controversy dominated the use of public funds for broadcasting. The threat of cutting public funds, in turn, served to spawn censorship of NPR's programming. Initially, NPR produced what were considered to be high-quality programs geared to the aural nature of the medium. These included such programs as the thirteen-part series "A Question of Place," discussion, and readings from foremost American thinkers.

Popular national programs on NPR include *Morning Edition*, a two-hour morning news program, *All Things Consid-*

ered, also two hours, an evening news show, and a number of variety programs available to affiliates across the country. In 1983, however, the network was almost bereft of funds, and only a loan from the Corporation for Public Broadcasting kept the network afloat, and a concerted fund-raising drive saved the system.

Local affiliates were drawn into the fund-raising effort, and they began to develop membership drives and to use commercial underwriters, a type of advertising. These advertisers were able to bring pressures on the stations, having a direct effect on the type of programs broadcast. For example, in 1994 NPR planned a series of commentaries from prison by death-row inmate and journalist Mumia Abu-Jamal, convicted in 1981 of the shooting death of a Philadelphia police officer. Pressure from police groups caused NPR to drop the broadcast.

In addition, the network has been accused of further censorship regarding Abu-Jamal himself: From May 1994 until August 1995 the network remained virtually silent about the case. According to critics, when NPR did do a report, it ignored many disputed facts about the shooting.

In 1993 and 1994 CAMERA (Committee for Accuracy in Middle Eastern Reporting in America) accused NPR of pro-Arab bias in its reporting of and omission of stories about the Arab-Israeli conflict. Specifically, CAMERA notes the network's failure to cover the goals and actions of Hamas and to cover the October, 1991, Teheran Conference, whose motto was "Israel must be destroyed."

In another case, James L. Nash, a moral theologian, was asked to serve on a panel on the role of homosexuals in American society as part of NPR's "Talk of the Nation." When Nash felt uncomfortable representing the religious right, he requested that a representative of that group be included in the panel. The producers made the judgment that the religious right was not interested in dialogue and rejected Nash's request. Nash criticized the panel in a subsequent magazine article. The Christian Coalition also expressed its concern at the panel's membership.

When NPR reporter Nina Totenberg reported Anita Hill's accusations of sexual harassment against Supreme Court nominee Clarence Thomas, Senator Orrin Hatch, a republican from Utah, stated that while other reporters from privately owned media outlets could protect their sources, she could not. Hatch reasoned that a recipient of federal funding, an agency is considered a public spokesperson. Ultimately, however, Totenberg was not forced to reveal the source of her information.

Hatch's viewpoint might seem to be supported by the 1991 *Rust v. Sullivan* decision of the Supreme Court, which ruled that government has the right to restrict the speech activities of those receiving government grants. This is viewed by many as a threat to the content of all public broadcasting and any institutions receiving federal funding.

Conservatives have long made NPR their target, calling for its elimination. They cite liberal bias and elitism as basis for their judgments, attacking National Public Radio as a tool of the Democratic Party. Republican leader Newt Gingrich claimed that the spectrum of cable channels now fill the need once met by NPR.

Funding threats remain a principal source of censorship of NPR, although 1995 funds provided only about 14 percent of affiliates' budgets. In 1995 $285 million was distributed to 650 radio stations and a small number of television outlets. Individual public radio stations send money back to NPR for annual dues and for syndicated programming.

The Republican Congress elected in 1994 set its sights on eliminating public radio completely from the federal budget. While unsuccessful in completely cutting funds for public radio, Congress cut them drastically, with further cuts slated for ensuing years. Although some individual public radio stations lobbied vigorously against the cuts, leaders at NPR seemed resigned to them. Some have proposed a broadcasting trust fund to finance public radio and television. A proposal to eliminate small stations where signals overlap has had lukewarm reception from affiliates. Such plans would create further censorship, particularly on the local level. Since only about 10 percent of NPR listeners actually contribute to the station drives, other critics suggest that it is among listeners that NPR and affiliates should look for funding.

Some in Congress have urged that public radio become more commercial, broadening the role of underwriters in funding. This, too, has been resisted by broadcasters, who see the result of such a move as being a further decline in the quality of programming under pressure from advertisers. Some programs draw a limited audience and would likely be eliminated if they were considered primarily for their economic value.

—*Patricia J. Huhn*

See also Abortion gag rule; Advertisers as advocates of censorship; Armed Forces Radio and Television Service; Dole, Robert; Fairness doctrine; Fear; Federal Communications Commission; Gag order; Pacifica Foundation; Public Broadcasting Act of 1967; Public Broadcasting Service; Radio.

BIBLIOGRAPHY

Thomas Looker's *The Sound and the Story: NPR and the Art of Radio* (Boston: Houghton Mifflin, 1995) focuses on the power of the medium and the internal workings of NPR. Although somewhat dated, *Fear in the Air, Broadcasting and the First Amendment: The Anatomy of a Constitutional Crisis* (New York: W. W. Norton, 1973) by Harry S. Ashmore, notes some of the censorship challenges to all broadcasting including federal attempts to cut finding in the CPB's early days. James Fallows' book *Breaking the News: How the Media Undermine American Democracy* (New York: Pantheon, 1995) discusses arguments that have been made to show that journalists who could have saved American public life have, in fact, contributed to its decline.

National security

DEFINITION: The safety of a nation or government from foreign dangers or domestic subversion, as defined by the government in power

SIGNIFICANCE: Protection of national security has historically been a common justification for rigid government censorship

The belief that political institutions should be protected by censorship is an ancient one. Although ancient Athens is often regarded as one of the first societies to value free speech, its government nevertheless condemned philosopher Socrates to death because his teachings were believed to be encouraging a group of antidemocratic aristocrats who wanted to establish tyranny. If this view is correct, the death of one of the most famous teachers in Western civilization resulted from censorship to preserve Athens' political security.

Most governments throughout history have seen dissenters as threats to be silenced. Organized policies of censorship for national security, however, did not begin until centralized nation-states emerged in early modern Europe, when England's Queen Elizabeth I began controlling her country's press through licensing. She believed that anyone who criticized her threatened the security of the state itself. The monarchs who followed Elizabeth prosecuted their critics under laws against seditious libel, believing that the safety of the state depended on the Crown.

The view that criticisms of monarchs or governments pose dangers to nations depends on the theory that political authority comes from the monarch or government. By the eighteenth century, political thinkers such as Thomas Erskine and Chancellor Camden in England, and Thomas Jefferson and James Madison in the United States, had begun to argue that governmental authority in fact comes from the citizens who make up nations. Therefore, they argued, the state cannot limit the rights of citizens to speak freely, even to prevent its own destruction.

National Security in U.S. History. Queen Elizabeth's censorship was chiefly concerned with protecting the security of the state from troublemakers among her own subjects. Modern authoritarian governments, such as the former Soviet Union, have continued this tradition. In the United States, where people generally recognize the right of citizens to alter or do away with their own political systems, national security censorship has usually been justified by claims of threats from foreign nations.

The first act of legal censorship in the United States, the Sedition Act of 1798, was intended to meet a perceived threat from a foreign power, revolutionary France. Many in the Federalist Party of President John Adams believed that their opponents in the Democratic-Republican Party were pro-French subversives who sought to overthrow the government. The Sedition Act established jail penalties and heavy fines for Americans who criticized the president or members of the government.

Most attempts at censorship for the sake of national security in the United States from the 1798 law until 1945 were undertaken during wartime. During the Civil War, for example, the governments of both sides attempted to control the press. In World War I, the Committee on Public Information headed by George Creel pressured newspapers into publishing only stories approved by the government. In 1940, as the United States was on the verge of entering World War II, Congress passed the Smith Act, which explicitly made it illegal to advocate overthrowing the government by force or to belong to organizations advocating overthrowing the government. The following year, the Office of Censorship was created to prevent the publication of information that might be useful to the enemy.

The National Security State. After World War II a number of developments combined to create the "national security state," a government constantly concerned with protecting its own security. New technologically advanced weapons, such as nuclear bombs, created a belief that such weapons had to be kept secret from enemies. Moreover, the United States was becoming engaged in an ideological struggle with the communist countries of the Soviet Union and China known as the Cold War. Finally, the U.S. government was much larger than it had been before the war and it had many government agencies responsible for protecting national security that had an impulse to become more active.

The U.S. government produced the atomic bomb through the ultra-secret Manhattan Project during the war. With the end of the war, the government felt that it needed to continue to keep the secret of the bomb. The Atomic Energy Act of 1946 was probably the most far-reaching restriction on publication of knowledge in American history. It prohibited publication of a wide range of information on the manufacture, production, and use of atomic energy. As late as 1979, the U.S. Department of Energy used the 1946 act to hold up publication of an article on the hydrogen bomb by *The Progressive* magazine, even though the article was based on information already publicly available.

Perceptions of a communist threat led to limitations on the freedoms of speech and publication within the United States. Some American communists were imprisoned under the Smith Act. In 1951 President Harry S Truman, prompted by the perceived menace of communism, gave all of the agencies of the executive branch the right to classify information as secret. Agencies charged with protecting national security not only collected information, but tried to prevent its spread.

The powers of the Federal Bureau of Investigation (FBI) increased greatly during the war, and after the war the FBI became the federal agency primarily charged with fighting suspected subversion within the United States. During the 1960's the FBI collected information on publishers, sources of funds, and staff members of "underground" newspapers opposed to the war in Vietnam. Many of these newspapers were forced out of business when the FBI put pressure on their advertisers.

The Central Intelligence Agency (CIA) and National Security Agency (NSA) are both highly secretive organizations created after the war to collect information. Employees of both organizations are required to sign lifetime agreements not to publish anything without prior permission from the relevant agency. In 1977 the CIA sued Frank W. Snepp III, a former agent, when Snepp published a book about his experiences in Vietnam. In a 1980 decision, the U.S. Supreme Court affirmed the CIA's right to require and enforce the lifetime censorship of Snepp and other agents. In 1983 President Ronald Reagan signed National Security Decision Directive 84, which required a broad range of government employees to sign lifetime security agreements.

Concerns about the increase in secret information collected on American citizens led to the passage of the Freedom of Information Act (FOIA) in 1966, which enabled citizens to obtain government information. However, access to government information narrowed in 1982, when President Reagan issued an executive order allowing agencies to reclassify information in order to avoid releasing it under the FOIA. In 1996 the CIA's refusal, on the grounds of national security, to release information on its involvement in the Nicaraguan drug trade led to charges of censorship. —*Carl L. Bankston III*

See also Atomic Energy Act of 1954; Central Intelligence Agency; Classification of information; Communist Party of the U.S.A.; Freedom of Information Act; "H-Bomb Secret, The"; National Security Decision Directive 84; Sedition; Sedition Act of 1798; Smith Act; *Snepp v. United States.*

Bibliography

Those interested in early national security censorship may consult *Freedom of the Press in England, 1476-1776: The Rise and Decline of Government Control* (Urbana: University of Illinois Press, 1965), by Fred S. Siebert. *Freedom at Risk: Secrecy, Censorship, and Repression in the 1980's* (Philadelphia: Temple University Press, 1988), edited by Richard O. Curry, concerns Reagan era censorship. *The U.S. Intelligence Community* (Cambridge, Mass.: Ballinger, 1985), by Jeff Richelson, describes the agencies that keep America's secrets. David Dickson's *The New Politics of Science* (New York: Pantheon, 1984) considers science in the national security state. Donna A. Demac's *Liberty Denied: The Current Rise of Censorship in America* (New Brunswick, N.J.: Rutgers University Press, 1990) provides useful information.

National Security Decision Directive 84 (NSDD 84)

Declared: March 11, 1983

Place: Washington, D.C.

Significance: This declaration extended to all federal government agencies the same strict restrictions on disclosure of classified information that previously applied to the Central Intelligence Agency (CIA)

Ronald Reagan won election to the presidency in 1980 by presenting himself as a citizen-politician, an outsider sent to Washington to restore government to its proper path. He and his conservative followers believed that both the media and agencies of the executive branch controlled by their liberal opponents were anxious to undermine the Republican administration's conservative programs. The Reagan Administration saw evidence of such hostility in the many "leaks" of government documents to the press—even though many of those complaining about such disclosures were believed to be among the biggest document leakers.

The administration issued NSDD 84 in response to a report by an interagency committee formed in 1982 by Attorney General William French Smith. The committee, which had representatives from the CIA and the departments of State and Defense, said that unauthorized disclosure of classified information was damaging U.S. national security interests. The directive required government employees to report all their media contacts to their agencies. It also mandated that all suspected leaks be formally investigated, and it authorized using polygraph tests in such probes.

NSDD 84 affected nearly four million persons, more than a million of whom were employed by private defense contractors. The directive also required more than 290,000 government employees who had access to certain levels of classified material to sign nondisclosure agreements requiring them to submit for clearance any lectures that they planned to give, or any articles or books—including fiction—that they wished to publish.

NSDD 84 caused an uproar among journalists, federal employee unions, civil liberties groups, and members of Congress. Critics resented the fact that such directives set government policies without going through normal legislative processes, and that they—unlike executive orders—did not have to be published in the *Federal Register*. These opponents feared that the reporting of media contacts and polygraph testing would lead to infringement of the rights of freedom of speech and of privacy. The prepublication review process raised questions of prior restraint and censorship.

In September, 1984, under pressure from Congress, the administration suspended NSDD 84's prepublication review provision, but left in place a 1981 requirement that all government employees with high-level security clearance sign contracts holding them to lifetime promises to submit material for prepublication review. A 1986 congressional study found that suspension of the NSDD 84's prepublication review requirement did not end censorship. In 1984 alone 21,718 books, articles, speeches, and other materials were submitted for agency prepublication review; a thousand more were submitted in 1985. By December 31, 1985, more than 240,000 persons had signed the agreement, in either its 1981 or 1983 version.

See also Central Intelligence Agency; Civil service; Classification of information; Intelligence Identities Protection Act; Meese, Edwin, III; National security; News media censorship; Off-the-record information; Prior restraint; Reagan, Ronald.

National Socialism (Nazism)

Date: 1933-1945

Place: Germany

Significance: National Socialism was banned in Germany and in a number of European countries after 1945, although it continues to be legal in the United States

Adolf Hitler, an Austrian born in 1889, joined a small, insignificant political party in Munich, Germany, in late 1919 and transformed it into the dynamic, racist organization that assumed power in Germany in January, 1933. Within six months of taking power, the Nazis abolished all other political parties and subordinated the press. On May 10, 1933, books that were anathema to the Nazis were publicly burned in Berlin. Modern art, labeled degenerate by the Nazis, was withdrawn from German galleries and 4,829 paintings and drawings were burned in secret in Berlin on March 20, 1939. National Socialism was also exported, first through the National Socialist German Worker's Party (the complete name of the Nazi Party) or sympathetic organizations and then through war.

National Socialism Before World War II. Before 1933 the Nazi Party was permitted to compete legally for political power in democratic Weimar Germany. The only serious attempt to outlaw the party occurred in 1922 when it was banned by most German states. The ban was approved by the German constitutional court in the spring of 1923, but Bavaria allowed Hitler to continue his political career. After Hitler's failed putsch in Munich in November, 1923, he was jailed for a year, but in February, 1925, he was permitted to reestablish the Nazi Party in Munich. Between 1925 and 1927, a number of German states prohibited Hitler from addressing public party rallies. Thereafter, no significant attempt was made to ban National Socialism in Germany.

The Nazi Party faced much greater legal obstacles outside Germany, especially in the United States, where it established branches in 1924. As a result of the Nazi Party's unpopularity in the United States, the party was dissolved there in 1933 and replaced by two substitute organizations, the Friends of the New Germany and the American-German Bund. Both organizations came under the scrutiny of Congressional committees, particularly the House Committee on Un-American Activities. Customs officials raided German ships in New York harbor on February 5, 1934, and confiscated Nazi propaganda material.

Several American state governments attacked National Socialism. In New Jersey a 1934 law prohibiting race incitement was used in November, 1938, to indict Ferdinand Hepperle, a printer and member of the Bund, because the authorities had discovered in his print shop pictures of caricatures of Jews inscribed with slogans "Vote Gentile—Buy Gentile." A New York state committee investigated Fritz Kuhn, the German American leader of the Bund. Kuhn was convicted of embezzlement of Bund funds in 1939, which effectively destroyed the Bund before it was outlawed in 1941.

Individuals who were members of the Bund or who expressed support for National Socialism were censored by American judicial authorities. In a divorce case in August, 1938, Judge P. H. Schwaba of the Superior Court of Chicago ordered a father to stop indoctrinating his two small sons with National Socialism and to refrain from using the phrase "Heil Hitler" in their presence. Another judge in Hackensack, New Jersey, told a group of German Americans in his naturalization court in November, 1938, that he would deny U.S. citizenship to anyone who was a member of the Bund. Two German-American Bund members in California were deprived of their U.S. citizenship in late 1940 and early 1941 for promoting Nazi literature in a bookstore.

Postwar Denazification. In contrast to the interwar period, when censorship of National Socialism was much more pervasive outside Germany, after 1945 the reverse was true. The Allies initiated a denazification program in 1945, which included a ban of the Nazi Party and trials for its former members. The two German states continued this policy after 1949. Until 1979 it was illegal for bookstores in West Germany to display Hitler's book *Mein Kampf* (1925-1927), and anyone caught raising an arm in a Hitler salute was subject to substantial fines.

Article 21 of the German Basic Law allows that country's Constitutional Court to ban a political party that rejects democracy. Other organizations that support National Socialism have been banned by the minister of interior. In October, 1952, a neo-Nazi party, the Socialist Reich Party, was outlawed by the Constitutional Court. Most neo-Nazi parties that emerged later, particularly after German unification in 1990, were small groups. The German Constitutional Court in March, 1995, refused to recognize these associations as legitimate political parties. Since 1989 the German government has banned ten small neo-Nazi organizations.

The efforts of German authorities have been frustrated by American and Canadian neo-Nazis who have smuggled printed Nazi propaganda material into Germany. Constitutional protection of free speech has enabled supporters of National Socialism to operate freely in the United States, and, to a degree, in Canada. George Lincoln Rockwell, the founder of the postwar American Nazi Party, initiated the policy of sending illegal Nazi material to England and Europe in the summer of 1962.

After the murder of Rockwell in 1967 two persons in particular have carried on his activities. Ernst Zündel, a German Canadian, was arrested in December, 1991, in Munich for taking material into Germany that denied that the Holocaust actually occurred. Zündel was also tried and convicted for the

Adolf Hitler addresses a Nazi rally in April, 1938. (Library of Congress)

same crime in Canada, but the Canadian Supreme Court overturned Zündel's conviction in August, 1992, because it limited his right of free speech. By contrast, the German Supreme Court ruled in April, 1994, that Holocaust revisionism was not protected by constitutional rights of freedom of speech. In February, 1996, Zündel's Nazi Internet site was blocked by the German authorities to prevent distribution of Nazi material.

Since 1971 Gary Lauck of Lincoln, Nebraska, has been the major distributor of Nazi material to Germany, a crime punishable by five years in prison in that country. Lauck, who was born in 1953 in Milwaukee, Wisconsin, was the propaganda leader of the National Socialist German Worker's Party/Exile Organization. After being arrested in Germany in 1976, Lauck moved his operations in Europe to Denmark, where the dissemination of Nazi material is not illegal unless it incites race hatred. Acting on a German warrant, he was arrested in Denmark and turned over to German authorities on September 5, 1995. —*Johnpeter Horst Grill*

See also Book burning; Degenerate Art Exhibition; Denmark; Holocaust, Jewish; *Mein Kampf*; Simon Wiesenthal Center; World War II.

Bibliography

Jackson J. Spielvogel, *Hitler and Nazi Germany: A History* (Englewood Cliffs, N.J.: Prentice-Hall, 1995), surveys the history of the Third Reich. The Nazi Party's attempts to organize outside Germany are examined in Leland V. Bell, *In Hitler's Shadow: The Anatomy of American Nazism* (Port Washington, N.Y.: Kennikat Press, 1973), and in Donald M. McKale, *The Swastika Outside Germany* (Kent, Ohio: Kent State University Press, 1977). Oron J. Hale, *The Captive Press in the Third Reich* (Princeton, N.J.: Princeton University Press, 1964), and Alan Steinweis, *Art, Ideology, and Economics in Nazi Germany: The Reich Chambers of Music, Theater, and the Visual Arts* (Chapel Hill: University of North Carolina Press, 1993), review Nazi efforts to censor the press and artistic activities after 1933. Thorough examinations of neo-Nazi organizations in post-1945 Germany and government attempts to ban neo-Nazi activities are presented by Rand C. Lewis, *A Nazi Legacy: Right Wing Extremism in Postwar Germany* (New York: Praeger, 1991), and Richard Stöss, *Politics Against Democracy: Right-wing Extremism in West Germany* (New York: Berg, 1991).

Native Americans

Definition: Descendants of the original inhabitants of the Americas prior to European contact

Significance: The attitude, values, and activities of dominant non-native cultures have sometimes led to the suppression of Native American freedoms of expression

The European and European-derived cultures that came to dominate the Americas in the centuries following the voyages of Christopher Columbus had an oppressive effect on Native American cultures. The acculturative forces unleashed by Eurocentric cultures ranged from extermination of native peoples and cultures to more subtle repressions of cultural expression.

Overt Repression: The Potlatch. In the 1880's, the Canadian government outlawed the potlatch, a ceremony central to the life of the Pacific Northwest coast Indians. At a potlatch ceremony, a chief would bestow lavish gifts upon his guests in exchange for their recognition of his claims to new titles, privileges, or prerogatives for himself and his family. A newly carved cedar totem pole would sometimes be erected as part of the event, during which religious and social histories would be retold, acted out, and passed on to the next generation. The potlatch was thus a driving force for artistic production and performance and was vital to the continuity of the Northwest Indians' identity as a people.

Government bureaucrats viewed the potlatch as wasteful, however, and missionaries saw it as pagan; these and other forces conspired against it. Active enforcement of the prohibition began in 1913, culminating in the arrest of twenty-nine participants in a Kwakiutl potlatch ceremony held on Village Island, British Columbia, in 1921. The government confiscated more than 450 ceremonial artworks ranging from masks to copper shields. After decades of lobbying, the prohibition was dropped in 1951. A cultural revitalization ensued, with a renaissance in Northwest Coast arts and crafts. Many of the confiscated items were finally returned to the Kwakiutl beginning in 1979.

Repression by Incidental Activities: Sacred Grounds. At the heart of Native American religion is the relationship between people and the earth. Numerous private and governmental activities have infringed on this equation. In 1978, for example, the U.S. Congress passed the American Indian Religious Freedom Act (AIRFA). Its preamble noted that the United States was not founded on any notion of religious freedom for Native Americans and that the nation had, deliberately or through ignorance or inadvertence, infringed on the free expression of Native American religions. The act directed government agencies to review their operations to reverse this history of insensitivity. Yet because it contained no sanctions, AIRFA had little practical impact.

For example, even after AIRFA's adoption, the U.S. Forest Service went to court to support development of a ski area in the San Francisco Peaks north of Flagstaff, Arizona. To the Hopi, these peaks are considered the home of the gods, the residence of the sacred Kachina spirits. The Forest Service also endorsed a project to build an observatory on Mount Graham in Arizona, a joint venture of the University of Arizona and the Vatican. The project was approved by the courts despite testimony that the site was a holy place to Apaches.

In one of the biggest setbacks to AIRFA goals, the U.S. Supreme Court ruled 6-3 in *Lyng v. Northwest Indian Cemetery Protective Association* (1988) that the Forest Service could build a logging road through territory sacred to the Yurok, Karok, and Tolowa tribes of northwestern California. The road traversed high country sites that were sacred in part precisely because of their privacy, silence, and undisturbed natural setting. In a strong dissenting opinion, Justice William J. Brennan, Jr., joined by Harry Blackmun and Thurgood Marshall, wrote: "I find it difficult . . . to imagine conduct more insensitive to religious needs than the Government's determination to build a marginally useful road in the face of uncontradicted evidence that the road will render the practice

Indians from the Muckleshoot Reservation begin a march to protest the state of Washington's encroachments on their fishing rights in 1966. (AP/Wide World Photos)

of respondents' religion impossible." In 1993, the Native American Rights Fund (NARF) estimated that there were at least forty-four sacred sites threatened by tourism, development, and resource exploitation.

In *Employment Division v. Smith* (1990), the Supreme Court agreed with the state of Oregon that the religious use of the hallucinogenic cactus peyote was not constitutionally protected. Peyote is a sacrament of the Native American Church. Despite this, in the majority opinion written by Justice Antonin Scalia, the Court found that such religious concerns are of no consequence when they conflict with "neutral" laws passed by the state against "criminal" activities. The U.S. Congress, attempting to curtail bureaucratic abuses of AIRFA, passed the Native American Free Exercise of Religion Act (NAFERA) in 1993 and an amendment in 1994. NAFERA specifically addressed peyote use in an attempt to reverse the effects of the *Smith* ruling.

Political Repression. A government-aided campaign to suppress political dissent by Native Americans took place on Pine Ridge Reservation in South Dakota from 1972 to 1976. Opposition to the policies of Bureau of Indian Affairs-backed tribal chairman Richard Wilson led to formation of the Oglala Sioux Civil Rights Organization (OSCRO), which invited members of the American Indian Movement (AIM) to the reservation to defend the rights of free speech. AIM members occupied the hamlet of Wounded Knee on February 27, 1973, and a seventy-one day siege ensued. The takeover was followed by a concerted effort by government agencies to crush OSCRO and AIM.

Charges were filed against 562 occupiers of Wounded Knee; only fifteen were ever convicted of anything. AIM leaders Dennis Banks and Russell Means were freed in 1974 by a federal judge who found gross misconduct by agents of the Federal Bureau of Investigation (FBI). Still, between mid-1973 and mid-1976, nearly seventy AIM members and supporters were killed on Pine Ridge. Many suspected that members of an armed gang funded by Wilson and known as the "Goon Squad" were responsible. In 1975, a gun battle on the reservation left two FBI agents and one AIM member dead. Leonard Peltier, an AIM activist, was charged, convicted, and sentenced to two life terms for the agents' deaths.

A detailed account of these events was published by Peter Matthiessen in his book *In the Spirit of Crazy Horse* (1983), which argued that Peltier was innocent. Soon thereafter, separate libel suits were filed against Matthiessen and his publisher, Viking Press, by South Dakota governor William Janklow and by FBI agent David Price. Threatening calls were received by bookstores and the publisher, which decided to recall the book. Viking destroyed its stockpiles and canceled plans for paperback or foreign editions. The lawsuits were dismissed in 1990, and Viking re-released the book in 1991. Still, Matthiessen's account had been kept from the public for seven years.

Stereotypes. Native Americans often feel that their portrayal in popular media breeds insensitivity to their rights and culture. The use of Indian names and images by athletic team mascots is one highly publicized area of debate. This issue peaked during the "politically incorrect" baseball World Series of 1995, which pitted the Cleveland Indians against the Atlanta Braves. Many Cleveland supporters pointed out that the team's nickname was chosen in a 1915 fan contest to honor Lewis M. Sockalexis, a Penobscot who had been the first Native American professional athlete. Detractors pointed out that Cleveland's cartoon image of the grinning "Chief Wahoo" could hardly be considered a tribute. Atlanta's "tomahawk chop" and onetime employment of a mascot known as "Chief Knockahoma" (who cavorted near a tipi after home runs), came under similar criticism.

Popular culture is replete with such images. There is Cherokee Red Soda, Pow Wow Cheese Puffs, and Native American Barbie, which was the best-selling component of Mattel's 1993 "Dolls of the World" series. A Native American Teenage Mutant Ninja Turtle was added to that popular children's television series. The Hopi protested a Kachina-shaped liquor decanter and a 1992 Marvel Comics publication in which Kachina figures were portrayed as criminals; both products were withdrawn. The Hopi also protested a 1991 film version of Tony Hillerman's *Dark Wind*, claiming it inaccurately portrayed Hopi culture; the film experienced a short release in video stores.

Activists had less success in stopping the sale of Original Crazy Horse Malt Liquor. The product's name was outlawed by Congress in 1992 as offensive to Native Americans, but a federal judge overturned the ban as a violation of the free-speech rights of the marketer. AIM began a national boycott of the product in July, 1995; moreover, some states continued to ban the product—not because of the name, but because its forty-ounce bottle was judged to be too big.

Stereotypes create an image in the popular mind that many Native American artists have found difficult to break. They are expected to conform or be labeled "nontraditional." Some successful exceptions include White Eagle in classic opera, Cherokee rap artist Litefoot, and Mohican singer-composer Bill Miller, whose music combines blues with native themes.

In 1990, Congress passed the Act to Promote Development of Indian Arts and Crafts, which criminalized the presentation of anything as "Indian-made" unless the maker was of at least one-quarter Indian descent or was federally recognized on tribal roll. The legislation created problems for many bona fide Indian artists who never formally enrolled or who otherwise failed to meet criteria. Cherokee artist Willard Stone, whose sculpture "Trail of Tears" is included in the Great Seal of the Cherokee Nation, never enrolled; the Muskogee museum in which it was displayed closed its doors the day after the act was passed. Stone's descendant, Jeanne Walker Rorex, was excluded from the American Indian Heritage Exhibition at the Philbrook Museum in Tulsa, Oklahoma, in 1992 for the same reason. Ironically, the act created a "purity police" and stifled the creative expression of many artists.

The attempt to retain and freely express Native American culture has been challenged by conflicting and even hostile values of the dominant majority. This tension has been occurring for more than five hundred years, and the struggle continues.

—Gary A. Olson

See also Chilling effect; Federal Bureau of Investigation; Libel; Multiculturalism; *Naked Amazon*; Political correctness; Race.

BIBLIOGRAPHY

Arts and the Northwest Coast are addressed in *Captured Heritage*, by Douglas Cole (Seattle: University of Washington Press, 1985). For AIRFA and related issues, see *Handbook of American Indian Religious Freedom*, Christopher Vecsey, ed., (New York: Crossroad Publishing, 1991). Peter Matthiessen's *In the Spirit of Crazy Horse* (New York: Viking Press, 1983) covers Pine Ridge events; the libel suits are discussed in an afterword by Martin Garbus included in the 1991 Viking Penguin edition. Also see Jon Wiener's "Murdered Ink," *The Nation* 256, no. 21 (May 31, 1993). Rights of indigenous peoples are monitored by the Native American Rights Fund (NARF), which produces the publication *Cultural Survival Quarterly*.

Natural Born Killers

TYPE OF WORK: Film

RELEASED: 1994

DIRECTOR: Oliver Stone (1946-   )

SUBJECT MATTER: An attractive young couple on a murderous roadtrip become media heroes

SIGNIFICANCE: Although the film was intended as a satire of the modern American fascination with violence, its makers had to cut its most graphic scenes of violence to prevent its receiving a commercially damaging film rating

In August, 1994, *Natural Born Killers*, a story by Quentin Tarantino with screenplay by David Veloz and Richard Rutowski, made its controversial debut. This satire of the media's and society's obsession with violence followed the travels of two lovers, Mickey (Woody Harrelson) and Mallory Knox (Juliette Lewis), on a sensational killing spree. During their reign of terror, a tabloid-television journalist (Robert Downey, Jr.) covers both the couple's actions and society's addiction to them. However, the violence within the movie earned it the controversial NC-17 (no children under 17) rating from the Motion Picture Association of America. Director Oliver Stone agreed to make cuts in the movie so that it would achieve an R rating and avoid the economic hardships that an

Juliette Lewis and Woody Harrelson play a young couple on a murder spree in Oliver Stone's violent satire Natural Born Killers. (Museum of Modern Art/Film Stills Archive)

NC-17 rating would cause. Movie theaters and newspapers often refused to show films rated NC-17, and television promotion for such films was prohibited. To compensate for the censoring in theaters, Stone released a "director's cut" version with the edited scenes back in, which went into video stores in 1995.

See also Film censorship; Motion Picture Association of America; *Pulp Fiction*; Violence.

Near v. Minnesota

COURT: U.S. Supreme Court
DATE: 1931
SIGNIFICANCE: This decision was the first U.S. Supreme Court case to apply the First Amendment's free press clause to the states and to apply the historical Anglo-Saxon legal ban on prior restraints to court injunctions against newspapers

Jay Near, a somewhat unsavory muckraking journalist, published an anti-Semitic, anti-Catholic, and anti-black weekly newspaper in Minneapolis, Minnesota. Among other things, it denounced police corruption, blaming it on "Jew gangsters." Angered Minneapolis officials asked state courts for an injunction to close the paper permanently, citing a state law that banned nuisances defined to include malicious newspapers. Near lost in local courts and on appeal to the Minnesota Supreme Court, but joined by the American Civil Liberties Union (ACLU) and American Newspaper Publishers Association, he appealed successfully to the U.S. Supreme Court.

The first major issue before the Court was whether the U.S. Constitution's First Amendment free press clause applied to the states, as well as to the federal government. The Court decided that the portion of the First Amendment relating to freedom of the press applied to states as well. They did so using the Fourteenth Amendment's clauses providing that no one could be "deprived of life, liberty, or property, without due process of law." The Court maintained that the First Amendment had such a crucial relationship to due process that states could not deprive the citizens of its benefits without denying them due process.

The second major issue was whether a court-granted injunction was a prior restraint within the meaning of the historic ban on prior restraints under Anglo-Saxon law. Classically, a prior restraint—as expressed by British jurist William Blackstone—occurred when newspapers had to secure government approval before they could publish anything. While the press might seem better protected by courts than by bureaucrats, the Court ruled that the two cases were so similar that they both were prior restraints and strongly suspect of violating free press.

Despite the despicable character of the views that Near had expressed, the Supreme Court rejected a prior restraint on his newspaper and, by extension, all newspapers. The result served as the basis for the Court's decision forty years later to allow publication in the Pentagon Papers case. Although the Court did not absolutely bar any prior restraints, it made them so suspect under the legal system that U.S. judges almost automatically reject government requests for injunctions against the press. The antipathy against prior restraints does not, however, apply with equal force to post restraints. These might include suits for damages from wrongful behavior such as defamation of character or libel.

See also Blackstone, William; Gag order; Obscenity: legal definitions; *Pentagon Papers, The*; Prior restraint.

New Worlds

TYPE OF WORK: Magazine
PUBLISHED: 1946- (intermittent)
SUBJECT MATTER: Science-fiction stories
SIGNIFICANCE: This influential British literary science-fiction magazine that ceased publication after Great Britain's largest chain of newspaper and magazine outlets refused to carry issues containing a serial with offensive language

The late 1960's and early 1970's witnessed a movement within science fiction that came to be known as the New Wave. New Wave writers sought to bring stylistic innovation and psychological complexity to a genre that was in many ways still firmly rooted in the pulp tradition from which it sprang. This movement was partly a response to widespread cultural and economic factors, such as a larger and more highly educated readership, with a growing distrust of the technocratic ideology that science fiction often seemed to celebrate. It was also a deliberate effort by a group of young science-fiction writers to bring new life to a genre that seemed in danger of stagnation.

The primary vehicle for many of these authors was *New Worlds*, a publication that had been in existence (in one form or another) since 1946. In its first eighteen years *New Worlds* had published fiction by such innovative writers as Brian Aldiss, J. G. Ballard, and John Brunner. In 1964 a twenty-four-year-old writer named Michael Moorcock assumed the editorship of the magazine and turned it into the flagship for a new kind of literary science fiction. Rather than perpetuating the formulaic but marketable style of traditional science fiction, Moorcock encouraged literary experimentation by publishing such original works as Thomas Disch's *Camp Concentration* and Brian Aldiss' *Barefoot in the Head*. Soon *New Worlds* became the focus for a wide-ranging reassessment of the genre's conventional style and orthodox attitudes.

Moorcock's policies met with both great success and violent opposition, each sometimes coming from unexpected quarters. *New World*'s success was more artistic than commercial, unfortunately, but an appeal to the Arts Council had produced a generous grant that enabled the magazine to remain afloat. This government-sponsored generosity was due, in part, to the magazine's supporters in the literary community, among whom were such prestigious writers as Edmund Crispin, Anthony Burgess, Angus Wilson, J. B. Priestley, and Marghanita Laski. Despite this support, however, *New Worlds* often came under fire for permitting obscene language and explicit sexual content, most notably in 1968, when the magazine began serializing *Bug Jack Barron*, Norman Spinrad's provocative near-future novel about racial exploitation, politics, and the media. As each new issue appeared, opposition grew; Spinrad was denounced as a "degenerate" in the House of Commons, and W. H. Smith, the largest chain of retail news agents in Britain, decided to stop carrying the magazine. Even with continued Arts Council support, the loss of such a significant portion of the market was too much for *New Worlds*, and the magazine ceased publication in 1970, continuing only as an irregularly appearing series of paperback anthologies, which ended in 1976.

In 1991 David S. Garnett launched a new version of *New Worlds* with the help of Michael Moorcock.

See also *Little Review, The*; Magazines; Obscenity: legal definitions.

New York Times, The

TYPE OF WORK: New York City newspaper
FOUNDED: 1851
SUBJECT MATTER: Daily news and editorial commentaries
SIGNIFICANCE: For more than a century *The Times* has been one of the most respected newspapers in the world, but it has faced several First Amendment challenges

During the Red Scares of the early 1950's, *The Times* published strong editorial attacks on Senator Joseph McCarthy's red-baiting activities, and in favor of school integration. Senator James O. Eastland of Mississippi retaliated in 1955 by launching an investigation of the paper through the Senate's Internal Security Subcommittee. Twenty-six subpoenas were issued to current and former *Times* employees suspected of being communists. When a few employees refused to answer the subcommittee's questions by citing the Fifth Amendment, the newspaper's response was less than courageous. Publisher Arthur Hays Sulzberger fired the employees on the grounds that they had "sensitive" jobs requiring "trust and confidence." Nevertheless, the newspaper proudly announced that "long after all that was known as McCarthyism is a dim, unwelcome memory, long after the last Congressional committee has learned that it cannot tamper successfully with a free press, *The New York Times* will still be speaking for the men who make it, and only for the men who make it, and speaking, without fear or favor, the truth as it sees it."

Nearly a decade later the *Times* achieved the rare distinction of having its name identified with a landmark court decision protecting freedom of the press. In *New York Times Co. v. Sullivan* (1964), the U.S. Supreme Court held that under the First Amendment, public officials and public figures could not recover for libel for the publication of false and defamatory statements, unless they proved that the statements were made with "actual malice," that is, with knowledge of falsity or in reckless disregard of the truth. The decision significantly expanded freedom of expression by insulating the press from libel suits used to censor news stories on controversial political and social issues.

Less than seven years later, the *Times* again found itself at the center of a landmark First Amendment case. On June 13, 1971, the paper's Sunday edition began publishing *The Pentagon Papers*, a seven-thousand-page top-secret government study of how the United States had gotten involved in the Vietnam War. One journalist has called the publication "probably the single largest unauthorized disclosure of classified documents in the history of the United States." After the Nixon Administration failed to obtain a preliminary injunction restraining further publication of the material, the case swiftly reached the U.S. Supreme Court, which decided in favor of the *Times*. In a *per curiam* opinion written by Justice William J. Brennan, Jr., the Court held that "any system of prior restraints of expression comes to this Court bearing a heavy presumption against its constitutional validity" and that the government had failed to meet its burden of proof. Nine individual opinions were issued. Justice Hugo Black wrote that "every moment's continuance of the injunctions against these newspapers amounts to a flagrant, indefensible, and continuing violation of the First Amendment."

Two decades later former U.S. solicitor general Erwin N. Griswold, who had represented the government before the Supreme Court in *The Pentagon Papers* case, conceded that "in hindsight, it is clear to me that no harm was done by publication of the Pentagon Papers." Far from causing harm, the *Times* had disclosed that successive administrations had misled Congress and the public about American involvement in the Vietnam War. The *Times* had indeed served the highest ideals of journalism and freedom of the press.

See also Black, Hugo; Brennan, William J., Jr.; *New York Times Co. v. Sullivan*; News media censorship; Newspapers; *Pentagon Papers, The.*

New York Times Co. v. Sullivan

COURT: U.S. Supreme Court

DECIDED: March 9, 1964

SIGNIFICANCE: This landmark Supreme Court ruling increased protections of the news media against libel charges made by public officials

On March 20, 1960, a group of African American ministers from Alabama paid to publish a full-page advertisement in *The New York Times* that sought support for the Civil Rights movement in the South, and for Dr. Martin Luther King, Jr., in particular. While accusing no one by name, the advertisement attacked the Montgomery, Alabama, police for performing a variety of illegal acts against black students. Some of the advertisement's allegations were subsequently found to be untrue.

L. B. Sullivan, an elected Montgomery city commissioner responsible for supervising the police, sued the *Times* and the Alabama ministers for libel in an Alabama court, claiming that the published attacks on the police were in effect attacks on him personally. The Alabama court ordered the *Times* to pay Sullivan a half million dollars in damages—at that time the largest libel judgment in Alabama history.

In the civil rights struggle of the 1950's and 1960's, the national media played a crucial role in informing the country as a whole about racial discrimination and injustice in the South. Sullivan's libel suit against the *Times* was considered by many journalists to be a ploy to censor the national media and discourage Northern reporters from covering the struggle to end racial segregation in the South.

On appeal, the Supreme Court of Alabama affirmed the decision against the newspaper. The *Times* then appealed the case to the U.S. Supreme Court which overturned the lower court decisions and created the "*New York Times* rule," or actual malice test. The *New York Times* rule states that under the constitutional guarantees of a free press it was necessary for a public official suing for defamation to prove malice by showing that the media defendants acted with malice in the publication of the allegedly libelous article. The Court defined malice as "the publishing of material knowing it to be false, or with a reckless disregard of whether it is true or false."

The Court concluded that although some of the claims made in the advertisement published in the *Times* were untrue, they were not published with actual malice as defined under the law. The Court ruled that publication of editorial advertisements of the type in question was an important outlet for disseminating information and ideas by persons who did not have easy access to the media. The Court's decision immediately relieved the *Times* and the ministers of the half-million-dollar damage judgment. The decision also had broader implications by removing the threat of large libel judgments against those who criticized racial segregation.

See also Alabama; Civil Rights movement; Court Cases; Defamation; Libel; *New York Times, The*; Police.

News broadcasting

DEFINITION: Delivery of news by radio, television, or other electromagnetic transmission methods

SIGNIFICANCE: In general, the broadcast media have been subjected to greater censorship than the print media

When the U.S. Congress passed the Radio Act of 1927 it did not grant the broadcast media the same freedoms that had applied to newspapers and other print media. The primary justifications for regulation of the broadcast industry, first through the Federal Radio Commission (FRC), and later through the Federal Communications Commission (FCC), have been the relative scarcity of available space on the radio and television frequency spectrums in combination with the larger philosophical belief that the airwaves belong to the public. The concept of public ownership of the airwaves has thus implied greater public—and less private—interest in what is broadcast on the airwaves. One person can privately produce a book; a broadcast, by definition, reaches many.

Through a competitive process, the FCC has licensed broadcast stations to operate "in the public interest, convenience, and necessity." The FCC always has defined a crucial part of this public interest requirement as the broadcasting of a variety of views on controversial issues of public importance. One of the reforms implemented by the Telecommunications Act of 1996 was to increase the periods of broadcasting licenses from five years for television stations and seven years for radio stations to eight years for both. However, the act also made it clear that renewal of licenses would depend, in large measure, upon the stations' fulfillment of the law's public interest programming requirement. Such an expectation of renewal was also to depend upon the broadcaster's possession of a clean record of compliance with other FCC regulations.

Since its formation in 1934 the FCC has utilized a combination of persuasion, intimidation, and the illusion of apparent consensus to influence programming decisions regarding news broadcasting. A major area of concern for regulators has been the possibility that radio and television station owners might allow only the broadcasting of those viewpoints on social issues which they favored, or the airing of opinions only of those political candidates whom they supported. Efforts to prevent censorship of divergent views by station owners has taken three main forms. The first was the fairness doctrine, which directly impacted programming decisions until the FCC abandoned the doctrine under the Reagan Administration in 1986. The second has been the personal attack rule, which originally was part of the fairness doctrine, and which the FCC has continued to enforce. The third area concerns the airing of political editorials.

The Fairness Doctrine. In 1927, 1933, and 1947, Congress tried unsuccessfully to legislate that broadcasters include contrasting views on important social issues in their news coverage. Even in the absence of such a law, however, the federal government declared that balanced coverage was a requirement of news broadcasting that serves the public interest. The old FRC made this point in 1929. The commission ruled that the requirement of fairness applies not only to coverage of political candidates but also "to all discussion of issues of importance to the public." The FCC made a similar statement in a case in 1945, when it reaffirmed "the duty of each station licensee to be sensitive to the problems of public concern in the community and to make sufficient time available, on a non-discriminatory basis, for a full discussion thereof."

The FCC officially implemented its controversial fairness doctrine in 1949 as part of an extensive report, which dealt primarily with rules pertaining to the broadcasting of editorials. The report emphasized the need for broadcasters to play a positive role in bringing about the balanced presentation of opposing viewpoints on important public issues. The fairness doctrine won sanction from Congress in 1959, when lawmakers amended section 315 of the Communications Act to exclude news coverage from the equal opportunity requirements pertaining to candidates for political office. While allowing this exclusion, Congress insisted that broadcasters still must perform according to "the obligation imposed upon them under this Act to operate in the public interest and to afford reasonable opportunity for the discussion of conflicting views on issues of public importance."

The fairness doctrine remained the most bitter issue in broadcast regulation until it finally was abandoned in 1986. Many broadcasters considered the doctrine to be a form of government censorship and a violation of their constitutional protections of freedom of expression and freedom of the press. Many other people believed, however, that requiring broadcasters to provide balanced coverage was the only way to assure such freedom of expression, because it was the only way to be sure that the public would be exposed to a diversity of viewpoints aired over a limited number of privately owned broadcast stations.

The matter came to a legal head in 1969, when the U.S. Supreme Court upheld the doctrine's constitutionality. In the Red Lion Broadcasting case, the justices rejected claims by opponents that the fairness doctrine violated the First Amendment rights of broadcasters by forcing them to include material in their news coverage which they might not otherwise include. The Supreme Court's unanimous ruling rested on the original justification for federal regulation of the broadcast industry as necessary to protect the public from one-sided coverage of significant issues. Justice Byron White summarized the Court's opinion by stating that the public's need for a diversity of viewpoints and information supersedes the broadcaster's right of free speech: "It is the right of the public to receive suitable access to social, political, esthetic, moral, and other ideas and experiences, which is crucial here."

The FCC's method of monitoring stations for violations of the fairness doctrine depended upon complaints by viewers or listeners. Such complaints had to include evidence of violations. Further, the evidence had to indicate a station's failure to provide balanced coverage of a controversial issue in the context of the station's overall programming, not just within a single program or in a single news story. In 1980 more than twenty-one thousand complaints pertaining to violations of the fairness doctrine, equal opportunity, and political broadcasting were filed with the commission. Many of those came from candidates for political offices or their supporters. Of that total, only six complaints resulted in warnings or sanctions against stations by the commission.

One celebrated instance of a fairness doctrine complaint occurred in 1984, when the Central Intelligence Agency (CIA) petitioned the FCC to sanction an American Broadcasting Company (ABC) network news show. The CIA objected to a story in which a Honolulu investment counselor had claimed to be a covert agent who thought that the agency wanted to have him killed. The ABC story included a denial by the CIA, so the complaint was dismissed by the FCC on the grounds that there was insufficient evidence of a violation of the fairness doctrine. This was, however, the first time that the FCC had been officially pressured by another agency of the federal government to retaliate for a news broadcast.

The tide turned against the fairness doctrine in the 1980's. The National Association of Broadcasters long had lobbied against the requirement. One reason was the perception of censorship and a violation of broadcasters' rights. Another reason was the belief that free-market competition with other stations in their own markets, rather than a fear of government reprisal, provided the best incentive for broadcasters to program thorough and balanced coverage of important issues to their audience. As it turned out, however, the most compelling reason, in the commission's view, was the argument that the requirement's practical effect on news broadcasting was exactly the opposite of its intended effect. Broadcasters contended that the fairness doctrine was stifling public debate on matters important to both local communities and the nation.

Rodney King confronts the news media before appearing in court in May, 1992. Repeated television broadcasts of an amateur videotape that had recorded his beating by Los Angeles police transformed an incident that might otherwise have gone unnoticed into a national cause célèbre. (AP/Wide World Photos)

The possibility of being accused of biased news coverage was causing broadcasters to avoid covering controversial issues. This problem was acute among small- and medium-market radio and television stations, which typically lacked resources to wage extended legal battles in the event of a complaint.

In 1986 the FCC decided to cease enforcement of the fairness doctrine. After an extensive evaluation, the commission concluded "that far from serving its intended purpose, the doctrine has a chilling effect on broadcaster's speech." The matter remained a source of controversy, however. Many members of Congress and others in politics favor a return of the fairness doctrine, which, among other things, tends to provide them more access to the airwaves. Since 1986 several unsuccessful attempts have been made in Congress to codify the fairness doctrine into law.

Personal Attack Rule. Although the FCC abandoned the fairness doctrine, it left intact a portion of that doctrine known as the personal attack rule, which was begun in 1967. This rule requires broadcasters to notify any persons or groups whose character, integrity, or other personal qualities have been attacked during broadcasts of views on public issues. Such notifications must occur within a week of the broadcasts, and the stations must provide attacked persons or groups with reasonable opportunities to respond on the air.

The personal attack rule exempts certain kinds of charges so that it will not interfere with news coverage of political campaigns and other public issues. Exempt are attacks made by political candidates or their supporters against other candidates and their supporters. Also exempt are newscasts, news interviews, and on-the-spot news coverage. The rule applies, however, to personal attacks made by anybody as long as those attacks are aired by the station, not just to attacks made by someone who works for the station itself. The constitutionality of the personal attack rule was upheld by the U.S. Supreme Court as part of its ruling in the Red Lion Broadcasting case.

Editorials. The airing of editorials always has been a controversial aspect of broadcast news and public affairs programming. Broadcasters usually consider editorials to be a right or even a public duty. Regulators, on the other hand, often have been concerned about the potential for excluding differing viewpoints. In 1941 the FCC angered broadcasters by ruling that they no longer could editorialize on their stations. The commission revised this ruling in 1949, and stipulated instead that broadcasters had to provide equal access to their airwaves for persons or groups who wished to present opposing viewpoints. The commission later took up the matter of political editorials as part of its implementation of the personal attack rule. Broadcast licensees who endorsed particular candidates were required to notify the candidates' opponents and offer reasonable opportunities for replies. In the event that a station editorial opposed a particular candidate, that candidate must also be given a chance to respond.

Overt Censorship. Although the Communications Act of 1934 specifically prohibited the FCC from censoring the content of news and other broadcasts, overt government and military censorship has occurred during times of international conflict. The government's argument to justify such actions has been that some restrictions to a free press are necessary in order to protect American troops, advance the war effort, prevent enemy agents from using the broadcast media in the United States to send and receive secret codes, and, generally, to ensure the nation's well-being.

During World War II the Office of Censorship was created by President Franklin D. Roosevelt, who insisted that its scope would be limited and that broadcasters would be called upon voluntarily to censor radio programs containing information which might be of value to the enemy. The National Association of Broadcasters complied with the call for voluntary censorship by issuing a wartime guide for radio stations. The code prohibited the broadcast of weather reports and weather-related data, except in cases of emergency, because it was feared that German navy commanders might use the information to plan attacks. The code also called for interview programs to be screened, and prohibited the broadcast of information relating to the location or movement of troops and vessels.

A major area of work for the Office of Censorship throughout the war was investigation of foreign-language programming on radio stations throughout the United States, especially around such large metropolitan areas as New York, Boston, Philadelphia, Detroit, Chicago, Los Angeles, and San Francisco. Station owners were required to have English scripts of the foreign-language programs in advance of broadcasts,

PUBLIC CONFIDENCE IN TELEVISION NEWS

In early 1994 a CNN/*USA Today*/Gallup Poll surveyed Americans to learn how much confidence they had in the news they were getting from television. The results revealed a significant drop in confidence from a poll taken the previous year:

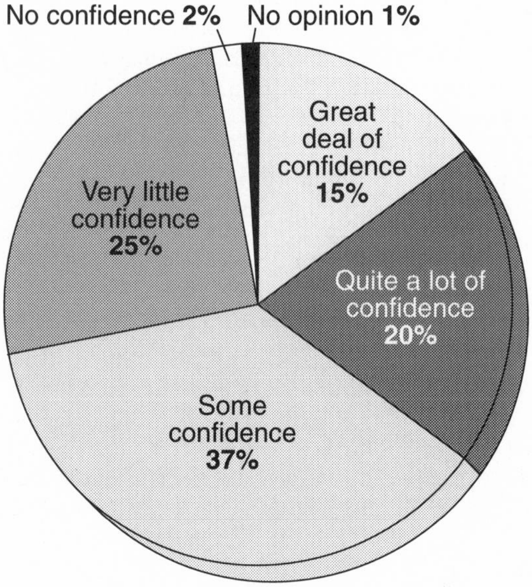

Source: The Gallup Poll: Public Opinion 1994. Wilmington, Del.: Scholarly Resources, 1995.

and station personnel were not allowed to depart from those scripts. Office of Censorship employees also were assigned to monitor American network news commentaries for any material that might compromise the war effort.

In 1990 and 1991 overt military censorship prevented Americans from gaining information from the broadcast news media about the origins and the developments of the Persian Gulf War. The military's insistence on pool coverage kept American reporters away from the front lines and reliant upon the government for video and other information about the conduct of the war. The tactic was a response to a pervasive belief among the military and some others in government that an unfettered American press was responsible for losing the Vietnam War by turning public opinion against the war.

One result of the shortage of independent video from the war was the heavy use of maps and graphic designs in broadcast news reports, along with Pentagon-supplied images of exploding "smart-bombs," which bore a remarkable resemblance to video games. The limitations placed on broadcast news gathering effectively made the war appear less real, less destructive, and less threatening to television viewers than probably otherwise would have been the case. Similar censorship of broadcast and other news outlets through the government's insistence on pool coverage occurred in the 1980's during the American invasions of Grenada and Panama. The trend led an angry Dan Rather of the Columbia Broadcasting System's news department to complain that "politicians have learned ways to intimidate individual reporters, news organizations, and the press in general."

Self-Censorship. A more subtle, yet important, form of censorship has always existed in ways in which broadcasters censor themselves. Robert McNeil, a prominent journalist with the Public Broadcasting System, commented on this phenomenon by observing that in the day-to-day broadcast of news, the public's right to know is qualified by what government officials "choose to tell them and by what information journalists, for a variety of reasons, choose to pursue." Noting that "secrecy is the oldest reality of government," McNeil claimed that relatively little modern news broadcasting could be considered investigative. Instead, reporters commonly simply condense information that they are given by sources—often government sources. This process results in the government, not the news media, directing the public's attention to areas that the government wants the public to be considering.

Certain qualities unique to broadcast news make it especially vulnerable to these subtle forms of self-censorship. One is the fast pace of most radio and television news formats, which allow little room for analysis, investigation, or questioning beyond a story's most basic elements. Because broadcast news typically reports both simple and complex stories through the time-limited format, there is little time for serious consideration of subtleties. The need for visual elements to illustrate stories adds another obstacle to television news reporting. Many stories, although important and stimulating, are not pursued because they would not provide sufficiently entertaining visual images. This accelerated, fleeting, and often superficial style has created, critics argue, a tendency in broadcast news to impart facts without necessarily establishing context—historical or otherwise. The energies of broadcast news reporters tend to be concentrated on the basic task of disseminating information, rather than on the arguably more important one of deepening the audiences' understanding of the significance of that information. —*Gerard Donnelly*

See also Blackstone, William; Cable News Network; Communications Act of 1934; Fairness doctrine; Federal Communications Commission; Gag order; News media censorship; Obscenity: legal definitions; *Pentagon Papers, The*; Press-radio war; Prior restraint; Radio; Television; Television networks; Vietnam War; World War II.

BIBLIOGRAPHY

Robert A. Liston's *The Right to Know: Censorship in America* (New York: Franklin Watts, 1973) offers insights into how the nature of the television news medium makes it vulnerable to censorship and coercion. A discussion of why the public interest requirements of stations were not changed by the abolition of the fairness doctrine can be found in Hugh Carter Donohue's *The Battle to Control Broadcast News: Who Owns the First Amendment?* (Cambridge, Mass.: MIT Press, 1989). Ford Rowan examines the fairness doctrine in *Broadcast Fairness: Doctrine, Practice, Prospects* (New York: Longman, 1984). *Mass Media Law*, by Don R. Pember (Dubuque, Iowa: Wm. C. Brown, 1987), provides an overview of the history of broadcast regulation, including the controversial fairness doctrine. Robert McNeil's comments about the process of broadcast news reporting were part of a speech broadcast by National Public Radio and available on "Robert McNeil and Dan Rather on the Media: What People Have the Right to Know and What They Don't" (Washington, D.C.: NPR Audio Cassette, 1981). John R. McArthur in *Second Front: Censorship and Propaganda in the Gulf War* (New York: Hill & Wang, 1992) explores the Bush Administration's manipulation of the broadcast news media leading up to and during the conflict. An excellent article about the radio industry's cooperation with government during World War II can be found in Ronald Garay's "Guarding the Airwaves: Government Regulation of World War II American Radio" in the *Journal of Radio Studies* 3 (1995-1996). The relative nature of terms such as free speech, freedom of expression, and freedom of the press comes under scrutiny in M. Ethan Katsh's *The Electronic Media and the Transformation of Law* (New York: Oxford University Press, 1989).

News media censorship

DEFINITION: The suppression of news reporting

SIGNIFICANCE: An informed, activist public is championed as the basis of democracy; censorship of the news media undermines democracy

Censorship has a long and scurrilous history that dates back to long before the invention of the printing press. Censorship's longevity has not contributed to a universal understanding of what censorship is or of the various forms in which it is manifested. Definitions of censorship are as varied and numerous as the scholars, politicians, and lexicographers who address the subject.

Historically, censorship can be placed into three basic categories: religious censorship, political censorship, and censorship of obscenities. Religion was an early source of censorship, with nonbelievers and infidels punished for blasphemy and heresy. Next came the censorship of unacceptable political ideas, with the disloyal renegades who disagreed with the prevailing powers being prosecuted for treason. In more recent times, punishment has been given to those who utter obscenities, distribute pornography, or even want to discuss safe sex.

Censorship of News. In the twentieth century a fourth important category—the censorship of news—came to be. Concurrent with the advent of television, the increasing value of information, and the power of advertising, news media censorship and self-censorship became a powerful influence. This critical form of censorship disturbs the free flow of news that warns a society of its problems. Without freedom of the press, a society becomes vulnerable to censorship of other forms, including religion, politics, and morals. Ironically, the United States, without equal in the twentieth century in terms of communications technology, appears to have suffered a breakdown when it comes to communications content. High technology does not guarantee a well-informed society.

As a result of late-twentieth century advances in communications technology, combined with the explosion in computer sciences, the average citizen became exposed to more information, at a greater speed, from throughout the world, as well as space, than had been available to political leaders not too many years before.

But the problem has not been with the quantity of information available, which sometimes seems to reach an overload level, but rather with the quality of that information. When a problem arises, there should be a warning signal—information—that alerts citizens that something is wrong that needs attention and resolution. An aware and informed populace could then influence its leaders to act upon that information in an effort to solve the problem. For such to happen, society needs a watchdog press to issue those warning signals. This should be the role of a free and aggressive press. Instead, critics have argued that the media have become the willing tools of the propagandists. Jacques Ellul warns in *Propaganda: The Formation of Men's Attitudes* (1968) that corporate, political, and military propagandists have become so skilled that the public is often not even aware it is being manipulated.

Media Monopoly. The primary sources of news and information for most people have come under the control of a small group. As media scholar Ben Bagdikian points out in *The Media Monopoly* (1992), fewer than twenty corporations controlled, at that time, most of the nation's mass media. Such a monopolistic control of the media promotes and enhances certain issues and individuals and provides limited or no coverage to other issues and individuals.

The media might not conspire to control the media messages, but there is little doubt that they share personal values and interests, which influence those messages. Thus, it is not surprising to find a variety of factors operating, when combined, that lead to the systematic failure of the news media to fully inform the public. While such is not an overt form of censorship, it is real and dangerous.

Reasons for Censorship. The traditional explanations for why some stories are not covered are plentiful. Sometimes a source for a story is not considered to be reliable. Other times the story does not have an easily identifiable beginning, middle, and end. Some stories are considered to be too complex for the general public. Stories are ignored because they have not been blessed by being told in *The New York Times*. Reporters and editors at other media outlets, electronic as well as print, know their news judgment is not going to be challenged when they produce and publish stories that someone else has already found important, a practice that leads to the herd phenomenon in journalism.

Another major factor contributing to media self-censorship is that the censored story is considered potentially libelous. There is no question that long and costly jury trials, and sometimes multi-million-dollar judgments against the media, have produced a massive chilling effect on the press. Another reason why some stories are not covered is that they do not fit the conventional definitions of news. This, of course, is why it is time for journalism to rethink its definitions of news. Real news is not repetitive, sensationalistic coverage of events that will raise ratings or circulation.

Real news is objective and reliable information about important events that affect the lives of the public. The widespread dissemination of such information helps people become better informed, and a better informed public can elect politicians who are more responsive to its needs.

The explanation for much of the censorship that occurs in the mainstream media is the media's bottom line. Corporate media executives perceive their primary, and often sole, responsibility to be to maximize profits, not inform the public. Many of the stories that can be cited as undercovered, overlooked, or censored are contrary in some way to the financial interests of publishers, owners, stockholders, or advertisers. Investigative journalism, moreover, is more expensive than the so-called public stenography school of journalism that came to dominate the field in the twentieth century. The mentality that pervades corporate media boardrooms pervades the newsroom.

News Media Censorship. Project Censored, the national news media research project founded in 1976, focuses on this new form of censorship and offers the definition of news media censorship:

First, it assumes that real and meaningful public involvement in societal decisions is possible only if a wide array of ideas are allowed to compete daily in the media marketplace for public awareness, acceptance, and understanding.

Next, it recognizes that the mass media, particularly the network television evening news programs, are the public's primary sources of information for what is happening in the world. If, however, the public does not receive all the information it needs to make informed decisions, then some form of news blackout is taking place.

In brief, then, news media censorship is defined as the suppression of news, whether purposeful or not, by any method—including bias, omission, under-reporting, or self-censorship—that prevents the public from fully knowing what is happening in the world.

A classic example of news media censorship is in the story of cigarette smoking and cancer.

Cigarettes and Cancer. In 1933 Dr. Raymond Pearl, of the Department of Biology at The Johns Hopkins University, launched a study of smokers to explore the influence of tobacco on human longevity. In 1938 he released the results of his study of seven thousand subjects, which concluded that tobacco shortens the life of everyone who uses it. The study, an early warning signal about the dangers of smoking, was ignored by the major news media. Journalist and media critic George Seldes recounts in *Never Tire of Protesting* (1968) how America's press suppressed that and other stories that reflected badly on a major advertiser, the tobacco industry.

In 1995 the American Medical Association, in a rare single-subject issue of the *Journal of the American Medical Association*, exposed the tobacco companies for their long cover-up of the hazards of smoking. The special issue and its extraordinary implications were well publicized in the national news media. The herd effect overcame the tendency to self-censorship.

In December, 1983, a decade earlier, the *New York State Journal of Medicine*, another well-respected medical journal, published a similar single-subject issue on the link between tobacco and cancer. The national news media ignored the story at that time. Since 1938, there were many stories about the dangers of tobacco that deserved, but did not receive, page-one treatment.

On January 16, 1939, Harold L. Ickes, Secretary of the Interior under Franklin D. Roosevelt, participated in a nationally broadcast Town Hall of the Air program. During the program, Ickes announced: "I understand that at Johns Hopkins University there is a very sensational finding resulting from the study of the effect of cigarette smoking that has not appeared, so far as I know, in any newspaper in the United States. I wonder if that is because the tobacco companies are such large advertisers."

Fighting News Media Censorship. In addition to Project Censored, a number of organizations have begun to fight news media censorship. Such groups include Article 19, First Amendment Congress, Fairness and Accuracy in Reporting, Freedom Forum, Media Alliance, National Coalition Against Censorship, People for the American Way, Student Press Law Center, and the Women's Institute for Freedom of the Press.

—Carl M. Jensen

See also Advertisers as advocates of censorship; Advertising as the target of censorship; Broadcast media; Junk food news; News broadcasting; Newspapers; Newsreels; Press-radio war; Project Censored; Project Censored Canada; Seldes, George; Smoking; Sports news.

Bibliography

Frank L. Mott's *American Journalism: A History of Newspapers in the United States Through 250 Years, 1690-1940* (New York: Macmillan, 1942) and Robert A. Liston's *The Right to Know: Censorship in America* (New York: Franklin Watts, 1973) are good starting points for any study of news media censorship in the United States. Kevin Boyle, ed., *Article 19: Information, Freedom, and Censorship* (New York: New York Times Books, 1988), examines the international human rights group that fosters free expression. In *Don't Blame the People* (New York: Random House, 1972), Robert Cirino discusses the various types of bias that affect news reporting. Carl Jensen's *Censored: The News That Didn't Make the News—and Why* (New York: Four Walls Eight Windows, 1995) is Project Censored's annual review of major stories that are underreported. Among George Seldes' many books *Never Tire of Protesting* (New York: Lyle Stuart, 1968) is a particularly interesting account of the censorship that he encountered as a journalist.

Newspapers

Definition: Printed summaries of news, usually prepared for mass public circulation

Significance: Throughout the world newspapers have long served as the public's most important sources of news, and have thus been primary targets of government efforts to control what the public knows

Governments have used a variety of methods to impose censorship on newspapers: legal restraints, economic and political constraints, secrecy, direct censorship, and force. Legal restraints take the form of constitutional restrictions on freedom of the press and press-related criminal laws. Economic and political constraints manifest in bribes and subsidies to journalists, favorable distribution of newsprint and government advertising, and restriction in the distribution of antigovernment papers. Under the secrecy constraint, governments practice censorship by disallowing access to public records and government sources. Many governments also impose direct censorship. Physical threats—including murders and assaults of journalists and arson—are not uncommon. Aside from governments, pressure and terrorist groups resort to intimidating newspapers around the world.

Africa. In comparison to other continents the African press is small. European colonial powers did little to stimulate the growth of newspapers and practiced censorship, which continued after the independence of African states. Governments have employed various tactics to keep the newspapers under control, including licensing of journalists and publications, controlling distribution of newsprint and government advertising, detaining reporters without charge or trial, imprisoning journalists, seeking security deposits from papers, using libel and criminal laws, and executing journalists. In the mid-1990's few African countries did not have press restrictions. In Botswana, Namibia, and South Africa, censorship had eased. Press freedom was prevalent in Cameroon, Kenya, and Zambia. Newspapers in Gabon, Mali, Sierra Leone, and Togo were not harassed very much, but strict controls remained in effect in Nigeria, Sudan, and Zaire.

The ruling party and military leadership controlled newspapers after Algeria attained independence from France. After the ouster of President Ben Bella in 1965 following a *coup d'état*, stringent censorship was introduced—including the suppression of two dailies. In the face of an armed conflict with Islamic groups, the government placed stringent controls on the press. For their transgressions, six newspapers were suspended for periods ranging from two weeks to six months in 1994, and copies of the most circulated Arabic-language daily were seized.

Newspapers in Nigeria have long fared badly. Having learned censorship methods from the British colonial regime, Nigeria applied them against critical newspapers. For example, after an election in 1965 two national newspaper editors were arrested for sedition and false publication and a number of other newspapers were banned for supporting the opposition. Censorship was imposed after a military coup in 1966. During the Biafran civil war from 1967 to 1970, censorship was placed on all papers. A series of coups since then hobbled the press. A press baron, Mashood Abiola, won the presidential election in 1993, but the ruler, General Ibrahim Babangida, annulled the election. In November, 1993, General Sani Abacha seized power and banned all newspapers belonging to Abiola and his supporters. Three of Nigeria's largest media businesses were shut down for seeking the reinstatement of Abiola as president, bringing about the cessation of fifteen leading papers. Further, detention was used as a censorship tool by the military governments from 1966 to 1979 and was revived by Abacha.

Under South Africa's white apartheid government newspapers were supposedly free of censorship, but the press was subjected to police raids and searches for printing critical news and commentary. With the advent of a black majority government of Nelson Mandela for the first time in 1994, newspapers attained a large degree of freedom.

The white minority government of Ian Smith imposed direct censorship on newspapers of what was then called Rhodesia in November, 1965. Newspapers protested by leaving blank spaces—showing where the government had censored—and stating that they were under censorship. In February, 1966, laws were enacted forbidding the newspapers from doing so. Moreover, newspapers were subjected to postpublication censorship during the Smith regime. Copies of newspapers on sale were confiscated and newspaper offices closed for criticizing the government. The same law remained under Zimbabwe's black majority government of Robert Mugabe, who came to power in 1980. The largest independent daily, the *Daily Gazette*, closed down in 1994 for financial reasons as it faced expensive libel suits and harassment from the secret police.

Asia and the Pacific. The history of newspaper publication is an ancient one; so is the legacy of censorship. China, where printing began and the first continuous newspaper appeared, along with North Korea and other Asian communist nations, has been subjected to strict press controls. The other Asian giant—India—has a record of censorship although it has attempted since its independence to allow press freedom. India's neighbors, Pakistan and Bangladesh, have seen considerable press restrictions. Censorship has been often imposed on the newspapers of the Pacific-Rim nations too. Japan has not seen any government censorship since World War II. Australia and New Zealand's newspapers have rarely been subjected to censorship.

China's papers have always been subjected to censorship. The emperors made sure that nothing was said of a critical nature against them. Little objective news reporting was carried out during the Sino-Japanese war because of stringent censorship. During the Chiang Kai-shek rule press controls remained in place. With the advent of the communist government in 1949, newspapers were brought under government control. All newspapers had to register and those found in opposition to the communist philosophy were denied permits, resulting in the closure of several hundred newspapers. The Soviet-style press concept became the norm, whereby newspapers had to toe the party line and receive clearance from the government to print sensitive news. In 1960 the Chinese newspapers were put under control of the Communist Party, with the first secretaries of the provincial party committees taking charge of the newspapers and many members of the party working as journalists. Although not experiencing communist-style control, Taiwanese newspapers remained under censorship during and after President Chiang Kai-shek's rule. From the late 1940's until the late 1970's, Taiwan remained under martial law. In 1958, a restrictive press law was enacted, bringing about self-censorship on the part of newspapers.

The *Bengal Gazette*, the first newspaper in India, began in 1780; it was immediately censored for criticizing the wife of the British governor general. Not only was the newspaper banned, its printing presses were also seized. Until the British left in 1947, newspapers were tightly regulated through licensing, press laws, and penal laws. Vernacular newspapers were especially censored because the colonial regime felt they were fomenting the independence movement. After independence, the most notable period of censorship was from 1975 to 1977 when Prime Minister Indira Gandhi declared a national emergency. Antigovernment newspapers came out with blank spaces to show the work of government censors; newspapers were banned; electricity was cut off to newspapers; and journalists were jailed. Political pressure groups have also acted as censors in Indian states, notably the Punjab and Kashmir, where rebellions against the government have taken place.

Censorship has been common for newspapers in Pakistan, especially under its series of military dictatorships. Pakistani newspapers have endured direct censorship, government control of newsprint and government advertising, registration of newspapers, demands for security deposits, prison terms for journalists, flogging of journalists, and the killing of journalists. Bangladesh has used most of these censorship tactics against its papers, learned from Pakistan as well as the British colonial authorities.

The Pacific Rim Nations. Countries such as Indonesia, Malaysia, Philippines, Singapore, and South Korea have opted for free-market economies, but criticisms of their governments have not been well tolerated. Thus, censorship has been common. In Indonesia, during the regime of President Sukarno, newspapers were kept under strict censorship. That continued under the regime of his successor, General Suharto, who took power in 1967. Anything critical about the national ideology was forbidden to be printed. More than twenty newspapers lost their licenses between 1973 and 1976, including the temporary closure of the daily *Sinar Harapan*. In 1994, the Suharto government banned three publications. Editors began practicing self-censorship.

In the Philippines, newspapers were the freest in Asia until 1972, when President Ferdinand Marcos declared martial law, took most of the important newspapers, and gave them to his cronies. He also established a media council to oversee the press. Even after martial law was withdrawn in 1981, newspapers avoided printing criticism about Marcos. In Singapore, rigid controls have long existed. The government has retained the right to ban critical papers. Search and seizure, without warrants, of banned newspapers have been also allowed. In 1982 a retired military officer was installed as a censor in the office of the *Strait Times*. The Official Secrets Act and the Internal Security Act made the editors practice self-censorship. Censorship has long prevailed for newspapers of both North and South Korea. Ever since the communists came to power in North Korea, newspapers were placed under very stringent Soviet-style censorship. In South Korea the number of newspapers was reduced in 1981. News has been subjected to military censorship. Journalists who have violated national security laws have been barred from practicing journalism for three years after they served their jail sentences. Moreover, access to public information has been disallowed if it obstructed official work or damaged public or private interests.

In Japan, after World War II, newspapers were allowed in the 1946 constitution's guarantee of press freedom. Japanese newspapers have, however, practiced self restraint, not printing anything that has gone against the national interest and the monarchy. Before World War II, the press experienced official censorship on many occasions. After the establishment of the first paper in 1862, the press operated under a certain degree of freedom, but newspapers were punished with fines, seizures of copies, and jail terms for reporters and editors. With the rise of the military to power in the 1930's the press was brought under complete control, allowed only the publication of material sanctioned by the authorities. This censorship continued until 1945 when American forces occupied Japan. Under American occupation, there was prepublication censorship, which was eased in 1948 and lifted in 1952. In Malaysia, the same kind of restrictions as those of Singapore have existed for Malaysian newspapers. Papers have faced loss of their licenses for printing distorted news dealing with communal problems or with law and order. In addition, newspapers have been disallowed from commenting on issues such as the national language, citizenship, and the special rights for Malays and the monarchy.

Europe. Until the end of World War II, censorship prevailed in one form or another in most of Europe. After 1945 censorship became routine for the newspapers in the communist nations, while Western Europe allowed almost total freedom of the press. With the collapse of communism in the late 1980's the threat of censorship became less obvious in all Europe.

In France, newspapers were under strict censorship during the reign of Napoleon. Although noted as being corrupt and openly receiving subsidies before World War II, French newspapers experienced direct censorship in the twentieth century when the Germans occupied France in 1940. During the German occupation, many papers continued publication under the direction of the Nazis; others closed down. Some others appeared as resistance papers. The staff of two such newspapers were executed by German firing squads. In 1958 the government of President Charles De Gaulle enacted Article 16 to the constitution, allowing the head of the state to take any action against the press. Further, legal restrictions have disallowed the publication of judicial, government, or military information unless cleared by the government.

Germany has also seen its share of censorship. The Weimar Republic's constitutional guarantee of press freedom was repealed in 1933 as Adolf Hitler came to power. The press was turned into a state entity and remained under strict censorship until his defeat. Under Allied occupation, American, French, and British military authorities licensed newspapers and forbade them to publish fascist and communist news and information. In 1950 the military authorities banned communist newspapers, as did the government of the Federal Republic of West Germany, which also forbade the publication of Nazi papers. Post-World War II newspapers have lived with the threat of being banned for publishing any false allegations against the military. The Soviet Union's control over East Germany influenced this zone's newspapers. Censorship was much stricter in the East than it was in the West.

Censorship was practiced in modern Greece even before the military seized power in 1967, allowing the government to seize and shut down newspapers. As a distributor of newsprint and government advertising, Greek governments have wielded economic leverage over the press. The return of civilian authorities in 1974 failed to return the newspapers to complete freedom. The restrictive laws of the military dictators remained in effect.

In Italy censorship for newspapers existed until 1848, when press freedom was specified in the constitution. That freedom started to erode after 1922 with the rise of the Fascist Party, which cowed the newspapers into supporting its policies. In 1924 newspapers were brought under control of the Fascist government through a decree that forbade the publication of any item that would embarrass the government. The defeat of Benito Mussolini in 1943 revived Italy's press freedom.

European communist nations followed the Soviet system of press control, in which criticism of the government and the Communist Party was disallowed because newspapers were looked upon as organs of the state and the party. Editors of the important newspapers also held important positions in the Communist Party. Detailed orders were issued to all newspapers on a regular basis. The first Russian paper, *Viedmosti*, appeared in Moscow in 1702 under the sponsorship of Peter the Great. From that first beginning and throughout the reign of the czars, the Russian press remained under constant censorship. However, newspapers attained more freedom with the dismantling of the Soviet Union and the democratization of eastern Europe after the collapse of the Berlin Wall in 1989.

Newspapers in Spain and Portugal have been subjected to direct censorship for most of the twentieth century. With the rise of Francisco Franco to power in 1936, Spanish newspapers were brought under the control of the government and many eliminated, especially through a law passed in 1938. Appropriate government departments telephoned their directives to the newspapers, while the information ministry approved all items to be printed. Any newspaper that dared to dissent was punished. For example, *Informaciones* had its newsprint quota reduced. After the death of Franco and the restoration of the monarchy, the press remained shackled because of the holdover bureaucrats from the previous regime. The newspapers of Portugal suffered the same fate as those of Spain when in 1926 the government first came under the control of Antonio Carmona and, after 1932, Antonio de Olivera Salazar. A 1936 decree placed censorship on Portuguese papers. Portugal dealt sternly with all signs of opposition until 1974, when the authoritarian regime was replaced and most press restrictions were lifted.

Great Britain. As early as the 1530's, recognizing the power of printing, King Henry VIII required printers to be licensed. In addition, prior restraint became a reality as printers refused to print anything offensive against the monarch, a practice that lasted for three hundred more years. Queen Elizabeth I devised a governmental body to punish transgressing printers severely. Selected imposition of taxes was employed to drive printers out of business. The law of seditious libel (criticism of the government) further kept the printers from criticism of the monarchy. James I used the Star Chamber to suppress the newssheets. British newssheets first appeared in 1621, with the *Oxford Gazette* (later called the *London Gazette*) becoming the first regularly published English newspaper in 1665. Throughout the fifteenth and sixteenth centuries restrictions on printers continued. By the end of the seventeenth century, restraints started to ease after poet John Milton's plea for freedom of the press in 1644 in *Areopagitica*. Official censorship has not been imposed since 1695, although a voluntary censorship was in place during World War II. Nevertheless, British newspapers have been subject to stern libel laws, the Official Secrets Act, and contempt of court restrictions.

Latin America. The first newssheet appeared in Lima, Peru, as early as 1594—a century before the appearance of the first newspaper in the United States—but it was not until 1773 that the first regularly published Latin American newspaper came out. The Spanish colonial authorities forcefully kept out dissension from the papers. Independence of the Latin American nations, however, failed to lift restraints from the papers. Governments have been intolerant of criticism, especially of public officials, a Spanish and Portuguese tradition. Authoritarian rule and political crises have provided the impetus for censorship on the Latin American press.

After 1930, when the military took over Argentina, newspapers faced censorship and a variety of other controls, such as withholding of newsprint. Censorship became very harsh as Juan Perón took over the reins of the government in 1946, continuing through 1955 until his overthrow. He shut down many papers, and his wife, Eva Perón, bought three of them. For its anti-Peronist stance, *La Prensa* was taken over in 1951 but restored to its owners after the fall of Perón. Disrespect for the president and other public officials was made punishable with a jail sentence with a maximum of three years. In 1962 the press was again subjected to stringent censorship as President Ongania took control of the government. Newspapers were closed and journalists jailed. In the mid-1990's the government of President Carlos Menem attempted to control the press by amending the penal laws and tightening the libel and defamation laws and making newspapers purchase $500,000 libel insurance.

Newspapers in Brazil have seen their share of censorship. Strict censorship was imposed on the press following the revolution in 1931. In February, 1956, two newspapers were seized. In 1967 a press law passed by the military government imposed censorship. It remained in the books in the 1990's, acting as a deterrent against critical newspapers. In Chile, the specter of censorship became a reality in 1931, when any writing against the national ideology was made an offense punishable by exile. After 1968 the Salvador Allende government began placing restrictions on Chilean newspapers. The military government that ousted Allende censored news about communists, Marxists, and leftists, and stories that questioned its legitimacy. In the mid-1990's the licensing of journalists was revived.

In Colombia, the arrival of President Gustavo Rojas Pinilla in 1953 brought about censorship to the point of closing down three newspapers, including Bogota's *El Tiempo*. For allegedly misreporting results of the presidential elections, censorship was imposed in the spring of 1970. Self-censorship has also been prevalent due to pressures from the drug barons. In Cuba, Fidel Castro's takeover brought Soviet-style press censorship, eliminating the private press. From a total of sixteen newspapers published from Havana before the revolution, four remained, with *Hoy* becoming the government mouthpiece. Journalists have practiced self-censorship, guided by the government and party leaders, in support of national development and party ideology. In Mexico, which claims the first newspaper in North America, *Gaceta*, in 1671, Mexican newspapers have seen censorship in tandem with national history. In spite of being guaranteed press freedom in the 1812 Spanish constitution, sixteen publications—including *El Pensador Mexicano*, were shut down. A newsprint distribution body was established in 1935 that has permanently withheld newsprint from six publications. In addition, the Comisión Calificadora de Publicaciones, with the government's blessing, put in a code of ethics—restricting newspapers from criticizing the government. In Venezuela, from the beginning of the twentieth century to 1958, newspapers had to contend with censorship. With the advent of dictatorships, censorship was reinstated several times. When the Communist Party was banned, the party's publications were prohibited. In late 1994 Latin America's most stringent licensing law of journalists was put into effect.

The Middle East. The first newspaper in this region began shortly after Napoleon Bonaparte introduced the printing press to Egypt at the end of the eighteenth century. However, the press enjoyed very little freedom because Middle Eastern rulers have seen newspapers as tools of nationalism and politics. Thus, papers have always been under government control. Iran, Israel, Jordan, Kuwait, Lebanon, Saudi Arabia, Turkey, and the United Arab Emirates have privately owned newspapers, but they have faced threats of censorship on a daily basis. Any criticism of the government and the monarchy has brought harsh recriminations. Algeria, Egypt, Iraq, Libya, and Syria have seen their newspapers nationalized or destroyed.

Press censorship was imposed in Egypt in 1939, when the British colonial regime declared martial law. In 1954 President Gamal Abdul Nasser lifted that censorship for a month before he clamped down again as the press criticized him. The Egyptian press was nationalized in 1960, and the ownership transferred to the only legal political party—the Arab Socialist Union—until the emergence in 1976 of a multiparty system in which only political parties could own newspapers. President Anwar Sadat set up a press council in 1975 to approve the publication of newspapers and license journalists. In response to criticism and armed Islamic opposition, the government of Hosni Mubarak attempted censorship through amendments to the Political Parties Law, prosecution of journalists in military courts, and other harassing tactics.

After visiting Turkey in 1867, Mark Twain commented on the proclivity of the country's Ottoman rulers to suppress newspapers in The Innocents Abroad *(1869), in which this illustration appeared.* (Arkent Archive)

The legacy of censorship is a long one in Iraq. In 1958 two newspapers, *Al Akhbar* and *Al Nas*, were shut down because they exhibited antinationalistic tendencies. Private papers have been disallowed. On coming to power, the ruling Ba'ath Socialist Party took over ownership of all newspapers. The Ministry of Information was given the right to distribute newsprint and advertising. Any dissent in the press has been suppressed with direct censorship and even execution of journalists. In Iran under the shahs, Iranian papers had very little freedom. The 1979 Islamic Revolutionary Government's constitution specified press freedom, but the acquisition of publishing licenses from the government has tempered the writings in Iranian newspapers. Israeli newspapers theoretically have not been subjected to censorship, but military censorship has prevailed since 1948 regarding the publication of national security information. In the occupied Palestinian territories Israel kept a tight leash on the press. Palestinian reporters were harassed, assaulted, imprisoned, and shot. Censorship eased on the Palestinian newspapers in 1994 as Israel and the Palestinians signed a peace treaty. Freedom of the press was guaranteed in Turkey's constitution, but the reality has been otherwise. Stringent press laws, government control of newsprint, and advertising have kept the press under control. A 1954 law provided for heavy fines and jail sentences for defaming public officials. In order to stem the Kurdish separatist movement, the Turkish Anti-Terror Law, which prohibited separatist propaganda, came in handy in the 1990's to punish the press. Papers have been shut down and issues confiscated.

Canada. The first Canadian newspaper, the *Halifax Gazette*, published in 1752 in Nova Scotia, came out in an atmosphere of censorship that lasted until the beginning of the nineteenth century. Unlike the United States, Canadian newspapers have faced a number of restrictive laws. Ontario and Nova Scotia directly adopted a provision of the British Libel Act of 1952 that made it unnecessary for using the plea of the truth as a defense in every allegation made. The law of contempt of court has kept Canadian papers from commenting about a trial in progress or the integrity of the judiciary. In 1959 the law was strengthened to keep out admissions or confessions in preliminary hearings. Canadian journalists have not enjoyed protection from revealing sources. Another press restraint is the revised section of the 1954 law of sedition that states that anybody who publishes and circulates writing that calls for extra-legal methods in the overthrow of the Canadian government has seditious intention.

United States. Similar to Canada, the newspapers in the United States began under censorship of the British colonial regime. Facing licensing, direct censorship, and seditious libel, in 1690 Benjamin Harris published the first American newspaper—*Publick Occurrences, Both Foreign and Domestick* without authority. No sooner did Harris bring out the paper, he fell victim of the colonial government's licensing act. The paper was banned, and he was put in prison. The punishment delayed the publication of the first true American newspaper for another fourteen years until the publication of the *Boston News-Letter*. In the 1720's, James Franklin, older brother of Benjamin Franklin, brought out the *New England Courant* without a license. For that and criticism of the colonial authorities and the church, James Franklin was cited for contempt and given a jail sentence. On his release from the prison, he continued to publish the newspaper while the government forbade him to do so. A grand jury, however, refused to charge him. Thus, the licensing law, despite being in the books, was unenforced. The authorities used the law of seditious libel against John Peter Zenger, who was hired by the opponents of colonial Governor William Cosby to bring out the *New York Weekly Journal* in 1733. For criticism of the governor's policies, Zenger was tried, and in 1735 a jury acquitted him at the urging of Zenger's lawyer, Andrew Hamilton, who told the jury that his client had indeed printed the offensive material against the governor but the material was true. Therefore, Hamilton argued that Zenger had not committed seditious libel. The government bowed again to public opinion, establishing the right to criticize public officials. In 1765 the British government attempted to control the American press through the passage in the British Parliament of the Stamp Act, which levied a stiff tariff on newspapers. Hardly any newspaper paid the tax. Ten years after the tax was imposed, the American colonies rebelled and the newspapers of the Revolutionary War fiercely supported the Revolution. With the birth of the United States of America, newspapers supporting the British regime stopped publication. The First Amendment to the U.S. Constitution guarantees that "Congress shall make no law . . . abridging the freedom of speech, or of the press." Nevertheless, Congress enacted the Sedition Act of 1798, which made criminal writing anything that was false, malicious, and scandalous and that defamed and brought disrepute to the government, members of Congress, or the president. Two years later the act was allowed to lapse. After a court applied Minnesota's gag law of 1925 against a Minneapolis newspaper for accusing city officials of corruption, the U.S. Supreme Court held the Minnesota law unconstitutional because it allowed prior restraint on publications, stating that suppression was more dangerous than any capricious attack on public officials in *Near v. Minnesota* (1931).

In 1971 the U.S. government attempted another imposition of prior restraint on newspapers. Earlier that year *The New York Times* acquired a government report on the Vietnam War and printed the first installment. The Department of Justice obtained a temporary restraining order, which the Supreme Court upheld. On hearing arguments, however, the Court lifted the injunctions and the Pentagon Papers were published by many newspapers. —*Niaz Ahmed Khan*

See also Colonialism; First Amendment; Junk food news; Military censorship; *New York Times, The*; News broadcasting; News media censorship; Newspapers, African American; Newspapers, student; Newspapers, underground; Newsreels; Pressure groups; Stamp Act; Zenger, John Peter.

Bibliography

A worldwide survey of censorship and other restraints on the press is examined on a yearly basis by the Committee to Protect Journalists in *Attacks on the Press* (1985-) through a brief background of each nation's press. Considered to be one of the definitive histories of American newspapers, Edwin Emery and Michael Emery's *The Press and America* (Englewood Cliffs, N.J.: Prentice-Hall, 1978) provides insights into the American press and the censorship history of Great Britain. Since 1952 the International Press Institute has issued a monthly magazine, the *IPI Report*, which features comprehensive, country-by-country freedom reports. John C. Merrill's *A Handbook of Foreign Press* (Baton Rouge: Louisiana State University Press, 1959) provides an excellent background of the international press, with many notable examples of censorship in each of the countries that existed then. Merrill has also edited a similar study, *A Survey of the World's Mass Media* (New York: Longman, 1995). This book also included the standing of the foreign broadcasting media. The survey covers more updated cases of censorship. Specifically written about the press of Third World nations, Ernest Lloyd Sommerlad's *The Press in Developing Countries* (University Park: Pennsylvania State University Press, 1966), along with a history of the press, provides many pertinent examples of censorship. A British periodical, brought out since 1972 by the Writers and Scholars Institute, is *Index on Censorship*, which notes censorship steps taken around the world.

Newspapers, African American

Definition: Newspapers specifically intended for African American communities

Significance: African American newspapers have been targeted for censorship; they have also published news that other newspapers have neglected

Freedom's Journal (edited and published by Samuel Cornish and John B. Russwurm beginning in 1827) is commemorated as the first newspaper issued by African Americans in the United States. The journal established a medium of expression for news about activities among African Americans and as editorial defense against attacks made by the *Daily Press of New York City* against free blacks. The journal was a mechanism to combat the censoring of African American experience. The African American press printed racial news that generally was left out of white newspapers. Black press censorship has included various schemes for screening either who may publish or what may be published.

The *Mirror of Liberty* was the first African American periodical published in New York (July, 1838). *The North Star*, the newspaper of the celebrated abolitionist Frederick Douglass, appeared in Rochester, New York, on December 3, 1847. African American newspapers evoked severe reactions from whites. Several cities tried to prevent the distribution of black newspapers. Representative of African American journalism's long tradition of protest, the *Defender*, an Arkansas paper, printed the daily review of brutality and outrage against African American expression. The *Defender* argued strenuously against the Black Codes of 1865. The codes were enacted to regulate the status and conduct of newly freed slaves. An Arkansas judge issued an injunction restraining circulation of the *Defender*, and two distributors of the paper were attacked and killed, although black newspapers in Arkansas were not sensational and declined to endorse radicalism. The black press in Arkansas in the decades following the Civil War advocated a philosophy of self-help and called upon the black community to prove itself worthy of advancement.

President Franklin Delano Roosevelt was encouraged to

indict some black editors for sedition, in order to curb the black press. Warren Brown was troubled by the aggressive tone of the black press. Brown's attack on the black press was published in December, 1942, in the *Saturday Review of Literature*. In his article, "A Negro Looks at the Negro Press," Brown did not advocate muzzling the black press, but he felt that the black press should not be encouraged in promoting hatred. Brown served Roosevelt as director of Negro Relations for the Council for Democracy.

The publication of a black newspaper in the South was a hazardous occupation. Black editors were threatened, assaulted, spat upon, inundated with vituperative remarks, and stymied by vicious gossip. Black editors complained not only of harassment from hostile whites but of mistreatment from blacks. Peddlers of black newspapers in the South were the objects of mob violence, and during World War II peddlers of black newspapers were forbidden access to army camps.

Historical Overview. African American newspapers published before emancipation include the *Weekly Advocate: The Spirit of the Times*, published in New York City from 1836 to 1842, and *The National Reformer* in Philadelphia. The *Colored American*, originally named the *Weekly Advocate*, was founded by Phillip A. Bell in 1837. Black editors of the era, including W. M. Trotter, editor of the *Boston Guardian* and T. T. Fortune of the *New York Age*, championed the freedom of the black press. The *Washington Bee*, the *Indianapolis World*, the *Philadelphia Tribune*, *The Cleveland Gazette*, and the *New York Age* experienced publication problems.

In 1940 200 black newspapers were in publication. In 1942 the Justice Department threatened about twenty editors with sedition charges, and many black papers found it difficult to obtain newsprint. The National Association for the Advancement of Colored People negotiated an unofficial settlement in which black papers tamed their criticism and were able to obtain essential supplies. Sengstacke Enterprises, the largest black newspaper chain in the nation, entered the newspaper business in the 1930's and resurged in the 1970's. Sengstacke's group made $5 million in overall sales in 1973. An older black paper, the *Baltimore Afro-American*, expanded from Baltimore to include editions catering to Newark, Philadelphia, Washington, D.C., and Richmond. During the 1990's the paper was run by John H. Murphy III, grandson of John Murphy, Sr., who founded the paper in 1892. Approximately one hundred black newspapers were in existence in 1975, and thirty-five of those had a circulation exceeding twenty thousand copies per issue. In the Southern white press, "colored

San Francisco police seize a truck belonging to The Black Panther *newspaper in November, 1968.* (AP/Wide World Photos)

news" was run in special editions. Such editions were marked with a star or red banner. These editions were never distributed in the white community, thus censoring by restricting dissemination. African Americans assumed that they were reading and purchasing the regular white newspaper.

Discriminatory voting requirements for blacks indirectly led to the creation of the New York City newspaper, *The Ram's Horn*. One of the more notable editorials was directed to enslaved blacks in the South and voiced outspoken opposition to slavery. Frederick Douglass' paper, *The North Star*, followed the death of *The Ram's Horn*. In his role as editor of *The North Star*, Douglass made special effort to increase his contact with blacks and their daily problems. His most severe editorials were directed toward blacks who passively accepted discrimination.

Since the 1970's, more than two hundred black newspapers ceased publication. In 1975, there remained only one major black daily, *The Chicago Defender*. In the late 1980's, there were more than 170 African American weekly newspapers being published in thirty-four states and the District of Columbia. Many black newspapers that once published national editions, such as *The Journal and Guide* of Norfolk, Virginia, *The Pittsburgh Courier*, and others, had to cease national distribution. Decreasing advertising revenue, poor circulation, and low subscription sales contributed to the decline of black newspapers. —*Lessie Bass Artis*

See also Abolitionist movement; African Americans; Civil Rights movement; Douglass, Frederick; Garvey, Marcus; Lovejoy, Elijah Parish; Newspapers.

Bibliography

Penelope Bullock's *The Afro-American Periodical Press 1838-1909* (Baton Rouge: Louisiana State University Press, 1981) records the historical development of black periodicals in the United States. Harry H. Ploski and James D. Williams' *The Negro Almanac: A Reference Work on the African American* (Detroit: Gale Research, 1989) serves as a guide to the newspapers, periodicals, broadcasters, and leaders of the African American media. Henry Lewis Suggs's *The Black Press in the South, 1865-1979* (Westport, Conn.: Greenwood Press, 1983) discusses significant contributions of editors state by state. Bernell Tripp's *Origins of the Black Press: New York, 1827-1847* (Northport, Alaska: Vision Press, 1992) describes the history of black newspapers and how these newspapers became a voice for African Americans.

Newspapers, student

Definition: News publications written and edited by students in secondary public schools and colleges

Significance: Student journalists have generally enjoyed less First Amendment protection than other journalists

Arguments favoring tight controls over school newspapers have usually centered around the responsibilities of high schools and colleges as legal publishers of school-sponsored publications and the fact that student journalists are immature and need guidance. Many school administrators do not trust teenagers to publish newspapers, even when adult advisers are overseeing their production. They are also concerned that some topics, such as homosexuality, drug abuse, teenage suicide, and premarital sex, are inappropriate for younger students.

Prior restraints on school papers have not been rare. In 1990 the Student Press Law Center in Washington, D.C., received requests for legal assistance from more than nine hundred college and high school organizations across the United States. That figure represented an increase of 51 percent over the previous year. Supporters of student press freedom have argued that college and high school publications should be tools of amateur journalists who are striving to become professionals. They believe schools should be the training ground for teaching students about the First Amendment, one of the most important sentences in U.S. law.

High School Newspapers. In 1974 the Robert F. Kennedy Foundation's Commission of Inquiry into High School Journalism issued a report that concluded most high school journalism teachers practiced censorship. This report was written after the 1969 U.S. Supreme Court decision in *Tinker v. Des Moines Independent Community School District*, in which the Court ruled that school principals may not stifle speech unless it is libelous, legally obscene, or would disrupt the educational process. The commission recommended that instead of censorship by school officials, First Amendment rights should be taught and practiced as part of high school journalism courses in the United States. The commission concluded: "Censorship is the fundamental cause of the triviality, innocuousness, and uniformity that characterize the high school press. It has created a high school press that in most places is no more than a house organ for the school administration."

Fourteen years after the 1974 report, the U.S. Supreme Court, in *Hazelwood School District v. Kuhlmeier* (1988), gave school officials greater latitude in controlling the content of student publications. The Court said: "A school need not tolerate student speech that is inconsistent with its basic educational mission. . . . A school must be able to set high standards for the student speech that is disseminated under its auspices—standards that may be higher than those demanded by some in the 'real' world—and may refuse to disseminate student speech that does not meet those standards." Thus the words "basic educational mission" entered the language regarding student newspapers.

After the Hazelwood decision some state legislatures passed laws designed to protect the press freedoms of student journalists. In California, for example, students of public school have the right to exercise freedom of speech and of the press, including the right to expression in official publications. States such as Colorado, Iowa, Kansas, and Massachusetts have passed similar student press freedom laws.

College Newspapers. U.S. courts have made distinctions between high school and college newspapers. The courts have varied their views about student publications in secondary schools since most students in such institutions are under the age of eighteen, and thus are legally children. At the college level, most students are adults; therefore, the courts have almost always extended full First Amendment protections to college newspapers.

State colleges and universities are not required to establish student publications or other forums for free expression; however, once a college has established a student newspaper, it cannot discontinue, repress, restrain, weaken, or remove its funding because of any content of the publication that is protected by the First Amendment. Prior restraint, including subtle as well as overt pressure, is not permissible against college newspapers.

While newspapers at colleges and universities appear to have more First Amendment protection than high school publications, they are not without their own censorship battles. For example, administrators at the University of Lowell in Massachusetts threatened student editors with arrest by university police because cartoons they published were described as sexist and racist. After consulting the school's attorney, the officials dropped the charges. In October, 1990, administrators at Our Lady of Holy Cross University in New Orleans confiscated and destroyed student newspapers that ran an advertisement for unsuccessful Senate candidate David Duke, a former Ku Klux Klan leader. The University of Denver shut down its student newspaper in June, 1990, because it published jokes deemed sexist by some in the campus community.

College school administrators have also tried to use a federal privacy law commonly known as the Buckley Amendment to deny student journalists access to campus crime reports. A federal court in *Bauer v. Kincaid* (1990), however, ruled that campus law enforcement records were not student education records, which are exempt from public access under the Buckley Amendment. Congress later passed the Campus Security Act of 1990, which requires private and public schools to compile, publish, and distribute annual reports providing information on the numbers of serious crimes occurring on school grounds.

Off-Campus and Online Newspapers. With advances in computer technology, a growing number of teenagers have founded underground, off-campus newspapers to avoid the editorial control of school administrators. The University of California at Berkeley *Daily Californian*, for example, severed its official ties with the university, and the University of Wisconsin has a large number of independent student newspapers. What an off-campus newspaper gains in liberty, however, it often loses in longevity. Most underground newspapers provide alternatives to student freedom of expression, but when their editors or core writers graduate and leave, the papers often die.

With the popularity of Internet, a global network of computerized information, high school and college newspapers started being electronically disseminated through the Internet during the 1990's. College newspapers such as *The Post* at Ohio University, *The Daily Illini* at the University of Illinois, and the *Iowa State Daily* at Iowa State University have begun to distribute their publications electronically over the Internet as well as in the traditional paper format. Many high school newspapers, such as the *Spokesman On-Line* at Wheeling High School in Illinois and the *Chatterbox* at Walnut Hills High School in Cincinnati, Ohio, also are being distributed electronically.

—Eddith A. Dashiell

See also Campus speech codes; Education; *Hazelwood School District v. Kuhlmeier*; Newspapers; Suicide; Yaqzan, Matan, affair.

BIBLIOGRAPHY

The Freedom Forum's *Death by Cheeseburger* (Arlington, Va.: Freedom Forum, 1994) assesses the state of scholastic journalism during the 1990's. *Captive Voices: The Report of the Commission into High School Journalism* (New York: Schocken Books, 1974) provides a historical overview of the student press. The Student Press Law Center's *Law of the Student Press* (Arlington, Va.: Student Press Law Center, 1995) analyzes the legal problems faced by student journalists, such as press freedom, libel, privacy invasion, copyright, confidential sources, adviser's rights, open records law, and advertising acceptability. George E. Stevens and John B. Webster's *Law and the Student Press* (Ames: Iowa State University Press, 1973) also surveys the history of student newspaper censorship. Louis E. Ingelhart has done extensive research in the area of press freedoms for high school and college newspapers; his works include: *Freedom for the College Student Press* (Westport, Conn.: Greenwood Press, 1985); *Press Law and Press Freedom for High School Students* (Westport, Conn.: Greenwood Press, 1986), and *Student Publications: Legalities, Governance, and Operation* (Ames: Iowa State University Press, 1993).

Newspapers, underground

DEFINITION: Small-scale newspapers with nonstandard means of distribution that flourished in the United States during the 1960's and 1970's

SIGNIFICANCE: Underground newspapers informed and amused many readers, but also sparked an offensive of government suppression that helped to destroy them

During the 1960's to 1970's more than four hundred underground newspapers were published throughout the United States. They were heirs to a tradition going back to nineteenth century European radicalism and American populist and socialist papers of the late 1890's and early 1900's. New York's *Village Voice* began as a beatnik underground newspaper in the mid-1950's. The 1960's-era underground press was directly linked to the 1964 founding of the highly successful *Los Angeles Free Press* and the youth and student movements of the mid- to late 1960's.

By the early 1960's censorship in the United States had relaxed, particularly in book publishing. This new atmosphere—together with new technology that made less expensive printing possible and growing discontent with mainstream media among youth—offered an opportune time to launch a new breed of newspapers. As rapidly as the papers arose, however, they declined in the mid-1970's. Changing times and bad management were in part to blame, but government surveillance, harassment, and unlawful attacks by government agencies also contributed.

Government attacks on the underground press were mostly autonomously orchestrated efforts of such bodies as the Federal Bureau of Investigation (FBI), the Central Intelligence Agency (CIA), the White House, the Internal Revenue Service, and local police departments. FBI efforts were part of the bureau's counterintelligence program, which viewed underground newspapers as part of a radical movement that threatened national security. CIA programs ranged from the agency's Operation Chaos program—which fostered spying on the underground press and various militant groups—to Project Resistance—which monitored and infiltrated underground newspapers and pressured record companies not to advertise in them.

There were public attacks as well. For example, a U.S. Senate subcommittee probed Liberation News Service's funding. Senator Thomas Dodd's 1970 Urban Terrorism Prevention Bill would have made it illegal to publish a periodical advocating the overthrow of the U.S. government. Most suppression was done privately, however. Some secret schemes were harassing, arresting, or assaulting newspaper staff members—from street vendors to editors; monitoring the finances of papers and their staffs; releasing false information or publishing fake underground newspapers to discredit real papers; and warning printers or distributors not to handle underground newspapers. For example, government documents show that a New York City distributor handling the Black Panther Party's weekly tabloid raised his rates after talking with federal agents. Newspapers were also raided for narcotics and their vendors were occasionally rousted.

The Los Angeles Free Press was targeted by California authorities in 1969 for exposing alleged misconduct by campus police and for revealing the identities of state narcotics agents. The agents and the state filed civil suits against the paper, and publisher Art Kunkin and reporter Jerry Applebaum were charged with receiving stolen property—copies of government documents. Both were convicted and fined, and the newspaper had to spend more than sixty thousand dollars of its limited funds to settle the various lawsuits out of court. In Milwaukee, Wisconsin, a freshly enacted obscenity ordinance was used to arrest *Kaleidoscope* editor John Kois, whose car and office were later shot at and bombed. A photographer was repeatedly arrested for disorderly conduct while he was working, and he and Kois were arrested and charged with conspiring with defendants in an antidraft trial that they were covering. Another editor was jailed for four months for refusing to divulge a news source to a grand jury.

In San Diego, California, several underground papers had their coinboxes confiscated in 1969 and 1970; thousands of copies of their papers were stolen, and dozens of their street vendors were arrested for littering and obstructing the sidewalks. Their offices were searched without warrants, ransacked, shot up, and burned. Staffers were arrested; there were also threats of violence, automobile tires were slashed, and a car was bombed.

In Philadelphia, the *Free Press* in 1970 reported that police threatened staff members with physical violence and beat one person. Police also arrested and detained other staffers, sometimes without charges being filed. The newspaper also reported that police broke into staffers' residences four times without warrants. The paper was also threatened with armed officers conducting obvious surveillance with as many as six cars at once.

Although underground newspapers usually won their court cases, they typically were driven out of business by their legal expenses. The mainstream media regarded underground newspapers as unseemly, leftist competitors, and remained largely silent on their struggles against government interference. *Washington Post* journalist Bob Woodward observed that the underground press was accurate in its accusations of government sabotage. However, without powerful defenders and economic resources, the newspapers could not survive in the face of government harassment.

See also Advocacy; Central Intelligence Agency; Draft resistance; Federal Bureau of Investigation; Free Speech Movement; News media censorship; Newspapers, African American; Newspapers, student; Police; Vietnam War.

Newsreels

Definition: Short films, exhibited in cinemas, of news

Significance: Newsreels, widely distributed from approximately 1911 to 1966, were objects of censorship

Undergoing self-imposed and external censorship, packaged newsreel footage reached American audiences for more than fifty years and shaped their views of events. Newsreels evolved with the motion picture industry, and two different philosophies shaped the newsreels' evolution. John Grierson and Robert Flaherty, for example, produced "objective" documentaries, the prototype of cinema verité, by editing raw footage into reels. Commercial studios, in contrast, produced "subjective" newsreels with methods similar to those of commercial film production.

A form of media censorship was common to such subjective newsreels. It involved selectively controlling the information in a newsreel to favor a particular position or deliberately altering information, including visual information, in order to create a desired impression. Pictures can lie as easily as words. Film media enhance such techniques with sound effects, narration, and music geared toward eliciting the desired emotional response. Commercial newsreels, the television of the day, often distorted events on which they reported.

The Newsreel Business. During the newsreel era, millions of Americans viewed silent and, after 1930, sound newsreels, an estimated one-half billion feet of film produced by major motion picture studios. The reels were made as part of an entertainment business—the film and theater industry. Shown locally in cinemas across the United States, newsreels served as fillers, sandwiched among serials, short subjects, and the feature films.

Accordingly, commercial studios treated motion pictures and newsreels as business products rather than as art. Used as tools for business ends, newsreels served to attract audiences to movie premieres and to publicize activities for motion picture stars. Emulating motion picture production, newsreels were produced, relative to later visual news presentations, in an overblown manner, complete with fanfare, marches, and music. Objective footage of controversial issues was less likely than footage that was aimed to please audiences with superficial and trivial images. Typical fare included beauty contests, fashions, sports, political news, stunts, disasters, and everyday events. Newsreels focused on the sensational aspects of catastrophes, disasters, and social events. Favoring shots with visual appeal, the makers of newsreels shunned interpreting complex events involving human suffering or social impact. After the footage (often staged action and usually shot without sound) was edited, narration, a musical score, and sound effects were added. Strikes, riots, hurricanes, and disasters were accompanied by dramatic narration, sound effects, and an intense musical score. Thus, the dictates of business competition among the major motion picture producers served as self-imposed censorship, as newsreels' coverage of events unfolding in the 1930's illustrate.

Examples of Newsreel Coverage. The 1930's Great Depression socially and economically affected most Americans; however, the mass media provided little factual news as the policy of media seemed to be to ignore the Depression's harsher realities. Early in the decade, five major companies dominated newsreel production. Although competition brought some realism to newsreels, evidently newsreels shielded realistic views about the Depression by avoiding complex stories involving its social impact. In general, 1930's motion pictures aimed to amuse audiences, to serve as escapism from Depression-evoked lifestyles. Likewise, newsreels mainly covered stories rife with images of soldiers, airplanes, stunts, and babies: apparent favorites among audiences. Still, by 1931, newsreels, although not challenging the existing social order, were covering more sober events.

Footage covering the Hunger March of 1931 illustrates aspects of a self-imposed censorship. Apart from the selected footage, which offered no visual explanation of the event's complexity, the narration describes the event and the demonstrations' purpose in non-objective, general terms. The marchers, among the 25 percent of an American unemployed workforce, are described as "Reds" and "troublemakers"; they are not shown in a favorable or neutral light. Newsreel footage, complemented frequently by jingoistic narration, highlights police measures taken against the people who blatantly exercise their First Amendment rights.

Likewise, the 1932 footage of the 25,000-man Bonus March in Washington, D.C., renders a similar treatment. World War I veterans, earlier authorized a pension by Congress, marched on Washington in protest to the announcement that the bonus would not be paid until 1945. Images appear to startle and confuse—entertain—the audience rather than provide factual information. Newsreel narration describes the march as a "war." A voice-over (accompanying visuals of "orderly" U.S. Army soldiers and "disorderly" marchers camped on "government property") informs viewers the Army was assembled to deal with the "riot," and attributes President Herbert Hoover, who insisted the Depression would "be over in sixty days," as relating the problem to "Reds" and "criminal elements" among the marchers' ranks. Hoover ordered soldiers to burn the camps and rout the marchers, and later issued an executive order limiting what cameramen could photograph. Cameramen complied or risked loss of their White House cards, which entitled newsreel crews to cover White House events.

The Film and Photo League, a radical group, offered an alternative view of Depression events through its production of the Workers Newsreel. The League, labeling itself a voice calling for relief from the Depression, said it wanted to shape and mobilize public consciousness of the Depression's impact. Not having access to local cinemas, Workers Newsreel, silent films with titles, were shown in private facilities—church basements, for example. Leo Seltzer, a film producer who joined the group in the early 1930's, used a hand-held camera to film what, he said, was actually being experienced. Though filming with a subjective focus, the Workers Newsreel offered exclusive coverage of some events, for example a mass demonstration in 1930 at Union Square in New York City. Although recorded, commercial footage of the Union Square demonstration, depicting violence and roughshod arrests, was not seen by the general public because the New York City Police Department censored it. Later, the Workers Newsreel staff acquired censored footage and exhibited it in its outlets.

Newsreel self-censorship continued into the 1950's as the emergence of nuclear weaponry and the implications of a Cold War stirred the nation's fear. Newsreel footage of the time neither questions nor explores the ramifications of such profound international incidents. Rather, it appears to have induced fear and elicited disturbing feelings among audiences, as jingoistic rhetoric and simplistic visuals preclude objective explanation of events.

By 1966, newsreel production had ceased. The demise of newsreels has generally been attributed to television.

—Gerald Boyer

See also Film censorship; News media censorship; Propaganda; War.

BIBLIOGRAPHY

The Reel World of News, part of the video series *A Walk Through the Twentieth Century with Bill Moyers*, produced and directed by David Grubin (WNET New York and KQED San Francisco, 1982); and *The Great Depression*, a seven-part video production of Blackside, Inc., in association with BBC-2, executive producer, Henry Hampton (WGBH Boston, 1993), provide illustrative examples of newsreel footage treatment of events recorded during the Depression. *The Film Experience: Elements of Motion Picture Art*, by Roy Huss and Norman Silverstein (New York: Dell Publishing, 1968), provides an overview of the evolution of the motion picture industry. *Media, Messages and Men: New Perspectives in Communication*, by John C. Merril and Ralph L. Lowenstein (New York: David McKay, 1971), provides an overview of basic issues in mass communication. *Censorship: The Knot That Binds Power and Knowledge*, by Sue Curry Jansen (New York: Oxford University Press, 1988), provides a general discussion of communication and society and the issue of censorship.

Nicholas I

BORN: July 6, 1796, Tsarskoye Selo, Russia

DIED: March 2, 1855, St. Petersburg, Russia

IDENTIFICATION: Emperor of Russia from 1825 to 1855

SIGNIFICANCE: The last autocratic czar of Russia, Nicholas believed that censorship was vital to existence of his empire

The last autocratic czar, Nicholas I assumed the Russian throne upon the death of his brother, Alexander I in 1825. Nicholas followed Alexander's reform movements in the beginning of his reign, but the revolutionary movement sweeping western Europe in 1830 prompted him to begin limiting, or censoring, the type of information that was being disseminated to the Russian people.

By 1848 Nicholas had created several imperial departments that bypassed the normal channels of Russian government and were answerable only to him. The department overseeing censorship was the "Third Department"—the political police. The revolutions of 1848 in Europe caused Nicholas to clamp down on the press and literature in order to protect his realm from unwelcome outside influences. By 1850 Nicholas' "censorship terror" campaign was at its height. Literature, music, and the press were severely controlled. Government control over the press was so tight that little information about the outside world was printed. Not only were Russian writers such as Alexander Pushkin and Nicholai Gogol censored, but writers such as Victor Hugo, Hans Christian Andersen, and Nathaniel Hawthorne were banned. Travel abroad was forbidden, and the teaching of European constitutional law and philosophy was eliminated. Even the censors had censors overseeing their work.

This tight censorship over all aspects of Russian life was only eased after Nicholas' death in 1855 and the defeat of Russia in the Crimean War.

See also Bakunin, Mikhail Aleksandrovich; Crimean War; Dostoevski, Fyodor; Gogol, Nikolai Vasilyevich; Hugo, Victor; Russia.

Nigeria

DESCRIPTION: Africa's most populous nation, located on the Gulf of Guinea

SIGNIFICANCE: In this country of divisions and volatile atmosphere, various organizations have dictated censorship policies

A country which has undergone tremendous political upheaval and divisions, and historically a large supplier of the slave trade, Nigeria sought independence from the British in 1945. Resolutions were finally drawn up by the 1950's which established three individual regions of Nigeria with parliaments similar to that of Britain. Independence came in 1960, but the three main rival ethnic groups fought for control.

In subsequent years, chaos and turmoil resulted in assassinations, a 1966 military takeover, and a civil war, during which Eastern Nigeria seceded to become the Republic of Biafra. Three years later the republic rejoined Nigeria. Stability was threatened by coups, changes in government between military to civilian, an imitation of the American system of government, political corruption, waste, abuse, and economic disasters. After 1979 the Federal Republic of Nigeria became a federation of nineteen states with a president acting as both head of state and head of government.

The barometer of censorship rose and fell with the changing political situation. The constitution of 1979 guaranteed freedom of the press. Media outlets proliferated. Newspapers included fifteen daily papers and twelve weeklies. There were twenty-five radio and twenty television stations.

At this juncture in the country's history, the press was thought to be relatively free. Nigerians had more access to the mass media and expressed their viewpoints in those outlets. However, in international reporting, the Nigerian Broadcasting Company (FRCN) and Nigerian Television (NTV) tended to conduct internal broadcasts in similar fashion and directed their reporting toward the National Party. Still, all the parties had access to what was generally considered the freest press in Africa. However, the outlets themselves often did not have capable reporters and know-how, and did not practice methods of self-censorship.

Under the military rule following a January 1, 1984, coup President Shehu Shagari of the National Party and his civilian government was deposed. General Mohammed Buhari took leadership of the country which had serious financial troubles, labor unrest, and increased corruption. Shortly after the takeover the government issued the Public Officers (Protection Against False Accusation) Decree which allowed for the federal military government to make its own laws unimpeded by the courts. Under this law no false information or ridicule of the government was allowed. Offenders received fines or jail sentences, were not entitled to appeals, and the reporting organization was to be closed for up to a year.

Economic censorship became another method used to place regulations on the media by restricting import licenses and thereby limiting the amount of paper supplied to the country. Newspapers had to cut production or were put out of business. A new constitution in 1989 created a two-party system run and financed entirely by the state. All former officeholders were banned from participating in elected office. Further, a clearance certificate had to be issued by the National Electoral Commission for any person wishing to run for office. In 1990 new president Ibrahim Babangida created two new parties, the only ones allowed by law.

See also Broadcast media; Death; News media censorship; Saro-Wiwa, Ken; Soyinka, Wole.

Nixon, Richard M.

BORN: January 9, 1913, Yorba Linda, California

DIED: April 22, 1994, New York, New York

IDENTIFICATION: Thirty-seventh president of the United States (1969-1974)

SIGNIFICANCE: Nixon was the only president who resigned to avoid impeachment for abuse of power and unconstitutional conduct

As president, Richard M. Nixon tried to suppress a wide range of political and personal expression, ranging from a sustained antipornography campaign to attempts to censor publication of the Pentagon Papers and other documents relating to the Vietnam War. Ultimately, his fear of the press, which, he believed, carried on a vendetta against him, would be a significant factor in his downfall.

Political Career. The child of Quaker parents, Nixon received his B.A. from Whittier College and won a scholarship to Duke University Law School, from which he was graduated in 1937. In 1946 after serving as a naval officer in World War II, he won election to the House of Representatives as a Republican from California, accusing his Democratic opponent of being soft on communism.

Nixon won national attention through his active role on the House Committee on Un-American Activities (HUAC), attacking alleged leftist influence in the film industry and pursuing an alleged communist conspiracy within the Truman Administration. In 1950 he successfully ran for the Senate in California, capitalizing on his anticommunist record and claiming that his Democratic opponent was a socialist because he supported the New Deal. Nixon's youth and national reputation led Dwight D. Eisenhower to select him as his vice-presidential running mate in 1952 and 1956.

After narrowly losing the 1960 presidential election to John F. Kennedy, Nixon returned to California, where in 1962 he ran for governor but was soundly defeated by Democrat Pat Brown. In a televised press conference, he raged at the press, accusing journalists of biased coverage that, he claimed, had led to his defeat, and announcing his retirement from politics. However, after moving to New York City, he campaigned widely for other congressional and state candidates, winning enough personal support to capture the 1968 Republican presidential nomination. The Vietnam War was then bitterly dividing the country, and Nixon won a narrow victory in the general presidential election.

Presidency. Nixon did not openly attack the press; instead, he used Vice President Spiro T. Agnew, who denounced the print and broadcast media as "effete snobs" whose liberal prejudice threatened the moral fabric of the country. Agnew's implied threat was that the administration would use the resources of the federal government to punish its critics in the media.

When the President's Commission on Obscenity and Pornography, originally appointed by President Lyndon Johnson, issued a report in 1970 that did not condemn pornography, Nixon reacted furiously. The commission proposed that laws prohibiting sale of erotic material to adults be repealed, while laws restricting access by children continue in force. Nixon repudiated the report, terming it morally bankrupt, and called for an intensification of state and federal censorship of pornography.

When he entered the presidency, Nixon was sure that a vast conspiracy existed among communist countries, the antiwar movement in the United States, and his American political opponents. He urged U.S. intelligence agencies to find evidence of this conspiracy by whatever means necessary. The Central Intelligence Agency (CIA) and the Federal Bureau of Investigation (FBI), however, found no evidence of foreign infiltration within the antiwar movement. In 1970 a frustrated Nixon approved a plan to centralize control of American intelligence agencies within the White House and remove significant constitutional protections of the civil liberties of American citizens; resistance from the FBI, however, caused Nixon to drop the idea.

Convinced that only absolute secrecy would permit him to attain his military and foreign policy goals, Nixon tried to prevent the American press and public from knowing what he was doing. This desire for secrecy extended to the other branches of government as well; to preserve the secrecy of bombing campaigns against the North Vietnamese in Cambodia, for example, Nixon sent false reports to the Senate.

Nixon's desire for secrecy and fear was not based entirely on dubious motives. He had entered office determined to open friendly relations with the People's Republic of China, for example, a move that reversed his own and the Republican Party's past positions. Secrecy was needed to permit him to reach an understanding with the Chinese leadership and startle the world in February, 1972, with a summit meeting in Beijing.

However, Nixon's general hatred of the press often had a negative influence on his judgment. A classic example is his reaction to the publication by *The New York Times* of *The Pentagon Papers* in June, 1971. Nothing in these volumes, which contained classified material on the prosecution of the Vietnam War during the Johnson Administration, involved Nixon. But he was so outraged at the thought of secret material being published that he ordered the Department of Justice to seek an unprecedented prior restraint injunction barring the *Times* from continuing publication of the classified documents. Nixon was overruled by the Supreme Court.

Unable to use the CIA or FBI to uncover the conspiracies which he felt surrounded him, and determined to stop classified documents and other secrets from being leaked to the press, Nixon decided to set up his own White House special investigations unit, which would soon become known as the "plumbers." Ordered to discredit Daniel Ellsberg, who had given the Pentagon Papers to the press, members of this unit broke into Ellsberg's psychiatrist's office in search of material which would be used to damage his reputation. White House aides, meanwhile, compiled an "enemies list" of politicians, reporters, and lawyers who had criticized the Nixon Administration. On October 19, 1972, Nixon's chief of staff, H. R. Haldeman, noted in his diary that Nixon "made the interesting point that after the election we will have awesome power with no discipline, that is, there won't be another election coming up to discipline us, and we've got to do our planning on that basis." Indeed, the enemies list would be put to use after the 1972 election, when Nixon would attempt to use such federal agencies as the Internal Revenue Service and Justice Department to further his own political goals.

Watergate and After. Nixon won the 1972 election, but before he could put his plans completely into effect, a break-in at the Democratic Party headquarters in the Watergate apartment building in Washington, D.C., became a major scandal. There is no evidence that Nixon knew in advance of the burglary and wiretap attempt, but it is clear that, once the intruders had been arrested, he directed an elaborate cover-up, attempting to use the CIA to thwart the FBI's investigation, authorizing "hush money" for the burglars, and encouraging his staff to mislead the press and members of Congress. However, the threat of long prison sentences led some conspirators to confess. As the cover-up unraveled, Nixon's role in the affair became public knowledge, confirmed by tapes that he had made of his conferences in the Oval Office. The House of

Representatives' Judiciary Committee voted to recommend impeachment. When it became clear that he would be convicted by the Senate of obstruction of justice and abuse of power, Nixon resigned from the presidency on August 9, 1974.

Newly installed President Gerald Ford quickly pardoned Nixon, ensuring that there would be no public trial of the former president. In retirement, Nixon worked tirelessly to rehabilitate his reputation, submitting to television interviews and writing seven books in an attempt to reclaim his image as a statesman. To a certain extent, he succeeded; he was often consulted on matters of foreign policy by succeeding presidents, and leaders of both parties eulogized him at his funeral. His attempts to curtail the activities of a free press, however, would prove a more troubling legacy. —*Milton Berman*

See also Central Intelligence Agency; Fear; House Committee on Un-American Activities; *Pentagon Papers, The*; Presidency, U.S.; President's Commission on Obscenity and Pornography; Prior restraint; Vietnam War; Watergate scandal.

Bibliography

Stephen E. Ambrose's three-volume biography, *Nixon: The Education of a Politician, 1913-1962*, *Nixon: The Triumph of a Politician, 1962-1972*, and *Nixon: Ruin and Recovery, 1973-1990* (New York: Simon & Schuster, 1987-1992), provides a detailed critical examination of Nixon's career. Joan Hoff-Wilson, the senior editor of the microform edition of Nixon's presidential papers, is more favorable in *Nixon Reconsidered* (New York: Basic Books, 1994), where she downplays the importance of Watergate and praises Nixon's domestic as well as foreign policy accomplishments. Nixon defends his actions in two memoirs, *RN: The Memoirs of Richard Nixon* (New York: Grosset & Dunlap, 1978) and *In the Arena: A Memoir of Victory, Defeat, and Renewal* (New York: Simon & Schuster, 1990). Carl Bernstein and Bob Woodward's two books on Nixon, *All the President's Men* (New York: Simon & Schuster, 1974) and *The Final Days* (New York: Simon & Schuster, 1976), are as fascinating as detective stories. The carefully documented account in Fred Emery, *Watergate: The Corruption of American Politics and the Fall of Richard Nixon* (New York: Times Books, 1994), however, provides a more reliable assessment of Nixon's role in Watergate. The daily entries in H. R. Haldeman, *The Haldeman Diaries: Inside the Nixon White House* (New York: G. P. Putnam's Sons, 1994), provide a chillingly detailed account of Nixon's devious and deceitful behavior as president.

Nolde, Emil

Born: August 7, 1867, Nolde, Germany

Died: April 15, 1956, Seebüll, West Germany

Identification: German expressionist painter

Significance: Nolde was featured prominently in the Nazis' Degenerate Art Exhibition of 1937, and most of his work was confiscated

Nolde was born Emil Hansen but changed his name on the occasion of his marriage to the Danish actress and musician Ada Vilstrup in 1902, taking the name of the town in northern Schleswig where he grew up. He tended toward impressionism in his early years, notably during his studies in Munich and Dachau in the 1890's. In the early 1900's he spent time in Paris and Berlin, briefly joining the circle known as *Die Brücke* in 1906, and acting as a founding member of the New Berlin Secession in 1910. He soon took Christian religious scenes as his subjects in a well-known series of paintings, but became fascinated with primitivism during an ethnological expedition to Russia and the Far East during 1913-1914.

Perhaps because of Nolde's "Volkish" ideas about art, which emphasized the spiritual and natural relation of race and landscape, or because of early support from Nazi cultural figures such as Alois Schardt and Alfred Rosenberg, the allegation has been widely accepted that Nolde joined the National Socialist Party officially in 1920—the same year as Adolf Hitler. This has, however, never been confirmed. On the other hand, Nolde has also often been excused as merely politically naïve, although he publicly stated that he believed in the racial superiority of the Nordic peoples. The question of his allegiance to Nazism has been, and remains, a matter of some controversy. In any case, expressionism as Nolde and others practiced it lost out to the demand for aesthetic and ideological purity in Germany in the 1930's.

In his autobiography Nolde suggests that he became persecuted by the Nazis because he refused to accept a high-level position in the Imperial Ministry of Culture, the *Reichskulturkammer*. In fact, the highest court of the Nazi Party investigated Nolde and determined in March, 1937, that he had never been a member of the party, thus rendering calls for his expulsion moot. This verdict is deceptive, however, because documentation unearthed in later years shows clearly that Nolde joined the party relatively late—not in 1920, but in 1934—although his membership was in the Danish National Socialist Party in northern Schleswig, which since the 1919 Versailles Treaty had belonged to Denmark.

Nolde attempted to justify himself and his art to the Nazi authorities for years after their denunciation of him, especially in 1937, after the Degenerate Art Exhibition in Munich. In the summer of 1939 he went as far as to write to Hitler's minister for propaganda, Joseph Goebbels, demanding the return of his confiscated work. Over a thousand of his paintings had been removed from German museums and galleries by that time. However, the *Reichskulturkammer* demanded that Nolde cease painting altogether and turn over his previous two years' work. Nolde continued to paint in secret at his isolated house in Seebüll. To avoid the detectable odor of oil paints, he switched to watercolors, and the police and Gestapo never found contraband in their visits to his residence. During this wartime period, which ended with Germany's surrender in 1945, Nolde secretly painted more than thirteen hundred aquarelles, which he called "unpainted pictures." These were the basis for a hundred large oil paintings made between 1945 and 1951.

Nolde never comprehended the National Socialist persecution of him, since he believed he himself had struggled, mostly alone, against foreign influences on contemporary German art. The Degenerate Art Exhibition placed his altar piece *Life of Christ* (1912) at the center of the first gallery on the upper floor and labeled it a mockery of the Divine. Otherwise the official objections to Nolde's expressionistic art were those applied to most modern art: that unconventional style is "impure" and "unhealthy," its images distorted and deformed. The exhibition leaders displayed almost thirty other paintings by Nolde to prove his degenerateness, including pictures of Frisian houses, sunflowers, and cows.

Already an old man by the time of his difficulties with the Nazis, Nolde died at his Seebüll home in 1956. The Nazis were more preoccupied with Nolde than with any other artist; he is the ironic example of the artist censored in spite of his expressed sympathy for the ideology of the regime.

Siegfried Lenz modeled his fictional character "Ludwig Nansen" on Nolde in his novel *The German Lesson* (1968).

See also Art; Degenerate Art Exhibition; Germany; Grosz, George; National Socialism.

Nonmailable matter laws

Definition: Laws that specify items not allowed to be deposited or carried in the mail

Significance: The U.S. Congress has the power to provide for a postal system, and regulation of the content of the mail is a major congressional power regarding the regulation of expression

Since the U.S. Congress first made provision for a postal service it has regularly sought to specify particular noxious items deemed unfit for transport through the mail. Sometimes the items have had little to do with the expression of ideas, as, for example, when Congress banned the mailing of items that might do physical damage to post office equipment or personnel in 1872 and firearms capable of being concealed in 1927. More often, however, nonmailable matter provisions have attempted to restrict communication in some fashion. Beginning with the declaration of obscene materials as nonmailable in 1865, federal lawmakers of their day have regularly expanded upon the nonmailable list. Congress, for example, declared lottery tickets unmailable in 1890. Film or pictorial representations of prize fights or other encounters of pugilists were declared unmailable in 1912. Materials that advocated treason or forcible resistance to any law of the United States were declared unmailable in 1917. Securities offerings for unregistered securities were declared unmailable in 1933, and information relating to obtaining a foreign divorce in 1939. A general list of nonmailable matter provisions has been codified in the United States Code and continues to include most of the provisions described above.

See also Communist Party of the U.S.A.; Comstock, Anthony; Comstock Act of 1873; Customs laws, U.S.; Lotteries; Postal regulations.

Northern Ireland

Description: Integral part of the United Kingdom that shares an island with the Republic of Ireland

Significance: Since the early 1970's the tense relationship between Protestant and Roman Catholic citizens has given rise to restrictions on free speech and censorship measures

Although settled by British Protestants in the seventeenth century, Northern Ireland did not come into political existence until the 1920 Government of Ireland Act. This act provided for separate Home Rule for two parts of Ireland with the North consisting of the six counties of Ulster and the rest encompassing three counties later known as the Republic of Ireland. After a protest by the Roman Catholic minority, the government of the United Kingdom suspended the provincial government in 1972 and imposed direct rule, on Northern Ireland. In a referendum vote, Protestants voted to remain under the United Kingdom's rule rather than join the Republic of Ireland.

In the aftermath Roman Catholics boycotted and hostilities ensued. Despite an attempt to place four Catholics on a coalition assembly, which replaced parliament and an eleven member executive committee, the assembly did not succeed. After the reinforcement of direct rule, violence erupted once more between Protestants and Catholics. This renewal erupted in decades of terrorism, bloodshed, and death. In 1985 an assembly formed which allowed the Republic of Ireland to have a voice in Northern Ireland's government in respect to unification of its two opposing religious factions. No unity was achieved and the assembly dissolved. Bloodshed ceased during a peace agreement between 1993 and 1996. Renewed violence occurred again in 1996.

Much of the censorship that occurred in Northern Ireland resulted from the prevailing violence. Terrorism posed a major threat and security tightened, which included daily searches to rout out terrorist activities by groups such as the Irish Republican Army (IRA), its legal political organization the Sinn Féin, and the Ulster Defense Association (UDA). Designed to aid in stemming the violence of the IRA, the Prevention of Terrorism (Temporary Provisions) Act of 1976 allowed for police to detain suspects for up to seven days. The 1978 Emergency Provisions Act was designed to protect government officials from becoming terrorist targets by banning the collection, recording, and publishing of any information regarding those officials. All segments of the media were prohibited from airing any view of terrorist groups, such as the IRA, and documentary programs were to be stopped if they portrayed these groups. Censorship on all media prevailed to ensure that these restrictions were enforced.

Security forces consisted of the British Army regiments, local police called the Royal Ulster Constabulary, and the Royal Ulster Rangers (RUC) or local Army. These groups have been criticized for their rough treatment of people during checks and searches. The prisons have also come under suspicion for treatment of prisoners that may be affiliated with terrorist attacks. Outside of terrorist threats, censorship followed other prohibitions according to earlier British laws.

See also Broadcast media; Devlin, Bernadette; Ireland; Irish Republican Army; News media censorship; Terrorism; United Kingdom.

Nova Scotia Board of Censors v. McNeil

Court: Supreme Court of Canada

Decided: January 19, 1978

Significance: This ruling held that a province could regulate the showing of films within its boundaries, but could not prescribe criminal punishments for showing films that it defines as indecent

After Nova Scotia's Board of Censors prevented the showing of the film *Last Tango in Paris* (1972) because it contained—among other things—a scene depicting sodomy, Gerald McNeil objected by filing a lawsuit. The province's supreme court, upon reviewing his objections, agreed with him and ruled that two elements of that province's statutes under its Theatres and Amusement Act of 1967 exceeded the powers of a provincial legislature. The court specifically objected to provisions in the Nova Scotia act that denied, on moral grounds, citizens the right to exercise freedom of choosing which films they viewed. This denial was not within the purview of the legislature of Nova Scotia, the court asserted, because it violated a section of the British North America Act of 1867, which gave the Canadian Parliament exclusive power over criminal matters.

The Supreme Court of Canada, however, ruled that "morality and criminality are not coextensive." The Court said the Nova Scotia statutory provisions regulating—sometimes on purely moral grounds—the exhibition, sale, and exchange of films can be distinguished from criminal codes in two ways. First, the statutes merely regulate a business or trade and do not define a crime. Secondly, the regulations are only preventive whereas criminal laws are penal or punitive.

Another of McNeil's objections was, however, upheld. Those provincial statutory provisions attempting to define indecency were, according to the Court, effectively identical to the Canadian criminal code provisions on indecency. Consequently, the Court ruled those provisions of Nova Scotia's law as beyond the powers of a provincial legislature.

McNeil also argued that Nova Scotia's laws denied fundamental Canadian freedoms, including those of association, assembly, speech, the press, conscience, and religion. Here the Court admitted that because no limitations on the Board of Censors was spelled out in the Theatres and Amusement Act of 1967, it was theoretically possible that the board has been granted broad powers to trample on fundamental Canadian rights. Nevertheless, to place such an extreme construction on the act required impugning the valid intent of the legislators, said the Court. Such an attack, in its view, could be grounded only in pure speculation, not a sufficient basis for overruling an 1878 ruling that all legislation—including provincial statutes—was to be presumed valid unless proven otherwise.

Although the high court ruled the Nova Scotia law's "indecency" provisions invalid, it said the rest of the 1967 act lay within the powers of the provincial legislature and were therefore a valid regulation of a business.

See also *Butler v. The Queen*; Canada; Community standards; Film censorship; *Last Tango in Paris*; Morality; Nudity; Obscenity: legal definitions; Obscenity: sale and possession.

Nuclear research and testing

DEFINITION: Investigations into energy released at the atomic level

SIGNIFICANCE: Governments have been most secretive and censorious regarding their nuclear programs, and have concealed the dangers of radioactivity from their people

In various countries, the public has been kept from being informed, or has been informed after the fact, regarding the developing and testing of nuclear weapons and powerplants. Scientific research and health and safety data have been suppressed.

The Manhattan Project, instigated by the United States in 1942, culminated in the first nuclear explosion on July 16, 1945, and inaugurated the nuclear age. The wartime secrecy surrounding nuclear weaponry continued in peacetime. The atomic bombs dropped by the United States on Hiroshima and Nagasaki, Japan, to force the close of World War II made public the reality of the nuclear age: Atomic bombs represented an enormous leap in the destructive weaponry available to states. The deliberate, complete, and rapid destruction of large countries became possible. Another power, the Soviet Union, quickly developed nuclear capability after the United States demonstrated that the weapons work.

From the end of World War II until the demise of the Soviet Union, the United States and the Soviet Union developed mammoth nuclear arsenals and engaged in mutual suspicion and hostility but not outright war; this period came to be called the Cold War. Both powers followed the rationale of deterrence theory, which relies on the understanding of Mutual Assured Destruction. According to the theory of Mutual Assured Destruction (which both powers evidently thought credible, since neither launched a nuclear attack during the Cold War), a nation starting a nuclear attack would be assured of its own destruction, because radar would give the nation being attacked enough warning to launch a devastating counterattack. Thus nuclear war was not winnable. Secrecy marked all aspects of nuclear weaponry during the Cold War.

Both superpowers were willing to overlook the human cost of atmospheric testing. Suppressed information has been classified in the United States, the former Soviet Union, and other nuclear countries as a matter of "national security," a mechanism that threatens those who publish leaked information with legal punishment. National security has been invoked on occasions in which the government has wished to be spared embarrassment or liability. The Partial Nuclear Test Ban Treaty (1963) moved testing underground, although the problem of unexpected release of radioactivity was documented.

The Atomic Energy Commission. The Atomic Energy Act of 1946 created the Atomic Energy Commission (AEC) to oversee the American nuclear arsenal and to monopolize nuclear research. Protests by scientists helped prevent direct military control of the AEC, but the free exchange of scientific information relating to nuclear devices was stopped. All data concerning the manufacture or utilization of atomic weapons, the production of fissionable materials, or the use of fissionable materials in the production of power became restricted. The military did not lead the AEC, but the Department of Defense classified nuclear information. By all accounts, fear of the Soviet Union superseded the AEC's safety concerns for soldiers present at testing sites and nearby civilians who suffered fallout exposure.

U.S. Testing Victims. Almost one hundred atmospheric tests were conducted at the Nevada Test Site between 1951 and 1958, which exposed U.S. citizens to the resulting radiation.

After a two-year moratorium with the Soviet Union, 135 more tests occurred prior to the Partial Nuclear Test Ban Treaty. Explosions were authorized only when wind patterns blew the contamination into the less populated areas of Utah, Arizona, and Nevada, rather than toward California. The "downwinders" were deemed to be, according to AEC documents, a "low-use segment of the population." AEC handbills promised that "no danger from or as a result of AEC test activities" would extend beyond the test site locale. The AEC's widely distributed booklet *Atomic Tests in Nevada* (1957) asserts that "Geiger counters . . . going crazy . . . may worry people unnecessarily. Don't let them bother you."

The United States tested thermonuclear (fusion) weapons in 1954 in the Pacific. Following the March 1, 1954, "Bravo" test of a fifteen-megaton (million tons) explosion on Bikini, wind currents carried contamination over the Marshall Islanders. The AEC's own monitors experienced radiation levels that exceeded their equipment's capacity to measure (at one hundred millirads per hour). The AEC's press release noted that the 236 exposed islanders were regarded as "well and happy."

Soldiers served as guinea pigs to assist the government in determining the effectiveness of soldiers exposed to nuclear effects. Between 250,000 and 500,000 U.S. soldiers were brought directly onto ground zero. The July 5, 1957, "Hood" shot was exploded 3,500 yards away from soldiers who had been given secret clearance status and classes at Camp Pendleton before being sworn to secrecy. Military authorities assured them that "Hood" was a "clean" device, although it measured seventy-four kilotons (thousand tons), and created massive fallout.

The vital question of what the health effects of repeated exposure to low-level radiation would be began to plague the AEC's credibility by the 1960's. Studies by Dr. John Gofman and Dr. Arthur Tamplin, as well as articles by Dr. Harold A. Knapp (AEC's Fallout Studies Branch) and Dr. Edward Weiss (U.S. Public Health Services), underscoring the dangers of low-level radiation as verified by the AEC's own secret 1950's data were censored. Gofman and Tamplin became critics of the AEC, which responded in kind. Later evidence seemed to confirm the critics' concerns. For example, Dr. Carl J. Johnson's study of 4,125 Utah downwinders published in the *Journal of the American Medical Association* in 1984 found 288 cancer cases, 109 more than the 179 predicted for a group of that size. Critics of the AEC came to the conclusion that the AEC had been willing to expose soldiers and uninfluential civilians to significant health risks in order to gather data.

Soviet Testing Victims. The Soviet Union's testing program has brutally devastated areas of the Kazakhstan Republic. Over 450 atmospheric nuclear explosions took place at the single "Polygon site" just west of the city of Semipalatinsk. The Soviet government never warned residents of radiation dangers or long-term health problems. When the twenty-six "ground explosions" at Semipalatinsk created toxic fallout levels, the Soviet Union escalated its published levels of acceptable exposure. As a result, some areas of central and eastern Kazakhstan contain significantly higher levels of radioactivity than found in Chernobyl after the reactor accident.

New York City feminists march in support of a nuclear-free planet in October, 1979. (Betty Lane)

Using previously classified information, Leonid Ilyin, director of the Institute of Biophysics at the Russian Federation's Public Health Ministry, concluded that the first Soviet blast, which took place at Semipalatinsk on August 29, 1949, was also the most lethal. The Kurchav Atomic Energy Institute determined that it exposed 200,000 people to radiation levels comparable to those experienced by the Japanese survivors at Hiroshima and Nagasaki. One result is that the region's rate of birth defects is ten times higher than that of Europe, Japan, or the United States. Declassified documents also reveal that six thousand local citizens were monitored but not treated for radiation effects in Semipalatinsk Clinic Number Four by doctors who were prohibited from revealing their findings.

Kazakhstan, independent after 1991, became the first country to close down a nuclear test site (Semipalatinsk), partly in response to a robust grassroots antinuclear movement, which called itself "Nevada-Semipalatinsk." No official compensation has been designated for survivors of Soviet testing.

U.S. Freedom of Information Act. Many victims of the U.S. testing program have received some compensation. The original Freedom of Information Act (1966) was amended in 1974 to force a timely bureaucratic response. Congressional mandates assisted the veterans who had been exposed to atomic tests in receiving benefits from the Department of Veterans Affairs in 1988, and extended limited compensation to civilians through the Radiation Exposure Compensation Act of 1990. The downwinders initially won the Allen case in Federal District Court in 1984. The court found a governmental liability for negligence. The Tenth Circuit Court of Appeals reversed the decision in 1987, citing the government's immunity from prosecution. The U.S. Supreme Court declined to review this decision in 1988. *—Nancy N. Haanstad*

See also Atomic Energy Act of 1954; Chernobyl disaster; Classification of information; "H-Bomb Secret, The"; Military censorship; Science; Soviet secret cities; Three Mile Island.

BIBLIOGRAPHY

The *Bulletin of the Atomic Scientists* (1946-   ) has credibly monitored and vigorously challenged official U.S. nuclear policy and misinformation. Howard Ball's *Justice Downwind: America's Atomic Testing Program in the 1950's* (New York: Oxford University Press, 1986) focuses on the legal struggle of the downwinders. Carole Gallagher's poignant photography and text depict the human cost of nuclear testing in *American Ground Zero: The Secret Nuclear War* (Cambridge, Mass.: MIT Press, 1993). John W. Gofman, a key AEC antagonist, presents his work in *Radiation and Human Health* (San Francisco: Pantheon Books, 1983). *Bombs in the Backyard* by A. Costandina Titus (Reno: University of Nevada Press, 1986) details the AEC's classification and control of nuclear information.

Nude dancing

DEFINITION: Public dancing for purposes of entertainment, or artistic or religious expression, in a state of undress

SIGNIFICANCE: Nude and topless dancing have long been subject to censorship

In the United States nude dancing in public places has drawn debate by pitting the First Amendment rights of free expression against the impact of such personal expressions on society. Dance involving full or partial nudity, or less clothing than is ordinarily worn, has been nearly universal in human cultures. It has been subject to censorship as well, often by religious authorities who fear that dance's sensuality will corrupt the morals of those who practice it or view it.

In the United States such practices have drawn intense debate. From the Puritans observing Native American ceremonial dance, to early twentieth century critics observing modern dance, to priests or parents protesting go-go bars in their neighborhoods, dance involving nudity has been scrutinized ardently. For some, it has provided avenues for entertainment, artistic expression, and even religious practice. For others, such dance is only a challenge to moral and religious beliefs about obscenity and sexuality.

Traditionally, dance has been primarily a female activity and thus has had a marginally valued role in society. Despite the skills and prowess dance requires, it has never gained the respect of similar activities practiced predominantly by men, such as athletics. As such, some advocates of nude and topless dancing argue that censorship of this activity is an effort to control the expression of women. From this perspective, censorship becomes a feminist issue involving First Amendment rights with implications generalizing to artistic, religious, and sexual expression. In contrast, some opponents of nude and topless dancing argue that it demeans women by objectifying them sexually. They suggest that the act of paying women to disrobe in public heightens the vulnerability of women everywhere and is an act of domination by men. Dancers are seen as victims forced to participate in this practice as a function of their vulnerable position in society. Thus, these opponents see censorship as an act which protects women from exploitation.

Still others have argued that nude and topless dancing are obscene practices that encourage immoral behavior. The impact of such practices on society is viewed as debasing and far outweighs the value that such self-expression or employment could provide for any individual. Such opponents link dance involving nudity to prostitution, pornography, sexual abuse, and alcohol and drug problems. It is seen as a pathway to morally repugnant practices involving impulsiveness, indulgence, and exploitation.

Known as burlesque, strip, exotic, go-go, nude, topless, bottomless, booth, striptease, and erotic dance, this cultural practice expanded in late twentieth century America. "Gentleman's clubs" and adult entertainment businesses featuring nude dance have increased in number to the point where they are represented on the stock market. Further, surveys as late as 1992 have indicated increasing acceptance of nudity by the public and the government. While restrictions exist insofar as the contexts in which such performances can be held (for example, behind glass walls, in adult-only settings, or with limits to alcohol sales), this practice appears to have found a stronghold despite its controversies.

See also Burlesque shows; Feminism; *Hair*; Nudity; *Oh, Calcutta!*; Wales padlock law.

Nudity

DEFINITION: Depictions of naked people in art, photography, film, and theatrical productions

SIGNIFICANCE: Nudity is the oldest and most common target of censorship

The naked body has long been the essential subject of artistic expression and the most frequent and persistent object of censorship. The taboos associated with nudity and the general disapproval of the practice of recreational nudism has created a moral justification for the censorship of images of nude men and women. Censors have disapproved of nudity even when no sexual activities are portrayed.

Ancient Greece and Rome. Nudity has played a vital role in the history of visual art. Early Greek sculptures known as kouroi featured handsome young male nudes. Roman art continued to use the nude figure as a symbol of strength and beauty. The advent of Christianity cast a pall of sin over sex and nudity, replacing pagan celebration of the human body as the mirror of divine perfection with the condemnation of nudity as shameful and immoral. The earliest censorship of nudity came in the form of church decrees prohibiting nude images except as part of mythological themes.

The power of art and self-expression persisted in the face of official censure. The works of Renaissance artists such as MichelangeloMichelangelo, Donatello, and Sandro Botticelli made plentiful use of nude figures. Nevertheless, great art was always vulnerable to disapproval from those in high places, as in 1558, when Pope Paul IV ordered that the genitalia of the nude figures in Michelangelo's *The Last Judgment* be painted over with drapery.

In every era, in every age, portrayals of nudity risk official condemnation. In 1769 the Royal Academy of London prohibited unmarried art students under twenty years of age from drawing female nudes using live models. In 1784 a nude Venus was banned in Philadelphia. In 1815 in New York City a nude painting was vilified as "a deplorable example of European depravity."

The Victorian period in England and America engendered strict standards of morality under which portrayals of nudity were not tolerated. The enactment of the Comstock Act of 1873 and obscenity laws codified social and religious taboos on nudity in the arts. In 1933 U.S. Customs seized books containing reproductions of Michelangelo's *The Last Judgment* (which were later released).

Hair* and *Oh, Calcutta! A brief nude scene in the musical *Hair* (which began on Broadway in 1967) was too much for the local officials who ran the municipal theaters in Chattanooga, Tennessee. In 1971, when the city denied permission to stage the show, the producers sued, claiming that the Chattanooga municipal theaters were a "public forum" where the city could not deny permission simply because it objected to the nude scenes in *Hair*. The U.S. Supreme Court agreed and ruled that the city had the burden of seeking a full and prompt adjudication of the issue before it could deny a permit.

Twenty years later, when Kenneth Tynan's *Oh, Calcutta!* (1969), a provocative revue featuring a variety of nude scenes, reached Chattanooga, the city fathers had learned their lesson. Lawyers for the city promptly went to court, arguing that the show violated city and state public indecency laws and was obscene. A local judge empaneled an advisory jury, which found the play patently offensive but not legally obscene, since the play had serious artistic value and lacked an appeal to prurient interest. The trial judge reluctantly concluded that "Whatever little value the play might have, the First Amendment normally protects against prior restraint where the production is not obscene under the legal test." As far as the public indecency charge was concerned, the judge deferred the issue on the grounds that the predicted illegal conduct had not yet occurred. *Oh, Calcutta!* ran without incident and there were no arrests for public nudity.

Nude Dancing. In 1991 the Supreme Court, in *Barnes v. Glen Theater, Inc.*, upheld the use of Indiana's general law against public nudity to ban nude barroom dancing. In particular, the case dealt with the state's requirement that dancers at the South Bend Kitty Kat Lounge wear G-strings and pasties. The judgment of the Court, written by Chief Justice William H. Rehnquist, was only joined in by Justices Sandra Day O'Connor and Anthony M. Kennedy. Justice Rehnquist reluctantly acknowledged that nude dancing was a form of artistic expression, whose primary message was "eroticism and sexuality." Noting that laws against public nudity were part of American history and traceable to "the Bible story of Adam and Eve," Rehnquist upheld the state's requirement of pasties and G-strings on the basis of its interest in "protecting order and morality," which would "not deprive the dance of whatever erotic message it conveys, it simply makes the message slightly less graphic."

Justice David H. Souter wrote a separate concurring opinion, arguing that nudity in entertainment could not be banned on the basis of vague notions of morality. Instead, he upheld the law because of the state's interest in combating the "harmful secondary effects" of nude bars, including "prostitution, sexual assault, and associated crimes." One commentator, Marjorie Heins, director of the American Civil Liberties Union's Arts Censorship Project, noted that "it didn't seem likely that these minor additions to the dancer's anatomy would have an appreciable impact on prostitution, sexual assault, or anything else that might occur in the vicinity of erotic dancing establishments" and doubted that there was any basis "for assuming that nude dancing caused sexual assault or prostitution, or that such problems would be reduced in an area if nude dancing were eliminated."

Justice Antonin Scalia upheld the ban on more direct grounds, without reliance on any secondary effects. He found that the Indiana law raised no First Amendment issue because it simply applied a neutral law against public indecency without any evidence that the state legislature intended to interfere with artistic freedom. Souter questioned Scalia's implication that theatrical nudity could constitutionally be banned. It was "difficult to see how the enforcement of Indiana's statute against nudity in a production of *Hair* or *Equus* somewhere other than an 'adult' theater would further the State's interest in avoiding harmful secondary effects." Heins calls Souter's

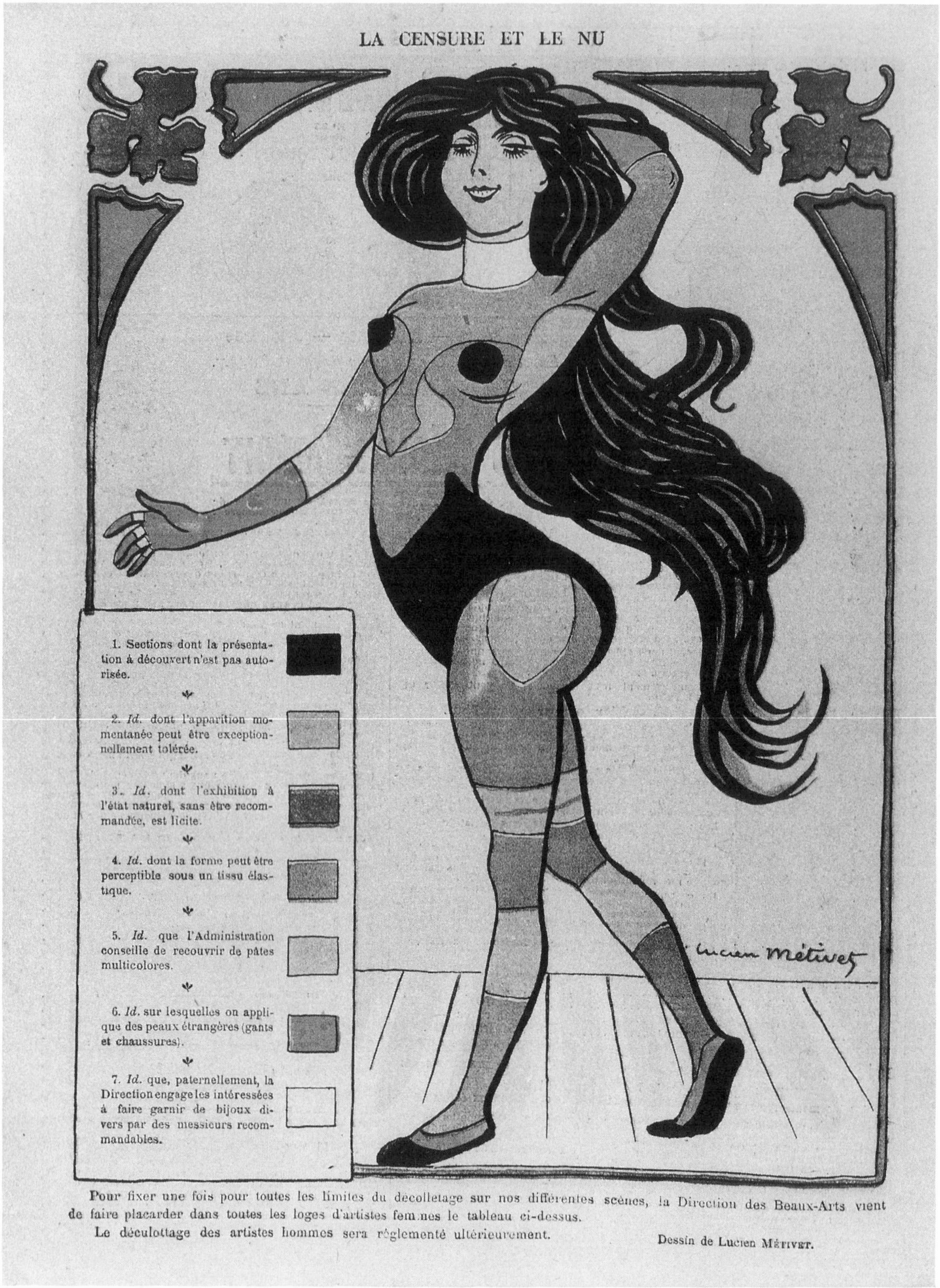
LA CENSURE ET LE NU
1. Sections dont la présentation à découvert n'est pas autorisée.
2. Id. dont l'apparition momentanée peut être exceptionnellement tolérée.
3. Id. dont l'exhibition à l'état naturel, sans être recommandée, est licite.
4. Id. dont la forme peut être perceptible sous un tissu élastique.
5. Id. que l'Administration conseille de recouvrir de pâtes multicolores.
6. Id. sur lesquelles on applique des peaux étrangères (gants et chaussures).
7. Id. que, paternellement, la Direction engage les intéressées à faire garnir de bijoux divers par des messieurs recommandables.
Lucien Métivet
Pour fixer une fois pour toutes les limites du décolletage sur nos différentes scènes, la Direction des Beaux-Arts vient de faire placarder dans toutes les loges d'artistes femmes le tableau ci-dessus.
Le déculottage des artistes hommes sera réglementé ultérieurement.
Dessin de Lucien Métivet.

In 1901 the French journal La Rire *("The Laugh") used this cartoon to satirize government censorship of nudity. Each section of the body is colored-coded to show which censorship restriction applied. For example, white areas could be shown without restriction, black areas could never be shown. Other colors indicated what clothing materials had to be used to cover flesh.* (Robert J. Goldstein)

view elitist, since it would "deprive Joe six-pack of the entertainment that classical dance and opera-goers could enjoy."

Public Funding of Public Nudity. During the uproar over the National Endowment for the Arts and public funding of controversial art, nude images played a prominent role. In 1990 Cincinnati museum director Dennis Barrie was criminally charged with obscenity (for exhibiting homoerotic photographs by the late Robert Mapplethorpe) and child pornography (for two photographs of children, also by Mapplethorpe). The case drew international attention and renewed the debate over whether nude images alone, unaccompanied by any sexual activity, could be legally obscene. After an extensive trial in which the defense called numerous art experts and the prosecution called one (who had worked on the children's television program *Captain Kangaroo*), the jury acquitted Barrie and the museum.

Another artist who came to prominence in the midst of the NEA controversy was Karen Finley. A provocative performance artist, Finley appeared on stage nude, using her body like a canvas, painting it with chocolate, red candies, alfalfa sprouts, and tinsel to dramatize "society's institutionalized debasement of women." When the NEA denied grants to Finley and three other artists, they sued, challenging the denials and the new decency standards imposed by Congress. In June, 1992, a federal court upheld Finley's claim, ruling that the "right of artists to challenge conventional wisdom and values is a cornerstone of artistic and academic freedom."

Thousands of years of nudity in art, theater, film, and photography, paralleled with thousands of years of efforts to censor nudity, reveal the power of the image of the nude body.

—*Stephen F. Rohde*

See also Community standards; Comstock Act of 1873; Film censorship; *Hair*; Mann, Sally; Men's magazines; Michelangelo; *Oh, Calcutta!*; *Playboy*; Pornography; Venus de Milo.

BIBLIOGRAPHY

William E. Hartman, Marilyn Fithian, and Donald Johnson, *Nudist Society: The Controversial Study of the Clothes-Free Naturist Movement in America* (Los Angeles: Elysium Growth Press, 1991), is a comprehensive and illustrated look at the nudist movement in America. The book contains insights into the societal forces that marginalize and condemn nudity and perpetuate the taboo against social and recreational nudism. Marjorie Heins, *Sex, Sin, and Blasphemy: A Guide to America's Censorship Wars* (New York: New York Press, 1993) is a lively and informative survey of key censorship issues by the executive director of the American Civil Liberties Union's Arts Censorship Project. Wendy McElroy, *XXX: A Woman's Right to Pornography* (New York: St. Martin's Press, 1995) is an outspoken and personal account of the adult entertainment industry. Marcia Pally, *Sex and Sensibility: Reflections on Forbidden Mirrors and the Will to Censor* (Hopewell, N.J.: Ecco Press, 1994) is a brief but enlightening look at the censorship of sexual imagery, with attention to feminist efforts to censor sexually explicit material and other issues. David G. Savage, *Turning Right: The Making of the Rehnquist Supreme Court* (New York: John Wiley & Sons, 1992) is a behind-the-scenes look at how U.S. Supreme Court justices have decided critical constitutional cases since Rehnquist became chief justice. Rodney A. Smolla, *Free Speech in an Open Society* (New York: Alfred A. Knopf, 1992) spans a wide range of major First Amendment issues.

NYPD Blue

TYPE OF WORK: Television program

BROADCAST: 1993-

CREATOR AND EXECUTIVE PRODUCER: Steven Bochco (1943-)

SUBJECT MATTER: Police drama that exposes the untidy lives and moral dilemmas of its detective protagonists

SIGNIFICANCE: Written as an adult drama, *NYPD Blue* has tested the boundaries of television standards by including street language and partial nudity

As the creator of such critically acclaimed television programs as *Hill Street Blues* and *LA Law*, Steven Bochco has made a career of creating gritty and tough adult programming. With *NYPD Blue*, Bochco wanted to push beyond where previous weekly shows had gone in regard to language and sexual activity. Before *NYPD Blue* even aired, conservative voices were speaking out against the show. Reverend Donald Wildmon of the American Family Association led a campaign against *NYPD Blue*. Some of the American Broadcasting Company (ABC) stations across the country decided against airing the premiere, while others decided against airing the show at all. The pilot episode contained a brief scene of lovemaking that included a glimpse of a woman's breasts, and dialogue that included such expressions as "douche bag" and "pissy little bitch."

The two main characters of the series were Detective John Kelly (David Caruso) and his partner Detective Andy Sipowicz (Dennis Franz). Set in New York, *NYPD Blue* revolved around more than the mere solving of criminal cases. The detectives wrestled with personal demons including bigotry and alcoholism. Caruso left the show over a salary dispute in 1994 and was replaced by Jimmy Smits as Detective Bobby Simone. Even with all the controversy of the show, *NYPD Blue* became highly popular and critically acclaimed.

Wildmon continued his crusade against the show by writing to the advertisers of the show and complaining about the so-called gross excesses of the upcoming episodes. ABC had a successful show on its hands, but it was unable to charge advertisers the amount it thought appropriate because of the controversy surrounding the show. *NYPD Blue* popularity continued, and it garnered numerous Emmy nominations and awards.

See also Advertisers as advocates of censorship; *Murphy Brown* controversy; National Federation for Decency; Nudity; Prior restraint; Television; Television networks.

O

Obituaries

DEFINITION: Published accounts of persons who have recently died

SIGNIFICANCE: Obituaries have frequently avoided unpleasant aspects of a person's life and death

American newspapers' obituary stories, usually written by cub reporters, contain three parts. First is the death story, which includes the deceased's name, age, time, date, place of death, cause of death, duration of last illness, address, professional and personal background, survivors, and funeral arrangements. Second, the funeral story adds such items as the name of the person conducting the funeral, special music, organizations participating, kind of service, official recognition, special tributes, bearers, place of burial, and miscellaneous information. Last, the deceased's biography includes career, achievements, and comments of associates and friends.

Total or partial censorship of obituaries is common practice under authoritarian and totalitarian governments. Deaths and executions of political opponents in prisons or concentration camps are usually hidden. Sometimes, as in the case of the death of German field marshal Erwin Rommel, the cause of death may be distorted. Rommel, a brilliant general, served Adolf Hitler in World War II, but became convinced by Hitler's delusional commands that Hitler was leading Germany to ruin. Rommel took part in a conspiracy to replace Hitler. When an assassination attempt (which Rommel had not endorsed) uncovered the conspiracy, Rommel was told to commit suicide or face trial. With the promise that his family would not be mistreated if he chose suicide, he took poison. Since he was a national hero, his death was attributed to a hemorrhage resulting from war wounds.

Censorship has been exercised by democratic governments in wartime. The World War II Office of Censorship, for example, issued detailed rules for news media to follow. Information on combat deaths withheld from publication included the exact location, time of death, and the specific unit of service. Peacetime government censorship has sought to hide deaths caused by government incompetence. At other times censorship aims to prevent panic by distorting the number of deaths caused by virulent disease.

Jessica Mitford, in *The American Way of Death* (1963), reports censorship of obituaries. Funeral homes and the florist industry were cooperating to deny requests from families to have printed in obituaries a phrase that typically read: "In lieu of flowers, the family requests that donations be sent to" a named charity. Other allied industries may have sought the withholding of aspects of obituaries not in the interests of their industry, such as the name of the hospital in which the person died.

Newspapers informally censor through editorial policy. Reporters are taught that decorum demands suppressing the gory details of violent deaths. Suicides may be reported euphemistically. Other occasionally omitted parts of obituaries include an embarrassing cause of death, place of death if such a place as an insane asylum or a brothel, past membership in unpopular organizations such as the Communist Party, criminal records, business or professional failures, previous marriages, illegitimate children, homosexuality, or lack of religious affiliation.

See also Advertisers as advocates of censorship; Biography; Death; Letters to editors; Mitford, Jessica; Newspapers; Office of Censorship, U.S.; Suicide.

Oboler, Eli M.

BORN: September 26, 1915, Chicago, Illinois

DIED: June 15, 1983, Pocatello, Idaho

IDENTIFICATION: American librarian

SIGNIFICANCE: Oboler was one of the leading voices against censorship among academic librarians

Oboler took a degree in library science in 1942, then served in the U.S. Army. In 1949 he began his three-decade career as librarian at Idaho State College (later University) in Pocatello, where he planned and supervised the building of two libraries (one of these is now named for him). He also served as president of the American Library Association, wrote hundreds of articles for journals and newspapers, conducted radio and television broadcasts about books and ideas, edited several library magazines, and published two books: *The Fear of the Word: Censorship and Sex* (1974) and *Defending Intellectual Freedom* (1980).

Advancing his opinions with humor and subtle wordplay, Oboler was called "the sharpest needle on campus." He could attack angrily and bluntly, and was equally likely to denounce censorship on his own campus, in his own state, in the nation and in the world. When Idaho State University named its library after Oboler in 1983, Judith Krug of the American Library Association said that Oboler, more than any other librarian, made public his support for intellectual freedom. He called the censor "the enemy of the truth," and quipped that "Man's stumbling climb from savagery to civilization is only impeded, not stopped, by the censor."

See also American Library Association; Freedom to Read Foundation; Libraries; Libraries, school; Library Bill of Rights.

Obscene Publications Acts

ENACTED: 1857, 1959, and 1964

PLACE: United Kingdom (national)

SIGNIFICANCE: These acts were among the major statutes in Great Britain aimed at controlling pornography and obscenity

One of the earliest obscenity statutes in British law, the Obscene Publications Act of 1857 is sometimes called Lord Campbell's Act, after the lord chief justice who proposed it in the House of Lords. Campbell's bill aimed to curb London's pornography trade. It did not create a new offense; instead, it gave authorities holding valid search warrants power to search private premises for obscene materials and to seize and destroy what they found. Despite some opposition to the bill because of the seemingly arbitrary power to censor that it would give to magistrates, Parliament passed the bill in 1857.

The crime of obscene libel had originally developed in English common law to restrict written materials whose religious or political content was objectionable because it was blasphemous, heretical, or seditious. Later the concept was extended to include works whose sexual content was objectionable. In 1727, for example, the Queens Bench Court convicted Edmund Curll of the common law offense of obscene libel for publishing *Venus in the Cloister or the Nun in Her Smock*, a book whose sexual content was considered objectionable.

The Obscene Publications Act of 1857 employed no precise definition of obscenity. In the 1868 case of *Regina v. Hicklin*, Lord Chief Justice Cockburn articulated a test of obscenity that remained the standard in British and American law for nearly a century. It defined as obscene any work that tended "to deprave and corrupt those whose minds are open to such immoral influences." According to Cockburn, it was the effect of the materials—not the author's intent—that mattered.

The Obscene Publications Act of 1959 replaced the Hicklin test with a new statutory definition of obscenity: an "article" was regarded as obscene if its overall effect tended "to deprave and corrupt persons who are likely, having regard to all relevant circumstances, to read, see or hear the matter contained or embodied in it." In practice, this definition—like the Hicklin test—was often disregarded. Real efforts to gauge the depraving and corrupting effects of allegedly obscene articles were rarely made.

The 1959 act eliminated the old common law offense of obscene libel and created the crime of publishing an obscene article or having it for the purpose of publication for gain. It also provided for the seizure by authorities of goods suspected of being obscene. One section of the act established a "public good defense," whereby articles otherwise considered obscene (that is, that they tended to deprave and corrupt) would not be subject to criminal prosecution or seizure if their publication could be "justified as being for the public good" because of their scientific, literary, or artistic value.

The Obscene Publications Act of 1964 sought to close several "loopholes" found in the 1959 act. It created the offense of "having an obscene article for publication for sale." It also broadened the definition of "article" so that photographic negatives were included.

See also Books and obscenity law; Courts and censorship law; Hicklin case; *Miller v. California*; Obscenity: legal definitions; Stag films; *Venus in the Cloister*.

Obscenity: legal definitions

DEFINITION: Legal definitions are what courts use to determine obscenity

SIGNIFICANCE: To convict someone of obscenity, a court must find that the alleged obscenity fits within a legal definition

The U.S. Supreme Court has long balanced other rights, including the public's presumed right to be protected from obscene materials, against the right of free expression. The press has a right to publish without prior restraint, but there is a corresponding right of adults to avoid being publicly assaulted by displays they regard as offensive. There is an even greater need to protect children from pornographic materials, which might damage their emotional development. Prior restraint is also allowed for pictures of sexual acts by children, as the U.S. Supreme Court made clear in *New York v. Ferber* (1982), and sex acts involving children are against the law in every U.S. jurisdiction. Filming an illegal sex act is also illegal, so such restraint is easy to define.

Regarding adult publications for private use at home, the Supreme Court has allowed some prior restraints, but it has had great difficulty in defining them, principally because of the strong constitutional presumption against prior restraint and because it is hard to define what is pornographic and what is not. The Court has consistently held that obscenity is not protected under the First Amendment, but the Court had had serious problems defining what is obscene.

First Definition Used in the United States. The first definition of obscenity was derived from the ruling of the British courts in the Hicklin case (*Regina v. Hicklin*, 1868). In the Victorian era, the British courts chose a broad definition of obscenity. A "tendency" in the material alleged to be obscene "to deprave and corrupt those whose minds are open to such immoral influences and into whose hands" the material "may fall," was sufficient to ban an entire work.

This definition was used by the authorities on the federal and state levels in the United States from its announcement until it was revised by the twentieth century federal courts. To say that it was used is not to say that it was not under attack. One critic, U.S. federal judge Curtis Bok, argued that the Hicklin rule "renders any book unsafe, since a moron could pervert to some sexual fantasy to which his mind was open the listings of a seed catalogue."

In the United States, the Hicklin definition survived until the 1930's, when Random House wanted to publish an uncut version of James Joyce's *Ulysses* (1922) and prepared a legal challenge to a U.S. Customs ban on the book. In the case, *United States v. One Book Entitled Ulysses* (1934), Judge John M. Woolsey ruled that the book was not obscene. When his reasoning was upheld by the Supreme Court, it became known as the Ulysses standard, which lasted until 1957. The most significant definitional change in the Ulysses standard was to abandon the notion that an isolated passage could render a work obscene. Woolsey held that a work could only be judged obscene if "the publication taken as a whole has a libidinous effect." Woolsey found that any work that was written deliberately as titillating pornography could be banned, but he asserted that the conclusion would have to be made by the "average person" who was defined as the close equivalent of the legal concept of the reasonable man.

First Modern Definition. The Supreme Court gave the first modern definition of obscenity in *Roth v. United States* (1957). The Court's first premise was that "All ideas having even the slightest redeeming social importance—unorthodox ideas, controversial ideas, even ideas hateful to the prevailing climate of opinion—have the full protection." With this first premise, the Court faced a difficult job of finding any way to block obscenity. The First Amendment has been interpreted to guarantee all ideas against any prior restraint except obscene ones. The definition of obscenity thus became crucial, but difficult. Chief Justice Earl Warren once said the definition of obscenity presented the Court with its most difficult area of adjudication. Obscenity was fully defined by the following phrase: "Whether to the average person applying contemporary community standards, the dominant theme of the material taken as a whole appeals to prurient interests."

"Prurient" was defined as "material having a tendency to excite lustful thoughts." However, the Court also asserted that "sex and obscenity are not synonymous." Obviously, the Court could not equate sex and obscenity without banning a whole range of artistic, medical, and scientific materials. While there is a certain logic in the Roth decision, the logic is achieved only by using words that themselves are not easy to define. Obscenity may be defined but the word "prurient" is also hard to define. What is meant by a community standard is also quite vague. Reaching judicial determinations on whether particular works do or do not fit within a definition made up of so many vague words is daunting. The Court has suffered the logical outcome of the vague definition: a flood of litigation that appeals to the Court for clarification. The Court has faced an extremely large number of obscenity cases being presented to it. Furthermore, its apparent agreement on the definition was short-lived.

By 1967, several distinct positions were evident. Associate justices Hugo Black and William O. Douglas maintained that the principle of no prior restraint is so strong that neither federal, state, nor local governments have any power to regulate any sexually oriented matter on the ground of obscenity. Associate Justice John Marshall Harlan took the diametrically opposed view that the federal government could control the distribution of pornography by using its enumerated powers, and that states were entitled to even greater freedom to ban any materials that state courts had reasonably found to treat sex in a fundamentally offensive manner under rational standards for judging such material.

A variety of other views were held by the other justices, and the remaining justices changed their statements so often that it is difficult to characterize their points of view. From 1967 until 1973, the court followed the practice in *Redrup v. New York* (1967). The Court granted reversals of convictions for the dissemination of obscene materials that at least five members of the Court, applying their separate tests, deemed not to be obscene. These reversals were *per curiam* (that is, they set no precedents) and were unsatisfactory because they did not include any accompanying opinions as guidance for lower courts. As do vague guidelines, *per curiam* decisions invite endless litigation.

At one point in the struggle to define pornography, Associate Justice Potter Stewart, with evident frustration, said of obscenity: "I can't define it, but I know it when I see it." This is an accurate description of what the Court was doing from 1967 to 1973, when it was forced to rely on *per curiam* decisions. The *per curiam* decisions were not working: It was unsatisfactory for all lower courts, prosecuting attorneys, police officers, defense attorneys, the producers of such materials, and the public.

The Miller Case. A new definition was offered in the case of *Miller v. California* (1973) and in a companion case *Paris Adult Theater 1 v. Slaton* (1973), when the Court revised its definition, which was no more adequate than the old. Since five justices voted for the definition, it became the new definitive holding (or leading case). The new definition made two major changes. First, it specifically rejected the standard "utterly without redeeming social value" established in *Memoirs v. Massachusetts* (1966) in favor of a broader standard that the obscene work must "appeal to the prurient interest in sex, which portray sexual conduct in a patently offensive way, and which, taken as a whole, do not have serious literary, artistic, political, or scientific value." Second, it rejected the notion that some kind of national "community standards" exists in favor of "community standards" determined by local areas. The Court explained: "our nation is simply too big and too diverse for this Court to reasonably expect that such standards could be articulated for all 50 states in a single formulation, even assuming the prerequisite consensus exists. To require a state to structure obscenity proceedings around evidence of a national 'community standard' would be an exercise in futility." Promptly some communities began defining obscenity very broadly. A Georgia community banned a nationally recognized film (*Carnal Knowledge*, 1971) because an actress in it exposed her "bare midriff." In *Jenkins v. Georgia* (1974), the Court was again faced with making a decision on a case-by-case basis.

Censorship and prior restraint are so alien to the American system that the Court has found it difficult to apply censorship in nearly any area. The Court acknowledges that society has rights to protect adults from unwanted public obscenity and to protect children, but the Court is uncomfortable with any form of prior restraint. It may be that there is no way to write a clear obscenity law.

—Richard L. Wilson

See also Books and obscenity law; Heresy; Hypocrisy; *Miller v. California*; Obscenity: sale and possession; Pornography; President's Commission on Obscenity and Pornography; Prior restraint; *Roth v. United States*.

BIBLIOGRAPHY

The best book of general scholarship on the subject is Henry J. Abraham and Barbara A. Perry, *Freedom and the Court* (New York: Oxford, 1994). For a very concise, thoughtful summary of all the reasons why it is so difficult to fashion a rule or definition of pornography, see Kent Greenawalt, "Pornography," in *Speech, Crime, and the Uses of Language* (New York: Oxford, 1989). One of the best edited casebooks for the general reader is Wallace Mendelson's *The American Constitution and Civil Liberties* (Homewood, Ill: Dorsey, 1981). An interesting broad overview of freedom of speech generally is Jeremy Cohen's *Congress Shall Make No Law* (Ames: Iowa State University, 1989).

Obscenity: sale and possession

DEFINITION: The marketing and ownership of materials that mainstream society regards as obscene

SIGNIFICANCE: The U.S. Supreme Court has protected the right to possess obscene materials in one's home, while allowing some censorship of obscene materials by jurisdictions using contemporary local community standards

In *Roth v. United States* (1957) the Supreme Court developed a complex doctrine defining obscenity and establishing rules that governed who may possess obscene material and under which circumstances it may be sold or distributed. The Court's doctrine on sale and distribution of obscene materials appears to contradict other decisions concerning its private possession.

Distribution to Adults. In *Roth*, the Court followed long standing precedent and ruled that obscene materials do not enjoy First Amendment protection, thus allowing the federal government to punish those who send such materials through the mail. State and local governments also may punish those individuals who sell, or who possess with the intent to sell, obscene materials. However, during the same year, the Court also maintained that Michigan could not punish individuals who made literature available to the adult population that would "manifestly tend to corrupt the morals of youth." Through *Butler v. Michigan* (1957), the Court declared that such a law would have the effect of reducing the entire population of Michigan to reading only what was fit for children.

In three separate cases in 1966 the Court attempted to clarify when states could punish individuals who distributed obscene materials. In *Memoirs v. Massachusetts* (1966), the Court explained that before a state may restrict a work, it must meet three conditions. First, the work's dominant theme, taken as a whole, must appeal to a prurient interest in sex. Second, the work must be patently offensive, violating contemporary community standards involving sexual matters. Third, the work must be utterly without any redeeming social value. In the companion case, *Ginsberg v. State of New York* (1968), the Court asserted that a state or locality may punish a distributor if the "commercial exploitation of erotica [is] solely for the sake of their prurient appeal," even if the work might not be obscene in other circumstances. Finally, the Court contended through *Mishkin v. New York* (1968), that obscene works distributed to certain "deviant" groups need only to appeal to the prurient interests of that group and not to society as a whole before the works can be restricted.

In *Miller v. California* (1973) the Supreme Court rejected a national community standard on obscenity and thus allowed communities to restrict works they felt were obscene. The *Miller* case refined the *Memoirs* definition of obscenity, and reduced the constitutional barriers limiting state attempts to regulate obscenity. With the *Miller* case, states and communities could regulate materials that they defined as obscene. However, although the Court allowed states broader regulatory powers concerning obscene materials, the Court overturned a conviction in *Jenkins v. Georgia* (1974) by asserting that local juries applying contemporary community standards are not free from First Amendment boundaries.

Distribution to Minors. The Supreme Court did not, however, allow states broad regulatory powers when it came to minors. Three cases illustrate the progression of the obscenity distribution doctrine regarding minors. In *Redrup v. New York* (1967), the Court stated that it would only uphold as constitutional those antiobscenity laws prohibiting distribution to juveniles, along with those prohibiting obscene materials from being foisted upon an unwilling audience. In *Ginsberg v. New York*, the Court clarified its stand on the distribution of obscene materials to minors, and declared that a state could only regulate obscene materials with respect to minors if that material satisfied three requirements. Above all, the work or material could have no redeeming social importance for minors. Additionally, the work had to have a predominant appeal to the prurient interest of minors, and the material had to be patently offensive to the prevailing community standards of what was suitable materials for minors.

The Court further justified this more conservative position on distribution concerning minors in 1982 with the decision in *New York v. Ferber*. With this case, the Supreme Court declared that states are "entitled to greater leeway in the regulation of pornographic depictions of children." Because the state "bears so heavily and pervasively on the welfare of children . . . it is permissible to consider these materials without first amendment protection." Although the Court regarded minors as a separate category concerning distribution, it maintained, through its decision in *Pinkus v. United States*, that a community could not include children in the concept of the "local community." Rather, when determining obscenity, communities could only punish the relevant forms of distribution.

Possession. When it came to the possession of obscene materials, the Supreme Court was not as conservative as it had been concerning the distribution of such materials. In *Stanley v. Georgia* (1969) the Court ruled that "the first and fourteenth amendment prohibit making mere private possession of obscene material a crime." While the states still retained broad powers to censor the sale of obscenity, these powers simply did not extend into the privacy of the home. To justify this position, a unanimous Supreme Court cited First Amendment protection for an individual to receive information and ideas, regardless of their social worth, and a right of privacy to possess materials which satisfy one's emotional and intellectual needs.

With the *Stanley* decision, the Court caught itself in a contradiction. If someone has the right to possess obscene materials in the privacy of the home, then logically someone else should have at least the limited right to sell or distribute that material to those with a right to privately possess it. After all, if according to the Court, one has the right to receive information or ideas regardless of their social worth, then prohibiting the distribution of such materials should be a violation of the right to receive the material.

Other lower courts saw this contradiction. The Supreme Court, however, refused to correct this contradiction, while reasserting through *United States v. Films* in 1972, that the right to privately possess obscene materials did not afford a "correlative right to acquire, sell, or import such material even for private use." The Court also rejected an argument that prohibition of possession was necessary to enforce a prohibition on the sale or distribution of such items. The right to read or observe, the Court stated, is dominant, and "its restriction may not be justified by the need to ease the administration of otherwise valid criminal laws." However, the Court still maintains that while one has the right to possess obscene materials, one does not necessarily have the right to acquire them.

—Thomas Clifton Greenholtz

See also Books and obscenity law; Community standards; *Miller v. California*; Obscenity: legal definitions; *Roth v. United States*.

Bibliography

Edward Shaughnessy's *A Standard for Miller: A Community Response to Pornography* (Lanham, Md.: University Press of America, 1980) provides an account of community enactment of laws banning obscenity after the Court's ruling in *Miller v. California. Censorship and the Public Morality*, by P. R. MacMillan (Aldershot, England: Gower, 1983) gives a comprehensive history of the banning of obscene materials in the United Kingdom and the United States. Edward de Grazia's *Censorship Landmarks* (New York: R. R. Bowker, 1969) is an excellent general reference book for new readers on obscenity case law.

Occult

Definition: Beliefs pertaining to mystical or deviant knowledge, such as those found in magic and witchcraft, that are unacceptable to mainstream religion or science

Significance: Opponents of new religious movements have often characterized these movements as evil and dangerous occult groups in order to legitimize their censorship and suppression

In the 1960's American society underwent a spiritual revolution that seemed to threaten conventional religions. The youth of that period alienated their parents by experimenting with lifestyles involving drug use, communal living, and Eastern mysticism. To retrieve their young, parental groups organized grassroots associations to combat and suppress new religious movements, which they termed "cults." The censorship of marginal religions, however, was not unique to this turbulent period. Labeling as "occult" any deviations from the norm has had a long and destructive employment.

Origins. Since the late Middle Ages, the term "occult" has continuously acquired meanings so vast as to render it almost useless for analysis. Coined by medieval alchemists to refer to their arcane arts such as magic and astrology, the word became a derogatory expression with the development of science in the seventeenth century. The rationalists of the eighteenth century Enlightenment wished to distinguish their disciplines from the medieval precedents: for example, alchemy/chemistry, astrology/astronomy, and numerology/mathematics. The earlier arts had long histories that began at the shamanistic dawn of human society. Urbanization and intense cultural exchange and contact gave birth to new universal religions. This development diminished the authority of local, and mainly rural, spiritual persons such as herbalists, witches, magicians, and nature worshipers. These traditions survived as an occult underground, which was censored and persecuted; striking instances were the Spanish Inquisition and the Salem witch trials.

The old arts did not die out with the rise of axial traditions such as Christianity, Islam, and Buddhism. They went underground and became secret, esoteric, and highly specialized. Monasticism and Gnosticism, Sufism, and Tantracism found places within, but separate from, the larger exoteric religions. A major difference between the two groups is the emphasis on experience/theosophy by the esoterists, and a focus on doctrine/theology by the exotericists. An occult formation also occurred in the Reformation with the simultaneous birth of Protestantism and Free Masonry. Throughout the modern period, since the eighteenth century, occultism and Romanticism have clashed with scientific rationalism. In addition, the latter, termed "secular humanism," became the focus of attack by Fundamentalist Christians in the mid-twentieth century.

Anticult Movements. The anticult movement (ACM) was created in the 1970's by a loose coalition of grassroots organizations initially concerned with "deprogramming" their children in new religious movements (NRMs) labeled "cults." This campaign captured the attention of mainstream church groups and local law enforcers. By the 1990's the Christian right sought to control the education of their youth through political activism in local school boards. Most of these attempts at censorship failed to convince the judicial establishment to violate constitutionally guaranteed freedoms. This, however, did not dampen the enthusiasm of ACMs.

ACMs such as the Parents' Committee to Free Our Sons and Daughters from the Children of God Organization (FREECOG)—later the Citizens Freedom Foundation (CFF), American Family Foundation, Cult Awareness Network, mounted a concerted effort against NRMs. These grassroots and vigilante-like groups charged the Reverent Sun Myung Moon's Unification Church, the Children of God, the Divine Light Mission, and the Hare Krishnas with kidnapping, enslavement, and "brainwashing." The Unification Church was the first movement targeted by the ACM. In the 1977 case of *Katz v. Superior Court of California*, a judge allowed a group of parents temporary conservatorship of five members of the church due to their adult children's alleged victimization by occult mind-control techniques. In the same year, the Vermont case of *Schuppin v. Unification Church* found parents claiming the enslavement of their daughter. In 1978 an Arizona church member resisted the guardianship of his father by a claim of violation of religious freedom in *Rankin v. Howard*. Most suits against the church were overturned on the grounds of religious freedom.

Legislative bills to curtail NRM activities were also unsuccessful. In 1979 the Pennsylvania legislature sought to limit the activities of the Unification Church, the Hare Krishnas, Scientology, and others. The bills of attainder—those that determine improper activities of a group—violated the due process clause of the Fourteenth Amendment. The separation of church and state prevents states from practicing attaint. Pennsylvania unsuccessfully introduced House Bill 406 in 1981, which refrained from mentioning religious groups. That same year, a similar fate fell upon Maryland's House Joint Resolution 67 and Massachusetts' House 5272. In 1982 the Supreme Court ruled that one religion could not be favored over any other.

The ACM has, however, had some success in challenging the operations of NRMs. In the "booth requirement" case, the U.S. Supreme Court ruled in 1981 that religious groups could be limited by states in the selling of merchandise and in the soliciting of funds. State fair officials in Minnesota required that the Hare Krishna sect contain its activities of fund raising and literature distribution to certain locations. Yet to be decided by the court is the performance of such activities at airports, bus stations, malls, and other public places.

Culture Wars. Censorship of the occult spread from persecution of NRMs to other aspects of culture, especially to education. These attempts were more successful due to stronger political activity. In the local and state elections of 1992, the Christian Coalition placed its candidates in 40 percent of the nation's contests, notably for school boards.

Beginning with objections to the Arm & Hammer baking soda logo of stars surrounding the Man in the Moon, the attack on the occult in culture spread to Halloween celebrations. Black cats and haunted houses, said to be rooted in satanic rituals by some religious fundamentalists, forced the banning of the holiday in schools across the country in 1993. Children were not consoled by a Fall Festival at an elementary school in Pine Island, Florida. Nor were students happy about the "Reading Is Fundamental Day" at a middle school in Banning, California, even though they were allowed to dress as their favorite book characters. The anti-Halloween alarm of groups such as Citizens for Excellence in Education located in Costa Mesa, California, pointed to the growing influence of evangelical Christianity's war on the occult in the 1990's.

The thrust of ACM influence in the nation's school boards threatened drastically to alter educational curricula. Among the three hundred words and phrases used by the National Congress for Educational Excellence to identify objectionable material are "occult" and "witchcraft." Books concerned with these themes, such as *The Exorcist* by William P. Blatty, *The Reincarnation of Peter Proud* by Max Ehrlich, and *Rosemary's Baby* by Ira Levin, have been routinely restricted by boards, which withhold funds for them or which refuse credit for reading them.

Assessment. NRMs have been censored for employing the same procedures used by groups as diverse as the military and the monastery. ACMs have attempted to censor all that does not conform to their narrow dogma. This has included all non-Western religious culture, contemporary psychological theory, evolution theory, and most popular culture found in films, recordings, and books. This activity has spread since the 1960's to include holidays, advertisements, school curricula, new religious movements, and other cultural manifestations. In the mid-1990's, its success, while significant, is by no means dominant. The legal system has yet to yield to its demands to curtail religious and individual freedom. Most mainstream churches see the attack on NRMs as an attack that could also be directed at themselves. —*William Howard Green*

See also Advertisers as targets of censorship; *Exorcist, The*; Fairy tales; Halloween; Leary, Timothy; Masonry; Moral Majority; Native Americans; Religion; Scientology, Church of; UFO evidence.

BIBLIOGRAPHY

James Webb's *The Occult Establishment* (La Salle, Ill.: Open Court Publishing, 1976) is one of the most comprehensive studies of the occult in modern times. Howard Kerr and Charles L. Crow, eds., *The Occult in America: New Historical Perspectives* (Urbana: University of Illinois Press, 1983), examines the study of the occult by sociologists and historians who seek to define and describe its influence in American culture. Thomas Robbins, William C. Shepherd, and James McBride, *Cults, Culture, and the Law: Perspectives on New Religious Movements* (Chico, Calif.: Scholars Press, 1985), gives a cogent account of the relationship between ACMs and NRMs from a legal perspective. Among the best sources for understanding the development and dynamics of ACM activity are Anson D. Shupe, Jr., and David G. Bromley, eds., *Anti-cult Movements in Cross-Cultural Perspective* (New York: Garland, 1994); *The New Vigilantes: Deprogrammers, Anti-Cultists, and the New Religions* (Beverly Hills: Sage Publications, 1980); David G. Bromley and Anson D. Shupe, Jr., *Strange Gods: The Great American Cult Scare* (Boston: Beacon Press, 1981). Edward A. Tiryakian, ed., *On the Margin of the Visible: Sociology, the Esoteric, and the Occult* (New York: John Wiley, 1974), gives a broad survey of the complex sociocultural phenomena subsumed by the term occult. James D. Tabor and Eugene V. Gallagher's *Why Waco?: Cults and the Battle for Religious Freedom in America* (Berkeley: University of California Press, 1995) is an analysis of one NRM that had a tragic end as a result of the flawed understanding of NRMs promoted by ACMs.

O'Connor, Sinead

BORN: December 8, 1967, Dublin, Ireland

IDENTIFICATION: Irish singer and songwriter

SIGNIFICANCE: O'Connor attracted strong public protests and was censored by a television network after she shredded a picture of Pope John Paul II on *Saturday Night Live*

In October, 1992, O'Connor sang on an episode of the television program *Saturday Night Live*. In the midst of her performance she exclaimed: "Fight the real enemy!" and then tore up a photograph of Pope John Paul II. Staunchly anti-Roman Catholic, O'Connor had previously protested the church's stance on abortion. The National Broadcasting Company (NBC) aired the complete incident; however, when the network later rebroadcast the episode, it replaced O'Connor's original segment with footage of her rehearsing for the broadcast. An NBC spokesperson stated that the network would never rebroadcast O'Connor's original performance.

Shortly after her appearance on *Saturday Night Live*, O'Connor appeared at New York City's Madison Square Garden in a benefit performance honoring Bob Dylan, but was booed off the stage by the crowd. Other protesters rented a steamroller and used it to crush some of her recordings in New York. The National Ethnic Coalition of Organizations, which

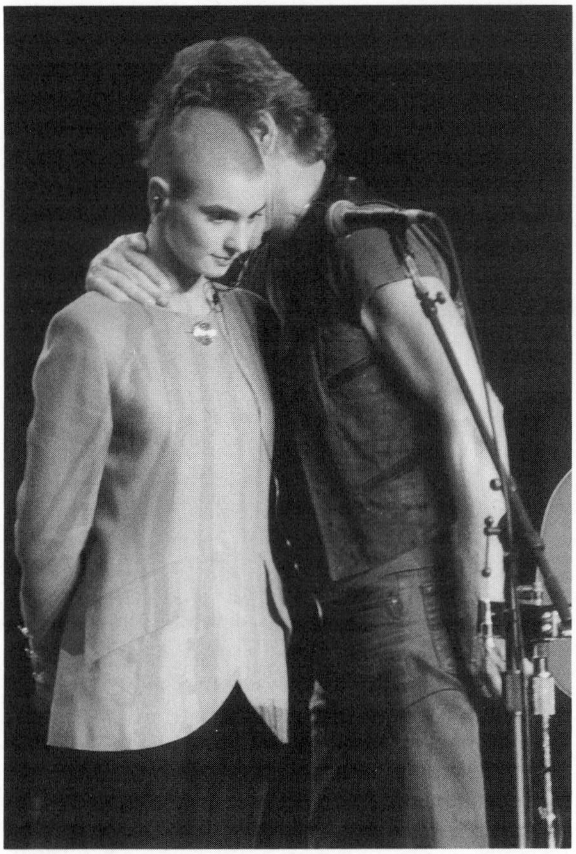

Kris Kristofferson comforts Sinead O'Connor as she is booed off a New York stage in her first public performance after shredding a photograph of the pope on Saturday Night Live *in late 1992.* (AP/Wide World Photos)

represents several ethnic organizations in the United States, placed a bounty on O'Connor albums, promising to donate ten dollars to charity on behalf of anyone who sent one of her records to the organization.

See also Ireland; Protest music; Religion; *Saturday Night Live*; Television networks.

Off-the-record information

Definition: Information given to news reporters with the understanding that it cannot be published or broadcast

Significance: News sources have been known to provide information off the record in order to inhibit its publication

Throughout the world thousands of people willingly allow their names to be quoted in newspaper and broadcast news stories every day. However, others refuse to talk to the press out of fear for their safety, reputations, or job security. Often, however, these same people agree to speak "off the record." That is, they will talk with reporters on condition that the reporters not use their names or publish what they say. Sometimes people agree to speak "on background"—that is, they permit reporters to use what they say, so long as the reporters do not reveal their names. Most journalists agree that sources cannot decide to go "off the record" after providing their information. For this reason, it is essential that sources get journalists to agree to accept their information as off the record before they are interviewed.

Journalists have sometimes complained that sources use off-the-record information as a ploy to censor news by forcing reporters to guarantee that their information will never be used in the press. Most journalism professionals believe, however, that agreeing not to publish or broadcast one source's off-the-record information does not ethically bar reporters from using such information to help them find other sources who will provide the same information on the record.

See also News media censorship; Press conferences; Privileged communication; Watergate scandal.

Offensive language

Definition: Vulgar, obscene, profane, or insulting words

Significance: Some words and forms of expression, by their nature, so readily offend certain people that language often becomes a target of censorship

The U.S. Supreme Court has held that some offensive language may be censored, but that political ideas are generally protected, even if communicated offensively. The larger category of offensive language may be separated into the topics of fighting words, symbolic speech, and hate speech. Sometimes these categories are taken to include profanity—irreverent utterances that offend the holders of certain religious beliefs. For example, the Federal Communications Commission attempted to regulate broadcasting indecency complaints by enforcing a federal statute that imposed fines and prison sentences on "whoever utters any obscene, indecent, or profane language by means of radio communication."

The classic case regarding fighting words is *Chaplinsky v. New Hampshire* (1942) in which the appellant addressed a city marshal as a "God-damned racketeer" and "a damned Fascist." The Supreme Court ruled that Walter Chaplinsky's words were unprotected by the First Amendment because they were fighting words, or words that "inflict injury or tend to incite an immediate breach of the peace." Because of this decision, governments may prohibit or punish such language as a breach of the peace.

The Court's decisions regarding symbolic speech also indicate what may and may not be censored. Symbolic speech is recognized by the Court as having First Amendment protection in certain circumstances and having the same impact as the spoken word. Because of offensiveness, the state of California prosecuted Robert Cohen for breach of the peace after he wore a jacket that had "Fuck the Draft" written on it inside a Los Angeles County Courthouse. The Court did not see Cohen's action as a breach of the peace, but instead communication of ideas. Conservative Supreme Court justice John M. Harlan, who authored the opinion in *Cohen v. California* (1971), stated in defense of Cohen's jacket that "one man's vulgarity is another man's lyric."

Hate speech is a form of offensive language characterized by malicious intent and the use of slurs or epithets against those of racial, ethnic, religious, or other groups. Hate speech is very closely related to fighting words in that it involves a

Online Vulgarity

An echo of Supreme Court justice John M. Harlan's 1971 dictum that "one man's vulgarity is another man's lyric" was heard in 1995. Late that year the popular online service America Online (AOL) announced that it was adding "breast" to the list of vulgar words it would not permit in bulletin board discussions. The announcement evoked immediate and loud protests, particularly from women using AOL's breast cancer bulletin board. Admitting that it had erred, AOL quickly announced that the word would be permitted, "as long as it is used in an appropriate manner."

personal attack. Because of its insulting and repugnant nature, hate speech is subject to censorship. The 1992 case of *R.A.V. v. St. Paul* tested the constitutionality of a law prohibiting hate speech. That law failed to meet with constitutional standards, as it required a content distinction in its enforcement.

Because offensive language affects the sensitivities of some individuals, censorship becomes an issue. However, the Court noted in the Cohen case that people cannot "forbid particular words without also . . . suppressing ideas." Unlike the speech uttered by Chaplinsky, the ideas expressed on Cohen's jacket were expressed to no one in particular. Rather, they communicated in general his political ideas. Based on such cases, the Court has acknowledged the distinction between language which is involved in the exchange of ideas and language which merely serves as a personal offense against another. Therefore, the greater the likelihood speech serves only to distress or provoke others, the lesser the likelihood it will be afforded constitutional protection.

See also Fighting words; First Amendment; Free Speech Movement; Hate laws; Political campaigning; Unprotected speech.

Office of Censorship, U.S.

Founded: December 14, 1941

Type of organization: Government agency office created when the United States entered World War II

Significance: This office coordinated voluntary and mandatory censorship policies, seeking to prevent disclosure of U.S. military secrets

Nine days after the United States entered World War II, President Franklin D. Roosevelt declared to the nation the necessity of censorship in times of war. "All Americans," he stated, "abhor censorship, just as they abhor war." But the president continued by noting that censorship was inevitable in a time of war and by observing that America was indeed at war. He therefore concluded that national security required military information of possible use to the enemy to be "scrupulously withheld at the source," and that laws prohibiting dissemination of such information had to be "rigidly enforced." To this end, he established the Office of Censorship by executive order on December 19, 1941. The office operated until abolished by an executive order on September 28, 1945.

The Office of Censorship's most important role in restricting the publication of sensitive military information was to propose in 1942 a voluntary system of media restraint in the form of a Code of Wartime Practices. This code consisted of guidelines to be adopted by the press. The code urged that information not be published that related to troop, ship, and plane movements, fortifications, weather conditions, casualty lists, damage to various military targets, transportation of war materials, and the movement of U.S. officials traveling abroad. In addition to the promulgation of this code, the Office of Censorship also had responsibility for inspecting mail and cable entering and leaving the United States and for censoring items that threatened national security.

The Code of Wartime Practices included a provision restraining news stories about new or secret military weapons. Perhaps the most dramatic and successful application of this provision was to news regarding development of the atomic bomb. Members of the press, being generally in support of U.S. involvement in World War II, were in the main willing partners with the government in maintaining voluntary censorship rules formulated by the Office of Censorship. This willingness included censorship of stories relating to research concerning atomic weapons. Although the blanket over this information was not complete and was pierced occasionally leaks concerning the bomb were relatively infrequent and never rose to a level sufficient to persuade government officials to elevate wartime censorship to the level of a mandatory code. The overwhelming willingness of the press to cooperate in this suppression of sensitive war-related news did not replicate itself in the wars that followed, perhaps because World War II was a conflict in which the nation's combative role was readily accepted by members of the media and the general public.

See also Military censorship; National security; News media censorship; Nuclear research and testing; War; World War II.

Official Secrets Act (Canada)

Enacted: 1939

Place: Canada (national)

Significance: This federal law provided penalties for unauthorized publication of classified government documents

The government of Prime Minister William Lyon Mackenzie King hastily introduced and passed the Official Secrets Act shortly after Canada entered World War II. The law was modeled directly on Great Britain's 1911 Official Secrets Act, with only a few words changed. It provided for fourteen-year jail sentences for anyone who released or retained classified government information without proper authorization. Of the twenty-one persons prosecuted under the law by 1985, only nine had been convicted.

Most persons charged under the act have been civil servants. The most famous case involved Peter Treu, an engineer working for the North Atlantic Treaty Organization (NATO). Treu was charged under the act with taking home official documents without permission; there was no evidence that he intended to pass the government files to a foreign power. After he was tried in secret, he was released on appeal. Nevertheless, he lost his

NATO job and was driven into bankruptcy by his legal fees.

Another famous case involved the *Toronto Sun* newspaper. In 1978 the *Sun* published details of a Royal Canadian Mounted Police document that had been classified "Top Secret." Although this document passed through many unauthorized hands before the newspaper published it, the government charged the newspaper under the Official Secrets Act. A judge eventually dismissed the charge; however, the newspaper still had to pay a large legal bill.

Since adoption of the Canadian Charter of Rights and Freedoms in 1982 the number of voices clamoring for revision of the Official Secrets Act has grown, but the law has remained in place.

See also Defense ("D") notices; Espionage; Licensing Act of 1662; National security; *Spycatcher*.

Official Secrets Act (U.K.)

Enacted: August 22, 1911

Place: United Kingdom (national)

Significance: This act has frequently been used by British governments to suppress publication of materials alleged to threaten the nation's security and vital interests

The Official Secrets Act (OSA) was originally passed by the British Parliament to deter spying and to establish legal procedures and penalties for those who betrayed Britain's national interests. The 1911 act—which was actually a substantial revision of a similar law passed in 1889—has been periodically amended, most notably in 1920 and 1939. Its most controversial provision, section 2, effectively prohibits the unauthorized disclosure of official information acquired by current or former governmental employees in the course of their work. The act also provides punishments for anyone who receives such information knowing that it has been passed on in violation of the law.

After the 1970's the OSA came under increasing attack. Civil libertarians were concerned about vague phrases in the act, such as "official information" and "national security," which could be variously interpreted. Historians believed that the government occasionally looked foolish in attempting to suppress books about events that had occurred far in the past and whose principal participants were dead. Above all, however, there was a growing suspicion that the OSA was being misused to suppress information exposing the incompetence, treachery, fiscal mismanagement, and blatant illegalities of government agents and agencies. This was particularly true of written materials that dealt with Britain's major security organizations, MI5 (counterintelligence) and MI6 (espionage abroad).

Perhaps the most celebrated case involving the OSA began in 1985, when the government of Prime Minister Margaret Thatcher attempted unsuccessfully to prevent Peter Wright, a former member of MI5, from publishing his memoirs, *Spycatcher*. Despite repeated protestations to liberalize the act by successive governments, no substantive reforms had been accomplished by the mid-1990's.

See also Defense ("D") notices; Espionage; Licensing Act of 1662; National security; Official Secrets Act (Canada); *Spycatcher*.

Oh, Calcutta!

Type of work: Musical stage play

Premiered: June 17, 1969

Creator: Kenneth Tynan (1927-1980)

Subject matter: Sketches and group musical numbers

Significance: This musical revue extended the boundaries of acceptable stage nudity, simulated sexual intercourse, and ribald humor in the American theater and London theater

Oh, Calcutta! premiered at the Eden Theater in New York City on June 17, 1969, and in London the following year. Originally devised by the drama critic, author, and journalist Kenneth Tynan, as "an evening of elegant erotica," it was conceived and directed by Jacques Levy during a period in America when sexuality was being extensively explored, both in the arts and the general population. As an enthusiastic admirer of the nightclub performances of Lenny Bruce, Tynan had always been a vociferous opponent of the theater censorship that existed in England from the mid-eighteenth century. In 1965 he wrote that governments effectively control artists in two ways, through direct censorship, and through withholding subsidies, thereby forcing the playwrights "to turn out lovable, undisturbing after-dinner entertainment." Tynan believed that erotic stimulation was a legitimate function of art, good or bad.

Oh, Calcutta! was basically a musical revue consisting of sketches and group musical numbers by various writers. However, the show included blatant nudity, simulation of sexual intercourse, and libidinous humor, all of which shocked the New York critics, who described it as hard-core pornography, brutalizing, degrading, tedious, and witless, but also "shatteringly effective." Audiences flocked to see the show. Besides enjoying long runs in New York and London, it was performed in cities throughout the world, though in Australia's South Australia and Victoria states performances were banned.

See also Australia; Baudelaire, Charles; Black, Hugo; Bruce, Lenny; Drama and theater; Nude dancing; Nudity.

O'Hair, Madalyn Murray

Born: April 13, 1919, Pittsburgh, Pennsylvania

Identification: Author and activist

Significance: A founder of several atheist organizations and the author of numerous books and pamphlets on atheism, O'Hair has vigorously opposed prayer and Bible reading in schools

O'Hair attended several colleges before receiving a bachelor's degree from Ashland College, Ohio, in 1948 and an LL.B. from Southwest Texas College of Law in 1953. While she was raising her children as atheists, she was infuriated to learn that her son's Baltimore school required him to recite the Lord's Prayer and attend Bible readings each morning. Claiming that her son was unconstitutionally discriminated against because of his religious beliefs, she sued in 1959 to have the district enjoined from requiring Bible reading and prayer.

O'Hair's case was appealed all the way to the U.S. Supreme Court, which joined it with the similar case, *Schempp v. School District of Abington Township (Pa.)*, and decided in her favor in 1963. The Court ruled that having students read the Bible aloud and recite the Lord's Prayer constituted religious exercises that were unconstitutional violations of the First and Fourteenth Amendments' ban on establishment of religion.

During the years that O'Hair's case was before the courts her family became targets of assault and harassment. Her son was attacked physically, her house was vandalized, and her car was destroyed. When the Court's decision became known, even more hate mail descended on her from across the country. Newspapers dubbed her "the most hated woman in America."

When a seventeen-year-old girl with whom O'Hair's (then named Murray) son was in love stayed at their house over her own parents' objections, the Baltimore police followed. A scuffle broke out, and O'Hair and her son, William Murray, were arrested and charged with assault and disorderly conduct. Believing they would never get a fair trial in Baltimore, the Murrays and the young woman, now married to William Murray, fled to Hawaii. After the Hawaiian courts upheld Maryland's extradition request, the Murrays moved to Mexico where Madalyn Murray met and married Richard O'Hair in 1965. Later the charges against her and her son were dismissed when she successfully challenged the grand jury indictments on the ground that Maryland law excluded atheists from serving on juries or being judges.

The O'Hairs moved to Austin, Texas, where O'Hair organized the Society of Separatists, later renamed American Atheists. It took another legal battle to force the Internal Revenue Service to grant a tax exempt status to her group, which published a magazine, *American Atheist*, and created the Atheist Library and Archive in Austin.

O'Hair has frequently appeared on radio and television talk shows as a spokesperson for atheism, and she began a series of lawsuits to try to end grants of tax money to religious schools

Madalyn Murray O'Hair in late 1969—around the time a court threw out her suit to prohibit U.S. astronauts from broadcasting their prayers and Bible readings from space. (AP/Wide World Photos)

and tax exemptions for churches. Despite hostile personal attacks by the media, and the hate mail and property vandalism that she and her family have suffered, O'Hair continued to propagandize for atheism, calling for increased separation of church and state, and protesting discrimination against unbelievers.

See also Atheism; Bible; Christianity; Fear; Heresy; Religion; School prayer.

O'Hara, John

BORN: January 31, 1905, Pottsville, Pennsylvania
DIED: April 11, 1970, Princeton, New Jersey
IDENTIFICATION: American novelist
SIGNIFICANCE: O'Hara's frank treatment of contemporary sexual mores helped make his books' popular, while attracting the attention of would-be censors

O'Hara's first novel, *Appointment in Samarra* (1934), was praised by many reviewers but castigated by others for its sexual outspokenness. Because the novel's setting, "Gibbsville," was clearly modeled on O'Hara's hometown of Pottsville, Pennsylvania, O'Hara was also criticized by his former neighbors for presenting the town in an unflattering light. The book was subsequently declared unmailable by the U.S. Post Office, although it continued to be sold openly in bookstores.

O'Hara's *Ten North Frederick* (1955) drew more censorship attempts than any of his other works. Detroit's police commissioner banned it from the city in early 1957, but O'Hara's publishers obtained a permanent injunction against the ban. That same year the book's paperback publisher, Bantam Books, was indicted for distributing obscene material in Albany, New York, O'Hara himself was also indicted, but the indictment was dismissed in circuit court the following year because jurors had been presented with only isolated passages of the book for consideration. This court ruling was an early application of the standard articulated in *Roth v. United States* in 1957. Meanwhile, the novel was also a target of legal challenges in Cleveland, Ohio, and Omaha, Nebraska.

See also Obscenity: legal definitions; Postal regulations; *Roth v. United States*; Vonnegut, Kurt.

O'Neill, Eugene

BORN: October 16, 1888, New York, New York
DIED: November 27, 1953, Boston, Massachusetts
IDENTIFICATION: American playwright
SIGNIFICANCE: Although O'Neill was called America's foremost dramatist, his plays were often attacked or banned from production because of their realistic language and sexual themes

For the first seven years of O'Neill's life he traveled with his parents, while his father toured the country as the star in a stage version of *The Count of Monte Cristo*. He attended boarding schools before entering Princeton University in 1906. After failing to complete his freshman year, he spent the next six years working on steamships and living a drunken, derelict existence in various ports between voyages.

In 1912 O'Neill contracted tuberculosis. While recovering in a sanitarium he began to write plays, mostly only one act long, dealing with people and subject matter that had never been depicted on the American stage—derelicts, prostitutes, and drunken sailors. In 1920 his first full-length play, *Beyond the Horizon*, impressed critics with its tragic realism and won him the first of his four Pulitzer Prizes.

Censors were not far behind. When *The Hairy Ape*, a play about the tragic life and suicide of a coal-stoker on a steamship, opened on Broadway in 1922, the police department filed a complaint with the magistrate's court alleging that its language was indecent and obscene. However, they failed to convince the magistrate who read the play and dismissed the complaint.

All God's Chillun Got Wings (1924) aroused even fiercer attacks when newspapers learned that O'Neill planned to cast a black man and a white woman as husband and wife, and that the wife would kiss her husband's hand on stage. The Hearst press led the assault, urging the mayor to prevent the play from opening on the ground that it might incite race riots; however, the mayor had no power to intervene. Wire services carried the story and bushels of hate mail from across the country—including threatening letters from the Ku Klux Klan—descended on O'Neill and the play's actors. Opening night was tense, but the feared riot never developed.

In 1925 the Manhattan district attorney tried to ban O'Neill's *Desire Under the Elms* as obscene, objecting to its portrayal of incest and infanticide. He did not succeed, but the play was banned in Boston by that city's mayor and in Great Britain by the Lord Chamberlain. When it was staged in Los Angeles, the entire cast was arrested and charged with putting on an immoral performance.

Not even O'Neill's receipt of the Nobel Prize for Literature in 1936 silenced his censors. Boston authorities prevented *The Iceman Cometh* (1946) from being seen in their city. *A Moon for the Misbegotten* (1947), the last of O'Neill's plays produced before his death, was attacked during its pre-Broadway tour. Pittsburgh's elite denounced it as vulgar and indecent. The Detroit police censor insisted on the removal of eight words he considered objectionable before permitting it to open. The play never made it to New York.

See also Drama and theater; Hearst, William Randolph; Lord Chamberlain; Miscegenation; Morality; Shaw, George Bernard.

Opera

Definition: Dramatic stage productions featuring orchestral music in which all parts for voices are sung

Significance: Because the drama, music, and stirring songs of opera can evoke strong emotional reactions from audiences, opera performances have been censored by governments afraid that audiences might be moved to dangerous actions

Over the centuries political authorities have frequently feared the power of operas and subdued them through censorship. Given the perceived ability of music and words to convey powerful political propaganda, to move emotions, and possibly to stir people to action, opera has long been viewed as a potentially subversive force requiring censorship controls wherever political regimes have been authoritarian.

Concerns that have led to censorship of the theater have also generally applied to opera. Indeed, there has been more censorship of the stage than of the printed word. Stage productions are unique in gathering together in public places large numbers of people, who may be mobilized for concerted action (whereas the printed word is usually consumed alone and in private). Live performances are more powerful in impact than readings of the same words. Furthermore, stage performances are accessible to the illiterate and usually feared poor, while print often is not.

Fear of Opera. Censorship of opera, an art form that originated in the seventeenth century, developed early. It began around 1770 in Austria and in 1737 in Great Britain. The mid-nineteenth century European revolutions especially convinced political authorities of the need for strict opera censorship, as outbreaks in both France and Belgium were partly blamed on opera crowds. The Belgian revolt against Dutch rule, for example, was widely attributed to mobs aroused by an August, 1830, performance of Daniel Auber's *La Muette de Portici* (1828). This opera portrayed a medieval rebellion against Spanish domination in Naples. Belgians who attended the opera in Brussels streamed into the streets, howling "Down with the Dutch!" and tearing down perceived symbols of Dutch oppression soon after the singers had cried out: "Let us unite and throw out the strangers, with one blow, save our country's freedom."

Fears of opera engendered by mid-nineteenth century revolutions were greatly reinforced in politically fragmented Italy, where opera houses became the centers of demonstrations demanding unity and independence. Audiences were often inspired by Giuseppe Verdi's operas—which, though set in foreign lands and remote times to avoid censorship, were nevertheless routinely understood by nationalistic Italian audiences as appeals for liberation from Austrian and papal tyranny. One Florentine censor dejectedly reported that the "perplexity of the censor is due to the public reaction" which gives performances an interpretation "over and above their literal meaning." When the English author Charles Dickens observed the same phenomenon at a Genoa opera, he concluded that the petty Italian tyrannies had created a situation in which "there is nothing else of a public nature at which [the Italians] are allowed to express the least disapprobation" and "perhaps they are resolved to make the most of this opportunity."

The Nature of Opera Censorship. Except perhaps in nineteenth century Italy, where opera was exceptionally important, opera censorship has rarely approached the level of stringency applied to the spoken drama. The first of several reasons is the higher cost of staging operas. Operas have frequently required state patronage and subsidies; under such conditions formal censorship has often not been required. Also, the amount of overtly political idea that can be conveyed within the framework of an opera libretto is severely limited. Finally, although the sensual power of music can add strength to the power of words, it can also overwhelm them. Thus, a play by Alexandre Dumas, *fils*, *La Dame aux camélias* (1852), was banned by the same nineteenth century English censor who simultaneously allowed the production of *La Traviata* (1853), Verdi's opera based on the same play. The censor explained that if there were "a musical version of a piece it makes a difference, for the story is then subsidiary to the music and singing." On the other hand, in Italy, where opera reigned supreme, a reverse logic appears to have applied: Verdi's opera, *Un Ballo in maschera* (1859), based on the 1792 assassination of Swedish king Gustav III, was forbidden by Roman censors until Verdi changed its setting to colonial Boston; however, ordinary plays on the same subject were allowed.

Opera censorship has usually reflected the particular concerns and fears of authoritarian regimes and the apparatus of repressive governmental controls has therefore fundamentally shaped the manner in which composers and librettists have written. Thus, in nineteenth century Europe, opera material challenging established government policy had to be suppressed; in such conditions most operas were set in remote and often imaginary pasts, focusing on highly romanticized events. In nineteenth century Italy, which was divided into a number of small states dominated by German-speaking Austria and the papacy, virtually all overt references to religion, nationalism, or anti-German sentiments were forbidden. Opera librettists naturally avoided politically censorable subject matter.

Nineteenth Century Italy. No doubt the height of modern opera censorship occurred in nineteenth century Italy. Even in operas that were clearly apolitical, censors generally forbade use of such words as "conspiracy," "fatherland," "liberty," "revolution," "slavery," "tyranny," and even "Italy." The results of such censorship were often ludicrous. For example, Milanese censors forced the heroine of Gaetano Donizetti's *Maria Padilla* (1841) to die of a "surfeit of joy" instead of committing suicide. Roman censors forced the heroine in Gioacchino Rossini's *L'Italiana in Algeri* (1813) to substitute the nonsensical "Think of your spouse!" for the original "Think of your country!"

Giacomo Meyerbeer's *Les Huguenots* (1836) is about the Catholic slaughter of Protestants in sixteenth century France. When it was performed in Rome in 1864, it was renamed *Renato di Crowenwald* and was rewritten to depict a struggle between powerful Dutch families in the early seventeenth century, with no hint of religious strife. In Austria the same opera was allowed only after it was renamed the *Ghibellines of Pisa* and altered so its libretto featured thirteenth century Italians singing a sixteenth century hymn by Martin Luther. In France the opera was allowed in the 1830's in Paris, but was banned from Protestant towns. Later, in Bolshevist Russia it was transformed into an opera about the failed 1825 Decembrist revolution against czarist autocracy.

Continental Opera. In the German-dominated but multinational Habsburg Empire Wolfgang Amadeus Mozart's *The Marriage of Figaro* (1786) was allowed only through the personal intervention of Emperor Joseph II, and his *The Magic Flute* (1791) was forbidden in 1795 as revolutionary propaganda. In the nineteenth century operatic depictions of conflict among ethnic groups and nationalities were strictly forbidden in the empire, and Hungarian, Polish, and Czech operas could not make overt appeals to nationalism. For this reason the great Czech medieval religious hero and martyr Jan Hus could not be depicted on the Czech stage during the first two-thirds of the nineteenth century (except during a short-lived revolution). Gioacchino Rossini's opera *William Tell* (1829) is the story of a revolt by the medieval Swiss against their Austrian overlords. Before it could be performed in the Habsburg Empire, its setting had to be shifted to Scotland, with English oppressors replacing Rossini's Austrians and Scotland's national hero, William Wallace, replacing Tell. In revolutionary and imperial France, as regime succeeded regime after 1789, all operas savoring of royalty were initially banned until 1815. After Napoleon Bonaparte met his final defeat at the Battle of Waterloo and the monarchy was restored, all mention of Napoleon was forbidden. Pierre-Augustin Beaumarchais' text for Antonio Salieri's opera *Tarare* (1787) had to be repeatedly changed as its hero transmuted from absolute monarch to republican ruler and then to constitutional monarch to keep up with the political winds.

In Nazi Germany, not only were all operas viewed as politically unacceptable banned (thus Alban Berg's *Wozzeck*, 1925, could not be performed for ideological reasons, a fate it also temporarily encountered in Soviet Russia), but all works by Jewish artists were forbidden—even Franz Werfel's German translations of the libretti to Verdi's operas could not be performed because of Werfel's Jewish ancestry. In Spain during the rule of Francisco Franco, Verdi's *Don Carlos* (1867) could not be performed apparently because it attacked the Roman Catholic church, one of its heros was a fervent advocate of liberty, and it was set in sixteenth century Spain.

Russia and Eastern Bloc Countries. In nineteenth century Russia, ruled by a brutal czarist autocracy supported by the Russian Orthodox church, no czar or ecclesiastic could be criticized or even depicted upon the opera stage (czars from the pre-Romanov dynasties could appear in spoken dramas, but, it was explained to composer Nikolai Rimsky-Korsakov that "it would be unseemly" if the czar of any dynasty were to "suddenly sing a ditty" in an opera). Rimsky-Korsakov's final opera, *The Golden Cockerel* (1907), an allegorical satire on the decay of the Russian autocracy was held up by censorship for two years, and then could be presented only in a mutilated version. Near its end, the opera's original text had the chorus sing: "What will the new dawn bring?" The censors changed the ominous "new dawn" to a "white dawn."

After the Russian Revolution of 1917, all favorable references to Russia's czarist heritage were effaced from opera. One typical result was that Mikhail Glinka's *A Life for the Czar* (1836) was renamed *Ivan Susanin*; it was rewritten so that instead of sacrificing for the founder of the Romanov dynasty (who disappeared entirely from the text), the opera's hero instead gives his life for the cause of Russian nationalism. Along similar politically directed lines, Giacamo Puccini's *Tosca* (1900) was performed under the new regime under the title *The Battle for the Commune*. In a 1925 Moscow performance, Georges Bizet's *Carmen* (1875) became a story about a communist woman who wins over a counterrevolutionary soldier and later transfers her affections to a Polish wrestler.

In Soviet-dominated Czechoslovakia, Bedrich Smetana's popular 1863 nationalist opera *The Brandenburgers in Bohemia*, which celebrated medieval Czech resistance to brutal German occupiers could not be performed until 1866 under Habsburg rule. After the Soviet Union's occupation of Czechoslovakia in 1968, it disappeared from the stage for sixteen years. In China planned performances of Puccini's *Turandot* (unfinished at his death in 1924) were canceled in Shanghai and Beijing in the aftermath of the 1989 massacre of democracy demonstrators in Beijing's Tiananmen Square. The cancellation was apparently due to the fact that the opera's tale of cruelty, torture, and executions is set in a legendary imperial China.

Perhaps no opera composer in history suffered more, both professionally and personally from censorship than Verdi. His private correspondence is filled with bitter diatribes directed against it. He termed the changes imposed by the censorship in Naples on *Un Ballo in maschera* an "artistic murder." When *La Traviata* was mangled by Roman censors—who wanted the character of the courtesan heroine Violetta to be "purified"—Verdi stormed that they had "ruined the sense of the drama. They made La Traviata pure and innocent. Thanks a lot! Thus, they ruined all the situations, all the characters. A whore must remain a whore. If the sun were to shine at night, it wouldn't be night any more. In short, they don't understand anything!" —*Robert Justin Goldstein*

See also Art; Drama and theater; Italy; *Mikado, The*; Music; *Times Film Corp. v. City of Chicago*.

Bibliography

There are no adequate general studies of opera censorship. Sections on opera censorship in nineteenth century Europe can, however, be found in Robert Justin Goldstein, *Political Censorship of the Arts and the Press in Nineteenth Century Europe* (New York: St. Martin's, 1989); David Kimbell, *Verdi in the Age of Italian Romanticism* (Cambridge, England: Cambridge University Press, 1981); Anthony Arblaster, *Viva la Liberta! Politics in Opera* (New York: Verso, 1992); Arnold Perris, *Music as Propaganda* (Westport, Conn.: Greenwood Press, 1985); and John Rosselli, *The Opera Industry in Italy from Cimarosa to Verdi* (Cambridge, England: Cambridge University Press, 1984). Walter Rubsamen's "Music and Politics in the Risorgimento," *Italian Quarterly* 51 (Spring-Summer, 1961), is informative on this key period of opera censorship. See also articles on censorship in dictionaries of opera.

Orwell, George (Eric Blair)

Born: June 25, 1903, Motihari, Bengal, India
Died: January 21, 1950, London, England
Identification: English novelist and journalist
Significance: Orwell wrote about the types of censorship that can be achieved through the manipulation of language by ruling elites in totalitarian societies

During the 1930's and 1940's, when few English socialists had awakened to the full horrors of Soviet totalitarianism under Joseph Stalin, Orwell was an exception. He was aware not only of the threat to intellectual freedom that totalitarianism—of the Left as well as the Right—posed, but also of the

One of Orwell's contributions to the English language is "Big Brother," a symbol of police state control over individual thought and expression. (Museum of Modern Art/Film Stills Archive)

peculiar nature of that threat: the totalitarian concept that the past is not unalterable, but can be continually re-created to suit prevailing orthodoxies. Censorship was then becoming a matter of the manipulation of language and thought, rather than such old-fashioned methods as public book-burnings or censors' blue pencils.

Orwell had some personal experience of the cruder forms of censorship. His mail was opened and some books were confiscated from his house in the atmosphere of fear that prevailed in England on the eve of World War II. Orwell's "London Letters" in *Partisan Review*, the first of which appeared in 1941, were subject to censorship by Great Britain's Ministry of Information. A passage in one of these essays referring to the possible lynching of German aviators who had parachuted into England was deleted. When Orwell worked for the British Broadcasting Corporation during the war he had to live with the possibility that his fairly innocuous broadcasts to India would be censored by eager bureaucrats, on the lookout for careless phrases.

Essays on Literature and Language. Orwell's views on censorship crystalized during World War II and bore fruit in his writings immediately afterward. In "The Prevention of Literature," an essay he published in January, 1946, he noted that intellectual liberty in England was under attack from three sources: totalitarians, monopolies (primarily radio and film), and bureaucracies. By the latter he meant particularly the

Ministry of Information and the British Council, which employed or financially aided writers, while assuming that the writers could have their opinions dictated to them. The particular focus of Orwell's essay, however, was on the intellectuals who should be the most vigorous in their defense of individual integrity, but who were not speaking out. He had in mind left-wing writers and intellectuals who had convinced themselves that it was not even desirable to tell the truth about certain contemporary events—usually anything that might put the Soviet Union in a negative light. They had accepted a kind of self-censorship, tacitly agreeing to put preservation of ideologies—the depravity of which they had not comprehended—before the need for objective truth.

Orwell had long been concerned about the nature of political writing. In his 1946 essay "Politics and the English Language," he claimed that political language had deteriorated to the point that it consisted mainly of euphemisms designed to draw veils over the real nature of events. Such language is heavy in abstractions so that unpleasant things may be said and events and actions may be described without any mental pictures accompanying them. Lies are made to sound truthful and murder respectable. This amounts to censorship through a kind of creeping bureaucratese.

The Nightmare Vision of *Nineteen Eighty-Four*. By the time Orwell came to write his major novel, *Nineteen Eighty-Four* (1949), his ideas had darkened into a sinister vision of the future. Within this novel England has become a totalitarian society in which every aspect of the lives of its citizens is controlled by the state and even the possibility of independent thought has been destroyed. Much of this oppression has been accomplished through the manipulation of language. A perverted and truncated form of English has been engineered, known as "Newspeak." The purpose of Newspeak is to make impossible any mode of thought that deviates from the official ideology of Ingsoc, or English Socialism. Undesirable words such as "justice," "morality," "religion," and "democracy" have simply been eliminated from the vocabulary. New words have been invented, and existing words have been stripped of secondary meanings. The range of thought has thus been diminished, and ambiguity of expression—and therefore thought—is no longer possible. Because Newspeak has not yet been fully established, cruder forms of enforcing orthodoxy are still necessary. This is achieved by the Thought Police, who root out all signs of "thoughtcrime."

In the nightmare society that Orwell envisioned, no one can ever contradict the ruling party's version of current or historical events. The party controls all records; the past, as recorded in newspapers, books, photographs, and films, is simply rewritten or remade ("rectified" in Newspeak) when this is considered necessary. For example, when economic output under a three-year plan does not match past forecasts (which is always the case), back issues of newspapers referring to earlier forecasts are simply altered. There is no need for overt censorship. Rather than suppress new information, the past is altered to conform with it. By this continuous process of alteration, every government prediction, every statistic, is made to seem correct. Whenever there is an obvious contradiction between the party's current version of an event and what was formerly declared to be the truth, party members engage in the practice of "doublethink." This is a Newspeak term that denotes the ability to hold two contradictory things in mind without acknowledging the contradiction—to forget a fact when necessary, to remember it again if necessary, and then to forget it once more when it is no longer required. If a heretical thought presents itself, party members are conditioned to blank it out instinctively in a process called "crimestop" in Newspeak.

As a prediction of the future, the vision of *Nineteen Eighty-Four* has not come true, but as a description of the thought processes of the totalitarian mind and those who fall subject to it, it is an unparalleled model. It shows the ultimate form of censorship: the manipulation of the mind so as to remove the very notion of an objective truth. In contrast, Orwell's own life and work stand as a testament to the preservation of truth and honesty in political life and writing. *—Bryan Aubrey*

See also British Broadcasting Corporation; British Broadcasting Standards Council; Euphemism; Historiography; Propaganda; Soviet Union; Trotsky, Leon; Wodehouse, P. G.; World War II; Zola, Émile.

BIBLIOGRAPHY

Michael Shelden's highly praised *Orwell: The Authorized Biography* (New York: HarperCollins, 1991) discusses all the censorship issues in Orwell's life. *The Collected Essays, Journalism, and Letters of George Orwell*, edited by Sonia Orwell and Ian Angus (4 vols., New York: Harcourt, Brace & World, 1968), gives invaluable insights into Orwell's day-to-day life as a working journalist. *Nineteen Eighty-Four: Text, Sources, Criticism*, edited by Irving Howe (New York: Harcourt, Brace & World, 1963), contains fifteen critical essays as well as suggestions for writing. Raymond Williams' *George Orwell* (New York: Viking Press, 1971) explores Orwell's "double vision" as a member of the ruling class who was committed to the cause of working people. *Critical Essays on George Orwell*, edited by Bernard Oldsey and Joseph Browne (Boston, Mass.: G. K. Hall, 1986), provides a wide range of perspectives on Orwell's work.

Our Bodies, Ourselves

TYPE OF WORK: Book
PUBLISHED: 1973
AUTHORS: Boston Women's Health Book Collective (BWHBC)
SUBJECT MATTER: Women's health
SIGNIFICANCE: Conservatives attempted unsuccessfully to suppress this well-researched, sexually explicit book about women's health and sexuality

Born of the women's liberation movement of the 1960's, *Our Bodies, Ourselves* was written from a feminist and leftist political perspective by women who believed that all women need full and accurate information about childbirth, abortion, birth control, sexuality, and other topics, in order to make informed decisions and lead full, healthy lives. The authors collected and evaluated comprehensive medical information, which they translated into nontechnical language; they also included many anecdotal experiences. The book has been used as a text in hundreds of high school and college courses. It has been revised many times, sold millions of copies, and been widely translated.

Since the revised 1976 edition was selected as one of the "Best of the Best" books for young adults by the American Library Association, *Our Bodies, Ourselves* has been the target of frequent, highly orchestrated attacks by conservative organizations, such as the Eagle Forum, Education Research Analysts, and the Moral Majority. These critics have claimed that the book is immoral, anti-Christian, and antifamily—charges which the BWHBC denies. By 1977 censors had used the book's explicit discussion of sexuality to attempt to have it banned from dozens of small-town libraries and schools in the Midwest, the South, and New England. Attempts at censorship increased dramatically during the Reagan Administration. Some librarians were pressured to remove the book, which was also deleted from order lists and stolen from libraries. In spite of such attempts, however, *Our Bodies, Ourselves* has continued to prove a popular guide to issues affecting the health and sexuality of women.

See also Boston; Eagle Forum; Feminism; Homosexuality; Libraries, school; Moral Majority; Morality; Sex education.

Outing

DEFINITION: Public exposure of another's secret homosexual orientation

SIGNIFICANCE: Alleging someone's homosexuality in print may expose the alleger to significant legal liability

Common forums for outing range from homosexual-oriented publications to mainstream metropolitan dailies. Proponents justify outing as a means of providing positive role models for gay youth, reinvigorating AIDS awareness, and exposing the hypocrisy of powerful people. They assert that the traditional press code of stifling information about the same-sex orientation of influential people is self-censorship that denies the legitimacy of homosexuality. Opponents respond that outing is a form of McCarthyism that treats privacy as a cheap commodity that may be traded for economic or personal gain.

A consensus has developed among journalists and editors that a decision to publish information about someone's sexual orientation should not be made lightly, and should turn on factors such as the newsmaker's status, the relevance of the information, and the level to which that information is in the public domain. In such circumstances, the media might view future discretion as futile and a form of censorship.

Many news executives remain uncomfortable with decisions to publish information about the sexual orientation of noted people. Aggrieved victims of outing may pursue an action for defamation, invasion of privacy, or infliction of emotional distress. For example, Oliver Sipple thwarted an assassination attempt on President Gerald Ford. Afterward many newspapers published articles intimating that Sipple was gay. He sued the *San Francisco Chronicle* for invasion of privacy. Although his suit was ultimately unsuccessful, publishers remain mindful of potential litigation costs and adverse judgments, and thus approach similar news stories cautiously.

See also Defamation; Homosexuality; Libel; Privacy, right to.

Outlaw, The

TYPE OF WORK: Film

RELEASED: 1943

DIRECTORS: Howard Hawks (1896-1977) and Howard Hughes (1905-1976)

SUBJECT MATTER: Outlaw Billy the Kid joins Doc Holliday to escape from a sheriff, despite their rivalry over a Mexican woman

SIGNIFICANCE: After the Motion Picture Producers and Distributors of America (MPPDA) revoked this film's Seal of Approval, Hughes filed an antitrust suit, the first real challenge to the film censorship code

Industrialist Howard Hughes began plans for *The Outlaw* in 1941, casting unknowns Jack Buetel as Billy the Kid and Jane Russell as a Mexican woman, Rio. In midproduction, Hughes fired director Howard Hawks and began directing himself, using the camera to emphasize Russell's ample bust. After negotiating with film censors, the film received the MPPDA's Seal of Approval on May 23, 1941; local censors, however, cut it severely, and Hughes postponed the film's release.

In 1943 *The Outlaw* opened in San Francisco's Geary Theater, playing to record crowds. Hughes blanketed the city with sexually provocative advertisements, causing public protests. The Legion of Decency condemned the film. Hughes withdrew it but continued advertising, and released it again in 1946. This time, the advertising was also condemned. Hughes sued the film industry's governing board, now called the Motion Picture Association of America (MPAA), claiming that it violated antitrust and restraint of trade laws and First Amend-

Release of The Outlaw *was delayed several years because of its producers' unabashed promotion of Jane Russell's physical attributes.* (Museum of Modern Art/Film Stills Archive)

ment free speech guarantees. Hughes lost the case and an appeal. On September 6, 1946, Hughes was ordered to remove the Seal of Approval from all prints. Canceled bookings followed. State boards in Massachusetts, Ohio, and Maryland banned the film, which was also banned in many cities and aroused criticism in Canada and Britain. Hughes took some cases to court and lost, although enough exhibitors showed the film to generate earnings of more than three million dollars by 1948. In 1949 a newly edited version regained the Seal of Approval; the Ohio ban, however, was not overturned until 1954.

See also Film censorship; First Amendment; Legion of Decency; Motion Picture Association of America.

Ovid

Born: March 20, 43 B.C.E., Sulmo, Italy

Died: 17 C.E., Tomis on the Black Sea (now Constanta, Romania)

Identification: Roman poet

Significance: The emperor Augustus charged Ovid with writing scandalous poetry and exiled him from Rome

In the year 8 C.E.—at the same time that the Roman emperor Augustus ordered his granddaughter Julia to leave Rome—Augustus also sentenced the poet Ovid to relegation for life in Tomis, a remote frontier seaport on the Black Sea. The full reasons for Ovid's banishment are obscure. Ovid himself wrote simply that his offenses included composing the *Ars Amatoria* and an unspecified "error"—which he insisted was not a crime. The apparent vindictiveness of his punishment suggests that Augustus regarded Ovid's "error" as a deep personal affront. Tomis was a Greek town, but life there was uncomfortable, dangerous, and totally cut off from the intellectual stimulation and personal contacts that Ovid had enjoyed in Rome.

The remoteness of Tomis made it easy for the imperial government to monitor Ovid's outside communications, but it did not keep him from writing. Nevertheless, he suffered mental distress that is reflected in the three major collections that he composed at Tomis. The *Tristia* and the *Epistulae ex Ponto* are addresses to the emperor and friends asking for forgiveness or intercession and begging permission to return to Rome. The *Ibis* is a book of curses directed against an unknown enemy.

Throughout his exile writings Ovid is deferential to Augustus, the man controlling his fate. In *Tristia* he accepts the justice of the emperor's punishment while describing a future pardon as a gift that must come from the Divine Emperor's sense of compassion; he also expresses an outward respect for the duties and responsibilities of the office. It is only in defense of his personal talent and creativity that Ovid allowed himself to criticize the emperor. He believed in the superiority and immortality of creative genius over raw political power, and believed that genius would eventually prevail.

Ovid's legacy to Roman literature was mixed. Seneca remembered him as an example of the power of talent. However, the cutting nature of Ovid's wit had little influence on Roman poets, with the exception of Martial. The stigma of exile stuck to Ovid's memory. In literary circles Ovid's ability to depict human emotions is legend, and he is remembered and read as the great preserver of Roman mythology and civic ritual, but his poetry from exile is often ignored. The proponents of courtly love in the Middle Ages cited Ovid as a titillating example of forbidden love, suspecting that a secret liaison with Julia provoked the emperor's anger. More often Ovid and his *Ars Amatoria* have been seen as the most immoral examples of an immoral age, and he has suffered condemnation at the hands of cultural moralists. For example, Christopher Marlowe's translation of Ovid was burned, and as late as 1928 the U.S. Customs Service was still seizing copies of the *Ars Amatoria*.

See also Cicero; Roman Empire; *Satyricon, The*; Seneca the Younger.

P

Pacifica Foundation

Founded: 1949

Type of organization: Nonprofit foundation that owns and operates a small group of community radio stations and a national radio news service

Significance: Pacifica has been at the forefront in the battle to preserve broadcasting as a forum for the presentation of nonmainstream programming

Pacifica was the pioneer in noncommercial community broadcasting, and its stations are known for their eclectic brand of programming. The Pacifica Foundation was a pioneer in the development of noncommercial, listener-supported community radio stations in the early days of FM radio, before the advent of National Public Radio and chain religious broadcasters. Community stations, found mostly in large metropolitan areas, are located mostly in the reserved frequencies between 88 and 92 MHz, are staffed mostly by volunteers, and feature an eclectic mix of nonmainstream music, news, and public affairs shows, and other spoken-word programming.

Pacifica was founded by Washington, D.C., radio journalist Lewis Hill, who had been a conscientious objector during World War II, in 1949. The foundation started its first radio station, KPFA, in Berkeley, California, in 1949 and 1954, respectively. The group expanded into Los Angeles with KPFK in 1959, and into New York in 1960 with WBAI. WPFT in Houston and WPFW in Washington, D.C., completed the chain in 1970 and 1977. Over the years, the foundation also helped groups in other cities start community stations. In fact, one Pacifica veteran, Lorenzo Milam, wrote a book called *Sex and Broadcasting* (1971) that combined musings about community radio with how-to advise on putting a station on the air. Pacifica also distributes a daily half-hour news program to noncommercial stations around the United States.

The tendency of the Pacifica Foundation stations has been to target fringe audiences not served by other stations, commercial or noncommercial, and to provide an outlet for alternative viewpoints. Not surprisingly, Pacifica has been the subject of dozens of listener complaints, investigations and enforcement actions by the Federal Communications Commission (FCC), and acts against its transmitters. Many of the complaints were brought by political conservatives, who alleged the stations had violated provisions of the FCC's fairness doctrine, which required all sides of controversial issues be addressed by broadcasters. Some of the complaints accused the stations of broadcasting offensive language.

WBAI and Filthy Words. Unquestionably the most famous of these offensive-language controversies was the so-called seven dirty words case of the 1970's, which made Pacifica a household name among legal scholars, media policy makers, free speech advocates, and other broadcasters. At approximately two o'clock in the afternoon of October 30, 1973, WBAI, as a part of a series of programs on uses of language, broadcast a twelve-minute recorded monologue from comedian George Carlin titled "Filthy Words." In the monologue, Carlin joked about the seven words not allowed on public airwaves. In spite of the fact the station aired a message before the monologue warning listeners of the possible offensive nature of the content, a man who said he had heard the program while riding in the car with his young son later complained to the FCC. The commission, while deciding not to punish the station, determined it had violated the U.S. Criminal Code by airing an indecent program. The FCC defined "indecent" as "language that describes, in terms patently offensive as measured by contemporary community standards for the broadcast medium, sexual or excretory activities and organs, at times of the day when there is a reasonable risk that children may be in the audience." In upholding the FCC ruling in *Federal Communications Commission v. Pacifica Foundation* (1978), the Supreme Court effectively carved out a new category of "offensive" speech that was subject to government restriction. Previously, only offensive speech found by the courts to be obscene was outside of the protection of the First Amendment. The FCC had never claimed the Carlin monologue met the rigorous obscenity test the justices had approved in *Miller v. California* (1973) but asserted that section 1464 of the criminal code, which forbids "any obscene, indecent, or profane language by means of radio communications," gave it the necessary regulatory authority.

Under pressure from broadcasters who feared some of their programming, particularly live news and talk programs, might meet what thus became known as the Pacifica test for indecency, the FCC eventually announced it would pursue only those complaints against stations for willful and repeated use of dirty language before 10:00 P.M.

KPFK and *Jerker*. Less than a decade after the landmark U.S. Supreme Court decision, Pacifica once again found itself the subject of an FCC indecency investigation, this time concerning programming on its Los Angeles station, KPFK. In 1986 its program "IMRU" (an acronym for "I am—are you?"), aimed at the lesbian and gay community, aired excerpts from the play *Jerker*, including a rather graphic portrayal of phone sex between two HIV-positive men. The FCC decided to use complaints about the program, along with those against Howard Stern's syndicated broadcasts and a song played on the University of California at Santa Barbara's station, as cases in support of its renewed efforts to crack down on broadcast indecency. The KPFK broadcast even was referred to the U.S. Department of Justice to determine if the government should bring more serious obscenity charges against the station, but the investigation eventually was dropped.

A federal appeals court did, nevertheless, give its blessing to the FCC's crackdown efforts, including the 1978 Pacifica standard some industry groups claimed was vague. In an effort to clarify what material the FCC would consider indecent, the Pacifica Foundation asked the FCC for a ruling on whether its stations' plans to broadcast excerpts from James Joyce's novel *Ulysses* (1922) would be considered indecent. The FCC, perhaps fearing it would be accused of prior restraint if it said the program would be indecent, declined to provide a ruling.

In the years since its 1987 indecency crackdown, most of the FCC's enforcement activities have concerned complaints about the shock radio of commercial air personalities such as Howard Stern. Although the Pacifica Foundation itself has not been the subject of any such recent actions, its name continues to be associated with government attempts to limit offensive broadcasts. —*Bruce E. Drushel*

See also Action for Children's Television; Carlin, George; Communications Act of 1934; Communications Decency Act; Federal Communications Commission; First Amendment; *Miller v. California*; Obscenity: legal definitions; Offensive language; Radio; Stern, Howard.

Bibliography

Janice Dee Gilbert, *Broadcasting in the Public Interest: Non-Commercial Radio and Television* (Monticello, Ill.: Vance Bibliographies, 1982) is available at many libraries and offers a useful listing of works on public radio and television. The title of Lorenzo W. Milam's *Sex and Broadcasting* (3d ed. Los Gatos, Calif.: Dildo Press, 1975) is misleading; more descriptive is its subtitle: *A Handbook on Starting a Radio Station for the Community*. The third edition is much more comprehensive than the first two, offering illustrative and often amusing anecdotes from the history of the Pacifica stations. Milam's *The Radio Papers, from KRAB to KCHU* (San Diego, Calif.: MHO & MHO Works, 1986) goes beyond Pacifica to other community radio organizations around the United States.

Padlock Act

Enacted: March 24, 1937
Place: Québec, Canada
Significance: A measure designed to suppress communist propaganda, this statute contradicted the Canadian tradition of freedom of political speech

Efforts begun by Canada's federal government to suppress communist activities during the Great Depression were joined in Québec by the provincial government of Maurice Duplessis. The so-called Padlock Act that his government passed in 1937 made it illegal for any person owning or occupying a house to use it, or to allow it to be used, to propagate "communism or bolshevism." The latter terms remained undefined, but Québec's attorney general was empowered to close for one year any building used to make such propaganda. The act also empowered the attorney general to confiscate and destroy any printed matter propagating communism or bolshevism. Persons convicted of distributing such material could be imprisoned for up to one year.

Pressure brought upon the federal government by trade unions and the liberal press to use its constitutional power to overturn the statute brought no results because the federal government was fearful of strengthening Duplessis' position in Québec. The law was subsequently variously applied, notably in closing down the communist newspaper *Combat* in 1947. In 1957, however, the Supreme Court of Canada declared the law unconstitutional on the grounds that it invaded the federal field of criminal law.

See also Canada; Censorship; Communism; Wales padlock law.

Paine, Thomas

Born: January 29, 1737, Thetford, Norfolk, England
Died: June 8, 1809, New York, New York
Identification: Anglo-American political pamphleteer
Significance: Paine was a fiery defender of individual liberties in writings that supported the American and French revolutions

Paine was the son of a Quaker small farmer and staymaker in Norfolk, England, who always acknowledged the influence of Quaker principles on his political ideas. At thirteen he entered his father's business, but after three years went briefly to sea. By the late 1750's he was again working as a staymaker. In 1761 he was appointed a government excise-tax agent, only to be fired four years later for making fraudulent reports. A letter of apology got him reinstated, however, and he got a new position in Lewes. Paine's pen first got him into trouble in 1772, when an organization of excisemen asked him to prepare a petition for higher wages. The pamphlet he wrote for them was distributed widely. In April, 1774, he was fired for being absent without leave, but the more likely explanation for his dismissal was his pamphlet.

The American Connection. Paine returned to London, where he met Benjamin Franklin, then acting as a representative of Great Britain's North American colonies. Their connection proved fruitful, for Paine arrived in America in November of 1774 with a letter of introduction that led to a position with Robert Aitken, a bookseller who was launching a magazine. Aitken's *American Museum* appeared in January, 1775, with Paine as a regular contributor and, after a brief while, its editor. Paine's strong political views were quickly apparent as he wrote essays attacking slavery and discrimination against women, and defending republican government. When the Revolutionary War began, supporters of independence asked Paine for a statement of their cause. His pamphlet *Common Sense* appeared in January, 1776. It denounced the tyranny of monarchy and championed the rights of individuals and virtues of republican government. Paine claimed to have sold 120,000 copies in four months, but he set its price so low that he lost money on its publication.

In the fall of 1776 Paine joined the Continental Army as an aide-de-camp to General Nathaniel Greene. His account of that fall's military retreat—which opened with the immortal line, "These are the times that try men's souls. . . ."—was the first of a series of pamphlets he titled *The American Crisis*. By the beginning of the following year, Paine was secretary to the Continental Congress. By the end of 1778 eight numbers of his series titled *The Crisis* had appeared.

Paine's outspokenness soon caused him trouble, however. Using secret documents seen during his official duties, he openly denounced malfeasance in connection with a French loan. Although he was correct, his indiscreet use of his sources cost him his job. Because he had continued to sell his political tracts at prices below their production costs, he was reduced to a clerkship and had to petition Pennsylvania's legislature for a loan to fund publication of his collected works. In November, 1779, Paine was appointed clerk of the Pennsylvania legislature. Over the following year he wrote three more pamphlets in *The Crisis* series. At the end of 1780 he resigned in order to write a history of the rebellion that he wished to take to England to expose the folly of Britain's opposing American independence. Although Paine did reach France, he did not get to England. Nevertheless, his fame continued to grow.

After the American Revolution. In 1784 the state of New York showed its gratitude to Paine by giving him an estate at New Rochelle that it had confiscated from a Tory; the U.S. Congress gave him three thousand dollars in 1785. Paine seemed established and secure. Although he continued to write about politics, he became interested in an idea for an iron bridge that he visited Europe to promote in 1787. The bridge idea came to nothing, but he was still in Europe when the French Revolution began.

The appearance of Edmund Burke's *Reflections on the Revolution in France* (1790) prompted Paine to write the first part of *The Rights of Man* (1791). This with the second part which followed later in the year was one of the clearest statements of the principles which underlay the ideals of the French revolutionaries. When he tried to publish the second part of his work in London, his printer was indicted for publishing subversive material—a charge to which he pled guilty. A few weeks later Paine escaped to France—sailing literally minutes before he would have been arrested. British authorities claimed the second part of Paine's work had been condemned because it was widely circulated—in contrast to the work's first part, which had reached only people who would not be unduly influenced. However, the clear difference was that during the months between each part's publication, respectable Englishmen had become concerned about the course of events in France. Paine refused to return to England for trial, making clear his indifference to certainty that he would be convicted in absentia. Further prosecutions of those selling and/or circulating *The Rights of Man* followed.

Reception in France. Meanwhile Paine was welcomed in France, made a citizen, and elected to the National Assembly. Following the abolition of the French monarchy in September, 1792, Paine was appointed to a committee to write a new constitution. However, he was soon in trouble because he openly opposed the execution of King Louis XVI. Initially protected by members of the Girondin Party, Paine became disillusioned with the Revolution. He began drinking heavily and withdrew from participation in the Convention, the body which had replaced the National Assembly. He was writing *The Age of Reason* when the fall of the Girondins and ascendancy of the Jacobins led by Maximilien Robespierre resulted in his arrest.

Fearing that he would be executed, Paine claimed U.S. citizenship, but the American ambassador to France, Gouverneur Morris, who had opposed the French Revolution, was uninterested in his case. Fortunately, a combination of illness and French governmental inefficiency protected Paine until James Monroe replaced Morris. Monroe's intervention and Robespierre's death combined to win Paine's release and restoration to the Convention. Despite Monroe's efforts, Paine was bitter about the paucity of American help in his hour of need and even denounced President George Washington.

The Age of Reason, which Paine finished while in prison, quickly attracted hostile attention. It was a defense of Deism, and it subjected the Bible to logical analysis. It was denounced as an atheist's manifesto. In June, 1797, the book's English publisher was convicted, and it became dangerous for anyone to publish Paine's work in Great Britain for some years thereafter.

Although Paine continued to write political pamphlets, his star had waned in France; in 1802 he returned to his New York estate. Although he had a friendly interview with President Thomas Jefferson, his welcome was muted because many of his old friends had been offended by *The Age of Reason*. Charges of sexual misconduct and drunkenness circulated; the former charges were largely, if not wholly lies, but the latter charges had some validity. Financial problems followed and by 1808 Paine was petitioning Congress for money and selling his New Rochelle home. —*Fred R. van Hartesveldt*

See also Atheism; Bible; *Citizen Tom Paine*; Franklin, Benjamin; Gibbon, Edward; Jefferson, Thomas; Revolutionary War, American; Voltaire.

Bibliography

R. R. Fennessy, *Burke, Paine and the Rights of Man* (The Hague: Nijhoff, 1963), argues that Burke and Paine actually agreed about the nature of the French Revolution, but differed strongly in how they felt about it. Leo Gurko's *Tom Paine: Freedom's Apostle* (New York: Crowell, 1957) is a popular biography that offers a good introduction to Paine's life and career. David Freeman Hawke's *Paine* (New York: Harper & Row, 1974), a biography based on solid scholarship, offers a penetrating analysis of Paine's ideas. Francis McConnell, *Evangelicals, Revolutionists, and Idealists: Six English Contributors to American Thought and Action* (New York: Abingdon-Cokesbury Press, 1942), includes a discussion of Paine; its other essays provide valuable context for understanding his place among those who helped shape American ideals. *The Life and Works of Thomas Paine* (New Rochelle, N.Y.: Thomas Paine National Historical Association, 1925) volume includes a biographical sketch by W. M. Van der Weyde and provides convenient access to Paine's most important writings.

Pakistan

Description: Independent south Asian republic that was part of British-ruled India until 1947

Significance: Among Asia's many independent modern countries, Pakistan has had a long and complicated history of censorship

The media in Pakistan have faced overt and covert censorship from the government and pressure groups. As an Islamic nation, with a 97 percent Muslim population, religious public opinion has been a powerful source of censorship. Having been a British colony, Pakistan shared a common censorship legacy with India until 1947, when the two countries became independent. After the birth of Pakistan, censorship continued for the media, literature, fine arts, and films.

Pakistan inherited the ministry of information and broadcasting and several press and press-related laws from the British such as the Official Secrets Act and printing and publishing licensing acts. From 1947 to the mid-1980's the ministry was accorded more power, and censorship laws were refined and newer ones added. One law, the Pakistan Safety Act, was promulgated in 1948—followed by its provincial counterpart the Punjab Safety Act. These laws were used to impose censorship on newspapers, telephones, and telegraphs when Pakistan's first martial law was declared on Lahore in 1953 to quell rioting between the majority Sunni and minority Ahmadiya Muslim sects.

During the ten-year regime of military commander Ayub Khan, who took power in a coup d'état in 1958, the government issued press advisories and press releases and furnished actual stories and speeches of public officials for acquiring support for its plans and policies. Further, the Press and Publications Ordinance, decreed in 1960 on the national level and in 1963 on the provincial levels, required approval from magistrates and security deposits for those publications that offended the government and Islam. To serve as the regime's mouthpieces, eleven newspapers were confiscated and run by the government-controlled National Press Trust.

In 1969 Ayub Khan handed power to the martial government general Yahya Khan, who found his predecessor's censorship tactics handy when he imposed censorship on the media from March 25 to December 16, 1971, the period of the civil war in East Pakistan, culminating in the creation of Bangladesh. In that strife, Pakistani forces killed several East Pakistani professors, eight journalists, and a film director for espousing anti-Pakistani sentiments.

For losing East Pakistan, Yahya Khan was forced to abdicate the government to Zulfiquar Ali Bhutto, who specified in the 1972 constitution freedom of the press similar to that of the First Amendment to the U.S. Constitution. Nevertheless, the Bhutto government rarely hesitated to act against the media. His successor General Zia-ul-Haq, who seized power in a coup d'état in 1977, imposed a blanket censorship on the press in 1979. In addition to hanging Bhutto, he shut down Bhutto's newspaper, *Muswaat*. Journalists who protested were jailed and four of them were flogged.

After Zia-ul-Haq's death in a plane sabotage in 1988, Pakistan returned to democracy—resulting in the repeal of the Press and Publications Ordinance and other press laws. However, the elected governments continued to publish five newspapers through the National Press Trust, to allocate newsprint, and to distribute government advertising. As the government's threats became veiled, intimidation from the Mohajir Qaumi Movement—a political party of Indian Muslim immigrants—heightened. This group used pressure against the media and the government in its quest to be recognized as Pakistan's fifth ethnic group.

Strict censorship has prevailed in broadcasting, literature, fine arts, and films. Broadcasting has in most part been a government monopoly. Cable News Network (CNN) broadcasts, carried by the privately owned television network, have drawn criticism from the government and viewers for anti-Pakistani reporting and advertising unsuitable for an Islamic audience. For blaspheming Islam, in 1988 Salman Rushdie's *The Satanic Verses* was banned. The film censor board ever since the British period has removed antigovernment messages and obscenity from both domestic and foreign films.

See also Bhopal disaster; Cable News Network; First Amendment; India; Islam; Nasrin, Taslima.

Panama, U.S. invasion of

DATE: December 20, 1989-January 6, 1990

PLACE: Panama

SIGNIFICANCE: This military conflict contrasts with the earlier U.S. invasion of Grenada and the later Persian Gulf War in being an example of a U.S. military operation in which relatively little press censorship was enforced

The generally amicable relations between the United States and Panama began to falter after Panamanian general Manuel Noriega came to power in Panama in 1987. Despite his history of involvement in drug trafficking, gun running, and money laundering, Noriega had been receiving support from the Central Intelligence Agency (CIA) as a friendly resource in Panama. However, relations between the two countries deteriorated rapidly after Noriega arranged the ouster of Panama's president Eric Delvalle and annulled the subsequent election of Guillermo Endara. Washington continued to distance itself from Noriega as both Panamanian domestic unrest and international opprobrium rose against Noriega. The growing instability in Panama raised American concern about the security of the Panama Canal, which was vital to international shipping. On December 20, 1976, President George Bush ordered U.S. troops into Panama with the ostensible purpose of seizing Noriega on drug-smuggling charges. After a two-week effort, which included Noriega's temporary sanctuary in the Vatican's local embassy building, American officials seized Noriega and took him to the United States to stand trial on drug-trafficking charges.

Several aspects of the invasion held the potential for embarrassing the U.S. government—not least of which was Washington's earlier support for Noriega. Moreover, the military operation itself had a number of embarrassing problems, including civilian deaths, and there were instances of Panamanian civilians protesting the American effort to "liberate" them. Despite these problems, the American news media were unusually supportive of the invasion, portraying it in a positive light—even in comparison with the media's coverage of the following year's Persian Gulf War. More significantly, there was little official effort to restrict or manage news coverage of the Panama invasion. The "press pool" system that would be used in reporting on the later Gulf War was not utilized in the Panama operation. American reporters and photographers were present at the invitation of the invasion force and had relatively free access to cover events. American press

Members of the U.S. occupying forces stand guard outside of the bombed-out headquarters of ousted Panamanian president Manuel Noriega. (AP/Wide World Photos)

coverage might therefore have been partly a product of self-censorship.

Although the U.S. government did not overtly hinder media access, there is some evidence that the Endara government—which the U.S. military returned to power after removing Noriega—worked to limit public negative portrayals of the military intervention by its American benefactors. Also, Noriega's numerous moral and political faults may have made portraying the invasion as a morality play almost irresistible. Finally, the relative swiftness of Noriega's defeat provided little time for antiwar sentiment to materialize.

See also Falkland Islands War; Grenada, U.S. invasion of; Haiti; Military censorship; Persian Gulf War; War.

Pankhurst, Emmeline

Born: July 14, 1858, Manchester, England

Died: June 14, 1928, London, England

Identification: Leader of a militant English movement to enfranchise women

Significance: Between 1905 and 1914 Pankhurst and her daughters, Christabel and Sylvia, battled a hostile British government to secure women's suffrage

Pankhurst grew up in the radical atmosphere of late nineteenth century Manchester, England, one of the sites of the Industrial Revolution, where her father established himself as a cotton manufacturer. She was encouraged to think for herself, read newspapers, and interest herself in current events. Her liberal and uncensored education inspired her devotion to progressive causes, especially those fostering the independence of women. In 1879 she married Dr. Richard Pankhurst, a lawyer and socialist, by whom she had five children. In 1893 she joined the Independent Labor Party. Disappointed by the party's hostility to women and its failure to take the censorship of women seriously, she began her own campaign for women's suffrage in 1903.

With the aid of her daughters, Pankhurst founded the Women's Social and Political Union (WSPU). Influenced by her strong-willed daughter Christabel, she adopted aggressive tactics, harassing Britain's Liberal government with invasions of the House of Commons, window-breaking, arson, and attacks on golf courses, art galleries, and politicians' homes. The government retaliated by arresting and imprisoning feminist protesters. In 1908 the WSPU campaign accelerated, with its members staging hunger strikes in prison and suffering forcible feeding that often ruined their health.

Sylvia Pankhurst later wrote a history of the women's suffrage movement which proved to be both sound history and a spirited defense of the cause against all forms of female censorship. Unlike her mother, who sought support among frustrated well-to-do women, Sylvia concentrated on the working classes, trying to broaden the movement, which was in danger of becoming captured by its middle-class organizers. After 1908 the WSPU began losing its influence and its funding base. As it succumbed to internal dissension, some prominent members, such as Dora Marsden, broke off to pursue broader issues of women's rights. By 1912 Emmeline Pankhurst was permanently estranged from her own daughters, who were pursuing increasingly militant actions to combat the censorship of women.

At the onset of World War I, Pankhurst abandoned her work for women's suffrage and joined forces with the political establishment, working closely with Lloyd George, Britain's minister of munitions. Even when the issue of women's suffrage was finally being settled in 1916-1918, Pankhurst maintained her distance from the negotiations, preferring to concentrate on recruiting men for the army. Some members of the suffrage movement regarded her actions as tantamount to self-censorship. Her remaining years were spent as a lecturer in North America. In 1926 she failed to win election to Parliament as a Conservative.

See also National Organization for Women; Women.

Parent Teacher Association (PTA)

Founded: 1897

Type of organization: Nonprofit and nonpartisan organization concerned with the well-being of children

Significance: As a body dedicated to protecting children from harmful influences, the PTA has occasionally advocated various forms of censorship

Long known as the Parent Teacher Association, the PTA began in 1897 as the National Congress of Mothers—a product of the "purity crusade" of the late nineteenth century. Influenced by the utopian and reformist moral ideologies then popular, the movement was formed to combat poverty and prostitution through educational and legal reform. The modern PTA involves itself in a wide range of social, economic, and moral issues, while working for laws for the care and protection of children and youth and fostering cooperation among the home, school, and public. This work has occasionally involved PTA branches in censorship controversies.

More than thirty thousand PTA branches—each organized on a national model—have formed at both public and private elementary and secondary schools. Small permanent staffs at state and national offices develop materials and support annual state and national conventions. Membership is open to parents of school children, teachers, care givers, and other persons who wish to support PTA goals. Local branches develop their own constitutions, following national guidelines, and develop programs to meet local school and community needs.

As a body advocating protection and promotion of children, the PTA has been placed in positions of being both an advocate and an opponent of censorship. When its members have testified before national and state legislatures against pandering pornography to children, the PTA has been accused of advocating censorship by civil libertarian groups. When its members have urged AIDS education in the schools, the PTA has fought against advocates of health education censorship. The national PTA has opposed school censorship in order to keep classrooms open and democratic. However, with seven million members in essentially autonomous local units, individual branches have occasionally taken opposite stances in order to make the PTA a vehicle for their own agendas—as in the Kanawha County, West Virginia, book-banning controversy during the 1970's. Local branches have also joined with other groups in antipornography campaigns.

See also Advocacy; Books, children's; "Cop Killer"; Education; Evolution; Gabler, Mel, and Norma Gabler; Kanawha County book-banning controversy; Libraries, school; Television, children's; Textbooks.

Parents' Alliance to Protect Our Children (PAPOC)

Founded: 1979

Type of organization: Profamily group opposed to secular humanism

Significance: This organization has tried to protect children from forms of manipulation that they believe occur in education and politics

Parents' Alliance to Protect Our Children (PAPOC) provides information and official opinions especially for education, on children's issues. Its members believe that children need to be protected from a public education that tries to turn them from traditional family values, and it has testified before the U.S. Department of Education on its research findings. The alliance conducts research into secular and religious life of the nuclear family with specific areas of interest being sex education, abortion and population control, curricula in public and private schools, legislation affecting the family, and censorship in music and education.

See also Eagle Forum; Education; National Federation for Decency; Secular humanism.

Parents' Music Resource Center (PMRC)

Founded: 1985

Type of organization: Nonprofit American child welfare and consumer rights watchdog group

Significance: The PMRC has prompted Senate hearings on the lyrics of popular music and has lobbied the Recording Industry Association of America

The PMRC was established in 1985 by Susan Baker, Tipper Gore, Pam Howar, and Sally Nevius. The founders, all married to prominent political and government leaders in Washington, D.C., were dubbed the Washington wives by the press. The four formed the PMRC to respond to the perceived rise in explicit lyrics in popular music. The PMRC objects to lyrics, videos, and concerts that are targeted at children and adolescents and that glamorize violence and substance abuse. In addition, the PMRC also censures lyrics and attendant performances that contain inappropriate references to Satanism, suicide, rape, misogyny, sadomasochism, racism, and sexism.

Representatives of the PMRC appeared on September 19, 1985, before the U.S. Senate Committee on Commerce, Science, and Transportation for a hearing on record labeling. Baker and Gore, the vice president and second vice president of the PMRC, testified that violent and obscene rock lyrics were unsuitable for minors. They argued that warning labels on music products would enable parents to monitor more effectively their children's musical choices. Their testimony led some senators, such as Democrat James Exon of Nebraska, to threaten restrictive legislation if the record industry did not remedy the problem. Shortly afterward, on November 1, 1985, the PMRC reached an agreement with the Recording Industry Association of America (RIAA). The RIAA promised that all music products containing graphic lyrics would be labeled with black-and-white stickers reading "Explicit Lyrics—Parental Advisory." In return, the PMRC agreed to desist from public attacks on the record industry for one year.

In 1995 the PMRC, headed by Barbara Wyatt, called for the RIAA to use a more comprehensive labeling system that would specifically identify why the labeled product was unsuitable for children. The PMRC argued for a multilevel label system, modeled on film ratings, that would identify the degree of graphic content found on music products. The PMRC also felt that there had been many recent releases that should have had stickers, and they urged the RIAA to more rigorously apply warning labels.

Along with monitoring the effectiveness of record labeling, the PMRC also serves as a clearinghouse for information on the deleterious effects that graphic lyrics and inappropriate subject matter in popular music have on children and adolescents.

See also Music; Pressure groups; Rap music; Rock 'n' roll music.

Paris, Council of

Date: 1210

Place: Paris, France

Significance: Roman Catholic church officials meeting in Paris prohibited the use of Aristotelian studies and non-Christian commentaries on Aristotle's works

The Council of Paris was a synodical meeting of French Catholic prelates convened by Peter of Corbeil, a church official. For several weeks the issues of heresy and authorized use of the metaphysical system of Aristotle were debated. Anti-Aristotelian council members opposed the reading and teaching of the Greek philosopher's cosmological scheme and Jewish and Muslim commentaries on his studies. They contended that Aristotelianism identified the "unmoved mover" or first cause as an impersonal being. They argued that in the Aristotelian order of the universe individual mortality and the eternal nature of the universe were incorrectly explained.

Council members who favored academic use of Aristotelianism noted the century-long European study of Aristotelian logic and the desirability of devising a bridge between Aristotelian thought and Divine revelation. The anti-Aristotelian members prevailed. A local ban was promulgated that prohibited the use of Aristotle's works, except those on logic, and related non-Christian commentaries in the presentation of private and public lectures in Parisian schools. Violators of the ban were to be excommunicated. Also, fourteen prominent scholars were accused of heresy.

In 1215 the prohibition was upheld by Roman legate Robert de Courçon. In 1231, however, Pope Gregory IX allowed the works of Aristotle to be studied throughout Europe if accurate texts were used. The end of the thirteenth century witnessed the efforts by Albertus Magnus and Thomas Aquinas to produce commentaries that reconciled Aristotelian reason and Christian faith, giving rise to the Scholastic movement.

See also Abelard, Peter; Alexandria library; Aristotle; Heresy; Lateran Council, Fourth.

Parker, Dorothy

Born: August 22, 1893, West End, New Jersey

Died: June 7, 1967, New York, New York

Identification: American short-story writer, poet, critic, and screenwriter

Significance: Parker was investigated by the Federal Bureau of Investigation (FBI) and the House Committee on Un-American Activities (HUAC), and was blacklisted by the movie industry because of her political activities

Dorothy Parker was the youngest child of J. Henry Rothschild, a prosperous Jewish clothing manufacturer, and Eliza A. Marston, a Scottish Presbyterian, who died while she was an infant. She was educated at the Blessed Sacrament Convent School, New York City. After her father's death in 1914 she tried freelance writing. In June, 1917, she married Edwin Pond Parker II, a young stock broker who soon volunteered as an ambulance driver in World War I. They were divorced in 1928, but Parker called herself Mrs. Dorothy Parker for the rest of her life.

Parker's witty and satiric remarks about people and events appeared frequently in New York City newspapers, making her famous for her lively repartee. She also contributed witty reviews of plays and books, along with light verse and short stories, to national magazines. In addition, she was a regular contributor to *The New Yorker*, from its second issue in 1925 until 1957, helping to establish the style of what became known as "the *New Yorker* short story." In 1934, with her second husband Alan Campbell, she went to Hollywood where they collaborated on twenty-two screenplays and were nominated for an Academy Award in 1947.

Meanwhile, the rise of Adolf Hitler and fascism in Europe alarmed Parker, who actively participated in several left-wing organizations during the 1930's. She helped found the Hollywood Anti-Nazi League and became national chairperson of the Joint Anti-Fascist Refugee Committee, which formed to aid those fleeing the fascist forces in the Spanish Civil War. These activities caused Parker problems in the late 1940's and 1950's as a red scare swept the United States.

In 1947 the *New York Daily News* claimed that HUAC planned to subpoena Parker, but she was never called to testify. In 1953 *The New York Times* reported that Senator Joseph McCarthy planned to call her as a witness. Again, however, she was not subpoenaed. In 1955 she testified briefly before a New York State Senate committee about the affairs of the Joint Anti-Fascist Refugee Committee. From the late 1940's until 1955 the FBI kept Parker under surveillance, eventually closing her file with the notation that she was not dangerous.

The late 1940's and 1950's were anxious decades for Parker. Accusations of being a member of the Communist Party—which she denied—led to her being blacklisted by movie producers, and she found it impossible to get new writing assignments. Although she did not suffer the fate of friends on the national board of the Joint Anti-Fascist Refugee Committee who went to jail for refusing to turn over records to HUAC, her inability to work in Hollywood caused her severe financial problems in the last decades of her life.

See also Blacklisting; Caricature; Communism; Federal Bureau of Investigation; House Committee on Un-American Activities.

Pascal, Blaise

Born: June 19, 1623, Clermont-Ferrand, Auvergne, France

Died: August 19, 1662, Paris, France

Identification: French writer and moralist

Significance: Pascal's works were burned and placed on the *Index Librorum Prohibitorum* because they questioned God's existence

A philosopher, mathematician, theologian, and visionary, Pascal wrote meditations on God and miracles that inspired the project of an apology or defense of the Christian religion (Catholicism) in his works. His innovations in mathematics included contributions to vacuum theory and the geometry of cycloid curves, and he helped create Paris' public omnibus carriage system.

During the 1650's Pascal grew interested in theology and moral philosophy. After undergoing a mystical experience at the convent at Port Royal in 1654, he retired from the world. He wrote his recollection of this mystical experience in a text called "The Memorial," which he sewed into his clothing in order always to have it with him. During 1656 he came out of retirement briefly to defend Antoine Arnauld from an attack by the Jesuits, publishing the *Lettres provinciales* (1656-1657), a series of letters defending Jansenism.

Pascal led a quiet life within the walls of Port Royal until his death in 1662. Eight years later a group of Jansenists edited and published *Pensées de M. Pascal sur la religion et sur quelques autres sujets* (commonly known as the *Pensées*), fragments salvaged from Pascal's unfinished work "Apologie de la religion catholique." Pascal's nephew believed that the order in which these fragments were discovered after his uncle's death made no sense, and he reorganized them in an order that seriously distorted Pascal's intentions. Only editions from the nineteenth century and later, which have been made from the original manuscripts, are trustworthy.

There was much controversy over the doctrines of the Dutch theologian Jansenius, who took positions on the issue of divine grace in human conduct that the papacy considered heretical. The central issues were that Jansenists did not believe in transubstantiation, the presence of Christ in the Eucharist, and were in effect, following Protestant theological doctrines. In 1657 a papal bull condemned Jansenism, creating a document termed the Formulary that was to be signed by all clergy. Although no serious action was taken at that time, by 1660, under pressure of the French government, *Lettres provinciales* was condemned and burned in the hands of the public executioner in September, 1660, and it was added to the *Index Librorum Prohibitorum.* Although Pascal's work was banned, it is considered to be the beginning of modern French prose in its brevity, tautness, and precision of style.

When the issue of the Formulary was revived, Pascal wrote strongly against signing, and broke off relations with Port Royal and Arnauld when the Jansenists decided to sign in order to save Port-Royal. Pascal's health declined after this period and he died at the age of thirty-nine.

See also Book burning; Christianity; Descartes, René; Gibbon, Edward; *Index Librorum Prohibitorum*; Reformation, the; Religion.

Pasternak, Boris

Born: February 10, 1890, Moscow, Russia
Died: May 30, 1960, Peredelkino, near Moscow, Soviet Union
Identification: Russian author
Significance: Pasternak received a Nobel Prize for *Doctor Zhivago*, but his novel could not be published in the Soviet Union and he was prohibited from further writing

Pasternak was a significant Russian poet, translator, and novelist. Although he lived through the decades of totalitarian rule under V. I. Lenin and Joseph Stalin, his literary work did not create controversy until he submitted his manuscript for *Doctor Zhivago* to a Soviet publisher in the 1950's. The editors concluded the novel was unsuitable for Soviet readers because its story about an idealistic young physician contained philosophical values and other descriptions that directly or indirectly ran counter to communist ideology. Events in the novel were accused of being unhistorical, as dictated by the commu-

Russian author Boris Pasternak with American composer Leonard Bernstein in September, 1959, shortly after the Soviet government forced Pasternak to decline the Nobel Prize. (AP/Wide World Photos)

nist literary theory of Socialist Realism.

Pasternak had not personally participated in political events during or after the 1917 Russian Revolution. He had been more of an observer than an activist, and his literary portrayal of the fictional Zhivago's ethical and moral standards was not intended as a political manifesto. However, the novel did express Zhivago's humane outlook that eventually was overwhelmed by the power and intellectual narrowness of a totalitarian ideology. This perspective constituted Zhivago's—and Pasternak's—crime against the state.

A short-lived period of greater cultural openness in the Soviet Union that had followed Stalin's death in 1953 ended by late 1956—the moment when Pasternak's manuscript was being considered for publication. After the Soviet publishers rejected it, it was published in Italy in 1957, and in English-language editions in 1958. The novel's imagery and message, and the circumstances behind its publication in the West, created great interest in the book and author. In 1958 Sweden's Nobel Committee selected Pasternak to receive the prestigious Nobel Prize in Literature.

News of Pasternak's novel being published in the West and his Nobel Prize elicited negative responses among the Soviet Union's bureaucratic leaders. The Soviet press accused Pasternak of pandering to foreign nations. His personal integrity was questioned, and some labeled him a traitor. When it came time for him to go to Sweden to accept his Nobel Prize, he was informed if he undertook the trip he might be prohibited from re-entering the Soviet Union. Widespread and excessive pressure led to his reluctant decision to reject the award.

In a revealing letter to Nikita Khrushchev, the general secretary of the Soviet Union's Communist Party, Pasternak said that expulsion from his country would be tantamount to death. He gave assurances of his loyalty to the Soviet Union and said he would accept whatever restrictions the state might impose on him. As a result, his opportunities to publish were ended and he had to live quietly until his death two years later. Only after the Soviet Union's collapse in 1991 did his novel appear in print in his country.

See also Communism; Gorbachev, Mikhail; Socialist Realism; Solzhenitsyn, Aleksandr; Soviet Union.

Paterson, Katherine

Born: October 31, 1932, Qing Jiang, China

Identification: Chinese American author of popular children's books

Significance: Paterson's books have been challenged or banned from classrooms and libraries in many cities in the United States

In December 1992, a parent of a fifth grader in Kansas objected to Katherine Paterson's *Bridge to Terabithia* (1977) for its language and its portrayal of a nontraditional family. The novel was withdrawn from classrooms. This book has also been challenged in Illinois, Michigan, Ohio, Pennsylvania, Georgia, Texas, and California, and it has appeared several times on the list of the ten most banned books in the United States. Other objections have centered on its portrayal of alleged "New Age" religion, disrespect for authority, theological treatment of death, and negative portrayals of Christianity. Another book, *The Great Gilly Hopkins* (1978), has been challenged in schools in North Carolina, Connecticut, and Texas for its use of profanity, obscenities, and derogatory remarks about God.

In an interview about censorship challenges to *Bridge to Terabithia*, Paterson noted, "As the daughter of missionaries, as a missionary myself, and as a minister's wife, I care deeply about the moral lives of children." Paterson believes that books are uniquely suited to develop children's inner strength and argues that censorship of children's books leads to children's "intellectual and spiritual poverty."

See also Banned Books Week; Books, children's; Impressions reading series.

Paul IV, Pope

Born: June 28, 1476, Italy

Died: August 18, 1559, Rome, Italy

Identification: Pontiff of the Roman Catholic church (1555-1559)

Significance: A member of the original Inquisition, Paul intensified Roman Catholic censorship and created the *Index Librorum Prohibitorum*

Cardinal Gian Pietro Carafa took the name Paul IV upon ascending to the papacy in 1555. He soon introduced significant repressive elements into the Roman Catholic Counter-Reformation, the crusade within the Church to reform itself and to oppose the spread of Protestantism. In 1542 Pope Paul III had established the Congregation of the Inquisition (also called the Holy Office), and then appointed Carafa and five other cardinals to the newly formed institution.

For a little more than a decade the activities of the Congregation of the Inquisition were almost exclusively confined to Italy and concerned mostly with theological questions of an academic nature. But when Carafa became pope, the geographical scope of the Inquisition was expanded. In Spain especially, Paul's vigorous pursuit of reform earned him the enmity of Protestants and Catholics alike. Here the Inquisition, although implemented by churchmen, became an instrument of King Philip II for imposing orthodoxy upon his Spanish subjects. In the process, thousands of reputed heretics were executed.

Paul also ordered the Congregation of the Inquisition to compile a list of books considered dangerous to faith and morals. In 1559 he published the first *Index Librorum Prohibitorum.* Catholics were forbidden to possess, read, or disseminate books on the *Index* without special permission. The last edition of the *Index* was published in 1948, but not until 1966 was it declared nonbinding by the church.

See also *Index Librorum Prohibitorum*; Reformation, the; Spanish Inquisition; Vatican.

Peckinpah, Sam

Born: February 21, 1925, Fresno, California

Died: December 28, 1984, Inglewood, California

Identification: American filmmaker

Significance: Because of the graphic depiction of violence in his films, Peckinpah was challenged by studio censors and later by the Motion Picture Association of America (MPAA)

Peckinpah began his screen career by writing episodes of such television westerns as *The Rifleman*, *The Westerner*, *Zane Grey Theatre*, and *Tombstone Territory*. He eventually moved behind the camera as an assistant and finally as a director, again starting with television westerns and episodes of *Route 66*. He later decided to apply his vision, again primarily of the western, to the wide screen, and his reputation was solid in Hollywood by 1960.

Peckinpah learned his first lessons about the power of the studios when he made *Major Dundee* (1965), a film starring Charlton Heston that Columbia expected to be a blockbuster. The studio was unconcerned with Peckinpah's vision or his style and ultimately cut almost twenty-five minutes from the film, either because it found the material extraneous or because it wanted a shorter film that would sell more easily. *Major Dundee* proved a box office flop, but it garnered good critical reactions across the country.

Peckinpah became best known for his quirky style and for his unique slant on history in such films as *Pat Garrett and Billy the Kid* (1973), *The Ballad of Cable Hogue* (1970), *Junior Bonner* (1972), and *Bring Me the Head of Alfredo Garcia* (1974). In addition, his 1962 film *Ride the High Country* began the vision presented in *The Wild Bunch* (1970), which is considered his most poetical film.

The Wild Bunch changed the way that Americans view their history. Peckinpah wanted a violent, ambivalent film with lots of blood; he produced so much blood, however, that some patrons at the film's opening screenings became violently ill. Peckinpah also introduced vile language and nudity. When he finished the film, he sent ten reels to the studio that he knew its officers would like. He did not, however, count on their sending a two-page synopsis of scenes to the MPAA, which told the studio that with revisions the film could get an R and not an X rating. The studio cut six scenes of various lengths (these were not restored until 1993, when the MPAA viewed the same material and granted the new cut an NC-17, also a noncommercial rating).

When Peckinpah went to England to film *Straw Dogs* (1971), he stayed away from western themes. Again, the MPAA wanted two scenes cut: a particularly brutal rape and a scene in which Dustin Hoffman throws a bear trap on a man's head. Peckinpah's theme was that a man's home is his castle, but again, the cuts were made.

Peckinpah died at fifty-nine, a sad and disillusioned genius, forever to be known for *The Wild Bunch* and his style of slow-motion action scenes. His violence in slow motion has been likened to ballet, and actors have defended his work as uniquely American.

See also *Blue Velvet*; Film censorship; Motion Picture Association of America; *Natural Born Killers*; Violence; *Wild Bunch, The*.

PEN

Founded: 1921

Type of organization: International writers' organization

Significance: PEN was formed to foster communication among writers, and to combat censorship

An acronym for "Poets, Playwrights, Editors, Essayists, and Novelists," PEN was founded by English writer Mrs. C. A. Dawson-Scott. Under the leadership of its first president, novelist and playwright John Galsworthy, PEN aggressively promoted cooperation among writers throughout the world. The organization has consistently supported the ideal of literature as freedom of expression, and has seen literature as a vehicle for stimulating and sustaining international good will. It deems any organization, government, or group seeking to limit the spread of literature or its free expression a force for censorship.

PEN leaders and members have mobilized several campaigns to free imprisoned writers, by writing letters to government authorities and by publishing reports and articles in the international press. PEN congresses have been held in settings both friendly and hostile to free speech and literature. Leaders of PEN such as former president Francis King have led delegations and arranged meetings in countries such as South Korea, where appeals have been made on behalf of imprisoned writers. Early PEN meetings in Eastern Europe protested the incarceration of writers critical of communist governments. In South Africa, PEN members worked for a fully integrated organization for writers. PEN has also been active in opposing Iran's sentence of death imposed on Salman Rushdie, whose novel *The Satanic Verses* (1988) was deemed blasphemous.

PEN has more than eighty affiliates around the world. The U.S. PEN chapter has been headed by such distinguished writers as Arthur Miller, Norman Mailer, and Susan Sontag. Mailer expressed the organization's view that because writers across the world can speak to one another more quickly than can governments, they can create bridges of cooperation. His own presidency, however, became controversial when he invited U.S. secretary of state George Schultz to address a PEN meeting in 1984. Many members felt the organization was compromised by inviting a speaker implicated in political actions that had contributed to the censorship of writers.

PEN's ongoing work includes educational programs and an annual censorship survey, an accounting of the fate of writers and their work throughout the world. To a large extent, PEN has functioned as a human rights organization—similar to Amnesty International—by publishing reports and letters signed by prominent writers calling attention to coercion of writers and the suppression of literature throughout the world. At the same time, PEN presidents have worked behind the scenes, negotiating with governments for the release of writers or petitioning officials for appeals of court cases and prison sentences.

See also Article 19; Blacklisting; Book publishing; Intellectual freedom; Rushdie, Salman.

Pentagon Papers, The

Type of work: Book

Published: 1971

Authors: Various government agencies

Subject matter: Documents from a secret U.S. Defense Department study of the origins of U.S. involvement in the Vietnam War

Significance: Publication of these papers over the objections of the U.S. government led to a landmark Supreme Court decision reaffirming that prior restraint is incompatible with constitutional guarantees of freedom of the press

The Pentagon Papers case is one of the most important cases involving freedom of the press. When Robert McNamara was secretary of defense during in the 1960's, he became disenchanted with U.S. involvement in the Vietnam War. Before he left office in 1968, he ordered a secret study of all Defense Department documents relating to how the United States had gotten involved in the war. The completed study contained three thousand pages of text and four thousand pages of documents—which collectively became known as the "Pentagon Papers."

The study and documents were kept secret (although not all its documents had been classified as secret) because they detailed several incidents in which McNamara and other national leaders had lied to Congress and the public about the U.S. entrance into the war. The study also disclosed that the United States had supported South Vietnamese military actions against North Vietnam before the 1964 Tonkin Gulf incident that could be regarded as provocative, if not illegal, under international law. Such actions could have been seen as having the North Vietnamese in their actions in the Tonkin Gulf incident, and, therefore could have made the U.S. retaliation a violation of international law, instead of an act of self-defense. The papers also included diplomatic documents between U.S. and foreign governments that were regarded as highly secret because they might embarrass other governments into retaliating for their disclosure by refusing to communicate with the United States. For all these reasons, the U.S. government naturally wanted to preserve the papers' secrecy, while every newspaper would have been eager to publish them.

Daniel Ellsberg, an employee of the Rand Corporation, a semiprivate U.S. Air Force "think tank," duplicated the documents and gave copies to *The New York Times*, the most prestigious American daily newspaper. All Rand employees were routinely required to have security clearances before they could examine the documents, and had to sign contracts promising not to violate their clearance as a condition of employment. Despite knowing the employment and criminal penalties for disclosing national secrets, Ellsberg felt that the Pentagon Papers contained information that the public had a right to know, even though giving them to a newspaper was equivalent to stealing government property.

The New York Times studied the papers and then, without notice to the government, printed some of them while stating they would publish the rest in installments starting on Sunday, June 17, 1971. The shock to high government officials was great. The newspaper's editors were aware of the questionable legality of their actions: They had possessed them for a long time, they did not return them to the U.S. government, and they clandestinely published them. Some government officials felt that the *Times* publishers were as much in violation of the law as Ellsberg.

The federal Justice Department prosecuted Ellsberg for stealing government documents, but failed to gain a conviction. Ellsberg's case was thrown out of court when it was discovered that President Richard Nixon had ordered a secret White House burglary team to break into his psychiatrist's office to search for information that would discredit Ellsberg. Acting under a law that prohibited the government from pressing a prosecution when the government itself has violated the law, the judge dismissed the case. After failing to convict Ellsberg, the Justice Department decided it would be futile to proceed against *The New York Times*.

Efforts to Stop Publication. Although conviction of Ellsberg after publication remained a possibility, the government wanted more: to stop the damaging information from getting into the hands of the public. It wanted prior restraint on publication. Naturally, the U.S. government believed it was protecting national security from an outrageous theft. Despite a strong argument that national security would be compromised, the U.S. government did not achieve a permanent prior restraint. Two days after the *Times* began publishing Pentagon Papers documents, U.S. attorney general John Mitchell sent Justice Department lawyers to a federal district court to obtain a temporary injunction against the paper. Anticipating such a result, someone gave copies of the Pentagon Papers to several other U.S. papers. Then, when the *Times* was enjoined from publishing them, *The Washington Post* started publishing them. When the U.S. government enjoined the *Post*, the *Boston Globe* began publishing them, and so on. After legal maneuvering, the cases were consolidated and appealed swiftly to the U.S. Supreme Court.

The Supreme Court voted 6-3 against the Nixon Administration. Although all nine justices—writing separate opinions—upheld the concept of no prior restraint, they disagreed on whether such restraint could be justified by the extraordinary circumstances in this case. Justices Hugo L. Black, William O. Douglas, and—to a lesser degree— William J. Brennan, Jr., essentially maintained that the principle of no prior restraint was so strong that the government should never censor the press; Black and Douglas also argued against even the temporary injunctions, although such orders have historically been common in American law. Justices Thurgood Marshall, Potter Stewart, and Byron White (who voted with the first three justices to allow publication of the Pentagon Papers) held that the presumption against prior restraint was too strong in this case, but held open the option that someday there might be a national emergency in which prior restraint might be justified. They pointed out that the Nixon Administration's case was further weakened because they had no law, duly passed by Congress, on which to rely, and that all the government could do was rely on a very weak legal argument that the president had a general power to protect the government from harm. Justices Warren Burger, Harry Blackmun, and John Harlan, voting against publication, maintained they were opposed to prior restraint but requested more time to look at the documents before making a final judgment whether a permanent restraining order should be issued.

By its 6-3 vote, the Court gave newspapers permission to publish the Pentagon Papers. However, because three "swing" justices expressed the view that there might be extreme circumstances in which prior restraint might be justified, there remained the possibility that a prior restraint might later be allowed. Nevertheless, publication of the documents was something that few, if any, other large countries would ever allow. *—Richard L. Wilson*

See also National security; *New York Times, The*; Nixon, Richard M.; Prior restraint; Tonkin Gulf incident; Vietnam War; Watergate scandal.

Bibliography

The original book form publication was edited by *The New York Times* staff under the title *The Pentagon Papers* (New York: Bantam Books, 1971). Documents on the U.S. negotiating procedure, a part of the original Defense Department study, were edited by George C. Herring, *The Secret Diplomacy of the Vietnam War: The Negotiating Volumes of the Pentagon Papers* (Austin: University of Texas, 1983). The best book covering the court case is Martin Shapiro's edited volume, *The Pentagon Papers and the Courts: A Study in Foreign Policy-Making and Freedom of the Press* (San Francisco: Chandler, 1972). The case is given prominent consideration in Lucas A. Powe, Jr., *The Fourth Estate and the Constitution: Freedom of the Press in America* (Berkeley: University of California, 1991), and in Wallace Mendelson's *The American Constitution and Civil Liberties* (Homewood,

Ill.: Dorsey, 1981). A later study that incorporates considerable evidence not available earlier is David Rudenstine's *The Day the Press Stopped: A History of the Pentagon Papers Case* (Berkeley: University of California Press, 1996).

Penthouse

TYPE OF WORK: Magazine
PUBLISHED: 1965- (England); 1969- (United States)
PUBLISHER: Bob Guccione (1930-)
SUBJECT MATTER: Men's magazine that has used sexually explicit pictures and controversial fiction and journalism
SIGNIFICANCE: This magazine's outspokenness and explicitness has made it a battleground for many issues involving the First Amendment

Robert (Bob) Guccione founded *Penthouse* after traveling through Europe as a struggling artist and settling in London in the early 1960's. He started the magazine with a bank loan equivalent to less than twelve hundred U.S. dollars. The magazine was an immediate success in Europe, and its first American edition sold 375,000 copies in 1969. By 1972 its worldwide circulation was 3.3 million copies, but by the 1990's it was down to 1.5 million.

Through its relatively brief history, *Penthouse* has had a variety of legal troubles. For example, its August, 1979, issue included a short story that provoked a lawsuit by Wyoming's candidate in the Miss America pageant. A jury awarded the beauty contestant twenty-five million dollars in punitive damages, but the award was overturned by an appeals court. The magazine was also involved in libel suits with the evangelist Jerry Falwell, singer-actress Cher, and the La Costa vacation resort. In 1976 the magazine's vice chairperson, Kathy Keeton, sued *Hustler* magazine claiming that she had been libeled in a case that led to a U.S. Supreme Court decision on jurisdictional grounds.

See also *Caligula*; *Hustler*; Junk food news; Libel; Men's magazines; Nudity; *Playboy*.

People for the American Way (PFAW)

FOUNDED: 1980
TYPE OF ORGANIZATION: Citizen group dedicated to fighting censorship and protecting First Amendment rights
SIGNIFICANCE: Originally founded to combat the procensorship philosophy of the Moral Majority, this organization has also promoted religious freedom, excellence in education, an independent judiciary, and free and open debate of public issues in the media

In 1980 television producer Norman Lear, with the support of a range of liberal, religious, educational, labor, and business leaders, founded PFAW to celebrate and protect First Amendment rights, tolerance, and diversity. This was a direct political reaction to gains made by conservative groups, most notably Jerry Falwell's Moral Majority. Early activities focused on maintaining religious freedom, not allowing fundamentalist Christians to impose their definitions and practices on entire communities through legislation or institutional directives. Soon PFAW took up the issue of censorship in the schools. It discovered and monitored an interlocking network of extremist organizations exerting influence on school boards and community leaders throughout America, involved in such projects as book banning, book burning, and curriculum restrictions.

In 1982 PFAW began publishing an annual survey of censorship and related challenges to public education. These surveys have generally followed a standard format: The first section analyzes general trends in censorship for the previous year; the second section gives a state-by-state listing of all reported attacks on the freedom to learn, with a short description of each. Since its founding, PFAW has documented a steady rise in censorship activities in the United States, and the American Library Association has estimated that for every censorship incident reported, four or five go unreported. For the 1994-1995 school year, for example, PFAW researchers confirmed 458 censorship challenges in schools throughout the United States, with the highest number reported in Texas, California, and Pennsylvania. In half of all the reported incidents, the challenged materials were subsequently removed or restricted in some way.

PFAW had an estimated membership of slightly more than

PFAW attorney Judith Schaefer (left) enters a federal court with Lisa Herdahl (center), whom she helped sue a Mississippi school district to stop it from broadcasting morning prayers into classrooms. PFAW won the suit in June, 1996. (AP/Wide World Photos)

300,000 in 1995. Through grassroots organizing, research, and public education it continued to speak out for pluralism, individuality, freedom of expression, freedom of religion, and tolerance. Through its corollary organization, the People for the American Way Action Fund, it has lobbied at all levels of government and provided legal advocacy. It has regional offices in New York; Los Angeles; and Boulder, Colorado; and state offices in Texas and Florida. The national office maintains an extensive research and video library of resources on religious right political groups and leaders.

See also First Amendment; Libraries, school; Moral Majority; Walker, David.

Performance art

Definition: Dramatic art typically presented outside the ordinary conventions of narration and acting, using themes and techniques of visual art, oratory, and the fine arts generally

Significance: The often confrontational presentations of performance art have made it a target of censorship for much the same reasons that art generally has been censored: offensive depictions, nudity, and controversy

Some define performance art as art in which an artist's own body becomes the medium, while others believe that performance art is only art that is unique to one location or limited to one performance. Performance art has come to be understood generally as art in which acts, rather than object, are central, and which does not fit other existing categories, such as dance or drama. It has roots in the street theater criticizing the Vietnam War and thus has a tradition of embracing controversy. By the 1990's performance art had diverged into a wide spectrum of public and private performances. Although some performance artists and scholars have argued that performance art must exist without the support of traditional arts venues, such as government grants or formal galleries, other artists have experienced no conflicts in applying for support from federal and state agencies.

Performance art festivals have been held in a number of cities around the globe. Cleveland, Ohio, for example, claimed to host the largest festival of performance art in the world. The city advertised that for their 1996 festival Kain Karawahn, an internationally known performance artist, would set the Cuyahoga River on fire. Performance art thus spanned the spectrum from the deliberately politically marginal, that is, performers who risked arrest for trespass or public indecency when they appeared, to artists who were comfortable working with established agencies for the entertainment of the mainstream public. Most scholars have agreed, however, that true performance art tests the boundaries of what is traditionally considered art. Such boundary testing has often led to censorship.

In the United States censorship of performance art occasionally has resulted in the arrests of artists on obscenity charges, but more often has resulted in denial of funding or threats of boycotts. In Santa Cruz, California, for example, feminists accused performance artist Fakir Mussafar of encouraging violence against women with a piece called "Torture Circus" in 1992. His performance segment consisted of one woman attaching feathers to another to symbolize her transformation into a bird. Protesters threatened to boycott commercial sponsors of the exhibit at the Bulkhead Gallery, which responded with a publicity campaign that warned of the dangers of censorship. In the end, the gallery lost only one sponsor.

Performance artist Karen Finley speaks out against the NEA, which denied her funding. (AP/Wide World Photos)

By the late twentieth century, American society was sufficiently open that censorship was often expressed financially, rather than by more direct means, but artists in conservative countries still ran the risk of severe penalties for challenging the status quo. In Cuba, for example, in 1989, performance artist Angel Delgado staged a piece titled "Sculptured Object" at the Havana Center for the Development of the Visual Arts. Intending for the work to protest censorship, he erected a circle of animal bones on the floor, placed the Cuban daily newspaper in the center, then dropped his pants and defecated on the newspaper. After state police arrested Delgado on a charge of "public scandal," he served six months in prison.

Delgado's piece typified much performance art both in being highly political and in testing what the public would accept as art. All art challenges viewers to experience the world in a new way, but performance art, through its use of confrontational techniques and politicized messages, has often been designed to offend. This offensive element has made it particularly vulnerable to censorship.

See also Art; Drama and theater; National Endowment for the Arts; Nudity; Street oratory; Warhol, Andy.

Persian Gulf War

Date: January 16, 1991-February 28, 1991

Place: The Arabian Peninsula and the Persian Gulf

Significance: The war included strict controls on the information allowed to the media

The Gulf War, which began as Operation Desert Shield to protect Saudi Arabia from Iraqi invasion and became Operation Desert Storm to liberate Iraqi-held Kuwait, involved world access to Persian Gulf oil. The United States fought to keep the mercurial Iraqi leader, Saddam Hussein, from military dominance in a sensitive region. Consequently, the United States began a military buildup in the region in August, 1990, after Iraq overran its small neighbor, Kuwait. United States and allied forces waged a massive air and ground assault on Iraq from January 16, 1991, to February 28, 1991. This assault liberated Kuwait but stopped short of total occupation of Iraq or removal of Saddam Hussein. The campaign involved serious censorship issues.

Generally, the restriction or manipulation of information in a free society during wartime has been viewed as acceptable when national or military security is at stake. It is viewed as unacceptable when information is restricted or manipulated for political purposes—such as protecting the images of military and civilian leaders. Generally too, the media and the wartime authorities conflict over the manner and degree of censorship.

The Vietnam War prompted American leadership to develop a new model for dealing with the media during subsequent conflicts. Vietnam had been the most open war in U.S. history. It was also the first television war. Brutal images flashed back to the United States the reality of war. Although political and military leadership had tried to influence the type and flow of information, the media were free to roam the war zone and talk to the troops. In a war without fronts, the count of enemy dead became the military yardstick by which success was measured. The media exposed the body count system as fantasy and folly. Some in the military blamed the media for damaging American morale to the extent that the war became unwinnable.

The new model for war coverage in an age of instant communication, based on the British practice during the Falkland Islands War of 1982, involved sanitizing visual images, controlling media access to military operations, censoring information that could upset civilians, and excluding journalists who filed unfavorable stories. True to the British model, during the U.S. invasion of Grenada in 1983 the media were simply held incommunicado until the operation was complete. During the Gulf War, this proved impractical, owing to the duration of the conflict. Not a single journalist, however, accompanied the first American troops to the Persian Gulf in August of 1990 (actual fighting did not begin until January, 1991), as the Department of Defense began to lay the groundwork for censorship. In September, 1990, the Department of Defense claimed that at least 250,000 Iraqi troops were massing in Kuwait to attack Saudi Arabia. President George Bush used this misinformation to "draw a line in the sand." No such buildup existed. Journalists at first accepted the military's word. As journalists arrived in the Persian Gulf, the military implemented the pool system for controlling the flow of information.

The pool system restricted journalists to group meetings with selected military units and accompanied by a military official. The military also instituted a security-review procedure, which constituted a prior restraint on the news. Escort guidelines further dictated that the media were allowed no "unilateral coverage" of events. Finally, all stories and photographs had to be cleared by the Pentagon.

The commanding U.S. field general, Norman Schwarzkopf, deflected all criticism of the system by claiming that he was merely following orders and referring all critics to the assistant secretary of defense for public affairs in the Pentagon. Schwartzkopf's own rules for dealing with the media were "Don't let them intimidate you"; "There's no law that says you have to answer all their questions"; "Don't answer any questions that in your judgment would help the enemy"; and "Don't ever lie to the American people."

As a junior officer in Vietnam, Schwartzkopf had had first-hand experience with the high command's insistence upon a body count. Consequently, as commander in the Persian Gulf, he angrily rejected any talk about body counts. He claimed that he was as forthcoming as he could be, and that he even had to intercede with the Saudis to ensure some media access to the war. Saudi Arabia and Kuwait were without any tradition of a free press. Officially, the Saudis and the Kuwaitis could not understand why censorship could not be complete. Schwartzkopf's command had to handle this situation delicately.

Politics, rather than military necessity, was the motive for much of the censorship in the Persian Gulf War. Washington insisted that it engaged in "precision bombing" using "smart" bombs during its forty-three day pounding of Baghdad, and doctored its photographic evidence accordingly. In fact, more than 90 percent of the bombs dropped were "dumb" bombs (those without guidance systems). Success was defined as avoiding civilian targets. Peter Arnett, a Cable News Network (CNN) correspondent who was allowed to broadcast from Baghdad, documented damage to civilian targets. He also verified the destruction of a plant that produced powdered milk for infants (the United States had insisted that the plant was used to produce biological weapons). The Iraqi government shadowed Arnett, but likely figured it was getting more propaganda value from his reports than the enemy was getting morale value. This introduced a new technological twist to modern warfare. A correspondent may broadcast live attacks on the enemy from the enemy's position; Arnett did so. Some viewed this, in the heat of war, as treasonous. Arnett was vilified in Washington. Senator Alan Simpson even went so far as to call him a "sympathizer" with the enemy. Whom Washington could not censor, it smeared.

War is ugly and any attempt to beautify it—such as showing only attractive videos of perfect hits with smart bombs—must have political implications. Presidential orders barred the media from Dover Air Force Base in Delaware when American caskets returned from the war zone. The military report minimizing the number of Iraqis killed became a sanitized account of how many tanks, planes, and pieces of equipment had been destroyed. Critics have claimed that these attempts to shield a free people from the consequences of their country's actions can have no justification as military security. They see this as a way of shielding political and military leaders from criticism. Clearly, a controversial and delicate balance exists between military security and freedom of information.

—Brian G. Tobin

See also Armed Forces Radio and Television Service; Falkland Islands War; Grenada, U.S. invasion of; Mexican-American War; Military censorship; Panama, U.S. invasion of; *Pentagon Papers, The*; Vietnam War; War.

Bibliography

In Peter Arnett, *Live from the Battlefield* (New York: Simon & Schuster, 1994), veteran war correspondent Arnett denies being used as a propaganda pawn and instead claims he chronicled the rapid deterioration of Iraqi society. Roger Cohen and Claudio Gatti, *In the Eye of the Storm: The Life of General H. Norman Schwartzkopf* (New York: Berkley Publishing Group, 1992), is a sympathetic portrait of a man who came from a prominent family. H. Norman Schwartzkopf, *It Doesn't Take a Hero* (New York: Bantam Books, 1993), argues that Vietnam caused a crisis of confidence within the American military, which Schwartzkopf aimed to cure if he could. In Jacqueline Sharkey, *Under Fire: U.S. Military Restrictions on the Media from Grenada to the Persian Gulf* (Washington, D.C.: Center for Public Integrity, 1991), the author suggests that because the military blamed the media for losing Vietnam, it has subsequently put unwarranted controls on media military coverage.

Pesticide industry

Definition: Manufacturers of petrochemicals designed to kill insects and other pests that threaten food crops and other plants

Significance: By withholding information concerning dangerous products and actively campaigning against those who attempt to obtain such information, the industry has made it difficult for consumers to determine what is safe to eat

Pesticides find their way into human food in three ways. Fruits and vegetables that are sprayed during growth contain small amounts of pesticides. Also, rinsing rainwater leaches pesticides through the soil and into groundwater, contaminating drinking water. Finally, erosion of contaminated soil into lakes and rivers pollutes fish, many of which are consumed by humans.

News coverage of pesticide misuse is rare, and where investigators have pursued the matter, chemical companies have actively engaged in suppressing pertinent information. Much of the problem of censorship of the negative aspects of pesticides lies in the fact that chemical companies realize huge profits in their manufacture, and in conjunction with the agrabusiness consortium, exert a great deal of pressure on state, local, and federal control agencies.

One case in point is the pesticide azinphos-methyl (AZM), which has poisoned fish in Louisiana. In 1991 that pesticide was responsible for one of the largest fish kills in U.S. history. Not only did the national news media bury the story, the federal Department of Agriculture and Forestry (DAF) withheld documents on pesticide spraying. When investigators attempted to secure those documents, the DAF withheld them. Another case concerns Rachel Carson's landmark book, *Silent Spring* (1962), which explained the bad effects of pesticides in detail. In response to Carson's book, the chemical industry developed a campaign to discredit both her and her findings.

In a tacit admission of dishonest and underhanded activities by the chemical industry in 1994, the president of Sandoz Agro, Inc., called for the industry to take "an honest and open approach to the solution of its problems." One can only infer that those "problems" are the negative impacts on the environment that pesticides have, and the loss of profits that the banishment of those pesticides would represent.

The argument in favor of the suppression of the negative aspects of pesticide use is predicated on the assumption that the public's general diet is essentially safe and healthy. All that would be accomplished by full disclosure of all of the less desirable factors in the use of pesticides would be needless fear and a general panic over what food was safe, and what food was not. The argument in favor of the full disclosure of all of the ramifications of pesticide use is that consumers have the right to know what they are ingesting. Also, this argument claims, the argument for censorship is based only on the assumption that the diet is an overall safe one, and that assumption might be incorrect.

See also Automobile safety news; Bhopal disaster; Congress, U.S.; Environmental education; Nuclear research and testing; Pharmaceutical industry; Project Censored; Toxic waste news.

Peyton Place

Type of work: Book

Published: 1956

Author: Grace Metalious (1924-1964)

Subject matter: Novel about the career of a young female novelist

Significance: This sexually explicit "bombshell" attacking small-town bigotry was a precursor to feminist literature

Peyton Place explicitly describes diverse sexual misconduct, sexual abuse, and violence in recounting the rise of a naïve and idealistic young woman writer. The name "Peyton Place" has passed into general American usage as a term for places and groups exhibiting similar conduct. The novel's principal character, Allison MacKenzie, and her story reflect author Grace Metalious' life and her own home town, Gilmanton, New Hampshire.

Shortly before Metalious published her novel, her interview with Hal Boyle was published. Reporters immediately invaded Gilmanton, aggressively questioning everybody. In reaction, Grace's husband, George Metalious, lost his position as principal of a local school. Public retaliation included threatening phone calls and letters, a death threat, and persecution of her children.

After its publication, *Peyton Place* became a best-seller, attracting widespread condemnation as obscene. Metalious

Lana Turner returns home to find her living room transformed into an adolescent passion pit in the film adaptation of Peyton Place. (Museum of Modern Art/Film Stills Archive)

further enraged opinion by denouncing small-town bigotry and bohemian conduct. Her book was banned in Fort Wayne, Indiana, and was blacklisted by the Rhode Island Commission. The Canadian Revenue Commission prohibited its importation as "of an indecent or immoral character."

A heavily revised film adaptation in 1957 met Hays Code standards for general release. An even more heavily revised television series ran on network television from 1964 to 1969.

See also Adultery; Customs laws, Canadian; Hays Code; Morality.

Pharmaceutical industry

DEFINITION: Companies that make and sell medications

SIGNIFICANCE: Drug companies have been the target of censorship in government restrictions on advertising and the instigators of censorship in attempts to suppress reports of side effects

Since prehistoric times human beings have used various substances to treat illnesses. This ancient practice became a major business at the start of the seventeenth century, when the first patents for medications were issued in England. The first drug patent in the United States appeared in 1796, and the industry expanded greatly during the nineteenth century. Companies made either "ethical drugs," now known as prescription drugs, or "patent medicines," now known as over-the-counter (OTC) drugs. Makers of ethical drugs usually supplied accurate information about their products to physicians and advertised only in medical journals. Makers of patent medicines, on the other hand, kept their formulas secret and relied on uncensored advertising to sell them to the public.

Censorship of Drug Advertising. Regulation of the pharmaceutical industry in the United States began on June 30, 1906, when the Food and Drug Act became law, creating the Food and Drug Administration (FDA). At first the FDA could only censor drug labels that could be proved false and fraudulent; it had no power over advertising. In October, 1937, 107 people died after taking an elixir that contained the poisonous substance diethylene glycol. In response, the Food, Drug, and Cosmetic Act became law on June 25, 1938, requiring that new drugs be proved safe. In the late 1950's and early 1960's deformed babies were born to pregnant women who had taken the sedative drug thalidomide, which was available in most European countries but not in the United States. In response, the Kefauver-Harris Amendments were signed into law on October 10, 1962, requiring that new drugs be proved effective and allowing the FDA to censor any advertisements for prescription drugs that it considered misleading. For example, in 1991 the FDA forced Syntex to discontinue advertising which implied that their anti-inflammatory drug Naprosyn might be able to halt the progression of joint degeneration in osteoarthritis.

Advertising for OTC drugs is usually regulated by the Federal Trade Commission (FTC). Since its creation in 1914 the FTC has censored countless print, radio, and television advertisements it judged misleading, including many for OTC drugs. The most famous example involves aspirin. During the 1960's, 1970's, and 1980's, the FTC fought many legal battles with aspirin manufacturers and succeeded in censoring some of the claims made in their advertising.

Sometimes the FDA, rather than the FTC, has censored advertising for OTC drugs used for serious illnesses. On January 28, 1988, the *New England Journal of Medicine* published the results of a study that indicated that small amounts of aspirin taken every other day reduced the risk of heart attack in healthy male volunteers. On January 29, Sterling, the manufacturer of Bayer aspirin, began publicizing this study in its advertisements. Other aspirin manufacturers soon did the same. The FDA stopped these advertisements because the FDA had not yet reviewed the study. On March 2, representatives of aspirin manufacturers met with Frank Young, a commissioner of the FDA, and agreed to stop promoting aspirin's ability to prevent heart attacks in healthy patients. They were allowed, however, to publicize the fact that aspirin could reduce the risk of a second heart attack in a patient who had already suffered one in the past, based on the results of an earlier study.

Censorship of Adverse Reactions. The World Health Organization has defined adverse drug reactions (ADRs) as any effects of medications taken at normal doses that are "noxious and unintended." Drug manufacturers are required to report all ADRs to the FDA during the testing of new drugs. They are also required to report any ADRs they learn about after the drug is marketed. Serious ADRs must be reported within fifteen days, but minor ADRs may appear in quarterly or annual reports.

On occasion drug manufacturers have censored ADR reports to the FDA. In 1980 Selacryn, used to treat high blood pressure, was removed from the market because of reports of liver damage. Criminal charges were brought against Smith, Kline, and French, the manufacturer of Selacryn, for reporting this serious ADR in a quarterly report rather than within the required fifteen days. A similar case involving the anti-inflammatory drug Oraflex, made by Eli Lilly, also resulted in criminal charges for the withholding of ADR information from the FDA. Oraflex was withdrawn from the market in 1982 after having been implicated in nearly one hundred fatal reactions.

One important case involved McNeil, a subsidiary of Johnson and Johnson, the world's largest health care conglomerate. On March 4, 1983, McNeil announced that it was withdrawing the anti-inflammatory drug Zomax from the market as a result of serious allergic reactions. A similar announcement was made on May 15, 1987, for the anti-inflammatory drug Soprol, due to pain as a side effect. A special investigation by the FDA found evidence of deficiencies in reporting ADRs. The FDA ordered Johnson and Johnson to take corrective actions but did not bring criminal charges.

A similar investigation of the sleeping pill Halcion, manufactured by Upjohn, was initiated in 1992, after Ian Oswold, a Scottish psychiatrist, accused the company of censoring data from its studies that would have linked Halcion to paranoia and agitation. Although Upjohn denied the charges and sued Oswold for libel, the drug was banned in the United Kingdom. The FDA did not ban the drug but required Upjohn to warn physicians to avoid high doses given over long periods of time. In 1994 the FDA's report was released, revealing that investigators had found evidence of misconduct.

Drug manufacturers have also attempted on occasion to prevent news reports of ADRs from appearing in the popular media. Such reports can have a devastating effect on sales, even if the reports are later shown to be inaccurate. The most famous example involves the antidepressant drug Prozac, manufactured by Eli Lilly. The media reported several lawsuits brought against the company alleging that the drug caused violent behavior. These lawsuits were often promoted by the Church of Scientology, which opposes medical treatment of psychiatric disorders. In 1991 the FDA decided that Prozac did not cause these problems.

The usual method used by drug companies to avoid the bad publicity associated with lawsuits involving ADRs is to settle such claims out of court, with opponents agreeing not to reveal information about the case. McNeil used this method in all but three of the more than six hundred lawsuits brought against its anti-inflammatory drug Zomax. Similar agreements led the research group Project Censored to list reports of the possibility of strokes caused by OTC diet pills containing phenylpropanolamine as one of the top twenty-five censored news stories of 1994. *—Rose Secrest*

See also Advertising as the target of censorship; Automobile safety news; Health epidemic news; Human Genome Project; Medical research; Project Censored; Scientology, Church of.

Bibliography

Advertising of OTC drugs is discussed in *The Aspirin Wars*, by Charles Mann and Mark L. Plummer (New York: Alfred A. Knopf, 1991). Censoring of ADR reports is included in Thomas Maeder's *Adverse Reactions* (New York: William Morrow, 1994) and in *Cured to Death* by Arabella Melville and Colin Johnson (Briarcliff Manor, N.Y.: Stein & Day, 1983). International aspects are discussed in *Bad Medicine: The Prescription Drug Industry in the Third World*, by Milton Silverman, Mia Lydecker, and Philip R. Lee (Stanford, Calif.: Stanford University Press, 1992).

Philippines

Description: Independent east Asian archipelagic nation

Significance: After a period of often brutal repression, the Philippines, like many new democracies, has struggled to establish a more open press and entertainment industry

After the Philippine islands became independent from the United States in 1946, they struggled to establish a democratic regime, with some success. They enjoyed a relatively vibrant press and political opposition was tolerated, until Ferdinand Marcos was elected president in 1965; he declared martial law in 1972. Marcos established a regime which had no parallel in Asia, in terms of suppression of speech. Eight thousand media members lost their jobs after Marcos declared martial law, and of eighteen newspapers published before 1972, only two survived.

Marcos established the Department of Public Information to ensure that news reports would have a positive national value. Anything that would influence people to oppose the government, to undermine morality, or to promote lawlessness or disorder, was strictly prohibited. All news, both broadcast and print, had to be cleared by the department. Because the government was fighting against an insurgency, all communist newspapers were illegal, while other journals were targeted by the military and right-wing groups for intimidation, resulting in the deaths of many journalists. One of the more subtle ways that Marcos established censorship was to promote, and sometimes force, the ownership of television stations and major newspapers by persons sympathetic to the government.

Martial law was lifted in January, 1981, and tolerance for media coverage of controversial issues increased. Reporters became more assertive, pursuing stories on governmental corruption and military abuse. Certain matters remained off-limits, however, and the Print Media Council and the Broadcast Media Council, established in 1974, continued to publish guidelines to encourage, along with the threat of intimidation, self-censorship.

In a bloodless coup in 1986, Marcos was driven from power and replaced by Corazon Aquino, wife of a slain journalist and candidate for president in elections the previous year. The Aquino government quickly dismantled much of the Marcos-era system of censorship. Opposition newspapers were encouraged, and the Philippine press returned to its traditionally vibrant and near licentious ways, as seventy-five daily newspapers soon appeared.

There remained some challenges, however. The system of licensure for reporters allowed for some censorship pressures. Many media outlets remained under the control of Marcos cronies. However, the artistic area continued to show improvement. In May, 1994, for example, President Fidel Ramos, who succeeded Aquino, ruled that the Steven Spielberg-directed film *Schindler's List* would be shown as made. The Philippine Movie and Television Review and Classification Board routinely deleted scenes it considered immoral, regardless of the consequences to the film. Spielberg refused to release his film in the Philippines unless it appeared as he made it. Ramos' ruling allowed the first legal public showing of explicit sex on film. Subsequently the government issued new, more liberal guidelines on film censorship.

See also Film censorship; Flag burning; Indonesia; Journalists, violence against; News media censorship; Police states; Sex in the arts; Spanish Empire.

Photocopying

DEFINITION: Photographic reproduction of documents and graphic images

SIGNIFICANCE: The modern development of high-speed, low-cost reproduction of printed information has had a revolutionary impact on the dissemination of ideas; however, copyright laws have limited the use of this technology

The U.S. Constitution empowers Congress to "promote the progress of science and the useful arts, by securing for limited times to authors and inventors the exclusive right to their respective writings and discoveries." Congress has done this by enacting a federal copyright law. The law was most recently rewritten in 1976. Copyright law allows authors and others to benefit economically from the fruits of their labor. The theory is that creative persons will be motivated to create new works, thus promoting society's interest in "the progress of science and the useful arts."

A doctrine called "fair use" attempts to balance the copyright holder's exclusive rights with other demands for access to copyrighted work. Researchers and educators often need to duplicate copyrighted materials. In determining whether a use is fair, courts consider four criteria: the purpose and character of the use, the nature of the copyrighted work, the amount and substantiality of the copying, and the effect of the use on the market for or value of the original. Many educators believe that copyright law impedes acquisition of important classroom materials.

Frustration over copyright law is not limited to educators; limitations on photocopying have had an impact on companies as well. In *Basic Books, Inc. v. Kinko's Graphics Corp.* (1991), a federal district judge found that photocopying book chapters for inclusion in classroom anthologies was not a fair use of copyrighted works. Kinko's had argued that the copies were for a nonprofit, educational purpose. The judge, however, did not see it that way. The court's decision was, according to copyright expert Kenneth D. Crews, "unquestionably directed primarily against Kinko's, and its profit motive within the framework of fair use." In another case, Texaco Corporation was sued in 1985 by a group of publishers who alleged that a company chemist had copied and filed a number of articles from scientific journals. At issue was whether such copying was a fair use or an infringement on copyrights. In the 1990's two federal courts sided with the publishers. The Texaco case caused many researchers to fear that the courts might restrict the free flow of information, while publishers were anxious for corporations to pay for their use of copyrighted materials.

See also Copyright law; Libraries; Photographic film processing; Printing.

Photographic film processing

DEFINITION: Commercial development and printing of film used by private individuals

SIGNIFICANCE: Laws requiring commercial film processors to report photographs that may indicate child abuse have led to conflicts over artistic expression, the role of private parties in law enforcement, and the right to privacy

Many people own cameras, but most do not own the equipment necessary to develop their photographs. Photographers typically rely upon commercial developing services to process their film. In hopes of apprehending child pornographers who make use of these services, many states have enacted laws that require commercial developers to report any photographs that depict children in an obscene fashion. These laws have been effective in the fight against child pornography, but they have raised significant questions concerning the nature of artistic expression, the right to privacy, and the responsibilities of businesses in aiding law enforcement officials in this effort.

The Crime Control Act of 1990 is the only federal law pertaining to child pornography and film processing. The law requires processors at federal installations or at installations on federal property to report indecent photos of children to appropriate authorities. The law does not cover most commercial photo processors in the United States, whose activities are instead regulated by the states. In order to assist film processors to comply with the patchwork of state laws concerning the issue, a professional association called the Photo Marketing Association International established guidelines used by many businesses. The guidelines recommend reporting photographs that depict minors performing sexual acts, receiving abuse, or displaying the genital or pubic area.

While the laws have led to the arrest and conviction of some pornographers, they have also led to legal difficulties for many parents who have nude photos of their children. State laws often fail to adequately define what constitutes a pornographic depiction, and in some instances processors have informed authorities about pictures of children that many parents do not consider explicit or exploitive.

Artists have also encountered difficulties with the laws. In a celebrated case in California, the Federal Bureau of Investigation seized the work of professional photographer Jock Sturges after a commercial developer reported finding negatives of nude girls. Sturges lost an important photography contract and found himself in a tense legal battle. A grand jury refused to indict Sturges and the charges were dropped. The Sturges case raised questions about the rights to artistic expression and laws regarding child pornography.

Commercial developers complain that state laws contain too many gray areas and are difficult to follow. Noting that in some states the failure to report suspicious photos is a crime punishable by stiff fines, processors argue that if they report a photograph that is later deemed not obscene they may face a lawsuit from the photographer. In addition, many large firms claim that it is impossible for their employees to check the content of the millions of photographs they handle each year.

The conflict between regulations intended to protect children and the rights of parents and artists to photograph nude minors is in many cases the result of poorly written and vague laws; however, the lack of a societal consensus as to the definition of pornography frustrates any resolution of the problem.

See also Mann, Sally; Photocopying; Pornography, child.

Picketing

DEFINITION: A form of protest involving people bearing placards who seek to inform hearers of their position in a dispute or to discourage hearers from patronizing particular businesses or institutions

SIGNIFICANCE: Picketing is frequently subjected to government restriction

Historically, picketing has been most closely associated with protests involving labor disputes. Picketing has also been used to communicate positions involving a variety of public issues. In the United States, the Supreme Court has upheld a wide variety of laws restricting picketing, but it has nevertheless recognized that this form of protest is entitled to some degree of First Amendment protection. Generally, the Court has allowed more substantial restrictions of labor picketing than picketing concerning public issues.

Labor Picketing. During the nineteenth century and the early years of the twentieth century, most Anglo-American judges considered labor picketing illegal. Since the common law prohibited combinations of merchants that created a monopoly in a particular area of trade, judges reasoned that combinations of workers were similarly contrary to law. Eventually, however, organized labor gained legal recognition under New Deal legislation proposed by President Franklin D. Roosevelt, and the Supreme Court soon followed this recognition by determining in *Thornhill v. Alabama* (1940) that states could not simply outlaw all forms of peaceful labor picketing.

The Supreme Court recognized that labor picketing might find some shelter under the First Amendment's mantle, but it continued to permit a number of restrictions on this form of protest. For example, the Court ruled that workers who were engaged in an illegal strike could be prevented from picketing outside their employers' premises with the intent of persuading other workers to join their illegal strike. Moreover, the Court held that workers could be prevented from engaging in certain secondary boycotts. In a secondary boycott, workers picket outside businesses which use products or engage in transactions with a business against which the workers have a more immediate grievance, such as the workers' employer. Generally, federal labor laws require workers to picket only businesses with which they have a direct dispute, and the Supreme Court has held that these laws do not violate the First Amendment.

Picketing as Social Protest. Outside the context of labor demonstrations, picketing has received a more cordial welcome within the law of the First Amendment. For example, in *National Association for the Advancement of Colored People v. Claiborne Hardware Co.* (1982), the Supreme Court upheld the right of black Mississippians to boycott and picket the premises of white merchants, even though the picketing produced occasional incidents of violence. The Court noted that the purpose of the picketing was to alter a social, political, and economic environment that had infringed upon blacks' civil rights and found that the First Amendment safeguarded the expression of this purpose. Similarly, in *Boos v. Barry* (1988), the Court struck down a District of Columbia ordinance that barred picketing within five hundred feet of a foreign embassy with signs that brought the foreign power into disrepute. The Supreme Court, however, has for some time recognized the power of government to enact reasonable restrictions on the time, place, and manner of delivering speech in public places, and it has allowed government bodies to enact these kind of restrictions with respect to picketing.

Antiabortion Picketing. Some examples of successful and unsuccessful attempts to restrict picketing involve protests of abortion clinics. In 1988 the Supreme Court upheld a ban on the "focused picketing" of a private residence. In *Frisby v. Schultz* (1988), groups of antiabortion protesters, sometimes numbering as many as forty, picketed several times over a few weeks the residence of a doctor who performed abortions. The Milwaukee suburb where the events occurred responded to the picketing by enacting an ordinance prohibiting protesters from picketing a particular residence. The Supreme Court ultimately held that this restriction on picketing served a legitimate purpose and that the picketers had other means of communicating their protests besides harassing the doctor at his residence.

In another case involving antiabortion protesters, the Supreme Court considered a number of restrictions on an antiabortion protest, upholding some of the restrictions but invalidating others. *Madsen v. Women's Health Center, Inc.* (1994) involved a state court injunction against protesters at a Florida abortion clinic. A state court judge had enjoined the protesters on a variety of points. The judge had barred protest within a thirty-six-foot buffer zone around the clinic entrance and driveway—a zone which included not only public streets but portions of private property adjacent to the clinic. The injunction imposed noise restrictions immediately around the clinic and barred the display of images that might be seen from the clinic. In addition, the judge ordered the protesters to refrain from approaching any person seeking the clinic's services within three hundred feet of the clinic unless the person approached indicated a desire to communicate with a protester. Finally, the judge's injunction prohibited the use of sound amplification equipment within three hundred feet of the homes of the clinic's staff and barred pickets and demonstrations within that zone. The Supreme Court, in reviewing these restrictions, ruled that the buffer zone as applied to the public streets was a reasonable means of keeping access to the clinic open, but that as applied to private property it violated without adequate justification the protesters' right to speak. The Court also upheld the noise restrictions around the clinic as reasonable in the light of the clinic's surgical activities and also upheld the restrictions on the use of sound equipment in residential areas. The Court, however, struck down the ban on images observable from the clinic, noting that patients disturbed by the contents of particular signs could easily pull the curtains on the clinic's windows. Moreover, the Court held

Dressed as the Grim Reaper, a member of Operation Rescue pickets a Planned Parenthood office in San Jose, California, in May, 1996. (AP/Wide World Photos)

that the no-approach zone and the prohibition against picketing or demonstrating within three hundred feet of the residences of clinic staff were simply too broad in their restriction of protected speech. In all, the *Madsen* decision illustrates the substantial degree to which government may impose limits on picketing to prevent picketers from unreasonably harassing the objects of their political or social displeasure. The case also reveals, however, that picketing continues to enjoy substantial First Amendment protection and may not be unduly restricted by government. —*Timothy L. Hall*

See also Assembly, right of; Boycotts; Labor unions; Marching and parading; Pressure groups.

Bibliography

For a general guide to the rights of protesters, including picketers, *The Right to Protest: The Basic ACLU Guide to Free Expression*, edited by Joel M. Gora et al. (Carbondale: Southern Illinois University Press, 1991), is a useful resource. The use of picketing in labor disputes is discussed in Peggy Kahn's *Picketing: Industrial Disputes, Tactics, and the Law* (London: Routledge & Kegan Paul, 1983) and Chris Ralph's *The Picket and the Law* (London: Fabian Society, 1977), both of which focus on British law. Susan A. Tacon's *Tort Liability in a Collective Bargaining Regime* (Toronto: Butterworths, 1980), which concentrates on Canadian law, includes a discussion of labor picketing. Barbara Carter, in *Pickets, Parents, and Power: The Story Behind the New York City Teachers' Strike* (New York: Citation Press, 1971), provides an interesting account of one particular labor dispute. For a general discussion of antiabortion protests, which routinely involve picketing, see Dallas A. Blanchard's *The Anti-Abortion Movement and the Rise of the Religious Right: From Polite to Fiery Protest* (New York: Twayne, 1994).

Pinky

Type of work: Film
Released: 1949
Director: Elia Kazan (1909-　　)
Subject matter: An African American woman who "passes" as white encounters prejudice in racially divided America
Significance: The banning of this controversial film in a small Texas town led to an important U.S. Supreme Court decision regarding due process

Ethel Waters (right) played the grandmother of Jeanne Crain (left) in Pinky, *a melodramatic exploration of racial identity.* (Museum of Modern Art/Film Stills Archive)

This film is a poignant look at racial attitudes in post World War II America. Jeanne Crain, a white actress, plays the title role of a "Negro" woman whose light skin allows her to be taken for "white." Director Elia Kazan explores the Southern community to which she returns after living as a white in the North. Southerner prejudices are illuminated in scenes in which her treatment by townspeople instantly changes when they realize that she is a "Negro." Northern prejudices also are illustrated by her fiancé, a white Boston doctor who loves her in spite of her color but realizes that their relationship cannot continue unless her race is kept secret.

The local Board of Censors in Marshall, Texas, denied a license for the film's release at a local theater. The owner showed the film anyway and was convicted of a misdemeanor. The ensuing legal case, *Gelling v. Texas*, reached the U.S. Supreme Court in 1951. The Court found that the board's ability to deny licenses to films simply because their character was judged "prejudicial" to the interests of local citizens was a violation of the due process clause of the Fourteenth Amendment. The board's action was found in a concurring opinion by Justice William O. Douglas to constitute prior restraint in which "thought is regimented, authority substituted for liberty, and the great purpose of the First Amendment to keep uncontrolled the freedom of expression defeated."

See also African Americans; Community standards; Douglas, William O.; Film censorship; Fourteenth Amendment; Miscegenation; Prior restraint; Race.

Plato

Born: 427 B.C.E., Athens, Greece

Died: 347 B.C.E., Athens, Greece

Identification: Ancient Greek philosopher

Significance: In describing the ideal state, Plato's *Republic* presents controversial views concerning the types of art that should be permitted in such a society

Plato's *Republic* advocates circumscribing the subject matter of fictional and religious narratives and recommends the expulsion of certain kinds of artists from the ideal state on the grounds of the power that art has to corrupt. The *Republic* differs considerably from Plato's *Ion*, in which art is not considered a potential danger to the state or the character of its citizens. The *Republic*, then, provides a series of arguments, some still voiced in modern times, that might be held to warrant censorship of certain forms of art.

The second and third books of Plato's *Republic* focus on narrative representations of gods and heroes, warning against portrayals that depict such figures as vicious or intemperate. Narratives of this sort might lead one to believe that the behavior and characteristics portrayed are as worthy as their possessors, and thereby provide a rationale for unjust conduct. Likewise, harrowing tales of Hades might make soldiers fear death, thereby disinclining them to risk battle. In each case, the narrative supplies a motivation for behavior undesirable in a citizen of the ideal state.

The power of drama and poetry is emphasized in book 10 of the *Republic*. Unjust characters are easier for the poet to imitate than just ones, and are thought to be more frequent and perhaps more popular subjects of representation. Thus, a poet or tragedian tends to embody inferior characteristics of the soul in his characters, a tendency that may weaken the moral judgments of an auditor or spectator, and that may even incline some to outright emulation.

Further, the capacity of poetry and drama to elicit emotion is regarded as evidence of their appeal to inferior parts of human nature that ought properly to fall under the rule of reason. Such responses lead to a breakdown of restraint and diminish the shame that should be felt upon indulging baser emotional impulses. To permit emotion to overwhelm judgment can set a precedent that is difficult to resist in other contexts.

As are the representations of the poet, those of the painter are also held to be at several removes from reason and truth. Representational painters do not imitate the forms or concepts of objects—a concept with which Plato holds them to be unacquainted. Neither do they represent the objects themselves. That exercise falls to the craftspersons, whose labors Plato regards as superior to those of the artist. The painter only represents a single appearance or aspect of a particular thing (which is in turn only a single embodiment or instantiation of a form), just as the poet only imitates an inferior aspect of a human being. Paintings are at the same remove from truth as shadows or mirror-images. Representational painting preys on a weakness in human nature, for it relies on a tendency to succumb to visual illusion in spite of reason, just as the emotions elicited by drama can be at odds with reason. Thus, both can lead to a contradiction within the soul.

The arts can, according to Plato, be thought to lead to a lack of understanding of things as they really are. They may consequently be regarded as a source of dangerous distortion, both of the truth and of an individual's own nature.

See also Aristotle; Art; Athens, ancient; Democritus; Drama and theater; Music; Poetry; Socrates.

Playboy

Type of work: Magazine

Published: 1953-

Publisher: Hugh Hefner (1926-   )

Subject matter: Male-oriented articles and stories and sexually provocative illustrations

Significance: As the most prominent men's magazine, *Playboy* helped to bring sex into the mainstream of popular culture, while pioneering in the struggle against censorship of print media

Promising a "pleasure-primer styled to the masculine taste," the inaugural issue of *Playboy* magazine was published in Chicago in November, 1953, by twenty-seven-year-old Hugh M. Hefner. Disclaiming any pretense "to solve any world problems or prove any great moral truths" but aiming only "to give the American male a few extra laughs and a little diversion from the anxieties of the Atomic Age," the premier issue, featuring actress Marilyn Monroe on its cover, sold an astounding fifty thousand copies and launched the most successful men's magazine in history. The new magazine combined tastefully provocative pictures of naked women with-naughty cartoons, short fiction, and articles on male fashion,

Publisher Hugh Hefner holds a cassette of Playboy*'s first "home video playmate" and a copy of the magazine's 1982 Christmas issue, which typifies* Playboy*'s efforts to project erotic sexuality and wholesomeness simultaneously.* (AP/Wide World Photos)

hi-fi (and later stereo) equipment, automobiles, restaurants, and other accoutrements of "the good life." According to Dr. Paul Gebhard of the Kinsey Institute, "Hefner's genius was to associate sex with upward mobility."

Beginning with Marilyn Monroe as the first issue's "Sweetheart of the Month," the centerfold, later renamed "Playmate of the Month," became the centerpiece of *Playboy*, and featured such women as film stars Jayne Mansfield, Brigitte Bardot, Gina Lollobrigida, Sophia Loren, and Anita Ekberg, as well as hundreds of unknown women.

Efforts to Suppress Playboy. *Playboy*'s early success drew immediate opposition from authorities. When the U.S. Post Office denied *Playboy*'s routine application for a second-class mailing permit, the magazine challenged the decision in court. *Playboy* won, and by June, 1956, was being delivered with the same mailing privileges as other magazines. Two years later Hefner was criminally charged with contributing to the delinquency of a minor when model Elizabeth Ann Roberts—the January, 1958, "Schoolmate Playmate"—proved to be only seventeen years old. However, the magazine had a signed release from her mother, so the charges were dropped for lack of evidence.

In 1959 *Playboy* deliberately invited controversy by publishing "The Pious Pornographers," a feature story chiding women's magazines for their sanctimonious use of sexy models, and "Rebel with a Caustic Cause," the first nationally published profile of comic Lenny Bruce, whose autobiography, *How to Talk Dirty and Influence People*, was later published by Playboy Press.

The Playboy Philosophy. In December, 1962, Hefner introduced "The Playboy Philosophy," a 150,000-word essay (serialized in twenty-five installments) defending the magazine against its "puritanical" critics and articulating a "new morality" espousing greater sexual freedom and opposing unwarranted government intrusion in people's private lives. Hefner discussed everything from censorship and abortion to capital punishment and divorce. After readers began joining the discussion, "The Playboy Forum" was established as a regular feature in July, 1963.

To institutionalize his political and social views in 1965, Hefner created the Playboy Foundation, which mounted legal challenges to obscenity statutes and restrictive sex laws. The foundation also helped fund a series of pro-choice lawsuits in abortion cases that culminated in the Supreme Court's *Roe v. Wade* decision, which legalized abortion. It supported sex research and education, including the work of Masters and Johnson, the Kinsey Institute, and the Sex Information and Education Council of the United States.

By the late 1960's *Playboy* had become synonymous with the "Sexual Revolution," but it was not until January, 1971, that it published photographs of a nude model that revealed a hint of pubic hair. While other "skin magazines," such as *Hustler* and *Penthouse*, became more sexually explicit, *Playboy* continually tried to position itself as a mainstream magazine, with photographs of beautiful naked women. *Playboy*'s claim to respectability prompted many readers to explain that they only read it for the interviews and articles, which admittedly were written by such prominent writers as Arthur Schlesinger, Jr., Kenneth Tynan, John Kenneth Galbraith, Garry Wills, David Halberstam, Hollis Alpert, V. S. Pritchett, Gay Talese, Norman Mailer, Alex Haley, John Updike, Joyce Carol Oates, James Baldwin, and Ray Bradbury—whose novel *Fahrenheit 451*, which first appeared in *Playboy*, described a dark future marked by pervasive censorship and book burning.

Targeted by Nixon and Reagan Administrations. Publishing important writers did not insulate *Playboy* from attack. Hefner was included on President Richard Nixon's infamous "enemies list," and he was investigated by the Internal Revenue Service, the Securities and Exchange Commission, and the Drug Enforcement Agency. The Justice Department under President Ronald Reagan awarded $750,000 to researcher Judith Reisman to study the question of child pornography in *Playboy*, *Penthouse*, and *Hustler*. Her report, which cited *Playboy* cartoonist Harvey Kurtzman's "Little Annie Fannie" as kiddie porn, was rejected by the Justice Department.

In the mid-1980's Attorney General Edwin Meese established a Commission on Pornography. When the commission wrote letters to the Southland Corporation, the owner of 7-Eleven convenience stores, intimating that by selling *Playboy* the company might be charged with trafficking in pornography, half the stores dropped the magazine out of fear of prosecution. *Playboy*, the American Booksellers Association, and other groups sued Meese and the commission, won a retraction, and then published a layout featuring female convenience store employees entitled "The Women of 7-Eleven."

Playboy Survives Court Challenge. In July, 1992, the Los Angeles County Fire Department issued a policy prohibiting "sexually oriented magazines, particularly those containing nude pictures, such as *Playboy*, *Penthouse* and *Playgirl*" from "all work locations, including dormitories, rest rooms and lockers." Represented by the American Civil Liberties Union, Fire Captain Steven W. Johnson filed a civil rights action seeking a declaration that the private possession, reading, and consensual sharing of *Playboy* was constitutionally protected under the First and Fourteenth Amendments. On October 25, 1994, a U.S. district court upheld his claims in *Johnson v. County of Los Angeles Fire Department*.

The court held that the content of *Playboy* was a "matter of public concern" and that Johnson's First Amendment right to read the magazine privately could only be overcome if the fire department could prove that in doing so, Johnson posed a material and substantial threat of disrupting the efficient operation of the fire station. After conducting the necessary balancing, the court rejected the claim that the reading of *Playboy* may result in "sex-role stereotyping" in the minds of the readers. "It is a fundamental principle of First Amendment law," wrote the court, "that the government cannot regulate material in order to prevent the readers from developing certain ideas." Furthermore, the court found that the fire department had "failed to prove that there is a connection between *Playboy* and 'sexual stereotyping,' and between 'sexual stereotyping' and sexual harassment." The court concluded that fire department officials "may not ban the reading of *Playboy* simply because they disagree with the manner in which *Playboy* portrays women."

The continued success of *Playboy* is a testament to the growing popular acceptance of sexual imagery in the face of persistent threats of censure and censorship from an uneasy coalition of conservatives and religious forces and procensorship feminists. No side in this debate has, however, shown any sign of letting up. *—Stephen F. Rohde*

See also Attorney General's Commission on Pornography; Bruce, Lenny; *Fahrenheit 451*; Feminism; Meese, Edwin III; Men's magazines; Nixon, Richard M.; Nudity; Obscenity: sale and possession; Pornography; Postal regulations; Sex education; Tax laws; Twain, Mark.

BIBLIOGRAPHY

Gretchen Edgre's *The Playboy Book: Forty Years* (Santa Monica, Calif.: General Publishing Group, 1994) is a complimentary pictorial history of *Playboy*'s first forty years. Marjorie Heins, *Sex, Sin and Blasphemy: A Guide to America's Censorship Wars* (New York: New York Press, 1993), contains a lively and informative survey of key censorship issues by a director of the American Civil Liberties Union's Arts Censorship Project. For an outspoken and personal account of the adult entertainment industry from a strong anticensorship perspective, see Wendy McElroy's *XXX: A Woman's Right to Pornography* (New York: St. Martin's Press, 1995). Marcia Pally, *Sex and Sensibility: Reflections on Forbidden Mirrors and the Will to Censor* (Hopewell, N.J.: Ecco Press, 1994) is a brief but enlightening look at the censorship of sexual imagery that examines why people censor. Rodney A. Smolla, *Free Speech in an Open Society* (New York: Alfred A. Knopf, 1992), is a highly readable discussion that spans the major First Amendment issues of the day.

Pledge of Allegiance

TYPE OF WORK: Oath
PUBLISHED: 1892
AUTHOR: (disputed)
SUBJECT MATTER: Affirmation of fidelity to the U.S. flag
SIGNIFICANCE: This statement of a national creed has at times been used as a litmus test of patriotism

The Pledge of Allegiance first appeared in the September 8, 1892, issue of the magazine *Youth's Companion*. It originally read, "I pledge allegiance to my flag and to the republic for which it stands, one nation indivisible, with liberty and justice for all." Censorship concerning the pledge has been mostly in the direction of prescribing, rather than proscribing. In the 1920's the phrase "my flag" was changed to "the flag of the United States of America." Until World War II, the correct method of reciting the pledge was to place the right hand over the heart, say, "I pledge allegiance," then extend the right arm toward the flag, palm up, and continue. That salute was deemed to be too much like the pro-Hitler "Sieg Heil" salute, however. Since then the hand has been left over the heart. In 1954, after Senator Joseph McCarthy and others attacked "godless communism," Congress added the words "under God" ("one nation, under God, indivisible").

Thanks to a 1943 decision by the U.S. Supreme Court in *West Virginia State Board of Education v. Barnette*, school children may not be required to recite the pledge. Nevertheless, in the 1988 presidential campaign Republican candidate George Bush successfully exploited the fact that his Democratic challenger, Michael Dukakis, had, as governor of Massachusetts, vetoed a bill that would have overridden that decision.

See also Jehovah's Witnesses; Loyalty oaths; *West Virginia State Board of Education v. Barnette*.

Poetry

DEFINITION: Polished, artistic speech, typically intended to generate emotional and intellectual response
SIGNIFICANCE: Poetry with sexual, spiritual, or psychological content causes controversy in public schools

Debate over which poetic works should be permitted to be read in high school English classes is of great concern to school board members, administrators, teachers, parents, and students. Poetry is censored primarily for three reasons: sexual content, spiritual beliefs and practices, and human psychology. Would-be censors claim that teachers select such material not for whatever artistic merit it possesses, but instead for its sensationalism and its ability to cause students to question the values taught by parents.

Sexuality. Challenges to poetry on the basis of its sexual content often center on treatments of premarital or extramarital sex. Censors and would-be censors have objected to poems that portray such acts favorably, or that fail to condemn such acts, or that simply in telling about such acts, focus on issues other than their moral wrongness. Anne Sexton's "Unknown Girl in the Maternity Ward" is an example. Some poems are banned on the basis of subtle genital-related symbolism as well as for more overt depiction of coition. Poems involving some type of sexual violence—rape, spouse abuse, molestation—are also objectionable to many people, especially since such poems usually cast women as victims. W. B. Yeats's poem "Leda and the Swan" and Robert Lowell's "To Speak of Woe That Is in Marriage" are two such poems.

In other cases, poetry has been banned for descriptions or suggestions of prostitution, incest, or homosexuality. Twentieth century poetry is particularly susceptible to attack on these grounds, as these issues are central to the twentieth century quest for meaning through sexual encounters. T. S. Eliot's "The Love Song of J. Alfred Prufrock," Allen Ginsberg's "Howl," and Adrienne Rich's "The Floating Poem," are among those frequently banned. Each of these poets is a primary figure in a period or school of poetry, so censoring their poems raises questions about a student's ability to draw intelligent conclusions about entire categories of poetry.

Spirituality. Censorship on the basis of spirituality frequently involves banning poets' entire canons or excluding whole movements. Censors target as pagan poetry that recalls or relies on Greek or Roman mythology; such poetry does not uphold Christian values. This argument extends to other mythological constructs, including the occultist work of W. B. Yeats and the Transcendental poetry of Ralph Waldo Emerson.

Poems by Emerson (a Christian minister) and others have been found especially objectionable by some because of the Eastern ideas upon which they are based.

Yet more ironic is censorship aimed at the poetry of Christian poets who struggle with the precepts of the Christian religion in order to come to terms with issues of personal faith. John Milton's *Paradise Lost* (1667), for example, which states that it seeks "to justify the ways of God to man," may be denounced as portraying sin and disbelief, because in the poem, Adam and Eve sin and Satan rebels. Although Milton's book is considered quite conservative by most, the very presence of spiritual doubt and speculation about the mercy of the Christian God is sufficient cause for others to push for its exclusion from high school curricula.

People who resist any questioning of religious faith especially object to many works of the late Victorian and early modern periods. Thomas Hardy (who was educated with an eye to the priesthood) and Gerard Manley Hopkins (an ordained Jesuit priest) are two British poets who express the despair that resulted from a society's theological underpinning being thrown into doubt by scientific advances. The kind of spiritual agony that Hopkins depicts in his "terrible sonnets," for example, is anathema to some censors. Those who argue for the inclusion of this sort of poetry in high school curricula claim that the very intensity of Hopkins' questioning indicates a mature spirituality—one not based on naïve acceptance of what a person has been taught to believe. Hardy, in addition to his open expression of religious doubt, makes fun of Victorian, Christian sexual mores in his poetry. Furthermore, some of the poetry of Charles Algernon Swinburne, for example, would likely draw criticism at even the most liberal high school.

Psychology. Similar to the resistance against poetic expression of religious doubt is the apprehension felt regarding an exploration of the human mind. The attitude of many censors is that censorship is necessary for safety; in the case of psychology, censorship has been called for on the argument that exploration of the human mind may lead to the questioning of religious doctrine, or of authority, or of established understanding. Such questioning can in turn lead to a rejection of authority.

Too much contemplation also potentially leads to depression and anxiety, sometimes even to insanity or suicide. Consequently, poetry that examines unhealthy states of mind or some aspect of death is considered detrimental to the well-being of young adults. Sylvia Plath's poems about suicide and depression, for example, may be censored on the grounds that adolescents may be unduly influenced by such poems.

Ramifications. The ramifications of censorship are manifold for teachers and students. Responsible teachers who attempt to offer their students rich ideas that foster incisive thinking often find censorship becoming, in their lives, something other than an abstract issue. Teachers often complain of being treated as subordinates incapable of sound judgment, and, to the dismay of the many teachers who may wish, for example, to teach an unexpurgated tale or two from *The Canterbury Tales* (1387-1400) or Walt Whitman's "I Sing the Body Electric," there are some other teachers who wish to teach their religious beliefs or their peculiar interpretations of history.

For many students, the classroom is the only forum for careful discussion of serious issues. Since most great poetry concerns itself with fundamental human experience, including sexuality, spirituality, and psychology, to eliminate poetry on such topics means that students are left with art that is not of the highest caliber. This problem impinges on academic performance: Students who have not studied "controversial" (that is, "real") literature typically do not perform as well on national standardized tests, which are based on great literature, as those students who do. Students who have read only the most inoffensive, unchallenging literature may be expected to have vocabulary that is underdeveloped and to have reasoning skills that are not as refined as those of students who have been grappling with complex psychological abstractions and artistic creations. Furthermore, students who have not studied the purportedly controversial poetry find college poetry courses formidable simply because such courses are much more complex than what the students studied in high school.

—Kimberly R. Myers

See also Akhmatova, Anna; Ferlinghetti, Lawrence; Ginsberg, Allen; Literature; Milton, John; Ovid; Sex in the arts; Shelley, Percy Bysshe; Swinburne, Algernon Charles; Whitman, Walt.

BIBLIOGRAPHY

Editor Anna S. Ochoa's *The National Education Association's Academic Freedom to Teach and to Learn: Every Teacher's Issue* (Washington, D.C.: NEA Professional Library, 1990) provides lucid essays on topics including "The Significance of and Rationale for Academic Freedom," the impact of censorship on teachers' professionalism, and a concise summary of litigation involving censorship. Joseph Bryson and Elizabeth Detty's *Legal Aspects of Censorship of Public School Library and Instructional Materials* (Charlottesville, Va.: Michie, 1982) provides a more basic overview of censorship in the public schools. For an earlier perspective on this issue, John Frank and Robert Hogan's *Obscenity, the Law, and the English Teacher* (Champaign, Ill.: National Council of Teachers of English, 1966) cites various people's responses to particular works. Arthur F. Ide's *Evangelical Terrorism* (Irving, Tex.: Scholars Books, 1986) focuses on censorship by Christian Fundamentalists, including Jerry Falwell and Pat Robertson.

Poland

DESCRIPTION: Eastern European country which began a transition from authoritarian to democratic government in the late 1980's

SIGNIFICANCE: Poland has experienced a typical transition from almost total suppression of freedom of expression under communism to a more open democratic system

Poland's history is characterized by periods of dominance by foreign powers. During these periods of external rule severe controls were often placed on any form of national expression, including use of the Polish language. During the period of Russian dominance, for example, censors would not allow the use of the word "Polish" in newspapers, and any appeal to Polish patriotism was strictly forbidden.

Between World War I and World War II, Poland was independent, and characterized by radical and sometimes vicious anti-Semitism, often government-supported, typical for Central Europe of that era. In 1939 Poland was once again partitioned, this time by Adolf Hitler's Germany and Joseph Stalin's Soviet Union. Hitler continued his Jewish extermination campaign in Poland, while Stalin repressed any move toward Polish independence.

With the Soviet army in place in Eastern Europe after 1945, Poland soon became a communist ally. In 1946 the institutional mechanism for controlling the media, designed to consolidate and maintain the power of the Communist Party, was established, the Central Office of Publications and Entertainment. This office developed a set of criteria to cover published and broadcast material, ranging from taboo subjects that were never to be mentioned under any circumstances, to sensitive topics that needed to be handled with extreme caution.

Despite these efforts, an independent press enjoyed success in Poland unequaled anywhere else in Eastern Europe. Some underground newspapers had circulations as high as twenty thousand. The Roman Catholic church, through the pulpit and through its own publications, such as *Universal Weekly*, also provided an independent voice. In the early 1980's the independent trade union, Solidarity, began to assert its growing political power. In July, 1981, the communist government passed the Act on Censorship, which provided ways for reducing the power of the censors, including an appeal process.

This freedom was short-lived, however, as General Wojciech Jaruzelski imposed martial law in December, 1981, suspending the freedoms that were beginning to develop, closing many newspapers and putting the broadcast media under military control. Martial law ended in 1983, and the government became increasingly tolerant of free expression. For example, *The Public Interest*, a dissident periodical which was first published in the late 1970's, received official permission to publish in May, 1987, the first nonstate, nonchurch magazine ever to appear legally in Eastern Europe under communism.

By April, 1990, after elections which gave the newly legalized Solidarity Party significant political power, state censorship was abolished, and the publishing and distribution monopoly broken up. This was followed by an explosion in the number of newspapers and magazines. The electronic media has been slower to respond to the elimination of censorship, however. All broadcast stations, television and radio, continue to belong to the state. Despite this, broadcast media are generally free.

See also Communism; National Socialism; News media censorship; Newspapers, underground; Stalin, Joseph.

Police

DEFINITION: Government law enforcement officers

SIGNIFICANCE: As the physical agents of law enforcement, members of police departments are often involved in censorship controversies

Police implement previously determined policies of censorship, and in some cases also engage in developing their own censorship as a result of the discretion that the law allots to the police methods. The police sometimes choose to become censors and are sometimes thrust into the role of censors. Police departments, as have bureaucracies generally, have been accused of internal censorship and secrecy that shields police wrongdoing.

The police are an agency of social control. They are constantly involved in a process of trying to guarantee that members of society conform to social norms as described in criminal codes. Although the police are not the only agency of social control (others include the family, the peer group, school, and religious institutions), they are usually the last resort for controlling abnormal behavior in the community.

The job of police becomes more difficult when a sizeable number of an area's population does not accept the police's definition of community norms. Typical censorship dilemmas have come into play when police must enforce policies that do not have widespread public support across the social, ethnic, racial, and economic sectors. For example, the removal of books from the school or public libraries, enforcing the ban on select films, and closing down adult pornographic entertainment centers all provide potential problematic censorship choices for law enforcement officials.

Discretion, Police Abuses, and Censorship. In the United States, police departments have become involved with issues of censorship when they attempt to enforce the laws of a city, county, or state government. In addition, the origin of a censorship incident may on occasion come directly from the police and not through any legislative initiative or chief executive's authority. For example, if a person is shouting threatening obscenities in the street, the police officer on the scene may choose to arrest or may choose to ignore the person. A police officer may also choose to arrest a man who was not shouting obscenities in the street but say that he was. Much police power, and abuse of power, lies in such discretion.

Although the police are the ones called upon to shut down a pornographic theater or arrest a bookstore owner, such acts of censorship, experts argue, are rare compared to practices that may be called internal censorship or maintaining silence about illegal acts committed by police as part of the enforcement of laws not related to censorship issues. Such acts include beatings, verbal abuse, arrest and search without probable cause, intimidation, perjury, and falsification of evidence. In all such cases, it is unlikely that the police officer who breaks the law will be punished unless another officer speaks against the first officer.

Critics have argued that a number of legal mechanisms help maintain the police behaviors that end in cover-up, denial, and a type of group censorship. A New York City attorney, Paul Chevigny, for example, argued that charges of disorderly conduct, resisting arrest, and felonious assault, or all three—together with a story to establish them—constitute a police system for covering up street abuses. Such legal devices provide the standard explanations for police brutality by some police in American law enforcement. Suppression of information that could lead to the truth has occurred in most urban police departments and county sheriff's offices as well. In the more sophisticated departments, police abuses rarely occur without the accompanying criminal charges to cover them, and little can be done to uncover, for example, a police beating unless the cover charges are modified or witnesses are found to help corroborate the testimony of the abused citizen. The videotaped record of Rodney King's beating at the hands of Los Angeles police in 1991 revealed how technological development could help expose internal police censorship and in doing so, heighten public awareness.

When addressing the concept of police and their record as censors, many police activities are inherently covert operations but are legitimate policies. Many times police investigators will not release critical information relating to a case if this is information only known to the perpetrator. Moreover, the withholding of information about suspects, victims, and witnesses is a form of necessary censorship that is done to protect the parties involved. Witness protection programs are representative of this type of censorship. Police agencies have sometimes been accused of being too careful about releasing crime information; for example, sometimes departments have not released information about serial rapists to the community, when critics argue that the benefits of such an announcement outweigh the negatives.

Throughout police procedure there is a deliberate effort to protect the process of an investigation. Techniques such as surveillance and wiretaps pose legal and ethical problems in a free and democratic society. Wiretaps are a common tool of information collection, as is the case with hidden video cameras and audio recorders. Police are required to show probable cause prior to planting these information collection devices, so as not to violate Fourth Amendment rights of citizens. There is definitely a reasonable expectation by citizens not to have their privacy violated. Likewise, the protection of minors is the reasoning behind the confidentiality of a minor's criminal records. It could be argued that evidence itself, kept under lock and key, is a form of legitimate censorship so that the evidence will be preserved in its original condition.

Censorship by police and sheriff officers has been practiced to some degree in most American communities. Censorship or the suppression, control, or restriction of expression of ideas believed dangerous to society may be found in both official and more subtle, nonofficial forms involving the participation of law enforcement officials. Any attempt by police in city and town government or sheriff's department in county government that stifles expression may constitute censorship. Numerous opportunities arise for censorship by the police either in their role of enforcer of specific laws or through their own discretion, when they may select to operate outside the law. There is evidence that most departments have a few bad apples, but it is important to understand why the police struggle to police themselves, and search for ways to discipline or purge such offenders from their ranks.

The Modern Police Department. The police power of the states is found in the Constitution and grants authority for each of these governments to provide for the "public health, welfare, and safety" of its citizens. Police departments, as an example of public bureaucratic growth, are partially a product of urbanization in America. The most important development of the nineteenth century in law enforcement was the birth of a modern professional urban police system during the period from 1844 to 1877. The antiquated watch and ward system (daytime constables and nighttime watchmen) was not able to respond to large scale rioting and increasing urban crime and disorder. The impetus for reform of the police system came from New York, Philadelphia, Boston and other cities that had been overrun with serious problems of criminal violence and rioting. Thus, the riot era of the 1830's to 1850's was a catalyst for the present professional urban police department and its paramilitary organizational system.

The police organizational culture provides an environment for various forms of censorship. It has been characterized by many scholars and practitioners as a closed and secretive group. Officers feel that they must act as a team and band together to protect themselves and the public from the criminal elements. Often this defensive behavior evolves into an us-against-them mentality, because many police tactics are not supported by a particular neighborhood they might patrol. Some residents in extreme cases may even view the police as an occupying army, without any appreciation of what police values may be. This negative image of the police has been most notable and most constant in the African American and Hispanic communities, but may also be found in other nations where one ethnic or racial minority group has been constantly the subject of retaliation and persecution by government authority controlled by the majority population. There was some hope that as the U.S. police forces became more diverse and thereby better reflected the racial, ethnic, and gender mix of the areas they patrol, they would be more responsive to change. While some positive steps of opening the closed society of the police brotherhood have evolved since the Kerner Commission's (1968) condemnation of police during the urban riots of the late 1960's, much evidence remains that major problems still exist; in the realm of censorship, a central problem that has been cited is self-censorship, specifically in which illegal acts by officers are not reported by other officers.

—G. Thomas Taylor

See also Assembly, right of; Community standards; Federal Bureau of Investigation; First Amendment; Fourteenth Amendment; Police states; Witnesses, protection of.

Bibliography

Jerome H. Skolnick's *Justice Without Trial: Law Enforcement in Democratic Society* (New York: John Wiley & Sons, 1966) provides insights on organizational and legal limits of the police from the author's own experience as a police detective. William A. Westley's *Violence and the Police: A Sociological Study of Law, Custom, and Morality* (Cambridge, Mass.: MIT Press, 1970) is a pioneering account of a midwestern city police department in the 1950's. James Q. Wilson's *Varieties of Police Behavior: The Management of Law and Order in Eight Communities* (New York: Atheneum, 1968) examines different styles of police discretion involved with police administration and the functions of patrol. An excellent inside account of the abuse of police authority is found in Paul Chevigny's *Police Power: Police Abuses in New York City* (New York: Pantheon Books, 1969). Three comprehensive U.S. government reports that study police include the report of a presidential commission on law enforcement and justice, *The Challenge of Crime in a Free Society* (New York: Avon Books, 1968), which makes recommendations about crime and the administration of the justice system; the Kerner Commission's *Report of the National Advisory Commission on Civil Disorders* (New York: Bantam Books, 1968), which studies the root causes of urban riots; and *Law and Order Reconsidered: Report of the Task Force on Law and Law Enforcement to the National Commission on the Causes and Prevention of Violence* (New York: Bantam Books, 1970), which analyzes and makes recommendations on violence in the United States. Harry W. More's *Behavioral Police Management* (New York: Macmillan, 1992) offers a police administration approach that focuses on organization behavior and personnel management concerns. Joel H. Henderson's *Crimes of the Criminal Justice System* (Cincinnati, Ohio: Anderson, 1994) discusses the criminal justice system and the administration of corrupt practices by police and the courts. Timothy Egan's *Breaking Blue* (New York: Alfred A. Knopf, 1992) provides detailed case studies of murder investigations, police murders, and police corruption in Pend Orielle County, Washington.

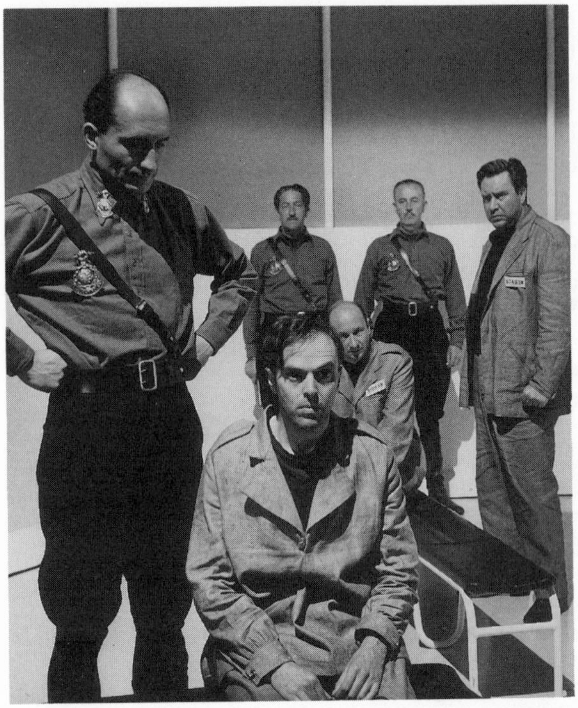

Officers of a totalitarian police state interrogate a man whose own children have denounced him for disloyalty to the state in this scene from the 1955 film adaptation of George Orwell's Nineteen Eighty-Four. (Museum of Modern Art/Film Stills Archive)

Police states

DEFINITION: Political systems controlled by leaders who rule by force

SIGNIFICANCE: Through the use of censorship and propaganda, police states seek to engender conformity within their societies

Police states are political systems generally characterized by dictatorial rule, whether the regime that rules is led by an individual, a family, a political party, or the military. A critical component common to police state rule is the desire to control the information flow to citizens through censorship and propaganda campaigns. The main reason a police state engages in such tactics is to maintain order and stability within the society. The leadership seeks to create an obedient and docile citizenry by restricting and shaping the mass media to which citizens are exposed. In such cases, the state is less likely to face challenges to its rule from society at large.

Types of Police States. There are two different types of police states: authoritarian and totalitarian. An authoritarian police state is primarily only interested in maintaining power. An authoritarian regime does not want to be challenged within the country it rules so it engages in censorship and propaganda to justify and glorify its rule, and to prevent potential rivals from having access to the masses through the media. Examples of authoritarian police states would be the regimes led by Saddam Hussein in Iraq and Muammar al-Qaddafi in Libya.

A totalitarian police state, much like an authoritarian one, is also concerned with the maintenance of power. Totalitarian police states, however, have an ideological element that authoritarian police states lack. Maintenance of power is not enough for a totalitarian police state; progress toward an ideal or a utopian goal that the regime has must also be made. The ideological goal of totalitarian police states can vary. For example, for Adolf Hitler, the leader of the Nazi Party that ruled Germany from 1933 until 1945, the goal was global domination by a master race. For Joseph Stalin, the leader of the Soviet Union from 1928 until 1953, the goal was advancement toward communism. No matter the goal, totalitarian police states harness the mass media in an attempt to make progress toward the ideal envisioned by the leadership of the regime.

Targets for Censorship and Propaganda. The objects of censorship and propaganda in a police state are numerous. Most important, perhaps, are the news media. Police states want their citizens to hear information about events from abroad or at home only if it supports the regime. As a result, the sources of news in police states are either state owned or tightly controlled by the state. Only information that is viewed favorably by the regime is allowed to be reported uncensored. News that the regime feels is problematic is either not allowed to be reported at all, or is altered to put the leadership in the best possible light. The enemies of the regime are placed in the worst possible light. Thus in a police state, all forms of news media, including television, radio, newspapers, and magazines, are in the service of the state.

Police states do not limit their censorship and propaganda activities to the news media. Any potential source capable of transmitting political messages to citizens is targeted. Music, dance, poetry, literature, plays, opera, films, paintings, and sculpture are all subjected to censorship and propaganda campaigns. Religion and religious practices are censored by the state. The leaders in police states have rewritten history and ordered languages and alphabets to be altered or eliminated. Textbooks and curricula taught in school become means by which to indoctrinate, socialize, and control.

Agents of State Control. The bureaucracy necessary to impose the degree of censorship and propaganda found in police states is extensive. There are two types of bureaucratic entities: state directed unions and guilds to produce material for public consumption, and the agencies and departments that censor all work produced, whether by an agent of the state or a private citizen.

The purpose behind creating unions and guilds is to channel the efforts of citizens with particular interests and skills into the service of the state. In police states, if an individual has the skills and desires to be an artist, for example, the regime will provide a job and a living provided the artist produces works favorable to the state. The artist is required to join the state guild and take orders from the representative of the regime that directs the guild. If the artist does not want to join the guild and wants to work independently, the police state will not necessarily frown upon it if the work being produced is not offensive to the regime. Artists working independently that produce work offensive to the state, however, will not be tolerated by the regime and inevitably face harassment and incarceration.

Whether an individual is working for the state or not, any work produced must be submitted for approval to censors in a police state. The censors have the right to alter or reject the work if they feel the interests and goals of the regime are not being appropriately served. Common tactics used by censors in police states include book burning, electronic jamming of television and radio, seizure and closure of unfavored publishing houses, and prohibitions on live broadcasts because of an inability to censor them.

Responses of Police State Citizens. The response of citizens living in police states to the censorship and propaganda efforts of their regime is often mixed. Typically, some embrace the regime and see the censorship and propaganda efforts as necessary and legitimate. Some take the state up on its offers of employment and personal advancement and commit themselves to the service of the state. Others do not support the state but are sufficiently intimidated and fearful of the state that they engage in self-censorship by not protesting. Finally, in every police state, despite the grandest efforts of the regime, opposition to the leadership does exist. Those who resist are quite courageous because their personal well-being is always at risk. One goal of the opposition in police states is to attack and discredit the policies of censorship and the propaganda campaigns sponsored by the state. To do so, the opposition circumvents the authorities by furtively producing material and information hostile to the regime. What is produced is then disseminated through underground networks of sympathizers to as wide an audience as possible. The hope of the opposition is that in time enough citizens in the society will become so disgusted with the regime that mass revolt will be possible and the overthrow of the police state will become a reality.

—Samuel E. Watson III

See also Art; Communism; Culture ministries; Death; Iraq; National Socialism; Propaganda; Solzhenitsyn, Aleksandr; Soviet Union; Stalin, Joseph; TASS; Voice of America.

BIBLIOGRAPHY

Brian Chapman's *Police State* (New York: Praeger, 1970) and Carl J. Friedrich's and Zbigniew Brzezinski's *Totalitarian Dictatorship and Autocracy* (Cambridge, Mass.: Harvard University Press, 1965) provide a comprehensive understanding as to why police states seek to censor as they do. Stephen J. Lee's *The European Dictatorships, 1918-1945* (New York: Methuen, 1987) offers a comparative account of the strategies and tactics that can be practiced by police states. Alan Bullock's *Hitler: A Study in Tyranny* (New York: Harper & Row, 1971) provides insight into the thinking and motivation behind a dictator's actions. Dilip Hiro's *Iran Under the Ayatollahs* (New York: Routledge, 1987) and Rudolf L. Tokes' *Dissent in the USSR* (Baltimore, Md.: The Johns Hopkins University Press, 1975) focus on the censorship practices in two individual police states.

Political campaigning

DEFINITION: Activities undertaken by political parties and candidates contesting public elections

SIGNIFICANCE: Three aspects of political campaigning have raised censorship issues: candidates' access to the media; government access to political party membership lists; and restrictions on campaign financing

Political campaigning has several important connections to issues of censorship. There is, for example, the matter of who actually belongs to parties and organizations, and how identifying members might infringe on their right to free speech. There are a number of issues relating to campaign financing. Historically, the fact that those wealthy enough to contribute to political campaigns have had their voices heard over those unable to make substantial contributions has been a form of censorship of the poor. Conversely, modern legislation restricting the amounts individual persons and groups can contribute to campaigns is another form of censorship. Finally, there is the matter of which candidates should be permitted time on the public airways—regardless of who pays for such time.

U.S. Political Campaigns and Broadcasting. Since 1934 the body that has governed the coverage of national political campaigns and political campaigning on the airways has been the Federal Communications Commission. Its "fairness doctrine," which was enforced until 1986, was an attempt to ensure that the views of certain groups or individuals were not censored by the refusal of television or radio stations to broadcast their campaign material. The policy was designed to ensure that balanced coverage greeted not only political campaign material, but campaign news reporting in general. In 1959, however, American lawmakers changed the section of the Communications Act of 1934 to remove news stories related to political candidates involved in a campaign from the balanced coverage requirement. The fairness doctrine remained controversial until its abandonment in 1986. Television and radio stations decried it as government imposed censorship while others saw the rules as one way of ensuring balanced coverage, or, at the least, that more than one voice was heard.

The issue of censorship and the airways remained important as late as the 1996 U.S. presidential election. H. Ross Perot, the presidential candidate leader of the Reform Party, sought to be included in the nationally broadcast debates between the two major-party candidates for the presidency, Democrat Bill Clinton and Republican Robert Dole. An election committee ruled, however, that Perot could be excluded because he did not have a realistic chance of winning the election. This decision prompted cries of censorship from Perot's campaign, which argued that its candidate's voice had been silenced.

Party Membership and U.S. Political Campaigning. In 1958 the state of Alabama tried to curtail the local civil rights work of the National Association for the Advancement of Colored People (NAACP); it demanded several sets of records from the organization. The NAACP turned over to the state all the requested documentation, except its membership lists—because it feared for the safety of those on the lists. A state judge held the organization in contempt and imposed a $100,000 fine. The organization appealed the case to the U.S. Supreme Court, which unanimously overturned the lower court decision. The Court ruled that the Alabama law violated the First Amendment rights of NAACP members freely to associate with each other. This case had clear implications for issues connected to political campaigning censorship.

During the 1980 U.S. presidential campaign supporters of President Jimmy Carter carry signs in Columbus, Ohio, belittling Republican challenger Ronald Reagan. (AP/Wide World Photos)

Financing of U.S. Political Campaigns. The financing of political campaigns in the United States has also had censorship implications. The U.S. Supreme Court's *Buckley v. Valeo* decision in 1976, for example, was described by journalist Elizabeth Drew as equating "freedom of speech with the spending of money." The case had its roots in the aftermath of the Watergate scandal in 1974, when the U.S. Congress passed a revised Federal Election Campaign Act covering campaign financing. The law called for public funding of presidential campaigns, spending limits for candidates seeking office, financial limits on donations by groups and individuals to campaigns, and—most controversially—prohibition of campaign spending of more than one thousand dollars by those uninvolved in any of the campaigns. These provisions were struck down in *Buckley v. Valeo*. Opponents of the campaign finance law felt that the limits it imposed on third parties infringed on freedom of speech. The Supreme Court agreed when it overturned the objectionable provisions of the law in January, 1976. At the same time, however, the Court upheld most of the law's other provisions. Congress passed a revised version in 1976.

Political Campaigning in Canada. Several countries besides the United States have dealt with issues of censorship and political campaigns. During the 1990's, for example, Japan proposed publicly financed election campaigns to prevent excessive influence on elections by the wealthy, and to end the censorship effect imposed on those who lacked the money to buy access to various forms of media.

Issues of political campaigns and censorship were also important in Canada during the 1980's and 1990's. In 1983 Canada's federal government introduced spending limits on interest groups and individuals outside of the political process. The following year an Alberta provincial court struck down the legislation on the grounds that it violated freedom of speech provisions included in Canada's Charter of Rights. Although this ruling was made by a single provincial court, the federal government under the leadership of Prime Minister Brian Mulroney did not appeal it. The nation's Chief Electoral Officer then ruled that no campaign spending limits applied anywhere in Canada. During the federal elections of 1988—in which the main issue was whether Canada should accept a free trade agreement with the United States—individuals and interest groups took advantage of the absence of spending restrictions by pouring large amounts of money into political campaigns. A last-minute advertising blitz by factions favoring free trade helped the governing Conservative Party win reelection.

The unprecedented involvement by outside political interests in a Canadian election campaign led the federal government to introduce a new law governing campaign spending in early 1993. This law, which was endorsed by the three main political parties, limited interest groups to contributions of a thousand dollars within any given four-week period. The legislation was widely denounced, especially by smaller political parties, which saw it as an infringement on their rights. The law did not last long, however. A court struck it down in June, 1993.

Some Canadian provinces elected to introduce their own laws governing political campaigns. The province of British Columbia, for example, passed a law allowing for a maximum of five thousand dollars to be spent by members of the public or third-party interests, either in support or against a political party. The law generated widespread opposition, including cries of censorship during British Columbia's 1996 provincial election when it was first enforced. One organization, the National Citizen's Coalition, circumvented the law by airing radio and television advertisements on American border stations. The National Citizen's Coalition had previously been instrumental in defeating the federal Canadian law that imposed similar restrictions. —*Steven R. Hewitt*

See also Canada; Communications Act of 1934; Congress, U.S.; Fairness doctrine; Federal Communications Commission; National Association for the Advancement of Colored People; Presidency, U.S.; Watergate scandal.

BIBLIOGRAPHY

Elizabeth Drew, *Politics and Money: The New Road to Corruption* (New York: Macmillan, 1983), offers a detailed discussion of *Buckley v. Valeo*. Kay Lehman Schlozman, ed., *Elections in America* (Boston: Allen & Unwin, 1987), is a general discussion of American political elections. Gary C. Jacobson's *Money in Congressional Elections* (New Haven, Conn.: Yale University Press, 1980) is a study of the role of financing in Congressional elections. Fred Gray, an attorney for the NAACP in its case against the state of Alabama, relates that story in *Bus Ride to Justice* (Black Belt Press, 1995). In "The Kindness of Strangers," *U.S. News and World Report* (October 10, 1994), Susan Headeen and David Bowermaster deal with the attempt to reform the financing of U.S. campaigns.

Political correctness

DEFINITION: A measure of social, cultural, intellectual, and political issues

SIGNIFICANCE: The terms "political correctness," "politically correct," and "PC" have been used to describe, often critically, attitudes and actions regarding social issues

Widely used in the United States after 1989, "political correctness" describes (with an inexactitude that people of various political opinions have exploited in their discussion of the term) a set of responses to various social issues. Critics have argued that political correctness is arbitrary and is the justification for the censorship of unpopular opinions; those who are attacked with charges of being politically correct have argued that those who belittle a cause as politically correct have political agendas of their own and seek to censor on their part. Examples are typically used to describe what is and what is not politically correct.

Politically correct speech arguably includes the use of carefully chosen words denoting ethnic and racial groups or sex; support of feminism; support of university speech codes and affirmative action; vigilance against hostility by white males toward women, racial and ethnic minorities, and homosexuals; and support of multiculturalism, including deemphasis of or hostility toward Western civilization. Politically incorrect behaviors arguably include championing Western civilization as superior to others; using disparaging terms for minorities and women, supporting national policies that favor big business, war, and the rich at the expense of the poor and of society generally; abusing the environment; and showing unconcern for social inequality. The debate over political correctness has a significant side; it hints at a widening cultural divide—and attempts to bridge it—in North American society and touches upon such issues as freedom of speech. It also has a frivolous side, having to do with jokes about smoking cigarettes, wearing real fur, and eating red meat.

Beyond the university, elements of political correctness are a pervasive aspect of much of American social, cultural, and economic life. Political correctness is found, for example, in kindergarten through twelfth-grade education, in hiring practices and sensitivity training in the workplace, in the storylines of Hollywood films, in television programming, in advertising, in magazine and textbook publishing, and in everyday speech and human relations.

Moral and political orthodoxies of PC, pervasive in American society, have led to various forms of censorship, including self-censorship. The influence of PC represents the coming to power of a 1960's generation influenced by liberationist thinking as well as those indirectly influenced by such thinking. In society at large, PC has important influence upon large portions of political and cultural life. The quest for political correctness, one of the hallmarks of which is tolerance for difference, has led, ironically, to open censorship, as in campus speech codes, and to more subtle restrictions on freedom of expression.

Roots of Political Correctness. The roots of political correctness are found in the Civil Rights movement of the 1950's and 1960's, which focused the nation's attention on injustices to blacks. Another root is the cultural revolution of the 1960's, combined with the movement opposing the Vietnam War. Among the most important roots of political correctness from the 1960's is feminism. Many feminists demanded conformity in the use of language. Feminists have argued, for example, that using "girl" for "woman," "men" for "people," or "mankind" for "humanity" is sexist and disparages women; critics of political correctness have argued that such usage has become taboo. Extremes of intolerance toward the perspectives prevalent in the antiwar and radical feminist movement carried over into the intolerance of PC and its impulse to silence opposing views. The moral certainty of PC led to sanctions against nonconformists.

Politically correct terms for certain groups became current. In the late 1960's it became politically incorrect to refer to African Americans as "colored" or as "negroes." Until the late 1980's the correct term was "black," when the politically correct term became "African American," despite a large percentage of blacks who objected. American Indians became Native Americans; homosexuals became gays; and Hispanics became Latinos. Once these terms became politically correct, freedom to use alternatives became rapidly circumscribed.

The ideology of political correctness first manifested itself as preferential ("affirmative action") policies for blacks, first justified as recompense for past injustices. Subsequently women, American Indians, Asians, Central Americans, and others were added, as nearly every group in American society—except heterosexual white males—claimed victim status that merited preferential treatment. At the same time, demands were made that nonconforming speech and writing be constrained by various sanctions, from the editorial scalpel or rejection to expulsion from college.

Political Correctness and the American University. The consequences of PC have been most apparent on American college campuses. There, PC has in many instances chilled the free expression of ideas and diminished the university's traditional ideal of disinterested search for truth. Critics argue that PC has ushered in a new ideological conformism in which restraints on free expression play a leading role in enforcing orthodoxy.

Where PC predominates—in liberal arts colleges, for example—emphasis on Western culture is replaced by greater attention to non-Western authors and perspectives, often deprecating Western culture as hegemonic and imperialist. Fewer Western classics are taught, and little-known works by women, minorities, and non-Europeans (often arguably of lesser quality) are added. Entire courses are geared to politically correct themes and conclusions. One university, for example, offered a course on one minority's hairstyles. Censorship issues are raised when dissent from the instructor's point of view is discouraged (by lower grades, ostracism, and harassment by fellow students). Such courses are often offered under the umbrella of multiculturalism.

Multiculturalism in schools and universities typically assails focus on the individual and raises the status of the group, attacks the West, and downgrades study of European culture, especially the cultural artifacts of white males. The expression of positive attitudes toward "dead white males" is widely discouraged.

Numerous instances of the application of sanctions to those not conforming to politically correct norms in the American university have been recorded. Some students have feigned compliance with PC to avoid sanctions. Open attempts to silence politically incorrect speech have been tolerated by university authorities. Some critics have termed PC "soft totalitarianism" because pervasive demands for "correct" speech and behavior have invaded nearly every facet of life and attempted to eliminate the distinction between public and private behavior, as expressed in the feminist slogan: "the personal is the political."

In this view, while sanctions in totalitarianism are carried out through terror, "soft" totalitarian sanctions against nonconforming faculty include harassment, threat of dismissal, tenure refusal, class boycotts, and hostile publicity. At Harvard University, for example, a history professor was repeatedly harassed by students who objected to his reading in class of the diary of a slave owner. When the university failed to support him, he stopped offering the course. Offenses by students have resulted in administrative harassment, poor grades, suspension, dismissal, and other sanctions. Rules have been unequally applied to students, with white males singled out for

Politically Incorrect Language and Politically Correct Alternatives

Incorrect	*Correct*
Handicapped, disabled person	Person with a disability
Impairment	Disablement
Deaf and dumb	Speech- and hearing-impaired
Mute	Speech-impaired
Blind	Visually impaired
Insane, crazy	Emotionally impaired
Normal	Able-bodied person
Crippled, spastic	Mobility-impaired
Fit, spell	Seizure
Mongolism	Down syndrome
Harelip	Cleft lip

sanctions for nonadherence to PC norms, while minority students have flaunted norms with impunity. At the University of Pennsylvania, minority students stole thousands of student newspapers that offended them. University administrators, including the president, failed to censure the students and instead admonished university guards who tried to stop the thefts. To justify and enforce PC, universities have adopted a variety of measures, some of which, especially speech codes, are censorship. That such codes have been successfully challenged in the courts on First Amendment grounds is evidence of the threat PC holds to free expression.

Political Correctness in Society at Large. While political correctness is sometimes conceived as primarily, or even entirely, a phenomenon of the university, it is widely encountered in society at large, in government, in the autonomous organizations of civil society, in cultural and economic affairs, and in myriad transactions of daily life. A pervasive PC influence in this regard is the widespread demand for inclusion, which means emphasis on representation of specified groups in all aspects of public life. Thus, representation of favored groups signals compliance with PC norms in electronic media, museum exhibitions, and newspapers and magazines.

Politically correct norms are common at all levels of government. At the federal level, controversies over PC have erupted at the American National History Museum in Washington, D.C., and other components of the Smithsonian Institution. Government departments or agencies in some states and metropolitan city governments endorse politically correct policies and are silent or openly hostile to opponents.

Cultural institutions have likewise been constrained to follow politically correct policies through political pressure, funding threats, and other sanctions. In the business world, many major corporations have instituted diversity programs whose stated purpose is sensitizing whites to a new work atmosphere incorporating minorities but whose effects includes subtle and overt demands for conformity to politically correct norms.

In education, manifestations of PC are common in high schools and in a variety of national organizations, such as the National Education Association and the National Council for the Social Studies (NCSS). At its annual meetings, the NCSS is known to refuse time to presenters of politically incorrect topics or to assign time when more participants have left. In these cases, measures are taken to ensure that the unorthodox receive little or no hearing. —*Charles F. Bahmueller*

See also Campus speech codes; Feminism; Multiculturalism; Race; Textbooks.

Bibliography

Political correctness is the subject of a growing body of literature. Many valuable articles are found in the periodical *Academic Questions*, published by the National Association of Scholars, Princeton, New Jersey. Two valuable books that examine diversity in higher education are John K. Wilson's *The Myth of Political Correctness: The Conservative Attack on Higher Education* (Durham, N.C.: Duke University Press, 1995) and Richard Bernsteinn's *Dictatorship of Virtue: Multiculturalism and the Battle for America's Future* (New York: Basic Books, 1994). The latter also looks at schools and newspapers. *The Partisan Review*'s special issue on political correctness (vol. 60, no. 4, 1993) presents numerous scholars' critical analysis of PC. David O. Sacks and Peter A. Thiel's *The Diversity Myth: "Multiculturalism" and the Politics of Intolerance at Stanford* (Oakland, Calif: The Independent Institute, 1995) makes a detailed inquiry into PC at a prominent university. Arthur M. Schlesinger, Jr.'s *The Disuniting of America: Reflections on a Multicultural Society* (Whittle Direct Books, 1991) presents a spirited critique of the effects of PC on education and culture in general.

Pornography

Definition: Explicit portrayal of human sexual activity, designed to produce sexual arousal

Significance: Attempts to censor sexually explicit materials have prompted extensive debate as to whether pornography constitutes expression that should be protected

Significant government interest in regulating and suppressing sexually explicit materials emerged at the beginning of the nineteenth century, when the mass production and distribution of sexually explicit writings and images first became economically feasible. Much of the subsequent debate concerning the legitimacy of government censorship of pornography has focused upon two issues. One is that of determining whether the widespread availability of pornography causes harm significant enough to warrant the abridgment of freedom involved in its censorship. The other is that of attempting to formulate a definition of pornography. Although these issues allow distinct formulation, inquiry into them is by no means unrelated; for decisions as to the harm inflicted by a certain phenomenon and proposals to regulate that phenomenon depend in large part upon the possibility of establishing fairly specific criteria for identifying the phenomenon in question.

Defining Pornography. No one, it seems, has done much better at defining pornography than U.S. Supreme Court justice Potter Stewart, whose legally unhelpful "I know it when I see it" (in his opinion on *Jacobellis v. Ohio*, 1964) has become famous. The statement illustrates two important points concerning the meaning of the word "pornography." The first part of Stewart's statement, the claim to be able to "know" pornography, points to the belief shared by many that the term refers to a phenomenon that can be readily identified with a high degree of reliability in most cases. The second part of Stewart's statement reflects the fact that it is extremely difficult to provide a precise definition for a phenomenon that occurs in many different mediums, in many different contexts, and expresses many different themes. A further complication concerning efforts to formulate a definition for "pornography" is that the term has both descriptive and evaluative content. The core of its descriptive content is found in the notion of a "sexually explicit portrayal intended to arouse sexually." Its evaluative content is found in its pejorative force, its tendency to cast a shadow of moral condemnation upon that to which it is applied. The problem that the pejorative nature of "pornography" poses for attempts to define the term is that any descriptive definition—such as Stewart's—is likely to be found wanting insofar as its descriptive content could be applied to material that a majority find in no way morally objectionable.

Given the difficulty of formulating a definition of "pornography," jurists have generally been unwilling to establish a set of criteria for its identification. Instead, the jurisprudential term of choice in dealing with the censorship of sexually explicit material has been "obscenity," a term that courts have been willing to define. The first attempt to do so is widely thought to have occurred in Great Britain in 1868 when Chief Justice Alexander Cockburn characterized as obscene material that would tend to "deprave and corrupt those whose minds are open to such immoral influences." This, the so-called Hicklin test, was adopted into U.S. law in 1879 (in *United States v. Bennett*), but has been subjected to extensive revision and modification in subsequent cases. Accordingly, more recent characterizations of the "obscene"—such as that offered in *Miller v. California* (1973)—differ significantly from the Hicklin test; nonetheless, the concept of obscenity continues to occupy a place of special prominence in legal battles over the censorship of pornography.

While the reluctance of courts to forge a definition of pornography is not surprising, it is somewhat surprising that jurists have found "obscenity" a more promising candidate for definition. "Obscenity" no less than "pornography" has pejorative force and thus would seem open to the same problems besetting attempts to define "pornography." Some light may be shed upon the jurisprudentially preferred status of "obscenity" by attending to the fact that "obscenity," unlike "pornography," does not have a readily identifiable descriptive core. This is significant insofar as the core of descriptive meaning central to pornography might allow for the uncritical application of the term to a variety of instances that really ought to be handled with a sensitivity to the complexities of the individual case. Lacking a dominant descriptive core, the term "obscen-

Brazen promotion of pornographic pleasures, such as those promised at this New York City theater, is more common in big cities than in small communities, where antipornography pressure groups wield greater influence. (AP/Wide World Photos)

Even in large cities antipornography feeling often translates into community action, as in this scene of New York City women marching against pornography in 1979. (Betty Lane)

ity" might be deemed less prone to such abuse. Its preferred status in legal decisions might, therefore, be an attempt to guard against a mechanical application of censorship guidelines that would uncritically erode the right to free speech.

Pornography and Free Speech. Despite the difficulties involved in formulating a fully satisfactory definition of pornography, it is generally agreed that pornography involves depictions or descriptions of a sexually explicit nature. Pornography is thus traditionally viewed as a form of expression or speech. Its censorship is, consequently, widely held to be a limitation of the right to free speech, a right commonly viewed as essential to the health of a democratic society. The mere fact, however, that the censorship of pornography does constitute a limitation of the right to free speech is not typically taken as absolutely conclusive grounds for maintaining that it should not be censored, for it is widely held that the right to free speech is not absolute. The First Amendment to the U.S. Constitution, for example, has been consistently understood by the U.S. Supreme Court as not protecting certain forms of injurious speech such as the "lewd and obscene, the profane, the libelous, and the insulting or 'fighting' words" (*Chaplinsky v. New Hampshire*, 1942). Thus it is that much of the debate about the legitimacy of government regulation of pornography has focused upon the issue of whether it constitutes speech that is sufficiently harmful to justify an abridgment of the civil right of free speech.

Pornography and Harm. Harms that have been alleged to be the fruits of pornography include but are not limited to the following: physical, psychological, moral, spiritual, social, and financial. Advocates of censorship have, for instance, variously argued that the widespread availability of pornography within a society can lead to a heightened frequency of sex crimes such as rape and child abuse (physical and psychological harms), the corruption of character (moral harm), the need for medical and psychological treatment (financial harms), an erroneous conception of human fulfillment (moral, psychological, and spiritual harms), and the erosion of the family unit (social harm). In evaluating the claim that pornography is injurious, it is therefore helpful to keep in mind that the harms alleged to be produced by pornography come in guises other than the merely physical. It is also helpful to think in terms of three distinct stages at which pornography is alleged to inflict harm: production, consumption, and pornographically induced action.

Production and Harm. The activity of producing pornography has been claimed to inflict harm upon those engaged in its production. This is most obvious in the case of child pornography, which involves the immediate and direct violation of the rights of the juvenile models and actors used to produce it. Prohibition of child pornography is, accordingly, one of the least controversial cases of legitimate government censorship; however, it is worth noting that the generally accepted legitimacy of outlawing child pornography is based not so much on the fact that the depictions involved therein are reprehensible; rather, it is based on the fact that the acts performed in the production of such pornography constitute serious breaches of criminal statutes. Illustrative in this regard was the U.S. Supreme Court's rationale for upholding the conviction of an Ohio man for possession of child pornography in *Osborne v. Ohio* (1990). The state's legislation was permissible, according to the court, insofar as its intent was not to control a person's private thoughts; rather, it was to protect children who might be used in the production of child pornography by pursuing measures to eradicate the demand for such materials.

Consumption and Harm. It has also been alleged that pornography, especially of the violent and degrading varieties, inflicts psychological damage and moral corruption upon those who consume it. These harms are deemed significant enough by some to warrant paternalistic censorship, censorship that would prohibit certain forms of pornography in order to prevent individuals from making choices by which they are likely to harm themselves. Just as a government may take a paternalistic interest in the physical welfare of citizens by legally mandating the use of helmets by motorcycle operators, so too a government might prohibit those things and activities that have a clear tendency to damage the moral character and psychological health of its citizens.

Setting aside the case of child pornography, in which society's concern is usually for the welfare of the child models, not the adult consumer, it is worth noting that the harms alleged to befall the producers and consumers of pornography have generally been deemed insufficient to support legislation that would ban pornography. One reason for this is that the types of harms most frequently claimed to befall these groups are either moral or psychological, and it is very difficult to formulate any precise way of establishing the nature and extent of such harms. Moreover, while democratic governments have shown some willingness to limit behavior for paternalistic reasons, they have generally been unwilling to regulate speech on similarly paternalistic grounds. For these reasons, many of those who advocate censorship do so on the nonpaternalistic ground that pornography is an indirect source of harms insofar as it disposes those who consume it to sexually victimize members of society.

Pornographically Induced Action and Harm. Dramatic illustration of pornography's alleged capacity to inflict indirect harm is found in the testimony of some sex offenders, who report that the consumption of violent pornography played an important role in their pursuit of criminally deviant behavior. One such individual—a man who confessed to the sexual molestation and murder of five boys—gave anonymous testimony to the U.S. Attorney General's Commission on Pornography (1985-1986) that pornography had caused him to lose "all sense of decency and respect for humanity and life."

The advantage of this approach to evaluating the regulation of pornography is that many of the alleged harms are criminal violations which are routinely tracked by governments and for which there is ample statistical data. The availability of data on crimes with a sexual component has not diminished the controversy concerning the extent to which pornography contributes to the commission of such crimes. There are at least two reasons for this. The first is that the statistical data is mixed. There are studies that indicate a direct relation between the consumption of sexually explicit materials and sex crimes; however, there are also studies which show an absence of a direct relation and sometimes even an inverse relation between the two. Against advocates of censorship, the last of these correlations has been used to defend what is sometimes called the "safety valve" theory of pornographic consumption. Proponents of this theory maintain that, far from inducing criminally deviant behavior, pornography may actually reduce it, since those predisposed to such behavior can use pornography as a victimless outlet for their deviant urges.

A second reason that the availability of data on crime rates has not resolved the controversy concerning the connection between pornography and crimes of a sexual nature is the fact that a statistical correlation does not necessarily correspond to a causal connection. Even if there were a clear statistical correlation, either positive or negative, between the availability of pornographic materials and criminally deviant behavior, this would not in itself establish that there was a causal relation between the two. That a substantial proportion of sex offenders are also consumers of pornography may only reveal that the consumption of pornographic materials and the commission of sex crimes are independently caused by some third factor, such as preexisting urges of a deviant nature. Conversely, a decrease in sex crimes following an increase in the availability of pornography may have nothing to do with a safety valve and may only reflect an increase in the difficulty of convicting sex offenders in a society that has become less restrictive in its laws regarding pornographic materials.

It is also worth emphasizing that even if a compelling statistical case could be made to show that pornography does lead to a heightened incidence of crimes of a sexual nature, it does not follow that a society will or should automatically ban the offending material. On this point, it is instructive to reflect on the fact that the United States government repealed the federally mandated fifty-five mile per hour speed limit in 1995 even though there was compelling statistical evidence to show that doing so would annually result in several thousand additional automobile-related fatalities. The people, who are free, wanted to drive faster and were willing to accept the consequences.

Pornography as Behavior. In 1984 the Indianapolis city council passed a civil rights ordinance the text of which begins by defining pornography as "the graphic sexually explicit subordination of women, whether in pictures or in words." The ordinance, originally drafted by feminists Catharine MacKinnon and Andrea Dworkin, then proceeds to list six kinds of sexually explicit portrayals of women that would constitute a violation of the civil rights of women. What is especially noteworthy about this ordinance is its characterization of pornography as the "subordination of women," a characterization that classifies pornography as behavior, not speech, and thereby removes the obstacle to regulating pornography imposed by the First Amendment. Ultimately, the ordinance was deemed unconstitutional by the Seventh U.S.

Circuit Court of Appeals, which ruled that the attempt to redefine pornography as a form of behavior was unconvincing and amounted to legal "sleight of hand" (*Hudnut v. American Booksellers Association, Inc.*, 1986). It is also worth noting that the MacKinnon-Dworkin attempt legally to prohibit pornography has itself been subjected to feminist critiques, which maintain that the practice of censorship has traditionally done significantly more to hurt than help the cause of women's rights. —*James Petrik*

See also *American Booksellers Association, Inc. v. Hudnut*; Attorney General's Commission on Pornography; Dworkin, Andrea; MacKinnon, Catharine A.; *Miller v. California*; Obscenity: legal definitions; Pornography, child; Women Against Pornography.

BIBLIOGRAPHY

The Invention of Pornography, edited by Lynn Hunt (New York: Zone Books, 1993) is an excellent collection of essays that traces the origins of the modern concept of pornography through the key phases of its development from 1500 to 1800. For a history of the regulation of pornography, an excellent resource is the *Final Report of the Attorney General's Commission on Pornography* (Washington, D.C.: U.S. Department of Justice, 1986). This report, compiled under the direction of U.S. Attorney General Edwin Meese III, is also one of the most comprehensive sources on pornography available. Susan Dwyer's *The Problem of Pornography* (Belmont, Calif.: Wadsworth Publishing, 1995) is a collection of influential essays on pornography that also includes a synopses of significant developments in Canadian and U.S. law. Of particular note are the essays by Andrea Dworkin and Catharine MacKinnon, advocates of feminist antipornography legislation. *Defending Pornography* by Nadine Strossen (New York: Scribner's, 1995) is an extended feminist critique of the antipornography legislation proposed by Dworkin and MacKinnon. An anthology noteworthy because of the balance of its selections is *Pornography: Private Right or Public Menace?* edited by Robert M. Baird and Stuart E. Rosenbaum (Buffalo, N.Y.: Prometheus Books, 1991).

Pornography, child

DEFINITION: Photographs, films, and other depictions of children engaged in sexual acts, of their genitalia

SIGNIFICANCE: Using children for pornographic purposes has been almost completely banned throughout the developed world

Child pornography has long been popular in some cultures. In England, for example, child pornography in art was popular in both the Romantic and Victorian eras. In France, it was briefly popular in the Neo-Classical period. In Scandinavian countries, considerable child pornography has been produced un-

New York City theater marquees reflect the strong appeal of child pornography. (AP/Wide World Photos)

derground. Artwork from eras before the late twentieth century has undergone revisionist criticism—from ancient Roman frescoes that are blatantly pornographic, to the work of modern photographers, including author Lewis Carroll. Most of this work is "grandfathered," however, that is, considered to be historical and not created for lascivious purposes.

Child pornography became a public issue in the 1970's, when various states in the United States began to revise their sex codes to define child abuse. Much of the discussion about child pornography originated in considerations of child abuse and the use of children who were runaways. Several important reports on the subject have linked child pornography with child prostitution, and several states have adopted separate statutes for such crimes. In 1977 a federal statute for child pornography was under consideration in the U.S. Congress. As law enforcement agencies encountered more and more runaways, and as social service agencies began to provide aid to their child clients, it was becoming clear that a significant number of children were being used for sexual purposes in the production of photographs, magazines, and films.

Allegations developed that organized crime was heavily involved in the production and distribution of child pornography, just as it was involved in adult prostitution. Meanwhile, the pornography exhibiting children disappeared from open markets as rumors of a federal statute began to circulate. Taking its place were depictions by young adults who seemed even younger, since the demand for such pornography had not been satiated. An Illinois legislative investigating commission issued a lengthy report on this subject, concluding that organized crime was not involved in the child pornography industry. The pornography that was available was coming from other sources.

Sources of Child Pornography. One of the easiest ways that child pornography was entering Western countries, such as the United States, Canada, Great Britain, and France, was through mail sent from Denmark. Also, since the end of the Vietnam War, several countries in Southeast Asia have become known for their sex industries. In Thailand, visitors could purchase time with young children to take pictures or make videos. To some extent sanctioned by their governments, Sri Lanka, the Philippines, Taiwan, Thailand, and Brazil have become notorious as producers of child pornography. Tours to these countries are arranged by organizations in the United States. U.S. police cannot eliminate such organizations; they can only monitor them, and they can do nothing when their members leave the country.

U.S. Law. In the United States, child pornography has been an issue in numerous court cases at all jurisdictional levels. Two of the best-known cases are *New Yorker v. Ferber*, a circuit court case, and *Osborne v. Ohio* (1990), a state supreme court case. Both involved freedom of expression, the other side of the child pornography definition. Finally, issues regarding parental rights to one's own children have also been litigated at all levels. Drafters of the federal statute wrestled with the language the new law would use. For example, mere nudity could not be considered pornographic. All agreed, however, that a child could be regarded as being involved in pornography without having to commit an actual sex act—especially children whose genitalia were showing. Child pornography presents a number of problems. One is to what extent parents, photographers, or other artists have the right to free expression in the production of art or personal representations of their own children.

In the last decade of the twentieth century, child pornography was being produced in Western countries by many people, some of whom were linked through the mails or with computers. They were easy for law enforcement officers to catch, as were those receiving child pornography from abroad. The most alarming trend in this area was the sanctioning by entire countries of the use of children for sexual purposes.

—*John Jacob*

See also Child Pornography Law; Customs laws, U.S.; Nudity; Photographic film processing; Pornography; Postal regulations; Sade, Marquis de.

Bibliography

C. David Baker's "Preying on Playgrounds: The Sexploitation of Children in Pornography and Prostitution" (*Pepperdine Law Review* 5, 1978, pp. 809-846) presents a primer for the reader first coming to these subjects, and the article's point of view is that children are stalked and preyed upon in this country. *The Report of the Commission on Obscenity and Pornography* (New York: Bantam Books, 1970) presents a broad overview of issues, but sections specifically talk about history and recommendations concerning child pornography. Joyce Greller's paperback book *Young Hookers* (New York: Dell, 1976) is a study of child and adolescent prostitutes that finds a common exposure to child pornography, child molestation, or both. Well worth reading is David Hechler's *The Battle and the Backlash: The Child Sexual Abuse War* (Lexington, Mass.: Lexington Books, 1988), a treatise on all elements of the various pornographic uses to which children are put.

Portnoy's Complaint

Type of work: Book

Published: 1969

Author: Philip Roth (1933-   )

Subject matter: Novel about a young Jewish man's obsession with sex

Significance: Censored primarily because of its comic treatment of masturbation, this best-selling novel helped to extend the limits of what is considered permissible in literature by treating a formerly taboo subject masterfully

Portnoy's Complaint, a long monologue narrated by a young Jewish man while in analysis, is prefaced by a definition of "Portnoy's Complaint" as a disorder in which "strongly felt ethical and altruistic impulses are perpetually warring with extreme sexual longings, often of a perverse nature." The book focuses on Portnoy's parents, his endless adolescent experimentation with masturbation, his youthful sexual encounters with girls, his varied sexual experiences with a model named Monkey, and his pilgrimage to Israel—all of which are punctuated by frequently obscene outcries against the guilt he feels for his sexual obsessions. Roth, who has defended himself and the book many times, claims it is full of dirty words because

Richard Benjamin (right) plays Philip Roth's sexually confused Portnoy in the 1972 film. (Museum of Modern Art/Film Stills Archive)

Portnoy wants to be free: "I wanted to raise obscenity to the level of a subject."

The book became a *cause célèbre* in 1969, commented on by social critics and stand-up comedians alike. Most objections to it came from Jewish groups and rabbis who called it "anti-Semitic" and "self-hating" and protested against libraries that put it on their shelves. It was seized in Australia in 1970 and 1971 by Melbourne officials, who filed obscenity charges against it and the bookseller who sold it.

See also Australia; Judaism; Libraries; Literature; Newspapers; Sex in the arts.

Postage stamps

DEFINITION: Government-issued adhesive or imprinted designs affixed to mail to indicate payment of postal charges

SIGNIFICANCE: Typically designed to commemorate persons and events, or to celebrate ideas, postage stamps have often been targets of both private and government censors

Most designs on postage stamps are reviewed by government advisory committees before the stamps are issued to the public. In the United States a twelve-to-sixteen-member body called the Citizens' Stamp Advisory Committee reviews stamp designs; it recommends subjects for postage stamps to the postmaster general and approves or disapproves the art work for each. All countries that participate in the Universal Postal Union have similar arrangements.

Occasionally an advisory committee approves a stamp design that becomes the subject of protests or censorship after the stamp is printed and released. Protests against stamp designs have ranged from objections to nudity to complaints about political, religious, and commercial content. In the United States, for example, a public outcry arose in 1887 when a stamp depicting the female figure of Liberty was issued. This stamp had been approved and printed before someone publicly noticed that Liberty's breasts were uncovered. The stamp was then redesigned with draping over Liberty's chest. During the 1930's a Dallas, Texas, stamp dealer was jailed for exhibiting in his store window French stamps with reproductions of famous French paintings, including several depicting nude women.

In February, 1952, the U.S. Post Office issued a three-cent stamp featuring the Baltimore & Ohio Railroad in a design commemorating the 125th anniversary of American rail transportation. This ostensibly harmless design provoked a law suit by a Pennsylvania trucking company requesting an injunction against the stamp because, it alleged, the stamp would unlawfully advertise one of its competitors. Production of the stamp was suspended and the matter was discussed on the floor of Congress. A federal judge eventually dismissed the case on the grounds that "it is not for the Courts to interfere in matters entrusted by Congress to the discretion of executive officers." Nevertheless, this incident had a clear impact on later commemorative stamps. Stamps commemorating the poultry, trucking, and automobile industries of the 1950's, for example, are known as "phantom" stamps because their designers carefully blended models into generic designs in order to avoid the appearance of the government's favoring any particular commercial companies.

In 1994, the U.S. government was pressured into suppressing a stamp designed to commemorate the fiftieth anniversary of the end of World War II. That stamp depicted the dropping of the atomic bomb on Hiroshima, Japan; news of its forthcoming release raised an outcry from both the Japanese government and members of the U.S. Congress. Eventually the stamp was replaced by one depicting Harry S Truman, who had been president of the United States at the end of the war.

See also Advertising as the target of censorship; Art; Nudity.

Postal regulations

DEFINITION: Laws regulating the fees and conditions for delivery of mail

SIGNIFICANCE: Because the mails have long been a key form of communicating printed materials they have been prime targets for censorship

Modern postal services owe their origins at least partially to the government urge to control the flow of information. In the sixteenth and seventeenth centuries, European governments gradually assumed control of postal delivery, both for the income to be derived from providing such service and out of a desire to have closer oversight of information flowing through their realms. Oversight of the mails has generally encouraged government officials to concern themselves with the contents of the materials transported by their postal services. The urge to censor and suppress mail traffic in particular items or ideas has sometimes proceeded from the perception that government was somehow complicitous with the originators of noxious items if it allowed its mails to be tainted with objectionable materials. Even without this sense of moral partnership as a source of censorial zeal, however, government officials have constantly been ready to use government monopoly of the mail to control traffic in particular items or ideas.

Nonmailable Matter Laws. In the United States, the chief source of power within the postal service to censor speech has lain in the variety of nonmailable-matter provisions that Congress has enacted over the past two centuries. Not all such laws were attempts to regulate the content of expression, however. The earliest nonmailable provision, enacted by Congress in 1797, was one preventing newspapers from depositing their papers in the mail for delivery before the ink on them had dried adequately. Other nonmailable provisions have concerned themselves with harmful objects of one sort or another. For example, a law enacted in 1872 banned articles such as explosives or poisons that might damage the postal service itself, and one passed in 1927 classified as nonmailable weapons that were capable of being concealed. Usually, however, when Congress has undertaken to declare specific materials unfit for the mails, it has targeted expression in one form or another. In 1865, for example, Congress declared obscene materials nonmailable—a provision that has remained intact, with minor revisions, since that time. Other nonmailable matters have included lottery tickets, which were banned in 1890; films or other graphic representations of prize fights, banned in 1912; writings advocating treason or forcible resistance to United States law, banned in 1917; and information relating to obtaining foreign divorces, banned in 1939.

The U.S. Post Office and Slavery. The first major attempt in the United States to use control of the mail as a form of censorship occurred under the shadow of the slavery controversy in the nineteenth century. In 1835 a newly formed antislavery society began a vigorous campaign of mailing abolitionist literature. Southern postal offices were inundated with abolitionist tracts, which many Southerners believed would land in the hands of slaves and lead to their violent revolt. The U.S. postmaster general, with the concurrence of President Andrew Jackson, informed postal officers that they need not deliver the tracts, except to those who had specifically subscribed to them. President Jackson suggested, in fact, that postmasters would do well to publish lists of any persons subscribing to the abolitionist papers and, by bringing them into disrepute, to discourage people from subscribing to such materials. Jackson also urged Congress to enact laws banning materials from the mail that were likely to incite slaves to riot. Although Congress ultimately declined to regulate the mails in the fashion sought by Jackson, several Southern states enacted laws in the 1830's criminalizing the mailing of "incendiary" or "inflammatory" (that is, "antislavery") writings.

Obscenity and the Mail. As early as 1865 Congress banned obscene books and publications from the mail, though without prescribing penalties for violations of the law. Not until a few years later, however, did the problem of obscenity in the mail gain prominence, thanks to the efforts of Anthony Comstock, who complained that men were being ruined by pornography. In association with a New York chapter of the YMCA Comstock engaged in his own private war against obscenity. In the early 1870's he determined to take his private war public, and he persuaded Congress to pass a law in 1873 that added stiff penalties to the previously enacted obscenity provisions, and which included in its nonmailable provisions a new prohibition against mailing items used to prevent conception or to procure abortions. That same year Comstock obtained a commission for himself as an enforcement agent for the Post Office. In the years following, he was a vigorous proponent and enforcer of nonmailable matter laws.

Since 1865 the U.S. Post Office—and its successor, the Postal Service—has wielded the provision relating to nonmailable obscenity in its various incarnations to censor many books regarded as serious literature. Books deemed nonmailable by the Post Office have included such classic works as Aristophanes' *Lysistrata* and Geoffrey Chaucer's *Canterbury Tales*, as well as the works of modern authors including Victor Hugo, Honoré de Balzac, Oscar Wilde, Ernest Hemingway,

Eugene O'Neill, D. H. Lawrence, John Steinbeck, William Faulkner, and F. Scott Fitzgerald. Curiously, books such as John O'Hara's *Appointment in Samarra* and Hemingway's *For Whom the Bell Tolls* could not traverse the mails, even though these books were displayed openly in bookstores around the country. As the decades of the twentieth century passed, however, the postmaster general's power to suppress literary works because of their asserted obscenity crumbled before a federal judiciary increasingly hostile to these claims. For example, in 1959 a publisher finally released in the United States an unexpurgated version of D. H. Lawrence's *Lady Chatterley's Lover*. The postmaster general responded by seizing copies of the book and labeling obscene not only the book but advertising circulars put out by the book club. A federal district judge presented with the case disagreed with the postmaster general's determination, and an appellate court sided with his order overturning the postmaster general's ban. Eventually, the Supreme Court removed a great deal of the bite of the nonmailable obscenity provision through its evolving definition of obscenity. In 1973 the Court held, in *Miller v. California*, that obscenity included only those works that the average person—applying community standards—would regard as appealing on the whole to prurient interest; such works would depict sexual conduct in a patently offensive manner, and, on the whole, lack any serious literary, artistic, political, or scientific value.

Fraud and the Mail. Beginning in 1872 Congress declared nonmailable various written materials intended to carry out fraudulent enterprises. By this original law, the postmaster general was authorized to issue a fraud order to a local postmaster forbidding payments on money orders drawn to firms engaged in fraud and to command the postmaster to return registered letters addressed to these firms to their original post offices with the word "Fraudulent" stamped on them. Over the years following this original provision, the Post Office Department retained significant power to frustrate the attempts of various schemers to further their fraudulent activities through the mail. Perhaps the most famous of these schemes to reach the U.S. Supreme Court was the one at issue in *Donaldson v. Read Magazine, Inc.*, decided in 1948. *Read Magazine* ran a series of puzzle contests during the 1940's that the postmaster general determined were actually elaborate schemes to separate puzzle enthusiasts from their money. Contestants were called upon to solve a series of puzzles, with an entry fee of a few dollars for each series. Since the puzzles were easily solved, contestants found themselves constantly advancing forward to a new round of puzzles and a new entry fee. The contest's final device for separating winners from the remaining contestants was to require submission of essays and award prizes to the authors of the best essays. When the postmaster general issued a fraud order against the magazine, the magazine brought suit claiming that this action violated numerous constitutional provisions, including the First Amendment's guarantee of free speech. The Supreme Court disagreed, however, finding that the postmaster general's determination of fraud was amply supported by the evidence, and concluding that protections against fraudulent uses of the mails were too deeply planted in the country's history to be uprooted by *Read Magazine*'s attempt to cloak itself in the sheltering folds of the First Amendment.

Postal Rates and Censorship. In 1874 Congress expanded the Post Office Department's power to regulate expression by authorizing it to grant lower, second-class mailing rates to certain newspapers and magazines that were devoted to literature, science, or the arts, or that were otherwise designed to advance "dissemination of information of a public character." Postmasters routinely used this power during the closing years of the nineteenth century and the first half of the twentieth century to reward or punish particular publications. During World War I, second-class rates were denied to several socialist papers, and a number of periodicals deemed by the postmaster general objectionable earned a similar treatment during World War II.

The use of the second-class mailing privilege to censor speech had its most famous illustration in a case involving *Esquire* magazine. *Esquire* had originally gained second-class mailing privileges in 1933, but the postmaster general challenged this privilege in the mid-1940's, alleging that *Esquire* was devoted neither to literature, nor science, nor the arts, and was not otherwise designed to advance "dissemination of information of a public character"; instead it was regularly filled with "smoking room" humor—that is, humor about sex. When its second-class rate was revoked in 1944, *Esquire* brought suit in a federal district court and eventually found an audience for its grievance with the U.S. Supreme Court. In *Hannegan v. Esquire* (1946), a unanimous Court found that the postmaster general had essentially censored *Esquire* not on the basis of whether it was about literature or art or some other information of public character, but simply because he had determined the periodical to be "bad." The American system of government, said the Court, was intended to oversee the widest variety of tastes and opinions, and—so long as material was not actually obscene—the postmaster general had no authority to enforce his own tastes upon the American people. *—Timothy L. Hall*

See also Abolitionist movement; Comstock, Anthony; Comstock Act of 1873; *Lady Chatterley's Lover*; *Miller v. California*; Nonmailable matter laws; Postage stamps; Sedition; Sex in the arts.

BIBLIOGRAPHY

Dorothy Ganfield Fowler's *Unmailable: Congress and the Post Office* (Athens: University of Georgia Press, 1977) offers an excellent historical account of the development of nonmailable matter laws in the United States. For a similar, though older account, which focuses on mail censorship from the late nineteenth century through the first half of the twentieth century, see *Federal Censorship: Obscenity in the Mail* by James C. N. Paul and Murray L. Schwartz (New York: Free Press of Glencoe, 1961). Wayne E. Fuller's *The American Mail: Enlarger of the Common Life* (Chicago: University of Chicago Press, 1972) and Gerald Cullinan's *The Post Office Department* (New York: Praeger, 1968) are historical surveys of the U.S. Post Office that include some discussion of censorship matters. *Confederate Postal History*, edited by Francis J. Crown, Jr. (Lawrence, Mass.: Quarterman Publication, 1976), is an older work that includes a brief but interesting chapter on Confederate censorship of southbound mail during the Civil War. *Governing Global Networks: International Regimes for Transportation and Communications*, by Mark W. Zacher with Brent A. Sutton (Cambridge, England: Cambridge University Press, 1996), contains a helpful chapter on modern international postal arrangements.

Presidency, U.S.

Definition: Head of state and of government of the U.S. federal government

Significance: Since the founding of the republic, chief executives have wrested with the question of how they should exercise their powers while also protecting the free exchange of information

Supreme Court Justice Potter Stewart once suggested that the Founders of the United States, suspicious of traditional organs of government, expected the nation's press to serve as "a fourth institution outside the government." Thus, the news media, from the early years of the republic, sought to play a special role, battling power hungry presidents and congresses. As Stewart explained, the press placed "an additional check" on the three official branches of government, which too often restricted basic freedoms. In their struggle with strong-willed government officials, the news media could depend on the U.S. Constitution as a bulwark against censorship and attacks prompted by the other branches of government.

Jefferson and the Press. Despite the wishes of the Constitution's framers and the strength of the First Amendment, presidents have historically viewed the press—and the freedoms demanded by the media—with wariness and, at times, outright hostility. This is especially evident in the transformation of the generally enlightened Thomas Jefferson. Before being elected president, Jefferson said: "Were it left to me to decide whether we should have a government without newspapers or newspapers without a government, I should not hesitate a moment to prefer the latter." After eight years of press criticism, however, Jefferson's defense of the "fourth institution outside our government" turned sour. The media's close examination of Jefferson's bold use of executive authority to purchase the Louisiana Territory, partisan bickering among Federalists and Jefferson's Democratic-Republican allies, questions about Vice President Aaron Burr's western exploits, Jefferson's advocacy of the economically ruinous Embargo Act, his pursuit of North Africa's Barbary pirates, his unorthodox religious beliefs, and his defense of a broad interpretation of executive privilege all caused Jefferson's views. He said that "the abuses of freedom of the press have been carried to a length never before known or borne by any civilized nation." He added bitterly, "Nothing can now be believed which is seen in a newspaper." While Jefferson did not actually suggest censorship, he considered the media to be an unworthy branch of government; presidents and their actions should be shielded from the prying eyes of inquisitive journalists.

Presidents and the press are by their very natures symbiotic, but also adversarial as they define each other's territory. They might need each other for promotional purposes but they can often abhor one another. Honeymoons between the two quickly deteriorate, amid charges of censorship and lust for power, into acrimonious divorces. Nowhere are the tensions in the president-press relationship better illustrated than during times of national conflict.

Lincoln and His Critics. During the Civil War, President Abraham Lincoln was unwavering in his determination to triumph on the battlefield and restore the union. Loosely interpreting his role as commander-in-chief, he suspended three hundred newspapers for "treason" or "disloyalty." One thousand people were arrested as Lincoln trampled on the Bill of Rights and censored the flow of information. In February, 1862, telegraph lines were placed under White House control. Federal officials seized the *Chicago Times* and the Philadelphia *Christian Observer*. One of Lincoln's critics, Ohio newspaper editor Edson Olds, was arrested and imprisoned for raising questions about the president's conduct of the war. While in jail, Olds was nominated to the Ohio legislature; he won and was released. Similarly, Philadelphia journalist Albert Broilean was imprisoned for criticizing Lincoln's 1862 State of the Union speech. After Broilean apologized to Lincoln, he gained his freedom. Suspending *habeas corpus*, censoring the press, and jailing outspoken journalists were, in Lincoln's opinion, sometimes permissible in times of what he called "extraordinary insurrection." Occasionally, arrest and incarceration were deemed insufficient in silencing press opposition. Clement Laird Vallandigham, co-owner of the *Dayton Empire*, was arrested by order of General Ambrose E. Burnside. At Lincoln's insistence, Vallandigham was transported behind Confederate lines and abandoned.

Few presidents suffered more from editorial abuse than Lincoln. Opposition editors and disappointed favor-seekers accused him in print of vicious deeds, which the patient president usually ignored. He was falsely accused of drawing his salary in gold bars, while his soldiers were paid in deflated greenbacks. He was charged with drunkenness while making crucial decisions, with granting pardons to secure votes, and with needless butchering of armies as a result of his lust for victories. Once he was accused of outright treason. Typical of his press detractors was the *La Crosse Democrat*, a Wisconsin weekly, which said of the draft: "Lincoln has called for 500,000 more victims."

On balance, however, Lincoln resisted the temptation to censor—or exile—his multitude of critics. Most of the punitive measures were taken not by the president but by military commanders such as General Burnside. For example, when Wilbur Storey, publisher of the *Chicago Times* questioned Lincoln's authority to issue the Emancipation Proclamation, Burnside ordered the newspaper padlocked. After a three-day cooling off period, Lincoln rescinded Burnside's military order. When put to the test, Lincoln thus defended the First Amendment and usually permitted the press to voice its criticism.

The Early Twentieth Century. By the beginning of the twentieth century, the executive branch's willingness to control the flow of information had increased. as William McKinley used the yellow journalism of the *New York World* and the

New York Journal to marshal public support for war with Spain. Similarly, Theodore Roosevelt grasped the fact that muckraking magazines such as *Collier's* and *Cosmopolitan*, could be useful tools in exposing unsanitary and unethical business practices. Thus, presidents and the media could at times form partnerships which aided both.

When America entered World War I in April, 1917, President Woodrow Wilson appointed a former newspaper editor, George Creel, to head the Committee on Public Information, a newly formed propaganda and censorship agency. Creel's management of domestic news censorship was based on a set of regulations prepared by the State, War, and Navy departments before the United States entered the war. These regulations, which the press voluntarily accepted, prohibited publication of such things as troop movements in the United States, ship sailings, and the identification of units being sent overseas.

However, the reporting of significant negative developments in the war were delayed because the War Department feared that such stories would damage the nation's confidence in the war effort. Reporters who published stories without clearing them had their credentials revoked and their access to battle fronts was restricted. At first, reporters could not visit the front lines. Gradually, these restrictions were lifted and accredited correspondents could even live among the troops.

During World War II, total military censorship prevailed. Every thing written, photographed, or broadcast was scrutinized by censors. Photographs of dead American soldiers were censored. Anything that did not meet the high command's consideration was deleted. Accreditation was used to enforce censorship. Correspondents were not allowed in the theaters of war unless they were accredited, and one of the conditions of accreditation was that the correspondent sign an agreement to submit all his copy to military or naval censorship. In some cases, heavy censorship distorted the news. For example, military censors refused to allow any mention of possible radiation effects of the atomic bombs dropped on Japan for three weeks after the August 1945 detonations.

Meanwhile, President Franklin D. Roosevelt created the Office of Censorship with Byron Price as its chief on December 18, 1941, pursuant to the War Powers Act. However, the Office of Censorship could only issue guidelines relevant to domestic news censorship.

The Late Twentieth Century. World War II was the last in which total military censorship prevailed. The change in the media-military relationship began during the Korean War, when what censorship that did occur was largely imposed at the source by senior officers. In December, 1950, General Douglas MacArthur's headquarters imposed full censorship, forbidding "any criticism of the Allied conduct of the war or 'any derogatory comments' about United Nations troops or commanders." General MacArthur expelled some seventeen correspondents from Japan for criticizing his policies. Censorship in Korea reportedly was so political in tone and so rigidly enforced that covert efforts were made by some reporters to avoid it.

During the Cuban missile crisis in the fall of 1962 reporters were not allowed to go on ships or planes deployed into the Caribbean to quarantine Cuba. The U.S. Naval base on Guantanamo, Cuba, was also closed to reporters during the midst of the crisis in October-November, 1962.

During the Vietnam War, reporters could travel relatively freely and combat coverage was not done by pools of reporters with military escort. In Vietnam, there were ground rules for press coverage designed to protect the security of military operations, and correspondents who violated those rules could have their press credentials lifted. But there was no formal security review or censorship. Nevertheless, censorship at the source reached its apogee in the Vietnam War. Reporters who did not have the trust of senior officers were given little information—especially as public support of the war evaporated.

Later President Richard M. Nixon's pursuit of leaks in his administration destroyed his presidency. During the Reagan Administration's 1983 invasion of Grenada, the Pentagon refused to let journalists accompany the invasion force or allow any journalist to travel to Grenada. At one point, four journalists reportedly were held incommunicado by the U.S. military. A defense industry journalist commented: "A dramatic chapter in history has gone unrecorded by objective newsmen because this administration chose a course that never was undertaken in the Civil War, World War I, World War II, and Korea. It kept reporters out of the action." Another journalist wrote: "The decision to deny access to press, radio and television reporters during the early stages of last October's operation in Grenada ran against the course not only of military precedent but of a history of considerable media freedom in covering American military conflicts that dates back to the Civil War. A lawsuit challenging the press restrictions was dismissed as moot when the invasion ended.

Ronald Reagan's direction of press access during the invasion of Grenada was expanded less than a decade later by President George Bush. After asserting to the U.S. Congress his constitutional powers to commit American troops, Bush instructed a tightly controlled system of press access to report events in the Middle East. On January 7, 1991, nine days before the Persian Gulf War began, a report in *The New York Times* complained that the Pentagon was imposing on journalists stricter restrictions than had been used during the Vietnam War. According to the *Times*, Pentagon officials justified the use of pools of reporters by "logistical difficulties in providing access to rapid American military operations." They justified security reviews on the ground that "tactical information useful to the enemy could be disseminated so quickly that it might endanger American operations."

In opposition to the press restrictions, the *Times* quoted Fred S. Hoffman, a former Pentagon spokesman, as saying that the press restrictions constitute "censorship by the Government and could be abused to protect the military from criticism or embarrassment." This charge raised the question of the extent to which the First Amendment's guarantee of freedom of the press permitted the government to impose restrictions on the press in wartime.

Press restrictions and clashes between the media and chief executives have occurred for over two centuries. Civil libertarians such as Jefferson have defended, even when they were the target of media scrutiny, the maintenance of a free and uncensored press. However, wars had repeatedly strained the unmolested flow of information, threatening the guarantees of the First Amendment. —*Joseph Edward Lee*

See also Bush, George; Civil War, U.S.; Congress, U.S.; Grenada, U.S. invasion of; Jefferson, Thomas; Kennedy, John F., assassination of; Korean War; Panama, U.S. invasion of; Persian Gulf War; Reagan, Ronald; Spanish-American War; Vietnam War.

Bibliography

For an old, but nonetheless thorough, analysis of the sometimes rocky relationship between chief executives and journalists, see James E. Pollard, *The Presidents and the Press* (New York: Macmillan, 1947). Philip Knightley's *The First Casualty* (New York: Harcourt, Brace, 1975) is a good introduction to the subject of press freedom during wartime. William Manchester, *The Glory and the Dream* (Boston: Little, Brown, 1973), is a readable examination of society during the period of FDR to Nixon. Major works placing individual presidents and their conceptions of the First Amendment into context include Stephen B. Oats' *With Malice Toward None: The Life of Abraham Lincoln* (New York: Harper and Row, 1977), Garry Wills' *Reagan's America: Innocents at Home* (Garden City, N.Y.: Doubleday, 1987), Wills' *Nixon Agonistes: The Crisis of the Self-Made Man* (Boston: Houghton Mifflin, 1979), and William Leuchtenburg's *In the Shadow of FDR: From Harry Truman to Bill Clinton* (Ithaca, N.Y.: Cornell University Press, 1994). Garry Wills's *Reagan's America* (Garden City, N.Y.: Doubleday, 1987) treats the Reagan Revolution's effect on society. In *Nightmare: The Underside of the Nixon Years* (New York: Viking Press, 1976), J. Anthony Lukas takes a troubling look at the paranoia that swirled around Richard Nixon.

President's Commission on Obscenity and Pornography

Date: October, 1967-September, 1970

Place: Washington, D.C.

Significance: This body created by Congress was the first federal commission seriously to study traffic in sexually explicit materials and its effects on people

Finding traffic in obscenity and pornography to be a matter of national concern, Congress passed Public Law 90-100 in October, 1967, creating an advisory council to study and recommend effective means for dealing with the problem. In 1968 President Lyndon B. Johnson appointed seventeen members to the commission. Congress specified four tasks for the Commission: to analyze laws controlling pornography and obscenity and to propose definitions of the latter, to determine the volume and distribution patterns of traffic in obscenity and pornography, to study the effects of pornography and obscenity, and to recommend appropriate action for controlling the traffic in such materials, consistent with respecting constitutional rights.

The commission noted the ambiguities surrounding the terms "obscenity" and "pornography" and their cognates. It avoided using "pornography" in descriptive contexts in its report, instead referring to the subject by expressions such as "explicit sexual materials" and "sexually oriented materials." The commission confined its attention to sexual obscenity. Also, given the common usage of the term "obscenity" in the law, the commission opted to apply that term only to legally prohibited sexual materials.

The commission did a survey of existing federal and state obscenity laws, a comparative study of obscenity laws in other countries, and a review of constitutional law pertaining to obscenity. It found that although the Supreme Court had held that obscene materials did not enjoy general protection under the First Amendment, grave difficulties attended the defining of "obscenity' in clear and practically useful terms. Federal and state statutes relied heavily on the so-called Roth test, which defined the obscene according to the three key, but problematic, elements of prurient interest, offensiveness, and lack of social value.

In its examination of the commercial traffic in obscenity and pornography, the commission observed the difficulty of determining with precision the size and scope of the industry. It claimed that the commercial market in sexually oriented materials was far smaller than many had estimated. It also discovered that there was no monolithic industry but rather several distinct markets and submarkets.

The commission developed a research program on the effects of exposure to explicit sexual materials. It used surveys, controlled experiments, and other empirical studies to explore how such exposure affected attitudes, aggressive behavior, and delinquency. The main and most significant conclusion tentatively drawn was that empirical research to date shows no evidence "that exposure to sexually explicit materials plays a significant role in the delinquent or criminal behavior among youth or adults."

Based primarily on this conclusion, a majority of commissioners recommended the repeal of all federal, state, and local legislation prohibiting the sale, exhibition, or distribution of sexual materials to consenting adults. It did recommend continued legislation restricting sale to young persons and regulating public display and unsolicited mailing. It discussed methods of dealing with explicit sexual material other than legal control, including sex education and organized citizen action. There were a number of separate statements by commission members, and a minority report issued by commissioners Morton Hill and Winfrey Link, which deemed the majority report "a Magna Carta for the pornographer." President Richard Nixon rejected the major recommendation of the report. The Supreme Court, headed by Chief Justice Warren Burger, issued a number of obscenity decisions in 1973 that showed no sign of influence by the report.

The report is nevertheless regarded as significant because it was the summary of one of the first systematic studies of the effects of obscenity and pornography undertaken. Social scientists perceive the findings as important but limited, in part because of the focus on nonviolent sexually explicit material. Feminist critics question the alleged harmlessness of pornography, especially given the violent, degrading, and misogynist character of much of the pornography that appeared starting in the early 1970's.

See also Attorney General's Commission on Pornography; Obscenity: legal definitions; Obscenity: sale and possession.

CENSORSHIP

List of Entries by Category

Subject headings used in list

BROADCASTING

BUSINESS AND ECONOMICS

CANADA

CENSORSHIP TOOLS

COURT CASES

DRAMA AND THEATER

EDUCATION

FAMILY AND SEXUALITY

FILM

FILMS

Amants, Les
And God Created Woman
Basic Instinct
Birth of a Nation, The
Blue Velvet
Caligula
Carnal Knowledge
Citizen Kane
Deep Throat
Ecstasy
Exorcist, The
Freaks
Front, The
Garden of Eden, The
I Am Curious—Yellow
King Kong
Kiss, The
Last Tango in Paris
Life and Death of Colonel Blimp, The
M
Man with the Golden Arm, The
Miracle, The
Mohammed, Messenger of God
Moon Is Blue, The
Naked Amazon
Natural Born Killers
Outlaw, The
Pinky
Pulp Fiction
Ronde, La
Titicut Follies
Who's Afraid of Virginia Woolf?
Wild Bunch, The

FORMS OF EXPRESSION

Advocacy
Armbands and buttons
Assembly, right of
Biography
Book publishing
Bumper stickers
Defamation
Draft-card burning
Draft resistance
Euphemism
Fighting words
Flag burning
Free speech
Hoaxes
Intellectual freedom
Leafletting
Libel
License plates, customized
Literature
Loyalty oaths
Marching and parading
Obscenity: legal definitions
Offensive language
Picketing
Pledge of Allegiance
Poetry
Political campaigning
Pressure groups
Privileged communication
Propaganda
Roman à clef
Slander
Street oratory
Symbolic speech
Translation
Unprotected speech
Wall posters

GOVERNMENT AND POLITICS

Abortion gag rule
Advocacy
Assembly, right of
Attorney General's Commission on Pornography
Books and obscenity law
Central Intelligence Agency
Chapultepec Declaration
Chilling effect
Civil service
Classification of information
Clear and present danger doctrine
Communism
Community standards
Congress, U.S.
Courtrooms
Courts and censorship law
Criminal syndicalism laws
Criminal trials
Culture ministries
Defamation
Democracy
Demonstrations
Draft-card burning
Draft resistance
Espionage
Examiner of plays
Federal Bureau of Investigation
Fighting words
Free speech
Gag order
House Committee on Un-American Activities
Judicial publication bans (Canadian)
Libel
Lord Chamberlain
Loyalty oaths
Marching and parading
Master of the Revels
National Endowment for the Arts
National Endowment for the Humanities
National security
Obscenity: legal definitions
Office of Censorship, U.S.
Pledge of Allegiance
Police
Police states
Political campaigning
Presidency, U.S.
President's Commission on Obscenity and Pornography
President's Task Force on Communications Policy
Pressure groups
Prior restraint
Prisons
Privileged communication
Propaganda
Right of reply
Sedition
Symbolic speech
Terrorism
United States Information Agency
Unprotected speech
Witnesses, protection of

HISTORICAL EVENTS AND ERAS

Abolitionist movement
Alexandria library
Armenian genocide
Athens, ancient
Basque separatism
Bay of Pigs invasion
Bhopal disaster
Chernobyl disaster
Chicago Art Institute furors
Civil Rights movement
Civil War, U.S.
Colonialism
Crimean War
Crop-ears
Cultural Revolution, Chinese
Dead Sea Scrolls
Defense ("D") notices
Degenerate Art Exhibition
Democratic National Convention of 1968
English Commonwealth
Falkland Islands War
First Hemispheric Conference on Free Expression
Free Speech Movement
Greek junta
Grenada, U.S. invasion of
"H-Bomb Secret, The"
Holocaust, Jewish
Iran-Contra scandal
Jeremiah's Book of Prophesies, burning of
Kanawha County book-banning controversy
Kennedy, John F., assassination of
Kent State shootings
Korean War
Lateran Council, Fourth
Maya books, destruction of
Mexican-American War
Military censorship
Mutual Broadcasting System scandal
My Lai massacre
National Socialism (Nazism)
Panama, U.S. invasion of
Paris, Council of
Persian Gulf War
Press-radio war
Publick Occurrences
Reformation, the
Revolutionary War, American
Roman Empire
Scopes trial
Simpson, O. J., case
Skokie, Illinois, Nazi march
Soviet secret cities
Spanish-American War
Spanish Empire
Spanish Inquisition
Temperance movements
Three Mile Island
Tiananmen Square
Tonkin Gulf incident
UFO evidence
Vietnam War
War
War of 1812
Watergate scandal
World War I
World War II
Worms, Edict of
Yaqzan, Matan, affair

LAWS

LIBRARIES

LITERATURE AND PUBLISHING

MUSIC AND DANCE

NEWS MEDIA

OBSCENITY AND INDECENCY

ORGANIZATIONS

PEOPLE: ARTISTS

PEOPLE: BROADCASTERS AND ENTERTAINERS

PEOPLE: JOURNALISTS AND PUBLISHERS

PEOPLE: JUSTICES AND LEGAL FIGURES

Black, Hugo
Blackstone, William
Brennan, William J., Jr.
Chase, Samuel
De Grazia, Edward
Douglas, William O.
Ernst, Morris Leopold
Frankfurter, Felix
Holmes, Oliver Wendell, Jr.
Warren, Earl

PEOPLE: MORAL CRUSADERS

Comstock, Anthony
Coughlin, Father Charles Edward
Cushing, Cardinal Richard James
Gabler, Mel, and Norma Gabler
Spellman, Cardinal Francis Joseph
Sumner, John
Torquemada, Tomás de

PEOPLE: MUSICIANS AND COMPOSERS

Baez, Joan
Beach Boys, the
Beatles, the
Bryant, Anita
Foster, Stephen Collins
Guthrie, Woody
Jackson, Michael
Khachaturian, Aram
Lennon, John
Lewis, Jerry Lee
Madonna
Mendelssohn, Felix
Morissette, Alanis
O'Connor, Sinead
Presley, Elvis
Prokofiev, Sergei
Robeson, Paul
Rolling Stones, the
Seeger, Pete
Shakur, Tupac
Shostakovich, Dmitri
2 Live Crew
Wagner, Richard
Weavers, the

PEOPLE: PHILOSOPHERS AND SCIENTISTS

Anaxagoras
Aristotle
Bentham, Jeremy
Confucius
Copernicus, Nicolaus
Darwin, Charles
Democritus
Descartes, René
Ellis, Henry Havelock
Erasmus, Desiderius
Galileo Galilei
Hume, David
Kant, Immanuel
Kropotkin, Peter
Leary, Timothy
Locke, John
Marcuse, Herbert
Marx, Karl
Mead, Margaret
Mercator, Gerardus
Plato
Rousseau, Jean-Jacques
Sakharov, Andrei
Sanger, Margaret
Seneca the Younger
Socrates
Swedenborg, Emanuel
Vesalius, Andreas

PEOPLE: POLITICAL FIGURES

Agnew, Spiro T.
Barnett, Ross Robert
Bush, George
Cicero
Devlin, Bernadette
Dole, Robert
Franklin, Benjamin
Giddings, Joshua Reed
Gorbachev, Mikhail
Helms, Jesse Alexander
Henry VIII
Hoover, J. Edgar
James I
Jefferson, Thomas
Lenin, Vladimir Ilich
Lyon, Matthew
Madison, James
Mandela, Nelson
Mao Zedong
Meese, Edwin III
Morison, Samuel Loring
Nicholas I
Nixon, Richard M.
Reagan, Ronald
Royal family, British
Seneca the Younger
Shih huang-ti
Stalin, Joseph
Stubbs, John
Talmadge, Eugene
Thurmond, Strom
Trotsky, Leon
Zhdanov, Andrei

PEOPLE: RELIGIOUS FIGURES

Abelard, Peter
Bacon, Roger
Biddle, John
Calvin, John
Coughlin, Father Charles Edward
Cushing, Cardinal Richard James
Farrakhan, Louis Abdoul
Ghazzali, al-
Hus, Jan
Hutchinson, Anne
Joan of Arc
King, Martin Luther, Jr.
Knox, John
Latimer, Hugh
Leighton, Alexander
Luther, Martin
Malcolm X
Mani
Muhammad
O'Hair, Madalyn Murray
Paul IV, Pope
Richelieu, Cardinal
Rutherford, Joseph Franklin
Savonarola, Girolamo
Smith, Joseph
Spellman, Cardinal Francis Joseph
Thomas à Kempis
Torquemada, Tomás de
Williams, Roger

PEOPLE: SOCIAL AND POLITICAL ACTIVISTS

Bakunin, Mikhail Aleksandrovich
Berrigan, Daniel, and Philip Francis Berrigan
Debs, Eugene
Devlin, Bernadette
Douglass, Frederick
Garvey, Marcus
Goldman, Emma
Gouzenko, Igor Sergeievich
King, Martin Luther, Jr.
Malcolm X
Mandela, Nelson
Martí, José Julián
Metzger, Tom
Mindszenty, József
Nader, Ralph
O'Hair, Madalyn Murray
Pankhurst, Emmeline
Sanger, Margaret
Sumner, John
Thomas, Norman
Woodhull, Victoria

PEOPLE: WRITERS, AMERICAN

Andrews, V. C.
Baldwin, James
Blume, Judy
Cabell, James Branch
Caldwell, Erskine
Chomsky, Noam
Cummings, e. e.
Dahl, Roald
Dreiser, Theodore
Dworkin, Andrea
Emerson, Ralph Waldo
Faulkner, William
Ferlinghetti, Lawrence
Franklin, Benjamin
Ginsberg, Allen
Helper, Hinton
Hemingway, Ernest
Hinton, S. E.
King, Stephen
Lewis, Sinclair
London, Jack
MacKinnon, Catharine A.
Mencken, H. L.
Miller, Henry
O'Hara, John
O'Neill, Eugene
Paine, Thomas
Parker, Dorothy
Paterson, Katherine
Sendak, Maurice
Silverstein, Shel
Sinclair, Upton
Southern, Terry
Steinbeck, John
Thoreau, Henry David
Twain, Mark
Vonnegut, Kurt
Webster, Noah

SCIENCE

WARS

WOMEN